P9-DCE-018

Readings in
American Foreign Policy

A Bureaucratic Perspective

Readings in American Foreign Policy

A Bureaucratic Perspective

Edited by

Morton H. Halperin *The Brookings Institution*
Arnold Kanter *The University of Michigan*

Little, Brown and Company *Boston*

COPYRIGHT © 1973 BY LITTLE, BROWN AND COMPANY (INC.)

ALL RIGHTS RESERVED. NO PART OF THIS BOOK MAY BE REPRODUCED IN ANY FORM OR BY ANY ELECTRONIC OR MECHANICAL MEANS INCLUDING INFORMATION STORAGE AND RETRIEVAL SYSTEMS WITHOUT PERMISSION IN WRITING FROM THE PUBLISHER, EXCEPT BY A REVIEWER WHO MAY QUOTE BRIEF PASSAGES IN A REVIEW.

LIBRARY OF CONGRESS CATALOG CARD NO. 72-4466

SECOND PRINTING

Printed simultaneously in Canada by
Little, Brown & Company (Canada) Limited

PRINTED IN THE UNITED STATES OF AMERICA

Contents

Part Four

Actions 351

Part Five

Interaction among Nations 385

Suggestions for Further Reading 431

Readings in American Foreign Policy

A Bureaucratic Perspective

Introduction

MORTON H. HALPERIN AND
ARNOLD KANTER

The Bureaucratic Perspective: A Preliminary Framework

Political scientists interested in events in the international arena have not reached anything approaching a consensus regarding the appropriate paradigm for the inquiry. On the contrary, there are very different views, often passionately advanced, as to what kind of analysis is most likely to produce satisfactory explanations of past events and/or reliable predictions of future events.

Most analysts agree on the basic questions to be asked — who are the relevant actors; what are their objectives; what stimuli do they respond to; how and why do things change? Differences between analysts over these very questions stem from fundamentally different perspectives. The "experts" cannot agree on what constitutes the most fruitful level of analysis nor where best to look for the answers.

ALTERNATIVE APPROACHES TO INTERNATIONAL POLITICS AND FOREIGN POLICY

Although the boundaries separating the branches of political science are vague and permeable, each of several of the approaches to the basic

1

questions can be associated with a particular branch. That branch called "international politics" concentrates on the interaction of designated actors, primarily nation-states, in the international system. The dynamics of the international system *qua* system are assumed to determine the international behavior of nations. Analyses of "international politics" consequently become investigations of systematic regularities and discontinuities and of corollary imperatives for nation-state behavior. In this "billiard ball" perspective, nations are treated more or less interchangeably, either passively yielding to the laws of the system or pursuing a common set of objectives (such as national security or territorial integrity).

Analysts adopting this perspective devote correspondingly little attention to the peculiarities of individual nation-states' foreign policies and, by implication, suggest that insights from the domestic political process of each country are relatively unimportant. Their approach implies that the wise researcher will consider the structure of the international system and the distribution of power among nations. For example, he will note whether the international system is unipolar, bipolar, or multipolar.

Students of the "foreign policy" branch concentrate on individual nation-states rather than adopting a system perspective. Foreign policy objectives usually are attributed to the specific nation as a whole or to the particular leaders of the country. In the former case, these goals are held to be substantially invariant with regard to the particular incumbent leadership — i.e., they are traditional, historical, or objective goals of foreign policy. In the latter case, a nation's foreign policy objectives are thought to be determined largely by the incumbent leaders. In either case, policymakers are assumed to be rational, value-maximizing individuals whose choices reflect a reasonable selection among alternative courses of action designed to achieve the desired objective.

Regardless of the source of a nation's objectives, the "foreign policy" approach implicitly assumes that, although individual nations have distinctive goals, a particular nation's *foreign* policy may usefully be studied in isolation from domestic policy and politics. The objectives of the actors are thought to be outside the borders of the country.

These twin assumptions permit an analyst to employ simple rules of inference to explain events in international affairs. Perhaps country X or its leader Y is observed to have done Z. Since it (or he) is rational, action Z must have been a means selected in the reasonable expectation that it would achieve a particular foreign policy objective. It then remains only to speculate on what goal was being sought with action Z.

More recently, attempts have been made to abolish, or at least to make flexible, the analytical boundary between foreign policy and domestic politics. Studies by Huntington, Hilsman, Schilling, Neustadt, and Allison focus on the policymaking process and emphasize that foreign policy decisions and actions may be viewed as a non-frivolous game — the result of the regulated interaction of several individuals and domestic organizations (usually intra-governmental) planning strategies, bargaining with one another, each struggling to achieve particular objectives. This approach directs attention away from the model of a value-maximizing individual and toward identification of the actual participants, their goals, and their bargaining resources. The perspective that guided the selection of the readings which follow is a variant of this approach.

We call our approach a *bureaucratic perspective* because it emphasizes the centrality of those individuals who are members of the national security bureaucracy. In the United States this means the President and that portion of the executive branch directly involved in decisions and actions affecting foreign policy and national security. We proceed on the assumption that the international environment permits a state to pursue a wide variety of goals and on the assumption that the predominant sources of a nation's behavior in the international arena are the organizations and individuals in the executive branch who are responding to opportunities for, and threats to, the maximization of their diverse interests and objectives. We believe that membership in the bureaucracy substantially determines the participants' perceptions and goals and directs their attention away from the international arena to intra-national, and especially intra-bureaucratic, concerns. Accordingly, we argue that a focus on the international objectives of a state is essentially misleading, in that the participants' attention primarily is focused on domestic objectives. Events in international affairs, according to this perspective, are most often the reflection of these internal concerns; the scholar requires an understanding of a nation's domestic political structure and of its national security bureaucracy in order to explain or predict the foreign policy actions it will take.

The bureaucratic perspective in this special sense implies (1) that change in the international environment is only one of several stimuli to which participants in the foreign policy process are responding (possibly among the weakest and least important) and (2) that events involving the actions of two or more nations can best be explained and predicted in terms of the actions of two or more *national bureaucracies* whose actions affect the domestic interests and objectives of the other bureaucracies involved. Both implications represent signficant departures from the conventional wisdom of studies of foreign policy and international politics.

The readings which make up this book concentrate on understanding the behavior of the United States in the postwar world in terms of the bureaucratic politics of foreign policy and national security. The framework sketched in the balance of this Introduction describes the process by which that part of the executive branch involved in foreign policy makes decisions and takes actions in the international arena. First the role of national security interests is discussed in the Introduction. Then the participants in the process are identified in terms of their positions in the bureaucracy, and the sources of their interests and objectives are discussed. Subsequently the process by which decisions are made comes under consideration. The strategies by which the participants seek to change the behavior of their government are described, and the clash of diverse goals is analyzed. When, still later, the actions of the government are discussed, the frailty of the relationship between decisions and actions is emphasized — and the gap between intentions and results. A final section explores interaction among nations.

The readings themselves were selected to illuminate aspects of the process of bureaucratic politics. Examples drawn from these articles are used to illustrate the major themes presented in this Introduction. All of the selections have been published elsewhere, and most were written from one of the more traditional perspectives. Accordingly, a brief note precedes each reading to relate it to a particular feature of bureaucratic politics. Inevitably, the literature is a richer source for some aspects of the approach than for others. The distribution of the articles is more a reflection of the availability of good readings than of the relative emphasis which the various points ideally deserve or require.

NATIONAL SECURITY AS A DECISIONMAKING GUIDE

Participants in the national security policy process believe that the policies and actions they should (and do) support promote the national security interest. Their perception of what constitutes that interest is in turn affected by their view of the world. In the postwar period a widely shared set of images of the functioning of the international system and the U.S. role in the world shaped the prevailing consensus on the requirements of American security.

These images combined perceptions of reality with preferences and objectives in an often conflicting set of beliefs. For example, it was widely held that in self-defense the United States had to maintain military superiority over the Soviet Union because the Soviet Union (because of Communism and/or Russian nationalism) was an aggressive nation. Any expansion of the area under Communist control was deemed to represent a serious challenge and had to be resisted because it would cast doubt on the credibility of American commitments. At the same time, these images of the respective roles of the Soviet Union and the United States were accompanied by a deep commitment to avoid a nuclear war.

Where a proposed course of action can be shown to be unambiguously necessary to preserve a shared objective, there is usually unanimous agreement. By the same token, widely shared images often lead to agreement on basic objectives and therefore to the exclusion of some options. Thus, in response to the Soviet launching in 1957 of the first Sputnik satellite, no one suggested that the United States simply yield leadership in strategic weapons and technology to the Soviet Union.

However, when the consequences of an action are ambiguous, which is most often the case, there is rarely agreement on what action to take, in spite of the shared images. For example, despite the general consensus that the United States needed to preserve its strategic deterrent and maintain its technological advantage over the Soviet Union after the Sputnik launching, President Eisenhower, Congressional leaders, and the heads of the military services all had very different notions of what course of action would achieve these objectives.

The differences arise, in part, from the inherent intellectual difficulty of the problems involved. Scholars without institutional interests or policy responsibility differ very substantially in their evaluation of what impact an American anti-ballistic missile (ABM) deployment might have on the Soviet-American arms race and on the possibility of nuclear war. Moreover, as Robert Jervis suggests in Part II of this book (pp. 113 ff), the individuals involved in the policy process have different personal experiences; they have had different educations; they remember different aspects of history and remember it in different ways. Their perceptions of reality and recommendations for action vary accordingly.

The set of shared images which has prevailed since World War II has established only very broad limits for policy deliberations: mutually incompatible policies and actions can and do fall within the limits set by common conceptions of the national security interest. Each participant is relatively free to give operational meaning to those conceptions, and, at any one time, there is a wide divergence among the members of the national security bureaucracy regarding what, in specific cases, the national security requires. Thus it is not enough to say that a nation's foreign policies seek to protect and enhance its national security. Such a statement has very little predictive power and offers a poor guide for policy advice. If we are to explain a nation's foreign policy decisions and actions, and if we are to be able to predict future decisions and actions, we must first identify the various participants of the national security bureaucracy, discover the sources of their particular perceptions of the national security, and seek to understand the process of interaction among them which yields the decisions and actions we observe.

PARTICIPANTS AND INTERESTS

Many discussions of American foreign policy assume either that officials in the government share a set of interests and work to accomplish an agreed set of goals or that the President determines policy and others seek to implement his decisions. Descriptions of "American" interests in Europe, for example, are often based on the assumption that actions by the American government affecting Europe are the result of unanimous "policy." Indeed, given the available data, such explanations may be the best we can provide in some cases.

However, as the readings collected here suggest, the reality is quite different. The individuals involved in decisionmaking do not see the problem in the same way, nor do they have the same interests. Each participant, because of his background and his particular role in the government, has access to different information and has different concerns. Each sees a different *face* of the issue. What is a budget issue to one participant will be a foreign relations issue to a second or a Congressional relations issue to a third.

Seeing different faces of an issue and having different interests, participants will have different *stakes* in the result and hence will take conflicting *stands*. That is why, in order to explain the reason for certain decisions, it is necessary first to specify who the participants were and what interests they had. For example, Richard Smith's case study (pp. 213 ff) suggests that to understand the decision to award the contract for the production of the TFX (later F-111) fighter aircraft to General Dynamics-Grumman, one must first recognize that a wide range of participants, including the Service secretaries, the Air Force, the Navy, the Secretary of Defense, influential Congressmen and Senators, and powerful defense contractors, all wished to influence the outcome (i.e., selection of the contractor). As each perceived the TFX issue, he saw a different face: a way to save money, a way to enrich a company and Congressional district, a fight to control the military services, a struggle to preserve organizational autonomy, etc. The participants' stakes in the outcome varied accordingly.

Similarly, for some of the participants, the question of whether to produce the Skybolt air-to-ground missile was a budget issue, for others it was a crisis in the Anglo-American alliance, and for still others it represented the continued survival of the manned bomber force. Even when participants see the same face in an issue, they may have different stakes. Thus both for Charles Hitch (the Pentagon comptroller) and for the Air Force, Skybolt was at least in part a budget issue. But their stakes were opposite: Hitch wanted to reduce the budget and therefore to cancel Skybolt, while the Air Force wanted to maximize its budget and therefore to continue the Skybolt program. Accordingly, a necessary prerequisite for the analysis of foreign policy decisions is to identify the participants, to discover the face of the issue they will see, and to understand their stakes in the outcome.

Participants

The President stands at the center of the foreign policy process in the United States. His role and influence over decisions are qualitatively different than those of any other participants. In any foreign policy decision widely perceived at the time to be important, the President will be a principal if not *the* principal figure determining the *general* direction of actions. It was President John F. Kennedy who made the decision to blockade Cuba, and President Lyndon B. Johnson who decided to oppose the defeat of the South Vietnamese government by committing U.S. combat troops.

Although the President is the principal decisionmaker on important foreign policy matters, he does not act alone. He is surrounded, on the one hand, by a large number of participants with whom he is more or less required by statute or tradition to consult (obligatory consultation) and, on the other hand, by those with whom he chooses to consult (discretionary consultation).

Regardless of who is President, Cabinet officers and heads of relevant agencies will be consulted because of their formal responsibilities and access to information. Law and custom dictate that among the Cabinet officers involved in foreign policy decisions almost always will be included the Secretary of State, the Secretary of Defense, the Director of Central Intelligence, and in economic matters the Secretary of the Treasury. The Joint Chiefs of Staffs will be consulted on defense budget issues and matters concerning the possible use of force. Officials from agencies such as AID and USIA and departments such as Agriculture and Commerce may become involved in economic decisions. In many cases American ambassadors and military commanders in the field are brought into the process for consultation.

Depending on the particular preferences of the incumbent President, certain members of the White House staff may also be consulted — specialists on national security or foreign policy, political advisers, speechwriters, and managers of the President's legislative program. President Eisenhower relied less on these advisers than did other Presidents. President Johnson drew on them for general foreign policy matters but not often for defense budget issues. President Nixon leans heavily on his adviser for national security affairs in all matters of foreign policy and national security.

Classifying Participants (I). The participants from the national security bureaucracy can be arrayed around the President at varying distances depending on the probability that they will be consulted by him. In detailed analyses of particular decisions it is useful to distinguish those participants who are regularly consulted (*senior* participants) and those who have access to the President only very infrequently or only through a senior participant (*junior* participants). It is important to note that whether a particular participant is senior or junior is only imperfectly related to the formal hierarchy of organization. Thus President Nixon's adviser for national security affairs clearly is a very senior participant but holds an office whose position in the formal hierarchy is, at best, unclear. More generally, a President's discretionary advisers are not necessarily located in formally high-ranking positions.

Although not formal members of the national security bureaucracy, individuals outside the executive branch have frequently been consulted by the President and have had significant influence on the shape of national security decisions and actions. Some Congressmen and Senators are senior participants, i.e., they are routinely contacted by the President for advice and support. These men are most often influential members or chairmen of the Congressional committees with direct responsibility for national security affairs (e.g., Armed Services, Foreign Relations, Appropriations, Atomic Energy). To the extent that Congress is the focus of the President's domestic political concerns, Congressmen and Senators who hold positions of leadership in their respective houses will be important participants even without direct legislative responsibilities for national security policy.

Individuals outside the government sometimes are participants in the national security policy process. Ostensibly private citizens who are the close personal confidants of the President are included in this category. Private interest groups, such as defense contractors, whose concerns are affected by foreign policy decisions will seek to influence the direction of policy. These groups may be consulted by the President from time to time but in any case are involved routinely through their contacts with the Congress. Other outsiders may be formally invited to participate in the process, although for limited periods of time and with narrowly defined responsibilities. The various Presidential commissions and study groups are examples.

The farther removed the outside participants are from routine involvement in the national security bureaucracy, the weaker their independent sources of bargaining power. This is especially striking in the case of ad hoc commissions and study groups. For example, neither the Gaither Committee nor the Rand study group on strategic bases was sufficiently influential to achieve its objectives without substantial assistance from regular members of the bureaucracy. The relative success of the Rand group and failure of the Gaither Committee can be attributed, in large measure, to their respective skills in forging alliances with important participants from the executive branch.

Guides to Interests

Since national security interests per se are essentially non-operational and therefore inadequate guides for action, most participants in the national security policy process turn to other sources for clues to the requirements of security and the best means to protect and enhance it. Other concerns and other interests become synonymous with the national security interest. These other interests may stem from the participant's organizational affiliation, his personal ambitions, and/or his evaluation of the domestic political climate.

Classifying Participants (II). Participants may be classified not only in terms of whether they are junior or senior but also in terms of how accurately their stands on a wide range of national security issues can be predicted from a knowledge of their organizational affiliation.

Career officials come naturally to believe that the health of their organization is vital to the nation's security. So also do certain individuals who are appointed by the President to senior posts in the Washington national security bureaucracy. In his chapter in this book (pp. 138 ff), William Jones attributes this inclination, at least in part, to the problems of communication and coordination endemic to any large organization.

The tendency of a Presidential appointee to identify his agency's success with the national security will depend on the individual, the strength of his prior convictions, and his definition of his role. However, the nature of the organization he heads will be of special importance: organizations vary in the extent to which positions of equivalent seniority constrain the behavior of role-occupants. For example, a Secretary of one of the military services usually will be strongly guided by the organizational interests of his service, since they ordinarily provide clear and coherent standards against which to measure success and failure. A Secretary of State, on the other hand, is likely to be less influenced by the organizational interests of his department and the foreign service, since these provide guidelines that are less clearcut and in many cases offer conflicting guides to the nation's security interest. These distinctions are supported by Robert Axelrod's findings in his interview study of the Military Assistance Program: the answers of most of his respondents could be predicted from their position in the bureaucracy, but the reliability of such predictions sharply declined in the case of certain high-ranking civilians (Axelrod's study is included here, pp. 154 ff.)

Participants whose stands on issues can be predicted with high reliability from a knowledge of their organizational affiliation will be termed *organizational participants,* and those for whom organizational membership is not a good predictor will be termed *players.* Thus an individual in the national security bureaucracy may be classified as either relatively junior or relatively senior and as an organizational participant or a player.

The higher the formal position occupied by the participant, the more likely it is that he will be classified as a senior participant and that he will behave like a player. There is not a perfect relationship, however, since the Chiefs of Staff of the military services and the Chairman of the Joint Chiefs are more usefully classified as senior organizational participants, and members of planning staffs who ordinarily occupy lower-ranking positions in the bureaucracy often should be classified as junior players.

Organizational Interests

Bureaucrats will examine any policy proposal, at least in part, to determine whether it will increase the effectiveness with which the mission of their particular organization can be carried out; their organizational responsibilities will help to define the face of the issue they see. For example, in examining a proposal for a new security commitment, the Office of Management and Budget (formerly the Budget Bureau) and the Comptroller's Office in the Pentagon gauge how it will affect their ability to keep down the defense budget. Treasury asks how its ability to maintain the U.S. balance of payments in equilibrium will be affected. State Department officials may assess the possible impact of the security arrangement on political relations with the country in question and its neighbors. The military services will weigh the possible effect of the proposal on their existing commitments. As Edward Katzenbach reports in his contribution to this book (pp. 172 ff), European cavalry officers viewed the increased firepower made possible by repeating rifles and machine guns not as an important addition to the nation's fighting capabilities but as a threat to the tradition of fighting mounted on horseback.

All organizations seek *influence*; many also have a specific *mission* to perform; and some organizations need to maintain expensive *capabilities* in order to perform their mission effectively. Organizations with missions seek influence to promote their missions. Those that also have large operational capabilities — like the armed forces — seek influence on decisions in part to maintain the capability necessary to perform their mission. They will see the face of an issue that affects their ability to justify the maintenance of these capabilities. Other organizations, such as the Office of International Security Affairs (ISA) in the Office of the Secretary of Defense and the Policy Planning Staff in the State Department, have neither large capabilities nor stable, organizationally defined missions. Hence their only constant organizational interest is in enhancing their influence for its own sake, because individuals in such organizations share with those in other organizations the belief that they can best judge the nation's security interests.

Organizations with missions strive to maintain or to improve their (1) essential role, (2) domain, (3) autonomy, and (4) morale. Organizations with high-cost capabilities are also concerned with maintaining or increasing their (5) budgets. These organizational objectives are the source of the stakes and stands of organizational participants.

1. Organizational "essence" refers to the notion held by members of an organization as to what the main capabilities and primary mission of the organization should be. For example, European cavalry commanders had great difficulty in adapting to technological advances in weaponry because, in their view, the essence of their mission permitted them to fight only while mounted on horseback. The American horse cavalry did not confront similar problems of adaptation because its doctrine allowed the cavalry to engage the enemy while dismounted. In some organizations, a view of the essence is shared by all of those in the same promotion and career structure. In other cases there is a difference of view. A large proportion of Air Force officers believe that the essence of their service involves flying aircraft in combat, either to bomb targets behind enemy lines or to engage enemy aircraft. The strenuous efforts to extend the life of the manned bomber, as reflected in the Skybolt missile and B-70 bomber programs, is an indication of their view of the Air Force's essence and their unwillingness to see the same strategic function performed by different weapons (the intercontinental ballistic missile, or ICBM) even though their service would retain major responsibility for the mission.

2. Concern about "domain" (or "roles and missions" when referring to the military services) arises from uncertainty about where the operations of one organization end and those of another begin. The conflict between the Air Force and Navy regarding responsibility for the strategic nuclear mission was intensified by the Navy's efforts in the 1940's to develop carrier-launched aircraft capable of dropping atomic bombs. Such disputes also can occur within organizations. For example, the TFX (now F-111) aircraft had its origins in the attempt by the Air Force Tactical Air Command to take over some of the responsibility for strategic bombing which had been the preserve of the Air Force Strategic Air Command.

3. Autonomy refers to the desire of an organization to have control over its own resources in order to preserve what it views as its essence and to protect its domain from encroachment. Thus the military services opposed the Gaither Committee's report because they feared that, although implementing its recommendations might mean larger budgets for their organizations, it would change the decisionmaking process in a way which would reduce their ability to control their own operations. Similarly, Robert Hunter reports that the other services unanimously supported the Air Force request for Skybolt, even though the missile represented a potential threat to their budgets, because they viewed the issue as a test case of civilian intrusion into areas in which the services had been operating autonomously. (Hunter's study appears on pp. 191 ff.)

4. Organizational morale encompasses those things which organizations come to believe are necessary to preserve the loyalty of all members. For example, the other branches of the Air Force supported the Strategic Air Command on the Skybolt issue in order to minimize intra-service conflict,

even though a favorable decision on Skybolt implied reduced funds for their own programs. Considerations of morale require, among other things, that what the organization is doing must look important in its own estimation, and it also means that serious attention must be given to problems of promotion.

5. Insofar as it is consistent with protecting and promoting their essence, organizations wish to maximize their budgets, both absolutely and in relation to the organizations with which they are in budgetary competition (e.g., each military service seeks to maximize its respective share of the Pentagon budget). Adequate budgets are needed to provide the resources necessary to accomplish the organization's mission and permit it to remain autonomous, independent of any of its bureaucratic competitors or its nominal superiors. Success in budgetary competition also contributes to an organization's reputation for influence.

Organizations with large and expensive capabilities (notably the military services) will be particularly concerned about budget decisions and about the budgetary implications of policy decisions. Organizations with missions but low-cost capabilities will be primarily concerned with policy decisions and their implications for missions. Thus the British Royal Navy opposed the substitution of Polaris missiles for Skybolt because it feared that the missile-firing submarines would be financed at the expense of programs with a higher Royal Navy priority. By contrast, the bureaucrats in ISA with responsibility for the Military Assistance Program were willing, and even eager, to see funds for that program reduced.

Domestic Interests

There is no doubt that domestic interests affect foreign policy decisions and actions. Nevertheless the view persists that such interests are and should be ignored in the shaping of foreign policy. The perception that such calculations are illegitimate in the foreign policy sphere leads to a reluctance to put forward explicit domestic political arguments in favor of a particular policy. Except for a single note passed between two of its members, the upcoming Congressional elections were not mentioned in the meetings of ExCom (the ad hoc Executive Committee of the National Security Council) during the 1962 Cuban missile crisis. Yet, outside the national security bureaucracy, the announcement that missiles had been discovered was greeted with suspicion of political motivations. Similarly, the debates over the Chinese Offshore Islands did not include an explicit discussion of how the American political environment, which included wide support for the Nationalist regime, would be affected by a serious challenge to Chiang Kai-shek. For the incumbent Conservative government in Britain, the cancellation of Skybolt represented a serious threat to Tory prospects for re-election, but the party's political future did not enter into the dialogue with the American government.

Domestic political concerns differ in their impact on Presidents and on the bureaucracy. They are much more likely to be included in the President's calculations as well as those of his senior political appointees (particularly the White House staff) than in those of career civil servants. Three kinds of domestic interests come to be interpreted by Presidents and their senior political appointees as serving the national security.

1. The first is getting and keeping office. Presidents easily come to believe that their re-election is in the national interest and that their ability to be re-elected could be adversely affected by a controversial foreign policy decision. For example, a President may be concerned about denying an opponent a key political issue such as a "missile gap." Alternatively a President may see a particular foreign policy decision as an effective appeal to a particular group of potential supporters such as textile manufacturers in the South or Jewish voters in New York. Contractors and labor unions frequently are affected by defense budget decisions, the TFX being a notable example.

2. Presidents and those who support them share with other bureaucratic participants a concern about maintaining their effectiveness — the ability to get things done. Stands on issues are affected in part by the desire to display influence — building a reputation for "winning" and avoiding a reputation for "losing." Thus a President and his supporters need to ask how a particular decision or action will affect his power. The desire to maintain and enhance influence leads to three rules:

(a) Avoid the appearance of failure. Presidents and their associates are reluctant to take on efforts that probably cannot succeed, for each defeat tarnishes their reputation for success and, consequently, diminishes the probability of success in the future.

(b) Avoid rows with Congress, the press, or the public. Even if the President is successful in the present instance, he may have paid too great a price in his own time as well as in antagonism, bitterness, and resentment. This was President Kennedy's assessment of his fight with Congress over the B-70 manned bomber.

(c) Develop a consensus of support for a particular policy. In seeking this wide support, Presidents may feel the need to maintain consistency. A particular decision should appear to be consistent with other decisions made by the administration. The decision by President Truman to defend Taiwan in 1950 was made because he felt that he could not get the public's support for his defense of Korea if, at the same time, he permitted Taiwan to be overrun. This was particularly the case because leading Congressional Republicans, as well as the Joint Chiefs of Staff, were more concerned about Taiwan than they were about Korea. Officials also feel bound by the precedents they inherit from their predecessors in office. The consistency in United States policy toward

Vietnam or the Offshore Islands through successive administrations has been attributed to pressures on Presidents for continuity of policy.

The desire for consensus may also lead the President to placate the bureaucracy or to appoint an administrator trusted by his opponents. Thus Harry Truman appointed a Republican to head the Marshall Plan.

3. Finally, domestic interests and foreign policy interact in the clash over the use of scarce resources. Although domestic political calculations may make him reluctant to do so in particular situations (for example, when such economizing implies reduced aerospace procurement or military base closings), the President usually desires to hold down spending on defense and foreign policy in order to avoid inflation and to have funds for other purposes.

Personal Interests

Participants have a variety of personal interests which they come to identify with national security and which shape their perception of what should be done. One can distinguish, as Anthony Downs has suggested, two groups among those individuals who are dominated by their personal interests and who come to see national security in these terms.[1] In one group are the "climbers" interested mainly in getting ahead and becoming more powerful. In the other are the "conservers" interested in maintaining what they have. A career bureaucrat primarily interested in job security will tend to be a "conserver." An appointed official for whom present participation in the national security bureaucracy is a means to a more ambitious end will probably be a "climber." Knowing whether a man is one or the other provides a clue to the personal interests that will color his view of national security.

Many "climbers," particularly those who come into the government for limited periods of time, have a desire to be effective, to be involved, and to be powerful. Others are concerned about being promoted and increasing their prestige. Still other officials, particularly those in high positions, may be concerned about the impact of decisions or actions on their own ability to gain elective office in the future or even about how they will look in the history books. This makes them anxious to accomplish any particular mission which they are given. It also leads them to seek the confidence and support of the President, to avoid "making waves," and to avoid standing alone against a developing consensus within the government.

"Conservers" are more concerned with keeping what they have. They are interested in convenience — that is, in avoiding decisions that would threaten their jobs, increase their workload, or upset their routine. In one of the selections included here (pp. 98 ff), James Thomson reports that

[1] See Anthony Downs, *Inside Bureaucracy* (1967), pp. 92–101.

the State Department's policy advice on Vietnam was constrained by career foreign service officers' memories of the fate of their colleagues who had given candid advice on China during the 1940's.

Faces, Stakes and Stands

In any specific case it is difficult to predict the exact mix of interests which will determine the face of a national security issue seen by the participant, his stake in its resolution, and his stand on it. However, a few simplifying generalizations can be offered.

Few career participants see any conflict between their personal interests and the objectives of the organization with which they are affiliated. A career official's view of what is in the national security interest is determined in large part by the shared images held within the organization in which he seeks promotion, as well as in the larger bureaucracies with which he comes in contact. He recognizes that if his organization prospers, he is more likely to be promoted and that his promotion may depend on his appearing to fight for the interests of his organization. As illustrated by Morris Blachman in "The Stupidity of Intelligence" (pp. 328 ff below) there was a widespread but probably only tacit agreement within the Air Force to overestimate the effectiveness of bombing North Vietnam: the organizational interests of the service required that interdiction appear to be effective, and the personal interests of its members required that the Air Force's organizational objectives be served. The absence of conflict among these sets of interests resulted in a highly — if spontaneously — coordinated effort to exaggerate bombing reports.

A participant less calculating and more selfless nevertheless may turn to his organization's interests and objectives for guides to stands on national security issues. Organizational interests tend to be more concrete and operational than general perceptions of national security and hence come to dominate the judgments of most career officials. William Jones suggests that an organizational participant is more aware of the good qualities of his own organization and more confident of its ability to accomplish a job. By contrast, he has only an imperfect understanding of other organizations, a mistrust for their intentions, and an awareness of their weaknesses. Thus it is reasonable for him to identify his organization's objectives with those of the nation. These analyses support Axelrod's finding that most officials' positions on issues can be predicted with high reliability from a knowledge of their organizational affiliation, regardless of the facts of a particular case. Such studies indicate that most members of the national security bureaucracy may be classified as organizational participants for the purposes of predicting their stands on issues.

However, non-career officials, particularly senior officials, in the national security bureaucracy are more likely to be players — that is, participants whose stands on issues cannot be reliably predicted from a knowledge of their organizational affiliation. Their perceptions of the national security interest are more likely to be dominated by images shared with society, their own experiences, and their historical memories. The position of senior officials in the bureaucracy nevertheless will affect the information which is called to their attention by subordinates and the faces of an issue they see. Their dependence on the organization that they manage for information and for definitions of interests and stakes will depend on the extent of operational responsibility they have and on their degree of contact with other individuals and organizations. A non-career official's definition of interests also will be affected by his conception of his role and of his relation to the President.

DECISIONS

Thus far, we have presented an image of numerous participants with divergent interests seeing differing faces of any issue. In examining any particular case, we need to understand not only what each participant wanted but also how these individuals sought what they desired. This leads to a consideration of *when* a participant may seek to change the pattern of governmental actions, the *constraints* within which the game is played, the strategies designed and implemented to effect the desired change, and the *bargaining advantages* which may be available.

The Impetus for Change

Given their interests and perspectives, participants are prone to believe that a large number of governmental actions ought to be altered. They also recognize, however, that the national security policy process would lapse into chaos and that they would fail if they sought to change everything they found undesirable. Thus mere preference does not determine which current policies and decisions will be challenged.

Participants will act to change decisions when (a) the expected probability of success increases and/or (b) the expected positive or negative payoffs shift substantially. For the purposes of the discussion, we will assume that the desired change requires a Presidential decision.

In a relatively few instances, the President, in his own interest and on his own initiative, raises an issue in order to make a decision. However, in general, Presidents do not address an issue unless one participant or a coalition makes a sustained effort to get him to do so.

For participants other than the President, the first problem is that a situation must occur which reopens an issue for a new decision. For certain classes of issues, this condition occurs *routinely*. The annual preparation of the defense budget, for example, virtually guarantees that, even in the absence of special efforts by any of the participants, a wide range of national security issues will receive Presidential scrutiny at least once a year.

A variety of less routine events may also create the necessary circumstances. Dramatic changes in the *actions of other nations* frequently create a situation in which new decisions appear feasible or even necessary. Sometimes the decision is closely related to those actions. For example, Communist Chinese pressures against the Offshore Islands forced a decision about whether or not the United States would defend those islands and, if so, whether it would use nuclear weapons. The relation between another nation's actions and the issues reopened for new decisions may be less direct. For example, when the Soviets detonated an atomic bomb in 1949, the debate over the pace of the American H-bomb program was reopened. At the extreme, the decision may be only peripherally related to the event. Thus the Joint Chiefs of Staff used the 1968 Tet offensive to press for a Presidential decision to mobilize reserve forces, a decision which they long had sought, less to increase the level of United States forces in Vietnam than to replenish the strategic reserves.

However, even dramatic changes in the international environment may produce no response among the participants, in part because they, like the horse cavalry, are inclined to interpret the lessons of experience according to their existing preconceptions. Axelrod found that his respondents in the Military Assistance Program agreed that the conflict between India and Pakistan held important lessons for MAP, but they could not agree on what those lessons were, and they acknowledged that no changes in their program were attributable to that experience.

In other cases, changes in *domestic mood* which affect participants' calculations of the domestic political consequences of a foreign policy decision may lead them to press for a particular decision. Also, changes in *personnel*, notably changes in administration, may lead to efforts to change a decision. This may be occasioned by the entrance of a new participant who is strongly committed to a different pattern of action, or it may occur because a participant who has effectively blocked a decision leaves the government. Accordingly, a change in Presidential administrations presents the opportunity to seek new decisions on a wide range of issues. When Kennedy replaced Eisenhower, the military services took advantage of the situation to renew their pressure for programs such as Skybolt and the nuclear-powered airplane which had been cancelled by the Republicans.

The Decision to Participate

Once an issue is raised, other participants in the process may recognize that an important individual or coalition is seeking a (Presidential) decision or that the President himself is prepared to make a decision. They then have to make a number of strategic estimates. The first calculation is to determine how their interests might be affected by the issue as they see it — to estimate their stakes in the outcome. They must consider what the range of decisions and changes in actions is likely to be. They must consider whether, if they beccme involved, they would be able to affect the decision and at what cost. In short, they must determine the intensity of their commitment and the scope of their involvement.

Some participants have no choice but to become involved. Because of their responsibilities they are directly concerned and find it impossible to opt out. The military services were inevitably involved in giving advice on whether the Offshore Islands could be defended and on whether the recommendations of the Gaither Committee made sense. Other officials are able to choose, since they will find it relatively easy either to become involved or to stay out. For example, because he saw it primarily as a choice among weapons systems and a defense budget issue, Secretary of State Dean Rusk played a minor role in the Skybolt decision and the ensuing crisis in Anglo-American relations. Perhaps more surprising, he chose not to become involved in most of the ExCom meetings during the Cuban missile crisis.

Where there is a choice, a participant's determination of whether to get involved depends on his calculation of the risks to his own personal interests and position, as well as his perception of national security interests. He is concerned about the time and energy involved in getting caught up in an issue, as well as the consequences to his reputation for effectiveness if he loses.

If a participant decides to get involved, he may plan a strategy — that is, a set of moves designed to produce the desired decision. Participants in the American government vary enormously in the degree to which they plan strategies. Many participants never plan, a few always plan, and the rest plan to a degree depending on the issue. In general, planning of this type is more likely to occur at lower levels.

The TFX decision is a good illustration of the extent to which various participants prepare strategies. The President and members of Congress appear to have done very little planning. The Air Force seems to have engaged in some calculations, but the Navy's strategy of postponement suggests more careful calculations. The elaborate strategies of the competing contractors, particularly their predictions regarding the power of the various intra-governmental participants and the resulting design of their contract bids, is a testament to how extensive strategic planning may become.

If they do plan, the participants' first step is to define their operational goal. They need to determine what decisions they hope to get made, by whom, and in what sequence. Next they must classify the other participants according to who has power with the President, who is likely to be neutral, who is an ally, and who is an opponent. It is then necessary to consider the kinds of arguments, the kinds of bargaining, and the kinds of coercive efforts that are required to achieve the desired decision. The resulting plans usually involve a series of *maneuvers* and *arguments* designed to influence the outcome. The maneuvers are directed first at determining the procedure by which an issue is raised, who should be involved, and how high up the ladder of organization the issue will go. Second, they are designed to influence the information presented to senior players. In each case, however, the range of choice is limited.

Constraints and Maneuvers

The national security policy process does not occur in an unstructured environment. In devising strategies to achieve desired outcomes, participants must take cognizance of the fact that they are *constrained* by a variety of factors, some of which derive from the laws and customs which govern the operation of the bureaucracy, others whose source lies in the images of international reality widely shared by members of the bureaucracy and/or the electorate, and still others which are attributes of any large and complex organization. Astute participants will design *maneuvers* which either seek to exploit an existing set of constraints for their advantage or try to modify constraints in order to increase the probability of success.

Two important classes of constraints which will be discussed in this section are (a) the rules of the game and (b) widely shared images of international reality. The corresponding maneuvers will describe (a) moves designed to exploit or alter the rules of the game, and (b) the arguments intended to maximize support on behalf of the desired decision. A third class of constraint — the limited performance of large and complex organizations — will also be addressed.

Rules of the Game. The rules of the game are the constitutional provisions, statutes, regulations, procedures, customs, traditions, etc. which organize the government and structure the process by which decisions are made and actions are undertaken: they are a device for arranging minds to work on a problem. The rules determine who has the "action" — who will be responsible for raising the issue and carrying the necessary papers through the government, whose concurrence will be needed before a decision is made, the alternate channels through which a piece of paper can be moved, and how high up in those channels one may (or must) go to get a decision on a particular issue.

In seeking to get the decision they want, participants engage in maneuvers within the limits imposed by the rules of the game. They recognize that the way the decision is made will affect the results — e.g., whether and in what form the issue gets to President. Among the key variables to be considered are who is involved in the process, whose views are reported to the President, and who is informed in advance that a decision is to be made.

Participants maneuver to involve those they think will favor their position and to exclude those they think will oppose it. Joseph Clerk's "The Art of the Memorandum," for example (included in this book on pp. 236 ff), describes several maneuvers based on the composition and circulation of memoranda designed to regulate participation in a particular game. Efforts to expand the number of participants may involve bringing additional members of the executive branch into the process. In other cases, maneuvers are an attempt to involve participants outside the bureaucracy, including Congress and interest groups. One method of expanding the number of participants is to leak information about an ongoing decision to the press so that other participants will be alerted to the issue. This happened, for example, after Eisenhower rejected the Gaither Committee report. Similar maneuvers were in evidence during the last stages of the decision to cancel Skybolt. The administration's announcement was timed to occur during a Congressional recess, presumably to foreclose the possibility that the Air Force's supporters in Congress would come to the assistance of the Strategic Air Command. In response, the Air Force timed the announcement of a "successful" test of the missile to coincide roughly with the administration's announcement that Skybolt was being terminated because of technical shortcomings. To counter the possibility of such leaks, participants may seek to restrict the involvement of others.

The rules of the game impose more or less narrow limits on participants who seek to change governmental actions. They always will permit some choice of behavior which defines the scope of potential maneuvers. Yet, the rules will necessarily have an important influence by affecting the decision to participate, i.e., who becomes involved, and whether he enters the game as an ally, opponent, or neutral. Thomson notes, for example, how certain rules of the game based on custom affected policymaking on Vietnam: as issues are perceived to be increasingly important, they are handled by bureaucrats of increasing rank. Consequently, as Vietnam became a salient issue, it was removed from the jurisdiction of relatively low-ranking experts on the area and made the responsibility of senior political appointees who had few specialized qualifications for the assignment.

The rules of the game vary in their permanence and in their application to particular cases: various administrations have applied different sets of rules to similar cases, and the same administration frequently varies certain rules under its control, depending upon the circumstances. One set of rules stems from Presidential directives, such as those that established the new National Security Council system under President Nixon in 1969. Still others come from directives issued by Cabinet officers. The customs and traditions of the bureaucracy, the participants' personal perceptions of their roles, and the nature of their personal relationships with the President are other sources of rules.

Some rules, such as those deriving from the American constitutional system, persist regardless of the particular incumbents. Most notable perhaps is the separation of powers which permits the Congress to constrain certain Presidential actions. Congressional legislation also helps to shape the rules of the game by requiring a specific subordinate official to make one or another kind of determination, by attempting to stipulate whom the President shall consult, or by specifying that the President personally must make a particular decision. For example, Congress has established a statutory membership for the National Security Council. While Presidents have been and are free to consult with other more informal bodies, the formal stipulation of membership affects who is consulted and when. Similarly, the formal procedures established by Congress for processing military assistance grants and sales dictate that several different organizations within the bureaucracy participate in each decision and must give their concurrence.

The more informal the rules, the more likely they are to be challenged or changed: acts of Congress are relatively permanent, whereas procedures imposed by a personal style of decisionmaking are relatively ephemeral. During the course of administration, participants seek to change the rules if they feel that the current set of rules is strongly biased against the kinds of decisions and actions that they seek. Usually the changes they desire are ones which would bring about either greater involvement on their own part in the decisionmaking process or reduced involvement by participants whose views they oppose. A new Secretary of Defense who has a very different notion of his role and how he should manage his department may drastically change the rules of decisionmaking within the Pentagon. Robert McNamara's early decisions on weapons systems such as the Skybolt, TFX, and the B-70 manned bomber were viewed by most participants as test cases which would determine the applicability and impact of the Secretary's changes in the rules for deciding which weapons to procure and from whom.

Getting to the President. A fundamental choice which participants may be able to make is whether or not an issue should be sent to the President. Participants frequently calculate that their prospects for success are enhanced if the President can be excluded or, at least, if Presidential involvement can be postponed to a more opportune time. As Vincent Davis notes in Part III of this book (pp. 261 ff), rather than go to President Truman with a request that the Navy be permitted to develop a nuclear weapons capability, Secretary of the Navy James Forrestal decided on his own authority to approve the aircraft modifications which enabled the service to begin its nuclear weapons program.

Participants have a tendency to compromise an issue among themselves rather than to submit it to the President. They do so in the belief that they can better protect their own organizational interest by getting a compromise which leaves other participants and themselves free to pursue their respective goals than by submitting the issue to unpredictable Presidential arbitration.

An issue will go to the President when (a) participants are unable to agree among themselves, (b) a senior participant believes he can secure a more favorable decision by taking the issue to the President, (c) the rules of the game require Presidential attention, or (d) the President has a strong personal interest in the issue.

Those who seek a Presidential decision face two problems. How and in what form shall they get the issue to the President? How shall they get him to make a decision?

The way in which an issue comes before the President—the face of the issue he sees — affects the decision that he makes. The rules of the game permit some choice: the same basic issue might come to the President in the form of a budget issue, or in the form of a sentence in a speech, or in the form of clearing a cable. The way it is raised will influence who in the White House is involved and whether the President sees it as a question of money, a question of policy, or a question of his relationship to a particular Cabinet officer.

There are a number of different maneuvers available to participants for bringing an issue to the President's attention. They may, for example, simply use existing formal channels, involving either consideration by the National Security Council or memoranda from the principal Cabinet officers to the President. In other cases, they may use more informal methods. For example, White House staff members, whether involved in foreign policy or not, are frequently used as channels to bring issues to the attention of the President. Sometimes this will be done informally before the issue comes up in formal channels; in other cases it will be a substitute for formal movement of the issue to the President. Other means used to bring issues to the President involve providing information to an allied country so that it will make a request which requires Presidential consideration, leaking information to the press or to the Congress, or simply making a public statement on an issue which then forces the matter to Presidential attention.

Once the issue gets to the President, the problem is not merely to get him to choose correctly, but to get him to choose at all. As Warner Schilling's description of Truman's minimal decision on the H-bomb program illustrates (pp. 240 ff), Presidents are notoriously reluctant to make binding decisions and tend to deal only with those problems which have a critical deadline. Thus the question for those who seek a Presidential decision is how to impose a deadline on the President or how to make the issue part of an existing Presidential deadline. Those who oppose a Presidential decision, on the other hand, will seek a delay by proposing additional clearances, or additional study, or the appointment of a commission to make a thorough study. As the history of the Gaither Committee suggests, Presidents themselves frequently resort to the tactic of appointing special commissions in order to postpone or avoid the necessity of making substantive decisions.

When the issue involves a budget item or when it is a matter of major concern, getting the President to act is no problem — he is routinely and unavoidably involved in the decisionmaking. By contrast, issues without built-in deadlines have difficulty gaining Presidential attention. In the case of the Offshore Islands, those favoring American withdrawal were able to get the issue to the President on only one occasion and even then had difficulty establishing a deadline.

Arguments. Thus far we have discussed maneuvers which exploit or modify the rules of the game with a view toward influencing the decision to participate and affecting the face of the issue perceived. These maneuvers logically (and usually temporally) precede another set of maneuvers designed primarily to affect the perceived stakes of those officials who participate. The latter class of maneuvers depend crucially upon controlling the substance and dissemination of information. Since the ostensible purpose of these maneuvers is, in one sense or another, to persuade other participants to support (or not oppose) the preferred stand, the information usually is presented in the form of rationales for action which we call *arguments.*

Participants may seek to maximize support on behalf of their position in basically three different ways. First they may seek to persuade someone that he has a stake in the issue. To do this, they stress information that will appeal either to the other party's sense of what is in the national security interest or to that party's more particular organizational, domestic, or personal interests.

Second, they may seek a bargain which will persuade a participant to give his support. They may, for example, offer to compromise: to alter the proposal in a way which reduces its cost to the interests of a particular participant. In other cases, the bargaining will involve logrolling: trade-offs between different issues.

Finally, participants may resort to coercion. They may try to convince an opposing participant that to make a substantial effort to alter the decision would affect his ability to accomplish things on other issues. By seeking to convince another participant that they have the power or ability to hurt his interests on other questions, they may persuade opponents to exit from the game (or reduce the probability that opponents initially will become involved).

Arguments also perform another function, closely related to that of persuasion. Particularly through what William Jones calls the formal communications channel within a bureaucracy, arguments are offered not only to persuade but also to communicate the stakes and stands of various participants. Since arguments designed to persuade are more familiar, we will concentrate our attention on the other purposes for which arguments are offered.

One of these is simply to fill in the blank. That is, under the rules of the game, proposals for new decisions must be accompanied by an explanatory memorandum presenting justifications. More specifically, in some cases the purpose of advancing arguments simply will be to demonstrate that there is a national security rationale for this proposal. Officials whose other interests incline them to support a proposal will need to be convinced that a responsible and reputable case can also be made for the national interest. The basic stakes of the participants in the Skybolt decision were obscured by focusing the public debate on technical feasibility and cost-effectiveness.

Another purpose of putting forward arguments is to signal strongly what one's policy preferences are. For example, when Eisenhower's principal advisers told him in 1958 that the loss of the Offshore Islands would have consequences greater than those which followed the capture of the Chinese mainland by the Communists, they were indicating to him not only what they thought he should do but also the strength of their commitment to the position being recommended.

Finally, arguments may be designed to present the appearance of a consensus not only on what decisions should be made but on the purpose. The Departments of State and Defense both supported an accelerated H-bomb program, but they did so for quite different reasons. However, these differences were not made clear to the President. Since participants will feel that the President is more likely to go along with their position if they all appear to favor it, they also are likely to seek agreement on a set of general arguments to which they can all subscribe. Participants advocating United States defense of the Offshore Islands did so for diverse reasons and could not agree on a set of specific arguments. As a result, a prediction of vague "dire consequences" was presented to the President.

In many cases a gap develops between the arguments put forward at one level and the arguments which actually persuade participants at another. Junior participants in the process are likely to focus on their conceptions of national security interest, as shaped by the organizational concerns of their agency. Presidents and senior participants are likely to have in mind a different notion of national security, more influenced by domestic politics and the history book, and by their relationships with other senior officials.

Thus, in internal Air Force debates, the case for intensified bombing of North Vietnam was argued in terms of the Air Force's competition with the Navy for the deep interdiction mission after the war. However, when pressing senior civilian participants for an expanded bombing role, the Air Force argued in terms of the bombing's effectiveness.

Just as maneuvers intended to influence the decision to participate and to affect the face of the issue perceived are limited by the rules of the game, arguments also are constrained. The most important constraints on arguments derive from widely shared images of international and domestic reality and commonly accepted standards which determine legitimate and unacceptable lines of argument.

Shared images provide an important constraint on what participants see and on what conclusions they draw from the evidence presented. Whatever their own beliefs, moreover, participants must shape their arguments for any particular case according to the shared images of the bureaucracy and society at the time. This reluctance to challenge unstated assumptions and conventional wisdom is related to what Thomson calls the "effectiveness trap": participants will not question the prevailing images lest they no longer be taken seriously, either in the present discussion or on future and unrelated matters. For example, in the early 1950's, those in the Department of State who advocated forcing the Chinese Nationalists off Quemoy and Matsu could not support their case by advancing the argument that this would result in a substantial improvement of relations between the United States and Communist China. Since improved relations between the two countries was not a widely shared goal, such an argument would have been counterproductive. Similarly, during the Cuban missile crisis Secretary of Defense McNamara quickly retreated from his initial recommendation that the United States do nothing about the Soviet missiles, for he recognized that he was in danger of being excluded from further effective participation in the decision.

A participant may, from time to time, seek to change the shared images in order to expand the range of arguments that can be used. However, images are so resistant to modification that he is likely to do so only when he feels that there is no other way to challenge decisions of importance to him and only if he feels that he has built a record of reasonableness and credibility sufficient to avoid his being dismissed as eccentric.

The use of arguments also is constrained by the existing rules of argument and by the language in which arguments must be cast. For example, at the time of the Gaither Committee report, the general assumption was that it was up to the military services, with their long experience and responsibility for carrying out military decisions, to decide whether particular defense programs were worthwhile. By the 1960's, as the TFX case suggests, a major change had taken place in the rules of argument, with systems analysis now playing a major role in determining the utility of weapons.

To this point, we have implicitly assumed that the participants who offer arguments have relatively complete and accurate information, particularly regarding the intentions and behavior of foreign countries. Of course, such intelligence in reality is rarely if ever either complete or accurate. An important constraint on the content of arguments as well as their effectiveness derives from the fact that most of the information about the world used by the national security bureaucracy is developed by large and complex organizations. How organizations operate greatly affects what information is made available to senior participants, when it comes to their attention, and in what context.

The job of intelligence gathering is enormously complex. It involves a very large number of organizations, each of which operates according to its own standard routines and operating procedures. Information does not pass quickly or unfiltered from the bottom of this system to the top. At each point "relevant" data must be identified, summarized, and passed up to higher levels. This not only takes time, but it means that information which senior participants might view as relevant may never reach them because junior participants with different interests and objectives may not see the faces of issues under debate among their superiors. Distortions in reporting the bombing campaign against North Vietnam are a particularly vivid example.

The standard procedures of organizations also affect the sort of options made available to policy officials. As Jones suggests, large and complex organizations are, by their very nature, inflexible and unresponsive to changing situations. When asked to produce options for a particular situation, organizations by and large will present alternatives which are consistent with the procedures and operating plans that they have developed. They generally will argue that options for which they have no plans are "infeasible" and will also insist that the details can be spelled out only by the organization itself. Because senior participants must depend on subordinate organizations for information and implementation, these arguments may be "persuasive" to senior participants even when they are not believed. To a significant degree, Kennedy's handling of the growing Vietnam problem was constrained by his dependence on the State Department's Bureau of East Asian and Pacific Affairs for non-military analysis and advice.

In some cases, participants seek to reduce organizational constraints by getting an existing organization to develop new options or by creating a new organization capable of implementing decisions. Efforts may also be made to change organizational constraints on the information-gathering process by creating a new organization such as the Central Intelligence Agency (established in 1947) or the Defense Intelligence Agency (set up by Secretary of Defense McNamara in 1961). To draw out some of the information sunk within the bureaucracy, submerged there either deliberately or inadvertently, efforts may also be made to change the procedures by which organizations report. Nevertheless, at any given time, the information and options available to senior participants will be heavily shaped by the routines and procedures of the organizations processing the information.

Decisions as System Outputs

Given participants with different interests who see different faces of an issue, given their maneuvering to affect what information is available to other participants and how the issue is decided, what determines which decisions are made? How does the process affect what is to be done and who is to do it?

Biases of the System. In part, decisions are biased by the constraints of the system. Even if all the participants were equal in the bargaining skills, the set of constraints which exist at any given time tends to skew the distribution of possible decisions, making some more likely than others. Thus some arguments will be more persuasive than others, particular options will be consistently offered and regularly selected, and the rules of the game will confer added bargaining advantages on certain participants.

A set of shared images determines what sort of actions participants will come to believe are in the national security interest and what kinds of arguments can be used in favor of these decisions. In the postwar United States the fact that there was a set of shared images about the need to contain Communist aggression, about the indivisibility of security, about the need to avoid appeasement, and about the need for military force to oppose Communist military expansion shaped the decisions made by Presidents on major issues. The system was biased in favor of decisions which could be supported by these kinds of arguments and against stands which were perceived to be counter to these doctrines.

The existing organizations and their procedures also shape what is to be done. The fact that the United States has a large Navy with aircraft carriers, that it has an Agency for International Development to give out aid, and that these and other organizations are structured in particular ways leads to support for particular policies and to capabilities for carrying out particular decisions. The system is heavily biased toward doing what its large organizations are eager and prepared to do.

The influence of individuals within the policy process consists of a blend of bargaining advantages conferred by the rules of the game, skill and will in using these advantages, and others' perceptions both of one's bargaining advantages and one's skill and will in using them.

The rules of the game are an important bias in the system because they result in an unequal distribution of bargaining advantages. An official who the rules stipulate must be consulted on a decision has greater influence than one who has to fight his way into the process. A rule which gives important powers to the Congress affects what can be accomplished in the executive branch as well. The different rules established by each President affect who has influence and access and how decisions are made. The rules also determine who has control over information and options and may, in some cases, provide a monopoly of expertise to certain participants.

Another form of bargaining advantage is the responsibility for implementing a decision. A participant who is to carry out a Presidential decision must be consulted and must be prepared to certify that the proposed action is feasible. Presidents find it difficult to order someone to do something that the latter said is infeasible or dangerous. This is particularly true for the armed forces, in that Presidents are reluctant to order combat operations which the responsible military commanders say are dangerous or unduly threaten American lives. Those responsible for implementation will also have the important bargaining advantage, at least in some cases, of being able to control deadlines.

The domestic political reality, as perceived by the participants in the process, also plays a major role in affecting the kind of decisions which emerge. All of the participants have a sense of what the society's shared images are. In addition, they are concerned about and dependent upon different groups within the society. Presidents will be concerned about political supporters and interest groups of importance in key states; members of the bureaucracy will be concerned about those interest groups within the society with which they have rapport. In the case of the Offshore Islands, for example, those who resisted any change of policy were able to bring to bear the weight of large, important groups that opposed any change in American China policy, while there were no comparable groups pressing for change.

Consequently, a key bargaining advantage conferred by the rules of the game in the United States is the ability to threaten to go beyond the executive branch, to appeal to the Congress, interest groups, or the general public in a way which may affect elections. Such a bargaining advantage manifests itself in the implicit threat to leak particular information or to resign from office. As Henry Kissinger indicates in one of the selections offered here (pp. 84 ff), the role of outsiders is less to introduce new information or ideas into the bureaucracy than to strengthen the position of some of the participants by giving their stand the stamp of approval of disinterested experts. This is one of the ways in which a Presidential commission can become a Presidential headache. Once the President has appointed a group of prestigious outside experts to make recommendations, he can ignore their advice only at great political peril.

Not every bargaining advantage derives from the rules of the game. Certain bargaining resources can be created and exploited by the participants themselves. For example, in making the choice about what to do, Presidents are also deciding who should do it. Accordingly, one form of bargaining advantage comes from a reputation for competence and willingness to obey orders. Staff skills, including the ability to draft effective memoranda, are also important in determining one's influence. In many cases Presidents in the postwar period have accepted Defense Department national security proposals because of the belief that this part of the government was more likely than was the State Department to be responsive to their needs.

A major set of bargaining advantages comes from personal attributes of particular participants. Perhaps the most important is the confidence of the President. Secretary of State Dean Acheson's principal advantage during the Truman administration was the knowledge that he had Truman's confidence and that the President was almost certain to support him on any issue. This resulted, in part, from Truman's perceptions that in order to enable his Secretary of State to operate effectively he had to support him and, in part, from the fact that Acheson was likely to be persuasive with the President on the merits of the issue. Thus Schilling attributes great influence to Acheson in shaping Truman's H-bomb decision.

Another personal attribute of considerable importance is the willingness and ability to assert one's prerogatives, even if doing so involves a certain amount of unpleasantness — including raising voices and banging tables. Axelrod found important differences among officials responsible for the Military Assistance Program in terms of their attitude toward interpersonal conflict. Participants who do not assert their prerogatives may well find that they are bypassed; others may be able to establish their right to involvement in particular decisions by making clear that, if they are not consulted or if their wishes are ignored, they are prepared to be nasty.

Finally, time, determination, and the willingness to seek responsibility and to act are important attributes affecting the influence of a participant in any particular case. Participants who do not have major ongoing responsibility, such as members of planning staffs, can pick a single issue and devote substantial time and determination to it. Many observers believe that the proposal for multi-national ship crews drawn from a number of NATO countries — the Multilateral Force (MLF) — got as far as it did because the State Department's Policy Planning Council was able to devote considerable time and effort to guiding the project through the bureaucracy while its opponents were preoccupied with other, more pressing responsibilities.

By virtue of the rules of the game, the President himself has the major advantage of formal responsibility and authority for most of the decisions to be made in the executive branch. On foreign policy questions the problem, from his perspective, is to get the issue to him in time and with the necessary information and options so that he can make a sensible choice, given his own interests. He must therefore create additional bargaining advantages for himself. These depend on his own skill in establishing rules to increase the probability that the issue will get to him in the way that he wants. He may, for example, deliberately assign overlapping responsibilities. They also depend on his willingness to assert his authority by hiring or firing people and by acting tough if necessary.

Decisions as Guides to Action

Our discussion of the national security bureaucracy has left the term "decision" deliberately undefined. From the context it is clear that "decision" has been used to mean "an authoritative determination that the stipulated member(s) should act in a specified manner." Conventional discussions of the policymaking process frequently concentrate on the manner in which decisions are reached and virtually exclude consideration of their subsequent implementation. Yet, most participants and analysts primarily are interested in the *actions* or outputs of governments and in the consequences or *outcomes* of those actions. Presumably the decision-making process is studied in the belief that decisions substantially determine actions and outcomes. However, this belief is frequently mistaken. Decisions are often imperfect predictors of governmental outputs, and actions can occur in the absence of decisions.

Although foreign policy decisions stipulate that someone should act in a specified manner, there usually is a wide range in the specificity of the directive. A significant proportion of foreign policy decisions do not explicitly direct well-defined actions. It might be useful to think of decisions arrayed along a continuum from least specific (with regard to directing actions) to most specific. At the one end of the continuum fall *policy decisions*, which in effect are statements of aspirations. At the opposite end fall *action decisions*, which explicitly direct particular participants to engage in a detailed set of activities.

Some examples may clarify this distinction. The United States may make a policy decision to promote European integration. This may be followed by a slightly more specific policy decision that Britain should be admitted to the Common Market. These policy decisions imply certain action decisions: e.g., the American ambassador in London should urge the British government to seek admission and the American ambassador to France should pressure the French to permit the British to join. Note that there still is considerable room for increased specificity in these action decisions. The specific communications have been left to the discretion of others. Notice also that the actions have yet to be performed — the ambassadors have yet to speak to their respective host governments. And the outcomes have yet to be observed — whether or not Britain becomes a member of the Common Market.

Another example is related to the Cuban missile crisis. Early in his administration, Kennedy made the policy decision to remove from the strategic arsenal those missiles vulnerable to a first strike. This led to a second policy decision that the liquid-fueled IRBM's installed in Europe should be phased out. To implement this policy decision, Kennedy made the action decision to remove American IRBM's from Turkey and directed the State Department to do so. However, the missiles remained in Turkey. At the time of the Cuban missile crisis, he personally discovered that foreign policy decisions, even a President's action decisions, often are poor predictors of governmental actions.

Despite the enormous time and effort which goes into the struggle over the decisions the President will make, in most cases the decisions which emerge are in no sense definitive. Often they are very general. They may be only statements of aspiration — vague policy decisions — or they may be somewhat more specific in that they assign a general action to a particular organization or individual. Even then, they are likely to leave considerable leeway as to who should act, what precisely they should do, and when they should do it. This is true for a number of reasons.

First, policymakers tend to assume that detailed instructions from them are unnecessary. Presidents, especially at the beginning of their terms, incline to think that what they order will be obeyed and obeyed faithfully. Hence, they believe, one needs only to give general direction and the decisions will be translated into effective actions. Even when Presidents learn that this is not true, they tend to feel that details are unimportant and that what really counts is the general thrust of policy.

Moreover, Presidents find that they lack the time and the expertise to draft detailed plans. When Kennedy ordered the blockade of Cuba in 1962, he left most of the details of implementation to the Navy. Until the British ambassador drew his attention to the fact, the President did not realize that the blockade had a much larger radius than he had intended, resulting in a sharp reduction of the time interval before Soviet vessels encountered United States ships.

Presidents also find that the legitimacy of providing great detail is questioned by operating agencies. These organizations assert that it is their responsibility to provide the detail, and they resist efforts by the President and by Cabinet officers to provide specifics. This is particularly true for the conduct of diplomatic negotiations and military operations. The Navy deeply resented Secretary McNamara's detailed questioning of its blockade procedures during the Cuban missile crisis and virtually expelled him from the Pentagon command post where the operation was being coordinated.

In some cases, generality and vagueness are used deliberately by the President. He may not want to be committed in great detail. He may see his decisions essentially as giving a hunting license to particular individuals to pursue a policy without having to commit himself to its effective implementation. In other cases, a President's compromise with his subordinates may prohibit him from spelling out in detail what he has decided. The compromise may be designed to gain adherence to a particular policy and to avoid harming the strongly felt interests of certain participants.

Presidents, as a rule, are likely to delay decisions on non-urgent matters in order to concentrate on pressing issues. They are also likely to decide as little as possible, leaving open the possibility of changing their position later. In many cases, this leads them to make narrow individual decisions on a number of different issues which come to them separately, even though an observer might feel that the decisions contradicted each other (or at least were not mutually supporting). Such a series of incremental, "minimal" decisions may culminate in what amounts to a major policy decision although no one of the decisions was made with this in view. The decision to support a crash program to develop and produce the hydrogen bomb is one such example. Similarly, the separate decisions taken in the days following the crossing of the 38th Parallel yielded an American commitment to defend South Korea although no single one of them necessarily implied that commitment.

Finally, Presidents frequently fear "leaks" and recognize that the more detail they give and the more they appear to be committed to a specific policy, the more likely somebody is to leak it. In international relations this reluctance to be explicit can lead to serious complications. For example, the Kennedy administration feared a serious adverse reaction from influential Congressmen if and when it announced the cancellation of Skybolt. This fear led the administration to be publicly vague and ambivalent about the program and prevented it from giving clear and explicit signals to the British regarding the missile's prospects. When cancellation finally was announced, many of the British felt they had been misled.

ACTIONS

Regardless of the motivation which leads to ambiguous decisions, the lack of complete specificity permits and often requires subordinates to exercise considerable discretion. To the extent that decisions allow discretion, they are poor predictors of governmental output; any analysis of the policy-making process that stops with decisions is incomplete. If we are to understand why a government behaves as it does, we must analyze what happens in the aftermath (or absence) of a Presidential decision.

Self-Executing Decisions

In most cases, once a President decides that some part of his government should do something, this decision is conveyed orally or in writing (in a non-public manner) to the official concerned, on occasion by the

President himself, but more likely by some member of the White House staff. This official in turn must draft implementing instructions to those who will actually do the work. Frequently this includes embassies and military commanders outside of Washington as well as subordinate officials in the major departments. Receipt of these instructions should theoretically result in the implementation of the actions which the President has decided upon. But at each stage of the process there are occasions for misunderstandings and mistakes and opportunities for discretion and non-compliance.

Opportunities for subordinate discretion are minimized and governmental outputs are most likely to resemble the President's intentions only in the severely restricted set of circumstances that permit the President to issue what Neustadt has called a "self-executing" order.[2] Such conditions require that the President's involvement in the process be unambiguous, that the decision which he makes be unambiguous, that his orders be widely publicized, that the men who receive it have control over everything and everyone needed to carry it out, and that they stand in no doubt of his authority to issue these orders.

Even in the absence of these ideal circumstances, other factors may induce an attempt at faithful compliance. The extent to which the government's actions implement Presidential decisions depends both on the willingness and ability of subordinates to fulfill the President's wishes and on the ability of the White House to check on subordinates' actions. Faithful compliance is most likely if it is relatively easy for the President to monitor actions or if there are known to be lower-ranking enthusiasts for the policy who are likely to monitor. The President's reputation for pressing for compliance and for punishing those who fail to obey is important in determining whether his decisions are loyally implemented. However, where those responsible for implementing the decision favor it and share the President's reasons for wanting to carry it out, they are likely to execute it faithfully regardless of the President's ability to detect and to punish disobedience.

The Struggle Over Implementation

But complete and faithful implementation of a Presidential decision remains the exception rather than the rule. More often than not, governmental outputs noticeably diverge from the President's expectations regarding the implementation of his decision. The gap between decision and follow-through results in part from the fact that compliance is not routinely forthcoming, particularly in cases where subordinates feel strongly about their positions and have a reasonable expectation of escaping detection and/or punishment. The gap results also in part from the fact that or-

---

[2] Richard E. Neustadt, *Presidential Power* (1960), p. 19.

ganizations are relatively inflexible instruments and that decisions frequently provide little or no guidance for action: even when there is a substantial effort to comply faithfully with a Presidential decision, there will be severe limits on "faithful compliance." Both forms of non-compliance — deliberate and inadvertent — derive from the fact that decisions are much more likely to be vague, ambiguous policy decisions than explicit, well-defined, self-executing action decisions.

One source of inadvertent non-compliance stems from the fact that the President himself may not know exactly what he wants done. A Presidential decision to consider seriously and sympathetically the recommendations of the Gaither Committee does not provide much guidance to his subordinates on how to react to its individual proposals. Moreover, those seeking to carry out the decision may not be aware of why and in what context the President decided as he did. In some cases, Presidents seek to keep this secret for fear of leaks or overcommitment. In other cases, a compromise may prevent them from making it known. But in any case, the gap between how the President looks at problems and how junior participants who are likely to carry out a decision see them produces a great divergence in their perceptions of the necessary details. In many cases, there simply will be confusion. Orders can be misinterpreted, misread, or not sent out; they can go to the wrong officials or to officials who will simply not understand that they are supposed to implement them.

In some cases, decisions may be conveyed to officials who have in the past been informed of other decisions which they see as incompatible. Hence their desire for faithful compliance with two directives may lead to a conflict causing them to alter what they have been told to do in one or both cases.

Finally, there will be important organizational constraints. When the action directed is a complicated one, it is carried out by an organization in ways that conform to one of the organization's existing plans of action. As Jones suggests, large organizations tend to be rigid, inflexible instruments incapable either of appreciating or implementing subtleties. As a result, execution may differ a good deal from what a President thought was going to be done.

Deliberate non-compliance derives from the fact that a Presidential decision does not end the conflict about what actions the United States should take. Participants still have very different interests, see different faces of the issues, have different stakes, and therefore have different notions as to what should be done. Because they see different aspects of the issue, they will interpret the decision differently and continue to fight the President's purpose, as well as his specific decisions. President Eisenhower discovered that his decision to cancel the atomic-powered airplane had little impact on the progress of the program. Indeed, he found himself making several decisions to terminate the project in the course of his administration.

Nevertheless, when Kennedy entered office in 1961, he was confronted with a program to develop a nuclear-powered aircraft.

Action games repeat many features of decision games. The action phase can become simply a new round in the process in which participants plan strategies, decide to opt in or out, and seek to find allies and overcome potential opponents. Those who favor the decision move to have it implemented as they want; those who oppose it try to block implementation. However, in this case, participants with responsibility for implementing the decision — primarily organizational participants — play a key role.

If deliberate non-compliance is possible, the key variable determining the degree of congruence between decision and action is whether or not the executors favor implementation. Albert Wohlstetter and the Rand study group on strategic bases apparently appreciated this fact. Since the Air Force would be responsible for implementation of the decisions the group favored, they made great efforts to win Air Force confidence and support for their recommendations. In fact, they did not go outside the Air Force to those officials formally responsible for approving the recommendations until the Air Force had adopted their report as its own. The Gaither Committee, on the other hand, seemingly gave only passing attention to designing its report to stimulate support among those participants who would be responsible for implementation.

In many cases, some or all of those who are supposed to implement a decision do not feel obliged to strive for faithful implementation. As Kennedy discovered during the Cuban missile crisis, his order that American IRBM's be removed from Turkey did not even lead to negotiations on their removal. In some cases, implementation may be overly zealous: those who receive a Presidential hunting license may carry the action further than the President intended. In other cases, those opposed to a policy fight back and seek a change in the Presidential decision or at least an exception for their organization. They may demand a meeting with the President; they may try to persuade other governments to protest the proposed action; or they may leak the information to the Congress or the press — all in the hope of reversing the decision.

Others opposed to a policy observe its letter but not its spirit. The 1970 Blue Ribbon Defense Panel's report on the reorganization of the Pentagon is replete with examples of how the intent of various legislation and successive reorganizations of the Defense Department has been circumvented. Efforts to reduce by law and regulation the impact of individual service perspectives on defense policy have been a failure.

Action in the Field

Although non-compliance occurs throughout the national security bureaucracy, a gap between decisions and actions is especially likely to be opened up by officials in the field — removed in time and distance from the President and senior participants in Washington. In general, compared with participants in Washington, officials in the field are even less willing to obey orders and less able to obey them faithfully, even when they choose to do so. They understand less of what the President wants and are less willing to respond. Not only do the actions of these participants highlight certain features of the process, but they often are the officials whose actions are most visible and most salient to foreign governments.

Officials in the field, particularly ambassadors and military commanders, tend to have a different perspective on issues than officials in Washington. They see these issues in terms of accomplishing their objectve — maintaining good relations with the local country or meeting their military responsibilities. They also tend to believe that Washington does not understand the problem, is out of touch with the realities of the situation in the local area, and does not respond properly to their suggestions, initiatives, and requests. Axelrod's interviews revealed that these field officials' suspicions may be essentially correct. Participants in Washington stated that those responsible for the Military Assistance Program in the field were relatively unimportant, when in fact Washington is dependent on the field for information, recommendations, and implementation. This underestimate of on-the-spot operations may also imply that Washington neglects to monitor their performance.

Participants in the field often have been only peripherally involved in the Washington decisions which they are asked to implement. Thus they are not fully informed about why the President decided what he did and the context in which he made that decision. In many cases, they are not sure whether indeed it was a Presidential decision, a Cabinet officer's decision, or a lower-level decision, since all cables come to them signed by the Secretary of State or the Secretary of Defense.

When confronted with decisions from Washington with which they do not agree, officials in the field engage in a number of different maneuvers. They may object to the proposed action, arguing that now is not the time to carry it out, or they may assert that it would be infeasible or counterproductive to do so. Alternatively, they may fail to do what they are ordered to do, in hope that Washington will not notice. In many cases this hope is justified. If they do feel the need to carry out the order, they may nevertheless depart from their instructions in a number of significant ways. For example, they may make a presentation to the host government in a very low key and yet report back that they made a major effort. It is possible that this is what Assistant Secretary Walter Robertson and Admiral Radford did when they went to Taiwan with instructions to persuade Chiang Kai-shek to withdraw from the Offshore Islands. Similarly, they may make the presentation to a different official than the one they were asked to consult — talking to a junior foreign ministry official, say, when they were supposed to talk to the head of government. Or they may simply do something other than what they were ordered to do and may or may not report what they have done back to Washington.

Actions need not be preceded by either policy decisions or action decisions. At times, officials in the field maneuver to accomplish their purposes in the absence of decisions from Washington. Instead of sending an issue to Washington for a decision, they may act without instructions. Alternatively, they may commit Washington to a policy by doing something in the field which forecloses the President's options. They may exploit visits to the area by high-level officials to get them to support their position, and then act as if there were now a commitment by the United States government. When they do consult Washington, they are likely to formulate messages along the lines of "Unless I hear to the contrary by a certain date, I will take a certain action." They count on the fact that Washington may be too busy or too preoccupied or too much in disagreement to send out a cable stopping them from taking the action that they propose to take.

Actions as System Outputs

The dominant bias in the American system is continuity. In the absence of some major disturbance which causes or allows them to change, officials, whether in the field or in Washington, will continue to do what they have been doing. Since continuity is the rule, our objective is to explain discontinuities.

Formal authority has some impact on what actions are taken, but even more important is control over resources and actual responsibility for implementation, as well as control over information regarding whether actions have in fact been carried out.

In those cases where a President does make a decision, the main thrust of what is done is generally in line with what the President orders. But the details stem largely from a combination of the objectives of the implementors and the constraints imposed by their organizations' repertoire of operating procedures. Where the line is drawn between general direction and specific detail will depend, not only on organizational constraints, but also on the President's interest and his willingness to commit his time and his public prestige.

A President has several options in seeking to increase the probability of compliance. He can, for example, utilize that organization or entity he thinks most likely to faithfully implement the decision. In many cases Presidents will send a White House official or private emissary to carry out diplomatic negotiations which they fear the State Department may not carry out faithfully or promptly. In other cases, they may create a whole new organization. Or they may create competition among existing organizations by assigning responsibility to more than one. In some cases, they will keep decisions or their reasons secret from those who might oppose the policy and who might leak the information to the press or Congress. However, in this case there is the dilemma that those who are not told of the policy are incapable of taking actions which will reinforce it.

The most effective Presidential weapon is personal involvement which demonstrates a willingness to be forceful and, if necessary, nasty. This personal involvement shows that the President cares, making it much harder for officials to resist doing what he has ordered. He can make an authoritative decision and, with the assistance of the White House staff, can monitor actions for compliance. When decisions are made in the name of senior participants other than the President, the frequency and degree of non-compliance will increase.

Just as the rules of the game bias decisions, they also bias actions by assigning responsibility for actions to particular organizations and individuals. The very existence of these organizations will affect the kinds of actions that are taken.

Actions also may change in the absence of any new policy decisions or action decisions. For example, changes in personnel may lead to changes in actions because a new official will interpret his instructions in a different way or will have a different set of interests than his predecessor.

In some cases, actions are taken deliberately by junior officials in an effort to present senior officials with a *fait accompli* or simply to carry out a policy on their own authority. On other occasions actions can be maneuvers designed to affect decisions. The Navy employed this maneuver when it decided on its own authority to develop a capability to make nuclear air attacks. Instead of seeking Presidential approval for such a program, the Navy confronted Truman with an already existing capability and merely requested funds to "improve" it.

Finally, actions may change in response to decisions made in other areas regarding ostensibly unrelated matters. For example, a decision to reduce the budget may imply changes in actions of which the decisionmaker was unaware.

INTERACTION AMONG NATIONS

Thus far, we have attempted to explain the process by which the American government makes foreign policy decisions and how this affects the actions of American officials. These foreign policy actions are designed to advance the national security interests of the United States as viewed by the participants. In some cases the actions are aimed at affecting the decisions and actions of other governments and hence are intended to affect outcomes — what happens in the world.

As was suggested in discussing interests, many of the objectives of each of the participants can be satisfied only at home. Political leaders of a nation rise and fall depending on whether they satisfy domestic needs. Individuals advance in the bureaucracy when they meet the standards set by political leaders or by career ladders. Organizations prosper or decline depending on the strength of their support in the bureaucracy and elsewhere within the nation. Such matters preoccupy participants in the foreign policy process. Perhaps because they are more immediate, threats to interests from rival organizations or from leading political groups seem much more real than threats from abroad.

Participants, of course, also bear national security interests in mind. No leader wants to see his nation attacked, and few desire to send their soldiers off to fight in distant wars. Some leaders are committed to a conception of world order. Several participants may have a wide range of interests beyond the borders of their nation. But whatever participants are concerned about, they are likely to see the battles as being won or lost mainly at home. This became obvious in the case of the Vietnam War.

It is not that actions of other nations do not matter, but rather that they matter mainly if and when they influence domestic and especially bureaucratic struggles. A participant's efforts to accomplish his objectives — whether to advance domestic political interests, organizational interests, personal interests, or national security interests — are sometimes affected by what he and other participants come to believe about the actions of other nations. A German Chancellor whose domestic position depends on his reputation for being able to get what the Federal Republic wants from the United States will be concerned about American actions that lead his colleagues and opponents to conclude that Washington no longer listens to him. An American President or Secretary of Defense who wishes to reduce defense spending will see that his position requires Soviet actions which permit him to argue that the nation's security can be protected with reduced forces. The Skybolt program was so crucial to the British government primarily because it was the heart of the Conservative Party's election pledge to maintain an independent nuclear deterrent.

Since actions by other nations can affect the stands that participants take, and thereby affect both decisions and outputs, we must consider how actions of other nations enter into the process of bargaining over decisions and actions. Therefore this next-to-last section of the Introduction outlines briefly the way in which the actions of officials in one nation are likely to affect the actions of officials in another.

In considering how actions of American officials affect the decisions and actions of foreign governments, we begin with the fact that other governments are, in at least one important respect, no different from the American government. They too consist of different participants with different interests and responsibilities who see different faces of an issue and struggle to get the decisions and actions they desire. As Neustadt shows in his comparison of the United States and Britain (see "White House and Whitehall," pp. 387 ff in the present volume), the relevant participants in other national security bureaucracies are not necessarily those officials with the same formal titles — function does not necessarily follow structure. But the communication between governments is not, as it is frequently painted, a dialogue between two rational individuals. Rather, actions of one government are simply one of the many elements that affect the struggle within the other over decisions and actions.

Nations affect the actions of one another less by physically compelling changes in behavior than by acting on one another's perceptions and expectations: interaction among nations is primarily a matter of threats, promises, and warnings designed to influence behavior by persuasion. Accordingly, the primary vehicle for the exercise of international influence takes the form of "signals" among international actors. Actions — the outputs of the national security bureaucracy — are the "signals," designed to persuade another nation to alter its behavior in the preferred direction. The bureaucratic perspective highlights the process of communication among nations.

Because the national security bureaucracy in any government is composed of a number of participants pursuing a wide range of objectives, individual participants not only have limited control over the sending of signals but also have relatively little control over which of their government's actions are recognized as signals and how they are interpreted. For the reasons discussed above, a significant proportion of a government's foreign policy actions are the result of activities whose primary objective is *not* to signal another international actor. Actions may simply be routine patterns of behavior carried on by large organizations. They may also be maneuvers in a decision game or actions by participants in the absence of decisions. Finally, they may be actions taken after a leader's decision but not related to influencing another nation. However, "signals" are, by their nature, in the eyes of the beholder. Many actions taken for bureaucratic or domestic objectives "leak" into the international arena and are interpreted as signals by participants in other national security bureaucracies. Not understanding the internal dynamics of the sender, being unable to distinguish between "deliberate" and "indeliberate" signals, seeking to maximize their information about an uncertain world and to secure the decisions and actions they desire, officials frequently offer mistaken or misleading interpretations of the actions of other nations.

Even when the sender is trying to communicate a signal, there are substantial barriers to clear and unambiguous transmission. First, the participant who designs a proposal intended to signal to another government is likely to put forward a signal which he knows to be less than optimally effective. This is because he has many objectives and must simultaneously address multiple audiences, both at home and abroad, besides the foreign government with which he is ostensibly communicating. He will be concerned about how the signal which he proposes to send will affect his own, more parochial interests.

Even when a participant is prepared to sacrifice his other objectives to the goal of sending a clear and unambiguous sign, that signal still is likely to be defective. As Jervis notes, individuals frequently fall victim to common misperceptions which lead them to overestimate the clarity of their communications. In particular, participants are inclined to believe that what is important to them is also important to the intended recipient of the message, that the latter share with the former the same background of concerns and information. They also tend to exaggerate the capabilities of recipients' intelligence organizations and assume that, when no effort has been made to conceal or distort, the signal will be clearly and completely received. Finally, the gap between decisions and actions means that carefully designing a signal does not insure that it will be accurately conveyed.

Complementary obstacles to clear communication exist in the national security bureaucracy of the intended recipient. Signals themselves will not routinely influence the behavior of officials of another nation. They ordinarily will affect behavior only if and when they are reported to senior participants by those, particularly in the foreign office or in the intelligence establishment, who are charged with observing, reporting, explaining, and predicting the actions of other nations. The observations of these individuals will be affected by the tendencies that all participants have to fit new information into existing attitudes and shared images. They will tend to notice what is consistent with their theories and to ignore the domestic and bureaucratic politics which shape the actions of another nation. The procedures of the organization, the ways in which it processes information, will affect what reaches senior participants, and when, as Graham Allison has shown in his analysis of the Cuban missile crisis (one of the readings gathered here, pp. 45 ff).

The barriers to communication described by Jervis are essentially technical obstacles. However, they are not the only impediments to effectively influencing behavior. The bureaucratic perspective which we have chosen for analyzing international affairs suggests that actions designed to persuade another government to alter its behavior will be effective primarily to the extent that they affect who is in power, the bargaining resources of the participants, the participants' perceptions of the face of the issue *they* confront, *their* stakes, and the appropriate stand. This implies that for a signal to be effective the sender must understand the bureaucratic politics of the recipient nation, must discover a participant in the latter whose own interests lead him to seek the decisions and actions the sender prefers, and must construct his action-signals so that the probability of the participant's success is increased.

For all these reasons, changes in the actions of one nation are quite likely to have unintended and unanticipated effects on the actions of others. Only very carefully designed strategies are likely to have any reasonable prospects for success. The concluding selection in this volume (pp. 419 ff), Richard Neustadt's memorandum to President Johnson on the Labour government's reaction to the proposal for the Multilateral Force, is a model for such a strategy, as well as astute policy advice.

Most of the approaches to the study of foreign policy and international politics emerge from compromises between the desire to generalize from findings and the desire to remain faithful to the intricacies of specific explanations. The bureaucratic perspective represents our calculation of the optimum trade-off. Much ink has been used in attempting to establish the "validity" of one approach or another, but "validity" is an inappropriate standard. Rather, the reader must ask himself which perspective supplies the most intuitively satisfying explanations and most accurate and complete predictions, i.e., which approach is the most useful and fruitful. Our judgment is apparent. We leave to the reader to decide whether we have been persuasive.

Part One
Overview

GRAHAM T. ALLISON

Conceptual Models and the Cuban Missile Crisis

The insights generated by the bureaucratic perspective as we have defined it are usefully demonstrated by comparing traditional analyses of familiar concepts and events with analyses which are sensitive to bureaucratic considerations. Graham Allison's landmark study of alternative conceptual models provides just such a demonstration.

Explanations, predictions, and policy evaluations are significantly influenced by the viewpoint of the analyst—the answers derived are largely dependent upon the questions asked. Because they assume that nations behave as unitary rational decisionmakers, most policy analysts (and even many advisers) devote little time and attention to the procedures and struggles which occur within the "black box" of the national security bureaucracy. However, as Allison shows, a shift of attention to the organizations and players that are part of that bureaucracy frequently yields explanations and predictions which differ from prescriptions derived from conventional perspectives. By illuminating the constraints on the President's freedom to decide, his dependence upon his nominal subordinates, as well as by emphasizing that particular government outputs may not reflect the exact intention of any single participant, including the President, the analytical approach to which we have given the rubric "bureaucratic perspective" constitutes a profitable supplement to other analytical approaches.

The Cuban missile crisis is a seminal event. For thirteen days of October 1962, there was a higher probability that more human lives would end suddenly than ever before in history. Had the worst occurred, the death of 100 million Americans, over 100 million Russians, and millions of Europeans as well would make previous natural calamities and inhumanities appear insignificant. Given the probability of disaster — which President Kennedy estimated as "between 1 out of 3 and even" — our escape seems awesome.[1] The event symbolizes a central, if only partially thinkable, fact about our existence. That such consequences could follow from the choices and actions of national governments obliges students of government as well as participants in governance to think hard about these problems.

Excerpted by the editors from the *American Political Science Review*, *63*, no. 3, (September 1969), pp. 689–718 by permission of the author and the American Political Science Association.

[1] Theodore Sorensen, *Kennedy* (1965), p. 705.

Improved understanding of this crisis depends in part on more information and more probing analyses of available evidence. To contribute to these efforts is part of the purpose of this study. But here the missile crisis serves primarily as grist for a more general investigation. This study proceeds from the premise that marked improvement in our understanding of such events depends critically on more self-consciousness about what observers bring to the analysis. What each analyst sees and judges to be important is a function not only of the evidence about what happened but also of the "conceptual lenses" through which he looks at the evidence. The principal purpose of this essay is to explore some of the fundamental assumptions and categories employed by analysts in thinking about problems of governmental behavior, especially in foreign and military affairs.

The general argument can be summarized in three propositions:

1. Analysts think about problems of foreign and military policy in terms of largely implicit conceptual models that have significant consequences for the content of their thought.[2]

Though the present product of foreign policy analysis is neither systematic nor powerful if one carefully examines explanations produced by analysts, a number of fundamental similarities emerge. Explanations produced by particular analysts display quite regular, predictable features. This predictability suggests a substructure. These regularities reflect an analyst's assumptions about the character of puzzles, the categories in which problems should be considered, the types of evidence that are relevant, and the determinations of occurrences. The first proposition is that clusters of such related assumptions constitute basic frames of reference or conceptual models in terms of which analysts both ask and answer the questions: What happened? Why did the event happen? What will happen?[3] Such assumptions are central to the activities of explanation and prediction, for in attempting to explain a particular event, the analyst cannot simply describe the full state of the world leading up to that event. The logic of explanation requires that he single out the relevant, important determinants of the occurrence. Moreover, as the logic of prediction underscores, the analyst must summarize the various determinants as they bear on the event in question. Conceptual models both fix the mesh of the nets that the analyst drags through the material in order to explain a particular

[2] In attempting to understand problems of foreign affairs, analysts engage in a number of related, but logically separable enterprises: (a) description, (b) explanation, (c) prediction, (d) evaluation, and (e) recommendation. This essay focuses primarily on explanation (and, by implication, prediction).

[3] In arguing that explanations proceed in terms of implicit conceptual models, this essay makes no claim that foreign policy analysts have developed any satisfactory, empirically tested theory. In this essay, the use of the term "model" without qualifiers should be read "conceptual scheme."

action or decision and direct him to cast his net in select ponds, at certain depths, in order to catch the fish he is after.

2. Most analysts explain (and predict) the behavior of national governments in terms of various forms of one basic conceptual model, here entitled the Rational Policy Model (Model I).[4]

In terms of this conceptual model, analysts attempt to understand happenings as the more or less purposive acts of unified national government. For these analysts, the point of an explanation is to show how the nation or government could have chosen the action in question, given the strategic problem that it faced. For example, in confronting the problem posed by the Soviet installation of missiles in Cuba, rational policy model analysts attempt to show how this was a reasonable act from the point of view of the Soviet Union, given Soviet strategic objectives.

3. Two "alternative" conceptual models, here labeled an Organizational Process Model (Model II) and a Bureaucratic Politics Model (Model III) provide a base for improved explanation and prediction.

Although the standard frame of reference has proved useful for many purposes, there is powerful evidence that it must be supplemented, if not supplanted, by frames of reference which focus upon the large organizations and political actors involved in the policy process. Model I's implication that important events have important causes, i.e., that monoliths perform large actions for big reasons, must be balanced by an appreciation of the facts (a) that monoliths are black boxes covering various gears and levers in a highly differentiated decisionmaking structure and (b) that large acts are the consequences of innumerable and often conflicting smaller actions by individuals at various levels of bureaucratic organizations in the service of a variety of only partially compatible conceptions of national goals, organizational goals, and political objectives. Recent developments in the field of organization theory provide the foundation for the second model. According to this organizational process model, what Model I categorizes as "acts" and "choices" are instead *outputs* of large organizations functioning according to certain regular patterns of behavior. Faced with the problem of Soviet missiles in Cuba, a Model II analyst identifies the relevant organizations and displays the patterns of organizational behavior from which this action emerged. The third model focuses on the internal politics of a government. Happenings in foreign affairs are understood, according to the bureaucratic politics model, neither as choices

---

[4] Earlier drafts of this argument have aroused heated arguments concerning proper names for these models. To choose names from ordinary language is to court confusion, as well as familiarity. Perhaps it is best to think of these models as I, II, and III.

nor as outputs. Instead, what happens is categorized as *outcomes* of various overlapping bargaining games among players arranged hierarchically in the national government. In confronting the problem posed by Soviet missiles in Cuba, a Model III analyst displays the perceptions, motivations, positions, power, and maneuvers of principal players from which the outcome emerged. . . .

The space available does not permit full development and support of such a general argument. Rather, the sections that follow simply sketch each conceptual model, articulate it as an analytic paradigm, and apply it to produce an explanation. But each model is applied to the same event: the U.S. blockade of Cuba during the missile crisis. These "alternative explanations" of the same happening illustrate differences among the models — *at work*.[5] A crisis decision, by a small group of men in the context of ultimate threat, this is a case of the rational policy model *par excellence*. The dimensions and factors that Models II and III uncover in this case are therefore particularly suggestive. The concluding section of this paper suggests how the three models may be related and how they can be extended to generate predictions.

MODEL I: RATIONAL POLICY

Rational Policy Model Illustrated

Where is the pinch of the puzzle raised by the *New York Times* over Soviet deployment of an anti-ballistic missile system? [6] The question, as the *Times* states it, concerns the Soviet Union's objective in allocating such large sums of money for this weapon system while at the same time seeming to pursue a policy of increasing détente. In President Johnson's words, "the paradox is that this [Soviet deployment of an anti-ballistic missile system] should be happening at a time when there is abundant evidence that our mutual antagonism is beginning to ease." [7] This question troubles people primarily because Soviet anti-ballistic missile deployment, and evidence of Soviet actions towards détente, when juxtaposed in our implicit model, produce a question. With reference to what objective could the Soviet government have rationally chosen the simultaneous pursuit of these two courses of actions? This question arises only when the analyst attempts to structure events as purposive choices of consistent actors.

---

[5] Each of the three "case snapshots" displays the work of a conceptual model as it is applied to explain the U.S. blockade of Cuba. But these three cuts are primarily exercises in hypothesis generation rather than hypothesis testing. Especially when separated from the larger study, these accounts may be misleading. The sources for these accounts include the full public record plus a large number of interviews with participants in the crisis.

[6] *New York Times*, February 18, 1967.

[7] *Ibid.*

How do analysts attempt to explain the Soviet emplacement of missiles in Cuba? The most widely cited explanation of this occurrence has been produced by two RAND Sovietologists, Arnold Horelick and Myron Rush.[8] They conclude that "the introduction of strategic missiles into Cuba was motivated chiefly by the Soviet leaders' desire to overcome . . . the existing large margin of U.S. strategic superiority.[9] How do they reach this conclusion? In Sherlock Holmes style, they seize several salient characteristics of this action and use these features as criteria against which to test alternative hypotheses about Soviet objectives. For example, the size of the Soviet deployment, and the simultaneous emplacement of more expensive, more visible intermediate-range missiles as well as medium-range missiles, it is argued, exclude an explanation of the action in terms of Cuban defense — since that objective could have been secured with a much smaller number of medium-range missiles alone. Their explanation presents an argument for one objective that permits interpretation of the details of Soviet behavior as a value-maximizing choice. . . .

Deterrence is the cardinal problem of the contemporary strategic literature. Thomas Schelling's *Strategy of Conflict* formulates a number of propositions focused upon the dynamics of deterrence in the nuclear age. One of the major propositions concerns the stability of the balance of terror: in a situation of mutual deterrence, the probability of nuclear war is reduced not by the "balance" (the sheer equality of the situation) but rather by the stability of the balance, i.e., the fact that neither opponent in striking first can destroy the other's ability to strike back.[10] How does Schelling support this proposition? Confidence in the contention stems not from an inductive canvass of a large number of previous cases but from two calculations. In a situation of "balance" but vulnerability, there are values for which a rational opponent could choose to strike first, e.g., to destroy enemy capabilities to retaliate. In a "stable balance" where, no matter who strikes first, each has an assured capability to retaliate with unacceptable damage, no rational agent could choose such a course of action (since that choice is effectively equivalent to choosing mutual homicide). Whereas most contemporary strategic thinking is driven *implicitly* by the motor upon which this calculation depends, Schelling explicitly recognizes that strategic theory does assume a model. The foundation of a theory of strategy is, he asserts: "the assumption of rational behavior — not just of intelligent behavior, but of behavior motivated by conscious calculation of advan-

[8] Arnold Horelick and Myron Rush, *Strategic Power and Soviet Foreign Policy* (1965). Based on A. Horelick, "The Cuban Missile Crisis: An Analysis of Soviet Calculations and Behavior," *World Politics* (April 1964). [Ellipses by Allison.]

[9] Horelick and Rush, *Strategic Power and Soviet Foreign Policy*, p. 154.

[10] Thomas Schelling, *The Strategy of Conflict* (1960), p. 232. This proposition was formulated earlier by A. Wohlstetter, "The Delicate Balance of Terror," *Foreign Affairs* (January 1959).

tages, calculation that in turn is based on an explicit and internally consistent value system.[11]

What is striking about these examples from the literature of foreign policy and international relations are the similarities among analysts of various styles when they are called upon to produce explanations. Each assumes that what must be explained is an action, i.e., the realization of some purpose or intention. Each assumes that the actor is the national government. Each assumes that the action is chosen as a calculated response to a strategic problem. For each, explanation consists of showing what goal the government was pursuing in committing the act and how this action was a reasonable choice, given the nation's objectives. This set of assumptions characterizes the rational policy model. . . .

Most contemporary analysts (as well as laymen) proceed predominantly — albeit most often implicitly — in terms of this model when attempting to explain happenings in foreign affairs. Indeed, that occurrences in foreign affairs are the *acts of nations* seems so fundamental to thinking about such problems that this underlying model has rarely been recognized: to explain an occurrence in foreign policy simply means to show how the government could have rationally chosen that action.[12] These brief examples illustrate five uses of the model. To prove that most analysts think largely in terms of the rational policy model is not possible. In this limited space it is not even possible to illustrate the range of employment of the framework. Rather, my purpose is to convey to the reader a grasp of the model and a challenge: let the reader examine the literature with which he is most familiar and make his judgment.

The general characterization can be sharpened by articulating the rational policy model as an "analytic paradigm" in the technical sense developed by Robert K. Merton for sociological analyses. . . . [13]

Rational Policy Paradigm

I. Basic Unit of Analysis: Policy as National Choice. Happenings in foreign affairs are conceived as actions chosen by the nation or national government. Governments select the action that will maximize strategic goals and objectives. These "solutions" to strategic problems are the fundamental categories in terms of which the analyst perceives what is to be explained.

---

[11] Schelling, *Strategy of Conflict*, p. 4.

[12] Sidney Verba's excellent essay "Assumptions of Rationality and Non-Rationality in Models of the International System" is less an exception than it is an approach to a somewhat different problem. Verba focuses upon models of rationality and irrationality of individual statesmen: in Klaus Knorr and Sidney Verba, *The International System* (1961).

[13] Robert K. Merton, *Social Theory and Social Structures* (rev. ed., 1957), pp. 12–16.

II. Organizing Concepts. A. National Actor. The nation or government, conceived as a rational, unitary decisionmaker, is the agent. This actor has one set of specified goals (the equivalent of a consistent utility function), one set of perceived options, and a single estimate of the consequences that follow from each alternative.

B. The Problem. Action is chosen in response to the strategic problem which the nation faces. Threats and opportunities arising in the "international strategic market place" move the nation to act.

C. Static Selection. The sum of activity of representatives of the government relevant to a problem constitutes what the nation has chosen as its "solution." Thus the action is conceived as a steady-state choice among alternative outcomes (rather than, for example, a large number of partial choices in a dynamic stream).

D. Action as Rational Choice. The components include:

1. Goals and Objectives. National security and national interests are the principal categories in which strategic goals are conceived. Nations seek security and a range of further objectives. (Analysts rarely translate strategic goals and objectives into an explicit utility function; nevertheless, analysts do focus on major goals and objectives and trade off side effects in an intuitive fashion.)

2. Options. Various courses of action relevant to a strategic problem provide the spectrum of options.

3. Consequences. Enactment of each alternative course of action will produce a series of consequences. The relevant consequences constitute benefits and costs in terms of strategic goals and objectives.

4. Choice. Rational choice is value-maximizing. The rational agent selects the alternative whose consequences rank highest in terms of his goals and objectives.

III. Dominant Inference Pattern. This paradigm leads analysts to rely on the following pattern of inference: if a nation performed a particular action, that nation must have had ends toward which the action constituted an optimal means. The rational policy model's explanatory power stems from this inference pattern. Puzzlement is relieved by revealing the purposive pattern within which the occurrence can be located as a value-maximizing means. . . .

The basic assumption of value-maximizing behavior produces propositions central to most explanations. The general principle can be formulated as follows: the likelihood of any particular action results from a combination of the nation's (1) relevant values and objectives, (2) perceived alternative courses of action, (3) estimates of various sets of consequences (which will follow from each alternative), and (4) net valuation of each set of consequences. . . .

The U.S. Blockade of Cuba: A First Cut [14]

The U.S. response to the Soviet Union's emplacement of missiles in Cuba must be understood in strategic terms as simple value-maximizing escalation. American nuclear superiority could be counted on to paralyze Soviet nuclear power; Soviet transgression of the nuclear threshold in response to an American use of lower levels of violence would be wildly irrational since it would mean virtual destruction of the Soviet Communist system and Russian nation. American local superiority was overwhelming: it could be initiated at a low level while threatening with high credibility an ascending sequence of steps short of the nuclear threshold. All that was required was for the United States to bring to bear its strategic and local superiority in such a way that American determination to see the missiles removed would be demonstrated, while at the same time allowing Moscow time and room to retreat without humiliation. The naval blockade — euphemistically named a "quarantine" in order to circumvent the niceties of international law — did just that.

The U.S. government's selection of the blockade followed this logic. Apprised of the presence of Soviet missiles in Cuba, the President assembled an Executive Committee (ExCom) of the National Security Council and directed them to "set aside all other tasks to make a prompt and intensive survey of the dangers and all possible courses of action.[15] This group functioned as "fifteen individuals on our own, representing the President and not different departments." [16] As one of the participants recalls, "The remarkable aspect of those meetings was a sense of complete equality." [17] Most of the time during the week that followed was spent canvassing all the possible tracks and weighing the arguments for and against each. Six major categories of action were considered.

1. Do nothing. U.S. vulnerability to Soviet missiles was no new thing. Since the U.S. already lived under the gun of missiles based in Russia, a Soviet capability to strike from Cuba too made little real difference. The real danger stemmed from the possibility of U.S. over-reaction. The U.S. should announce the Soviet action in a calm, casual manner thereby deflating whatever political capital Khrushchev hoped to make of the missiles.

This argument fails on two counts. First, it grossly underestimates the

---

[14] As stated in the introduction, this "case snapshot" presents, without editorial commentary, a Model I analyst's explanation of the U.S. blockade. The purpose is to illustrate a strong, characteristic rational policy model account. This account is (roughly) consistent with prevailing explanations of these events.

[15] Sorensen, *Kennedy,* p. 675.

[16] *Ibid.,* p. 679.

[17] *Ibid.*

military importance of the Soviet move. Not only would the Soviet Union's missile capability be doubled and the U.S. early warning system out-flanked. The Soviet Union would have an opportunity to reverse the strategic balance by further installations and indeed, in the longer run, to invest in cheaper, short-range rather than more expensive longer-range missiles. Second, the political importance of this move was undeniable. The Soviet Union's act challenged the American President's most solemn warning. If the U.S. failed to respond, no American commitment would be credible.

2. Diplomatic pressures. Several forms were considered: an appeal to the UN or OAS for an inspection team, a secret approach to Khrushchev, and a direct approach to Khrushchev, perhaps at a summit meeting. The United States would demand that the missiles be removed, but the final settlement might include neutralization of Cuba, U.S. withdrawal from the Guantanamo base, and withdrawal of U.S. Jupiter missiles from Turkey or Italy.

Each form of the diplomatic approach had its own drawbacks. To arraign the Soviet Union before the UN Security Council held little promise since the Russians could veto any proposed action. While the diplomats argued, the missiles would become operational. To send a secret emissary to Khrushchev demanding that the missiles be withdrawn would be to pose untenable alternatives. On the one hand, this would invite Khrushchev to seize the diplomatic initiative, perhaps committing himself to strategic retaliation in response to an attack on Cuba. On the other hand, this would tender an ultimatum that no great power could accept. To confront Khrushchev at a summit would guarantee demands for U.S. concessions, and the analogy between U.S. missiles in Turkey and Russian missiles in Cuba could not be erased.

But why not trade U.S. Jupiters in Turkey and Italy, which the President had previously ordered withdrawn, for the missiles in Cuba? The U.S. had chosen to withdraw these missiles in order to replace them with superior, less vulnerable Mediterranean Polaris submarines. But the middle of the crisis was no time for concessions. The offer of such a deal might suggest to the Soviets that the West would yield and thus tempt them to demand more. It would certainly confirm European suspicions about American willingness to sacrifice European interests when the chips were down. Finally, the basic issue should be kept clear. As the President stated in reply to Bertrand Russell, "I think your attention might well be directed to the burglars rather than to those who have caught the burglars.[18]

3. A secret approach to Castro. The crisis provided an opportunity to separate Cuba and Soviet Communism by offering Castro the alternatives "split or fall." But Soviet troops transported, constructed, guarded, and

---

[18] Elie Abel, *The Missile Crisis* (1966), p. 144.

controlled the missiles. Their removal would thus depend on a Soviet decision.

4. Invasion. The United States could take this occasion not only to remove the missiles but also to rid itself of Castro. A Navy exercise had long been scheduled in which Marines, ferried from Florida in naval vessels would liberate the imaginary island of Vieques.[19] Why not simply shift the point of disembarkment? (The Pentagon's foresight in planning this operation would be an appropriate antidote to the CIA's Bay of Pigs!)

Preparations were made for an invasion, but as a last resort. American troops would be forced to confront 20,000 Soviets in the first Cold War case of direct contact between the troops of the super powers. Such brinksmanship courted nuclear disaster, practically guaranteeing an equivalent Soviet move against Berlin.

5. Surgical air strike. The missile sites should be removed by a clean, swift conventional attack. This was the effective counter-action which the attempted deception deserved. A surgical strike would remove the missiles and thus eliminate both the danger that the missiles might become operational and the fear that the Soviets would discover the American discovery and act first.

The initial attractiveness of this alternative was dulled by several difficulties. First, could the strike really be "surgical"? The Air Force could not guarantee destruction of all the missiles.[20] Some might be fired during the attack; some might not have been identified. In order to assure destruction of Soviet and Cuban means of retaliating what was required was not a surgical but rather a massive attack — of at least 500 sorties. Second, a surprise air attack would of course kill Russians at the missile sites. Pressures on the Soviet Union to retaliate would be so strong that an attack on Berlin or Turkey was highly probable. Third, the key problem with this program was that of advance warning. Could the President of the United States, with his memory of Pearl Harbor and his vision of future U.S. responsibility, order a "Pearl Harbor in reverse"? For 175 years, unannounced Sunday morning attacks had been an anathema to our tradition.[21]

6. Blockade. Indirect military action in the form of a blockade became more attractive as the ExCom dissected the other alternatives. An embargo of military shipments to Cuba enforced by a naval blockade was not without flaws, however. Could the U.S. blockade Cuba without inviting Soviet reprisal in Berlin? The likely solution to joint blockades would be the lifting of both blockades, restoring the new status quo, and allowing the Soviets additional time to complete the missiles. Second, the possible

[19] *Ibid.*, p. 102.
[20] Sorensen, *Kennedy*, p. 684.
[21] *Ibid.*, p. 685. Though this was the formulation of the argument, the facts are not strictly accurate. Our tradition against surprise attack was rather younger than 175 years. For example President Theodore Roosevelt applauded Japan's attack on Russia in 1904.

consequences of the blockade resembled the drawbacks which qualified the air strike. If Soviet ships did not stop, the United States would be forced to fire the first shot, inviting retaliation. Third, a blockade would deny the traditional freedom of the seas demanded by several of our close allies and might be held illegal, in violation of the UN Charter and international law, unless the United States could obtain a two-thirds vote in the OAS. Finally, how could a blockade be related to the problem, namely, some 75 missiles on the island of Cuba, approaching operational readiness daily? A blockade offered the Soviets a spectrum of delaying tactics with which to buy time to complete the missile installations. Was a *fait accompli* not required?

In spite of these enormous difficulties, the blockade had comparative advantages: (1) It was a middle course between inaction and attack, aggressive enough to communicate firmness of intention, but nevertheless not so precipitous as a strike. (2) It placed on Khrushchev the burden of choice concerning the next step. He could avoid a direct military clash by keeping his ships away. His was the last clear chance. (3) No possible military confrontation could be more acceptable to the U.S. than a naval engagement in the Caribbean. (4) This move permitted the U.S., by flexing its conventional muscle, to exploit the threat of subsequent non-nuclear steps in each of which the U.S. would have significant superiority.

Particular arguments about advantages and disadvantages were powerful. The explanation of the American choice of the blockade lies in a more general principle, however. As President Kennedy stated in drawing the moral of the crisis:

> Above all, while defending our own vital interests, nuclear powers must avert those confrontations which bring an adversary to a choice of either a humiliating retreat or a nuclear war. To adopt that kind of course in the nuclear age would be evidence only of the bankruptcy of our policy—of a collective death wish for the world.[22]

The blockade was the United States' only real option.

MODEL II: ORGANIZATIONAL PROCESS

For some purposes, governmental behavior can be usefully summarized as action chosen by a unitary, rational decisionmaker: centrally controlled, completely informed, and value-maximizing. But this simplification must not be allowed to conceal the fact that a "government" consists of a conglomerate of semi-feudal, loosely allied organizations, each with a substantial life of its own. Government leaders do sit formally, and to some extent in fact, on top of this conglomerate. But governments perceive problems

---

[22] *New York Times,* June 11, 1963.

through organizational sensors. Governments define alternatives and estimate consequences as organizations process information. Governments act
as these organizations enact routines. Government behavior can therefore
be understood according to a second conceptual model, less as deliberate
choices of leaders and more as *outputs* of large organizations functioning
according to standard patterns of behavior.

To be responsive to a broad spectrum of problems, governments consist of large organizations among which primary responsibility for particular areas is divided. Each organization attends to a special set of problems
and acts in quasi-independence on these problems. But few important problems fall exclusively within the domain of a single organization. Thus
government behavior relevant to any important problem reflects the independent output of several organizations partially coordinated by government leaders. Government leaders can substantially disturb, but not
substantially control, the behavior of these organizations.

To perform complex routines, the behavior of large numbers of individuals must be coordinated. Coordination requires standard operating
procedures: rules according to which things are done. Assured capability
for reliable performance of action that depends upon the behavior of
hundreds of persons requires established "programs." Indeed, if the
eleven members of a football team are to perform adequately on any
particular down, each player must not "do what he thinks needs to be
done" or "do what the quarterback tells him to do." Rather, each player
must perform the maneuvers specified by a previously established play
which the quarterback has simply called in this situation.

At any given time, a government consists of existing organizations, each
with a fixed set of standard operating procedures and programs. The behavior of these organizations — and consequently of the government —
relevant to an issue in any particular instance is, therefore, determined
primarily by routines established in these organizations prior to that
instance. But organizations do change. Learning occurs gradually, over
time. Dramatic organizational change occurs in response to major crises.
Both learning and change are influenced by existing organizational
capabilities. . . .

Organizational Process Paradigm[23]

I. Basic Unit of Analysis: Policy as Organizational Output. The happenings of international politics are, in three critical senses, outputs of
organizational processes. First, the actual occurrences are organizational

---

[23] The formulation of this paradigm is indebted both to the orientation and insights
of Herbert Simon and to the behavioral model of the firm stated by Richard Cyert
and James March, *A Behavioral Theory of the Firm* (1963). Here, however, one is
forced to grapple with the less routine, less quantified functions of the less differentiated elements in government organizations.

outputs. For example, Chinese entry into the Korean War — that is, the fact that Chinese soldiers were firing at UN soldiers south of the Yalu in 1950 — is an organizational action: the action of men who are soldiers in platoons which are in companies, which in turn are in armies, responding as privates to lieutenants who are responsible to captains and so on to the commander, moving into Korea, advancing against enemy troops, and firing according to fixed routines of the Chinese Army. Government leaders' decisions trigger organizational routines. Government leaders can trim the edges of this output and exercise some choice in combining outputs. But the mass of behavior is determined by previously established procedures. Second, existing organizational routines for employing present physical capabilities constitute the effective options open to government leaders confronted with any problem. Only the existence of men equipped and trained as armies and capable of being transported to North Korea made entry into the Korean War a live option for the Chinese leaders. The fact that fixed programs (equipment, men, and routines which exist at the particular time) exhaust the range of buttons that leaders can push is not always perceived by these leaders. But in every case it is critical for an understanding of what is actually done. Third, organizational outputs structure the situation within the narrow constraints of which leaders must contribute their "decision" concerning an issue. Outputs raise the problem, provide the information, and make the initial moves that color the face of the issue that is turned to the leaders. As Theodore Sorensen has observed: "Presidents rarely, if ever, make decisions — particularly in foreign affairs — in the sense of writing their conclusions on a clean slate . . . The basic decisions, which confine their choices, have all too often been previously made." [24] If one understands the structure of the situation and the face of the issue —which are determined by the organizational outputs — the formal choice of the leaders is frequently anticlimactic.

II. Organizing Concepts. A. Organizational Actors. The actor is not a monolithic "nation" or "government" but rather a constellation of loosely allied organizations on top of which government leaders sit. This constellation acts only as component organizations perform routines.[25]

B. Factored Problems and Fractionated Power. Surveillance of the multiple facets of foreign affairs requires that problems be cut up and parceled out to various organizations. To avoid paralysis, primary power must accompany primary responsibility. But if organizations are permitted to

[24] Theodore Sorensen, "You Get To Walk to Work," *New York Times Magazine*, March 19, 1967. [Ellipsis by Sorensen.]

[25] Organizations are not monolithic. The proper level of disaggregation depends upon the objectives of a piece of analysis. This paradigm is formulated with reference to the major organizations that constitute the U.S. government. Generalization to the major components of each department and agency should be relatively straightforward.

do anything, a large part of what they do will be determined within the organization. Thus each organization perceives problems, processes information, and performs a range of actions in quasi-independence (within broad guidelines of national policy). Factored problems and fractional power are two edges of the same sword. Factoring permits more specialized attention to particular facets of problems than would be possible if government leaders tried to cope with these problems by themselves. But this additional attention must be paid for in the coin of discretion for *what* an organization attends to and *how* organizational responses are programmed.

C. Parochial Priorities, Perceptions, and Issues. Primary responsibility for a narrow set of problems encourages organizational parochialism. These tendencies are enhanced by a number of additional factors: (1) selective information available to the organization, (2) recruitment of personnel into the organization, (3) tenure of individuals in the organization, (4) small-group pressures within the organization, and (5) distribution of rewards by the organization. Clients (e.g., interest groups), government allies (e.g., Congressional committees), and extra-national counterparts (e.g., the British Ministry of Defense for the Department of Defense, ISA, or the British Foreign Office for the Department of State, EUR) galvanize this parochialism. Thus organizations develop relatively stable propensities concerning operational priorities, perceptions, and issues.

D. Action as Organizational Output. The pre-eminent feature of organizational activity is its programmed character: the extent to which behavior in any particular case is an enactment of pre-established routines. In producing outputs, the activity of each organization is characterized by:

1. Goals: Constraints Defining Acceptable Performance. The operational goals of an organization are seldom revealed by formal mandates. Rather, each organization's operational goals emerge as a set of constraints defining acceptable performance. Central among these constraints is organizational health, defined usually in terms of bodies assigned and dollars appropriated. The set of constraints emerges from a mix of expectations and demands of other organizations in the government, statutory authority, demands from citizens and special interest groups, and bargaining within the organization. These constraints represent a quasi-resolution of conflict — the constraints are relatively stable, so there is some resolution. But conflict among alternative goals is always latent; hence, it is a quasi-resolution. Typically, the constraints are formulated as imperatives to avoid roughly specified discomforts and disasters.[26]

[26] The stability of these constraints is dependent on such factors as rules for promotion and reward, budgeting and accounting procedures, and mundane operating procedures.

2. Sequential Attention to Goals. The existence of conflict among operational constraints is resolved by the device of sequential attention. As a problem arises, the subunits of the organization most concerned with that problem deal with it in terms of the constraints they take to be most important. When the next problem arises, another cluster of subunits deals with it, focusing on a different set of constraints.

3. Standard Operating Procedures. Organizations perform their "higher" functions, such as attending to problem areas, monitoring information, and preparing relevant responses for likely contingencies, by doing "lower" tasks — for example, preparing budgets, producing reports, and developing "hardware." Reliable performance of these tasks requires standard operating procedures (SOP's). Since procedures are "standard," they do not change quickly or easily. Without these standard procedures, it would not be possible to perform certain concerted tasks. But because of standard procedures, organizational behavior in particular instances often appears unduly formalized, sluggish, or inappropriate.

4. Programs and Repertoires. Organizations must be capable of performing actions in which the behavior of large numbers of individuals is carefully coordinated. Assured performance requires clusters of rehearsed SOP's for producing specific actions, e.g., fighting enemy units or answering an embassy's cable. Each cluster comprises a "program" (in the terms both of drama and computers) which the organization has available for dealing with a situation. The list of programs relevant to a type of activity, e.g., fighting, constitutes an organizational repertoire. The number of programs in a repertoire is always quite limited. When properly triggered, organizations execute programs; programs cannot be substantially changed in a particular situation. The more complex the action and the greater the number of individuals involved, the more important are programs and repertoires as determinants of organizational behavior.

5. Uncertainty avoidance. Organizations do not attempt to estimate the probability distribution of future occurrences. Rather, organizations avoid uncertainty. By arranging a *negotiated environment*, organizations regularize the reactions of other actors with whom they have to deal. The primary environment, relations with other organizations that comprise the government, is stabilized by such arrangements as agreed budgetary splits, accepted areas of responsibility, and established conventional practices. The secondary environment, relations with the international world, is stabilized between allies by the establishment of contracts (alliances) and "club relations" (U.S. State and U.K. Foreign Office or U.S. Treasury and U.K. Treasury). Between enemies, contracts and accepted conventional practices perform a similar function — for example, the rules of the "precarious status quo" which President Kennedy referred to in the missile crisis. Where the international environment cannot be negotiated, organizations

deal with remaining uncertainties by establishing a set of standard "scenarios" that constitute the contingencies for which they prepare. For example, the standard scenario for Tactical Air Command of the U.S. Air Force involves combat with enemy aircraft. Planes are designed and pilots trained to meet this problem. That these preparations are less relevant to more probable contingencies, e.g., provision of close-in ground support in limited wars like Vietnam, has had little impact on the scenario.

6. Problem-Directed Search. Where situations cannot be construed as standard, organizations engage in search. The style of search and the solution are largely determined by existing routines. Organizational search for alternative courses of action is problem-oriented: it focuses on the atypical discomfort that must be avoided. It is simple-minded: the neighborhood of the symptom is searched first; then, the neighborhood of the current alternative. Patterns of search reveal biases which in turn reflect such factors as specialized training or experience and patterns of communication.

7. Organizational Learning and Change. The parameters of organizational behavior mostly persist. In response to non-standard problems, organizations search and routines evolve, assimilating new situations. Thus learning and change follow in large part from existing procedures. But marked changes in organizations do sometimes occur. Conditions in which dramatic changes are more likely include: (1) Periods of budgetary feasts by purchasing additional items on the existing shopping list. Nevertheless, if committed to change, leaders who control the budget can use extra funds to effect changes. (2) Periods of prolonged budgetary famine. Though a single year's famine typically results in few changes in organizational structure but a loss of effectiveness in performing some programs, prolonged famine forces major retrenchment. (3) Dramatic performance failures. Dramatic change occurs (mostly) in response to major disasters. Confronted with an undeniable failure of procedures and repertoires, authorities outside the organization demand change, existing personnel are less resistant to change, and critical members of the organization are replaced by individuals committed to change.

E. Central Coordination and Control. Action requires decentralization of responsibility and power. But problems lap over the jurisdictions of several organizations. Thus the necessity for decentralization runs headlong into the requirement for coordination. (Advocates of one horn or the other of this dilemma — responsive action entails decentralized power vs. coordinated action requires central control — account for a considerable part of the persistent demand for government reorganization.) Both the necessity for coordination and the centrality of foreign policy to national welfare guarantee the involvement of government leaders in the procedures of the organizations among which problems are divided and power shared. Each organization's propensities and routines can be disturbed by government leaders' intervention. Central direction and persistent control of organizational activity, however, is not possible. The relation among organizations, and between organizations and the government leaders depends critically on a number of structural variables including: (1) the nature of the job, (2) the measures and information available to government leaders, (3) the system of rewards and punishments for organizational members, and (4) the procedures by which human and material resources get committed. For example, to the extent that rewards and punishments for the members of an organization are distributed by higher authorities, these authorities can exercise some control by specifying criteria in terms of which organizational output is to be evaluated. These criteria become constraints within which organizational activity proceeds. But constraint is a crude instrument of control. . . .

F. Decisions of Government Leaders. Organizational persistence does not exclude shifts in governmental behavior. For government leaders sit atop the conglomerate of organizations. Many important issues of governmental action require that these leaders decide what organizations will play out which programs where. Thus stability in the parochialisms and SOP's of individual organizations is consistent with some important shifts in the behavior of governments. The range of these shifts is defined by existing organizational programs.

III. Dominant Inference Pattern. If a nation performs an action of this type today, its organizational components must yesterday have been performing (or have had established routines for performing) an action only marginally different from this action. At any specific point in time, a government consists of an established conglomerate of organizations, each with existing goals, programs, and repertoires. The characteristics of a government's action in any instance follows from those established routines, and from the choice of government leaders — on the basis of information and estimates provided by existing routines — among existing programs. The best explanation of an organization's behavior at t is $t - 1$; the prediction of $t + 1$ is t. Model II's explanatory power is achieved by uncovering the organizational routines and repertoires that produced the outputs that comprise the puzzling occurrence.

IV. General Propositions. A number of general propositions have been stated above. In order to illustrate clearly the type of proposition employed by Model II analysts, this section formulates several more precisely.

A. Organizational Action. Activity according to SOP's and programs does not constitute far-sighted, flexible adaptation to "the issue" (as it is conceived by the analyst). Detail and nuance of actions by organizations are determined predominantly by organizational routines, not government leaders' directions.

1. SOP's constitute routines for dealing with *standard* situations. Routines allow large numbers of ordinary individuals to deal with numerous instances, day after day, without considerable thought, by responding to basic stimuli. But this regularized capability for adequate performance is purchased at the price of standardization. If the SOP's are appropriate, average performance, i.e., performance averaged over the range of cases, is better than it would be if each instance were approached individually (given fixed talent, timing, and resource constraints). But specific instances, particularly critical instances that typically do not have standard characteristics, are often handled sluggishly or inappropriately.

2. A program, i.e., a complex action chosen from a short list of programs in repertoire, is rarely tailored to the specific situation in which it is executed. Rather, the program is (at best) the most appropriate of the programs in a previously developed repertoire.

3. Since repertoires are developed by parochial organizations for standard scenarios defined by that organization, programs available for dealing with a particular situation are often ill-suited.

B. Limited Flexibility and Incremental Change. Major lines of organizational action are straight, i.e., behavior at one time is marginally different from that behavior at $t - 1$. Simpleminded predictions work best. Behavior at $t + 1$ will be marginally different from behavior at the present time.

1. Organizational budgets change incrementally — both with respect to totals and with respect to intra-organizational splits. Though organizations could divide the money available each year by carving up the pie anew (in the light of changes in objectives or environment), in practice, organizations take last year's budget as a base and adjust incrementally. Predictions that require large budgetary shifts in a single year between organizations or between units within an organization should be hedged.

2. Once undertaken, an organizational investment is not dropped at the point where "objective" costs outweigh benefits. Organizational stakes in adopted projects carry them quite beyond the loss point.

C. Administrative Feasibility. Adequate explanation, analysis, and prediction must include administrative feasibility as a major dimension. A considerable gap separates what leaders choose (or might rationally have chosen) and what organizations implement.

1. Organizations are blunt instruments. Projects that require several organizations to act with high degrees of precision and coordination are not likely to succeed.

2. Projects that demand that existing organizational units depart from

their accustomed functions and perform previously unprogrammed tasks are rarely accomplished in their designed form.

3. Government leaders can expect that each organization will do its "part" in terms of what the organization knows how to do.

4. Government leaders can expect incomplete and distorted information from each organization concerning its part of the problem.

5. Where an assigned piece of a problem is contrary to the existing goals of an organization, resistance to implementation of that piece will be encountered. . . .

The U.S. Blockade of Cuba: A Second Cut

Organizational Intelligence. At 7:00 P.M. on October 22, 1962, President Kennedy disclosed the American discovery of the presence of Soviet strategic missiles in Cuba, declared a "strict quarantine on all offensive military equipment under shipment to Cuba," and demanded that "Chairman Khrushchev halt and eliminate this clandestine, reckless, and provocative threat to world peace." [27] This decision was reached at the pinnacle of the U.S. government after a critical week of deliberation. What initiated that precarious week were photographs of Soviet missile sites in Cuba taken on October 14. These pictures might not have been taken until a week later. In that case, the President speculated, "I don't think probably we would have chosen as prudently as we finally did." [28] U.S. leaders might have received this information three weeks earlier — if a U-2 had flown over San Cristobal in the last week of September.[29] What determined the context in which American leaders came to choose the blockade was the discovery of missiles on October 14.

There has been considerable debate over alleged American "intelligence failures" in the Cuban missile crisis.[30] But what both critics and defenders have neglected is the fact that the discovery took place on October 14, rather than three weeks earlier or a week later, as a consequence of the established routines and procedures of the organizations which constitute the U.S. intelligence community. These organizations were neither more nor less successful than they had been the previous month or were to be in the months to follow.[31]

[27] U.S. Department of State, *Bulletin,* XLVII, pp. 715–720.

[28] Arthur Schlesinger, Jr., *A Thousand Days* (1965), p. 803.

[29] Sorensen, *Kennedy,* p. 675.

[30] See U.S. Congress, Senate, Committee on Armed Services, Preparedness Investigation Subcommittee, *Interim Report on Cuban Military Build-up,* 88th Cong., 1st sess., 1963, p. 2; Hanson Baldwin, "Growing Risks of Bureaucratic Intelligence," *Reporter* (August 15, 1963), pp. 48–50; Roberta Wohlstetter, "Cuba and Pearl Harbor," *Foreign Affairs* (July 1965), p. 706.

[31] U.S. Congress, House of Representatives, Committee on Appropriations, Subcommittee on Department of Defense Appropriations, *Hearings,* 88th Cong., 1st sess., 1963, pp. 25 ff.

The notorious "September estimate," approved by the United States Intelligence Board (USIB) on September 19, concluded that the Soviet Union would not introduce offensive missiles into Cuba.[32] No U-2 flight was directed over the western end of Cuba (after September 5) before October 4.[33] No U-2 flew over the western end of Cuba until the flight that discovered the Soviet missiles on October 14.[34] Can these "failures" be accounted for in organizational terms?

On September 19 when USIL met to consider the question of Cuba, the "system" contained the following information: (1) shipping intelligence had noted the arrival in Cuba of two large-hatch Soviet lumber ships, which were riding high in the water; (2) refugee reports of countless sightings of missiles, but also a report that Castro's private pilot, after a night of drinking in Havana, had boasted: "We will fight to the death, and perhaps we can win because we have everything, including atomic weapons"; (3) a sighting by a CIA agent of the rear profile of a strategic missile; (4) U-2 photos produced by flights of August 29, September 5 and 17 showing the construction of a number of SAM (surface-to-air missile) sites and other defensive missiles.[35] Not all of this information was on the desk of the estimators, however. Shipping intelligence experts noted the fact that large-hatch ships were riding high in the water and spelled out the inference: the ships must be carrying "space-consuming" cargo.[36] These facts were carefully included in the catalogue of intelligence concerning shipping. For experts sensitive to the Soviets' shortage of ships, however, these facts carried no special signal. The refugee report of Castro's private pilot's remark had been received at Opa Locka, Florida, along with vast reams of inaccurate reports generated by the refugee community. This report and a thousand others had to be checked and compared before being sent to Washington. The two weeks required for initial processing could have been shortened by a large increase in resources, but the yield of this source was already quite marginal. The CIA agent's sighting of the rear profile of a strategic missile had occurred on September 12; transmission time from agent sighting to arrival in Washington typically took 9 to 12 days. Shortening this transmission time would impose severe

[32] R. Hilsman, *To Move a Nation* (1967), pp. 172–173.

[33] Subcommittee on Department of Defense Appropriations, *Hearings,* p. 67.

[34] *Ibid.,* pp. 66–67.

[35] For (1) Hilsman, *op. cit.,* p. 186; (2) Abel, *op. cit.,* p. 24; (3) Department of Defense Appropriations, *Hearings,* p. 64; Abel, *op. cit.,* p. 24; (4) Department of Defense Appropriations, *Hearings,* pp. 1–30.

[36] The facts here are not entirely clear. This assertion is based on information from (1) "Deparment of Defense Briefing by the Honorable R. S. McNamara, Secretary of Defense, State Department Auditorium, 5:00 P.M., February 6, 1963" (a verbatim transcript of a presentation actually made by General Carroll's assistant, John Hughes), and (2) Hilsman's statement in *To Move a Nation,* p. 186. But see R. Wohlstetter's interpretation, "Cuba and Pearl Harbor," p. 700.

cost in terms of danger to sub-agents, agents, and communication networks.

On the information available, the intelligence chiefs who predicted that the Soviet Union would not introduce offensive missiles into Cuba made a reasonable and defensible judgment.[37] Moreover, in the light of the fact that these organizations were gathering intelligence not only about Cuba but about potential occurrences in all parts of the world, the informational base available to the estimators involved nothing out of the ordinary. Nor, from an organizational perspective, is there anything startling about the gradual accumulation of evidence that led to the formulation of the hypothesis that the Soviets were installing missiles in Cuba and the decision on October 4 to direct a special flight over western Cuba.

The ten-day delay between that decision and the flight is another organizational story.[38] At the October 4 meeting, the Defense Department took the opportunity to raise an issue important to its concerns. Given the increased danger that a U-2 would be downed, it would be better if the pilot were an officer in uniform rather than a CIA agent. Thus the Air Force should assume responsibility for U-2 flights over Cuba. To the contrary, the CIA argued that this was an intelligence operation and thus within the CIA's jurisdiction. Moreover, CIA U-2's had been modified in certain ways which gave them advantages over Air Force U-2's in averting Soviet SAM's. Five days passed while the State Department pressed for less risky alternatives such as drones [unmanned aircraft] and the Air Force (in Department of Defense guise) and CIA engaged in territorial disputes. On October 9 a flight plan over San Cristobal was approved by COMOR [Committee on Overhead Reconnaissance] but to the CIA's dismay, Air Force pilots rather than CIA agents would take charge of the mission. At this point details become sketchy, but several members of the intelligence community have speculated that an Air Force pilot in an Air Force U-2 attempted a high altitude overflight on October 9 that "flamed out," i.e., lost power, and thus had to descend in order to restart its engine. A second round between Air Force and CIA followed, as a result of which Air Force pilots were trained to fly CIA U-2's. A successful overflight took place on October 14.

This ten-day delay constitutes some form of "failure." In the face of well-founded suspicions concerning offensive Soviet missiles in Cuba that posed a critical threat to the United States' most vital interest, squabbling between organizations whose job it is to produce this information seems entirely inappropriate. But for each of these organizations, the questions

[37] See Hilsman, *To Move a Nation*, pp. 172–174.

[38] Abel, *Missile Crisis*, pp. 26 ff; Edward Weintal and Charles Bartlett, *Facing the Brink* (1967), pp. 62 ff; Preparedness Investigation Subcommittee, *Cuban Military Build-up*; J. Daniel and J. Hubbell, *Strike in the West* (1963), pp. 15 ff.

involved the issue: *"Whose* job was it to be?" Moreover, the issue was not simply which organization would control U-2 flights over Cuba but rather the broader issue of ownership of U-2 intelligence activities — a very long-standing territorial dispute. Thus though this delay was in one sense a "failure," it was also a nearly inevitable consequence of two facts; many jobs do not fall neatly into precisely defined organizational jurisdictions; and vigorous organizations are imperialistic.

Organizational Options. Deliberations of leaders in ExCom meetings produced broad outlines of alternatives. Details of these alternatives and blueprints for their implementation had to be specified by the organizations that would perform these tasks. These organizational outputs answered the question: What, specifically, *could* be done?

Discussion in the ExCom quickly narrowed the live options to two: an air strike and a blockade. The choice of the blockade instead of the air strike turned on two points: (1) the argument from morality and tradition that the United States could not perpetrate a "Pearl Harbor in reverse"; (2) the belief that a surgical air strike was impossible.[39] Whether the United States *might* strike first was a question not of capability but of morality. Whether the United States *could* perform the surgical strike was a factual question concerning capabilities. The majority of the members of the ExCom, including the President, initially preferred the air strike.[40] What effectively foreclosed this option, however, was the fact that the air strike they wanted could not be chosen with high confidence of success.[41] After having tentatively chosen the course of prudence — given that the surgical air strike was not an option — Kennedy reconsidered. On Sunday morning, October 21, he called the Air Force experts to a special meeting in his living quarters where he probed once more for the option of a *surgical* air strike.[42] General Walter C. Sweeny, Commander of Tactical Air Forces, asserted again that the Air Force could guarantee no higher than ninety percent effectiveness in a surgical air strike.[43] That "fact" was false.

The air strike alternative provides a classic case of military estimates. One of the alternatives outlined by the ExCom was named "air strike." Specification of the details of this alternative was delegated to the Air Force. Starting from an existing plan for massive U.S. military action against Cuba (prepared for contingencies like a response to a Soviet Berlin grab), Air Force estimators produced an attack to guarantee success.[44]

---

[39] Schlesinger, *A Thousand Days,* p. 804.
[40] Sorensen, *Kennedy,* p. 684.
[41] *Ibid.,* pp. 684 ff.
[42] *Ibid.,* pp. 694–697.
[43] *Ibid.,* p. 697; Abel, *Missile Crisis,* pp. 100–101.
[44] Sorensen, *Kennedy,* p. 669.

This plan called for extensive bombardment of all missile sites, storage depots, airports, and, in deference to the Navy, the artillery batteries opposite the naval base at Guantanamo.[45] Members of the ExCom repeatedly expressed bewilderment at military estimates of the number of sorties required, likely casualties, and collateral damage. But the "surgical" air strike that the political leaders had in mind was never carefully examined during the first week of the crisis. Rather, this option was simply excluded on the grounds that since the Soviet MRBM's in Cuba were classified "mobile" in U.S. manuals, extensive bombing was required. During the second week of the crisis, careful examination revealed that the missiles were mobile, in the sense that small houses are mobile: that is, they could be moved and reassembled in 6 days. After the missiles were reclassified "movable" and detailed plans for surgical air strikes specified, this action was added to the list of live options for the end of the second week.

Organizational Implementation. ExCom members separated several types of blockade: offensive weapons only, all armaments, and all strategic goods including POL (petroleum, oil, and lubricants). But the "*details*" of the operation were left to the Navy. Before the President announced the blockade on Monday evening the first stage of the Navy's blueprint was in motion, and a problem loomed on the horizon.[46] The Navy had a detailed plan for the blockade. The President had several less precise but equally determined notions concerning what should be done, when, and how. For the Navy the issue was one of effective implementation of the Navy's blockade — without the meddling and interference of political leaders. For the President, the problem was to pace and manage events in such a way that the Soviet leaders would have time to see, think, and blink.

A careful reading of available sources uncovers an instructive incident. On Tuesday the British ambassador, Ormsby-Gore, after having attended a briefing on the details of the blockade, suggested to the President that the plan for intercepting Soviet ships far out of reach of Cuban jets did not facilitate Khrushchev's hard decision.[47] Why not make the interception much closer to Cuba and thus give the Russian leader more time? According to the public account and the recollection of a number of individuals involved, Kennedy "agreed immediately, called McNamara, and over emotional Navy protest, issued the appropriate instructions." [48] As Sorensen records, "in a sharp clash with the Navy, he made certain his will

[45] Hilsman, *To Move a Nation*, p. 204.
[46] See Abel, *op. cit.*, pp. 97 ff.
[47] Schlesinger, *A Thousand Days*, p. 818.
[48] *Ibid.*

prevailed." [49] The Navy's plan for the blockade was thus changed by drawing the blockade much closer to Cuba.

A serious organizational orientation makes one suspicious of this account. More careful examination of the available evidence confirms these suspicions, though alternative accounts must be somewhat speculative. According to the public chronology, a quarantine drawn close to Cuba became effective on Wednesday morning, the first Soviet ship was contacted on Thursday morning, and the first boarding of a ship occurred on Friday. According to the statement by the Department of Defense, boarding of the *Marcula* by a party from the *John R. Pierce* "took place at 7:50 A.M., E.D.T., 180 miles northeast of Nassau." [50] The *Marcula* had been trailed since about 10:30 the previous evening.[51] Simple calculations suggest that the *Pierce* must have been stationed along the Navy's original arc which extended 500 miles out to sea from Cape Magsi, Cuba's easternmost tip.[52] The blockade line was *not* moved as the President ordered and the accounts report.

What happened is not entirely clear. One can be certain, however, that Soviet ships passed through the line along which American destroyers had posted themselves before the official "first contact" with the Soviet ship. On October 26 a Soviet tanker arrived in Havana and was honored by a dockside rally for "running the blockade." Photographs of this vessel show the name *Vinnitsa* on the side of the vessel in Cyrillic letters.[53] But according to the official U.S. position, the first tanker to pass through the blockade was the *Bucharest*, which was hailed by the Navy on the morning of October 25. Again simple mathematical calculation excludes the possibility that the *Bucharest* and the *Vinnitsa* were the same ship. It seems probable that the Navy's resistance to the President's order that the blockade be drawn in closer to Cuba forced him to allow one or several Soviet ships to pass through the blockade after it was officially operative.[54]

This attempt to leash the Navy's blockade had a price. On Wednesday morning, October 24, what the President had been awaiting occurred. The 18 dry-cargo ships heading towards quarantine stopped dead in the water. This was the occasion of Dean Rusk's remark, "We are eyeball to eyeball, and I think the other fellow just blinked." [55] But the Navy had another interpretation. The ships had simply stopped to pick up Soviet submarine escorts. The President became quite concerned lest the Navy —

[49] Sorensen, *Kennedy*, p. 710.
[50] *New York Times,* October 27, 1962.
[51] Abel, *Missile Crisis*, p. 171.
[52] For the location of the original arc, see *ibid.*, p. 141.
[53] *Facts on File*, XXII (1962), p. 376.
[54] This hypothesis would account for the mystery surrounding Kennedy's explosion at the leak of the stopping of the *Bucharest*. See Hilsman, *To Move a Nation*, p. 45.
[55] Abel, *Missile Crisis*, p. 153.

already riled because of Presidential meddling in its affairs — blunder into an incident. Sensing the President's fears, McNamara became suspicious of the Navy's procedures and routines for making the first interception. Calling on the Chief of Naval Operations in the Navy's inner sanctum, the Navy Flag Plot, McNamara put his questions harshly.[56] Who would make the first interception? Were Russian-speaking officers on board? How would submarines be dealt with? At one point McNamara asked Anderson what he would do if a Soviet ship's captain refused to answer questions about his cargo. Picking up the Manual of Navy Regulations the Navy man waved it in McNamara's face and shouted, "It's all in there." To which McNamara replied, "I don't give a damn what John Paul Jones would have done; I want to know what you are going to do, now.[57] The encounter ended on Anderson's remark: "Now, Mr. Secretary, if you and your Deputy will go back to your office, the Navy will run the blockade."[58]

MODEL III: BUREAUCRATIC POLITICS

The leaders who sit on top of organizations are not a monolithic group. Rather, each is, in his own right, a player in a central, competitive game. The name of the game is bureaucratic politics: bargaining along regularized channels among players positioned hierarchically within the government. Government behavior can thus be understood according to a third conceptual model not as organizational outputs, but as outcomes of bargaining games. In contrast with Model I, the bureaucratic politics model sees no unitary actor but rather many actors as players, who focus not on a single strategic issue but on many diverse intra-national problems as well, in terms of no consistent set of strategic objectives but rather according to various conceptions of national, organizational, and personal goals, making government decisions not by rational choice but by the pulling and hauling that is politics.

The apparatus of each national government constitutes a complex arena for the intra-national game. Political leaders at the top of this apparatus plus the men who occupy positions on top of the critical organizations form the circle of central players. Ascendancy to this circle assures some independent standing. The necessary decentralization of decisions required for action on the broad range of foreign policy problems guarantees that each player has considerable discretion. Thus power is shared.

The nature of problems of foreign policy permits fundamental disagreement among reasonable men concerning what ought to be done. Analyses yield conflicting recommendations. Separate responsibilities laid on the

[56] See *ibid*, pp. 154 ff.
[57] *Ibid.*, p. 156.
[58] *Ibid.*

shoulders of individual personalities encourage differences in perceptions and priorities. But the issues are of first order importance. What the nation does really matters. A wrong choice could mean irreparable damage. Thus responsible men are obliged to fight for what they are convinced is right.

Men share power. Men differ concerning what must be done. The differences matter. This milieu necessitates that policy be resolved by politics. What the nation does is sometimes the result of the triumph of one group over others. More often, however, different groups pulling in different directions yield a resultant distinct from what anyone intended. What moves the chess pieces is not simply the reasons which support a course of action, nor the routines of organizations which enact an alternative, but the power and skill of proponents and opponents of the action in question.

This characterization captures the thrust of the bureaucratic politics orientation. If problems of foreign policy arose as discrete issues, and decisions were determined one game at a time, this account would suffice. But most "issues," e.g., Vietnam or the proliferation of nuclear weapons, emerge piecemeal, over time, one lump in one context, a second in another. Hundreds of issues compete for players' attention every day. Each player is forced to fix upon his issues for that day, fight them on their own terms, and rush on to the next. Thus the character of emerging issues and the pace at which the game is played converge to yield government "decisions" and "actions" as collages. Choices by one player, outcomes of minor games, outcomes of central games, and "foul-ups" — these pieces, when stuck to the same canvas, constitute government behavior relevant to an issue.

The concept of national security policy as political outcome contradicts both public imagery and academic orthodoxy. Issues vital to national security, it is said, are too important to be settled by political games. They must be "above" politics. To accuse someone of "playing politics with national security" is a most serious charge. What public conviction demands, the academic penchant for intellectual elegance reinforces. Internal politics is messy; moreover, according to prevailing doctrine, politicking lacks intellectual content. As such, it constitutes gossip for journalists rather than a subject for serious investigation. Occasional memoirs, anecdotes in historical accounts, and several detailed case studies to the contrary, most of the literature of foreign policy avoids bureaucratic politics. The gap between academic literature and the experience of participants in government is nowhere wider than at this point.

Bureaucratic Politics Paradigm

I. Basic Unit of Analysis: Policy as Political Outcome. The decisions and actions of governments are essentially intra-national political outcomes: outcomes in the sense that what happens is not chosen as a solution to a problem but rather results from compromise, coalition, competition, and confusion among government officials who see different faces of an issue; political in the sense that the activity from which the outcomes emerge is best characterized as bargaining. . . . National behavior in international affairs can be conceived as outcomes of intricate and subtle, simultaneous, overlapping games among players located in positions, the hierarchical arrangement of which constitutes that government. These games proceed neither at random nor at leisure. Regular channels structure the game. Deadlines force issues to the attention of busy players. The moves in the chess game are thus to be explained in terms of the bargaining among players with separate and unequal power over particular pieces and with separable objectives in distinguishable subgames.

II. Organizing Concepts. A. Players in Positions. The actor is neither a unitary nation, nor a conglomerate of organizations, but rather a number of individual players. Groups of these players constitute the agent for particular government decisions and actions. Players are men in jobs.

Individuals become players in the national security policy game by occupying a critical position in an administration. For example, in the U.S. government the players include "Chiefs": the President, Secretaries of State, Defense, and Treasury, Director of the CIA, Joint Chiefs of Staff, and, since 1961, the Special Assistant for National Security Affairs;[59] "Staffers": the immediate staff of each Chief; "Indians": the political appointees and permanent government officials within each of the departments and agencies; and *"Ad Hoc* Players": actors in the wider government game (especially "Congressional Influentials"), members of the press, spokesmen for important interest groups (especially the "bipartisan foreign policy establishment" in and out of Congress), and surrogates for each of these groups. Other members of the Congress, press, interest groups, and public form concentric circles around the central arena — circles which demarcate the permissive limits within which the game is played.

Positions define what players both may and must do. The advantages and handicaps with which each player can enter and play in various games stems from his position. So does a cluster of obligations for the performance of certain tasks. The two sides of this coin are illustrated by the position of the modern Secretary of State. First, in form and usually in fact, he is the primary repository of political judgment on the political-

---

[59] Inclusion of the President's Special Assistant for National Secruity Affairs in the tier of "Chiefs" rather than among the "Staffers" involves a debatable choice. In fact he is both super-staffer and near-chief. His position has no statutory authority. He is especially dependent upon good relations with the President and Secretaries of Defense and State. Nevertheless, he stands astride a genuine action-channel. The decision to include this position among the Chiefs reflects my judgment that the Bundy function is becoming institutionalized.

military issues that are the stuff of contemporary foreign policy; consequently, he is a senior personal adviser to the President. Second, he is the colleague of the President's other senior advisers on the problems of foreign policy, the Secretaries of Defense and Treasury, and the Special Assistant for National Security Affairs. Third, he is the ranking U.S. diplomat for serious negotiation. Fourth, he serves as an administration voice to Congress, the country, and the world. Finally, he is "Mr. State Department" or "Mr. Foreign Office," "leader of officials, spokesman for their causes, guardian of their interests, judge of their disputes, superintendent of their work, master of their careers." [60] But he is not first one, and then the other. All of these obligations are his simultaneously. His performance in one affects his credit and power in the others. The perspective stemming from the daily work which he must oversee — the cable traffic by which his department maintains relations with other foreign offices — conflicts with the President's requirement that he serve as a generalist and coordinator of contrasting perspectives. The necessity that he be close to the President restricts the extent to which, and the force with which, he can front for his department. When he defers to the Secretary of Defense rather than fighting for his department's position — as he often must — he strains the loyalty of his officialdom. The Secretary's resolution of these conflicts depends not only upon the position but also upon the player who occupies the position.

For players are also people. Men's metabolisms differ. The core of the bureaucratic politics mix is personality. How each man manages to stand the heat in his kitchen, each player's basic operating style, and the complementarity or contradition among personalities and styles in the inner circles are irreducible pieces of the policy blend. Moreover, each person comes to his position with baggage in tow, including sensitivities to certain issues, commitments to various programs, and personal standing and debts with groups in the society.

B. Parochial Priorities, Perceptions, and Issues. Answers to the questions: "What is the issue?" and "What must be done?" are colored by the position from which the questions are considered. For the factors which encourage organizational parochialism also influence the players who occupy positions on top of (or within) these organizations. To motivate members of his organization, a player must be sensitive to the organization's orientation. The games into which the player can enter and the advantages with which he plays enhance these pressures. Thus propensities of perception stemming from position permit reliable prediction about a player's stances in many cases. But these propensities are filtered through

[60] Richard E. Neustadt, Testimony, United States Senate, Committee on Government Operations, Subcommittee on National Security Staffing, *Administration of National Security*, March 26, 1963, pp. 82–83 (88th Cong., 1st sess.).

the baggage which players bring to positions. Sensitivity to both the pressures and the baggage is thus required for many predictions.

C. Interests, Stakes and Power. Games are played to determine outcomes. But outcomes advance and impede each player's conception of the national interest, specific programs to which he is committed, the welfare of his friends, and his personal interests. These overlapping interests constitute the stakes for which games are played. Each player's ability to play successfully depends upon his power. Power, i.e., effective influence on policy outcomes, is an elusive blend of at least three elements: bargaining advantages (drawn from formal authority and obligations, institutional backing, constituents, expertise, and status), skill and will in using bargaining advantages, and other players' perceptions of the first two ingredients. Power wisely invested yields an enhanced reputation for effectiveness. Unsuccessful investment depletes both the stock of capital and reputation. Thus each player must pick the issues on which he can play with a reasonable probability of success. But no player's power is sufficient to guarantee satisfactory outcomes. Each player's needs and fears run to many other players. What ensues is the most intricate and subtle of games known to man.

D. The Problem and the Problems. "Solutions" to strategic problems are not derived by detached analysts focusing coolly on *the* problem. Instead, deadlines and events raise issues in games and demand decisions of busy players in contexts that influence the face the issue wears. The problems for the players are both narrower and broader than *the* strategic problem. For each player focuses not on the total strategic problem but rather on the decision that must be made now. But each decision has critical consequences not only for the strategic problem but for each player's organizational, reputational, and personal stakes. Thus the gap between the problems the player was solving and the problem upon which the analyst focuses is often very wide.

E. Action Channels. Bargaining games do not proceed randomly. Action channels, i.e., regularized ways of producing action concerning types of issues, structure the game by pre-selecting the major players, determining their points of entrance into the game, and distributing particular advantages and disadvantages for each game. Most critically, channels determine "who's got the action," that is, which department's Indians actually do whatever is chosen. Weapon procurement decisions are made within the annual budgeting process; embassies' demands for action cables are answered according to routines of consultation and clearance from State to Defense and White House; requests for instructions from military groups (concerning assistance all the time, concerning operations during war) are composed by the military in consultation with Defense, State, and White House; crisis responses are debated among White House, State,

Defense, CIA, and Ad Hoc players; major political speeches, especially by the President but also by other Chiefs, are cleared through established channels.

F. Action as Politics. Government decisions are made and government actions emerge neither as the calculated choice of a unified group nor as a formal summary of leaders' preferences. Rather the context of shared power but separate judgments concerning important choices determines that politics is the mechanism of choice. Note the *environment* in which the game is played: inordinate uncertainty about what must be done, the necessity that something be done, and crucial consequences of whatever is done. These features force responsible men to become active players. The *pace of the game* — hundreds of issues, numerous games, and multiple channels — compels players to fight to "get other's attention," to make them "see the facts," to assure that they "take the time to think seriously about the broader issue." The *structure of the game* — power shared by individuals with separate responsibilities — validates each player's feeling that "others don't see my problem" and "others must be persuaded to look at the issue from a less parochial perspective." The *rules of the game* — he who hesitates loses his chance to play at that point, and he who is uncertain about his recommendation is overpowered by others who are sure — pressure players to come down on one side of a 51-49 issue and play. The *rewards of the game* — effectiveness, i.e., impact on outcomes, as the immediate measure of performance — encourage hard play. Thus most players come to fight to "make the government do what is right." The strategies and tactics employed are quite similar to those formalized by theorists of international relations.

G. Streams of Outcomes. Important government decisions or actions emerge as collages composed of individual acts, outcomes of minor and major games, and foul-ups. Outcomes which could never have been chosen by an actor and would never have emerged from bargaining in a single game over the issue are fabricated piece by piece. Understanding of the outcome requires that it be disaggregated.

III. Dominant Inference Pattern. If a nation performed an action, that action was the *outcome* of bargaining among individuals and groups within the government. That outcome included *results* achieved by groups committed to a decision or action, *resultants* which emerged from bargaining among groups with quite different positions, and *foul-ups*. Model III's explanatory power is achieved by revealing the pulling and hauling of various players, with different perceptions and priorities, focusing on separate problems, which yielded the outcomes that constitute the action in question.

IV. General Propositions. 1. Action and Intention. Action does not presuppose intention. The sum of behavior of representatives of a government relevant to an issue was rarely intended by any individual or group. Rather separate individuals with different intentions contributed pieces which compose an outcome distinct from what anyone would have chosen.

2. Where you stand depends on where you sit.[61] Horizontally, the diverse demands upon each player shape his priorities, perceptions, and issues. For large classes of issues, e.g., budgets and procurement decisions, the stance of a particular player can be predicted with high reliability from information concerning his seat. In the notorious B-36 controversy, no one was surprised by Admiral Radford's testimony that "the B-36 under any theory of war, is a bad gamble with national security," as opposed to Air Force Secretary Symington's claim that "a B-36 with an A-bomb can destroy distant objects which might require ground armies years to take." [62]

3. Chiefs and Indians. The aphorism "where you stand depends on where you sit" has vertical as well as horizontal application. Vertically, the demands upon the President, Chiefs, Staffers, and Indians are quite distinct.

The foreign policy issues with which the President can deal are limited primarily by his crowded schedule: the necessity of dealing first with what comes next. His problem is to probe the special face worn by issues that come to his attention, to preserve his leeway until time has clarified the uncertainties, and to assess the relevant risks.

Foreign policy Chiefs deal most often with the hottest issue *de jour*, though they can get the attention of the President and other members of the government for other issues which they judge important. What they cannot guarantee is that "the President will pay the price" or that "the others will get on board." They must build a coalition of the relevant powers that be. They must "give the President confidence" in the right course of action.

Most problems are framed, alternatives specified, and proposals pushed, however, by Indians. Indians fight with Indians of other departments; for example, struggles between International Security Affairs of the Department of Defense and Political-Military of the State Department are a microcosm of the action at higher levels. But the Indian's major problem is how to get the *attention* of Chiefs, how to get an issue decided, how to get the government "to do what is right."

In policymaking then, the issue looking *down* is options: how to pre-

[61] This aphorism was stated first, I think, by Don K. Price.
[62] Paul Y. Hammond, "Super Carriers and B-36 Bombers," in Harold Stein (ed.), *American Civil-Military Decisions* (1963).

serve my leeway until time clarifies uncertainties. The issue looking *sideways* is commitment: how to get others committed to my coalition. The issue looking *upwards* is confidence: how to give the boss confidence in doing what must be done. To paraphrase one of Neustadt's assertions which can be applied down the length of the ladder, the essence of a responsible official's task is to induce others to see that what needs to be done is what their own appraisal of their own responsibilities requires them to do in their own interests. . . .

The U.S. Blockade of Cuba: A Third Cut

The Politics of Discovery. A series of overlapping bargaining games determined both the *date* of the discovery of the Soviet missiles and the *impact* of this discovery on the administration. An explanation of the politics of the discovery is consequently a considerable piece of the explanation of the U.S. blockade.

Cuba was the Kennedy administration's "political Achilles' heel." [63] The months preceding the crisis were also months before the Congressional elections, and the Republican Senatorial and Congressional Campaign Committee had announced that Cuba would be "the dominant issue of the 1962 campaign." [64] What the administration billed as a "more positive and indirect approach of isolating Castro from developing, democratic Latin America," Senators Keating, Goldwater, Capehart, Thurmond, and others attacked as a "do-nothing" policy.[65] In statements on the floor of the House and Senate, campaign speeches across the country and interviews and articles carried by national news media, Cuba — particularly the Soviet program of increased arms aid — served as a stick for stirring the domestic political scene.[66]

These attacks drew blood. Prudence demanded a vigorous reaction. The President decided to meet the issue head-on. The administration mounted a forceful campaign of denial designed to discredit critics' claims. The President himself manned the front line of this offensive, though almost all administration officials participated. In his news conference on August 19, President Kennedy attacked as "irresponsible" calls for an invasion of Cuba, stressing rather "the totality of our obligations" and promising to "watch what happens in Cuba with the closest attention." [67] On September 4, he issued a strong statement denying any provocative Soviet action in Cuba.[68] On September 13 he lashed out at "loose talk" calling for an

---

[63] Sorensen, *Kennedy*, p. 670.
[64] *Ibid.*
[65] *Ibid.*, pp. 670 ff.
[66] *New York Times*, August, September, 1962.
[67] *New York Times*, August 20, 1962.
[68] *New York Times*, September 5, 1962.

invasion of Cuba.[69] The day before the flight of the U-2 which discovered the missiles, he campaigned in Capehart's Indiana against those "self-appointed generals and admirals who want to send someone else's sons to war." [70]

On Sunday, October 14, just as a U-2 was taking the first pictures of Soviet missiles, McGeorge Bundy was asserting:

> I *know* that there is no present evidence, and I think that there is no present likelihood that the Cuban government and the Soviet government would, in combination, attempt to install a major offensive capability.[71]

In this campaign to puncture the critics' charges, the administration discovered that the public needed positive slogans. Thus Kennedy fell into a tenuous semantic distinction between "offensive" and "defensive" weapons. This distinction originated in his September 4 statement that there was no evidence of "offensive ground-to-ground missiles" and warned "were it to be otherwise, the gravest issues would arise." [72] His September 13 statement turned on this distinction between "defensive" and "offensive" weapons and announced a firm commitment to action if the Soviet Union attempted to introduce the latter into Cuba.[73] Congressional committees elicited from administration officials testimony which read this distinction and the President's commitment into the *Congressional Record.*[74]

What the President least wanted to hear, the CIA was most hesitant to say plainly. On August 22 John McCone met privately with the President and voiced suspicions that the Soviets were preparing to introduce offensive missiles into Cuba.[75] Kennedy heard this as what is was: the suspicion of a hawk. McCone left Washington for a month's honeymoon on the Riviera. Fretting at Cap Ferrat, he bombarded his deputy, General Marshall Carter, with telegrams, but Carter, knowing that McCone had informed the President of his suspicions and received a cold reception, was reluctant to distribute these telegrams outside the CIA.[76] On September 9 a U-2 "on loan" to the Chinese Nationalists was downed over main-

---

[69] *New York Times*, September 14, 1962.

[70] *New York Times*, October 14, 1962.

[71] Cited by Abel, *Missile Crisis*, p. 13.

[72] *New York Times*, September 5, 1962.

[73] *New York Times*, September 14, 1962.

[74] Senate Foreign Relations Committee; Senate Armed Services Committee; House Committee on Appropriation; House Select Committee on Export Control.

[75] Abel, *Missile Crisis*, pp. 17–18. According to McCone, he told Kennedy, "The only construction I can put on the material going into Cuba is that the Russians are preparing to introduce offensive missiles." See also Weintal and Bartlett, *Facing the Brink*, pp. 60–61.

[76] Abel, *Missile Crisis*, p. 23.

land China.[77] The Committee on Overhead Reconnaissance (COMOR) convened on September 10 with a sense of urgency.[78] Loss of another U-2 might incite world opinion to demand cancellation of U-2 flights. The President's campaign against those who asserted that the Soviets were acting provocatively in Cuba had begun. To risk downing a U-2 over Cuba was to risk chopping off the limb on which the President was sitting. That meeting decided to shy away from the western end of Cuba (where SAM's were becoming operational) and modify the flight pattern of the U-2s in order to reduce the probability that a U-2 would be lost.[79] USIB's unanimous approval of the September estimate reflects similar sensitivities. On September 13 the President had asserted that there were no Soviet offensive missiles in Cuba and committed his administration to act if offensive missiles were discovered. Before Congressional committees, administration officials were denying that there was any evidence whatever of offensive missiles in Cuba. The implications of a National Intelligence estimate which concluded that the Soviets were introducing offensive missiles into Cuba were not lost on the men who constituted America's highest intelligence assembly.

The October 4 COMOR decision to direct a flight over the western end of Cuba in effect "overturned" the September estimate, but without officially raising that issue. The decision represented McCone's victory for which he had lobbied with the President before the September 10 decision, in telegrams before the September 19 estimate, and in person after his return to Washington. Though the politics of the intelligence community is closely guarded, several pieces of the story can be told.[80] By September 27, Colonel Wright and others in DIA believed that the Soviet Union was placing missiles in the San Cristobal area.[81] This area was marked suspicious by the CIA on September 29 and certified top priority on October 3. By October 4 McCone had the evidence required to raise the issue officially. The members of COMOR heard McCone's argument but were reluctant to make the hard decision he demanded. The significant probability that a U-2 would be downed made overflight of western Cuba a matter of real concern.[82]

The Politics of Issues. The U-2 photographs presented incontrovertible evidence of Soviet offensive missiles in Cuba. This revelation fell upon

---

[77] *New York Times*, September 10, 1962.

[78] See Abel, *op. cit.*, pp. 25–26; and Hilsman, *To Move a Nation*, p. 174.

[79] Department of Defense Appropriations, *Hearings*, p. 69.

[80] A basic but somewhat contradictory account of parts of this story emerges, *Ibid.*, pp. 1–70.

[81] Department of Defense Appropriations, *Hearings*, p. 71.

[82] The details of the 10 days between the October 4 decision and the October 14 flight must be held in abeyance.

politicized players in a complex context. As one high official recalled, Khrushchev had caught us "with our pants down." What each of the central participants saw, and what each did to cover both his own and the administration's nakedness, created the spectrum of issues and answers.

At approximately 9:00 A.M., Tuesday morning, October 16, McGeorge Bundy went to the President's living quarters with the message: "Mr. President, there is now hard photographic evidence that the Russians have offensive missiles in Cuba." [83] Much has been made of Kennedy's "expression of surprise." [84] but "surprise" fails to capture the character of his initial reaction. Rather, it was one of startled anger, most adequately conveyed by the exclamation: "He can't do that to *me!*" [85] In terms of the President's attention and priorities at that moment, Khrushchev had chosen the most unhelpful act of all. Kennedy had staked his full Presidential authority on the assertion that the Soviets would not place offensive weapons in Cuba. Moreover, Khrushchev had assured the President through the most direct and personal channels that he was aware of the President's domestic political problem and that nothing would be done to exacerbate this problem. The Chairman had *lied* to the President. Kennedy's initial reaction entailed action. The missiles must be removed.[86] The alternatives of "doing nothing" or "taking a diplomatic approach" could not have been less relevant to *his* problem.

These two tracks — doing nothing and taking a diplomatic approach — were the solutions advocated by two of his principal advisers. For Secretary of Defense McNamara, the missiles raised the spectre of nuclear war. He first framed the issue as a straightforward strategic problem. To understand the issue, one had to grasp two obvious but difficult points. First, the missiles represented an inevitable occurrence: narrowing of the missile gap. It simply happened sooner rather than later. Second, the United States could accept this occurrence since its consequences were minor: "seven-to-one missile 'superiority,' one-to-one missile 'equality,' one-to-seven missile 'inferiority' — the three postures are identical." McNamara's statement of this argument at the first meeting of the ExCom was summed up in the phrase, "a missile is a missile." [87] "It makes no great difference," he maintained, "whether you are killed by a missile from the Soviet Union or Cuba." [88] The implication was clear. The United States should not initiate a crisis with the Soviet Union, risking a significant probability of nuclear war over an occurrence which had such small strategic implications.

[83] Abel, *Missile Crisis*, p. 44.
[84] *Ibid.*, pp. 44 ff.
[85] See Richard Neustadt, "Afterword," *Presidential Power* (1964).
[86] Sorensen, *Kennedy*, p. 676; Schlesinger, *A Thousand Days*, p. 801.
[87] Hilsman, *To Move a Nation*, p. 195.
[88] *Ibid.*

The perceptions of McGeorge Bundy, the President's Assistant for National Security Affairs, are the most difficult of all to reconstruct. There is no question that he initially argued for a diplomatic track.[89] But was Bundy laboring under his acknowledged burden of responsibility in Cuba I? Or was he playing the role of devil's advocate in order to make the President probe his own initial reaction and consider other options?

The President's brother, Robert Kennedy, saw most clearly the political wall against which Khrushchev had backed the President. But he, like McNamara, saw the prospect of nuclear doom. Was Khrushchev going to force the President to an insane act? At the first meeting of the ExCom, he scribbled a note, "Now I know how Tojo felt when he was planning Pearl Harbor."[90] From the outset he searched for an alternative that would prevent the air strike.

The initial reaction of Theodore Sorensen, the President's Special Counsel and "alter ego," fell somewhere between that of the President and his brother. Like the President, Sorensen felt the poignancy of betrayal. If the President had been the architect of the policy which the missiles punctured, Sorensen was the draftsman. Khrushchev's deceitful move demanded a strong counter-move. But like Robert Kennedy, Sorensen feared lest the shock and disgrace lead to disaster.

To the Joint Chiefs of Staff the issue was clear. *Now* was the time to do the job for which they had prepared contingency plans. Cuba I had been badly done; Cuba II would not be. The missiles provided the *occasion* to deal with the issue: cleansing the Western Hemisphere of Castro's Communism. As the President recalled on the day the crisis ended, "An invasion would have been a mistake — a wrong use of our power. But the military are mad. They wanted to do this. It's lucky for us that we have McNamara over there."[91]

McCone's perceptions flowed from his confirmed prediction. As the Cassandra of the incident, he argued forcefully that the Soviets had installed the missiles in a daring political probe which the United States must meet with force. The time for an air strike was now."[92]

The Politics of Choice. The process by which the blockade emerged is a story of the most subtle and intricate probing, pulling, and hauling; leading, guiding, and spurring. Reconstruction of this process can only be tentative. Initially the President and most of his advisers wanted the clean, surgical air strike. On the first day of the crisis, when informing Stevenson of the missiles, the President mentioned only two alternatives: "I suppose

---

[89] Weintal and Bartlett, *Facing the Brink*, p. 67; Abel, *Missile Crisis*, p. 53.
[90] Schlesinger, *A Thousand Days*, p. 803.
[91] *Ibid.*, p. 831.
[92] Abel, *op. cit.*, p. 186.

the alternatives are to go in by air and wipe them out, or to take other steps to render them inoperable." [93] At the end of the week a sizeable minority still favored an air strike. As Robert Kennedy recalled: "The fourteen people involved were very significant. . . . If six of them had been President of the U.S., I think that the world might have been blown up." [94] What prevented the air strike was a fortuitous coincidence of a number of factors — the absence of any one of which might have permitted that option to prevail.

First, McNamara's vision of holocaust set him firmly against the air strike. His initial attempt to frame the issue in strategic terms struck Kennedy as particularly inappropriate. Once McNamara realized that the name of the game was a strong response, however, he and his deputy Gilpatric chose the blockade as a fallback. When the Secretary of Defense — whose department had the action, whose reputation in the Cabinet was unequaled, in whom the President demonstrated full confidence — marshaled the arguments for the blockade and refused to be moved, the blockade became a formidable alternative.

Second, Robert Kennedy — the President's closest confidant — was unwilling to see his brother become a "Tojo." His arguments against the air strike on moral grounds struck a chord in the President. Moreover, once his brother had stated these arguments so forcefully, the President could not have chosen his initially preferred course without, in effect, agreeing to become what RFK had condemned.

The President learned of the missiles on Tuesday morning. On Wednesday morning, in order to mask our discovery from the Russians, the President flew to Connecticut to keep a campaign commitment, leaving RFK as the unofficial chairman of the group. By the time the President returned on Wednesday evening, a critical third piece had been added to the picture. McNamara had presented his argument for the blockade. Robert Kennedy and Sorensen had joined McNamara. A powerful coalition of the advisers in whom the President had the greatest confidence, and with whom his style was most compatible, had emerged.

Fourth, the coalition that had formed behind the President's initial preference gave him reason to pause. *Who* supported the air strike — the Chiefs, McCone, Rusk, Nitze, and Acheson — as much as *how* they supported it, counted. Fifth, a piece of inaccurate information, which no one probed, permitted the blockade advocates to fuel (potential) uncertainties in the President's mind. When the President returned to Washington Wednesday evening, RFK and Sorensen met him at the airport. Sorensen gave the President a four-page memorandum outlining the areas of agree-

93 *Ibid.*, p. 49.
94 Interview, quoted by Ronald Steel, *New York Review of Books*, March 13, 1969, p. 22.

ment and disagreement. The strongest argument was that the air strike simply could not be surgical.[95] After a day of prodding and questioning, the Air Force had asserted that it could not guarantee the success of a surgical air strike limited to the missiles alone.

Thursday evening, the President convened the ExCom at the White House. He declared his tentative choice of the blockade and directed that preparations be made to put it into effect by Monday morning.[96] Though he raised a question about the possibility of a surgical air strike subsequently, he seems to have accepted the experts' opinion that this was no live option.[97] (Acceptance of this estimate suggests that he may have learned the lesson of the Bay of Pigs — "Never rely on experts" — less well than he supposed.) [98] But this information was incorrect. That no one probed this estimate during the first week of the crisis poses an interesting question for further investigation.

A coalition, including the President, thus emerged from the President's initial decision that something had to be done: McNamara, Robert Kennedy, and Sorensen's resistance to the air strike; incompatibility between the President and the air-strike advocates; and an inaccurate piece of information.[99]

CONCLUSION

. . . The preliminary, partial paradigms presented here provide a basis for serious re-examination of many problems of foreign and military policy. Model II and Model III cuts at problems typically treated in Model I terms can permit significant improvements in explanation and prediction.[100] Full Model II and III analyses require large amounts of information. But even in cases where the information base is severely limited, improvements are possible. Consider the problem of predicting Soviet strategic forces. In the mid-1950's, Model I calculations led to predictions that the Soviets would rapidly deploy large numbers of long-range bombers. From a Model II perspective, both the frailty of the Air Force within the Soviet military establishment and the budgetary implications of such a buildup would have led analysts to hedge this prediction. Moreover, Model II would have pointed to a sure, visible indicator of such a buildup: noisy struggles among the Services over major budgetary shifts. In the late

[95] Sorensen, *Kennedy*, p. 686.
[96] *Ibid.*, p. 691.
[97] *Ibid.*, pp. 691–692.
[98] Schlesinger, *A Thousand Days*, p. 296.
[99] Space will not permit an account of the path from this coalition to the formal government decision on Saturday and action on Monday.
[100] A number of problems are now being examined in these terms both in the Bureaucracy Study Group on Bureaucracy and Policy of the Institute of Politics at Harvard University and at the Rand Corporation.

1950's and early 1960's, Model I calculations led to the prediction of immediate, massive Soviet deployment of ICBM's. Again a Model II cut would have reduced this number because in the earlier period strategic rockets were controlled by the Soviet ground forces rather than an independent service, and in the later period, this would have necessitated massive shifts in budgetary splits. Today, Model I considerations lead many analysts both to recommend that an agreement not to deploy ABM's be a major American objective in upcoming strategic negotiations with the USSR, and to predict success. From a Model II vantage point, the existence of an ongoing Soviet ABM program, the strength of the organization (National Air Defense) that controls ABM's and the fact that an agreement to stop ABM deployment would force the virtual dismantling of this organization make a viable agreement of this sort much less likely. A Model III cut suggests that (a) there must be significant differences among perceptions and priorities of Soviet leaders over strategic negotiations, (b) any agreement will affect some players' power bases, and (c) agreements that do not require extensive cuts in the sources of some major players' power will prove easier to negotiate and more viable.

The present formulation of paradigms is simply an initial step. As such it leaves a long list of critical questions unanswered. Given any action, an imaginative analyst should always be able to construct some rationale for the government's choice. By imposing, and relaxing, constraints on the parameters of rational choice (as in variants of Model I) analysts can construct a large number of accounts of any act as a rational choice. But does a statement of reasons why a rational actor would choose an action constitute an explanation of the *occurrence* of that action? How can Model I analysis be forced to make more systematic contributions to the question of the determinants of occurrences? Model II's explanation of t in terms of $t - 1$ is explanation. The world is contiguous. But governments sometimes make sharp departures. Can an organizational process model be modified to suggest where change is likely? Attention to organizational change should afford greater understanding of why particular programs and SOP's are maintained by identifiable types of organizations and also how a manager can improve organizational performance. Model III tells a fascinating "story." But its complexity is enormous, the information requirements are often overwhelming, and many of the details of the bargaining may be superfluous. How can such a model be made parsimonious? The three models are obviously not exclusive alternatives. Indeed the paradigms highlight the partial emphasis of the framework — what each emphasizes and what it leaves out. Each concentrates on one class of variables, in effect, relegating other important factors to a *ceteris paribus* clause. Model I concentrates on "market factors": pressures and incentives created by the "international strategic market place." Models II and III focus on the internal mechanism of the government that chooses in this environment. But can these relations be more fully specified? Adequate synthesis would require a typology of decisions and actions, some of which are more amenable to treatment in terms of one model and some to another. Government behavior is but one cluster of factors relevant to occurrences in foreign affairs. Most students of foreign policy adopt this focus (at least when explaining and predicting). Nevertheless, the dimensions of the chess board, the character of the pieces, and the rules of the game — factors considered by international systems theorists — constitute the context in which the pieces are moved. Can the major variables in the full function of determinants of foreign policy outcomes be identified? . . .

HENRY A. KISSINGER

Bureaucracy and Policymaking: The Effects of Insiders and Outsiders on the Policy Process

In the following essay, written before he became President Nixon's national security adviser, Henry Kissinger affirms "that there is no such thing as an American foreign policy" and "that if one wants to understand what the government is likely to do, one has to understand the bureaucratics of the problems." Kissinger's description of foreign policy decisionmaking stresses that the "decisions" which are observed are in fact either the output of semi-autonomous organizations within the foreign policy bureaucracy or the outcome of interaction among these organizations. He observes that the ostensible decisionmakers are unlikely to become involved in an issue unless and until there is conflict among the component organizations. Senior players, who are usually short-term political appointees, frequently are insensitive to the bureaucratic realities of foreign policy decisionmaking. They share, with most outsiders, the mistaken belief that persuading the President to issue an order is all that is required to change policies and actions. The result is either that they are ineffective or that they are actually exploited by their formal subordinates.

An awareness of the "bureaucratics" of foreign policy decisionmaking also places the role and function of outside advisers in a new light. As Kissinger notes, the utility of outsiders lies less in their ability to generate fresh and exciting proposals than in the simple fact that their advocacy of a particular policy does not necessarily involve them in the bureaucratic

Reprinted from Henry A. Kissinger and Bernard Brodie, *Bureaucracy, Politics, and Strategy,* Security Studies Paper No. 17, (Los Angeles: University of California Security Studies Project, 1968), pp. 1–14, by permission of the authors.

battle. That is, serious bureaucrats are inclined to view outside advisers less as wise men than as a potent resource to be used in their own intra-bureaucratic maneuvers and arguments.

This role of outside advisers makes them vulnerable to the same fate as Kissinger's policy planners: being thought irrelevant, harmless, and not to be taken seriously. A comparison of the experiences of two groups of outsiders—the Gaither Committee and the Rand Corporation (pp. 275 ff.)— illuminates the bureaucratic process and supplies important clues to the sources of effectiveness for outsiders in the foreign policy process.

The most frequent question that one is asked when abroad, or by people who are concerned with international affairs and have not seen policy made, is "What is American policy?" Foreign policy is additionally complicated in the contemporary period by the fact that the actual decision-making process leads to a fragmentation of the decisions. Also, research and intelligence organizations, either foreign or national, attempt to give a rationality and consistency to foreign policy which it simply does not have. I have found it next to impossible to convince Frenchmen that there is no such thing as an American foreign policy, and that a series of moves that have produced a certain result may not have been planned to produce that result.

Foreigners looking at American policy have a tendency to assume that anything that happened was intended and that there is a deep, complicated purpose behind our actions. I wish this were true, but I don't believe that it is. In fact, I think that in any large bureaucracy it probably cannot be true, and this is probably the case with the Soviet Union also. We probably ascribe more consistency to Soviet foreign policy than really exists. The only foreign country which I believe has understood American policy making at all well is Great Britain. Most foreign countries that deal with us wait until we have done something and then try to prove to us that what we have done is either illegal or undesirable.

Once the American decision-making process has disgorged an answer, it becomes technically very difficult to change the policy because even those who have serious doubts about it become reluctant to hazard those doubts in an international forum. There is no telling what would come out of a re-evaluation of existing measures. If one wishes to influence American foreign policy, the time to do so is in the formative period, and the level is the middle level of the bureaucracy — that of the assistant secretary and his immediate advisers. That is the highest level in which people can still think. Above that, the day to day operation of the machine absorbs most of the energy, and the decisions that are made depend very much on internal pressures of the bureaucracy. Great Britain seems to me to have correctly identified this and attempts to influence us through a whole set of personal relationships. This does not prevent such things as the Skybolt Affair and others, so it is not an infallible process, but the British system works better than that of any other foreign country.

Why is it so difficult to change policy? Part of the reason is mechanical, and part of it seems to me to be psychological. The mechanical reason is that as the bureaucracy becomes large and complex, more time is devoted to running its internal management than in divining the purpose which it is supposed to serve. The two things tend to merge in the minds of the top decisionmakers.

When I first started advising at high levels of the government in the early days of the Kennedy Administration, I had the illusion that all I had to do was walk into the President's office, convince him I was right, and he would then naturally do what I had recommended. There were a number of things wrong with this view. Most of the people who advise the President are plausible, so he constantly sees individuals who sound very convincing. His time is so budgeted and the pressures on him are so great that it is almost impossible for him to know whether he should listen to one convincing individual or the other.

Also, even if by chance I persuaded him that his whole bureaucracy was wrong and I was right, he would then have the next problem of going about implementing what had been suggested. And that is not a negligible issue. There is only so much that even the President can do against the wishes of the bureaucracy, not because the bureaucracy would deliberately sabotage him but because every difficult issue is a closed one. The easy decisions are made at subordinate levels. A closed issue is characterized by the fact that the pros and cons seem fairly evenly divided and/or because the execution really depends on certain nuances of application. Unless you can get the willing support of your subordinates, simply giving an order does not get very far.

I have reason to believe, for example, that after the Nassau meeting President Kennedy intended to extend to France the same sort of consideration that had been given to Britain at Nassau. Indeed, he was prepared to put France into the same position, with some nuclear assistance as well, since that formal offer would not have meant anything unless France had some help on its nuclear warheads. It is also clear that the State Department and certain groups in the Defense Department were opposed to this. In order not to force this issue, President Kennedy kept his intention relatively vague. Why fight the State Department before you even know what de Gaulle will accept? There existed a wide margin within which the State Department people could operate in interpreting their directives, not because they were deliberately trying to undermine the President's intentions, but because they sincerely did not understand his intention. Certainly, one of the contributing factors to the failure of our post-Nassau diplomacy was the fact that while presidential emissaries were saying one thing to the French, State Department embassies were saying something else to other European countries. Leaving aside the question of whether Kennedy's intention was correct, one can nevertheless illustrate the difficulty that even a president can encounter when moving in a certain direction without the willing and perhaps even enthusiastic support of most of his bureaucracy.

When the bureaucracy is as large and fragmented as it is, decisions do not get made until they appear as an administrative issue. One cannot convince a high level official that he has a problem until it appears unambiguously in the form of an administrative conflict. There is no such thing, in my view, as a Vietnam policy; there is a series of programs of individual agencies concerned with Vietnam. These programs are reconciled or not, as the case may be, if there is a conflict between the operating agencies. In the areas where there is no conflict between agencies, it would be very unusual to get a high level consideration of a problem. When conflict exists, the environment becomes receptive. For example, when General Westmoreland asked for 200,000 troops, that forced a high level review. But the day to day operations of a war or of an alliance diplomacy will not generally engage the President and the Secretary of State.

In the late 1950s it was axiomatic among my colleagues that the United States was lacking a sense of national purpose, though in the early 1960s this was remedied. The top officials are too busy to deal with anything except the several thousand cables that arrive in Washington every day. Typically, they are too busy to plan ahead. Planning involves conjectures about the future and hypothetical cases. They are so busy with actual cases that they are reluctant to take on theoretical ones. As an illustration: in 1963 or 1964 the Policy Planning Staff of the State Department produced a long document about American national purposes which somebody leaked to the Senate Foreign Committee. That Committee subsequently called Secretary of State Rusk to testify about this document. That was the first time that Mr. Rusk had ever read it, and his feelings are easy to imagine. This is the typical fate of policy planning in the State Department. In my experience I do not recall a single instance in which, when a decision had to be made at a high level, a policy planning paper was discussed or a member of the policy planning staff was asked to join. I report this as an empirical fact. I don't believe it has happened in the Vietnamese war at all.

I think most policy planning staffs in our government are created as sops to administrative theory and spend their time projecting the familiar into the future. They are not used for real innovation or even for developing criteria by which one can judge progress properly. This creates considerable rigidities. The executives become extremely conscious of the morale of their staffs.

Modern policy makers face a problem which is quite unique. I recently wrote an article about the foreign policy of Bismarck and discovered in the process that the German Foreign Office in the 1870's had exactly four permanent officials, roughly the scale at which all foreign offices operated at the turn of the century. It would never have occurred to any cabinet minister as late as the outbreak of World War II that he knew less about his problems than his subordinates. Yet, in the contemporary world, policy makers have to make decisions on a range of issues in which they may not give many hours to the same problems that their experts have spent years studying. This creates a congenital insecurity and a quest for administrative consensus behind which executives take refuge. It also leads to a situation in which, rather than the executives using the bureaucracy, the opposite may be true: the bureaucracy often tries to use the executives. I think the history of the MLF is a good example.

Our governmental process works reasonably well in relation to specific technical issues and also when there is an adversary procedure. If one department is strongly for something and another department opposed, then the President or cabinet officer has a chance of elaborating an overall purpose. The system goes awry if you have a small, dedicated, unopposed group. I would argue that the MLF was put over by five or six highly motivated, highly intelligent individuals, in a government where a considerable number of people were indifferent and nobody was really opposed. The process by which it was done involved, at least in its early phases, a fairly deliberate manipulation by the bureaucracy of the senior executives.

For example, sentences were put into a Presidential speech which in themselves were perfectly sensible, but the full import of which was perhaps not understood. These were then used to start study groups which were subsequently used to present a new claim for a little more progress, and so on until the point where the prestige of the United States had become heavily committed to something the implications of which, in my judgment, had never been submitted to the adversary procedure. No systematic case was made for the opposition to the MLF during the most formative period of the relevant U.S. policy.

Because of this gap between expertise and decision making, a great deal of communication occurs by means of a briefing. Now, briefings reward theatrical qualities. They put a premium on the ability to package information and to present a fore-ordained result. Every briefer worth his salt says, "Interrupt me at any point with a question." Usually the victim of the briefing is very proud if he can formulate a question. The briefer has heard the question a hundred times before, and it is like throwing a fast ball across the middle of the plate to Mickey Mantle. He gives a glib response which is overwhelming. All this creates a state of mind where the policymaker may have the uneasy feeling of knowing he is being taken, even though he doesn't quite know how. This magnifies the sense of insecurity.

Because management of the bureaucracy takes so much energy and precisely because changing course is so difficult, many of the most important decisions are taken by extra-bureaucratic means. Some of the key decisions are kept to a very small circle while the bureaucracy happily continues working away in ignorance of the fact that decisions are being made, or the fact that a decision is being made in a particular area. One reason for keeping the decisions to small groups is that when bureaucracies are so unwieldy and when their internal morale becomes a serious problem, an unpopular decision may be fought by brutal means, such as leaks to the press or to congressional committees. Thus, the only way secrecy can be kept is to exclude from the making of the decision all those who are theoretically charged with carrying it out. There is, thus, small wonder for the many allegations of deliberate sabotage of certain American efforts, or of great cynicism of American efforts because of inconsistent actions. In the majority of cases this was due to the ignorance of certain parts of the bureaucracy, rather than to malevolent intent. Another result is that the relevant part of the bureaucracy, because it is being excluded from the making of a particular decision, continues with great intensity sending out cables, thereby distorting the effort with the best intentions in the world. You cannot stop them from doing this because you do not tell them what is going on.

Now, finally, this explains why sometimes outsiders can play an influential role. In the majority of cases, the outsider will say nothing that the bureaucracy has not already developed on the inside. The most frequent question that one is asked, if one is a consultant in Washington, is: "Have you had any new ideas lately?" This notion that foreign policy consists in constantly sparking new ideas, as if constant originality is the essence of foreign policy, is in itself open to question. I do not believe that de Gaulle is a considerable statesman because he comes up with a new thought every Thursday. Most ideas that masquerade as new ideas in Washington have been around for quite a long time. The utility of the outsider is that he can inject at a higher level certain ideas that have been around. He is not part of the bureaucratic battle. He is not a problem person whom the decision-maker has to placate. He can be listened to without the implications that are almost inseparable from listening to the bureaucracy. One corollary conclusion I would draw is that the outside adviser should never advise unless his opinion is asked, and he should get out as soon as it is delivered. When he himself becomes an advocate of his policies, that is, as soon as he becomes a bureaucratic problem, he loses his effectiveness, and he is gradually degraded to the level of other bureaucrats.

The tendencies which seem to me to be inherent in the nature of modern bureaucracy tend to be compounded in the United States by the particular cast of mind of our top policy makers, many of whom come from the legal profession. Lawyers are notoriously reluctant to take on hypothetical cases. All planning involves hypothetical cases and therefore there is a tendency among the legal professionals to deal with problems on their merits.

Secondly, the lawyers and some of our business executives are comfortable only with adversary proceedings; without them, they don't know how to guide policy. In the areas where I have seen American negotiations being carried out, I do not recall a detailed negotiating position ever existing before a date for the conference was set. And this reluctance to spell out what we are after is due to the fact that professional negotiators want to see what the other side has to offer before they commit themselves. Therefore, in periods of preliminary diplomacy, our position is very rigid and tough, but this changes rapidly when a negotiator has been appointed because he acts as spokesman for the other side. It is not his problem to worry about the overall picture. He worries about the success of the negotiations, and you make the negotiations succeed by taking very seriously into account what the other side has to say. Therefore, one notices a tendency in American foreign policy to spasms of rigidity and spasms of tactical flexibility.

Another group that deserves mention is the business executives whom Secretary McNamara excluded to some extent. They have the conviction that their special skill consists in making decisions between administratively produced proposals on the basis of some general rule of thumb or a strong will. Within the government they lack the familiar framework of the experience they have accumulated over a long period with their businesses. They become as often prisoners of the bureaucracy as its leaders.

In all of these observations I must consider Secretary McNamara as an exception — a man of unusual intelligence, toughness of mind, and long range conceptions. In his case, however, a number of very serious problems existed. One was a very curious bent for theoretical combat which would allow him to leave no stupid argument go unchallenged, even if no practical conclusion followed from it. Secondly, he had a tendency to want to be right at all times and to be so far superior to most people with whom he was arguing that he would win even without fully convincing them. I feel that Secretary McNamara gained control over procurement and over procurement-type decisions in the Pentagon at the eventual cost of losing control over major policy decisions. He lost control over these because he not only unified the Defense Department (which is one of his great achievements) but he also managed to unify the military services in a common dislike of the sort of control he was exercising, so that for the first time the civilians were confronted with unified JCS views on most policy issues. As long as the JCS remained divided, a certain element of civilian choice existed, but when they became united and started seeing every issue theologically as defending their special prerogative, McNamara's profundity in analysis had to give way to a very practical problem: how many times a month could he go to the mat with the JCS? He had to decide very deliberately which issues he could confront them with. If one wants to explain why it is that McNamara's theories about the war in Vietnam were not always matched by implementation, especially toward the end, the primary reason was that he felt that confronted with issues of ABM, troop deployment, force levels, renewal of the strategic force, and Vietnam strategy, he could only handle so many of these cases simultaneously. He picked those which he thought were crucial at the moment. Therefore, McNamara does not illustrate the general observations with which I started, but he nevertheless shows that it is not enough to be in charge of a Department. The management of the bureaucracy does tend to play a very large role.

[Dr. Kissinger's remarks were followed by a question and answer period which is reprinted below.]

COMMENT: I think your indictment of Mr. McNamara is correct, but too narrow. The problem with Mr. McNamara is that he lacks an appreciation of the unifying influence of theory (be it political, mathematical, or economic) and he deals too much in the concrete. This is his flaw, but let us give him his due. What he did in one year was change the war plan of the United States, communicate this unequivocally to our allies, who found it a magnificent reinforcement of our commitment abroad, and assert command over the most stubborn parts of the military bureaucracy.

MR. KISSINGER: Let me comment briefly. I did not mean to say that McNamara addressed himself only to procurement. McNamara, in the nature of the decisions that had to be taken during the first four years of his being in office, addressed himself primarily to general doctrinal issues and to putting some sense and order into the problem of force levels of the various services. He did this with extraordinary ability. In the process, whether avoidably or unavoidably, and largely unavoidably, he made so many enemies that in the actual conduct of policy he then had to pick his objectives. I disagree with you when you say that the doctrine he developed was considered by our allies as a magnificent reinforcement of the American commitment. I consider it a taking on of a theoretical argument that had no great consequence and produced considerable difficulty. However, that is a question of judgment that any defense secretary has a right to make and has nothing to do with the bureaucratic process. I feel that political sensitivity was not included among McNamara's great qualities and therefore he would not always be conscious of the political impact abroad of theoretical arguments he was making. I often felt he was doing things with which I agreed but in such a way as to be counterproductive. However, that was a question of personality rather than of structure.

QUESTION: Could you comment on the ways in which a new president may or may not be able to shake the inertia of the system in regard to the problem of Vietnam?

MR. KISSINGER: I have the impression that much of Vietnam is going to be shaken up before a new President comes in. As a general rule, I believe a new President, in the areas where he wants to effect change, must do so within the first four months. He need not complete it within this time, but he must give enough of a shake to the bureaucracy to indicate that he wants a new direction and he must be brutal enough to demonstrate that he means it.

It was easy under the Eisenhower administration to ridicule the formalism of the decisionmaking process. In effect, it was somewhat ridiculous — there were many documents which were really diplomatic treaties between the various departments, and which enabled each department to do what it had wanted to do in the first place. But it had the great advantage of a regular procedure for getting decisions made. Under Kennedy this procedure was dismantled, and he substituted for it a sort of nervous energy and great intellectual activity, which worked well because he was an enormously intelligent man, surrounded by a very lively group of people, so that all sorts of ideas were floating into the very receptive White House. The drawback under the Kennedy Administration was that there really was no regular procedure to getting things done, except on crisis issues, because you never could be sure who was being heard in addition to the constituted people, who did not always present their cases in the presence of the others who disagreed with them. It was a somewhat amorphous process. Under Johnson you had the disorganization of Kennedy without the intellectual excitement, and with somewhat of a fear of the President superimposed on it. The organizational problem seems to be to combine the procedural regularity of Eisenhower with the intellectual excitement of Kennedy. Whether that is possible, I do not know.

Eisenhower tended to operate almost exclusively with the National Security Council machinery, and he had divided the responsibility so that the current NSC business would be conducted by the staff secretary, while the planning side was conducted by the chief of the NSC staff. The operations coordinating board was the undersecretary's and was supposed to implement the planning decisions of the National Security Council. The drawback of the NSC as it was run under President Eisenhower was that it was terribly formalistic. One way to tell they really weren't doing anything was to take their papers, write down the opposite of what they had said, and see that this involved no policy choice. One is not saying anything by advocating that it is in the American interest to have a pro-

American government in country X. No one would argue that it is in our interest to have an anti-American government there. It turned into a series of abstract platitudes which were not very effective.

Kennedy used the NSC primarily as a sounding board; it rarely made important decisions. He had something called the Committee of Principals which met when concrete decisions had to be made — such as the Berlin crisis. There was no regular staff work for these meetings; it was all done on an ad hoc basis, on a very substantial intellectual level.

Johnson is compulsively secretive and will not say what he thinks, so it is very hard to discover people who think they know what he wants. There is less of a premium on coming up with new ideas under him. I think something like the Committee of Principals, or the National Security Council with a staff of McGeorge Bundy qualities is needed. There is a staff which keeps groping and is not primarily a diplomatic instrument.

Probably what is needed is something similar to what McNamara did in the Defense Department, that is, to try to establish some criteria by which to judge success and failure. McNamara got control of the Defense Department by flooding the various agencies with questions which they had to answer and which gave him good information. It took several years to bring home to them that the usual bureaucratic double-talk wouldn't go. Something like that is needed in the national security area, where it is much more difficult to establish, because the criteria are more elusive. There isn't any clear notion of what the American national interest is, and this presents a great problem. Most of the traditional concepts of balance of power just don't apply to the contemporary theory of national interest. To develop criteria in this sort of intellectual vacuum is very difficult.

All the thinking of balance of power has been related to territorial control. You could judge whether there was an equilibrium by what country changed allegiance. We live in a curious period in which territorial control may not be that important. We have good categories for resisting what we call aggression. Leaving the issue of whether we are correct in our assessment that the Vietnamese war was Chinese instigated — which I don't happen to believe — one would still be able to argue that no conceivable territorial gain of Communist China in Vietnam, or for that matter in Southeast Asia, could compare in terms of augmentation of its strength with the acquisition of nuclear weapons so far as concerned its impact on the international situation. We have some criteria for judging one, and none for the other.

It is hard to argue that any area is essential for American survival from the purely physical point of view, but there is such a thing as a psychological, moral balance. What would it do to the U.S. to be completely isolated, irrelevant to the rest of the world, even if we had enough of a nuclear arsenal to prevent a physical attack? This is an area in which I have not seen any very systematic thinking, although it is a chief problem in international equilibrium to which we have to address ourselves.

QUESTION: This is really on a broader scale. Mr. Kissinger, must we worry about neutralization until the time and place has been set? Don't we have within the bureaucracy some kind of planning for negotiations?

MR. KISSINGER: There are two parts to plans: first, to get them; second, to have to take them seriously. We have more plans than we have plans that are taken seriously. Take the problem of negotiations on an issue that is highly controversial and may even have political implications. No doubt some planning paper gets prepared, maybe even an interagency one. Yet the people involved have in the back of their minds the question: why should they fight with that issue now? It will be just as bloody later on, but at least they will be paying the price then for a possible result. Why fight it as a purely theoretical issue? And therefore my experience with any sort of negotiating plan shows that usually we'll get a multiplication of tough positions. Nobody wants to take on the unpleasant role of advocating major changes; nobody wants to be called before a Congressional committee. Therefore, that sort of plan, if you're talking about a negotiating plan, is very abstract and theoretical.

Secondly, in my experience, which is limited, it rarely receives the serious attention of the principals. Either the principals won't look at it at all or they will look at it in a way that requires no practical consequence. They won't do it in a way that requires implementation to follow, and this is especially true if there is no one who has a primary responsibility for it — if it is simply said that it would be a good thing to have a negotiating position but there is no one whose own bureaucratic success depends on having one.

QUESTION: Do you feel that negotiation is good in and of itself?

MR. KISSINGER: Do I think so? Don't apply what I said to Vietnam, although some aspects of it would apply. The tendency is to say that something is either a military problem or a diplomatic problem—and if it's a diplomatic problem, then it's the State Department's job. The State Department, probably for reasons of the background of its personnel that one could go into, tends to approach it on a largely tactical level. They'll develop a position, they'll want to see what the other position is, then they'll see what is negotiable. The difference between what is negotiable and what is desirable may be very wide. And if you don't know what is desirable and operate only on the basis of what is negotiable, you really encourage the other side to take a very extreme position. If the other side knows that you're going to compromise considerably, they are encouraged to take an extreme rather than a conciliatory position. So the problem with the State Department approach to most negotiations is that it is entirely tactical.

QUESTION: Could you comment, please, on the seizing of the *Pueblo* by North Korea?

MR. KISSINGER: It was quite an intelligence coup for the other side to get the equipment and all of these people. I think it also shows the extent to which we have become overextended by the Vietnamese war. It would have been inconceivable five years ago that North Korea could capture an American ship, tow it into Wonsan, and that absolutely nothing would happen. In our public discussion we say we must get it through diplomacy — well, diplomacy unrelated to other things can't achieve a great deal, and we can't do many other things because of Vietnam. Another thing the *Pueblo* incident illustrates or highlights to me is the following: I always thought it was a mistake to get South Korea involved in Vietnam for many reasons, one of which was the fact that at any level the outcome of the Vietnamese war was not likely to be very agreeable to Seoul, even before the Tet offensive. Besides, it created additional incentives to what is already a very tough regime in North Korea to get itself involved. But I have no brilliant solution on how to get these people back.

QUESTION: I have a double-barrelled question. Would we do better without a monumental State Department? It seems we do better if we have a small number of chairmen and officials than a huge array, or are they necessary? The State Department is habitually accused of being tedious and of not producing anything. Is that a plausible accusation?

MR. KISSINGER: I must say I hold the view that we are so overstaffed that it makes thinking almost impossible. When you have in embassies abroad individuals assigned to particular small groups, each of them filing endless reports, the result is that no senior official can possibly read everything that comes in — no new official in turn will say that he has nothing to report, so the machine keeps churning on. I've often been struck by the fact that when a U.S. embassy would use me to get people in that weren't easily accessible, there would be about twelve Americans hanging over these people taking down practically every word, so that they could include it in their reports the next day rather than to let it develop in a more normal way. I think the handling of all of this material does make it more difficult to reflect. Which part you cut out is a big problem, because the world has become more complicated and you have to know more things. On the whole, if we could get rid of the bottom half of the Foreign Service we might be better off.

Now about the State Department. There is a definite problem in the State Department, and it consists of many factors. One is that State Department training is in the direction of reporting and negotiation, not of thinking in terms of national policy. They are trained to give a very good account of what somebody said to them. They can give a much less good account of what this means. Also, if an officer works on the Iran desk, he can tell you every detail about Iran. Then he gets transferred to another job and you can never get him to talk about Iran again, but he will know everything about Austria or whatever.

Another quality that is rewarded is a certain negotiation skill. But what is not encouraged in the State Department hierarchy, though it is in a military hierarchy, is an assumption of responsibility and the tendency to think of problems from the vantage point of a higher level. I think the first eight to ten years of a State Department man's career tend to be such as to drive the more imaginative and more purpose-oriented people out of it. When I look at people that I see engaged in it at lower levels, I think this is probably true that they are the least adventurous.

QUESTION: Can you make some comment on the role of intellectuals in the bureaucracy?

MR. KISSINGER: I don't think you relate intellectuals to the bureaucracy as one undifferentiated group. For example, in the preparation of the strategic posture document it was the practice — as least on some occasions — to call in outside intellectuals to help in the preparation. And there they were useful on their merits, just as if they had been in the bureaucracy. They were not being called in just because they could referee the disputes but because of their expertise in a particular field. Other intellectuals are called in not because anyone cares about their opinion but because they are judged to be useful in defending the policy elsewhere. This has the risk that if the policy changes, you have made yourself a critic. Other intellectuals are called in in order to give some moral reinforcement to the decision maker who really has heard all arguments already but would like to hear an outsider say the same thing. Thus there are many different roles that outsiders play. Sometimes outsiders are called in because it is the only way of keeping knowledge of certain things from getting too widely diffused in the bureaucracy.

QUESTION: There is in your presentation a kind of pessimistic historical inevitability in the American policy process. One almost has the impression that policy making by lottery might be almost as good, if not better. What then do you feel is rational and correct about the policy process as you have known it, and do you think there are improvements to be made?

MR. KISSINGER: I don't think policy by lottery would be better, but I think that if one wants to understand what the government is likely to do, one has to understand the bureaucratics of the problems. The ways in which intellectuals from the outside often go wrong are several: one is that they judge a policy by its plausibility to them without taking into account that the policy maker is responsible not only for the best thing that can happen but also for the worst thing and that many ideas cannot be implemented not because they are bad but because the consequences of their failure would be too great. Another is that for the policy maker the most difficult problem is the problem of conjecture. That is, when the scope for action is great, the knowledge on which to base this action is relatively small. When the knowledge is great, the scope for action has already disappeared. So you have to act on the basis of an assessment which you cannot prove true when you make it. It involves a moral and psychological act as much as an intellectual act.

And finally, there is the inherent dynamism of the political and bureaucratic process itself. In that sense, there is a certain necessity about this. If you do not know how this process operates, it is very difficult to predict on the basis of abstract rationality how it is going to come out. The reason why this particular problem is magnified is, it seems to me, that only in the rarest cases is there a relationship between high position and great substantive knowledge. Most of our elective officials had to spend so much of their energy getting elected that they can give relatively little attention to the substance of what they are going to do when they get elected. And therefore you get the curious phenomenon of people deciding to run for high office first and then scrambling around for some intellectuals to tell them what their positions ought to be. In many cases it is not that the intellectuals are used merely as speech writers for positions that the policy makers already have; it is literally the case that you are starting with a *tabula rasa*, and that the position the political leader takes is much influenced by the type of intellectual that sometimes quite accidentally winds up in his entourage.

The top policy makers usually do not know that they have a problem until they have an administrative issue. They often show enormous reluctance to guide the project, because they are not really sure in what direction they want to guide it. Now de Gaulle has a conception of policy, and I would therefore not say that he is the prisoner of his administrative apparatus. The opposite may be the problem there: that this policy verges on the capricious. But still, the typical political leader of the contemporary managerial society is a man with a strong will, a high capacity to get himself elected, but no very great conception of what he is going to do when he gets into office. This is true of many of the cabinet officials as well, and in this sense, although I don't accept your notion of inevitability, I am pessimistic about the ability of modern bureaucratic society to manage a world which is quite discontinuous with its previous experience, and especially to do so with generosity and vision. I am not saying it's technically impossible, but the challenges are so much greater.

JAMES C. THOMSON

How Could Vietnam Happen? An Autopsy

In retrospect, the policy process which led to increasing United States involvement in Vietnam reveals bureaucratic politics at work. Participants with divergent objectives, constrained by their images of reality and by organizational limits, interacted to yield a substantial American commitment to South Vietnam — even though, Thomson argues, such a commitment originally seems to have been the intention of few if any of them.

The United States' approach toward Vietnam in the early 1960's was constrained by images of reality which were widely shared both within the national security bureaucracy and among the general public. Some of the images regarding the aims of Communism, China, and the Soviet Union were held by most of the pool from which senior participants were drawn. Other images, with an institutional base such as the Bureau of East Asian and Pacific Affairs, inherited from the previous administration, represented an important organizational constraint. The future careers of the foreign service officers assigned to the Bureau were largely dependent upon accepting and pursuing the then existing policy. To the extent that the Kennedy administration relied upon the State Department for its Vietnam policy, it had little alternative but to depend upon the Bureau of East Asian and Pacific Affairs. Members of the administration attuned to domestic political considerations cautioned against any sharp departures from past policy toward Asia, thereby reducing any inclination to overhaul the Bureau. Similar considerations of domestic politics led to ever more extreme public justifications for the U.S. involvement, and these justifications resulted in deepening the commitment and increasing the costs of withdrawal.

Even those participants who did not share the widely held images usually were unwilling to challenge them. In part, this derived from personal interests combined with a memory of the price paid by those who had candidly reported their assessment of the situation in China after the war. Even those participants who were prepared to sacrifice their careers (if necessary) were, nevertheless, constrained by what Thomson calls the "effectiveness trap." They recognized that if the arguments they advanced openly challenged widely shared images and assumptions, they ran the substantial risk of not being listened to, not only on Vietnam but also on other, unrelated issues in the future. Finally, those who did dare to challenge policy usually had little effect other than to assure senior players that all the options had been considered.

A peculiarity of public bureaucracies further insulated senior players from alternative perspectives and contributed to a perpetuation of the status quo. Substantive experts in a policy area usually are relatively junior players, whereas most senior players are selected for reasons other than

Reprinted from *The Atlantic Monthly* (April, 1968). Copyright © 1968 by The Atlantic Monthly Company, Boston, Massachusetts. Reprinted with permission.

their substantive expertise and previous professional training. This leads
to the perverse result that as an issue is perceived to be increasingly
critical, it passes from the scrutiny of the experts up to the politically
appointed generalists. Thus, as Vietnam became more critical, control
passed to decisionmakers whose images of reality and over-simplifications
of history went unchallenged by those with a substantive knowledge of the
area.

As a case study in the making of foreign policy, the Vietnam War will
fascinate historians and social scientists for many decades to come. One
question that will certainly be asked: How did men of superior ability,
sound training, and high ideals—American policy-makers of the 1960s
— create such costly and divisive policy?

As one who watched the decision-making process in Washington from
1961 to 1966 under Presidents Kennedy and Johnson, I can suggest a
preliminary answer. I can do so by briefly listing some of the factors that
seemed to me to shape our Vietnam policy during my years as an East
Asia specialist at the State Department and the White House. I shall deal
largely with Washington as I saw or sensed it, and not with Saigon, where
I have spent but a scant three days, in the entourage of the Vice President,
or with other decision centers, the capitals of interested parties. Nor will I
deal with other important parts of the record: Vietnam's history prior to
1961, for instance, or the overall course of America's relations with
Vietnam.

Yet a first and central ingredient in these years of Vietnam decisions
does involve history. The ingredient was *the legacy of the 1950s* — by
which I mean the so-called "loss of China," the Korean War, and the Far
East policy of Secretary of State Dulles.

This legacy had an institutional by-product for the Kennedy Administration: in 1961 the U.S. government's East Asian establishment was undoubtedly the most rigid and doctrinaire of Washington's regional divisions
in foreign affairs. This was especially true at the Department of State,
where the incoming Administration found the Bureau of Far Eastern
Affairs the hardest nut to crack. It was a bureau that had been purged of
its best China expertise, and of farsighted, dispassionate men, as a result
of McCarthyism. Its members were generally committed to one policy
line: the close containment and isolation of mainland China, the harass-
ment of "neutralist" nations which sought to avoid alignment with either
Washington or Peking, and the maintenance of a network of alliances with
anti-Communist client states on China's periphery.

Another aspect of the legacy was the special vulnerability and sensitivity of the new Democratic Administration on Far East policy issues. The
memory of the McCarthy era was still very sharp, and Kennedy's margin

of victory was too thin. The 1960 Offshore Islands TV debate between Kennedy and Nixon had shown the President-elect the perils of "fresh thinking." The Administration was inherently leery of moving too fast on Asia. As a result, the Far East Bureau (now the Bureau of East Asian and Pacific Affairs) was the last one to be overhauled. Not until Averell Harriman was brought in as Assistant Secretary in December, 1961, were significant personnel changes attempted, and it took Harriman several months to make a deep imprint on the bureau because of his necessary preoccupation with the Laos settlement. Once he did so, there was virtually no effort to bring back the purged or exiled East Asia experts.

There were other important by-products of this "legacy of the fifties":

The new Administration inherited and somewhat shared *a general perception of China-on-the-march* — a sense of China's vastness, its numbers, its belligerence; a revived sense, perhaps, of the Golden Horde. This was a perception fed by Chinese intervention in the Korean War (an intervention actually based on appallingly bad communications and mutual miscalculation on the part of Washington and Peking; but the careful unraveling of that tragedy, which scholars have accomplished, had not yet become part of the conventional wisdom).

The new Administration inherited and briefly accepted *a monolithic conception of the Communist bloc*. Despite much earlier predictions and reports by outside analysts, policy-makers did not begin to accept the reality and possible finality of the Sino-Soviet split until the first weeks of 1962. The inevitably corrosive impact of competing nationalisms on Communism was largely ignored.

The new Administration inherited and to some extent shared *the "domino theory" about Asia*. This theory resulted from profound ignorance of Asian history and hence ignorance of the radical differences among Asian nations and societies. It resulted from a blindness to the power and resilience of Asian nationalisms. (It may also have resulted from a subconscious sense that, since "all Asians look alike," all Asian nations will act alike.) As a theory, the domino fallacy was not merely inaccurate but also insulting to Asian nations; yet it has continued to this day to beguile men who should know better.

Finally, the legacy of the fifties was apparently compounded by an uneasy sense of a worldwide Communist challenge to the new Administration after the Bay of Pigs fiasco. A first manifestation was the President's traumatic Vienna meeting with Khrushchev in June, 1961; then came the Berlin crisis of the summer. All this created an atmosphere in which President Kennedy undoubtedly felt under special pressure to show his nation's mettle in Vietnam — if the Vietnamese, unlike the people of Laos, were willing to fight.

In general, the legacy of the fifties shaped such early moves of the new

Administration as the decisions to maintain a high-visibility SEATO (by sending the Secretary of State himself instead of some underling to its first meeting in 1961), to back away from diplomatic recognition of Mongolia in the summer of 1961, and most important, to expand U.S. military assistance to South Vietnam that winter on the basis of the much more tentative Eisenhower commitment. It should be added that the increased commitment to Vietnam was also fueled by a new breed of military strategists and academic social scientists (some of whom had entered the new Administration) who had developed theories of counterguerrilla warfare and were eager to see them put to the test. To some, "counter-insurgency" seemed a new panacea for coping with the world's instability.

So much for the legacy and the history. Any new Administration inherits both complicated problems and simplistic views of the world. But surely among the policy-makers of the Kennedy and Johnson Administrations there were men who would warn of the dangers of an open-ended commitment to the Vietnam quagmire?

This raises a central question, at the heart of the policy process: Where were the experts, the doubters, and the dissenters? Were they there at all, and if so, what happened to them?

The answer is complex but instructive.

In the first place, the American government was sorely *lacking in real Vietnam or Indochina expertise*. Originally treated as an adjunct of Embassy Paris, our Saigon embassy and the Vietnam Desk at State were largely staffed from 1954 onward by French-speaking Foreign Service personnel of narrowly European experience. Such diplomats were even more closely restricted than the normal embassy officer — by cast of mind as well as language — to contacts with Vietnam's French-speaking urban elites. For instance, Foreign Service linguists in Portugal are able to speak with the peasantry if they get out of Lisbon and choose to do so; not so the French speakers of Embassy Saigon.

In addition, the *shadow of the "loss of China"* distorted Vietnam reporting. Career officers in the Department, and especially those in the field, had not forgotten the fate of their World War II colleagues who wrote in frankness from China and were later pilloried by Senate committees for critical comments on the Chinese Nationalists. Candid reporting on the strengths of the Viet Cong and the weaknesses of the Diem government was inhibited by the memory. It was also inhibited by some higher officials, notably Ambassador Nolting in Saigon, who refused to sign off on such cables.

In due course, to be sure, some Vietnam talent was discovered or developed. But a recurrent and increasingly important factor in the decision-making process was *the banishment of real expertise*. Here the underlying cause was the "closed politics" of policy-making as issues become hot: the more sensitive the issue, and the higher it rises in the bureaucracy, the more completely the experts are excluded while the harassed senior generalists take over (that is, the Secretaries, Undersecretaries, and Presidential Assistants). The frantic skimming of briefing papers in the back seats of limousines is no substitute for the presence of specialists; furthermore, in times of crisis such papers are deemed "too sensitive" even for review by the specialists. Another underlying cause of this banishment, as Vietnam became more critical, was the replacement of the experts, who were generally and increasingly pessimistic, by men described as "can-do guys," loyal and energetic fixers unsoured by expertise. In early 1965, when I confided my growing policy doubts to an older colleague on the NSC staff, he assured me that the smartest thing both of us could do was to "steer clear of the whole Vietnam mess"; the gentleman in question had the misfortune to be a "can-do guy," however, and is now highly placed in Vietnam, under orders to solve the mess.

Despite the banishment of the experts, internal doubters and dissenters did indeed appear and persist. Yet as I watched the process, such men were effectively neutralized by a subtle dynamic: *the domestication of dissenters.* Such "domestication" arose out of a twofold clubbish need: on the one hand, the dissenter's desire to stay abroad; and on the other hand, the nondissenter's conscience. Simply stated, dissent, when recognized, was made to feel at home. On the lowest possible scale of importance, I must confess my own considerable sense of dignity and acceptance (both vital) when my senior White House employer would refer to me as his "favorite dove." Far more significant was the case of the former Undersecretary of State, George Ball. Once Mr. Ball began to express doubts, he was warmly institutionalized: he was encouraged to become the in-house devil's advocate on Vietnam. The upshot was inevitable: the process of escalation allowed for periodic requests to Mr. Ball to speak his piece; Ball felt good, I assume (he had fought for righteousness); the others felt good (they had given a full hearing to the dovish option); and there was minimal unpleasantness. The club remained intact; and it is of course possible that matters would have gotten worse faster if Mr. Ball had kept silent, or left before his final departure in the fall of 1966. There was also, of course, the case of the last institutionalized doubter, Bill Moyers. The President is said to have greeted his arrival at meetings with an affectionate, "Well, here comes Mr. Stop-the-Bombing . . ." Here again the dynamics of domesticated dissent sustained the relationship for a while.

A related point — and crucial, I suppose, to government at all times — was *the "effectiveness" trap,* the trap that keeps men from speaking out, as clearly or often as they might, within the government. And it is the trap that keeps men from resigning in protest and airing their dissent outside the government. The most important asset that a man brings to bureaucratic life is his "effectiveness," a mysterious combination of training, style, and connections. The most ominous complaint that can be whispered of a bureaucrat is: "I'm afraid Charlie's beginning to lose his effectiveness." To preserve your effectiveness, you must decide where and when to fight the mainstream of policy; the opportunities range from pillow talk with your wife, to private drinks with your friends, to meetings with the Secretary of State or the President. The inclination to remain silent or to acquiesce in the presence of the great men — to live to fight another day, to give on this issue so that you can be "effective" on later issues — is overwhelming. Nor is it the tendency of youth alone; some of our most senior officials, men of wealth and fame, whose place in history is secure, have remained silent lest their connection with power be terminated. As for the disinclination to resign in protest: while not necessarily a Washington or even American specialty, it seems more true of a government in which ministers have no parliamentary backbench to which to retreat. In the absence of such a refuge, it is easy to rationalize the decision to stay aboard. By doing so, one may be able to prevent a few bad things from happening and perhaps even make a few good things happen. To exit is to lose even those marginal chances for "effectiveness."

Another factor must be noted: as the Vietnam controversy escalated at home, there developed *a preoccupation with Vietnam public relations as opposed to Vietnam policy-making.* And here, ironically, internal doubters and dissenters were heavily employed. For such men, by virtue of their own doubts, were often deemed best able to "massage" the doubting intelligentsia. My senior East Asia colleague at the White House, a brilliant and humane doubter who had dealt with Indochina since 1954, spent three quarters of his working days on Vietnam public relations: drafting presidential responses to letters from important critics, writing conciliatory language for presidential speeches, and meeting quite interminably with delegations of outraged Quakers, clergymen, academics, and housewives. His regular callers were the late A. J. Muste and Norman Thomas; mine were members of the Women's Strike for Peace. Our orders from above: keep them off the backs of busy policy-makers (who usually happened to be nondoubters). Incidentally, my most discouraging assignment in the realm of public relations was the preparation of a White House pamphlet entitled *Why Vietnam*, in September 1965; in a gesture toward my conscience, I fought — and lost — a battle to have the title followed by a question mark.

Through a variety of procedures, both institutional and personal, doubt, dissent, and expertise were effectively neutralized in the making of policy. But what can be said of the men "in charge"? It is patently absurd to suggest that they produced such tragedy by intention and calculation. But it is neither absurd nor difficult to discern forces at work that caused decent and honorable men to do great harm.

Here I would stress the paramount role of *executive fatigue*. No factor seems to me more crucial and underrated in the making of foreign policy. The physical and emotional toll of executive responsibility in State, the Pentagon, the White House, and other executive agencies is enormous; that toll is of course compounded by extended service. Many of today's Vietnam policymakers have been on the job for from four to seven years. Complaints may be few, and physical health may remain unimpaired, though emotional health is far harder to gauge. But what is more seriously eroded in the deadening process of fatigue is freshness of thought, imagination, a sense of priorities and perspective — those rare assets of a new administration in its first year or two of office. The tired policy-maker becomes a prisoner of his own narrowed view of the world and his own clichéd rhetoric. He becomes irritable and defensive — short on sleep, short on family ties, short on patience. Such men make bad policy and then compound it. They have neither the time nor the temperament for new ideas or preventive diplomacy.

Below the level of the fatigued executives in the making of Vietnam policy was a widespread phenomenon: *the curator mentality* in the Department of State. By this I mean the collective inertia produced by the bureaucrat's view of his job. At State, the average "desk officer" inherits from his predecessor our policy toward Country X; he regards it as his function to keep that policy intact — under glass, untampered with, and dusted — so that he may pass it on in two to four years to his successor. And such curatorial service generally merits promotion within the system. (Maintain the status quo, and you will stay out of trouble.) In some circumstances, the inertia bred by such an outlook can act as a brake against rash innovation. But on many issues, this inertia sustains the momentum of bad policy and unwise commitments — momentum that might otherwise have been resisted within the ranks. Clearly, Vietnam is such an issue.

To fatigue and inertia must be added the factor of internal confusion. Even among the "architects" of our Vietnam commitment, there has been persistent *confusion as to what type of war we were fighting* and, as a direct consequence, *confusion as to how to end that war*. (The "credibility gap" is, in part, a reflection of such internal confusion.) Was it, for instance, a civil war, in which case counter-insurgency might suffice? Or was it a war of international aggression? (This might invoke SEATO or UN commitment.) Who was the aggressor — and the "real enemy"? The Viet Cong? Hanoi? Peking? Moscow? International Communism? Or maybe "Asian Communism"? Differing enemies dictated differing strategies and tactics. And confused throughout, in like fashion, was the question of American objectives; your objectives depended on whom you were fighting and why. I shall not forget my assignment from an Assistant Secretary of State in March, 1964; to draft a speech for Secretary McNamara which would, *inter alia*, once and for all dispose of the canard that the Vietnam conflict was a civil war. "But in some ways, of course," I mused, "it *is* a civil war." "Don't play word games with me!" snapped the Assistant Secretary.

Similar confusion beset the concept of "negotiations" — anathema to much of official Washington from 1961 to 1965. Not until April, 1965, did "unconditional discussions" become respectable, via a presidential speech; even then the Secretary of State stressed privately to newsmen that nothing had changed, since "discussions" were by no means the same as "negotiations." Months later that issue was resolved. But it took even longer to obtain a fragile internal agreement that negotiations might include the Viet Cong as something other than an appendage to Hanoi's delegation. Given such confusion as to the whos and whys of our Vietnam commitment, it is not surprising, as Theodore Draper has written, that policymakers find it so difficult to agree on how to end the war.

Of course, one force — a constant in the vortex of commitment — was that of *wishful thinking*. I partook of it myself at many times. I did so especially during Washington's struggle with Diem in the autumn of 1963 when some of us at State believed that for once, in dealing with a difficult client state, the U.S. government could use the leverage of our economic and military assistance to make good things happen, instead of being led around by the nose by men like Chiang Kai-shek and Syngman Rhee (and, in that particular instance, by Diem). If we could prove that point, I thought, and move into a new day, with or without Diem, then Vietnam was well worth the effort. Later came the wishful thinking of the air-strike planners in the late autumn of 1964; there were those who actually thought that after six weeks of air strikes, the North Vietnamese would come crawling to us to ask for peace talks. And what, someone asked in one of the meetings of the time, if they don't? The answer was that we would bomb for another four weeks, and that would do the trick. And a few weeks later came one instance of wishful thinking that was symptomatic of good men misled: in January, 1965, I encountered one of the very highest figures in the Administration at a dinner, drew him aside, and told him of my worries about the air-strike option. He told me that I really shouldn't worry; it was his conviction that before any such plans could be put into effect, a neutralist government would come to power in Saigon that would politely invite us out. And finally, there was the recurrent wishful thinking that sustained many of us through the trying months of 1965–1966 after the air strikes had begun: that surely, somehow, one way or another, we would "be in a conference in six months," and the escalatory spiral would be suspended. The basis of our hope: "It simply can't go on."

As a further influence on policymakers I would cite the factor of *bureaucratic detachment*. By this I mean what at best might be termed the professional callousness of the surgeon (and indeed, medical lingo — the "surgical strike" for instance — seemed to crop up in the euphemisms of the times). In Washington the semantics of the military muted the reality of war for the civilian policy-makers. In quiet, air-conditioned, thick-carpeted rooms, such terms as "systematic pressure," "armed reconnaissance," "targets of opportunity," and even "body count" seemed to breed a sort of games-theory detachment. Most memorable to me was a moment in the late 1964 target planning when the question under discussion was how heavy our bombing should be, and how extensive our strafing, at some midpoint in the projected pattern of systematic pressure. An Assistant Secretary of State resolved the point in the following words: "It seems to me that our orchestration should be mainly violins, but with periodic touches of brass." Perhaps the biggest shock of my return to Cambridge, Massachusetts, was the realization that the young men, the flesh and blood I taught and saw on these university streets, were potentially some of the numbers on the charts of those faraway planners. In a curious sense, Cambridge is closer to this war than Washington.

There is an unprovable factor that relates to bureaucratic detachment: the ingredient of *crypto-racism*. I do not mean to imply any conscious contempt for Asian loss of life on the part of Washington officials. But I do mean to imply that bureaucratic detachment may well be compounded by a traditional Western sense that there are so many Asians, after all; that Asians have a fatalism about life and a disregard for its loss; that they are cruel and barbaric to their own people; and that they are very different from us (and all look alike?). And I *do* mean to imply that the upshot of such subliminal views is a subliminal question whether Asians, and particularly Asian peasants, and most particularly Asian Communists, are really people — like you and me. To put the matter another way: would we have pursued quite such policies — and quite such military tactics — if the Vietnamese were white?

It is impossible to write of Vietnam decisionmaking without writing about language. Throughout the conflict, words have been of paramount importance. I refer here to the impact of *rhetorical escalation* and to the *problem of oversell*. In an important sense, Vietnam has become of crucial significance to us *because we have said that it is of crucial significance*. (The issue obviously relates to the public relations preoccupation described earlier.)

The key here is domestic politics: the need to sell the American people, press, and Congress on support for an unpopular and costly war in which the objectives themselves have been in flux. To sell means to persuade, and to persuade means rhetoric. As the difficulties and costs have mounted, so has the definition of the stakes. This is not to say that rhetorical escalation is an orderly process: executive prose is the product of many writers, and some concepts — North Vietnamese infiltration, America's "national honor," Red China as the chief enemy — have entered the rhetoric only gradually and even sporadically. But there is an upward spiral nonetheless. And once you have *said* that the American Experiment itself stands or falls on the Vietnam outcome, you have thereby created a national stake far beyond any earlier stakes.

Crucial throughout the process of Vietnam decision-making was a conviction among many policy-makers: that Vietnam posed a *fundamental test of America's national will*. Time and again I was told by men reared in the tradition of Henry L. Stimson that all we needed was the will, and we would then prevail. Implicit in such a view, it seemed to me, was a curious assumption that Asians lacked will, or at least that in a contest between Asian and Anglo-Saxon wills, the non-Asians must prevail. A corollary to the persistent belief in will was a *fascination with power* and an awe in the face of the power America possessed as no nation or civilization ever before. Those who doubted our role in Vietnam were said to shrink from the burdens of power, the obligations of power, the uses of power, the responsibility of power. By implication, such men were soft-headed and effete.

Finally, no discussion of the factors and forces at work on Vietnam policy-makers can ignore the central fact of *human ego investment*. Men who have participated in a decision develop a stake in that decision. As they participate in further, related decisions, their stake increases. It might have been possible to dissuade a man of strong self-confidence at an early stage of the ladder of decision; but it is infinitely harder at later stages since a change of mind there usually involves implicit or explicit repudiation of a chain of previous decisions.

To put it bluntly: at the heart of the Vietnam calamity is a group of able, dedicated men who have been regularly and repeatedly wrong — and whose standing with their contemporaries, and more important, with history, depends, as they see it, on being proven right. These are not men who can be asked to extricate themselves from error.

The various ingredients I have cited in the making of Vietnam policy have created a variety of results, most of them fairly obvious. Here are some that seem to me most central:

Throughout the conflict, there has been *persistent and repeated miscalculation* by virtually all the actors, in high echelons and low, whether dove, hawk, or something else. To cite one simple example among many: in late 1964 and early 1965, some peace-seeking planners at State who strongly opposed the projected bombing of the North urged that, instead, American ground forces be sent to South Vietnam; this would, they said, increase our bargaining leverage against the North — our "chips" — and would give us something to negotiate about (the withdrawal of our forces) at an early peace conference. Simultaneously, the air-strike option was urged by many in the military who were dead set against American participation in "another land war in Asia"; they were joined by other civilian peace-seekers who wanted to bomb Hanoi into early negotiations. By late 1965, we had ended up with the worst of all worlds: ineffective and costly air strikes against the North, spiraling ground forces in the South, and no negotiations in sight.

Throughout the conflict as well, there has been *a steady give-in to pressures for a military solution* and only minimal and sporadic efforts at a diplomatic and political solution. In part this resulted from the confusion (earlier cited) among the civilians — confusion regarding objectives and strategy. And in part this resulted from the self-enlarging nature of military investment. Once air strikes and particularly ground forces were introduced, our investment itself had transformed the original stakes More air power was needed to protect the ground forces; and then more ground forces to protect the ground forces. And needless to say, the military mind develops its own momentum in the absence of clear guidelines from the civilians. Once asked to save South Vietnam, rather than to "advise" it, the American military could not but press for escalation. In addition, sad to report, assorted military constituencies, once involved in Vietnam, have had a series of cases to prove: for instance, the utility not only of air power (the Air Force) but of supercarrier-based air power (the Navy). Also Vietnam policy has suffered from one ironic by-product of Secretary McNamara's establishment of civilian control at the Pentagon: in the face of such control, interservice rivalry has given way to a united front among the military — reflected in the new but recurrent phenomenon of JCS unanimity. In conjunction with traditional congressional allies (mostly Southern senators and representatives) such a united front would pose a formidable problem for any President.

Throughout the conflict, there have been *missed opportunities, large and small, to disengage ourselves from Vietnam on increasingly unpleasant but still acceptable terms.* Of the many moments from 1961 onward, I shall cite only one, the last and most important opportunity that was lost: in the summer of 1964 the President instructed his chief advisers to prepare for him as wide a range of Vietnam options as possible for postelection consideration and decision. He explicitly asked that all options be laid out. What happened next was, in effect, Lyndon Johnson's slow-motion Bay of Pigs. For the advisers so effectively converged on one single option — juxtaposed against two other, phony options (in effect, blowing up the world, or scuttle-and-run) — that the President was confronted with unanimity for bombing the North from all his trusted counselors. Had he been more confident in foreign affairs, had he been deeply informed on Vietnam and Southeast Asia, and had he raised some hard questions that unanimity had submerged, this President could have used the largest electoral mandate in history to de-escalate in Vietnam, in the clear expectation that at the worst a neutralist government would come to power in Saigon and politely invite us out. Today, many lives and dollars later, such an alternative has become an elusive and infinitely more expensive possibility.

In the course of these years, another result of Vietnam decision-making has been *the abuse and distortion of history*. Vietnamese, Southeast Asian, and Far Eastern history has been rewritten by our policy-makers, and their spokesmen, to conform with the alleged necessity of our presence in Vietnam. Highly dubious analogies from our experience elsewhere — the "Munich" sellout and "containment" from Europe, the Malayan insurgency and the Korean War from Asia — have been imported in order to justify our actions. And more recent events have been fitted to the Procrustean bed of Vietnam. Most notably, the change of power in Indonesia in 1965–1966 has been ascribed to our Vietnam presence; and virtually all progress in the Pacific region — the rise of regionalism, new forms of cooperation, and mounting growth rates — has been similarly explained. The Indonesian allegation is undoubtedly false (I tried to prove it, during six months of careful investigation at the White House, and had to confess failure); the regional allegation is patently unprovable in either direction (except, of course, for the clear fact that the economies of both Japan and Korea have profited enormously from our Vietnam-related procurement in these countries; but that is a costly and highly dubious form of foreign aid).

There is a final result of Vietnam policy I would cite that holds potential danger for the future of American foreign policy: *the rise of a new breed of American ideologues who see Vietnam as the ultimate test of their doctrine*. I have in mind those men in Washington who have given a new life to the missionary impulse in American foreign relations: who believe that this nation, in this era, has received a threefold endowment that can transform the world. As they see it, that endowment is composed of, first, our unsurpassed military might; second, our clear technological supremacy; and third, our allegedly invincible benevolence (our "altruism," our affluence, our lack of territorial aspirations). Together, it is argued, this threefold endowment provides us with the opportunity and the obligation to ease the nations of the earth toward modernization and stability: toward a full-fledged *Pax Americana Technocratica*. In reaching toward this goal, Vietnam is viewed as the last and crucial test. Once we have succeeded there, the road ahead is clear. In a sense, these men are our counterpart to the visionaries of Communism's radical left: they are technocracy's own Maoists. They do not govern Washington today. But their doctrine rides high.

Long before I went into government, I was told a story about Henry L.

Stimson that seemed to me pertinent during the years that I watched the Vietnam tragedy unfold — and participated in that tragedy. It seems to me more pertinent than ever as we move toward the election of 1968.

In his waning years Stimson was asked by an anxious questioner, "Mr. Secretary, how on earth can we ever bring peace to the world?" Stimson is said to have answered: "You begin by bringing to Washington a small handful of able men who believe that the achievement of peace is possible.

"You work them to the bone until they no longer believe that it is possible.

"And then you throw them out — and bring in a new bunch who believe that it is possible."

Part Two

Participants and Interests

ROBERT JERVIS

Hypotheses on Misperception

Jervis' discussion of misperception can be classified as falling into the realm of Allison's Model I. Nevertheless he presents many insights which are relevant to the bureaucratic perspective. In particular he shows how images of reality impose constraints on the play of bureaucratic politics in two important ways.

First, a participant's images constrain not only what is perceived, but also how it is interpreted and the selection of an appropriate response. Individuals perceive what they expect and are inclined to reinterpret or discard data in order to preserve their preconceptions rather than adjust their images to take account of new information. This means that an actor's images of reality are highly resistant to change and therefore tend to persist over long periods of time. Since information from the international environment tends to be especially ambiguous, the images held by foreign policy decisionmakers are inclined to be particularly inflexible and resistant. The relatively common backgrounds and generational experiences of the participants lead to a substantial congruence in their perceptions of international relations, a congruence which in turn further rigidifies their images through a process of mutual reinforcement.

Second, the fact that a given group of policymakers shares the same rigid images regarding the international environment suggests that a bureaucratic participant intent on advancing a certain policy must construct his arguments in terms of these images whether or not he personally holds them. If an advocate presents data which cannot be accommodated by prevailing images, that information is likely to be ignored. If the advocate reveals assumptions regarding the nature of reality which do not conform to prevailing assumptions, *he* is likely to be ignored. Thus advocates of "negotiating from positions of strength" differ from proponents of unilateral efforts at tension reduction primarily in their perceptions of Soviet intentions. However, if the latter group expects to be effectively persuasive, it would be well advised to construct its recommendations to conform to the more widely accepted assumptions of the former. Similarly, efforts to affect the behavior of another nation should begin with an understanding of that nation's dominant images of international relations in general and of the potential "influencer" in particular.

The latter sections of Jervis' essay cast light on the difficulty that participants in one nation have in conveying clear signals to participants in another nation. Participants tend to overestimate the degree to which their signals are getting through and are reluctant to alter their images of the intentions of other nations.

Reprinted from *World Politics*, 20, 3 (1968), pp. 454–479. Copyright 1968 by Princeton University Press. Reprinted by permission of Princeton University Press.

In determining how he will behave, an actor must try to predict how others will act and how their actions will affect his values. The actor must therefore develop an image of others and of their intentions. This image may, however, turn out to be an inaccurate one; the actor may, for a number of reasons, misperceive both others' actions and their intentions. In this research note I wish to discuss the types of misperceptions of other states' intentions which states tend to make. The concept of intention is complex, but here we can consider it to comprise the ways in which the state feels it will act in a wide range of future contingencies. These ways of acting usually are not specific and well-developed plans. For many reasons a national or individual actor may not know how he will act under given conditions, but this problem cannot be dealt with here.

I. PREVIOUS TREATMENTS OF PERCEPTION IN INTERNATIONAL RELATIONS

Although diplomatic historians have discussed misperception in their treatments of specific events, students of international relations have generally ignored this topic. However, two sets of scholars have applied content analysis to the documents that flowed within and between governments in the six weeks preceding World War I. But the data have been put into quantitative form in a way that does not produce accurate measures of perceptions and intentions and that makes it impossible to gather useful evidence on misperceptions.[1]

The second group of theorists who have explicitly dealt with general questions of misperception in international relations consists of those, like Charles Osgood, Amitai Etzioni, and, to a lesser extent, Kenneth Boulding and J. David Singer, who have analyzed the cold war in terms of a spiral of misperception.[2] This approach grows partly out of the mathematical theories of L. F. Richardson[3] and partly out of findings of social and cognitive psychology, many of which will be discussed in this research note.

[1] See, for example, Ole Holsti, Robert North, and Richard Brody, "Perception and Action in the 1914 Crisis," in J. David Singer (ed.), *Quantitative International Politics* (1968). For a fuller discussion of the Stanford content analysis studies and the general problems of quantification, see my "The Costs of the Quantitative Study of International Relations," in Klaus Knorr and James N. Rosenau (eds.), *Contending Approaches to International Politics* (1969).

[2] See, for example, Osgood, *An Alternative to War or Surrender* (1962); Etzioni, *The Hard Way to Peace* (1962); Boulding, "National Images and International Systems," *Journal of Conflict Resolution,* III (June 1959), 120–131; and Singer, *Deterrence, Arms Control, and Disarmament* (1962).

[3] See Richardson's *Statistics of Deadly Quarrels* (1960) and *Arms and Insecurity* (1960). For nonmathematicians a fine summary of Richardson's work is Anatol Rapoport's "L. F. Richardson's Mathematical Theory of War," *Journal of Conflict Resolution,* I (September 1957), 249–299.

These authors state their case in general, if not universal, terms, but do not provide many historical cases that are satisfactorily explained by their theories. Furthermore, they do not deal with any of the numerous instances that contradict their notion of the self-defeating aspects of the use of power. They ignore the fact that states are not individuals and that the findings of psychology can be applied to organizations only with great care. Most important, their theoretical analysis is for the most part of reduced value because it seems largely to be a product of their assumption that the Soviet Union is a basically status-quo power whose apparently aggressive behavior is a product of fear of the West. Yet they supply little or no evidence to support this view. Indeed, the explanation for the differences of opinion between the spiral theorists and the proponents of deterrence lies not in differing general views of international relations, differing values and morality,[4] or differing methods of analysis,[5] but in differing perceptions of Soviet intentions.

II. THEORIES — NECESSARY AND DANGEROUS

Despite the limitations of their approach, these writers have touched on a vital problem that has not been given systematic treatment by theorists of international relations. The evidence from both psychology and history overwhelmingly supports the view (which may be labeled Hypothesis 1) that decision-makers tend to fit incoming information into their existing theories and images. Indeed, their theories and images play a large part in determining what they notice. In other words, actors tend to perceive what they expect. Furthermore (Hypothesis 1a), a theory will have greater impact on an actor's interpretation of data (a) the greater the ambiguity of the data and (b) the higher the degree of confidence with which the actor holds the theory.[6]

For many purposes we can use the concept of differing levels of perceptual thresholds to deal with the fact that it takes more, and more unambiguous, information for an actor to recognize an unexpected phenomenon than an expected one. An experiment by Bruner and Postman determined "that the recognition threshold for . . . incongruous playing cards (those with suits and color reversed) is significantly higher than the

---

[4] See Philip Green, *Deadly Logic* (1966); Green, "Method and Substance in the Arms Debate," *World Politics,* XVI (July 1964), 642–667; and Robert A. Levine, "Facts and Morals in the Arms Debate," *World Politics,* XIV (January 1962), 239–258.

[5] See Anatol Rapoport, *Strategy and Conscience* (1964).

[6] Floyd Allport, *Theories of Perception and the Concept of Structure* (1955), p. 382; Ole Holsti, "Cognitive Dynamics and Images of the Enemy," in David Finlay, Ole Holsti, and Richard Fagen, *Enemies in Politics* (1967), p. 70.

threshold for normal cards." [7] Not only are people able to identify normal (and therefore expected) cards more quickly and easily than incongruous (and therefore unexpected) ones, but also they may at first take incongruous cards for normal ones.

However, we should not assume, as the spiral theorists often do, that it is necessarily irrational for actors to adjust incoming information to fit more closely their existing beliefs and images. ("Irrational" here describes acting under pressures that the actor would not admit as legitimate if he were conscious of them.) Abelson and Rosenberg label as "psycho-logic" the pressure to create a "balanced" cognitive structure — i.e., one in which "all relations among 'good elements' [in one's attitude structure] are positive (or null), all relations among 'bad elements' are positive (or null), and all relations between good and bad elements are negative (or null)." They correctly show that the "reasoning [this involves] would mortify a logician." [8] But those who have tried to apply this and similar cognitive theories to international relations have usually overlooked the fact that in many cases there are important logical links between the elements and the processes they describe which cannot be called "psycho-logic." (I am here using the term "logical" not in the narrow sense of drawing only those conclusions that follow necessarily from the premises, but rather in the sense of conforming to generally agreed-upon rules for the treating of evidence.) For example, Osgood claims that psycho-logic is displayed when the Soviets praise a man or a proposal and people in the West react by distrusting the object of this praise.[9] But if a person believes that the Russians are aggressive, it is logical for him to be suspicious of their moves. When we say that a decision-maker "dislikes" another state, this usually means that he believes that that other state has policies conflicting with those of his nation. Reasoning and experience indicate to the decision-maker that the "disliked" state is apt to harm his state's interests. Thus in these cases there is no need to invoke "psycho-logic," and it cannot be claimed that the cases demonstrate the submission of "emotional consistency for rational consistency." [10]

The question of the relations among particular beliefs and cognitions can often be seen as part of the general topic of the relation of incoming bits of information to the receivers' already established images. The need to fit data into a wider framework of beliefs, even if doing so does not

[7] Jerome Bruner and Leo Postman, "On the Perceptions of Incongruity: A Paradigm," in Jerome Bruner and David Krech (eds.), *Perception and Personality* (1949), p. 210. [All ellipses and connective interpolations in this chapter by Jervis.]

[8] Robert Abelson and Milton Rosenberg, "Symbolic Psycho-logic," *Behavioral Science,* III (January 1958), 4–5.

[9] Osgood, *Alternative to War,* p. 27.

[10] *Ibid.,* p. 26.

seem to do justice to individual facts, is not, or at least is not only, a psychological drive that decreases the accuracy of our perceptions of the world, but is "essential to the logic of inquiry." [11] Facts can be interpreted, and indeed identified, only with the aid of hypotheses and theories. Pure empiricism is impossible, and it would be unwise to revise theories in the light of every bit of information that does not easily conform to them.[12] No hypothesis can be expected to account for all the evidence, and if a prevailing view is supported by many theories and by a large pool of findings it should not be quickly altered. Too little rigidity can be as bad as too much.[13]

This is as true in the building of social and physical science as it is in policy-making.[14] While it is terribly difficult to know when a finding throws serious doubt on accepted theories and should be followed up and when instead it was caused by experimental mistakes or minor errors in the theory, it is clear that scientists would make no progress if they followed Thomas Huxley's injunction to "sit down before fact as a mere child, be prepared to give up every preconceived notion, follow humbly wherever nature leads, or you will learn nothing." [15]

[11] I have borrowed this phrase from Abraham Kaplan, who uses it in a different but related context in *The Conduct of Inquiry* (1964), p. 86.

[12] The spiral theorists are not the only ones to ignore the limits of empiricism. Roger Hilsman found that most consumers and producers of intelligence felt that intelligence should not deal with hypotheses but should only provide the policymakers with "all the facts" (*Strategic Intelligence and National Decisions* [1956], p. 46). The close interdependence between hypotheses and facts is overlooked partly because of the tendency to identify "hypotheses" with "policy preferences."

[13] Karl Deutsch interestingly discusses a related question when he argues, "Autonomy . . . requires both intake from the present and recall from memory, and selfhood can be seen in just this continuous balancing of a limited present and a limited past. . . . No further self-determination is possible if either openness or memory is lost. . . . To the extent that [systems cease to be able to take in new information], they approach the behavior of a bullet or torpedo: their future action becomes almost completely determined by their past. On the other hand, a person without memory, an organization without values or policy . . . — all these no longer steer, but drift: their behavior depends little on their past and almost wholly on their present. Driftwood and the bullet are thus each the epitome of another kind of loss of self-control . . ." (*Nationalism and Social Communication* [1954], pp. 167–168). Also see Deutsch's *The Nerves of Government* (1963), pp. 98–109, 200–256. A physicist makes a similar argument: "It is clear that if one is too attached to one's preconceived model, one will miss all radical discoveries. It is amazing to what degree one may fail to register mentally an observation which does not fit the initial image . . . On the other hand, if one is too open-minded and pursues every hitherto unknown phenomenon, one is almost certain to lose oneself in trivia" (Martin Deutsch, "Evidence and Inference in Nuclear Research," in Daniel Lerner (ed.), *Evidence and Inference* [1958], p. 102).

[14] Raymond Bauer, "Problems of Perception and Relations Between the U.S. and the Soviet Union," *Journal of Conflict Resolution,* V (September 1961), pp. 223–229.

[15] Quoted in W. I. B. Beveridge, *The Art of Scientific Investigation* (3d ed.; 1957), p. 50.

As Michael Polanyi explains, "It is true enough that the scientist must be prepared to submit at any moment to the adverse verdict of observational evidence. But not blindly. . . . There is always the possibility that, as in [the cases of the periodic system of elements and the quantum theory of light], a deviation may not affect the essential correctness of a proposition. . . . The process of explaining away deviations is in fact quite indispensable to the daily routine of research," even though this may lead to the missing of a great discovery.[16] For example, in 1795, the astronomer Lalande did not follow up observations that contradicted the prevailing hypotheses and could have led him to discover the planet Neptune.[17]

Yet we should not be too quick to condemn such behavior. As Thomas Kuhn has noted, "There is no such thing as research without counterinstances."[18] If a set of basic theories — what Kuhn calls a paradigm — has been able to account for a mass of data, it should not be lightly trifled with. As Kuhn puts it: "Lifelong resistance, particularly from those whose productive careers have committed them to an older tradition of normal science [i.e., science within the accepted paradigm], is not a violation of scientific standards but an index to the nature of scientific research itself. The source of resistance is the assurance that the older paradigm will ultimately solve all its problems, that nature can be shoved into the box the paradigm provides. Inevitably, at times of revolution, that assurance seems stubborn and pig-headed as indeed it sometimes becomes. But it is also something more. That same assurance is what makes normal science or puzzle-solving science possible."[19]

Thus it is important to see that the dilemma of how "open" to be to new information is one that inevitably plagues any attempt at understanding in any field. Instances in which evidence seems to be ignored or twisted to fit the existing theory can often be explained by this dilemma instead of by illogical or nonlogical psychological pressures toward consistency. This is especially true of decision-makers' attempts to estimate the inten-

---

[16] *Science, Faith, and Society* (1964), p. 31. For a further discussion of this problem, see *idem,* pp. 16, 26–41, 90–94; Polanyi, *Personal Knowledge* (1958), pp. 8–15, 30, 143–168, 269–298, 310–311; Thomas Kuhn, *The Structure of Scientific Revolutions* (1964); Kuhn, "The Function of Dogma in Scientific Research," in A. C. Crombie (ed.), *Scientific Change* (1963), pp. 344–369; the comments on Kuhn's paper by Hall, Polanyi, and Toulmin, and Kuhn's reply, *idem,* 370–395. For a related discussion of these points from a different perspective, see Norman Storer, *The Social System of Science* (1960), pp. 116–222.

[17] "He found that the position of one star relative to others . . . had shifted. Lalande was a good astronomer and knew that such a shift was unreasonable. He crossed out his first observation, put a question mark next to the second observation, and let the matter go" (Jerome Bruner, Jacqueline Goodnow, and George Austin, *A Study of Thinking* [1962], p. 105).

[18] Kuhn, *Structure of Scientific Revolution,* p. 79.

[19] *Ibid.,* pp. 150–151.

tions of other states, since they must constantly take account of the danger that the other state is trying to deceive them.

The theoretical framework discussed thus far, together with an examination of many cases, suggests Hypothesis 2: scholars and decision-makers are apt to err by being too wedded to the established view and too closed to new information, as opposed to being too willing to alter their theories.[20] Another way of making this point is to argue that actors tend to establish their theories and expectations prematurely. In politics, of course, this is often necessary because of the need for action. But experimental evidence indicates that the same tendency also occurs on the unconscious level. Bruner and Postman found that "perhaps the greatest single barrier to the recognition of incongruous stimuli is the tendency for perceptual hypotheses to fixate after receiving a minimum of confirmation. . . . Once there had occurred in these cases a partial confirmation of the hypothesis . . . it seemed that nothing could change the subject's report." [21]

However, when we apply these and other findings to politics and discuss kinds of misperception ,we should not quickly apply the label of cognitive distortion. We should proceed cautiously for two related reasons. The first is that the evidence available to decision-makers almost always permits several interpretations. It should be noted that there are cases of visual perception in which different stimuli can produce exactly the same pattern on an observer's retina. Thus, for an observer using one eye the same pattern would be produced by a sphere the size of a golf ball which was quite close to the observer, by a baseball-sized sphere that was further away, or by a basketball-sized sphere still further away. Without other clues, the observer cannot possibly determine which of these stimuli he is presented

---

20 Requirements of effective political leadership may lead decisionmakers to voice fewer doubts than they have about existing policies and images, but this constraint can only partially explain this phenomenon. Similar calculations of political strategy may contribute to several of the hypotheses discussed below.

21 "Perceptions of Incongruity," p. 221. Similarly, in experiments dealing with his subjects' perception of other people, Charles Dailey found that "premature judgment appears to make new data harder to assimilate than when the observer withholds judgment until all data are seen. It seems probable . . . that the observer mistakes his own inferences for facts" ("The Effects of Premature Conclusion Upon the Acquisition of Understanding of a Person," *Journal of Psychology*, XXX [January 1952], pp. 149–150). For other theory and evidence on this point, see Bruner, "On Perceptual Readiness," *Psychological Review*, LXIV (March 1957), pp. 123–152: Gerald Davison, "The Negative Effects of Early Exposure to Suboptimal Visual Stimuli," *Journal of Personality*, XXXII (June 1964), pp. 278–295; Albert Myers, "An Experimental Analysis of a Tactical Blunder," *Journal of Abnormal and Social Psychology*, LXIX (November 1964), pp. 493–498; and Dale Wyatt and Donald Campbell, "On the Liability of Stereotype or Hypothesis," *Journal of Abnormal and Social Psychology*, XLIV (October 1950), pp. 496–500. It should be noted that this tendency makes "incremental" decisionmaking more likely (David Braybrooke and Charles Lindblom, *A Strategy of Decision* [1963]), but the results of this process may lead the actor further from his goals.

with, and we would not want to call his incorrect perceptions examples of distortion. Such cases, relatively rare in visual perception, are frequent in international relations. The evidence available to decision-makers is almost always very ambiguous since accurate clues to others' intentions are surrounded by noise[22] and deception. In most cases, no matter how long, deeply, and "objectively" the evidence is analyzed, people can differ in their interpretations, and there are no general rules to indicate who is correct.

The second reason to avoid the label of cognitive distortion is that the distinction between perception and judgment, obscure enough in individual psychology, is almost absent in the making of inferences in international politics. Decision-makers who reject information that contradicts their views — or who develop complex interpretations of it — often do so consciously and explicitly. Since the evidence available contains contradictory information, to make any inferences requires that much information be ignored or given interpretations that will seem tortuous to those who hold a different position.

Indeed, if we consider only the evidence available to a decision-maker at the time of decision, the view later proved incorrect may be supported by as much evidence as the correct one — or even by more. Scholars have often been too unsympathetic with the people who were proved wrong. On closer examination, it is frequently difficult to point to differences between those who were right and those who were wrong with respect to their openness to new information and willingness to modify their views. Winston Churchill, for example, did not open-mindedly view each Nazi action to see if the explanations provided by the appeasers accounted for the data better than his own beliefs. Instead, like Chamberlain, he fitted each bit of ambiguous information into his own hypotheses. That he was correct should not lead us to overlook the fact that his methods of analysis and use of theory to produce cognitive consistency did not basically differ from those of the appeasers.[23]

---

[22] For a use of this concept in political communication, see Roberta Wohlstetter, *Pearl Harbor* (1962).

[23] Similarly, Robert Coulondre, the French ambassador to Berlin in 1939, was one of the few diplomats to appreciate the Nazi threat. Partly because of his earlier service in the USSR, "he was painfully sensitive to the threat of a Berlin-Moscow agreement. He noted with foreboding that Hitler had not attacked Russia in his *Reichstag* address of April 28. . . . So it went all spring and summer, the ambassador relaying each new evidence of the impending diplomatic revolution and adding to his admonitions his pleas for decisive counteraction" (Franklin Ford and Carl Schorske, "The Voice in the Wilderness: Robert Coulondre," in Gordon Craig and Felix Gilbert [eds.], *The Diplomats* [1963], pp. 573–574). His hypotheses were correct, but it is difficult to detect differences between the way he and those ambassadors who were incorrect, like Neville Henderson, selectively noted and interpreted information. However, to the extent that the fear of war influenced the appeasers' perceptions of Hitler's intentions, the appeasers' views did have an element of psycho-logic that was not present in their opponents' position.

A consideration of the importance of expectations in influencing perception also indicates that the widespread belief in the prevalence of "wishful thinking" may be incorrect, or at least may be based on inadequate data. The psychological literature on the interaction between affect and perception is immense and cannot be treated here, but it should be noted that phenomena that at first were considered strong evidence for the impact of affect on perception often can be better treated as demonstrating the influence of expectations.[24] Thus, in international relations, cases like the United States' misestimation of the political climate in Cuba in April 1961, which may seem at first glance to have been instances of wishful thinking, may instead be more adequately explained by the theories held by the decision-makers (e.g., Communist governments are unpopular). Of course, desires may have an impact on perception by influencing expectations, but since so many other factors effect expectations, the net influence of desires may not be great.

There is evidence from both psychology[25] and international relations that when expectations and desires clash, expectations seem to be more important. The United States would like to believe that North Vietnam is about to negotiate or that the USSR is ready to give up what the United States believes is its goal of world domination, but ambiguous evidence is seen to confirm the opposite conclusion, which conforms to the United States' expectations. Actors are apt to be especially sensitive to evidence of grave danger if they think they can take action to protect themselves against the menace once it has been detected.

III. SAFEGUARDS

Can anything then be said to scholars and decision-makers other than "Avoid being either too open or too closed, but be especially aware of the latter danger"? Although decision-makers will always be faced with ambiguous and confusing evidence and will be forced to make inferences about others which will often be inaccurate, a number of safeguards may be suggested which could enable them to minimize their errors. First, and most obvious, decision-makers should be aware that they do not make "unbiased" interpretations of each new bit of incoming information but rather are inevitably heavily influenced by the theories they expect to be verified. They should know that what may appear to them as a self-evident

---

[24] See, for example, Donald Campbell, "Systematic Error on the Part of Human Links in Communications Systems," *Information and Control,* I (1958), pp. 346–350; and Leo Postman, "The Experimental Analysis of Motivational Factors in Perception," in Judson S. Brown (ed.), *Current Theory and Research in Motivation* (1953), pp. 59–108.

[25] Dale Wyatt and Donald Campbell, "A Study of Interviewer Bias as Related to Interviewer's Expectations and Own Opinions," *International Journal of Opinion and Attitude Research,* IV (Spring 1950), pp. 77–83.

and unambiguous inference often seems so only because of their preexisting beliefs. To someone with a different theory the same data may appear to be unimportant or to support another explanation. Thus many events provide less independent support for the decision-makers' images than they may at first realize. Knowledge of this should lead decision-makers to examine more closely evidence that others believe contradicts their views.

Second, decision-makers should see if their attitudes contain consistent or supporting beliefs that are not logically linked. These may be examples of true psycho-logic. While it is not logically surprising nor is it evidence of psychological pressures to find that people who believe that Russia is aggressive are very suspicious of any Soviet move, other kinds of consistency are more suspect. For example, most people who feel that it is important for the United States to win the war in Vietnam also feel that a meaningful victory is possible. And most people who feel defeat would neither endanger U.S. national security nor be costly in terms of other values also feel that we cannot win. Although there are important logical linkages between the two parts of each of these views (especially through theories of guerrilla warfare), they do not seem strong enough to explain the degree to which the opinions are correlated. Similarly, in Finland in the winter of 1939, those who felt that grave consequences would follow Finnish agreement to give Russia a military base also believed that the Soviets would withdraw their demand if Finland stood firm. And those who felt that concessions would not lead to loss of major values also believed that Russia would fight if need be.[26] In this country, those who favored a nuclear test ban tended to argue that fallout was very harmful, that only limited improvements in technology would flow from further testing, and that a test ban would increase the chances for peace and security. Those who opposed the test ban were apt to disagree on all three points. This does not mean, of course, that the people holding such sets of supporting views were necessarily wrong in any one element. The Finns who wanted to make concessions to the USSR were probably correct in both parts of their argument. But decision-makers should be suspicious if they hold a position in which elements that are not logically connected support the same conclusion. This condition is psychologically comfortable and makes decisions easier to reach (since competing values do not have to be balanced off against each other). The chances are thus considerable that at least part of the reason why a person holds some of these views is related to psychology and not to the substance of the evidence.

Decision-makers should also be aware that actors who suddenly find themselves having an important shared interest with other actors have a tendency to overestimate the degree of common interest involved. This

[26] Max Jakobson, *The Diplomacy of the Winter War* (1961), pp. 136–139.

tendency is especially strong for those actors (e.g., the United States, at least before 1950) whose beliefs about international relations and morality imply that they can cooperate only with "good" states and that with those states there will be no major conflicts. On the other hand, states that have either a tradition of limited cooperation with others (e.g., Britain) or a strongly held theory that differentiates occasional from permanent allies [27] (e.g., the Soviet Union) find it easier to resist this tendency and need not devote special efforts to combating its danger.

A third safeguard for decision-makers would be to make their assumptions, beliefs, and the predictions that follow from them as explicit as possible. An actor should try to determine, before events occur, what evidence would count for and against his theories. By knowing what to expect he would know what to be surprised by, and surprise could indicate to that actor that his beliefs needed reevaluation.[28]

A fourth safeguard is more complex. The decision-maker should try to prevent individuals and organizations from letting their main task, political future, and identity become tied to specific theories and images of other actors.[29] If this occurs, subgoals originally sought for their contribution to higher ends will take on value of their own, and information indicating possible alternative routes to the original goals will not be carefully considered. For example, the U.S. Forest Service was unable to carry out its original purpose as effectively when it began to see its distinctive competence not in promoting the best use of lands and forests but rather in preventing all types of forest fires.[30]

Organizations that claim to be unbiased may not realize the extent to which their definition of their role has become involved with certain beliefs about the world. Allen Dulles is a victim of this lack of understanding when he says, "I grant that we are all creatures of prejudice, including CIA officials, but by entrusting intelligence coordination to our central intelligence service, which is excluded from policy-making and is married to no particular military hardware, we can avoid, to the greatest possible extent, the bending of facts obtained through intelligence to suit a particular occupational viewpoint." [31] This statement overlooks the fact that the CIA has developed a certain view of international relations and of

[27] Raymond Aron, *Peace and War* (1966), p. 29.

[28] Cf. Kuhn, *Structure of Scientific Revolutions*, p. 65. A fairly high degree of knowledge is needed before one can state precise expectations. One indication of the lack of international relations theory is that most of us are not sure what "naturally" flows from our theories and what constitutes either "puzzles" to be further explored with the paradigm or "anomalies" that cast doubt on the basic theories.

[29] See Philip Selznick, *Leadership in Administration* (1957).

[30] Ashley Schiff, *Fire and Water: Scientific Heresy in the Forest Service* (1962). Despite its title, this book is a fascinating and valuable study.

[31] Dulles, *The Craft of Intelligence* (1963), p. 53.

the cold war which maximizes the importance of its information-gathering, espionage, and subversive activities. Since the CIA would lose its unique place in the government if it were decided that the "back alleys" of world politics were no longer vital to U.S. security, it is not surprising that the organization interprets information in a way that stresses the continued need for its techniques.

Fifth, decision-makers should realize the validity and implications of Roberta Wohlstetter's argument that "a willingness to play with material from different angles and in the context of unpopular as well as popular hypotheses is an essential ingredient of a good detective, whether the end is the solution of a crime or an intelligence estimate." [32] However, it is often difficult, psychologically and politically, for any one person to do this. Since a decision-maker usually cannot get "unbiased" treatments of data, he should instead seek to structure conflicting biases into the decision-making process. The decision-maker, in other words, should have devil's advocates around, just as, as Neustadt points out,[33] the decision-maker will want to create conflicts among his subordinates in order to make appropriate choices, so he will also want to ensure that incoming information is examined from many different perspectives with many different hypotheses in mind. To some extent this kind of examination will be done automatically through the divergence of goals, training, experience, and information that exists in any large organization. But in many cases this divergence will not be sufficient. The views of those analyzing the data will still be too homogeneous, and the decision-maker will have to go out of his way not only to cultivate but to create differing viewpoints.

While all that would be needed would be to have some people examining the data trying to validate unpopular hypotheses, it would probably be more effective if they actually believed and had a stake in the views they were trying to support. If in 1941 someone had had the task of proving the view that Japan would attack Pearl Harbor, the government might have been less surprised by the attack. And only a person who was out to show that Russia would take objectively great risks would have been apt to note that several ships with especially large hatches going to Cuba were riding high in the water, indicating the presence of a bulky but light cargo that was not likely to be anything other than strategic missiles. And many people who doubt the wisdom of the administration's Vietnam policy would be somewhat reassured if there were people in the government who searched the statements and actions of both sides in an effort to prove that

[32] *Pearl Harbor,* p. 302. See Beveridge, *Art of Scientific Investigation,* p. 93, for a discussion of the idea that the scientist should keep in mind as many hypotheses as possible when conducting and analyzing experiments.

[33] Richard Neustadt, *Presidential Power* (1960).

North Vietnam was willing to negotiate and that the official interpretation of such moves as the Communist activities during the Têt truce of 1967 was incorrect.

Of course all these safeguards involve costs. They would divert resources from other tasks and would increase internal dissension. Determining whether these costs would be worth the gains would depend on a detailed analysis of how the suggested safeguards might be implemented. Even if they were adopted by a government, of course, they would not eliminate the chance of misperception. However, the safeguards would make it more likely that national decision-makers would make conscious choices about the way data were interpreted rather than merely assuming that they can be seen in only one way and can mean only one thing. Statesmen would thus be reminded of alternative images of others just as they are constantly reminded of alternative policies.

These safeguards are partly based on Hypothesis 3: actors can more easily assimilate into their established image of another actor information contradicting that image if the information is transmitted and considered bit by bit than if it comes all at once. In the former case, each piece of discrepant data can be coped with as it arrives and each of the conflicts with the prevailing view will be small enough to go unnoticed, to be dismissed as unimportant, or to necessitate at most a slight modification of the image (e.g., addition of exceptions to the rule). When the information arrives in a block, the contradiction between it and the prevailing view is apt to be much clearer and the probability of major cognitive reorganization will be higher.

IV. SOURCES OF CONCEPTS

An actor's perceptual thresholds — and thus the images that ambiguous information is apt to produce — are influenced by what he has experienced and learned about.[34] If one actor is to perceive that another fits in a given category he must first have, or develop, a concept for that category. We can usefully distinguish three levels at which a concept can be present or absent. First, the concept can be completely missing. The actor's cognitive structure may not include anything corresponding to the phenomenon he is encountering. This situation can occur not only in science fiction but also

[34] Most psychologists argue that this influence also holds for perception of shapes. For data showing that people in different societies differ in respect to their predisposition to experience certain optical illusions and for a convincing argument that this difference can be explained by the societies' different physical environments, which have led their people to develop different patterns of drawing inferences from ambiguous visual cues, see Marshall Segall, Donald Campbell, and Melville Herskovits, *The Influence of Culture on Visual Perception* (1966).

in a world of rapid change or in the meeting of two dissimilar systems. Thus China's image of the Western world was extremely inaccurate in the mid-nineteenth century, her learning was very slow, and her responses were woefully inadequate. The West was spared a similar struggle only because it had the power to reshape the system it encountered. Once the actor clearly sees one instance of the new phenomenon, he is apt to recognize it much more quickly in the future.[35] Second, the actor can know about a concept but not believe that it reflects an actual phenomenon. Thus Communist and Western decision-makers are each aware of the other's explanation of how his system functions but do not think that the concept corresponds to reality. Communist elites, furthermore, deny that anything *could* correspond to the democracies' description of themselves. Third, the actor may hold a concept, but not believe that another actor fills it at the present moment. Thus the British and French statesmen of the 1930's held a concept of states with unlimited ambitions. They realized that Napoleons were possible, but they did not think Hitler belonged in that category. Hypothesis 4 distinguishes these three cases: misperception is most difficult to correct in the case of a missing concept and least difficult to correct in the case of a recognized but presumably unfilled concept. All other things being equal (e.g., the degree to which the concept is central to the actor's cognitive structure), the first case requires more cognitive reorganization than does the second, and the second requires more reorganization than the third.

However, this hypothesis does not mean that learning will necessarily be slowest in the first case, for if the phenomena are totally new the actor may make such grossly inappropriate responses that he will quickly acquire information clearly indicating that he is faced with something he does not understand. And the sooner the actor realizes that things are not — or may not be — what they seem, the sooner he is apt to correct his image.[36]

Three main sources contribute to decision-makers' concepts of international relations and of other states and influence the level of their perceptual thresholds for various phenomena. First, an actor's beliefs about his own domestic political system are apt to be important. In some cases, like

[35] Thus when Bruner and Postman's subjects first were presented with incongruous playing cards (i.e., cards in which symbols and colors of the suits were not matching, producing red spades or black diamonds), long exposure times were necessary for correct identification. But once a subject correctly perceived the card and added this type of card to his repertoire of categories, he was able to identify other incongruous cards much more quickly. For an analogous example — in this case, changes in the analysis of aerial reconnaissance photographs of an enemy's secret weapons-testing facilities produced by the belief that a previously unknown object may be present — see David Irving, *The Mare's Nest* (1964), pp. 66–67, 274–275.

[36] Bruner and Postman, "Perceptions of Incongruity," p. 220.

that of the USSR, the decision-makers' concepts are tied to an ideology that explicitly provides a frame of reference for viewing foreign affairs. Even where this is not the case, experience with his own system will partly determine what the actor is familiar with and what he is apt to perceive in others. Louis Hartz claims, "It is the absence of the experience of social revolution which is at the heart of the whole American dilemma. . . . In a whole series of specific ways it enters into our difficulty of communication with the rest of the world. We find it difficult to understand Europe's 'social question'. . . . We are not familiar with the deeper social struggles of Asia and hence tend to interpret even reactionary regimes as 'democratic.' " [37] Similarly, George Kennan argues that in World War I the Allied powers, and especially America, could not understand the bitterness and violence of others' internal conflicts: ". . . The inability of the Allied statesmen to picture to themselves the passions of the Russian civil war [was partly caused by the fact that] we represent . . . a society in which the manifestations of evil have been carefully buried and sublimated in the social behavior of people, as in their very consciousness. For this reason, probably, despite our widely traveled and outwardly cosmopolitan lives, the mainsprings of political behavior in such a country as Russia tend to remain concealed from our vision." [38]

Second, concepts will be supplied by the actor's previous experiences. An experiment from another field illustrates this. Dearborn and Simon presented business executives from various divisions (e.g., sales, accounting, production) with the same hypothetical data and asked them for an analysis and recommendations from the standpoint of what would be best for the company as a whole. The executives' views heavily reflected their departmental perspectives.[39] William W. Kaufmann shows how the perceptions of Ambassador Joseph Kennedy were affected by his past: "As befitted a former chairman of the Securities Exchange and Maritime Commissions, his primary interest lay in economic matters. . . . The revolutionary character of the Nazi regime was not a phenomenon that he could easily grasp. . . . It was far simpler, and more in accord with his own premises, to explain German aggressiveness in economic terms. The Third Reich was dissatisfied, authoritarian, and expansive largely because her economy was unsound." [40] Similarly it has been argued that Chamberlain was slow to recognize Hitler's intentions partly because of the limiting

[37] *The Liberal Tradition in America* (1955), p. 306.

[38] Kennan, *Russia and the West under Lenin and Stalin* (1962), pp. 142–143.

[39] DeWitt Dearborn and Herbert Simon, "Selective Perception: A Note on the Departmental Identification of Executives," *Sociometry*, XXI (June 1958), pp. 140–144.

[40] "Two American Ambassadors: Bullitt and Kennedy," in Craig and Gilbert, *The Diplomats*, pp. 358–359.

nature of his personal background and business experiences.[41] The impact
of training and experience seems to be demonstrated when the background
of the appeasers is compared to that of their opponents. One difference
stands out: "A substantially higher percentage of the anti-appeasers
(irrespective of class origins) had the kind of knowledge which comes
from close acquaintance, mainly professional, with foreign affairs." [42]
Since members of the diplomatic corps are responsible for meeting threats
to the nation's security before these grow to major proportions and since
they have learned about cases in which aggressive states were not recognized as such until very late, they may be prone to interpret ambiguous
data as showing that others are aggressive. It should be stressed that we
cannot say that the professionals of the 1930's were more apt to make
accurate judgments of other states. Rather, they may have been more
sensitive to the chance that others were aggressive. They would then
rarely take an aggressor for a status-quo power, but would more often
make the opposite error.[43] Thus in the years before World War I the per-

---

[41] Hugh Trevor-Roper put this point well: "Brought up as a businessman, successful in municipal politics, [Chamberlain's] outlook was entirely parochial. Educated
Conservative aristocrats like Churchill, Eden, and Cranborne, whose families had
long been used to political responsibility, had seen revolution and revolutionary
leaders before, in their own history, and understood them correctly; but the Chamber-
lains, who had run from radical imperialism to timid conservatism in a generation of
life in Birmingham, had no such understanding of history or the world: to them the
scope of human politics was limited by their own parochial horizons, and Neville
Chamberlain could not believe that Hitler was fundamentally different from himself.
If Chamberlain wanted peace, so must Hitler" ("Munich — Its Lessons Ten Years
Later," in Francis Loewenheim [ed.], *Peace or Appeasement?* [1965], pp. 152–153).
For a similar view, see A. L. Rowse, *Appeasement* (1963), p. 117.

But Donald Lammers points out that the views of many prominent British public
figures in the 1930's do not fit this generalization (*Explaining Munich* [1966],
pp. 13–140). Furthermore, arguments that stress the importance of the experiences
and views of the actors' ancestors do not explain the links by which these influence
the actors themselves. Presumably Churchill and Chamberlain read the same history
books in school and had the same basic information about Britain's past role in the
world. Thus what has to be demonstrated is that in their homes aristocrats like
Churchill learned different things about politics and human nature than did middle-
class people like Chamberlain and that these experiences had a significant impact.
Alternatively, it could be argued that the patterns of child-rearing prevalent among
the aristocracy influenced the children's personalities in a way that made them more
likely to see others as aggressive.

[42] *Ibid.* (Lammers), p. 15.

[43] During a debate on appeasement in the House of Commons, Harold Nicolson
declared, "I know that those of us who believe in the traditions of our policy, . . .
who believe that one great function of this country is to maintain moral standards in
Europe, to maintain a settled pattern of international relations, not to make friends
with people who are demonstrably evil . . . — I know that those who hold such
beliefs are accused of possessing the Foreign Office mind. I thank God that I possess
the Foreign Office mind" (quoted in Martin Gilbert, *The Roots of Appeasement*
[1966], p. 187). But the qualities Nicolson mentions and applauds may be related to
a more basic attribute of "the Foreign Office mind" — suspiciousness.

manent officials in the British Foreign Office overestimated German aggressiveness.[44]

A parallel demonstration in psychology of the impact of training on perception is presented by an experiment in which ambiguous pictures were shown to both advanced and beginning police-administration students. The advanced group perceived more violence in the pictures than did the beginners. The probable explanation is that "the law enforcer may come to accept crime as a familiar personal experience, one which he himself is not surprised to encounter. The acceptance of crime as a familiar experience in turn increases the ability or readiness to perceive violence where clues to it are potentially available." [45] This experiment lends weight to the view that the British diplomats' sensitivity to aggressive states was not totally a product of personnel selection procedures.

A third source of concepts, which frequently will be the most directly relevant to a decision-maker's perception of international relations, is international history. As Henry Kissinger points out, one reason why statesmen were so slow to recognize the threat posed by Napoleon was that previous events had accustomed them only to actors who wanted to modify the existing system, not overthrow it.[46] The other side of the coin is even more striking: historical traumas can heavily influence future perceptions. They can either establish a state's image of the other state involved or can be used as analogies. An example of the former case is provided by the fact that for at least ten years after the Franco-Prussian War most of Europe's statesmen felt that Bismarck had aggressive plans when in fact his main goal was to protect the status quo. Of course the evidence was ambiguous. The post-1871 Bismarckian maneuvers, which were designed to keep peace, looked not unlike the pre-1871 maneuvers designed to set the stage for war. But that the post-1871 maneuvers were seen as indicating aggressive plans is largely attributable to the impact of Bismarck's earlier actions on the statesmen's image of him.

A state's previous unfortunate experience with a type of danger can sensitize it to other examples of that danger. While this sensitivity may

[44] George Monger, *The End of Isolation* (1963). I am also indebted to Frederick Collignon for his unpublished manuscript and several conversations on this point.

[45] Hans Toch and Richard Schulte, "Readiness to Perceive Violence as a Result of Police Training," *British Journal of Psychology,* LII (November 1961), p. 392 (original italics omitted). It should be stressed that one cannot say whether or not the advanced police students perceived the pictures "accurately." The point is that their training predisposed them to see violence in ambiguous situations. Whether on balance they would make fewer perceptual errors and better decisions is very hard to determine. For an experiment showing that training can lead people to "recognize" an expected stimulus even when that stimulus is in fact not shown, see Israel Goldiamond and William F. Hawkins, "Vexierversuch: The Log Relationship Between Word-Frequency and Recognition Obtained in the Absence of Stimulus Words," *Journal of Experimental Psychology,* LVI (December 1958), pp. 457–463.

[46] Kissinger, *A World Restored* (1964), pp. 2–3.

lead the state to avoid the mistake it committed in the past, it may also lead it mistakenly to believe that the present situation is like the past one. Santayana's maxim could be turned around: "Those who remember the past are condemned to make the opposite mistakes." As Paul Kecskemeti shows, both defenders and critics of the unconditional surrender plan of the Second World War thought in terms of the conditions of World War I.[47] Annette Baker Fox found that the Scandinavian countries' neutrality policies in World War II were strongly influenced by their experiences in the previous war, even though vital aspects of the two situations were different. Thus "Norway's success [during the First World War] in remaining non-belligerent though pro-Allied gave the Norwegians confidence that their country could again stay out of war." [48] And the lesson drawn from the unfortunate results of this policy was an important factor in Norway's decision to join NATO.

The application of the Munich analogy to various contemporary events has been much commented on, and I do not wish to argue the substantive points at stake. But it seems clear that the probabilities that any state is facing an aggressor who has to be met by force are not altered by the career of Hitler and the history of the 1930's. Similarly the probability of an aggressor's announcing his plans is not increased (if anything, it is decreased) by the fact that Hitler wrote *Mein Kampf*. Yet decision-makers are more sensitive to these possibilities, and thus more apt to perceive ambiguous evidence as indicating they apply to a given case, than they would have been had there been no Nazi Germany.

Historical analogies often precede, rather than follow, a careful analysis of a situation (e.g., Truman's initial reaction to the news of the invasion of South Korea was to think of the Japanese invasion of Manchuria). Noting this precedence, however, does not show us which of many analogies will come to a decision-maker's mind. Truman could have thought of nineteenth-century European wars that were of no interest to the United States. Several factors having nothing to do with the event under consideration influence what analogies a decision-maker is apt to make. One factor is the number of cases similar to the analogy with which the decision-maker is familiar. Another is the importance of the past event to the political system of which the decision-maker is a part. The more times such an event occurred and the greater its consequences were, the more a decision-maker will be sensitive to the particular danger involved and the more he will be apt to see ambiguous stimuli as indicating another instance of this kind of event. A third factor is the degree of the decision-maker's personal involvement in the past case — in time, energy, ego, and position. The last-

[47] Kecskemeti, *Strategic Surrender* (1964), pp. 215–241.
[48] Fox, *The Power of Small States* (1959), p. 81.

mentioned variable will affect not only the event's impact on the decision-maker's cognitive structure, but also the way he perceives the event and the lesson he draws. Someone who was involved in getting troops into South Korea after the attack will remember the Korean War differently from someone who was involved in considering the possible use of nuclear weapons or in deciding what messages should be sent to the Chinese. Greater personal involvement will usually give the event greater impact, especially if the decision-maker's own views were validated by the event. One need not accept a total application of learning theory to nations to believe that "nothing fails like success." [49] It also seems likely that if many critics argued at the time that the decision-maker was wrong, he will be even more apt to see other situations in terms of the original event. For example, because Anthony Eden left the government on account of his views and was later shown to have been correct, he probably was more apt to see as Hitlers other leaders with whom he had conflicts (e.g., Nasser). A fourth factor is the degree to which the analogy is compatible with the rest of his belief system. A fifth is the absence of alternative concepts and analogies. Individuals and states vary in the amount of direct or indirect political experience they have had which can provide different ways of interpreting data. Decision-makers who are aware of multiple possibilities of states' intentions may be less likely to seize on an analogy prematurely. The perception of citizens of nations like the United States which have relatively little history of international politics may be more apt to be heavily influenced by the few major international events that have been important to their country.

The first three factors indicate that an event is more apt to shape present perceptions if it occurred in the recent rather than the remote past. If it occurred recently, the statesman will then know about it at first hand even if he was not involved in the making of policy at the time. Thus if generals are prepared to fight the last war, diplomats may be prepared to avoid the last war. Part of the Anglo-French reaction to Hitler can be explained by the prevailing beliefs that the First World War was to a large extent caused by misunderstandings and could have been avoided by farsighted and non-belligerent diplomacy. And part of the Western perception of Russia and China can be explained by the view that appeasement was an inappropriate response to Hitler.[50]

---

[49] William Inge, *Outspoken Essays* (First Series, 1923), p. 88.

[50] Of course, analogies themselves are not "unmoved movers." The interpretation of past events is not automatic and is informed by general views of international relations and complex judgments. And just as beliefs about the past influence the present, views about the present influence interpretations of history. It is difficult to determine the degree to which the United States' interpretation of the reasons it went to war in 1917 influenced American foreign policy in the 1920's and 1930's and how much the isolationism of that period influenced the histories of the war.

V. THE EVOKED SET

The way people perceive data is influenced not only by their cognitive structure and theories about other actors but also by what they are concerned with at the time they receive the information. Information is evaluated in light of the small part of the person's memory that is presently active — the "evoked set." My perceptions of the dark streets I pass walking home from the movies will be different if the film I saw had dealt with spies than if it had been a comedy. If I am working on aiding a country's education system and I hear someone talk about the need for economic development in that state, I am apt to think he is concerned with education, whereas if I had been working on, say, trying to achieve political stability in that country, I would have placed his remarks in that framework.[51]

Thus Hypothesis 5 states that when messages are sent from a different background of concerns and information than is possessed by the receiver, misunderstanding is likely. Person A and person B will read the same message quite differently if A has seen several related messages that B does not know about. This difference will be compounded if, as is frequently the case, A and B each assume that the other has the same background he does. This means that misperception can occur even when deception is neither intended nor expected. Thus Roberta Wohlstetter found not only that different parts of the United States government had different perceptions of data about Japan's intentions and messages partly because they saw the incoming information in very different contexts, but also that officers in the field misunderstood warnings from Washington: "Washington advised General Short [in Pearl Harbor] on November 27 to expect 'hostile action' at any moment, by which it meant 'attack on American possessions from without,' but General Short understood this phrase to mean 'sabotage.' " [52] Washington did not realize the extent to which Pearl Harbor considered the danger of sabotage to be primary, and furthermore it incorrectly believed that General Short had received the intercepts of the secret Japanese diplomatic messages available in Washington which indicated that surprise attack was a distinct possibility. Another implication of this hypothesis is that if important information is known to only part of the government of state A and part of the government of

---

[51] For some psychological experiments on this subject, see Jerome Bruner and A. Leigh Minturn, "Perceptual Identification and Perceptual Organization," *Journal of General Psychology*, LIII (July 1955), pp. 22–28; Seymour Feshbach and Robert Singer, "The Effects of Fear Arousal and Suppression of Fear upon Social Perception," *Journal of Abnormal and Social Psychology*, LV (November 1957), pp. 283–288; and Elsa Sippoal, "A Group Study of Some Effects of Preparatory Sets," *Psychology Monographs*, XLVI, No. 210 (1935), pp. 27–28. For a general discussion of the importance of the perceiver's evoked set, see Postman, "Motivational Factors in Perception," p. 87.

[52] *Pearl Harbor*, pp. 73–74.

state B, international messages may be misunderstood by those parts of the receiver's government that do not match, in the information they have, the part of the sender's government that dispatched the message.[53]

Two additional hypotheses can be drawn from the problems of those sending messages. Hypothesis 6 states that when people spend a great deal of time drawing up a plan or making a decision, they tend to think that the message about it they wish to convey will be clear to the receiver.[54] Since they are aware of what is to them the important pattern in their actions, they often feel that the pattern will be equally obvious to others, and they overlook the degree to which the message is apparent to them only because they know what to look for. Those who have not participated in the endless meetings may not understand what information the sender is trying to convey. George Quester has shown how the German and, to a lesser extent, the British desire to maintain target limits on bombing in the first eighteen months of World War II was undermined partly by the fact that each side knew the limits it was seeking and its own reasons for any apparent "exceptions" (e.g., the German attack on Rotterdam) and incorrectly felt that these limits and reasons were equally clear to the other side.[55]

Hypothesis 7 holds that actors often do not realize that actions intended to project a given image may not have the desired effect because the actions themselves do not turn out as planned. Thus even without appreciable impact of different cognitive structures and backgrounds, an action may convey an unwanted message. For example, a country's representatives may not follow instructions and so may give others impressions contrary to those the home government wished to convey. The efforts of Washington and Berlin to settle their dispute over Samoa in the late 1880's were complicated by the provocative behavior of their agents on the spot. These agents not only increased the intensity of the local conflict but led the decision-makers to become more suspicious of the other state because they tended to assume that their agents were obeying instructions and that the actions of the other side represented official policy. In such cases both sides will believe that the other is reading hostility into a policy of theirs which is friendly. Similarly, Quester's study shows that the attempt to limit bombing referred to above failed partly because neither side was able to

[53] For example, Roger Hilsman points out, "Those who knew of the peripheral reconnaissance flights that probed Soviet air defenses during the Eisenhower administration and the U-2 flights over the Soviet Union itself . . . were better able to understand some of the things the Soviets were saying and doing than people who did not know of these activities" (*To Move a Nation* [1967], p. 66). But it is also possible that those who knew about the U-2 flights at times misinterpreted Soviet messages by incorrectly believing that the sender was influenced by, or at least knew of, these flights.

[54] I am grateful to Thomas Schelling for discussion on this point.

[55] Quester, *Deterrence before Hiroshima* (1966), pp. 105–122.

bomb as accurately as it thought it could and thus did not realize the physical effects of its actions.[56]

VI. FURTHER HYPOTHESES FROM THE PERSPECTIVE OF THE PERCEIVER

From the perspective of the perceiver several other hypotheses seem to hold. Hypothesis 8 is that there is an overall tendency for decision-makers to see other states as more hostile than they are.[57] There seem to be more cases of statesmen incorrectly believing others are planning major acts against their interest than of statesmen being lulled by a potential aggressor. There are many reasons for this which are too complex to be treated here (e.g., some parts of the bureaucracy feel it is their responsibility to be suspicious of all other states; decision-makers often feel they are "playing it safe" to believe and act as though the other state were hostile in questionable cases; and often, when people do not feel they are a threat to others, they find it difficult to believe that others may see them as a threat). It should be noted, however, that decision-makers whose perceptions are described by this hypothesis would not necessarily further their own values by trying to correct for this tendency. The values of possible outcomes as well as their probabilities must be considered, and it may be that the probability of an unnecessary arms-tension cycle arising out of misperceptions, multiplied by the costs of such a cycle, may seem less to decision-makers than the probability of incorrectly believing another state is friendly, multiplied by the costs of this eventuality.

Hypothesis 9 states that actors tend to see the behavior of others as more centralized, disciplined, and coordinated than it is. This hypothesis holds true in related ways. Frequently, too many complex events are squeezed into a perceived pattern. Actors are hesitant to admit or even see that particular incidents cannot be explained by their theories.[58] Those events not caused by factors that are important parts of the perceiver's image are often seen as though they were. Further, actors see others as more internally united than they in fact are and generally overestimate the degree to which others are following a coherent policy. The degree to which the other side's policies are the product of internal bargaining,[59]

---

[56] *Ibid.*

[57] For a slightly different formulation of this view, see Holsti, "Images of the Enemy," p. 27.

[58] The Soviets consciously hold an extreme version of this view and seem to believe that nothing is accidental. See the discussion in Nathan Leites, *A Study of Bolshevism* (1953), pp. 67–73.

[59] A. W. Marshall criticizes Western explanations of Soviet military posture for failing to take this into account. See his "Problems of Estimating Military Power," a paper presented at the 1966 Annual Meeting of the American Political Science Association, p. 16.

internal misunderstandings, or subordinates' not following instructions is underestimated. This is the case partly because actors tend to be unfamiliar with the details of another state's policymaking processes. Seeing only the finished product, they find it simpler to try to construct a rational explanation for the policies, even though they know that such an analysis could not explain their own policies.[60]

Familiarity also accounts for Hypothesis 10: because a state gets most of its information about the other state's policies from the other's foreign office, it tends to take the foreign office's position for the stand of the other government as a whole. In many cases this perception will be an accurate one, but when the other government is divided or when the other foreign office is acting without specific authorization, misperception may result. For example, part of the reason why in 1918 Allied governments incorrectly thought "that the Japanese were preparing to take action [in Siberia], if need be, with agreement with the British and French alone, disregarding the absence of American consent," [61] was that Allied ambassadors had talked mostly with Foreign Minister Motono, who was among the minority of the Japanese favoring this policy. Similarly, America's NATO allies may have gained an inaccurate picture of the degree to which the American government was committed to the MLF because they had greatest contact with parts of the government that strongly favored the MLF. And states that tried to get information about Nazi foreign policy from German diplomats were often misled because these officials were generally ignorant of or out of sympathy with Hitler's plans. The Germans and the Japanese sometimes purposely misinformed their own ambassadors in order to deceive their enemies more effectively.

Hypothesis 11 states that actors tend to overestimate the degree to which others are acting in response to what they themselves do when the others behave in accordance with the actor's desires; but when the behavior of the other is undesired, it is usually seen as derived from internal forces. If the *effect* of another's action is to injure or threaten the first side, the first side is apt to believe that such was the other's *purpose*. An example of the first part of the hypothesis is provided by Kennan's account of the activities of official and unofficial American representatives who protested to the new Bolshevik government against several of its actions. When the Soviets changed their position, these representatives felt it was largely

---

[60] It has also been noted that in labor-management disputes both sides may be apt to believe incorrectly that the other is controlled from above, either from the international union office or from the company's central headquarters (Robert Blake, Herbert Shepard, and Jane Mouton, *Managing Intergroup Conflict in Industry* [1964], p. 182). It has been further noted that both Democratic and Republican members of the House tend to see the other party as the one that is more disciplined and united (Charles Clapp, *The Congressman* [1963], pp. 17–19).

[61] George Kennan, *Russia Leaves the War* (1967), p. 484.

because of their influence.[62] This sort of interpretation can be explained not only by the fact that it is gratifying to the individual making it, but also, taking the other side of the coin mentioned in Hypothesis 9, by the fact that the actor is most familiar with his own input into the other's decision and has less knowledge of other influences. The second part of Hypothesis 11 is illustrated by the tendency of actors to believe that the hostile behavior of others is to be explained by the other side's motives and not by its reaction to the first side. Thus Chamberlain did not see that Hitler's behavior was related in part to his belief that the British were weak. More common is the failure to see that the other side is reacting out of fear of the first side, which can lead to self-fulfilling prophecies and spirals of misperception and hostility.

This difficulty is often compounded by an implication of Hypothesis 12: when actors have intentions that they do not try to conceal from others, they tend to assume that others accurately perceive these intentions. Only rarely do they believe that others may be reacting to a much less favorable image of themselves than they think they are projecting.[63]

For state A to understand how state B perceives A's policy is often difficult because such understanding may involve a conflict with A's image of itself. Raymond Sontag argues that Anglo-German relations before World War I deteriorated partly because "the British did not like to think of themselves as selfish, or unwilling to tolerate 'legitimate' German expansion. The Germans did not like to think of themselves as aggressive, or unwilling to recognize 'legitimate' British vested interest." [64]

Hypothesis 13 suggests that if it is hard for an actor to believe that the other can see him as a menace, it is often even harder for him to see that issues important to him are not important to others. While he may know

[62] *Ibid.*, pp. 404, 408, 500.

[63] Herbert Butterfield notes that these assumptions can contribute to the spiral of "Hobbesian fear. . . . You yourself may vividly feel the terrible fear that you have of the other party, but you cannot enter into the other man's counter-fear, or even understand why he should be particularly nervous. For you know that you yourself mean him no harm and that you want nothing from him save guarantees for your own safety; and it is never possible for you to realize or remember properly that since he cannot see the inside of your mind, he can never have the same assurance of your intentions that you have" (*History and Human Conflict*, [1951], p. 20).

[64] Sontag, *European Diplomatic History 1871–1932* (1933), p. 125. It takes great mental effort to realize that actions which seem only the natural consequence of defending your vital interests can look to others as though you are refusing them any chance of increasing their influence. In rebutting the famous Crowe "balance of power" memorandum of 1907, which justified a policy of "containing" Germany on the grounds that she was a threat to British national security, Sanderson, a former permanent undersecretary in the Foreign Office, wrote, "It has sometimes seemed to me that to a foreigner reading our press the British Empire must appear in the light of some huge giant sprawling all over the globe, with gouty fingers and toes stretching in every direction, which cannot be approached without eliciting a scream" (quoted in Monger, p. 315). But few other Englishmen could be convinced that others might see them this way.

that another actor is on an opposing team, it may be more difficult for him to realize that the other is playing an entirely different game. This is especially true when the game he is playing seems vital to him.[65]

The final hypothesis, Hypothesis 14, is as follows: actors tend to overlook the fact that evidence consistent with their theories may also be consistent with other views. When choosing between two theories we have to pay attention only to data that cannot be accounted for by one of the theories. But it is common to find people claiming as proof of their theories data that could also support alternative views. This phenomenon is related to the point made earlier that any single bit of information can be interpreted only within a framework of hypotheses and theories. And while it is true that "we may without a vicious circularity accept some datum as a fact because it conforms to the very law for which it counts as another confirming instance, and reject an allegation of fact because it is already excluded by law," [66] we should be careful lest we forget that a piece of information seems in many cases to confirm a certain hypothesis only because we already believe that hypothesis to be correct and that the information can with as much validity support a different hypothesis. For example, one of the reasons why the German attack on Norway took both that country and England by surprise, even though they had detected German ships moving toward Norway, was that they expected not an attack but an attempt by the Germans to break through the British blockade and reach the Atlantic. The initial course of the ships was consistent with either plan, but the British and Norwegians took this course to mean that their predictions were being borne out.[67] This is not to imply that the interpretation made was foolish, but only that the decision-makers should have been aware that the evidence was also consistent with an invasion and should have had a bit less confidence in their views.

The longer the ships would have to travel the same route whether they were going to one or another of two destinations, the more information would be needed to determine their plans. Taken as a metaphor, this inci-

---

[65] George Kennan makes clear that in 1918 this kind of difficulty was partly responsible for the inability of either the Allies or the new Bolshevik government to understand the motivations of the other side: "There is . . . nothing in nature more egocentrical than the embattled democracy. . . . It . . . tends to attach to its own cause an absolute value which distorts its own vision of everything else. . . . It will readily be seen that people who have got themselves into this frame of mind have little understanding for the issues of any contest other than the one in which they are involved. The idea of people wasting time and substance on any *other* issue seems to them preposterous" (*Russia and the West,* pp. 11–12).

[66] Kaplan, *Conduct of Inquiry,* p. 89.

[67] Johan Jorgen Holst, "Surprise, Signals, and Reaction: The Attack on Norway," *Cooperation and Conflict,* No. 1 (1966), p. 34. The Germans made a similar mistake in November 1942 when they interpreted the presence of an Allied convoy in the Mediterranean as confirming their belief that Malta would be resupplied. They thus were taken by surprise when landings took place in North Africa (William Langer, *Our Vichy Gamble* [1966], p. 365).

dent applies generally to the treatment of evidence. Thus as long as Hitler made demands for control only of ethnically German areas, his actions could be explained either by the hypothesis that he had unlimited ambitions or by the hypothesis that he wanted to unite all the Germans. But actions against non-Germans (e.g., the takeover of Czechoslovakia in March 1939) could not be accounted for by the latter hypothesis. And it was this action that convinced the appeasers that Hitler had to be stopped. It is interesting to speculate on what the British reaction would have been had Hitler left Czechoslovakia alone for a while and instead made demands on Poland similar to those he eventually made in the summer of 1939. The two paths would then still not have diverged, and further misperception could have occurred.

WILLIAM M. JONES

On Decisionmaking in Large Organizations

That national security policy is, to a large degree, the output of complex organizations rather than the decisions of individuals has important consequences for behavior of the participants in the bureaucracy and for the decisions and actions which emerge. Even if all the actors are intelligent, dedicated, selfless men, the fact that they are members of large-scale complex organizations frequently has a deleterious impact on the decisions and actions which result.

Because each component organization within the national security bureaucracy is itself composed of large numbers of people, certain compromises in performance are necessary to achieve the necessary interpersonal coordination which is required if the organization is to be able to operate at all. In particular, organizations are inclined to place a high premium on consistency of behavior over time in order to establish a reliable pattern of mutual expectations among their members. The same considerations lead organizations to prefer simple instructions and uncomplicated procedures of operation. From the perspective of a senior participant, however, the organizations on which he depends appear to be rigid and inflexible, unable or unwilling to be responsive to his needs. He finds that they can undertake only those activities which they have prepared for and cannot improvise or innovate. Complex instructions become simplified, and subtle reasoning is translated into stark imperatives. These organizational characteristics frequently result in outputs which vary substantially from what the senior participant had in mind and told his subordinates to do.

Abridged by the editors from *On Decisionmaking in Large Organizations* (Santa Monica: The Rand Corporation, March 1964) with permission.

Views or conclusions contained in this Memorandum should not be interpreted as representing the official opinion or policy of the United States Air Force.

Since an organization's formal communications channels are an inaccurate representation of that organization's processes and procedures, and because only experienced members of the organization ordinarily are privy to the informal and personal communication channels, communication between organizations within the national security bureaucracy is very difficult, and coordination is likely to be highly deficient. Because one organization usually doesn't understand how another operates, the latter frequently appears to be incompetent or incapable in the eyes of the former. These organizational problems create pressures for each organization to seek to maximize its autonomy of operations and to minimize its dependence on other groups.

The consequences of these basically structural deficiencies lead to organizations which (1) bias their recommendations and options toward their particular capabilities and in favor of activities which will allow them to operate autonomously, (2) try to maximize their influence over and participation in decisions, and (3) resist implementing decisions which imply costs to particular organizational objectives. The problems which attend the existence and interaction of complex organizations illustrate the limits on the ability of senior participants to secure the behavior they desire and the actions they intend.

I. THE APPROACH TO BE USED

In the development of this description of organizational decisionmaking, the writer has drawn primarily on his experiences and observations as a staff officer in a number of military headquarters. As a result, this discussion is directed toward directive-type decisionmaking organizations such as one finds in the Executive Branch of the U.S. government. Discussions with associates experienced in other types of large organizations lead the writer to believe that most of the factors discussed here are to be found in any large organization, with some variation in the importance of several elements.

In describing the patterns and processes of organizational decisionmaking, actual or hypothetical examples will occasionally be cited. These should be considered as illustrations of the element being discussed rather than proof of the validity of this particular construct.

The organization decisionmaking process is a product of the very complex communications process among individual decisionmakers in the organization.[1] The following assumptions will be used to simplify and give structure to a description of the process:

(1) Much of the phenomena in the decisionmaking processes of large

---

[1] Throughout this Memorandum the word "communications" is used to mean the interchange of thoughts and opinions between people. "Communications equipment" or "communications systems" is used to mean electronic or mechanical devices designed to support this interchange.

organizations can be explained without assuming the existence of any irresponsible, stupid, undedicated, or uncaring members. Stated positively, whenever the expression "large organization" is employed in this discussion, the members are assumed to be serious, dedicated, responsible, and intelligent officials.

(2) The communications process between the members of a large organization, and between large organizations, can be described by categorizing the process as occurring at three levels: formal, subformal, and personal.

(3) Certain additional facts and events can be explained by assuming that all organization members can be categorized as being either oriented toward centralization or toward decentralization in their views on how their organization should manage its processes.

The remainder of this discussion develops and illustrates the ideas embodied in the above assumptions, attributing certain commonly seen organizational phenomena to their interaction, and draws a few tentative implications for the structuring of military command and control systems.

II. COMMUNICATIONS IN AND BETWEEN LARGE ORGANIZATIONS

In discussing intrastaff and interstaff communications channels, three levels will be assumed: the *formal,* the *subformal,* and the *personal.* This categorization into three levels of what is, in fact, a highly complex spectrum has been adopted so as to make the subject manageable although its artificiality and arbitrariness are recognized.

Formal Communications

The formal communications channel is the explicit level. At this level, one finds published organization charts, standing operating procedures, formal orders and directives, formal periodic reports, and so on. The substance of the messages communicated at this level is marked as being, officially, a matter for the record. This is the structure that is manipulated when a change in organizational procedures is made. Being overt, it serves as a useful guide to a first point of contact when communications must be established among subordinates on two large staffs. The strength of and in fact the necessity for, communications at this level are related to its official nature. The substance of the messages passed in the formal channel (and at the formal level) makes the taking of certain actions and the making of certain decisions "legal." Being explicit and having the aspect of legalizing, communications at the formal level tend to be somewhat slow in their development and passage through a large staff or organization. When a number of ongoing activities of a slightly discrepant nature must all be made legal in one formal message (a frequent event when more than one staff element is involved in originating the message), one can observe a great deal of care being exercised in wording the message so as to allow for adequate latitude in interpretations.

Whereas the formal level is the structure most apparent to an outsider, a careful observer will soon become aware that much of importance to the understanding of organizational attitudes and activities lies beneath this surface.

Subformal Communications

The subformal communications channel is the level at which activities and attitudes are much less explicit. It is characterized by the "our way of doing things" that develops around the formal organization structure. The undirected or partially directed patterns of communications linkages that develop between subunits of large organizations are in this level. These linkages are usually related to certain subjects or actions. (For example, Plans *always* coordinates with Operations on base acquisition matters.) The subformal communications and the rules governing their use are organizational necessities as they permit a certain latitude in operation within the formal structure and allow for personality variations that cannot be reflected in the formal organization.

To be effective in his job a subordinate official must know and observe these rules and procedures. Being mostly unspecified, these subformal rules are learned by experience and example and, during his learning period, the newcomer to the organization may have a number of unpleasant experiences. Violation of these unwritten "rules of the road" is certain to arouse resistance and, if persisted in, active antagonism.

As suggested above, there are many gradations in the subformal level. Permanent, interstaff committees and published directives that require coordination are, in a sense, formal recognition of the subformal operations and frequently grow out of preexisting subformal activities. The subformal rules, in any active organization, are continuously changing and therefore the learning process is always going on. The rate of change is usually slow, however, and accommodation to the changes is relatively easy. The freedom to ignore the rules or establish new rules varies with the position of the official within the organization although there are always practical limits to this freedom. A new commander can be expected to make changes in the subformal pattern but his ability to make such changes rapidly is limited by the ability of the organization to adjust to the change.[2]

---

[2] It is assumed here that the purpose for which the organization was formed is of sufficient importance to preclude a deliberately accepted period of disorganization as a reasonable option.

Once an insider has gained an adequate "feel" for the subformal communications pattern of his organization he is likely to view the prospect of a sharp change, imposed from above or from the outside, with considerable distaste. His functional needs have urged him into the pattern, and his emotions are likely to be aroused by the prospect of change and a resulting period of reduced effectiveness. Objective discussion of projected changes is made difficult because many of the features of the subformal pattern are unadmitted and, to some extent, are unconscious habits.

Because the subformal attitudes and activities are strong operative factors in the accomplishment of objectives within an organizational framework, and because they are usually learned by experience and example, they represent an important but unknowable element to an outsider. A sensitive observer will be aware that they exist, may suspect that he knows some of the rules, but is unlikely to know the degree of importance the insider attaches to them.

Personal Communications

The personal communications channel is, for the purposes of this discussion, defined as that level at which an organization functionary, in communicating with an insider or an outsider, deliberately reveals something of his own attitude toward the activities of his own organization. This does not mean, exclusively, the network of friendships that develop within an organization but rather that pattern of low-key shop talk that goes on behind formal and subformal activities. Within a large staff it is observable primarily as a type of interelement communications that is used to keep the participants aware of what is going on. The "coffee cup conversations" between friends and acquaintances within a large organization characterize this level. The observer can usually detect the personal level in a conversation between two functionaries by the advent of expressions like "Personally, I think . . ."; "My boss would skin me if he heard me say this but . . ."; "My outfit is planning to . . . but I feel . . ."; and "I don't know if I can sell it to my outfit but I'll try."

Although the specific connections in the nexus of personal channels are usually uncontrolled in an organization, there are quite specific rules as to how they may be used. In general, the personal channels within a staff may be safely used only for the passage of information, not for "action type" direction. The friendly tip, dropped during a period of shop talk at the "19th hole," is designed to direct the attention of the recipient to a subject. Proper organizational procedures require that the information be verified (using subformal or formal channels) before action is taken. Protection of the source is frequently important. Personal level communications, while they exist between echelons in the staff, tend to be degraded between people occupying significantly different ranks since "good ethics" dictate that shop secrets must be protected and a person in a subordinate position must, for safety's sake, avoid the appearance of violating this dictum.

The outsider is likely to be surprised at the speed with which the personal channel, "the rumor mill," operates in a large staff. This speed is the result of the lack of control and the absence of any built-in verification mechanism, insofar as the organization is concerned.

Effective communications and coordination between large staffs are difficult matters due to a mutual lack of detailed knowledge of each other's current communication patterns and the rules under which they operate. Being an insider on one staff does nothing to change one's status as an outsider on another. In fact, if the two organizations are competitive (and large organizations communicating with each other characteristically are), the communications block is likely to be formidable.

Use of Communication Levels

In their attempts to communicate and coordinate with each other, large organizations are rather rigidly confined to the formal level, with some superficial elements of the subformal and the personal.

The introduction of the new budgeting procedure in the Department of Defense is an excellent case study that demonstrates some of the difficulties. Without describing either the prior or the new procedures or commenting on their merits and failings, one can simply observe that there was a sharp change in the formal organizational arrangements for handling this procedure. The old procedure had, over time, developed a well-recognized pattern of organization and communication at the subformal level. The sharp change in the formal system shattered many of the subformal arrangements and necessitated a rather unpleasant period of adjustment. Those functionaries on the headquarters staffs whose job it was to express their service's requirements in proposed budget form had previously known the offices and functionaries in the OSD [Office of the Secretary of Defense] with whom they should interact in an attempt to "sell" their package. Without suggesting that they were always pleased with the results of such interactions, it can be noted that they generally understood the subformal operations they had to perform in the attempt to accomplish their job.

With the advent of the new system this knowledge of operations was removed and a period of trial and error, false starts, and general confusion ensued. It is also worth noting that the pace with which the new system has gained operating efficiency has been closely related to (and in the view of this writer, dependent upon) the rate at which a new subformal pattern has developed. Finally, it should be observed that the existence of personal connections between the staffs that existed before, during, and after the change had little or no effect in the smoothing of the transition.

Another case in point might be the interactions between a service headquarter's staff and the headquarters of a major subordinate command. . . . The major subelements of a large staff have only vague notions about the operations of the other elements. Therefore, one should expect that the notions about the headquarters staff one finds in a command headquarters will be considerably distorted (and vice versa). Again we see the resultant lack of mutual predictability. Notice that in this situation we can identify strong ties in the formal structure and numerous links in the personal, but still the misunderstandings exist.

It is in this context that one can observe quite sharply the rules that divide the subformal and the personal. Information about ongoing decisions in the headquarters staff is rapidly transmitted to major command headquarters via personal contacts, but an officer from a command headquarters can only cause embarrassment to himself and to his acquaintances by trying to exploit this connection to steer the decisions.

You are formally responsible to the Deputy Chief of Staff for monitoring the status and capabilities of the Service components of the Unified and Specified Commands as well as certain uncommitted Service elements. Readiness status must be measured against something, and conventionally it is measured against the various contingency plans of the Unified and Specified Commanders. Your function urges you not only to insure that your estimates of Service capabilities are accurate but also to exert such influence and authority as you have to keep these capabilities at high level.

Your immediate superior exercises two major functions. He is responsible to the Chief of Staff for your functions and that of your colleagues, certain other Directors. He also is a member of a committee under the Joint Chiefs of Staff.

His superior, the Chief of Staff, also has two jobs. In his unilateral capability he is responsible to the Secretary of Defense, through the Service Secretary, for the management of Service resources. As a member of the JCS, he is one of the senior military advisors to the Secretary of Defense and the President and is responsible for providing strategic direction to the Armed Forces of the United States.

Your normal round of activities involves frequent conversations with your subordinates and their staff officers on such matters as they bring to your attention. Officers from other elements of the staff frequently seek concurrence in proposed decisions and actions that would have an effect on your job and the resources you monitor. Usually they will be accompanied by members of your Directorate who will recommend for or against the requested concurrence. Occasional staff meetings are held by your superior during which you receive guidance for future decisions, and you hold occasional meetings of your staff to pass this information along. You are also frequently called upon to sit on various boards and panels to consider matters that have implications for many of the Directorates across the Service Staff.

III. An Insider's View of a Decisionmaking Staff

To further illustrate the assumptions developed thus far, this section will focus on organizational activities from the insider's view. For this view we will use a hypothetical Director of Operations on the headquarters staff of a military service.[3] The reader is requested to adopt the attitude that our hypothetical officer is a serious, dedicated, intelligent, and responsible individual. In addition, it is important to this construct that similar attributes be conceded to all people occupying positions of responsibility.[4] Given such a concession, little violence will be done to the notions expressed if the reader substitutes any other functionary in the organization up to and including the Chief of Staff. To a considerable extent, the same general observations made below can be applied to any functionary in any large governmental organization; however, care should be used in applying some of the ideas to organizations where the personnel are likely to have significantly lesser feelings of identity.

To aid in the suggested exercise in empathy, the term "you" will be used to designate the hypothetical functionary whose attitudes and activities are to be discussed.

You are the Chief of a Directorate under a Deputy Chief of Staff. Directly under you are a group of Deputy Directors for various special activities, various divisions, and branches.

To the outsider you may appear to be involved in a daily mass of trivia, dialogues, and meetings. From your viewpoint, however, your numerous contacts are opportunities to influence the direction of the organization effort. Within this plethora of daily interactions and decisions you are urged into certain patterns of action by your sense of your responsibilities, your responsibility to the nation, to your Service, to your immediate superior, and to the members of your own organization. Notice here the existence of opportunities for internal conflicts. Your resolution of such conflicts is a personal matter and is dependent on the situation under consideration.

Having had much experience on various military staffs, you are urged in your daily decisions toward a consistent pattern. You understand (pos-

[3] No attempt is being made here to describe precisely the functions of an actual position on a real staff. The intent is to outline a context in which the development of attitudes can be illustrated. The consequences of organizational overlaps are not discussed here. Our hypothetical officer might also be a Methodist, a Mason, and a member of the neighborhood bowling team. These connections, while they may have certain effects, are not considered to be of serious consequence to the ideas expressed in this Memorandum.

[4] Of course, not all incumbents of positions of authority are consistently serious, dedicated, intelligent, and responsible. It is, however, the belief of the writer that all or most of the decisions that to an outsider appear ill advised or ill timed can be explained without recourse to a scapegoat on the staff.

sibly without consciously thinking about it) that your staff cannot function in support of you unless you are somewhat predictable to them. (Your superior must be consistent in his expressed views concerning things that influence your area of responsibility if he is to give you freedom, within bounds, to operate effectively.) To the outsider you may present a picture of a confirmed bureaucrat in your resistance to new and "better" ideas, but to you this resistance is the result of balancing a theoretical gain against the practical necessity of keeping your staff functioning effectively.

Another factor being urged upon you continuously is the need to "keep it simple." To insure that your staff understands your views toward certain policy matters, many subtle variations that you may well understand will have to be omitted from your formal communications. A policy statement or published plan that contains numerous "if this — then that" considerations can produce confusion at the time it is to be implemented simply because of a wide divergence in view as to what the situation really is at the time. To the outsider this can result in the appearance of stupidity or "black and white" thinking, but to you it is the only way to operate effectively.[5]

In summary to this point, your job is one of decisionmaking in a management organization. The normal pattern of activities is such that your opportunities to make or influence obviously important decisions are much less frequent than your opportunities to make numerous small decisions. Most of your influence on the direction of the organization is the result of these numerous, small decisions. Consistency in the making of these decisions is, you feel, necessary for effective staff work and coordination. In addition, consistency enhances your influence on the over-all organizational decisionmaking since your beliefs as to what should be done are best expressed by a consistent pattern.

Your decisions, as anyone's, are based on your prediction of the consequences if they are implemented. In the making of these predictions an important factor is the effect it will have on your organization and the probable reactions of other staff elements and associated agencies. Your ability to predict and therefore influence the probable attitudes and activities of other staff elements and associated agencies is degraded by your

---

[5] An interesting side note at this point is that every external communication and observable action of a functionary tends to convey a caricature. While a functionary may be aware that his images of adjacent staff elements are caricatures, he tends to believe the images of those elements with which he has infrequent interaction. We leave to the reader's imagination the picture of the typical Department of State functionary one sometimes hears sketched by military officers. The writer gains some wry amusement, if no satisfaction, from evidence that the image of the typical military officer drawn by Department of State personnel is equally unflattering. The important thing to notice here is that the absence of any significant volume of interagency communication at other than the formal level makes this type of attitude inevitable. As a result, interagency relations tend to vary from distrust to active controversy.

lack of adequate communications with them as compared with your daily communications with your own staff. Your communications with your staff are usually at the subformal, interactive level. Your communications with other staff elements tend toward the formal level. The result is that your predictions are based on mental images that can be grossly inaccurate. Finally, and quite important, you are not conscious of many of these influences.

Some outsiders have occasionally expressed bafflement because of the failure of the Services to accept the notion that decisions on weapon systems procurement are best approached as a sequential process. The construct developed here may shed some light on this "failure." Again placing yourself in the position of the Director of Operations, consider a proposed system development being coordinated through the staff. You recognize that you may only have this one opportunity to influence the decision. The next decision in the sequence may well be made through other channels. Given your confidence in your view of the future and your lack of confidence in the other, little-known decision channels, you are urged to make (or at least influence) all foreseeable decisions at that time. Because every other functionary in the staff has similar urges, the result tends to be a complete systems decision with all foreseeable decisions made at the outset. In short, the notion of setting up a sequential decision process is acceptable to an individual only if he believes he will have opportunities in the future to make the decisions implied.

Decisions related to future strategies may be bedeviled by this same factor. As a serious, responsible official you are likely to have a vague discomfort with a strategy that suggests, "If they do this, then we'll do either that or the other." Implied here is an idea that someone will be making the decision at the time and that someone is not likely to be you. Your reaction is to conjure up reasons for not adopting such a strategy.

IV. Time, Time Horizons, and Decisionmaking

Decisionmaking within a large, military management structure such as a Service headquarters staff has many interesting features. To the outsider the appearance can be one of considerable divergences of view and resulting confusion. To the insider, our hypothetical functionary, decisionmaking is a way of life and a manyfaceted activity.

For the purposes of this discussion, it should be assumed that all of the organizational decisions made by our "ideal" functionary are made in an over-all, comprehensive context. He may have to resolve conflicts between his beliefs as to what is in the best interest of the nation, his service, his staff, and himself. Notice here that his decision may well be based on his judgment of what the nation, his Service, he and his staff *should* be doing rather than being based on what it *is* doing at the time. This is not meant to suggest any serious possibility of insubordination or violation of directives from superiors. What is meant here is that, *until such time as a final decision is made*, our ideal functionary will feel free to attempt to influence the decision in the direction he feels is proper.

One facet of the decision process is the functionary's sense of how closely he is coupled to the decision of the moment. His knowledge that a specific decision is in the process of being made is a result of the information available to him from his formal, subformal, and personal sources. His sense of being or not being potentially influential in the process is affected by all three levels. For example, our hypothetical Director of Operations might hear through a personal channel of a recommendation for action being developed in the Directorate of Personnel. He might then verify the accuracy of the information through subformal channels and express opposition to the proposal to his superior through formal channels. His recommended opposition or alternative must be presented in such a way that it will be favorably considered. For personal and career reasons and for the sake of his own organization, he must try to avoid placing himself and his superior in a position that appears unacceptable or ridiculous to top management.

Another feature of the decision process is the view that our hypothetical functionary has of his capabilities and those of his staff as contrasted with his views of the capabilities of other staff functionaries and their staffs. Because of his daily interactions with his own organization, he has an appreciation of their abilities to weigh the many, widespread factors involved in developing a decision or recommended action. He has much less frequent interactions with some of the other functionaries and their staff, and his main source of information about their internal processes is their formal outputs. As a consequence, he is likely to feel that his organization is much more qualified to make the "proper" recommendation if they had available the required data.[6]

One question that is not unusual in the mind of our hypothetical functionary is whether the formal responsibilities and authority of his position authorize him to make and initiate implementation of his decisions or whether he should translate his decisions into a recommendation to his superiors. This determination is not as simple as it might seem to an outsider. The formal organization chart and job descriptions are only a general guide. The specific nature and detailed degree of latitude available is learned (developed) over time. (Our hypothetical functionary is likely

---

[6] This feeling, maintained over time, may partially explain the forces at play that produce a tendency toward "empire building," an outsider's expression. It takes people to acquire and maintain data. It may also help explain the inordinately widespread and detailed information requirements placed on manual and electronic reporting systems.

to have certain inaccuracies in his views of the actual authority exercised by other functionaries with whom his interactions are infrequent.)

Timing factors and time horizons enter into the decisionmaking process in many ways when viewed in an organizational context. In formulating a recommendation to his superior (or in arriving at a decision to order some action), our hypothetical functionary must estimate the time required to obtain approval, to send the implementing messages and, finally, the time required by the recipient of the orders to execute the directed actions. Simultaneously, he predicts, from his then current information, the likely course of events he wishes to alter so that the recommended (or ordered) action will be appropriate.[7]

Closely related to this predictive process is the problem of selecting a time horizon. Many of the misunderstandings that develop between staff sections (or parallel organizations) arise because, although the two organizations have similar predictions of "things likely to come," they are focusing their attention on a different time in the future. One recommended action might lead to short-term improvements followed by adverse results at a later date, whereas another recommendation might be expected to have opposite results. Inter-organizational arguments can often be seen to develop and to continue for lengthy periods without the contenders ever becoming aware of the fact that they are not using a similar time horizon.

Given the honest organizational egotism of our hypothetical officer, one can frequently observe a rush to "nail down" a decision before a "less reliable" competitive staff can interfere.

V. Crisis Phenomena

National crises, insofar as one can describe them in a general way, are marked as periods in which apparently vital, national decisions *must* be made.[8] "What can be done?" "What should be done?" and "How should we go about doing it?" become the dominant questions.

Characteristically, different elements of a large organization will display crisis phenomena at different times, *even if all subelements have continuous access to all the available information about the situation.* Each staff element monitors or controls different forces that may be applied to the situation. These different forces have different time lags before they

---

[7] This feature of deciding on the basis of extrapolation and estimated time lags will be discussed later in more detail.

[8] "Crisis — the point of time when it is decided whether an affair or course of action must go on, or be modified, or terminate," *Webster's New International Dictionary,* Second Edition. The reader may prefer the medical definition, "that change in a disease which indicates whether the result is to be recovery or death; also a striking change of symptoms attended by an outward manifestation as by an eruption or sweat."

can be brought to bear on the situation. It follows that each subelement is likely to judge the seriousness of the growing situation against its own ability to deal with it at the time.

Initial Phase of the Crisis

The over-all effect, when viewed from the position of the central decisionmaker, is that he is likely to receive, from one of his top subordinates, a first indication that a decision is desperately needed. Quite possibly, the rest of his subordinates will recommend a "wait and see" approach. If the situation continues to develop one can expect more and more of the top subordinates to start pressing for a decision as time goes on.

The required decisions are (in the viewpoint adopted in this study) organizational decisions and most of the phenomena associated with the noncrisis decision processes become readily observable during a crisis. Responsible officials feel powerfully moved to recommend *their* solutions. Each recommendation is likely to be related to the use of the organization controlled by the recommending official simply because that is the capability in which he has the greatest confidence. The desire for information increases inordinately as the feeling of the gravity of the situation makes the formulation of the *right* recommendation a vital matter. Time horizons are likely to contract sharply. Stresses develop in the attempt to get the "right" decision made in sufficient time to permit the effective use of the "right" organization as the "tools" available to different authorities vary in the speed with which they can be effectively employed. Controllers of specialized organizations that are affected by any one proposal may have strong desires to achieve coordination with other such organizations. However, the implementation of these desires may be frustrated by counterproposals from the other organizations. An additional communications barrier can be the fact that, prior to the crisis, the organizations trying to coordinate may have had a history of conflict and controversy.

Given the strong feelings that develop in the perceived gravity of the situation, the motivations toward dealing with people and organizations in which one has confidence become very great. Authorities will often turn to persons and organizations in which they have such confidence even though, in the normal course of events, these people and organizations have little connection with the now acute problems at hand.

Working against these forces of confusion are those people and organizations (and thank heaven for them) that, while recognizing the gravity of the situation, make no attempt to become involved in the decision process unless asked. They recognize that the additional confusion so created is likely to be more harmful than any possible ill effects of a decision arrived at without their participation.

In general one can describe this initial phase of the crisis — the "What should we do?" and "What can we do?" phase — as a period in which old formal patterns are ignored, new subformal patterns rapidly develop, and personal interactions take on a much more important function in organization and interorganizational activities.

Decisions in the Implementation Phase

Following a decision made by the national executive authority, the large, subordinate organizations enter a phase of implementation, a period characterized by a myriad of detailed implementive decisions. It is important that the knowledge be widely disseminated that the decision has been made as well as the nature of the decision itself, else much of the organizational effort will be directed toward developing unneeded recommendations. A tentative "We will take one step, then look and see" type of decision is organizationally troublesome as it sets the stage for implementation-type decisions based on ideas of what the nation should do, rather than being based on what it is doing. Of course, such national decisions are usually and properly of "a first step" nature. Also, the desire to deny enemy access to national intentions makes it difficult to settle the organizations into a pattern of implementation. Some confusion will continue to be present until the selected course of action becomes apparent. Even at that time, many of our serious, responsible functionaries, continuing their strong belief that the course of action selected is likely to result in undesirable consequences for the nation, are likely to exploit many of the channels available to them to influence future decisions.

One characteristic phenomenon of crisis situation is "by-passing." This is the procedure, either by communications or by conference, of establishing contact between a superior and a subordinate separated by one or more functionaries in the formal structure. The higher-level superior can feel driven to such a procedure by his urgent desire for timely information and a resulting desire to shorten his communications channel. The "by-passed" authorities are certain to resent such a procedure as it eliminates them from the decision process, a happenstance that no responsible functionary can accept without concern. Persistent fears will be felt that the superior, using such a personal level channel, will violate the unwritten rules of the organization, that the personal channel is for information not orders, and that the superior will fail to recognize that the information is unverified in the organizational sense. Finally the by-passed officers will feel, quite understandably, that their ability to direct possible future action properly is degraded by their having been denied some important information.

One observation or generalization can be made about crisis decisionmaking that is significant to control system development. It is that those people and organizations that have a history of frequent interaction (and therefore a reasonable degree of mutual predictability) tend to achieve coordination more expeditiously than those people or organizations that have no such history.

VI. CENTRALIZATION VERSUS DECENTRALIZATION: TRENDS AND ISSUES

The Trend Toward Centralization

One frequently hears assertions that the advent of mass destruction weaponry and the speed with which it can be brought into play make a trend toward centralized control both inevitable and proper. The writer believes that the trend toward centralization of detailed decisionmaking, contrary to the usual assertion, is directly related to the development of rapid, high-volume communications gear and modern data handling equipment. The desires for detailed information and for detailed control of the operating forces in periods of national crisis are probably little stronger in the leaders of today than in the national leaders of a century ago. The significant difference lies in their differing capabilities to influence ongoing events. The availability of high-speed, high-capacity communications systems has made centralization versus decentralization a subject of controversy in military organizational plans. The issue has changed from a question of mechanical feasibility to a question of organizational efficiency.

To make this complex subject somewhat more manageable, the assumption will be made that decisionmakers can be categorized as one of two types. These two "types" are illustrated by a certain amount of exaggeration. It is recognized that most or all actual functionaries should be positioned somewhere between the extremes described.[9]

Type I: The Manager

One type of decisionmaker views himself as the manager of a decision-making organization. He relies upon differences in view among his subordinates to keep him informed and to provide opportunities for directing the organization.

In practice the manager must take steps to ensure that he is not entirely dependent upon his immediate subordinates for information upon which to base his decisions. The special information-gathering organizations that support the decisionmaking structure will also report to the central

---

[9] These opposed views can be found coexisting in every organization functionary. To attribute a single set to any actual official is, of course, quite unfair. In practice, one can observe officials changing their styles of operations as a function of the changing external situation.

decisionmaker on the situation external to his organization. The manager's visits to and inspection of subordinate groups are used to develop his own opinion about the attitudes and capabilities of his organization. The status reports that flow upward to him through his organization give him an opportunity to observe how his policy directives are being implemented, and provide a basis for estimating the consequences of a change in policy in the future.

The style of operation of this type of leader is characterized by a deliberate withdrawal or self-isolation from the details of the day-to-day operations. He will frequently sacrifice his own preferred objectives and ways of proceeding in favor of those recommended by his subordinates if the expected end result is not too different from his goals.

In crisis situations, with the resulting bargaining with his peers (the heads of comparable organizations — possibly the enemy), he will tend to negotiate about objectives and goals rather than about detailed activities, because, in his view, his control of detailed activities is imprecise. The solutions of his organization to crisis problems will tend to lie well inside of previously laid plans *because the preparation of his organization for action is an important element in his bargaining considerations.*

Type II: The Decisionmaker

This type views himself as literally *the* decisionmaker. His role, as he views it, is to direct his organization by ensuring that the right decisions are made and the right actions are taken throughout the structure. He tends to view his organization as an implementing device rather than a decisionmaking structure.

The point of view of the organization head who is oriented toward detailed centralized control is best observed and appreciated in situations where he is bargaining with his counterpart in another operation. Implicit in the bargaining (or threatening) process is the promised ability to do or refrain from doing certain things. Part of the "bargaining" process, when dealing with a potential (or in some cases actual) military enemy, can be the actual movements of military forces. Here again we can see a requirement for detailed control so that the desired "message" can be transmitted to the opponent. Viewed in this light, it is apparent that such control of detailed activities from the highest level can become necessary.

The information flow in support of this type of decisionmaking is likely to be directed toward identifying an area needing decision and, subsequently, providing detailed data for decisionmaking.

The Weaknesses and Strengths of the Extremes

An organization controlled by a "manager" is slow to adapt itself to changed requirements. The interactive decisionmaking process is time consuming and inherently resistant to innovation. The manager himself is vulnerable to collusion among his subordinates since he relies upon them for indications as to when decisions must be made as well as for data upon which to make a decision. The strength of this type is that the decisions that are made are organizationally feasible and, in fact, anticipated.

An organization controlled by a "decisionmaker" is expected to adapt to changes more rapidly, although with considerable friction. The one-man type of decisionmaking is inherently much faster than that of the manager, and the decisionmaker is not very vulnerable to "capture" by his subordinates. The weaknesses inherent to this style of operation are, however: (1) the lack of organizational preparation, in the form of preliminary contributions to the decision, makes the implementation of the decisionmaker's plans a time consuming affair; and (2) one-man decisionmaking places a very high premium on selecting the right man to head the organization. . . .

ROBERT AXELROD

Bureaucratic Decisionmaking in the Military Assistance Program: Some Empirical Findings

The role of organizational interests and the consequences of bureaucratic interaction are revealed in interviews by Robert Axelrod with Washington officials whose responsibilities include administering the Military Assistance Program (MAP). Although MAP is funded at more than a billion dollars annually, most of those involved in the program's administration have additional and frequently more important responsibilities. This diversity encourages the participants to see different faces of a MAP issue and to take different stands.

The power of organizational interests in determining stakes and stands is supported by the finding that the officials interviewed were inclined to predict the stands taken by their colleagues on an agency-by-agency basis, independent of the personalities involved, i.e., knowledge of a participant's organizational affiliation ordinarily was all that was needed for the respondents to guess his position. Moreover, since agency positions were seen to be substantially unaffected by the specific facts of the case, the respondents were prepared to predict the stakes and stands of their colleagues, independent of the particular substantive issue under consideration. Most

Figures, table, and appendix have been omitted. Reprinted from Robert Axelrod, *Bureaucratic Decisionmaking in the Military Assistance Program: Some Empirical Findings* (Santa Monica: The Rand Corporation, October, 1968) with permission.

Views or conclusions contained in this study should not be interpreted as representing the official opinion or policy of the United States Air Force or ISA.

striking, however, was the finding that these predictions were, in fact, highly accurate and very reliable: except for the senior players, organizational affiliation is an excellent predictor of a participant's stakes and stands, and these stands do not vary much from case to case.

The interviews also suggest that the list of proposals offered by the respondents to deal with a problem rarely if ever included mutually exclusive alternatives. Thus an agency might be prepared to support any number of the several proposals offered. This style of bureaucratic problem-solving facilitates logrolling solutions to problems and helps to explain how organizational actors with diverse interests and objectives can form a coalition in support of a single program.

Axelrod also found that the proposals put forward by the various agencies were bargaining positions taken vis-à-vis competing agencies. The agency's recommendations were intended more to move the resultant decisions in a preferred direction than to depict a carefully designed program to which the agency was unalterably committed. Viewing agency policy positions and the interaction among them in this manner helps to explain how the decisions and actions which finally do emerge may have been the intention of no single player or organization.

Finally, it is interesting to note that, as a result of his analysis and appraisal of his conceptual framework, Axelrod urges the adoption of a bureaucratic perspective approach for further research.

I. INTRODUCTION

The purpose of this study is to inquire into the decisionmaking process of bureaucracies. More specifically, the purpose is to explore three questions:

(a) How are alternatives generated?
(b) What are the bargaining relationships between different parts of a bureaucracy?
(c) How do organizations learn?

I selected a single functional area, the Military Assistance Program (MAP), with which I was already familiar, and conducted a small survey of twenty-five officials in the various agencies that deal with the program. . . .

This research had the modest task of trying to improve understanding of how the process does, in fact, work and not to provide recommendations on how the process can be improved. Furthermore, this study reports empirical findings and discusses some of their implications, but it does not provide a definitive theoretical framework that can incorporate all the results.

Uniqueness of the Military Assistance Program

Every program has many distinctive features that make its decision-making process different from the process in other areas. For the present purposes, the two most distinctive aspects of MAP are that it is both political and military, and that it is shrinking.

The fact that MAP does not fall neatly into either a political or a military framework has several important implications. First, success in the program is particularly hard to measure. Second, the rationale for specific parts of the program is sometimes far from clear. Finally, the political-military character of MAP means that responsibility for the program is diffuse, with a number of peripheral agencies playing strong roles.

The second distinctive feature of MAP is that it is a shrinking program. For example, in Fiscal Year 1961 the new obligational authority was $1.9 billion, but in FY 1964 it was only $1.0 billion, and for FY 1968 the President has requested only $.6 billion. These figures exaggerate the extent of the cutback, because in recent years Vietnam-related expenses have been excluded from the program, and sales are replacing grants to a growing extent. Nevertheless, the size of the program has certainly been reduced faster than an incremental theory would predict.

Despite a rapid cutback in the size of the program, the decision process should not be thought of as an example displaying pathological features normally associated with shrinking programs. The reasons are not hard to find: (a) the top people in the program, the Secretary of Defense and his Assistant Secretary for International Security Affairs, have favored a reduction in the program; (b) the policymakers in Washington are thousands of miles away from where a cutback is most agonizing; and, most important, (c) the very high rate of job rotation in and out of the program means that no official in Washington is likely to lose a job if MAP has fewer funds the following year.

The Organizational Setting

A central office in MAP is that of the Assistant Secretary of Defense for International Security Affairs (ISA). ISA is a relatively small organization made up of both civilians and military men. The three parts that concern us are the Office of the Director of Military Assistance (ODMA), which is primarily a facilitator of grant aid; the various regional offices that do most of the programming of the grant part of the program; and International Logistics Negotiations (ILN), which handles the sales of arms. The Secretary of State has the authority by law to determine the value of military assistance programs to individual countries, and this authority had been delegated to the Administrator of the Agency for International Development (AID). Besides ISA, State, and AID, the other agencies that play significant roles are the National Security Council (NSC), the Bureau of the Budget (BoB), and the Joint Chiefs of Staff (JCS). To keep the study manageable, I have limited the survey to these six agencies.

Among them, these agencies incorporate nearly all of the decisionmaking processes of MAP insofar as it takes place within the Executive Branch in Washington. The other agencies that play a role from time to time include the Import-Export Bank, the Treasury Department, and the Office of the Assistant Secretary of Defense for Systems Analysis. Outside of Washington the country teams in the field are important. In addition to the Executive Branch, Congress, the American public, and the governments of the recipient countries all help shape outcomes. The military services also have an input, but most of it is channeled through either the Joint Chiefs of Staff or country teams. Not all of the decision process for MAP takes place within the Executive Branch in Washington.

MAP Procedures

To understand the decisionmaking process, one must have at least a rough idea of the procedural as well as the organizational setting of a program. MAP has two sets of procedures, one for grants and one for sales. These procedures can get quite complex; a thick volume called the *Military Assistance Manual* prescribes some of them, and other are part of a less formal set of rules. The following skeleton description indicates how these procedures typically operate:

Grants
1. ISA gives dollar and policy guidelines, with State and AID approval
2. Country teams write rolling five-year plan
3. Unified commands approve
4. JCS forwards
5. ISA approves
6. BoB holds hearings
7. Congress allocates money
8. ISA reprograms during the year.

Sales
1. Recipient government makes a request
2. Country team comments
3. State approves
4. ILN negotiates

Sales can usually be arranged much quicker than grants can. Typically, the programming of a grant item will take eighteen to twenty-four months. The shorter set of procedures for sales frequently allows them to be concluded within six months. Of course, with increased speed comes reduced coordination. Thus, many of the agencies that play an active role in determining the shape of the grant part of the program have difficulty in influencing what, and how much, is sold to whom. Although most arms sales are made to industrialized nations of Europe and hence need not concern us in this study, the arms sales to underdeveloped nations form a significant and growing segment of the Military Assistance Program.

The Survey Sample

The respondents were selected on the basis of their official positions so that the sample would have an appropriate distribution within each of four attributes: agency, region, rank, and civil-military. . . .

Each of the four attributes was correctly distributed with respect to the others. For example, respondents dealing with each of the regions were drawn for several different agencies. The added restrictions of cross-distributions meant that the sample was not random in the strict sense, but was instead a highly controlled, stratified sample designed to include the correct distribution and cross-distribution of each of the four attributes.

Caveats

Two caveats that have already been discussed are that the decision process in MAP has several distinctive features stemming from the political-military character and that only the part of the process was examined that takes place within the executive branch in Washington. Another is that a survey relies on the respondents' perceptions. However, the interview schedule was designed to elicit information on specific actions the respondent himself had taken, and for many purposes — such as which problems are felt to be serious and which alternatives are live options — perceptions are exactly what matter.

A final caveat is that the results are based on only twenty-five interviews. This limitation is mitigated to some extent by the good distribution of the respondents and by their openness. Their openness is exemplified by the fact that I received the "party line" only once, and a number of times I was told about sensitive proposals that have not yet surfaced even within the bureaucracy. Still another factor mitigating the effects of the small sample is that the number of people working on the program is not very large anyway. As a very rough approximation, the sample included 8 of the top 15 people, 9 of the next 15, and 8 of the next 100 officials dealing with the program in the Executive Branch in Washington. In other words, the survey was very roughly a one-in-three sample of some generalized notion of influence in the program. Finally, despite the fact that only twenty-five interviews were conducted, some results are overwhelming.

II. ALTERNATIVE GENERATION

The question of how alternatives are generated can best be approached in the broader context of how problems are perceived and dealt with. . . .

Type of Problem

There were no big surprises on the types of problems raised, so the results can be given quickly. The problems can be divided into those referring to policy and those referring to process. Under policy problems, only one-third were based on insufficient funds, which is considerably fewer than expected. On the other hand, half of the respondents mentioned Congress as one of the two most important problems facing the Military Assistance Program.

There were fewer process problems, and nearly all of these dealt with either the need for more analysis or the need for other parts of the Executive Branch to attain an understanding of things as the respondent sees them. The difference between a problem of analysis and one of understanding is that analysis means the respondent admits the need for more information, while insufficient understanding means someone else in the Executive Branch is supposed to need more information because he does not understand something.

Origin of Proposals

Next come the more interesting questions about where problems and proposals come from. After the respondent mentioned a problem, I intended to ask how that problem came to his attention. It nearly always turned out to be a foolish question. For example, if the problem was that Congress was not providing sufficient funds, one could hardly ask how that came to his attention. In fact, for only four people was there a clear answer . . . to the question of how it came to his attention.

After eliciting proposals for what can be done about the problem, I intended to take the most specific proposal and ask the respondent whether he devised it, or where it came from. Once again, this was often a foolish question. As an example, consider the following problem and proposals offered by an arms salesman:

Problem: There is an increasing sense of no urgency with respect to military capabilities around the world.

Proposals:
1. More public statements emphasizing the problem;
2. More reasonable sales terms to promote sales;
3. More technical assistance;
4. Better relations between our military services and the services of the recipients;
5. A posture of "understanding insistence" (which I take to mean, "we understand your problems, but do it our way").

This example is unusual in that the problem is stated with very wide applicability, and the list of proposals is rather long, but it serves to illustrate how useless it can be to ask the origin of a proposal.

. . . For less than a quarter of the problems did the respondent give a source for the origin of either of his proposals. These sources were divided between the staff in the field or a recipient government (three times), his own immediate office (three times), and himself (five times).

The numbers are obviously not a good indication of where proposals really do originate. Not once was another agency in Washington given credit for devising a proposal. Furthermore, three proposals credited to the field or a recipient government must be a very drastic underestimate of their role in formulating problems and suggesting what can be done about them. Answers to a later question about the role of the country team indicate that the field plays a major role in virtually every part of the policy process except the final making of a binding decision: they give information on such things as local threat and the recipient's ability to handle various types of equipment; they predict the recipient's reactions to possible American policies; they warn of future issues; they suggest a five-year plan that meets policy and dollar guidelines; and they are in charge of implementing the program. Nevertheless, the field is rarely given credit for originating a proposal.

Indeed, rarely is anyone given credit for devising a proposal, and rarely does a problem come to one's attention from a distinct source. The reason for this seems to be that problems and proposals are regarded as "obvious," and do not require a burst of originality to uncover. The example of a sense of no urgency with respect to military capabilities, and the suggestion that more public statements are needed, illustrates this.

But to say that most problems and proposals do not have distinct sources because they are regarded as obvious raises the question of why some are obvious and not others, and why what is obvious to one man is far from clear to another. Perhaps the explanation is that problems and proposals are multiply determined: problems that are raised only once are probably not often regarded as serious, and it seems that proposals that are suggested by only one person are not often retained as salient options. So the problems and proposals that are regarded as most significant have been brought to the respondent's attention in many different ways and therefore rarely have distinct sources.

Multiple determination helps explain another unanticipated result. When asked if there were any problems that are not sufficiently recognized, only six people were able to name one. This is a surprisingly low number in view of the complexity of the program. The explanation is probably the one offered spontaneously by a number of respondents, namely, that all the important problems are recognized as problems but do not always get the attention or action they merit. This supports the notion that the perceived significance of a problem is related to the multiplicity of ways in which it is brought to one's attention. Thus, although there is no precise consensus among officials on which are the most serious problems, nearly everyone believes that each of the problems they find significant are at least recognized as problems by most of the others.

Types of Proposals

In exploring the first major question — how alternatives are generated — some evidence and its implications on the nature of the generation process has been examined. The next issue is, Exactly what is being generated? When a typical respondent suggested several things in response to the questions, "What can be done about this problem?" and "What else can be done?" what structure does his list of proposals have?

One possibility, and the one that we tend to think of first, is that the proposals will contain a short list of mutually exclusive alternatives. The actual results are clear enough to require almost no comment: the respondents rarely think in terms of mutually exclusive alternatives. Instead, the most common structure by far allows a list of proposals to be implemented in any combination. The earlier example illustrates the point. Just because more public statements are given does not mean that more reasonable sales terms cannot also be given. And if either or both of these proposals were implemented, they would not preclude any of the other suggestions. The various tools or instruments at one's disposal are rarely conceptualized as mutually exclusive packaged alternatives; instead they retain their separate identities. This is true even for the senior officials within the Office of the Secretary of Defense, despite McNamara's strong emphasis on the value of distinct alternatives to the decisionmaking process.

III. BARGAINING RELATIONSHIPS

The second major question the survey was designed to explore was the bargaining relationships between different parts of the bureaucracy. Specific items in the interview schedule were included to provide data on the competitiveness of the bargaining process, the individual styles of the respondents, the perception of influence, and the attributed policy positions of the various agencies.

Competitiveness of the Process

The results on the competitiveness of the bargaining process contain no surprises. There is usually interagency disagreement.

Not infrequently there is also disagreement within one's own agency. Compromise is sometimes easy and sometimes hard. When asked what happens if one agency gets what it has been advocating, almost half of the respondents said the others can be pretty well satisfied too; half said the others cannot also be satisfied, and a few said that the others cannot also win but at least they can feel they have had a fair hearing.

Individual Styles

More interesting are the two questions on individual styles. These were quite often answered with an expression that seemed to mean, "That's a ridiculous question — everyone knows what the answer is." But then half the people answered one way, and half answered the other way.

. . . A bit more than half of the officials said that if they had final authority to make a decision they would not sacrifice much effort in trying to get general agreement. The others stressed the importance of making sure the other parts of the Government find the decision acceptable. Answers ranged from a colonel who said he had been brought up to make decisions and he did not want a lot of "garbage input" from other agencies, to an AID official who said that no single person could make the best decision because he would not have enough information, and that general agreement is sometimes necessary so as not to force anyone to lose too much.

[The respondents were asked:] "Some people enjoy taking part in conflicts or disputes between agencies, and others don't want to get involved. How about you?" Half the people answered one way and half the other, but I got the feeling that behind their replies was the attitude that anyone with any intelligence would know what the answer was. For example, of two officials in ISA, one said that of course he did not enjoy conflicts and tried to avoid them, although he welcomed an exchange of facts, opinions, and judgments by other people gripped with the same problems. The other official said that he enjoyed conflict a lot; it made life worth living; matching of wits was fun. Another ISA respondent even said that the decisionmaking process was an Hegelian dialectic, with a thesis, antithesis, and synthesis.

Perception of Influence

Two opposing theories exist about how officials perceive influence. One view says that everyone will say that he just contributes to the process but the decisions are actually made elsewhere. The opposite theory was exemplified by one of the respondents who said the MAP policy process is like 10,000 red ants on a log floating downstream, each thinking he is guiding the log. Actually neither theory is supported by the evidence collected in this survey.

Outside of the Executive Branch in Washington, the country teams were thought of as playing a significant role by two-thirds of the respondents, and Congress was unanimously regarded as being a very important power to contend with in the Military Assistance Program. In fact, when asked about whether the top policymakers worry much about the public, almost everyone spontaneously changed the terms of the question and said the top people certainly do worry about Congress.

Agency Positions

Perhaps the most surprising result of this study is that stereotyped policy positions for the various agencies involved in the Military Assistance Program are seen to be:

1. Independent of personality;
2. Predictive;
3. Reliable;
4. Independent of the issue; and
5. Simplifiable into two dimensions.

First, stereotypes of agency positions can be applied to an agency quite independently of specific personalities. For example, when respondents were asked what other parts of the Executive Branch think should be done about the problem the respondent raised, they were able to reply on an agency-by-agency basis. Although many people drew distinctions between one part of an agency and another, no one said that he was unable to specify agency positions because it all depended on personalities. Sometimes people said that they did not want to speak for other agencies, but once I assured them that I was also going to talk to people in those agencies, they were quite willing to attribute policy preferences to them.

Second, these attributed preferences are predictive. A large proportion of the respondents felt that they could predict what each of the other agencies would say on a given problem.

Third, they were reliable. Of the more than one hundred policy positions attributed to other agencies and to one's own agency, over 90 percent were consistent with each other.[1]

Fourth, and most surprising, the positions were independent of the issue at hand. To give a fictitious example, what the Philippine desk officer in the State Department thinks AID will say to a proposal to give more planes to the Philippines will nearly be similar to what a general in the JCS will expect AID to say about having more tanks sent to Peru. Furthermore, when an AID official dealing with the Near East is interviewed, the problems he thinks are important and the proposals he offers to deal with them will almost certainly be consistent with the expectations of the desk officer and the general. It rarely matters who you see or what issue they are

---

[1] This excludes positions attributed to the ISA regions for reasons explained below.

discussing; stereotyped agency positions exist, they are used for predictions, and they are actually correct.

Fifth, the stereotyped positions can be represented in terms of two policy dimensions. The more important dimension is pro-weapons versus anti-weapons. The operative question here is whether the agency favors more weapons for countries such as Peru, Ethiopia, or Korea. The second dimension is pro-grants versus pro-sales. Here the question is whether the agency favors more grants or more sales within a given program. To return once again to the arms salesman in the ILN subagency of ISA and his sample problem, it is not hard to see that his concern with a sense of "no urgency" with respect to military capabilities reflects a pro-weapons attitude, and his proposal for "more reasonable" sales terms reflects a pro-sales attitude. Of course, what classifies as a pro-weapons or pro-sales attitude is relative to what others are advocating, so that the same opinion may have meant quite different things in 1957 than it does in 1967.

Although most problems that the respondents raised were more specific than this example, it was often easy to determine the respondent's position on the two policy dimensions, as well as positions he attributed to other agencies. Nearly all issues could be described in terms of these two dimensions.

Within ISA three subagencies are distinguishable: ODMA, which is primarily a facilitator of grant aid; the regional offices, which do most of the programming of grants; and ILN, which handles the sales. This gives six agencies (or subagencies) in which more than one person was interviewed: ODMA, ISA regions, ILN, State, AID, and JCS. There is a very high degree of consensus on the positions of each of these agencies on each dimension, except for the ISA regions for which there is no clear consensus. . . . Only 9 of the 104 codable positions are inconsistent with the positions [attributed to each of] these five agencies. . . .

Information was not solicited for the separate divisions of ISA, but enough was obtained to distinguish the positions of ODMA, the regions, and ISA. Although no systematic data were obtained for the position of the Bureau of the Budget, my previous personal experience leads me to believe that it is safe to assume BoB is anti-weapon and pro-sales. Not shown . . . because of insufficient evidence is the position of the NSC (which I would guess is pro-sales) and the top of ISA (which seems near the center but somewhat anti-weapon and pro-sales).

If it is possible to position agencies in a policy space, then research on bureaucratic bargaining may not be quite as difficult as has often been supposed. For example, the isolated position AID has in the policy space [pro-grant, anti-weapon] may explain (at least in part) the earlier finding that no one attributed much power to AID. As still another example, the similar policy positions of State and JCS suggest a possible explanation of why the political and military rationales for the program stay blurred. Finally, the distribution of agencies in the policy space suggests that the main cleavage in the Washington bureaucracy is probably between State and JCS (with the support of ODMA) on one hand and on the other the ISA regions.

Lest the reader take this optimistic theme too seriously, let him beware of limitations on an analysis of bargaining in MAP based on agency stereotypes. First, the ISA regions were placed in the center because there was not a clear consensus on where they belonged. Second, due to insufficient data, the top echelon of ISA was not placed at all (although they are, I believe, similar to the regions on most issues). Thus, the most important parts of the bureaucracy cannot be reliably described by simple stereotypes. Third, even reliable predictions on agency positions do not indicate how hard a given agency will fight on a given issue. One criterion for how hard someone is expected to fight is how important the issue is to him, but another criterion is whether he thinks fighting will help him improve the outcome. One agency can usually guess what another agency will advocate on any given issue, but predicting how hard they will fight is much more difficult. This uncertainty is one of the things that keeps bureaucratic politics exciting. Another important reason why agency stereotypes cannot give the full richness to the bargaining process is that there is a conviction throughout the bureaucracy that there *is* such a thing as the national interest, and the job of all government officials is to discover it and promote it. But even after all this is said, the existence of reliable agency policy stereotypes, which do not depend on the particular issue at hand and which can be represented in a simple two-dimensional space, bodes well for the study of bargaining in bureaucracies.

The existence of a policy space in which agencies are positioned may also be useful in explaining the earlier finding that officials do not think in terms of mutually exclusive packaged alternatives. Why should they? They do not need to know how far they want the policy to move, only the direction in which they want it to go. For example, the arms salesman in ILN is pulling for more generous sales terms, but he does not have to decide just how generous — at least not until he wins a number of bureaucratic fights and is in danger of getting sales terms more generous than even he wants. If packaging of alternatives is often unnecessary for an official, it suggests that when it is done — that is, when someone recommends a specific point in the policy space rather than just a direction or a vague area — this may be based on bargaining considerations and not represent what his first preference is at all. Thus, the specific form in which a proposal gets packaged as an alternative may depend more on an estimate of bargaining strength than on the merits of that particular proposal. Furthermore, the official may be quite willing to give up one alternative and advocate another as his perception of his prospects changes. If the re-searcher is looking for a stable aspect of this process he is more likely to find it in the general direction in which each agency is pulling, rather than in the specific alternative each proposes.

Other implications for the nature of the alternative generation process follow from the obvious thought that the policy space of MAP is not "lumpy" and may not be lumpy for other programs either. However, if the space is continuous rather than lumpy, common notions such as "an individual can only conceptualize three or four outcomes at once" must be put aside. Anyone can think of a whole range of outcomes. If proposals are packaged (for example, *three* public speeches next month and *one-half percent* lower interest rate on sales payments) then obviously little effort is required to unpack this alternative and make another one (for example, *two* speeches and *three-fourths percent* lower). Once again, this suggests that alternative generation may be an elusive aspect of the policy process.[2]

IV. ORGANIZATIONAL LEARNING

How do organizations learn? That is to say, how do they use experience to adapt their behavior? The approach to the question of organizational learning was to ask the respondents a series of questions about two recent events — the war between India and Pakistan in 1965, and the 1967 Near East war. The India/Pakistan war was chosen because it was thought to be such a major negative stimulus to MAP that organizational learning would be fairly easy to identify. The survey provided abundant evidence that the war between India and Pakistan was certainly regarded as a major disaster for MAP by the respondents. Both sides used American-supplied military equipment against each other, and Congressional and public support for the entire Military Assistance Program was eroded to such an extent that several other problems mentioned by the respondents date their origin to this war. Another reason the India/Pakistan war was used is that enough time has elapsed (two years) to determine whether any lessons are likely to be applied elsewhere, but the crisis is still recent enough so that any such applications are not likely to have been forgotten.

The Near East war of 1967 was chosen because it bore certain similari-ties (an arms race; a war with American equipment being used on both sides; a rapid American response of an arms cutoff, and so on), and because the interviews could be conducted three to six weeks after hostili-

---

[2] Of course if the issue is whether to build a fixed or variable geometry airplane, the space is lumpy. Nevertheless, there are many important policy variables left that are inherently continuous, such as how *many* dollars will be spent over what *length* of time and for how *many* planes.

ties began and while the repercussions were still reverberating in Washington. . . .

Nearly everyone thought there were lessons for MAP from the India/Pakistan war, and nearly everyone was able to cite other instances in which the lesson could be applied. But when asked if the program had been modified there, less than half could say yes, and when the reasons for these modifications were examined, most of the modifications turned out to be not by choice of the Executive Branch but rather because of such things as Congressional funding cuts. Only three respondents were able to give an example of a modification in another country's program that was a result of the Executive Branch's application of a lesson of the India/Pakistan war.

When asked if the India/Pakistan experience helped meet the new problems raised by the Near East crisis, the vast majority of the respondents asserted that one event was not relevant to the other. However, one State Department official who was personally involved in both said that some old papers were pulled out and did prove useful, and many things were recalled from memory. However, he said that the usefulness of the previous experience was primarily in smoothing channels within the American Government and in helping to expedite the implementation of policy rather than in providing lessons for the new policy to use. Two high officials in JCS and ISA who also participated in both crises gave similar accounts.

When asked about the Near East crisis, most respondents did think there were lessons for MAP, and these lessons were applicable elsewhere. There was a dropoff in the number who responded positively to the question of whether any of these other programs should be modified, and only five people thought their suggestions for modifications were not likely to meet much disagreement. In other words, a consensus on how MAP should be modified elsewhere to take into account lessons of the Near East is completely lacking. This result parallels the finding that only three people were able to cite a modification in some other part of the world that was an application of the India/Pakistan war that was initiated by the Executive Branch.

It should not be concluded from these figures that no one learned anything. After all, Congress certainly changed its behavior and became much more critical of all of MAP after the India/Pakistan war. And the executive department officials I talked with cited examples of other countries applying lessons from that war also. An example, cited in *Aviation Week and Space Technology*, is given below:

> One setback to U.S.-Iran relations was the lesson the Shah learned in the September 1965 fighting between India and Pakistan. The U.S. cut off spare and other military supplies to Pakistan, another Moslem

country. "The Shah then realized we could cripple his war machine by cutting off spares," explained a U.S. official. This prompted him to seek other sources of supply, which led to the barter agreement with the Soviets.[3]

Of course there was some learning in the Executive Branch in Washington. The programs directly involved in both wars were dramatically changed (at least in the short run), and some details concerning the implementation of policy were learned in one crisis and applied in the next. But many of the respondents would have agreed with a junior ISA official whose first thought was, "I suppose there are lessons, but I'm not sure we learned any of them."

What, then, was the difficulty? The location of the bottleneck can be specified with some assurance for the India/Pakistan case. The event was seen to be very unfortunate for MAP, there *were* lessons, these lessons *were* seen to be applicable elsewhere, but then it seems nothing was done by the bureaucracy to modify the other programs where these lessons applied.

There are a host of possible explanations for this peculiar pattern. One might say that there were, in fact, modifications elsewhere, but that the respondents refused to admit it because that would be equivalent to admitting they did not understand their own programs before. Or one could give a variety of explanations as to why there was no adaptation. The first of these is the obvious possibility that they knew the lessons beforehand and, hence, did not have to make any modifications. For example, two magazine editorials published a week before the interviewing began pointed out lessons of the Near East crisis, but the lessons conformed to what each magazine had been advocating long before this crisis. According to *Aviation Week and Space Technology*:

> The major political lesson, which still seems to escape many people in Washington, is that the Soviet leaders' policy is as ferociously anti-American as ever, and they will go to almost any lengths short of a direct nuclear war to implement their implacable hatred of the West.[4]

The *Saturday Review* stated:

> Fundamentally, a lesson to be learned from recent events is that any attempt to make peace or keep peace, or any attempt to invoke law, must rest on abstract, objective concepts of justice, self-evident to a world consensus if not to some of those directly affected.[5]

Both editorials saw a lesson that was applicable elsewhere, but their lesson was hardly something new to them and hence need not have led to any

[3] *Aviation Week and Space Technology,* August 7, 1967, p. 54.
[4] *Aviation Week and Space Technology,* June 26, 1967, p. 11.
[5] *Saturday Review,* June 24, 1967, p. 20.

modification in their previous attitudes. Perhaps the same was true for the respondents.

Still other possibilities abound. Perhaps individuals did learn something new, but no modifications were made in the programs because different individuals learned different things. Perhaps the individual lessons were consistent, but for any given program there were so many other policy considerations and commitments that the lessons had to be ignored. Perhaps sheer inertia in the bureaucracy made it easier to continue with current plans rather than accept short run costs to apply a lesson that might lower the probability of another war. Or perhaps the lessons were not applied because no heads rolled in the State Department or Defense Department after the India/Pakistan fiasco.

There is one explanation, however, that is consistent with a number of these seemingly contradictory possibilities. This explanation employs the concept of multiply determined policy, which was found to be useful earlier in explaining why problems and proposals did not have clear sources. Perhaps the experience of India/Pakistan or the Near East war did indeed indicate good reasons for making modifications in other programs, but there are also dozens of other reasons that arise every year for making modifications in every program. And, in fact, modifications are made in almost every year in almost every program. But for a respondent to say, for example, that a certain change was made in a Latin American program *because* of the India/Pakistan experience would be overstating the case to the point of gross distortion. Still, that experience may have been one of the many factors leading to change, and in this special sense learning may have taken place. This interpretation is supported by the kinds of words the respondents used to describe the effect of the India/Pakistan experience: "it underlined the lesson that . . .", "it was a ghost that haunted us," or "since then we have been more cautious about. . . ." These terms suggest that a major negative stimulus can contribute to determining future behavior without being the sole cause of some modification.

The finding can be related to the earlier discussions of alternatives and bargaining. Perhaps the learning of lessons from a crisis takes the form of modifications in the relative seriousness with which a wide variety of problems and alternatives are taken, rather than directly in the form of modifications in programs. Bargaining relations need not be changed even by a serious crisis, because different agencies might draw different lessons each consistent with its own previous policy position.

V. STUDYING BUREAUCRATIC DECISIONMAKING

This study began with three simple questions: how are alternatives generated?; what are the bargaining relationships between different parts of the bureaucracy?; and how do organizations learn? The research findings demonstrate that in some ways these questions rest on false assumptions. For example, the proposals generated are not mutually exclusive alternatives, the generation process rarely provides distinct sources for proposals, and even though a lesson is perceived and seen to be widely applicable it need not lead to identifiable modifications in programs.

This suggests the need for a new set of questions that will take these findings into account. In addition, other findings about how proposals are dealt with and how agencies bargain provide insights into just how these questions might be formulated. The purposes of the new questions are to help guide future research into bureaucratic decisionmaking and to organize the information gathered on how decisionmaking works in MAP.

The new questions are shown below;[6] as innocuous as they seem, each relies on several very strong assumptions:

Main Question
    (A) What governmental outputs emerge?
    (B) from what efforts to alleviate which problems?
    (C) by which agencies in what manner?

A. Rational
    What governmental objectives are sought through what governmental policies?
B. Organizational Process
    What demands increase, and what instruments are used to decrease the seriousness of what problem on whose list?
C. Bureaucratic Politics
    Which agencies use what tactics to pull with how much effort in what policy space on which issues in what direction?

The main question assumes that officials conceptualize their jobs as involving the alleviation of problems. This assumption is consistent with the evidence from the present study, but conceivably in other programs the main task might be the grasping of opportunities. The third part of the main question assumes that agencies are cohesive with respect to shared preferences and common action. Again, this assumption is valid for MAP but is still a very strong assumption. One thing the main question does not assume is that decisions are made. Instead, the phrase "governmental outputs emerge" is meant to suggest that important outcomes may occur without anyone making a deliberate decision. To avoid begging the question of whether decisions are the crucial unit of analysis, the subject of the new set of questions is "what happens in a bureaucracy."

The first specific question incorporates a rational conception of what

---

[6] Graham Allison helped me formulate these questions.

happens by asking "what governmental objectives are sought through what governmental policy?" This question assumes that the bureaucracy can be described as a unitary rational actor doing a means-end analysis to determine its behavior. Clearly, this assumption is almost always false, and is certainly not true for MAP. Nevertheless, for a first look at what is happening in a given program, the question of what governmental objectives are sought through what policies is a useful one. In the case of MAP, the overall objectives and policy are set forth in the annual Presidential statement to Congress on the foreign aid bill. For a more incisive examination of a program one must understand what happens within the bureaucracy. The questions on organizational process and bureaucratic politics should help in this regard.

The organizational process question, as formulated here, asks "what demands increase and what instruments are used to decrease the significance of what problems on whose list?" This question assumes that officials have lists of problems that can be ordered by their importance, that demands that tend to increase the priority of certain problems are made on the official, and he has certain instruments of government policy that he consciously tries to use to alleviate different problems. All these assumptions are supported by the evidence for MAP. Note, however, that the organizational process question does not assume that alternatives are generated.

The answer for MAP to the organizational process question comes in several parts. The demands come largely from the field and Congress, with the importance of each demand evaluated largely in terms of the official's conception of the mission of his agency. Instruments to deal with problems are suggested by many different sources, or are implicit in the definition of the problem. Two instruments that are often important are the reallocation of money and the reallocation of one's own time. One's own time can be used to buy a better analysis of the problem (to increase the efficiency of the other instruments) or for advocacy (to persuade or bargain with other agencies). All in all, instruments are not very effective. For example, more public speeches, more generous sales terms, and more technical assistance will probably not go very far if the problem is an increasing sense of "no urgency" with respect to military capabilities around the world. The problem may be alleviated to some extent, but it will remain a serious problem. Finally, each person's list of problems reflects his agency's goals. Although there is no precise consensus among officials on which are the most serious problems, few people believe that all the problems they find serious are not at least recognized as problems by most of the others. The relative seriousness with which different problems are taken may be modified as a result of lessons learned from a crisis.

The specific question on bureaucratic politics that the MAP findings suggest is: "Which agencies use what tactics to pull with how much effort in what policy space on which issues in what direction?" This formulation assumes that there exist agency positions that are largely independent of personalities and specific issues. It also assumes these positions can be represented in a simple policy space. These assumptions do, indeed, work for MAP. The policy space has a pro-weapons/anti-weapons dimension and a sales/grants dimension, and the positions of the various agencies have been determined. What is still not understood is how hard an agency will pull on a given issue, and what particular tactics will be employed.

EDWARD L. KATZENBACH

The Horse Cavalry in the Twentieth Century: A Study in Policy Response

Career members of large organizations typically take stands on issues in terms of the predicted consequences for their organization's interests and objectives. The experiences of the horse cavalry branch of the armies of Europe and the United States illustrate how organizational perspectives frequently dominate responses to technological and strategic developments. Considerations of organizational survival, views of its "essence," concern for its autonomy, and attention to the morale of its members combine to explain the organization's behavior in a changing environment.

The persistence of the horse cavalry in the face of several developments in weapons technology and the experiences of two world wars stands as testimony to the strength of organizational survival as a motivation. Organizational perspectives are highly resistant to change: rather than asking whether the changing situation implied altering or abolishing particular functions, the cavalry sought to incorporate these potential challenges into existing routines, practices, and doctrine. The consequences of the development of new weapons such as the tank and airplane were substantially determined by the interests and objectives of the organizations concerned. Thus, at the turn of the century, the future role of the newly developed machine gun was largely dependent on whether the weapon was made part of the infantry or of the cavalry. Each branch, in turn, believed that its organizational future would be substantially affected by whether or not the new weapon was assigned to it.

Considerations of organizational "essence" and the morale of its members further constrained the cavalry's responsiveness. European cavalrymen, whose view of their mission did not include fighting while

Excerpted by the editors from *Public Policy*, 8 (1958), pp. 120–149 with permission.

dismounted, vehemently resisted adopting advances in firepower lest the horse degenerate into being merely a mode of transport. The apparent progressiveness of the U.S. cavalry was due less to flexibility and sophisticated analysis than to different but equally inflexible organizational doctrines.

The long survival of the cavalry as a combat arm also illustrates the limits on analysis and problem-solving as techniques for resolving disputes. The obsolescence of the horse cavalry was merely overwhelmingly plausible, never unambiguously proven. The lessons of experience in combat (and simulated combat maneuvers) were in the eyes of the beholder and served more as a fund for arguments by both sides on behalf of their respective positions than as sources of data designed to resolve the differences. In the absence of compelling and mutually accepted analysis, the outcomes were dominated by bargaining among the participants and the power relationships between them. The position of the cavalry as an elite branch within an army and with its influential supporters in the political arena beyond the military substantially accounts for its prolonged organizational success.

THE PROBLEM

Lag-time, that lapsed period between innovation and a successful institutional or social response to it, is probably on the increase in military matters. Moreover, as the tempo of technological change continues to quicken, it is likely that lag time will increase as well. This is understandable: the kind of readjustment in terms of doctrine, organization, and training that the ballistic missile will demand of those who have flown manned aircraft from land and sea simply shocks the imagination. Atomics, supersonics, electronics of widely differentiated capabilities make the problem of successful institutional absorption most difficult.

Of course, at first there would seem to be a paradox here. As weapons systems have become more complex, the lead-time needed to bring them from the drawing board to the assembly line has become markedly longer. On the basis of the longer lead-time one might hypothesize that the institutional lag might lessen inasmuch as prior planning would seem eminently more possible. It might even be surmised that the institutional response might be made to coincide with the operational readiness of new weapons. To date, however, military institutions have not been able to use this lead-time effectively because real change has so outdistanced anticipated change. Moreover, there is not the urgency that there should be in the military to make major institutional adjustments in the face of the challenge of new weapons systems, if for no other reason than that the problem of testing is so difficult. Just as in the academic world it is well-nigh impossible to *prove* that any change in curriculum would enable future leaders to think more clearly than those with a classical education, so in the military it is quite impossible to *prove* that minor adjustments in a traditional pattern of organization and doctrine will not suffice to absorb technological innovations of genuine magnitude.

Furthermore the absence of any final testing mechanism of the military's institutional adequacy short of war has tended to keep the pace of change to a creep in time of peace and, conversely, has whipped it into a gallop in time of war. The military history of the past half century is studded with institutions which have managed to dodge the challenge of the obvious. The Coast Artillery continued until the middle of World War II, at least in the United States. Other such institutional anomalies will spring to mind. But the most curious of all was the horse cavalry which maintained a capacity for survival that borders on the miraculous. The war horse survived a series of challenges each of which was quite as great as those which today's weapons systems present to today's traditional concepts. Like the mollusk, the horse cavalry made those minor adjustments that time dictated absolutely. Then it continued to live out an expensive and decorous existence with splendor and some spirit straight into an age which thought it a memory. Indeed it is difficult to conceive of an institution that underlines so sharply the relativity of the concept of obsolescence. In times such as these when today's weapons are already out-of-date and there is therefore a daily need for reassessing our military institutions' response to them, the strange and wonderful survival of the horse cavalry may amount to something more than a curiously alarming anachronism.

The horse cavalry has had to review its role in war four times since the end of the nineteenth century in the face of four great changes in the science of war: the development of repeating automatic and semi-automatic weapons, the introduction of gasoline and diesel-fueled engines, the invention of the air-borne weapon, and the coming of the nuclear battlefield. Each new challenge to the horse has been, of necessity, seriously considered. Each has demanded a review of doctrine, a change in role and mission. And in each review there have been, of necessity, assumptions made as to the relevance of experience to some pattern of future war. The role and mission of service or branch or unit must, after all, be based on some reasoned view of men's future reactions under the circumstances of war — when man is at his most unreasonable. Indeed, the paradox of military planning is that it must be reasonably precise as to quite imprecise future contingencies.

By the year 1900, or thereabouts, the clip-fed breech-loading repeating rifle was in the hands of the troops of all the major powers. The French Lebel had been adopted in 1886 after a decade of squabbling — the most difficult weapons to adopt or to change are the simplest: sword, lance, bayonet, rifle — the improved Mauser in 1898, and the United States Springfield in 1903. The Lee-Enfield, the Ariska, the Mannlicher-Carcano, all rifles which were to become familiar to millions in two world wars, had been developed by the beginning of the century and either were or were about to go into production.

Self-firing automatic weapons were also on the assembly lines of the world's armament makers. Hiram Maxim had registered the last of a famous series of machine gun patents in 1885. By the time (1904–1905) of the Russo-Japanese War the guns of Maxim and Hotchkiss were in national arsenals everywhere, or almost everywhere, for the expense of new weapons was rapidly shrinking the ranks of those powers which could be considered "great." At roughly the same time it had been found that the use of glycerine in the recoil mechanism of artillery pieces enabled these to remain aimed after being fired. This in turn meant that the artillery piece itself became a rapid fire (20 rounds per minute) weapon. The French "Seventy-Five," perhaps the most famous of all artillery pieces, was shortly to be in production. Firepower, in short, had a new meaning.

For the elite of the armies of the world, the cavalry, each of these developments would seem to have been nothing short of disaster. For that proud and beautiful animal, the horse, has a thin skin and a high silhouette, and its maximum rate of speed on the attack is only 30 m.p.h. Especially in conjunction with barbed wire, automatically manufactured since 1874 and in military use at the end of the century, it is difficult to imagine a target more susceptible to rapid fire.

The cavalry had always considered itself to have a variety of missions. The cavalry was the good eye of the infantry. It was taught to collect, and if necessary to fight for, information about the enemy. The cavalry protected friendly, and harried enemy flanks and rear. It covered any necessary withdrawal. It was used in pursuit of defeated enemy. And above and beyond all else, the cavalry was used to charge the faltering, the weary, or the unwary, to deliver the *coup de grace* with the *arme blanche*: with cold steel, with saber or lance, to "crown victory" as the proud phrase went.

It was clear that the introduction of the automatic and the semi-automatic weapon would make some cavalry missions more difficult. But there was no doubt in any cavalryman's mind, and there was little doubt in the minds of most others, that most cavalry missions would have to continue simply because there was no viable substitute. The horse was transport, and the horse was mobility. A group of horsemen could cover a hundred miles in twenty-four hours with a load of around 225–250 pounds. The beast was reasonably amphibious; at least it could swim rivers. To scout, to patrol, to cover flank, rear and withdrawal, to raid — these missions remained untouched.

There remained, however, one really great problem area. Did automatic fire relegate the horse to a transport role or should it still be considered as part of a weapons system? At the time the problem was never stated quite this simply. Indeed it was never stated simply at all, but in essence this was the issue from roughly the end of the Boer War until World War I. The reason why the question so divided men was this: Cavalry as an arm was an integrated weapon made up of horse, man and cold steel fighting as one. If horses were to be considered simply as transportation, and if man and horse were to be separated for the fire fight, then the cavalry as an arm would no longer exist. Only mounted infantry would remain.[1]

On the issue of the relationship between horse and man hung a number of subsidiary issues. Should the horseman be armed with the new automatic weapons? If so, he would have to be dismounted in action, for the horse, as differentiated from the elephant, is a most unsatisfactory gun platform. Yet to deprive cavalry of the new weapons would be to deprive the weapons of mobility. And if the horse could no longer be used to charge the new guns, then of what possible use was honed steel, e.g., lance and sword, even if one took into serious account the last ditch defense of it, to wit that it was "always loaded"? Finally, and here one comes to the most burning question in any issue of military policy — the effect of change on morale. If the cavalry were deprived of its cold steel, would it lose that fine edge of morale, that élan without which of course it simply would not be "cavalry," no matter what its mission?

There should have been some way to learn through experience just what could and could not be done with the cavalry with and against the new weapons. There were, after all, two wars of some importance during the period under consideration — the Boer War (1898–1901) and the Russo-Japanese (1904–1905). In both, cavalry and repeating and automatic weapons were used. Each fall, moreover, there were great maneuvers in each country of Europe. Present at each were foreign observers with, at least by modern standards, a free run of the field of action. Why was it then that there could be no final decisions on these matters?

The answer lies in the number of variables. For instance, before the problem of the cavalry armament could even be tackled, the difficult question had to be answered as to what the rapid-fire weapons could do and should be doing.

There was agreement that a given weapon, *if* kept supplied with ammunition, could be fired for a given period of time, *if* it could be kept in action, i.e., was *not* knocked out by, say, long-range artillery fire, at a certain rate of fire, and that the firing might or might not be worthwhile depending on the availability of targets, i.e., enemy tactical doctrine. In short for each demonstrable fact there was an awkwardly intangible "if" which could neither be properly accounted for nor possibly forgotten.

If into the balance of judgment concerning the machine gun was thrown

---

[1] Perhaps this will be better understood if a modern analogy is cited — the substitution of missile for manned aircraft, for example.

the urgent problem of its resupply and its vulnerability to long-range artillery fire, then a rational conclusion might be reached that the weapon was primarily defensive in character and should be dug into the earth, into a well sandbagged bunker, there to pour forth its withering fire into an attacking force. Yet if, on the other hand, it was concluded that the withering fire of the weapon made it ideal to use on the surprise target, the target of opportunity on the enemy flank, then the weapon became offensive. If an offensive weapon, then the machine gun could well be designated a cavalry weapon. If defensive, then was it not an infantry, or even an artillery weapon? Of course this initial decision was a serious one for it might well determine the future of the weapon. Once assigned to an organization, a branch or arm of a service, it was at least likely that the weapon's development would be stunted except in line with the mission of the unit to which it was assigned. . . .

So in the period between 1900 and 1914 the immediate problem was to conceptualize the mission or missions of the machine gun and the tactics of the new clip-fed, bolt-action rifle and the automatic gun. The second problem was to decide the future tactics and armament of cavalry in view of the concept arrived at. What actually happened was that the new was absorbed into old organizational and tactical concepts, and nothing of the old was rejected. The reasoning from country to country may, however, be of lasting interest. The matter of the cavalry *charge* provides an excellent focal point.

THE CHARGE

. . . Reasons why the charge was continued varied from one country to another. But basically it was continued because the cavalry liked it. In virtually all countries the cavalry was a club, an exclusive one, made up at the officer level of those who could afford to ride when young, hunt, dress, and play polo when older. The impression that one absorbs from contemporary cavalry reviews, from the pictures, the social columns, the interests expressed in the less than serious articles, together with the portrait of the cavalryman in the contemporary novel, is of a group of men who were at once hard-riding, hard-drinking, and hard-headed. Its leadership was derived from the countryside rather than from the city. The cavalry was the home of tradition, the seat of romance, the haven of the well-connected. New York City's Squadron A, the proud majors in the Prussian Cavalry Reserve, the French Horse Breeders' Association, all had a built-in loyalty to the cavalry, and if the Chief of Cavalry said that the charge was still feasible, he had important backing. So it was that in Europe the charge was still considered not only feasible but a future way of war.

American cavalrymen, however, thought that European cavalry had much to learn. And in many respects the U.S. "Red Necks" were quite the most realistic of the world's cavalries in the period just prior to World War I. To be sure, they retained the saber charge, executing it with the same straight saber, a thrust weapon, used by the Canadian cavalry. But in the years from just before World War I until just after World War II the U.S. Cavalry preferred to practice the charge with the Colt semi-automatic .45 pistol. (The pistol charge was never actually used in battle. The last battle charge of the U.S. Cavalry seems to have been in the Philippines during the insurrection of 1901.) Of course it might be argued that to put a .45 in the hands of a man on a horse was simply to mount the inaccurate on the unstable, but given the argument that the essence of the charge was its psychological impact, the sound of the .45 might have had an effect comparable to the sight of saber or lance.

But what the U.S. Cavalry did have that others did not was a genuine appreciation of the importance of dismounted action. It is this which is given the more elaborate treatment in the regulations, and it is this that the trooper really expected to be the rule in combat. But was this the result of a thoughtful analysis of the new weapons or something else? . . .

The U.S. cavalryman had a tradition quite different from that of any of the Europeans. He had always done the bulk of his fighting on his feet. Therefore there was no break in tradition for him to recognize the revolution in firepower for the great change it was. Cavalry during the Civil War most frequently fought dismounted, although clashes between cavalry were fought with the sword, and in the wars against the Indians cavalrymen also dismounted to fight with the aimed accurate fire quite unattainable on horseback. Horses were considered transportation, and the ground was considered a respectable substance on which to fight a battle. U.S. cavalry-men did not feel morally obligated to die on a horse — which European cavalrymen did. In short, the U.S. Cavalry reacted to the new firepower as it did because its history and its tradition made it quite natural for it to do so. In Europe the cavalry history of the U.S. Civil War was scarcely known until the very late eighteen hundreds, and hence the relevance of that war to cavalry problems was largely overlooked. Or given European experience and tradition, would a study of the Civil War have made any real difference?

Of all the cavalry arms of the world that which seems in retrospect to have been the furthest behind the times was that of the German Empire. The German Cavalry had adopted the lance for all ninety-three of its cavalry regiments in 1890 instead, as was true in the mid-nineteenth century, of having only one in four so armed. . . .

Why was it that such serious students of war as the Germans are reputed to have been were in general quite so oblivious to the impact of the new firepower? There seem to have been several reasons. The first and most important was the attitude of Emperor William II towards cavalry. A young U.S. Cavalry lieutenant who witnessed German maneuvers in the fall of 1903 was frankly appalled by it. He noted the total lack of realism in the great rolling charges of the cavalry against both rifle and artillery. And he noted too the fact that the Kaiser was so proud of his cavalry that his umpires, knowing their place, pronounced the charges successful!! In Germany, in short, the well-known penchant of the Emperor for the charge undoubtedly did much to insulate the Germans from any serious thought of change.

There was, however, another reason as well. Even after seeing machine guns fired in the late 1880s, the German General Staff refused to take them seriously. Their reason lay in their misreading of their own experience with the *mitrailleuses* during the war of 1870–1871 when these were badly misused. The fact that past experience happened to be irrelevant did not make it any less important, however, and it was not until 1908 that the machine gun was given the serious attention in Germany that it so obviously deserved. Even then it was only the infantry that recognized the importance of the new automatic weapons. Cavalry units, although armed with them, did not take them very seriously. German cavalry went trotting off to war in 1914, pennons flying from their lances, just as units of French infantry went off to war in red trousers, and for much the same reason; psychological effect. For the real effect of cavalry was, when on the charge, a psychological one, and was generally admitted as such. It was the role of the charge to break the enemy's will, and what could do this more effectively than a charge by lancers? The same argument was used by those who wanted to keep the infantry in red pants. They advanced the proposition that the sense of belonging was the essence of group spirit, and group spirit in turn was the touchstone of the will to fight, the ingredient that won battles. They added the corollary that nothing gave units the sense of oneness that did red trousers, and that therefore camouflaged material would actually sabotage national security. Red pants and lances were both subject to this unshakable *quod erat demonstrandum.*

So tradition, personal predilection, and misinterpreted past experience kept the cavalry charge alive in Germany. The experiences of the British after the Boer War likewise suggests how difficult it is to test the relevance of one's own experience in war. . . .

THE RELEVANCE OF EXPERIENCE

A U.S. Cavalry officer noted on a trip to Aldershot in 1903 that "Every change is made entirely with reference to the Boer War and the Boer country, as though future wars would be fought under the same conditions." [2] But what this observer should also have noted was that there was a wide division of opinon as to just what that war proved and how genuinely relevant it really was. This problem of the interpretation of experience was not a new one in the historiography of military operations, and is a continuing one. When, after all, is a war or even a battle an aberration from an established norm? And who is to say with any precision just what a "norm" is? When war is won in a battle rather than in a series of battles, such a norm could be established with some semblance of reality. But by its very nature modern war is made up of a series of battles, a cumulative effect. Battles, if not war itself, are decisive in only a limited sense.[3] Furthermore, it has been increasingly true in wars from the Civil War to the Korean episode that what is the correct doctrinal application of force in one area at one time is not always correct for some different time and place. But the very urgency of having a doctrine to teach, of having to write regulations to insure that degree of unity of approach without which no hierarchy can be fully effective, has militated against that flexibility of thought which is only realistic given the differing circumstances under which battles are fought in modern war.[4]

Like other modern wars the Boer War was made up of a series of actions no one of which was decisive. The Boers, fine shots and fine horsemen, used their horses as transportation. In effect they fought as mounted infantry, employing the mobility of the horse in combination with the aimed firepower of infantry. They possessed all the advantages of great space and a friendly and embattled population, and the British were hard put to it to bring them to terms. But these were virtually the only points on which there was any agreement whatsoever. What did the facts mean, if anything?

Two of Great Britain's best known military figures, Lord Roberts, the British Chief of Staff, and Field-Marshal Sir John D. P. French, Cavalry Commander in Africa and, in 1914, Commander-in-Chief of the British Expeditionary Forces, led two factions within the army whose views of the future of cavalry were in direct opposition. . . .

Lord Roberts believed simply that the "main lesson" to be learned from the Boer War and the Russo-Japanese War was that "knee to knee, close order charging is practically a thing of the past." He qualified his opinion somewhat. "There may be, there probably will be, mounted attacks, preferably in open order against Cavalry caught unawares, or against broken

---

[2] Frank R. McCoy, "Notes of the German Maneuvers," *Journal of the U.S. Cavalry Association,* XIV (January 1904), 30–31.

[3] See the suggestive essay on the indecisiveness of war in John Holland Rose, *The Indecisiveness of Modern War and Other Essays* (1927).

[4] Thus German air-tank doctrine won the battle of France and made it possible for Hitler to dance his jig at Réthondes. But this same doctrine never took the Nazis to Omsk and was irrelevant to the problem of taking London.

Infantry," he wrote. But even these mounted attacks, he said, should be carried out with the rifle, rather than with steel.[5] These ideas he actually wrote into the British regulations, *Cavalry Training*, in 1904.

. . . The general argument, as one can imagine, was first that lances and sabers were not killing men in war, and, second, that infantry and mounted infantry were killing, when dismounted, cavalrymen. Three wars — the U.S. Civil War, the Boer War, and the Russo-Japanese War — were cited as proof of the contention. In retrospect this point of view hardly needs explanation. It seems quite obvious to think that the armaments which took the warrior off his feet and put him on his belly would by the same token take him off his charger and put him on the ground.

For a time Lord Roberts was Commander-in-Chief of the British Army, and his views were thus imposed for a brief moment on the generals. What this meant in effect was that the lance disappeared in Britain between 1903 and 1906. But Lord Roberts proved unpopular, and as is the way with unpopular leaders, he was eased gently out of office in quite short order, to become a disturbing shadow amongst their eminences in the House of Lords. And the lance came back into use in 1906 to remain for better than two decades — until 1927, to be precise.

Sir John French, an officer whom one of the most distinguished of Great Britain's War Secretaries, Lord Haldane, called "a real soldier of the modern type" [6] was an old Hussar. He had entered the army through the Militia and had thus avoided Sandhurst and the mental training this would have involved. For Sir John the experience of the Boer War was disturbing only because a number of his colleagues had been disturbed by it. As he thought over this experience, his final assessment as of the very eve of World War I was that "It passes comprehension that some critics in England should gravely assure us that the war in South Africa should be our chief source of inspiration and guidance, and that it was not normal." [7]

The Field-Marshal's reasoning was very simple. First, he said, "The composition and tactics of the Boer forces were as dissimilar from those of European armies as possible," and he added that "Such tactics in Europe would lead to the disruption and disbandment of any army that attempted them." [8] Second, he noted that in South Africa both unlimited space and the objective of complete submission of the enemy made it a most unusual war. Third, he maintained that the British had not at the time developed proper means for remounting the cavalry with trained horses.[9] But to say

---

[5] Erskine Childers, *War and the "Arme Blanche"* (1910). With an introduction by the Right Hon. Field-Marshal Earl Roberts, V.C., K.G., p. xii.

[6] Richard Burdon Haldane, *An Autobiography* (1929), p. 295.

[7] General Fredrich von Bernhardi, *Cavalry* (1914), with a Preface by Field-Marshal Sir J. D. P. French, p. 9.

[8] *Ibid.*, p. 9.

[9] *Ibid.*, pp. 10 ff.

this is really to say nothing at all. It is only by uncovering Sir John's basic premises that there is really any possibility of understanding his view of his own experience.

Perhaps Sir John summarized his own thinking best when he wrote sometime during the course of 1908 that "The Boers did all that could be expected of Mounted Infantry, but were powerless to crown victory as only the dash of Cavalry can do." [10] It was the "dash of Cavalry" of which Sir John was thinking. There is ample evidence to document the point. If cold steel were thown away as "useless lumber," he wrote, ". . . we should invert the role of cavalry, turn it into a defensive arm, and make it a prey to the first foreign cavalry that it meets, for good cavalry can always compel a dismounted force of mounted riflemen to mount and ride away, and when such riflemen are caught on their horses, they have power neither of offence nor of defence and are lost." [11] Based on this analysis of the effect of rapid fire on mounted cavalry action, he deduced that the proper role of cavalry was first to fight the battlefield's greatest threat, i.e., the enemy cavalry. "The successful cavalry fight confers upon the victor command of the ground." [12] This, he said, was a job for cold steel. Only when the enemy cavalry was out of action did he think that the cavalry would rely more on the rifle than on steel — which is not to say that he ruled "out as impossible, or even unlikely, attacks by great bodies of mounted men against other arms on the battlefield." [13]

So it was that Sir John and his followers decided that the experience of recent wars was irrelevant. The Boer War was not relevant because it had not been fought in Europe and because the Boers had not been armed with steel as were cavalries in Europe. The war in Manchuria between the Russians and the Japanese was irrelevant not only because it had not been fought in Europe, but also because the cavalry used there had been badly mounted, rode indifferently, and, above all, were poorly trained, i.e., in dismounted principles. "They were," wrote Sir John, "devoid of real Cavalry training; they thought of nothing but of getting off their horses and shooting. . . ." [14] From one principle, note, Sir John never deviated: *Unless the enemy cavalry was defeated, the cavalry could not carry out its other responsibilities.* And there was a corollary of this, to wit: *"Only cavalry can defeat cavalry,"* cavalry being defined of course as "a body of horsemen armed with steel."

Sir John, however wrong he may have been in his estimate of the fire-

[10] From his Introduction to the English edition of Lt. Gen. Frederick von Bernhardi, *Cavalry in Future Wars* (1909), p. x.

[11] Bernhardi, *Cavalry,* p. 11.

[12] *Ibid.,* p. 13.

[13] *Ibid.,* p. 15. See also A. P. Ryan, *Mutiny at the Curragh* (1956), pp. 97–100, for a further elaboration of Sir John's views.

[14] Bernhardi, *Cavalry in Future Wars,* p. xxiii.

power revolution of his day, made one point of real consequence when he insisted that the cavalry should keep its mind on a war likely to be fought — which a war in Manchuria, the United States, or South Africa was not. To talk about wars which are likely seems eminently sensible, although there are times when the unlikely ones are given rather more attention than they warrant depending on what set of premises are in search of some wider acceptance.[15] To cite a recent example, the war in Korea in 1950–1952 provided what seemed to the U.S. Air Force to be irrelevant experience because bombers were not effectively used. To the U.S. Navy and Marine Corps, on the other hand, it seemed very relevant indeed because Korea was a peninsula admirably suited to the projection of naval power. To the U.S. Army it presented a whole new way of thinking: that limited war involving ground troops might well be the way of the future despite and because of the horrors of nuclear exchange.

THE LIMITS OF A WEAPONS SYSTEM EVALUATION

But even if history in terms of recent war experience seemed irrelevant for one reason or another to the problem of the charge, it is hard to believe that war is a science so limited that means could not be found to test in practice the effectiveness of the charge, that a conclusive study could not be made of charges made in a variety of patterns, in different formations, and with different weapons against simulated "enemy formations." But the simple truth is that nothing is more difficult to test than a weapon's effectiveness. (This should be patently obvious to anyone who, during the late 1950s, troubled himself to inquire into the missile development claims of the several U.S. armed services.) Maneuvers, like wars, take place after all under certain sets of conditions, and who is to say, therefore, what is their meaning?

There is a grievously large number of intellectual stumbling blocks in first setting up and then later evaluating any test experience. For example, during the summer of 1936 the U.S. Infantry maneuvered against the U.S. Cavalry at Fort Benning, Georgia. As the problem started, the cavalry rode and the infantry trucked to the given maneuver area. The motor vehicles being rather faster than the horses, the infantry had ample time to get into position first. This proved a most frightening advantage. The infantry, well camouflaged, waited with some excitement while the cavalry were allowed to pass concealed forward infantry units. Only when the advance units of cavalry hit the main units of infantry did the infantry's stratagem become apparent. It was at that moment that the infantrymen rose shouting from entrenched positions waving bed sheets. The horses thought their

---

[15] The difficulty is readily admitted that wars seem either "likely" or "unlikely" depending upon whether the perspective is past or future.

Day of Judgment had arrived as ghosts rose over the battlefield, and what followed is best left to the imagination.

To infantrymen the maneuver proved conclusively that trucks gave the infantry a mobility with which the cavalry could not hope to compete and that when minus multicolored uniforms and not drawn up in drill formation, the infantry made unsatisfactory cavalry targets. Yet to the cavalrymen — and this raised a furor that still stays in men's minds — the whole exercise only proved that infantrymen were practical jokers. The problem, that is to say, of "proving out" doctrine in the field of maneuver is distressingly difficult. . . .

FACTORS IN INSTITUTIONAL SURVIVAL

The Role of History

On the morrow of victory after World War I, a member of the House of Commons rose to criticize the Secretary of War, Mr. Winston Churchill. He noted that the cavalry was at "practically the same figure as before the war, and yet if I should have thought anything had been proved by the War, it was that cavalry was less useful (than) we had previously thought it was going to be." [16] . . .

There would seem to be no reasonable doubt but that in the minds of the doughboy, the *poilu* or Tommy Atkins, the day of the horse was over. The cavalryman had been called a number of things during the war, "Pig-sticker," the "Rocking Horseman," etc., which indicated what the infantry thought of his contribution. But to the cavalryman himself the cavalry was not dead, and the history of the Great War was never written really in meaningful terms. To him the role of the horseman in the victory became swollen with the yeast of time. Indeed, in cavalry historiography, the role of the horse in World War I was most emphasized at that moment in time when the cavalry was most threatened in army reorganization plans, between 1934 and 1939.

The cavalry had been used in the First World War. The Germans used it extensively on that last stronghold of the cavalryman, the eastern frontier. The British and French used it extensively in 1914 during the retreat from Le Mans during late August and early September. Indeed the largest item of export from Great Britain to its forces on the Continent for the war as a whole was horse fodder — which goes to show that the expression "eat like a horse" is a simile of substance! For the most part the cavalry fought dismounted, but it did fight mounted as well. It did charge machine guns. In one case the Canadians charged a group of German machine guns, and came out unscathed, so great was the surprise achieved when the

[16] *125 H.C. Deb. 25*, pp. 1366 ff.

horsemen charged, blades bared. And it was used mounted as late as 1918. Indeed, this claim has been made for its work at that time — by a cavalryman: "It may or may not be true to say that we (the allies) should have defeated the Germans just the same in the autumn of 1918, even without our cavalry. But it is certainly true that, had it not been for that same cavalry, there would have been no autumn advance at all for the Germans would have defeated us in the spring."

But the campaign which did more to save the horse cavalry than any other was not fought in Europe at all. It was fought on the sands of Palestine — at Gaza, at Beersheba, at Jerusalem — and it was fought in part, and indeed in large part, with the lance. It was as dashingly romantic as anything that happened during that singularly drab war, and strong drink it was to the cavalry. In a sense it kept the cavalry going for another quarter century. There was irony in this for the most eager of the cavalrymen, men of the stamp of Sir John French, had for a decade defended the cavalry regulations on the basis of the forecast of their utility for the big war on the continent, only to have the cavalry successfully used only on the periphery of the great battlefields.

So experience, that most revered of teachers, continued to couch the "lessons" of war in a certain studied ambiguity. The horse retained that place in warfare which it had had for a thousand years — in the minds of its military riders.

Mission Justification for the Future, 1920–1940

On the eve of World War II the General Officers of the U.S. Army were, next to those of Poland, Rumania and possibly the USSR, most convinced of the continuing utility of the horse. The French had four divisions of mixed horse and mechanized cavalry. The Germans had a debated number of horses and mechanized cavalry, for use largely as reconnaissance. The British were converting from oats to oil as rapidly as possible.

A number of problems immediately present themselves. A first very general question must be asked of the cavalrymen themselves: What did they consider their mission to be in the period between 1920 and roughly 1935 when the development of both plane and tank had reached the stage at which their future development could be foreseen with some clarity, and at which therefore some reasonable readjustment of forces to the fact of their existence could be expected. How can one account for those great differences in thinking between the responsible staffs of the larger nations during the years between 1935 and the outbreak of war in 1939?

With the introduction of each new weapon into the arsenal of any power the future is more difficult to see than it was previously. Each of the four revolutions in warfare which have occurred in this century have made policy determination that much more difficult. One of the reasons for this is that each new weapons system is so quickly idealized by those who control it. Those situations which frustrate its usefulness are left for those out of control to exaggerate. The bomber pilot remembers that he can destroy the hub of industry, and forgets that he has only a very limited capacity to win a war against a self-sustaining countryside. He thinks of Germany rather than of China. The tankman remembers the plains cut by roads and forgets the jungles cut by rivers. The anti-whatever-it-is-man — the anti-tank, the anti-air — thinks of the power of the defense over that of the offense. The crystal ball has been shattered by technology. It was fractured by 1900, but this only became quite evident after the First World War.

The basic argument of the cavalrymen in their journals and in their manuals in the period between the great wars was an absolutely sound one. They argued in essence that new weapons obviated only those with like characteristics. They argued that while a better tank scrapped a worse one, the tank as a weapons system could not replace the horse until such time as it could perform all the missions of a horse. Whether these missions were worthwhile was seldom considered.

Many of the arguments which cavalrymen of all nations advanced to substantiate their claims as to their future role in war will be recognized by any student of recent military history as a version of what one can only describe as standardized clap-trap. One was the argument that, since most of the world was roadless, "To base our transportation needs solely upon conditions existent in the comparatively tiny proportion of the earth's surface containing roads . . . is putting too many eggs in the same basket." [17] This will be recognized as a cavalry variant on the navy contention that "since the world is 60 per cent water . . . ," and the air contention that "since air surrounds the earth and the shortest distance between two points. . . ." Another argument familiar to all military historians came up again and again in the journals. This one was to the effect that mechanical aids and auxiliaries end by neutralizing each other, an argument which in its most outrageous form had the anti-tank weapon returning the battlefield to the horse. "It is quite within the bounds of possibility that an infantry anti-tank weapon may be produced which will make tanks useless as weapons of attack," wrote one enthusiast [18] in a vein not unlike that used by airmen against seamen at roughly the same moment in time. The difficulty of supplying tanks was brought up as the supply problem is brought up as a limitation on each new weapons system. And, of course, the essentially experimental nature of tanks — "as yet untried" is the term — raised its head perennially and everywhere.

[17] Major Malcolm Wheeler-Nicholson, *Modern Cavalry* (1922), p. VII.
[18] Anonymous, "Oil and Oats," *Cavalry Journal* (British), XVIII (January 1938), p. 31; Col. Sir Hereward Wake, "The Infantry Anti-Tank Weapon," *Army Quarterly*, XVII (January 1929), p. 349.

But there were other problems and more serious ones. If the tank could be made to replace the cavalry on the charge, did that mean that the tank could take over all the other cavalry missions: reconnaissance, raids, flank protection in rough country? Could the plane be made to supplement the tank in such a way that the two used in combination could effectuate a complete substitution for the horse? Or would some kind of combination of horse and tank, and plane and tank be a future necessity? And if this were so with whom would the control lie, with tankmen or horsemen or pilots? And finally if this was a problem of phasing out the horse, what factors should govern the timing of this phasing?

These questions do not seem to have been asked with any precision largely perhaps because they edged too closely on the emotion-packed matter of prestige, on the one hand, and on an essentially insoluble organizational problem on the other. Naturally armor wanted maximum independence as do those who service and fire any weapon. The tankman wanted a command of his own, just as the machinegunner wanted his own battalion, the artillery its own regiment, the horse cavalry its own division and the airman his own service. And this is logical for in a decentralized structure growth is faster as imagination is given a freer rein. But the difficulty is that, war being all of one cloth, each weapon component also wishes to control elements of the others. And this is why the sparks flew between arms in the period between the World Wars, and before the First and after the Second. Where, as in Germany and Great Britain, armor was given its independence, it thrived. Where, as in the United States and Poland, the Cavalry (Horse) remained in control, tank doctrine never grew roots. But where, as in France, mechanized and horse were joined together in what at first blush seemed to be a happy marriage, a unity was forced which was pitifully inadequate from every standpoint.

For the man on the horse there was much greater difficulty in understanding the tank than in understanding the rapid-fire weapon. Perhaps this could be expected since tank and horse were competitors for the same missions. Certainly the limpid eye and high spirit of the one and the crass impersonal power of the other was enough to render partisans of the one quite helpless when it came to understanding the military views of the other, quite as helpless indeed as the seabased fighter is to understand the landbased or the airbased and their view of world geography.

Practicality and the Concept of the Balanced Force

One finds the horse cavalryman making the same points over and over again. He stressed the tanks' need for spare parts, without taking into consideration that one of the greatest difficulties of the cavalry was that horses do not have spare parts. He stressed the lack of mobility of the tank along mountain trails without mention of the appalling problem of getting horses overseas — they have a tendency to pneumonia, together with a soft breast which becomes raw and infected with the roll and pitch of the ship. Whereas the point was occasionally made that the Lord took care of the resupply of horses — i.e., that while factories could be bombed out, sex could not — no mention was ever made that in wartime as in peace He still took four or five years to produce each animal. And, finally, although the horse was claimed to have certain immunities to gas warfare, the peculiar problems of getting gas masks on the poor beasts were omitted.

Yet whether partisans were ankle deep in the sands of prejudice or not, there were certain aspects of the relationship between horses and planes, and horses and tanks which were so obvious that they could hardly be missed. However low and slow it flew, the plane would not be a substitute for a still lower and still slower man on a horse. And the plane could not penetrate forests, and neither, within limits, could tanks. So there was, and indeed there still is, a gap between what the horse can do and what the plane and the tank can do. But admitting the gap, there still remained the most vexing problem of all — to wit whether that gap was worth filling and if so how. And this was something which each general staff decided somewhat differently and for itself. . . .

Concepts of Modernization

One cannot help but be impressed with the intellectual isolation in which the U.S. armed forces operated in the 1930s. The *Journal of the U.S. Cavalry Association* paid almost no attention to mechanization throughout the period. Compared to the military periodicals on the continent, the U.S. journal seems curiously antiquated. And because there was so little critical thinking going on within the service, it is not surprising that there was virtually no thinking going on in Army ordnance either, for ordnance, after all, works on a demand basis, and if there is no demand, there is likely to be no new hardware. In the United States there was in short no intellectual challenge.

Not only were there no pressures to change cavalry thinking from inside the arm, there were no pressures from outside either. United States industry was never anxious to sell to the services during the depression years or before. They were no more willing to put money into military research and development than were the services or the Congress. The few Secretaries of War who can be considered adequate were interested in the managerial aspects of their office and not in matters which they considered "purely military." And finally there was a not inconsiderable pressure for the status quo in the Congress. The U.S. had some ten millions of horses, and government spending in this direction, little though it was, was a chief source of revenue to all the many horse breeders, hay growers, and saddlemakers.

In Great Britain, the situation was markedly different. Although the British had their branch journals — the tankers founded their own in 1937 — they also had one great advantage in having two journals which were more generally read. The first was the *Army Quarterly* which published on all topics of concern to the army as a whole, and the other was *The Journal of the Royal United Service Institution* which crossed service lines. Into these journals there poured articles from a singularly able, and remarkably prolific and dedicated group of publicists of whom J. F. C. Fuller and Captain Basil H. Liddell Hart are simply the best known. Officers in the British Empire were simply unable to escape, as were U.S. officers, from challenge. Thus from 1936 onwards there was an increasingly strong movement in favor of conversion to oil. Furthermore this was helped rather than hindered by the stand taken by many in Parliament. For Parliament was at least conscious of *The Times* military correspondent, Liddell Hart, and the battle he was waging for mechanized warfare, a form of warfare which would, so he thought, limit and shorten future wars by making them more rapid, hence shorter and cheaper than the war of the trenches. To be sure there were those who, like Admiral of the Fleet Sir Roger Keyes, took a position against the reduction of cavalry. But they were in the minority. Most felt that the Household Cavalry and two mounted regiments still left in Egypt in 1939 were probably two too many. A statement made by Mr. Duff Cooper on the very eve of the war while defending the conversion of the army to mechanization may also explain British willingness to change. Duff Cooper mentioned the lack of horses which would be subject to wartime draft.

The overall development of French cavalry thinking between the wars is plain enough. What they did was to absorb the new machines of war into old doctrine. Instead of allowing the characteristics of new weapons to create new doctrine, the French General Staff simply gave them missions to fulfill that were within the old framework. Thus tanks were made subordinate and supporting weapons to the infantry, and subordinate and supporting weapons to the cavalry. In a sense the French achieved what General Herr of the U.S. Cavalry wanted to achieve, except that the French did look forward to complete mechanization at some future date, which Herr did not. And the *Revue de Cavalerie,* a strange hodge-podge of oats, history and oil, reflects this point of view.

The German experience was somewhat different again. Whereas the French looked back to the stalemate at Verdun, the great achievement of defensive weapons, the Germans looked back to the great offensives of 1918 and to the very near miss of the Schlieffen plan in 1914. Particularly in the case of the younger officers the great objective was regaining the lost means of offensive. A defeated army, the Germans were in a position to start once more from the beginning. To be sure there was a very difficult period of struggle with German horse cavalrymen, but those in Germany with an interest in tanks had an advantage which those in the democracies did not. They had the interest of the Chief of State. When Hitler saw Panzer units in action, he said repeatedly, "That's what I need! That's what I want to have!" [19] To Hitler they were the keystone in a concept of total war.

The *Revue de Cavalerie* stopped publication during the war and never appeared again. The British *Cavalry Journal* disappeared forever as well. Only the *Journal of the U.S. Cavalry Association* continued to appear. Its heroes were the horse-drawn artillery which landed on Guadalcanal, the animals flown over the Burma "Hump" into China, the U.S. units which were remounted on Italian Cavalry horses in Italy and German horses in Germany; the great heroes were the only real cavalry left — the Cossacks. Duly noted was how greatly needed were horse cavalry during the battles in Normandy and elsewhere.

In his closing chapter of *He's in the Cavalry Now* Brig. Gen. Rufus S. Ramey, a former commander of the U.S. Cavalry School, concluded in 1944, "Currently we are organizing and training adequate mechanized horse cavalry for field employment." [20] His was the final testament. The last old Army mule, except for the West Point Mascot, was retired in 1956. The horse cavalry had been disbanded five years before.

New Item

In 1956 the Belgian General Staff suggested that for the kind of dispersed war which low yield atomic weapons necessarily create, the horse, which in Europe could be independent of depots, should be reintroduced into the weapons system.[21] . . .

[19] General Heinz Guderian, *Panzer Leader* (1952), p. 30.

[20] Ramey, *He's in the Cavalry Now* (1944), p. 190. There were 60,170 animals in the U.S. Forces on December 31, 1943.

[21] "Belgians Hit U.S. Concept of Atomic War," *Christian Science Monitor,* August 25, 1956.

ROBERT E. HUNTER

The Politics of U.S. Defense 1963: Manned Bombers versus Missiles

The fate of the RS-70 manned bomber and of Skybolt air-to-ground missile during the early years of the McNamara administration of the Pentagon are good examples of the process of bureaucratic politics at work in the area of weapons procurement. Hunter's analysis emphasizes the central role of organizational interests in defining the face of the issue perceived by the Air Force, its stake in the decision, and the stand it took. The struggle between the services and the Secretary of Defense illustrates the play of maneuvers and argument as the adversaries jockey to secure a favorable outcome.

The development of missiles had, by the early 1960's, posed an unmistakable challenge to the future of manned bombers and, correspondingly, to the future of the most powerful branches of both the Air Force and the Navy. For both the bomber pilots of the Strategic Air Command (SAC) and naval aviators, the problem was to protect their organizational essence — flying high-performance aircraft in combat — and therefore to devise a new rationale which would permit their organizations to continue with a minimum of adjustment. The naval aviators accommodated the threat posed by missiles by simply redefining the mission of the carrier forces to make them noncompetitive with strategic missiles. This redefinition in no way limited their claims for newer, better carriers to launch ever more sophisticated aircraft.

No such easy way out was open to the bomber pilots of SAC for whom (at least prior to Vietnam) there was no foreseeable limited war mission. To SAC, the B-70 follow-on bomber and Skybolt missile represented efforts to preserve the strategic role of the manned bomber in the missile age. The renaming of the B-70 to RS-70 represented an effort to find a new mission not competitive with ICBM's.

Other organizational interests combined to stimulate valuable support from other branches and services for the SAC pilots' objectives. The three services were interested in minimizing inter-service conflict. They wished to sustain morale and maximize their budgets, and they desired to reduce their vulnerability to outside (civilian) interference. The services' mutual interest in preserving their respective organizational autonomy allowed them to submerge their competition for scarce funds and to present a united front in support of the SAC position in opposition to increasing pressures for civilian domination.

Since organizational interests are considered to have no legitimate role

This material originally appeared in the March 1963 issue of *The World Today,* the monthly journal published by the Royal Institute of International Affairs, London. Reprinted by permission.

in national security decisions, maneuvers and arguments to achieve SAC's objectives were justified in terms of other criteria — in particular, the technical feasibility of the proposed weapons. Thus the administration pointed to the repeated failures of Skybolt in test firings as the reason for cancelling the project. In an effort to trap the administration in its own arguments, the Air Force announced a successful test at the conclusion of the Nassau conference with Britain, evidencing a willingness to exacerbate a crisis in Anglo-American relations in order to protect its organizational essence. The administration sought to reduce future embarrassments by cutting off funds for future testing. All of this was played out during a Congressional recess — an administration attempt to kill the project before the Air Force could call upon its supporters in Congress.

Hunter's analysis may be most significant for what it omits; neither the Soviet Union nor any other security threat is mentioned in the course of explaining and interpreting these national security decisions. His interpretation is complete without such factors.

The reader's attention also is directed to several of the footnotes, which are themselves a rich source of insight into the objectives and maneuvers of the various participants.

The return of Congress to Washington soon after the new year often brings with it the prospect of a confrontation between the Administration and Congress over issues that have been raised, but not resolved, either at the tail-end of the preceding session or during the autumn hiatus in Congressional activities.

This year one very important confrontation can be expected in the controversial and sensitive area of defense policy. Among the various differences on defense matters between the executive and legislative branches, two complex and interrelated problems stand out. The first involves the Air Force's projected new bomber — dubbed the RS-70 (the *Valkyrie*) — that was designed to extend the life of the manned bomber for strategic missions well into the 1970s, despite the phasing-out of the 2,000 B–47s, B-52s, and B-58s (the *Hustlers*). Production of the last two weapons systems ceased late last year despite Congressional objections; the B-47 is already being "phased out." In March 1962, in a period of tense personal negotiations between Mr. Kennedy and leading Congressmen — most notably Georgia's Carl Vinson, forty-eight-year veteran of the House of Representatives and Chairman of the Armed Services Committee — the President agreed, in the famous "Rose-Garden Compromise," that the Defense Department would reconsider its decision to eliminate the multimillion-dollar bomber from the nation's projected nuclear arsenal. In exchange, Representative Vinson agreed that Congress would merely "authorize," rather than "direct," the President to expend unwanted funds on the new weapons system.

Following the Rose-Garden Compromise, Congress appropriated $362.6 million for the RS-70 in the fiscal year 1963, which began on July 1, 1962. This was $191.6 million more than the $171 million asked for by the Secretary of Defense, Mr. McNamara. Indeed, the funds requested by Mr. McNamara were designed only for the development stage of the program, with a maximum of three prototype aircraft being produced; the funds appropriated by Congress would have provided partial funding for six aircraft. Furthermore, the funds requested by Mr. McNamara would have come from the $180 million appropriated by Congress for the RS-70 in the preceding fiscal year but not spent by the Defense Secretary. As a result of the Rose-Garden Compromise, however, the $362.6 million Congressional appropriation for the fiscal year 1963 was considerably less than many Congressmen had earlier intended. For example, the Senate version of the appropriations bill called for an expenditure of $491 million — the amount requested by the Strategic Air Command (SAC) despite the objections of the Defense Secretary. Led by Representative Vinson, the House trimmed its version of the appropriations bill to $223.9 million. In the House-Senate Conference, the figure of $362.6 million was agreed as a compromise, but a proviso was added that more funds should be diverted to the RS-70 project from Defense Department emergency funds, if technical advances made such diversion profitable.

In practice, "technical difficulties" have postponed the flight test of the first prototype RS-70 from December 1962 at least until April of this year. Furthermore, so far this fiscal year the Defense Department has refused to authorize the expenditure of $141.6 million appropriated for the RS-70 — in other words, the Defense Department has spent $221 million or $50 million more than it had proposed. The "cost" of the Rose-Garden Compromise to the Administration, therefore, at least in terms of avoiding possible, but unspecified, Congressional retaliation against the 1962 Presidential Program, appears to have been $50 million (although the Defense Department would undoubtedly have preferred to have saved *all* of the $362.6 million; indeed, no new funds have been requested for the RS-70 in the Budget for the fiscal year 1964, which begins in July). The total cost of the Defense Department's refusal to spend RS-70 funds (funds that have been "impounded")[1] has yet to be measured. This year's impounding of funds will probably provoke another relatively innocuous Congressional appropriation of funds wanted by SAC for the RS-70. These funds will again be rejected by the Secretary of Defense in his efforts to speed up the

---

[1] Before funds appropriated by Congress can be spent by Administration agencies, the President must direct the Director of the Budget to apportion the funds — divide them into four parts to be spent during the four quarters of the fiscal year. If the President will not direct apportionment, funds may not be spent and have been "impounded."

transition from manned bombers to missiles. In addition, however, the Administration's stand on the RS-70 issue may have to be paid for in terms of Congressional votes on non-military legislation.

The other problem, closely related to the first and much more significant in its implications for international politics, involves the cancellation last December of the Air Force's *Skybolt* missile project. This issue may bring even more vehement protests from Congress as some leading Congressional defense authorities have promised, partly because they regarded Administration support for *Skybolt* as part of the price of the RS-70 settlement, on an "either-or" basis.

Skybolt was designed to be a solid-fuelled "stand-off" missile with a range of 1,000 nautical miles. It would have been mounted beneath the wings of B-52 Hs, as well as beneath the wings of British *Vulcan* bombers, thus prolonging the life of these bombers and of the SAC bomber force, especially if the RS-70 is finally and decisively rejected. On December 6, the Department of Defense stated that *Skybolt* was "not needed" by the Air Force because of the ability of the *Minuteman* missile to hit any *Skybolt* target from U.S. soil. Later, arriving in London for talks with Britain's Defense Minister prior to a "final" decision to cancel *Skybolt*, Mr. McNamara stated: "It is no secret . . . that all five flight tests [of *Skybolt*] attempted thus far have failed and production costs have climbed sharply." [2] Thus, the Defense Secretary's staff had judged *Skybolt* to be of too little military value (because its role could be played by a weapon system not dependent on a vulnerable, inaccurate bomber launching-platform), too far from technical perfection, and too expensive to justify its continued development and planned production. Following so closely the crisis over the RS-70 (with some Congressmen assuming that the Administration would support *Skybolt*), the prospect of a conflict over *Skybolt*, both within the Administration and between Administration and Congress, accentuates the seriousness of the *Skybolt* affair, at least in terms of the intra-governmental politics of U.S. defense policy.

THE DOCTRINAL CONFLICT

There are [several] fundamental political conflicts involved in the RS-70 and *Skybolt* controversies. The first is doctrinal: what is to be the role of manned aircraft in the future nuclear retaliatory arsenal of the United States? Is there a role for these planes in the era of missiles, or, as the Defense Secretary contends (recalling the slow and costly demise of the battleship), should the transition to a missile-dominated strategic nuclear force be accomplished as quickly and cheaply as possible?

[2] *New York Times* (international edition), December 12, 1962. [All ellipses in this chapter by Hunter.]

The gradual shift of service emphasis from manned bombers to missiles has been rapidly accelerated since the launching of the first Soviet *Sputnik* in October 1957. This has created a basic conflict between, on the one hand, vested interests absorbed with the refinement of manned bombers, together with sincere proponents of "mixed" [3] nuclear retaliatory forces, and, on the other, innovators who foresee the need for the U.S. armed forces to become missile-centered sooner rather than later.[4] As with any vested interest, the supporters of manned bombers within the military services and in private industry had the advantage in early confrontations with their rivals. But as a larger portion of high-level service personnel in the Air Force and Navy (the services primarily responsible for U.S. nuclear retaliatory capability) have recognized the inevitability of missile dominance, as well as the political opportunities for securing a sizeable share of strategic weapons procurement funds, the balance of power has swung the other way.[5] Similarly, the proliferation of missile projects, with their economic stimulation of otherwise declining aircraft companies, has had its influence on the attitude of manufacturers towards strategic doctrine. Companies formerly dependent upon aircraft defense contracts are now finding that they can do well in the missile field; entire new industries, developed to meet the needs of missile and space research, have grown up with no ties to the aircraft vested interests.

The technical and strategic obsolescence of manned bombers is affecting the Air Force and the Navy in significantly different ways. Within the Navy, which has always prided itself on its strategic flexibility, a potentially explosive conflict between the aircraft-carrier Navy and the rapidly emerging and popular *Polaris* submarine Navy has been channelled to the benefit of both groups. Towards the end of the 1950s, the primary function of the aircraft-carrier was redirected from a strategic nuclear retaliation role to a multiple-threat, predominantly "limited-war" role. With comparatively few difficulties, the doctrine of the aircraft-carrier has been altered to embrace

---

[3] A "mixed" force is a mixture of armaments to accomplish the same objective with the intent of confusing and complicating enemy defenses. A mixed nuclear retaliatory force might include manned bombers based in the United States and Europe, *Polaris* missiles, *Minuteman* (or *Atlas* and *Titan*) missiles, and low-flying pilotless bomber-missiles like the planned nuclear ram-jet, *Pluto*.

[4] Some of these innovators argue that "overkill" — super-saturation bombing capability — adds nothing to and may even detract from a nuclear deterrent. SAC has long been a proponent of "redundancy" in nuclear-weaponry, partly in order to increase the significance of SAC in the overall defense budget. A return to this politically valuable concept, following a period when "finite" — counter-city — deterrence was stressed, may result from McNamara's counter-force concept. This concept presumably requires larger striking forces than does finite deterrence.

[5] With the removal of two squadrons of *Jupiter* missiles from Italy and one from Turkey — thirty and fifteen missiles respectively — the Army's role as a strategic (as opposed to tactical) nuclear power will come to an end. Until December 1956, the Army was to have developed the missile for the *Polaris* project.

types of warfare where the use, or even the threat, of nuclear weapons would be inappropriate (although aircraft-carriers could still be employed in strategic nuclear warfare).

Within the Air Force a similar problem presented itself, namely, what to do about a large and powerful — in strategic and political terms — nuclear bomber force in the face of missile technology. Unfortunately for the Air Force, SAC's large, long-range bombers could not be adapted to limited war missions as readily as could the smaller, less costly aircraft-carrier planes that can fly either nuclear strike missions or ground-support missions from mobile bases close to targets. Because of the difficulties of converting long-range bombers to other uses, the conflict within the Air Force and the Defense Department over the phasing-out of SAC's manned bombers has been and may continue to be prolonged and extremely costly.

The first-line hope of the bomber interests in this battle was the B-70, unenthusiastically received during an early round of bargaining within the Defense Department during the Eisenhower Administration (President Eisenhower impounded $195 million of a $345 million B-70 appropriation in the fiscal year 1960). The Kennedy Administration, after a brief acceptance of the Air Force super-bomber, also arrived at the conclusion that the B-70 was only a "manned missile," and consequently restricted the B-70's rate of development. When presented for approval again last year, however, the B-70 had been renamed the RS (Reconnaissance-Strike)-70, and had supposedly become "more than a bomber. [It] could be used for flying radar detection and as a missile-hurling base." [6] Presumably these functions would include surveillance of bomb damage, location of additional targets, and on-the-spot decision-making as well as the long-range launching of *Skybolt*-type weapons. Like the Navy, the Air Force had apparently tried to create a new role for its manned bombers that would both help to preserve the prestige of SAC and mitigate the effects of a wasteful internal struggle between manned aircraft vested interests and missile system innovators during the slow transition into the new technology.

With the slowdown imposed by the Defense Department on the development of the RS-70, the *Skybolt* missile came to represent SAC's last technological argument for manned bombers as opposed to missiles. *Skybolt* was originally conceived as a manned-bomber answer to the second-strike *Polaris* solid-fuelled missile system, in much the same way that *Minuteman* was designed to be the missile Air Force's solid-fuelled answer to the popular Navy weapons system. With the cancellation of *Skybolt* (if this decision is not in some way reversed by Congress) the triumph of

[6] *New York Times*, March 9, 1962.

missiles over manned bombers will be speeded up by several years, with a consequent large saving in dollars; Mr. McNamara has estimated the cost of the RS-70 at $10,000 million and the saving on *Skybolt* at $2,000 million. In the view of advocates of mixed nuclear retaliatory forces, however, this dollar-saving would mean the sacrifice of over-all military effectiveness.[7]

The nature of the Air Force counter-attack against the Administration's attempt to end the *Skybolt* controversy before Congress could mobilize any sort of effective counter-action was partially revealed during the first week in January. It was announced that the Air Force was studying ways of using the knowledge gained in the *Skybolt* program for other purposes, with the missile itself perhaps becoming the vehicle for advanced space probes. This possible use of *Skybolt* represents in the long run the same kind of change of mission that characterized the change of the B-70 to the RS-70 and the (more successful) change of the aircraft-carrier into a predominantly limited-war weapon.[8] In the short run, the provision of an alternative use for *Skybolt*, in the hope that the program would be at least temporarily continued, makes the parallel between *Skybolt* and the RS-70 even more complete. Not only have both programs been opposed by the Administration for similar strategic and political reasons, but also the *Skybolt* program — if continued in any form at all — could be presented to Congress as a continuing program although in a state of incipient decline, just as the RS-70 program was presented last year when it was successful in obtaining Congress' support. With a dead program, on the other hand, what help could the supporters of *Skybolt* expect from Congress; what good would funds do for a dead program? The timing of the *Skybolt* cancellation — with orders to stop work being hastily given before the return of Congress to Washington — was presumably designed to stymie Air Force lobbying with Congress.

In the Defense Department argument against *Skybolt* early in December, technical difficulties, soaring costs, and diminishing military value were put forward. Because of the overriding character of the conflict over the role of manned bombers, however, arguments concerning the technical feasibility or even the expense (within reason) of the *Skybolt* project were

[7] Secretary McNamara, on the other hand, has pointed out that Defense Department plans include the mixed-force concept — and the hundreds of remaining SAC aircraft — for the 1964–68 period. SAC advocates, however, do not regard these plans as taking into account the need for manned bombers in the 1970s, nor do they allay their suspicions of Defense Department planners, already suspect because of the *Skybolt* decision.

[8] In late December, a possible compensation for the Air Force's loss of *Skybolt* appeared in the decision by the Defense Department to release $24 million — a small fraction — of impounded funds that had been appropriated for the *Pluto* missile. Politically, this decision may reduce the Air Force reaction to the *Skybolt* cancellation.

basically irrelevant. Had there been no technical, and hence fiscal, complications, the McNamara decision, founded on the opinion that *Skybolt* "combined the weaknesses of the bomber and the missile, and would have had the lowest accuracy, reliability, and yield of any of our strategic missiles," [9] would probably have been the same. The significance of *Skybolt's* technical difficulties lay in the timing of the cancellation; it came at a time when technical difficulties added political leverage to the Defense Department's case against manned bombers. In face of the five successive flight test failures of *Skybolt,* the Air Force argued that the *Thor* missile (now a successful space booster) and the now highly successful *Polaris* A-1 missile had also been plagued with early difficulties, and that the failures of even the *Polaris* A-3 missile were keeping pace with the *Skybolt* failures.[10] Furthermore, on December 22, the day after the conclusion of the Nassau Conference (in a test twice postponed by Washington, apparently to prevent an embarrassing success during a conference founded partially on *Skybolt's* lack of success), the Air Force claimed a successful *Skybolt* firing, "very close" — presumably within one nautical mile — to the full programmed range. In its desperation the Air Force was attempting to sabotage U.S. policy at the highest level. Abandoning the implied logic that test results connote technical feasibility, the Defense Department (Deputy Secretary Roswell Gilpatric) promptly countered that one success in six tests was not conclusive. Despite the objections of the Air Force and the Douglas Aircraft Company, *Skybolt's* prime contractor, the Department of Defense then suspended all further tests, presumably because further testing could not justify a review of the decision to cancel.[11]

Within a week, the desperation of the Air Force became even more apparent, and the implication that test failures equaled infeasibility, or at least "unacceptable" delays in development, reappeared. The Defense Department announced that the earlier Air Force statement had not been authorized and that the "successful" flight had actually been a failure, with a computed flight error (since the missile, test-launched without a nose cone, had burned up on re-entry) of between fifty-seven and ninety nautical miles. To this the Air Force replied — and this argument would have had some justification, had earlier claims not been made — that accuracy had not been a test objective. Whether the test was actually a success can

[9] *Times* (London), January 31, 1963.

[10] In a maneuver not uncommon in the fierce competition between supporters of rival weapons systems, one Air Force source was reported to have contended that only one of the five tests had been a "failure"; the other four had been "partial successes," a phrase that has come to possess little meaning. The *Polaris* A-3, incidentally, succeeded at the seventh attempt on February 7, 1963.

[11] Cancellation of further tests may also have been designed to prevent further embarrassing successes. Testing, indeed, does not necessarily prove either technical feasibility or infeasibility.

never be known, since the definition of criteria for success cannot be agreed upon.

The rationale for the cancellation of *Skybolt*, partly based on the argument of technical infeasibility, diminishes still more when viewed against the opinion of the Joint Chiefs of Staff that the project could have been completed.[12] Even the JCS Chairman, General Maxwell B. Taylor, former military adviser to President Kennedy in the White House, was reported to have supported *Skybolt's* technical feasibility, although he opposed the missile's further development on other grounds.[13] The clue to the decision to cancel perhaps lies in the lack of publicity, prior to the Defense Department announcement on December 6, concerning the technical difficulties encountered by the program.[14] The overwhelming technical and fiscal arguments suddenly advanced against *Skybolt* in December lead one to speculate that these arguments did not carry as much weight in the actual decision to cancel as political considerations in the doctrinal dispute, manned bombers versus missiles.[15] Long-range technical considerations, of course, militate against the perpetuation of the manned bomber, but the sudden cancelling of this particular project, thereby shortening the timetable for phasing-out manned bombers by several years, was probably occasioned by the appearance of a political opportunity. The Defense Secretary used his position and skills to enforce a decision that, rightly or wrongly, the Kennedy Administration had charged him to make, despite opposition from the military and from Congress, which wishes to share in such decisions.

[12] In addition, the cost of missile programs has long been something of an unknown quantity, with final costs often far outstripping original predictions. If *Skybolt* had been favored on other grounds, therefore, the cost factor would have been relatively insignificant. On the other hand, the complications posed by the agreement with Britain made technical and fiscal arguments all the more necessary. The 1959 agreement on *Skybolt* between President Eisenhower and Mr. Macmillan was reported to have hinged upon "the success of the project" (*New York Times* [int. ed.], December 14, 1962). Only technical infeasibility or spiralling costs — not strategic obsolescence — could, therefore, be cited to the British as grounds for cancellation.

[13] *New York Herald Tribune* (European ed.), January 7, 1963.

[14] According to Mr. Thorneycroft, "it was not until the beginning of November that Mr. McNamara, while assuring me that no decision would be taken without the fullest consultation, informed me that the future of the weapon was under review." *New York Times* (int. ed.), December 18, 1962.

[15] This argument further leads one to speculate that the revision of the relationship between the United States and the United Kingdom that grew out of the "*Skybolt* Affair" was an afterthought that was essentially independent of the doctrinal battle in Washington over the future of *Skybolt* in particular and the SAC bomber force in general. If this is the case, the implications of U.S. inability to deliver promised weapons to her allies or to consider her allies' political needs, because of domestic disputes among vested interests, are obvious. This may be one of the high costs of inter-service rivalry.

THE CONFLICT OF ORGANIZATION

The second fundamental conflict that is involved in the RS-70 and *Skybolt* controversies is one of organization: will resistance on the part of the separate military services to the Defense Department's plans for centralization prevent Secretary McNamara from accomplishing his grand design, which is to rationalize America's defense organization? Secretary McNamara has previously run into stiff opposition on the question of centralization of power in his immediate office — opposition from Congress over, among other things, the so-called "muzzling of the military"; from the press over curbs on interviews with Pentagon personnel; from Army Secretary Elvis J. Stahr, Jr., who, on retirement, charged the Defense Secretary with "overreaching in personal control"; and from industry over proposals to regulate salaries reimbursable from "non-competitive" government research and development contracts.

The question of the RS-70 and *Skybolt* may represent a sticking-point in the issue of centralization of control, beyond which service interests are not at present willing to proceed. If this is so, it would help to explain the common stand of the service chiefs within the JCS in favor of *Skybolt* — even before the "successful" *Skybolt* launching on December 22 — whereas a self-interested reaction of the individual services would have been expected to place the Air Force Chief of Staff (General Curtis LeMay, former head, and still leading supporter, of SAC) in opposition to the Chief of Naval Operations (Admiral George W. Anderson, Jr.) and the Army Chief of Staff (General Earle G. Wheeler).[16] Indeed, expectations of support from the other services — as well as from the missile Air Force — might well have contributed to the timing of the Defense Secretary's decisions to delay the RS-70 (presumably to "study it to death") and to cancel *Skybolt*. In the former instance, as Mr. McNamara explained last March: "The Secretaries and chiefs of the other [than Air Force] services . . . never supported the B-70 for full-weapon system development or procurement and, indeed, many vigorously opposed it." [17] Defense Department references to the JCS position on *Skybolt*, on the other hand,

---

[16] In terms of inter-service competition for funds and for doctrinal superiority, the Chief of Naval Operations could be expected, unless some "bargain" were struck, to oppose the SAC bombers in favor of funds for *Polaris,* the Navy weapon in the same budget category; the Army Chief of Staff, to oppose *Skybolt* in favor of increased conventional strength; the Air Force Chief of Staff — if he were other than LeMay — to have mixed feelings. He would probably support *Skybolt* because it was an Air Force project but would be beset by loyalties to Air Force missilemen.

[17] Quoted by Senator William Proxmire in the Senate, June 13, 1962. There had been support from the services for the development (as opposed to production) of the B-70, when the Navy's *Polaris* needed Air Force support. (See Senate Armed Services Committee, *Hearings,* 1961.)

have been minimized and the JCS position may have been discounted as merely an expression of feeling against centralization.

The attitude of General Taylor, who supported Mr. McNamara's decision on non-technical grounds, could also be interpreted in terms of the issue of centralization. He had retired in 1960 from the position of Army Chief of Staff over a doctrinal disagreement in the JCS, and had recently been called back to uniform from his position as President Kennedy's personal military adviser.[18] Presumably, therefore, he could have been expected to take more of a Kennedy–McNamara stand on the question of centralization than the three service chiefs.[19]

Resistance from the military against centralization of control within the Office of the Secretary of Defense has also led to misgivings about the making of decisions on weapons systems on a "cost-effectiveness" instead of "military-judgment" basis — that is, comparing the cost of a weapons system in relation to its effectiveness with the cost and effectiveness of a competing weapons system. As in the case of the RS-70 and *Skybolt*, however, the terms in which effectiveness is expressed vary. If one assumes the dominance of missile technology, then manned bomber systems are at a disadvantage. If one assumes the need for mixed nuclear retaliatory forces, then manned bombers must be allowed an added, subjective quantity of effectiveness; as has been argued, economy must not stand in the way of military security. Where there is agreement over doctrine, therefore, cost-effectiveness can be a useful tool (given the difficulties of estimating costs); where there is disagreement over doctrine, cost-effectiveness becomes merely a means of obscuring the politics of disagreements, based on subjective, but not necessarily unimportant, strategic philosophies and on vested interests.

As a result of the RS-70 and *Skybolt* controversies, where doctrinal clashes and bargaining over military alternatives have tended to be buried beneath a mass of purportedly objective evidence, the resolve of those in the services — and in Congress — who oppose the Defense Department's

---

[18] General Taylor's ". . . failure to win Administration support of heavy investments in the *Nike Zeus* Project contributed to his retirement from the Army two years ago." *New York Times* (int. ed.), December 13, 1962. The importance of service political strength in doctrinal conflicts is reflected in the observation that, although the Chairman of the JCS is committed to the *Nike Zeus* anti-missile missile, the administration has not yet permitted it to be produced, nor has Congress reacted to administration obstinacy as in the cases of the RS-70 and *Skybolt*.

[19] General Taylor's replacement of the previous JCS Chairman, Army General Lyman Lemnitzer, now Supreme Commander of NATO, may have been an attempt by the Administration to add top-level military support to Mr. McNamara's efforts for centralization; the *Skybolt* stand of the other three JCS members may, therefore, have reflected resistance to such an alliance. Indeed, General Taylor had expressed strong views on centralization in his book written in retirement, *The Uncertain Trumpet* (1960).

policy of centralization may be strengthened. Centralization has so far not eliminated bargaining: until and unless it does so, the use of "objective" arguments to obscure bargained or subjective premises will still be an effective weapon — for good or evil — in the hands of whoever can muster the most impressive expert opinion on his behalf.[20]

RONALD STEEL

The Kennedys and the Missile Crisis

Steel's review essay of Robert Kennedy's book on the Cuban missile crisis suggests that considerations of domestic politics are never absent from the calculations of senior players even during the most urgent foreign policy crisis. His description of the ExCom meetings highlights (1) the importance of domestic politics for the form and timing of the United States' response and (2) the norm which stipulates that such considerations may not be put forth as arguments in support of a foreign policy position.

The Kennedy administration, politically sensitive to the issues of the strategic balance of power and Cuba, confronted the missile crisis in the weeks immediately preceding the 1962 Congressional elections. Although strategic analysts might agree with McNamara's opinion that the military balance of power between the United States and the Soviet Union had not been affected, the same could not be said for the balance of power in the soon-to-be-elected House of Representatives.

The importance of domestic political factors is suggested by the fact that when Eisenhower was informed of the existence of the missiles, he became suspicious of Kennedy's political motives. Similarly, when the British ambassador was told, he replied that, in the absence of very firm evidence, his countrymen would share Eisenhower's suspicions. There is reason to believe that these suspicions were at least partly correct. For McNamara the issue was one of strategic deterrence; so he could counsel that the United States do nothing. But Kennedy's problem was different. When informed of the missiles, he is said to have exclaimed: "He [Krushchev] can't do that to me!" McNamara's advice did not address his problem and was rejected out of hand. The urgency in securing a Soviet commitment to remove missiles already in Cuba and the extreme reluctance to agree to the quid pro quo of removing United States IRBM's from Turkey reflect the face of the issue Kennedy perceived.

---

[20] Senator Leverett Saltonstall (Republican, Mass.) stated in the Senate, June 13, 1962: "Dr Brown [Director, Defense Research and Engineering] took a dim view of the RS-70 program. The military strongly recommended its accelerated development. One may place his faith in whomever he desires."

Excerpted with permission from *The New York Review of Books.* Copyright © 1969 by NYREV, Inc.

But, with the exception of the note Dillon passed to Sorensen, the domestic political consequences of the crisis were never specifically addressed in the ExCom meetings. It would have been "political folly" for JFK to have done so. Yet, as Steel suggests, the ever present but never voiced political calculations may have influenced the analysis and interpretation of the intelligence data which revealed the missiles' existence. The administration almost did not want to discover missiles in Cuba until after the elections.

Participants in the national security bureaucracy feel obligated to serve the national security interests of their country. But the vagueness of what that interest requires or allows impels them to substitute more concrete criteria. The domestic political consequences of foreign policy actions is one such standard.

It was a time in Khrushchev's memorable phrase, "when the smell of burning hung in the air." Robert Kennedy's account of those thirteen days in 1962 from October 16, when he and his brother were presented with proof that the Russians were secretly building long-range missile bases in Cuba, until October 28, when the Kremlin agreed to dismantle them, shows the view from the inside by one of the key participants. Written with economy and directness, *Thirteen Days* is a valuable historical document with all the elements of a thriller.

This short, terse memoir — bloated by the publisher with superfluous introductions, photographs, and documents — does not, of course, tell the whole story of the missile crisis. There is a good deal about the events leading up to the crisis that is gone over too lightly or deliberately clouded over. The clash of personalities and ambivalent motives is muted and the tone rather detached. But behind the measured prose we see the spectacle of rational minds swayed by passions and the euphoria of power, governmental machinery breaking down into the struggle of individual wills, and decisions affecting the future of humanity made by a handful of men — the best of whom were not always sure they were right. A disturbing description of decesion-making in the nuclear age, this posthumous work also offers a revealing glimpse of an enigmatic man who might have bridged the gap between the old politics and the new.

We have come to take the balance of terror so much for granted that it is hard to imagine any situation in which the two super-powers would actually use their terrible weapons. Yet more than once during those thirteen days it seemed as though the unthinkable might actually occur. SAC bombers were dispersed to airfields throughout the country and roamed the skies with their nuclear cargoes. At one point President Kennedy, fearful that some trigger-happy colonel might set off the spark, ordered all atomic missiles defused so that the order to fire would have to come directly from the White House.

The first showdown came on the morning of October 24, as Soviet ships approached the 500-mile quarantine line drawn around Cuba. "I felt," Robert Kennedy wrote of those terrible moments, "we were on the edge of a precipice with no way off. . . . President Kennedy had initiated the course of events, but he no longer had control over them." [1] Faced with this blockade, the Russian ships turned back, and the first crisis was surmounted. No more missiles could get into Cuba. But what of the ones already there that Russian technicians were installing with feverish haste? President Kennedy was determined that they had to be removed immediately, and on Saturday, October 27, sent his brother to tell Soviet ambassador Dobrynin "that if they did not remove those bases, we would remove them." The Pentagon prepared for an air strike against the bases and an invasion of Cuba. "The expectation," Robert Kennedy wrote of that fateful Saturday, "was a military confrontation by Tuesday."

We know, of course, how it turned out. On Sunday morning the message came through that Khrushchev would withdraw the missiles in return for a US pledge not to invade Cuba. Kennedy had pulled off the greatest coup of his career — the first, and one hopes the last, military victory of the nuclear era. Not a shot was fired, although we came a good deal closer to war than most people realized at the time, or have cared to think about since.

It was a victory not only over the Soviets, but over many of Kennedy's own advisers who favored a more militant course from the start. The drama was played out among a hastily assembled group, which later took on the formal title of the Executive Committee of the National Security Council, that met several times a day in the White House. The sessions were frequently stormy, although the lines were loosely drawn at first. Several of the participants, according to Robert Kennedy, shifted their opinion "from one extreme to the other — supporting an air attack at the beginning of the meeting and, by the time we left the White House, supporting no action at all." A few, such as Dean Acheson and Douglas Dillon, were hawks from the start, and argued for what they euphemistically called a "surgical strike" against the air bases. They were eventually joined by John McCone, General Maxwell Taylor, Paul Nitze, and McGeorge Bundy. Favoring a more moderate course, which settled around a naval blockade to be "escalated" to an attack on the bases only if absolutely necessary, were the doves, led by Robert Kennedy and Robert McNamara, and including George Ball, Roswell Gilpatric, Llewellyn Thompson, and Robert Lovett.

Dean Rusk, for the most part, avoided taking a stand, or even attending the sessions. The Secretary of State, in Robert Kennedy's caustic words,

[1] [Prior to the final abridgement, all ellipses and interpolations by Steel.]

"had other duties during this period and frequently could not attend our meetings." It would be interesting to know what these duties were. Robert Kennedy does not elaborate, although he does offer the further intriguing aside that "Secretary Rusk missed President Kennedy's extremely important meeting with Prime Minister Macmillan in Nassau because of a diplomatic dinner he felt he should attend." That was the meeting, one will remember, where President Kennedy agreed to help out Harold Macmillan (author of one of the two Introductions to this volume) on the eve of the British elections by turning over Polaris missiles to Britain after the Skybolt fiasco that had embarrassed the Tories. De Gaulle, predictably, was furious, declared that Britain still valued her trans-Atlantic ties above her European ones, and vetoed her entry into the Common Market. The Nassau accord was a colossal error of judgment that an astute Secretary of State should have been able to prevent — had he not been too busy attending diplomatic dinners.

Some of the hawks were, of course, predictable. It is not surprising that the Joint Chiefs of Staff were eager to use their expensive hardware. "They seemed always ready to assume," Robert Kennedy wrote, "that a war was in our national interest. One of the Joint Chiefs of Staff once said to me he believed in a preventive attack against the Soviet Union." Nor is it surprising that Dean Acheson, among the most recalcitrant of the cold warriors, should have come down on the side of the military. "I felt we were too eager to liquidate this thing," Elie Abel reports him as saying in *The Missile Crisis.* "So long as we had the thumbscrew on Khrushchev, we should have given it another turn every day. We were too eager to make an agreement with the Russians. They had no business there in the first place." Ever since his crucifixion by Congress during the Alger Hiss affair, Acheson has become increasingly reactionary and eager to prove his toughness towards the Communists. His bomb-first-and-talk-later argument found receptive ears in such pillars of the Eastern Republican Establishment as Douglas Dillon, John J. McCloy, and McGeorge Bundy.

Many who were not aware of the drama being played out in the White House during those thirteen days, however, will be surprised to find Robert Kennedy as the leader of the doves and the moral conscience of his brother's Administration. Although he does not dramatize his own role, we learn from his account and those of others that he argued against a first strike as contrary to American traditions. "My brother," Abel quotes him as saying, "is not going to be the Tojo of the 1960s." This impassioned plea against a Pearl Harbor in reverse moved even Maxwell Taylor. The general, Abel quotes one of the participants as commenting, "showed what a moral man he is by recommending that we give the Cubans twenty-four hours' advance notice — and then strike the missile bases."

The other outstanding dove of the deliberations was the man in charge of the military establishment, Robert McNamara. The Secretary of Defense, in Kennedy's words, "became the blockade's strongest advocate" and argued that a "surgical air strike . . . was militarily impractical." McNamara was not only a consistent dove, fighting off the belligerent advice of his service chiefs, but disputed the prevailing view that the Russians were trying to upset the strategic balance between East and West. "A missile is a missile," Abel and others have quoted him as saying. "It makes no difference whether you are killed by a missile fired from the Soviet Union or from Cuba." Observing that the Russians had ICBMs and that the only effect of the Cuban-based intermediate-range missiles would be to reduce by a few minutes our warning time in case of attack, McNamara's advice, in effect, was to sit tight.

However valid such advice might have been from a military point of view, it was quite unacceptable politically. John F. Kennedy was especially vulnerable on Cuba, having used it as an issue against Nixon during the 1960 campaign, and then having suffered the ignominy of the Bay of Pigs. The Republicans were pressing him hard on his "do-nothing" policy toward Castro, and former Senator Keating of New York was leading a wolf pack in charging that the Russians were turning Cuba into a base for offensive weapons. Kennedy as Democratic Party leader could not tolerate Soviet missiles in Cuba, even if the civilian head of the Pentagon could.

"If the missiles," Roger Hilsman, head of intelligence in the State Department and then Assistant Secretary of State for the Far East, comments in his book, *To Move a Nation,* "were not important enough to justify a confrontation with the Soviet Union, as McNamara initially thought, yet were 'offensive,' then the United States might not be in mortal danger, but the administration most certainly was." And, according to John Galbraith, then ambassador to India, "once they [the missiles] were there, the political needs of the Kennedy administration urged it to take almost any risk to get them out."

Did we, then, nearly go up in radioactive dust to shore up the Kennedy Administration's fading image before the November, 1962, elections? Not necessarily, for if the missiles did not upset the strategic balance, even a President less image-conscious than John F. Kennedy could not easily accept such an abrupt change in the status quo — least of all in the Caribbean. "To be sure," Theodore Sorensen observed in his *Kennedy,* "these Cuban missiles alone, in view of all the other megatonnage the Soviets were capable of unleashing upon us, did not substantially alter the strategic balance *in fact.* . . . But that balance would have been substantially altered *in appearance* [italics in original]; and in matters of national will and world leadership, as the President said later, such appearances contribute to reality." In fact, Kennedy himself leaned heavily on the prestige argument when he announced the blockade to the nation on October 22.

> This sudden, clandestine decision to station strategic weapons for the first time outside of Soviet soil is a deliberately provocative and unjustified change in the status quo which cannot be accepted by this country, if our courage and our commitments are ever to be trusted again by either friend or foe.

Elevating his rhetoric, as usual, above the needs of the occasion, Kennedy set the stage for a direct military confrontation.

He was acutely conscious of any questioning of his courage, and with the ashes of the Vienna encounter with Khrushchev still in his mouth and another Berlin crisis brewing, he had to get the missiles out of Cuba. But did he have to get them out before the end of October? What would have happened had he negotiated with Khrushchev instead of issuing the ultimatum — delivered to Ambassador Dobrynin on Saturday evening, October 27, by Robert Kennedy — that "we had to have a commitment by tomorrow that those bases would be removed." What would have happened had the negotiations dragged on for a few weeks and some kind of quid pro quo were arranged?

The Russians, of course, would have had the already delivered missiles in place by then. But their withdrawal could still be negotiated and, in any case, the continuation of the blockade would have brought Castro to his knees within a few months. Assuming that the missiles had to be removed, was it necessary, in Robert Kennedy's words, "to have a commitment by tomorrow?" At the time a good many people believed Kennedy had politics in mind during the missile crisis. General Eisenhower, when informed by McCone about the discovery of the missiles, "took a skeptical view," according to Abel, "suspecting perhaps that Kennedy might be playing politics with Cuba on the eve of Congressional elections." The thought also crossed the mind of Kennedy's old chum, David Ormsby-Gore, then British ambassador to Washington, who felt that "British opinion must somehow be persuaded that the missile crisis was the real thing, not something trumped up by the President for vote-getting purposes." Nor did the elections go unnoticed by the participants in the Executive Committee. I. F. Stone has pointed out Sorensen's comment that during one of the meetings a Republican member passed him a note saying:

> Ted — have you considered the very real possibility that if we allow Cuba to complete installation and operational readiness of missile bases, the next House of Representatives is likely to have a Republican majority? This would completely paralyze our ability to react sensibly and coherently to further Soviet advances.

It is not to denigrate John F. Kennedy's patriotism to assume that he was aware of such possibilities. Nor is it to question the motives of those who took part in those exhausting, often stormy, meetings during the thirteen days. It would have been political folly for Kennedy to have broached the subject of the elections before the Executive Committee, where it would have fallen on a good many unsympathetic ears, and it is exceedingly unlikely that the question was ever formally raised. Nor did the participants believe they were behaving by the rules of partisan politics when they decided that the missiles had to be removed immediately. But of the fourteen-odd people who participated in most of the meetings, only a few — Sorensen, Robert Kennedy, and, of course, the President — could be considered politicians. As politicians who had to fight elections, as leaders of the party which was about to be tested at the polls, they could not have been oblivious to what was going to happen in early November — even if they never mentioned it in the meetings, or to one another.

To do nothing about the missiles, as McNamara's position would imply, or to take the issue to the United Nations, or to compromise by trading the Soviet missiles in Cuba for the obsolete American missiles in Turkey, would have been bad politics at that particular time. Obsessed by his image, Kennedy feared that Khrushchev would not take him seriously if he again backed down in Cuba. This questioning of "our courage," he believed, could tempt the Russians to a policy of adventurism, perhaps in Central Europe. Indeed, the first reading of the missile crisis was that Khrushchev was preparing to force a Berlin settlement on his own terms. Thus did considerations of high strategy and party politics reinforce one another and convince Kennedy that the Russian withdrawal had to be complete, unilateral, and secured by the end of October.

The question of a quid pro quo revolved around the American missiles in Turkey and Italy. These had been placed there five years earlier during the Eisenhower Administration's panic over the Sputnik. Designed to re-dress the strategic balance during a time when the US had no reliable ICBMs, these relatively primitive liquid-fuel missiles had become, in Hilsman's words, "obsolete, unreliable, inaccurate, and very vulnerable." Shortly after his inauguration Kennedy asked that they be removed and was discouraged by the State Department. He raised the question again in early 1962, and despite objections that the Turks disapproved, instructed Dean Rusk to negotiate the removal of the missiles. "The President," Robert Kennedy has written, barely concealing his contempt for Dean Rusk, "believed he was President and that, his wishes having been made clear, they would be followed and the missiles removed."

But his instructions were not carried out, and Kennedy discovered that the obsolete Turkish missiles had become a bargaining foil for Khrushchev.

"We will remove our missiles from Cuba, you will remove yours from Turkey," read the note received from the Kremlin on the morning of Saturday, October 27. ". . . The Soviet Union will pledge not to invade or interfere with the internal affairs of Turkey; the US to make the same pledge regarding Cuba." This note, with its quid pro quo, added a new condition to the emotional message received the night before, in which the Soviet Premier indicated he would pull out the missiles in return for a US promise not to invade Cuba.

Adding Turkey to the bargain filled the White House advisers with consternation — not least of all because it appeared perfectly fair. "The proposal the Russians made," in Robert Kennedy's words, "was not unreasonable and did not amount to a loss to the US or to our NATO allies." Categorically to reject such a trade would make the US seem vindictive and threaten the support of its allies — none of whom had any wish to be dragged into nuclear war over the issue of Cuba. But to accept the trade would be to invite accusations of weakness and dishonor by the Republicans. Kennedy, needless to say, was furious at the State Department for putting him in such a vulnerable position.

The Kremlin was not the first to raise the issue of trading the Cuban bases for the Turkish ones. In his column of Thursday, October 25, Walter Lippmann suggested a diplomatic solution to get the missiles out of Cuba:

> There are three ways to get rid of the missiles already in Cuba. One is to invade and occupy Cuba. The second way is to institute a total blockade, particularly of oil shipments, which would in a few months ruin the Cuban economy. The third way is to try, I repeat, to negotiate a face-saving settlement . . . . I am not talking about and do not believe in a "Cuba-Berlin" horse trade . . . . The only place that is truly comparable with Cuba is Turkey. This is the only place where there are strategic weapons right on the frontier of the Soviet Union . . . . The Soviet military base in Cuba is defenseless, and the base in Turkey is all but obsolete. The two bases could be dismantled without altering the world balance of power.

This position had already been argued by Adlai Stevenson who, according to Robert Kennedy, on October 20 "strongly advocated what he had only tentatively suggested to me a few days before — namely, that we make it clear to the Soviet Union that if it withdrew its missiles from Cuba, we would be willing to withdraw our missiles from Turkey and Italy and give up our naval base at Guantanamo Bay." With this suggestion Stevenson went a good deal further than Lippmann, who never included Guantanamo in the trade. This won Stevenson the wrath of several of the participants, including Robert Kennedy, who prevailed upon his brother to send John J. McCloy to the UN to handle the Russians during the missile crisis. But time healed some of Robert Kennedy's wrath, and in *Thirteen Days* he wrote:

> Stevenson has since been criticized publicly for the position he took at this meeting. I think it should be emphasized that he was presenting a point of view from a different perspective than the others, one which was therefore important for the President to consider. Although I disagreed strongly with his recommendations, I thought he was courageous to make them, and I might add they made as much sense as some others considered during that period.

Stevenson's proposal was not so heretical as it was treated at the time, or in the inside stories that appeared shortly after the missile crisis. Kennedy was prepared to give up the Turkish bases, but for political reasons could not make it a quid pro quo — although there is some reason to think that he might have done so *in extremis.* On Saturday — when the Russians sent their second note calling for the Turkey-Cuba base trade — Kennedy, according to Abel, told Roswell Gilpatric to prepare a scenario for removing the missiles from Turkey and Italy, and have it ready for the meeting that night. That evening he sent his brother to Ambassador Dobrynin with the demand that the Russians had to promise to withdraw the missiles from Cuba by the following day. The Joint Chiefs of Staff were preparing to bomb the missile sites on Tuesday. Dobrynin, according to Abel, "gave it as his personal opinion that the Soviet leaders were so deeply committed they would have to reject the President's terms."

But while he ruled out an explicit deal, Robert Kennedy told the Soviet ambassadors that there need be no problem about the Turkish missiles. "President Kennedy," he said to Dobrynin, "had been anxious to remove those missiles from Turkey and Italy for a long period of time . . . and it was our judgment that, within a short time after this crisis was over, those missiles would be gone." Dobrynin sent on the message to Moscow; President Kennedy, at his brother's suggestion, accepted the more moderate first message from Khrushchev and ignored the second Kremlin note: and an apprehensive Washington awaited the Kremlin's response as plans proceeded for an air strike against the Cuban bases. On Sunday morning the word came through that the missiles would be withdrawn in return for a simple US pledge not to invade Cuba. The worst crisis of the Cold War was over. But even at this moment of triumph, some were not satisfied. "On that fateful Sunday morning when the Russians answered they were withdrawing their missiles," Robert Kennedy revealed, "it was suggested by one high military adviser that we attack Monday in any case." . . .

Part Three

Decisions

RICHARD AUSTIN SMITH

TFX: The $7-Billion Contract That Changed the Rules

The design of a new major weapons system and the selection of a contractor to produce it reveal in bold relief the bureaucratic politics of national security policy. The history of the TFX (now the F-111) aircraft is no exception. The major participants in the national security bureaucracy, along with their allies in Congress and the defense industry, became actively involved in the controversy surrounding which manufacturer was to get the TFX contract. Each of the participants saw a different face, and each had different stakes in mind when he viewed "the" TFX issue.

For Robert McNamara, TFX was a test case for his efforts to bring rationality and economy to weapons procurement and to demonstrate to the military services that he intended to exercise an active role in areas which previously had been their exclusive domain. Both the Air Force and the Navy also saw TFX as a test case as well as an effort by the Secretary of Defense to sacrifice performance to economy. The two services were united in their resistance to a common aircraft which, in their view, would be optimized for none of the missions they envisioned. Resistance to the principle of commonality was generalized into a fear that TFX was merely the opening phase in the civilians' campaign to reduce or destroy each service's organizational autonomy. The Air Force feared that the Navy would view the TFX as a threat to the aircraft carriers' roles and missions and would delay the project to death. The Navy feared that the Air Force would dominate the TFX project with the result that the Navy would have to buy a plane it did not want and would not be permitted to build the plane it believed was needed. For the defense contractors, the TFX promised to be a particularly lucrative contract for the winner and possible economic extinction for the losers. Those participants in the executive branch and in Congress attuned to domestic political considerations focused on the local economic impact of the contract award.

Since their corporate success depends upon it, defense contractors are particularly sensitive observers of bureaucratic politics. The diverse corporate strategies chosen by Boeing and by General Dynamics-Grumman represent their different estimates of McNamara's impact on existing patterns of civil-military interaction. Boeing bet that, in the end, not much would change; General Dynamics-Grumman bet that the new Secretary would have a significant impact but that the services would retain a very important voice. Thus, Boeing traded commonality for capability and pursued the traditional tactic of "buying in" with underestimates of projected costs. General Dynamics-Grumman gave somewhat more attention to the principle of commonality and displayed less optimism in its costs estimates. In what may have been its most astute move, General Dynamics

Excerpted by the editors from *Fortune* (March-April, 1963) with permission.

recognized that the services would continue to exercise a virtual veto power even if their positive powers of contractor designation were constrained. Accordingly, General Dynamics, an "Air Force" contractor, collaborated with Grumman, a popular "Navy" contractor. It was a perceptive assessment. The Navy, fearing that the Boeing proposal would result in a virtual capitulation to Air Force requirements (and incidentally threaten Navy procurement procedures), persistently maneuvered to reverse the recommendations of the Source Selection Boards, giving General Dynamics-Grumman the time it needed to catch up and, perhaps inadvertently, conferring crucial support on McNamara's position.

The world of defense procurement stretches across some 10 percent of U.S. production and whole hemispheres of geography, but its fortunes rise and fall with the moves and moods of its single customer in Washington. It has only begun to feel the impact of an epochal defense contract awarded four months ago, the first step in a $7-billion outlay for design and production of a fighter plane known as the TFX, or Tactical Fighter Experimental. Nine airframe companies and three engine manufacturers were initially involved in the battle over this joint Navy–Air Force plane, before Boeing and the team of General Dynamics and Grumman were selected for an unprecedented sudden-death play-off lasting ten months. When it was over, General Dynamics–Grumman had won the airframe part of the contract (expected to reach $4.2 billion by 1970), Pratt & Whitney had run away with a potential billion-dollar order for the engines, and Defense Secretary Robert Strange McNamara had wrought a profound shift in what might be called the realpolitik, the working strategy, of U.S. weapon procurement.

For some time after taking office, McNamara had cast about for a way to drive home his concept of "value engineering" in the tradition-encrusted procurement system of the U.S. armed services. He took a dim view of the old relationships between particular services, or branches, and their suppliers. He was less than tolerant of interservice rivalry, and generally gave single-service recommendations a hard going-over no matter how heavy in rank the earnest military pleader. He believed firmly that task forces of Defense Department civilian specialists, viewing rival claims with above-the-battle objectivity, could make broader, sounder judgments in many areas. And he had a conviction that the nation could save hundreds of millions by coordinating its weapon procurement, and an equal amount through "cost effectiveness" measurement of rival programs.

In the TFX, a multipurpose airplane that is likely to shape the future of military-aircraft development, he found a vehicle to put wings on his approach, and before the contract was awarded he had created a situation of unprecedented, and perhaps unexpected, magnitude.

The design of the aircraft was enormously complicated, as we shall see.

By requiring a virtual breakthrough in the state of the art, it put the contractors under the sort of pressures that defense firms can come to expect in the day of fewer but more complicated weapon systems. Moreover, the stakes were huge. The biggest fighter-plane program since World War II, perhaps the last consequential one for manned military aircraft, it had drawn almost every major airframe company into the battle at one time or another. . . .

The odds on a successful program were enormously long. McNamara himself was gambling — that he could get the Navy and the Air Force to accept a common aircraft (though each was prepared to go through hell and high water to win a separate, tailor-made TFX of its own). He was also gambling that he could get the contractors to design such a plane when this ran directly counter to their long-standing — and profitable — habit of giving the separate services what each wanted. Moreover, he was betting he could save $1 billion by having one TFX for both services, and had boldly called his shot by making that potential billion-dollar saving the showpiece of his cost-effectiveness program.

With so much money at stake, with the whole airframe industry hungry for business, and thousands of jobs hanging in the balance, politics was everywhere. A politician's choice lay in pushing the interests of his constituents or explaining why he hadn't during the next election campaign. Openly pushing for Grumman, which is located on Long Island, was Congressman Otis Pike from Long Island. Allied with him was the entire Texas congressional delegation, particularly Representative Jim Wright of Fort Worth. Also presumably in G.D.'s corner was Vice President Lyndon B. Johnson, whose predilection for the made-in-Texas label had early prompted some Pentagon cynics to rename the TFX the LBJ. As for Boeing, it had the powerful backing of Senator Warren Magnuson, considered the best horse trader in the U.S. Senate, and of Senator Henry Jackson, whose dedication to the affairs of the Seattle-based plane maker prompted some to refer to him as "the gentleman from Boeing."

. . . Necessarily, the story must be told from many viewpoints, for everyone — the armed services, the airframe companies, the politicians, the engine manufacturers, the Pentagon — saw things according to his own special lights, but the start, at least, was simple enough. The TFX story began as a gleam in the eye of General F. F. Everest, in 1959 the incoming commander of the Air Force's Tactical Air Command.

At that time the industry itself was working on advanced fighter planes, a result of having nosed around the Air Force to see what was wanted and needed. The new commander, however, was about to put the companies on a radically different tack. On Hank Everest's mind was a fighter-bomber that would meet the new and tougher conditions that he envisioned for the mid-sixties. . . .

Every military program is in competition with every other for funds, and in the last year of the Eisenhower Administration the reigning nuclear-deterrent rationale had put conventional weapons under a particularly heavy burden of proof. Everest's evidence [of the technical feasibility of his proposal], however, convinced even the bomber-minded skeptics in the Air Force high command, and with top-rank endorsement he had little trouble in "energizing" the airframe industry. Essentially, Everest told the companies that the TFX was the only aircraft likely to be built in operational numbers, despite agitation for the celebrated B-70 bomber. While he couldn't promise when — or if — Congress would vote the funds ("that's the smartest thing I ever said"), here was a real business opportunity. He hardly needed to point out that advance planning on the TFX, with its variable-sweep wing, would give an airframe company a headstart on the most promising technology for a multipurpose supersonic jet transport.

Thus by late April a joint conference of the Air Research and Development Command, the Tactical Air Command, and NASA had agreed on a program for the TFX: total cost would be $2.2 billion, R. and D. cost for sixteen test aircraft $338 million, first flight May, 1963, date of operational availability October, 1965 — all assuming a go-ahead in October, 1960. The Air Force routinely approved the development plan and the operational requirement, then went through the formalities of winning verbal consent from the D.O.D.'s Director of Defense Research and Engineering to proceed with the selection of a source (contractor) for development of the weapon. Two Air Force-attuned companies, meanwhile, were running out ahead of the formalities — Boeing, in particular. It had worked [on] a variable-sweep delta-wing design of its own, and by this time both Boeing and Republic Aviation had completed TFX wind-tunnel tests and were well along on full-scale mock-ups. But just at the moment when the schedule called for the go signal, all of this forehandedness was dashed by an order from Defense Research and Engineering to hold up on source selection pending review by Defense Secretary Thomas Gates Jr. On the eve of national elections, the Eisenhower Administration was reluctant to commit its successors to costly, far-reaching new military programs.

It was months before Gates's successor, Robert McNamara, got around to reviewing the TFX with his new R. and D. team, but when he did he came to some sweeping conclusions. First, the plane was the kind of weapon that coincided perfectly with his ideas about "controlled response," i.e., that our arsenal should contain a number of options to all-out nuclear war, one of which was the selective, tactical use of atomic weapons. The TFX, as he saw it, would be able to get in under enemy radar at speeds too great for foreseeable ground-to-air missiles (assuming the Russian versions were no more likely to knock down a plane flying at treetop level at better than 0.9 mach than comparable U.S. weapons). Second, turning Hank Everest's enthusiasm for the TFX to unexpected ends, McNamara made the decision that a plane of such versatility could be made to fill the requirements of the Army and Navy as well as the Air Force and, as the first fighter designed for tri-service requirements, thus become the cornerstone of his effort to cut costs.

This major conclusion, when transformed into policy, changed the whole course of events for the TFX. The Army, with limited and specialized combat-plane needs, managed to slip out of the TFX program (and went quietly off to work on aircraft of its own, a much simpler, lighter, and cheaper affair called the VAX). But the Navy and the Air Force were stuck with what seemed a pretty arbitrary and doctrinaire upstairs decision. Hank Everest was incensed at the Secretary's ruling. He foresaw an interminable argument on technical details among Air Force, Navy, and Defense Department experts. Moreover, still bearing scars of ancient battles with the Navy, Everest and his Air Force group feared the Navy might seize the occasion to delay the TFX to death. "The Navy's problem was different," said Everest recently. "Carriers can do the ferrying. The Navy didn't need the plane and we thought they would see the TFX as a threat. If someone else can operate without relying on this forty-knot barge called a carrier, it demolishes the carrier. Carriers did do a great job in the Pacific, but the TFX could make them less important: four hours to Europe vs. four days, from base to the Mediterranean."

The Navy was just as unhappy as Everest, but not for the reasons he ascribed. Its problem *was* different. It had long ago established the fact that it needed relatively lighter planes for carrier landings (thus would need a 55,000-pound TFX, compared to the 75,000-pound Air Force design) with stronger tail sections (to take the arresting gear). Additionally, the Navy's tactical needs were so different that a common plane could be achieved only by limiting one service or the other on capabilities. The Navy, for example, insisted that the TFX be no longer than fifty-six feet, to fit the carrier elevators. This made for a short, relatively fat fuselage. But the Air Force fuselage had to be narrow and long — its optimum length worked out to upwards of seventy feet — if it were to meet that service's basic requirements. Every increase in frontal area above forty square feet effectively increased fuel consumption. A short, fat fuselage would rob the TFX of its extreme ferry range and would shorten the time it could spend at supersonic speed at treetop level. The latter was a matter of great concern to the Air Force because its mission called for long-distance flight over missile-defended terrain. The Navy, on the other hand, would much rather have had longer loiter time over the missile-free expanses of open ocean, with only short-range supersonic boosts for interception or attack. How consequential these divergences were can be seen in the fact that the Navy's ultimate triumph in cutting the TFX fuselage down to size caused a serious reduction in the Air Force's treetop-level capability. The Air Force wanted an 800-mile radius of operation with 400 miles of that at mach 1.2; it had to settle for the same radius with only 200 miles supersonic. Nevertheless, McNamara made the bi-service concept stick. So far as he was concerned, the T in TFX stood not so much for "Tactical" as "Togetherness."

The new concept sent the contractors scurrying to revise their strategies. The preliminary strategy of a top defense contractor is to try to anticipate, say, Air Force thinking about new weapons and then get in early. ("If you don't get in at the birth," as one veteran vice president recently declared, "you're dead.") A period of intensive "brochuresmanship" usually follows, with contractors' representatives paying regular visits to Air Force people at Wright-Patterson and other key commands, not because it's the season to be jolly, but to be of tangible help in working out developmental problems. "You can't be effective," said a Boeing vice president, "unless you understand what the problems are; the military aren't interested in working with you unless you have something to contribute. In the case of the TFX, we sent representatives to TAC's field operations all over the world to get firsthand information on needs. We even wrote a description of how TAC operates, which the Air Force ordered for training programs at Randolph Field. It was a manual on the whole system — maintenance, spares, even the skills required of the people who will do the maintenance job."

Obviously, in the early stages of TFX, Boeing's energies and those of the other interested contractors (Republic, Lockheed, North American, McDonnell, Douglas, Chance Vought, Northrop, Grumman, and General Dynamics) had been concentrated on keeping the Air Force happy. After the Air Force's preliminary Work Statement, each company had spent anywhere from $1 million to $3,500,000 in trying to meet or anticipate Air Force requirements. Boeing had even gone so far in trying to increase its lead as to prepare a contract proposal on a dry-run basis, a task that demanded the total energies of a hundred people for more than two months. But with the Navy forcibly injected into the picture, all strategies had to be adjusted to a whole new set of imponderables.

Since there would be tremendous, and perhaps impossible, technical difficulties in designing one plane to meet the divergent requirements of the Navy and the Air Force, the airframe companies' own sense of realpolitik provoked some interesting front-office questions: Would it be better strategy to favor the Air Force in design since the Air Force would be buying 1,500 TFX's vs. only a couple of hundred for the Navy? Anyway, wasn't the Navy powerful enough politically to defeat McNamara and eventually win a special TFX of its own? Or would McNamara get enough support to make the TFX a symbol of his push for unification of the services, and was he likely to use it to put the military professionals in their places by making the civilian decision stick? Were the nickel-and-dime economies of the automobile business going to be imposed on the armament industry? How long would McNamara be around anyway? Washington had averaged a new Defense Secretary every eighteen months. After weighing all these factors, most of the companies must have found in McNamara's favor because most began to work for both an impartial resolution of Air Force–Navy requirements and a judicious balance of performance and cost. Republic teamed up with Chance Vought, which had a long history of producing naval aircraft. Douglas and McDonnell eventually went into partnership. General Dynamics joined forces with Grumman.

G.D.'s alliance with this "Navy company" was of tremendous importance in view of the final result; it now had a partner whose planes had made more than half of all the takeoffs and landings on carriers. Moreover, the Navy knew that, with Grumman in the deal, there would be a concerted effort to meet naval requirements. As J. T. Cosby, TFX program manager at General Dynamics in Fort Worth, recollected: "Grumman made no bones about standing up for what they thought were the Navy's requirements. We learned early in the game that the Navy was a strong group, and even though the number of its planes was smaller than that of the Air Force, it knew very well how to make its feelings known."

By the same token, Boeing made a serious miscalculation. It had ignored partnership feelers put out by Grumman, deciding to go it alone. In effect, it was guessing that there would ultimately be two planes, an Air Force TFX and a Navy TFX, and so would concentrate on meeting the Air Force requirements. And, unfortunately, the primacy Boeing gave to pleasing the Air Force shortly led it into another fateful misjudgment, this time on the choice of the engine.

The engine competition for the TFX — the winner would walk away with a billion-dollar contract in its hip pocket — was among three companies. Pratt & Whitney was pushing its TF-30, a Navy-sponsored power plant on which that service had already spent $30 million (it was to have been installed in the canceled Douglas Missileer, a subsonic fighter). General Motors' Allison Division offered the Rolls-Royce Spey engine, already operational on the British de Havilland transport, and redesigned by Allison to increase its performance. General Electric's initial entry was the J79, also operational as the power plant for McDonnell's Navy fighter, the F-4B, and the Air Force's F-4C. After looking over these engines, which would be a crucial element in performance and design, one of the six competing teams had chosen the Allison, the other five, including Boeing, had picked Pratt & Whitney's modified TF-30.

General Electric was left out in the cold. But even though G.E. knew that the airframe companies were already designing around the respective competitive power plants — and would be most reluctant to change — the company got to work on a new engine design, the MF295, of significantly superior performance. G.E. carefully timed the release of the news for August, 1961.

The strategy was simple and daring. G.E. expected that in October the Defense Department would issue its Request for Proposal and its specifications for bids on the TFX. G.E. also banked on its ability to sell the military on including the MF295 in its list of acceptable engines. And it figured (correctly) that the time between August and October was too short for either Allison or Pratt & Whitney to top the new design. Of course the MF295 was a "paper" engine — i.e., a design fortified by a few components from other G.E. power plants. Its development would also be time-consuming, a factor of considerable importance in an aircraft already months behind schedule. But the MF295 was several hundred pounds lighter than the Allison or Pratt & Whitney engine, and was smaller both in length and in diameter. This promised relief from the crushing limitation on weight, and it also permitted the narrower fuselage so critical to the Air Force's supersonic requirements. Moreover, G.E. did a brilliant selling job — with the military, with NASA, and with the propulsion division at Wright-Patterson. The result was that in the October specifications Wright-Patterson declared the MF295 eligible for the TFX competition.

This development prompted more strategy huddles in the various airframe plants. Some temperature taking immediately took place. Was Wright-Patterson's inclusion of the MF295 simply a localized result of inspired G.E. "brochuresmanship," or should it be taken as evidence of the services' genuine respect for the engine? The word got back that "the Air Force" was "very high" on the MF295. Boeing, which had been designing the TFX around the heavier Pratt & Whitney for two and a half years, then decided to switch to the MF295. The gamble looked eminently reasonable at the time. True, it usually takes about five years to come up with a pretty well "worked out" engine, but this clear inability to meet TFX's time schedule was counterbalanced by the probability that other difficulties with the TFX would make additional time available. The prospects for better performance were compelling. Moreover, the operational words were "Air Force" and "very high." Other contractors apparently shared Boeing's views for North American, McDonnell, Lockheed, Douglas — indeed everyone except Republic, Chance Vought, and General Dynamics–Grumman — eventually switched to the MF295.

McNamara's October 1 Request for Proposal and the accompanying Work Statement signaled the official start of the great race. The finish line for TFX designs was set for December 6, nine and a half weeks away. Crammed into 250 pages of the Work Statement were the rigorous requirements: the expected performance, the logistics and support demands, and the type of environment the aircraft would have to function in. Each contractor was required to specify how he intended to make the plane, which of the three eligible engines he would use, the costs involved, the dates on which he would guarantee to reach such milestones as first flight and operational availability, how much subcontracting there would be and to whom, and so on ad infinitum, even to the names of the top people to be assigned to the job.

Simply responding to all this within the time limit would be enormously difficult, but the difficulty was compounded by the subtle requirements of contract gamesmanship. One stratagem that had worked more than once, for example, was to "buy into" a program with a proposal below cost; then renegotiate more favorable terms at contract signing time or at still later stages. Even with TFX an incentive contract (with profit scaled to accurate estimates and performance) the temptation for below-cost bidding was great: belts had been pulled pretty tight in the airframe industry — Bell had already all but starved to death — and a low bid might be the deciding factor. Yet balanced against this was the possibility that the computer corps in the Defense Department might spot a starvation bid for what it really was, a potential cost overrun. Cost overruns had become a very sore point with McNamara; he had recently discovered that final costs on major systems over a period of years had exceeded the original estimates by between 300 and 1,000 percent.

It might also seem sound strategy for a contractor to try to keep as much as possible of the TFX production "in house" — substantial economies could be effected in tooling costs, and training time for labor could be minimized. Yet here, too, there was an important offsetting factor. The competition for the TFX would certainly be close, perhaps a tie; in the latter case *sub*contracting could play a decisive political role. As a Douglas executive explained it: "The only place where politics is important is if two contractors are neck and neck — then subcontracting has political advantages and can swing to the best political merchandiser. We tried to lock up a substantial part of our TFX bid with subcontracts in Missouri and Oklahoma [which the late Senator Robert Kerr intended to make a lodestone for defense industry], as well as in California.[1] Boeing followed its usual strategy of subcontracting some 50 to 60 percent to dependable suppliers, albeit with an eye on the politically important distressed areas. G.D.–Grumman kept flexible — and perhaps increased its political leverage — by having two or three runners-up in each subcontracting category and postponing final selection until the last minute.

Paramount to all of these time-honored considerations, however, was

---

[1] [Interpolation by Smith.]

the problem of commonality in this joint Air Force–Navy project. Each service was pressing for attention to its unique requirements while Secretary McNamara insisted on maximum interchangeability. Sure, McNamara was legally in command but the plane makers had learned the hard way that weapons seldom emerge from the chrysalis of development into full-blown production unless they have the active support of the military professionals. Nowhere was this commonality aspect of the race more carefully thought out than in the councils of the two hungriest competitors, Boeing and G.D.–Grumman.

General Dynamics, it so happened, was more disposed toward commonality as a philosophy than was Boeing. In building the Air Force's supersonic bomber, the B-58, G.D. had gone all out trying to please the generals. It got precious little for its pains; after bright promises that the B-58 might become the workhorse of the Strategic Air Command, the A.F. top brass limited it to only two wings. Moreover, G.D. had spent lots of time studying multipurpose weapons (in a vain attempt to interest TAC, the Air Defense Command, and SAC in the B-58) and thought the McNamara concept made a lot of sense.

"We read the Work Statement," said Frank Davis, president of G.D.'s Fort Worth division, "as putting significant emphasis on commonality. We went to a great deal of trouble to have a common structure, and paid some weight penalties to do it — some performance penalties as well, on both Navy and Air Force versions."

Boeing's strategy was not so much to oppose McNamara as it was to design for the Navy and the Air Force *better* planes than their individual requirements called for. It would thus bank on the hope that the best plane would be irresistible, regardless of commonality — making the most of its big lead in variable-wing design over the rest of the industry. A tremendous amount of effort would be put in the Air Force version of the TFX, for that had primacy in Boeing's view, but the separate Navy version would also be made as attractive as possible (within the limits of Boeing's lack of experience in designing modern Navy fighters). If all this had to be done at the sacrifice of McNamara's dream of a single blended plane, then so be it. Boeing was ready to gamble that the old way, pleasing the services, was still the best way, and that a bi-service TFX would ultimately be recognized as impractical. Hadn't the Navy, even after the Work Statement was out, moved heaven and earth in vainly trying to insert a requirement that its version be able to do 0.6 mach at 35,000-foot altitudes, a speed that would virtually have put the plane into a stall?

So with its service-oriented approach, its selection of the new G.E. engine, and its gamble on plenty of time to work out the engine "bugs," Boeing cut quite a different figure from its chief rival, G.D.–Grumman.

In the midst of its careful planning, Boeing began to notice that quite a lot of people were saying that its efforts were foredoomed to failure, no matter what. Indeed, these prophecies were coming so thick and fast that the company began noting them in a special scrapbook. One of its executives would report that some brass hat in the Pentagon had hinted G.D.–Grumman was going to beat Boeing out of the contract, regardless of design. Another would hear that selection of the Pratt & Whitney engine was a foregone conclusion, and this would weigh heavily against Boeing. Then there was the Texas politician who had reportedly been whispering that the Navy would hold out for a "better" design than Boeing's, and that meant one from G.D.–Grumman.

Undoubtedly the common denominator of most of these rumors was the assumption that G.D.–Grumman had more powerful political backing than Boeing and that politics would be decisive. The Texans indeed seemed to be lined up in force. Aside from Lyndon Johnson and hard-working Congressman Wright of Fort Worth, Navy Secretary Fred Korth came from Fort Worth, and his predecessor in the job, John Connally, was the newly elected governor of Texas. Moreover, the G.D.–Grumman combination put Texas hand in hand with New York (and Teddy Kennedy was busy trying to persuade Grumman to expand into Massachusetts). But Boeing's friends from Washington state and Midwest (Wichita) were busy too in the White House and the Pentagon.

The fact seems to be that insofar as political influence was concerned there was an immense difference between ritual and results. Congressmen habitually go through a sort of formalistic dance in behalf of their constituents, waltzing over to the White House to plead their case before Kenneth O'Donnell or Lawrence O'Brien, then doing a brisk fox-trot with one of the Pentagon's congressional liaison men or even an assistant secretary. Letters of special pleading usually follow, and when it's over all concerned can say with perfect honesty, "We gave the matter every consideration." Where these representations are more than ritualistic and do carry considerable weight within the Pentagon is in circumstances of real economic hardship. But in the case of the TFX, Congressman Wright could hardly hope to win any special consideration for General Dynamics on grounds that loss of the contract would be a severe blow to the economy of Fort Worth. McNamara's Office of Economic Adjustment, set up to gauge the impact of military procurement on sixty cities across the nation, had already informed him that if Boeing lost the TFX, Wichita would be just as hard hit as Fort Worth. The political battle appeared to be a standoff.

By early December, 1961, the nine weeks of frantic activity came to an end for Boeing, G.D.–Grumman, and the other six remaining contractors (only Northrop of the original starting ten had dropped out). The days of computer time and wind-tunnel testing, the trade-offs in design, the compromises and intricate strategies had been synthesized into printed proposals, typically 1,500 pages long and five feet in height. The proposals were shipped off to Wright-Patterson and followed by the engineers who were to give the oral summations. At Wright-Patterson there was none of the good fellowship usual to industry get-togethers, for it had been growing increasingly clear that the U.S. had too many airframe companies with too little business. Competitive stances were maintained, even down to drawing straws for the order of position (the lead-off spot was bad — the audience wasn't warmed up — but being "tail-end Charlie" was even worse, for by then the military knew enough to ask questions that would curl a man's hair). The presentations were completed in three days.

Then it was the military's turn to sweat. The first job fell to the evaluation teams, each assigned to cover a particular section in all the proposals (such as avionics, costs, or logistics). Billeted together behind barbed wire and armed guards, the teams began their round-the-clock operation: a comparative rating of each element of each proposal both from the standpoint of what the contractor had said he could do and what the teams thought his performance would be. Roughly a month later they presented their findings to the TFX Source Selection Board.[2]

Boeing had done spectacularly well on performance. The company's design for its Air Force model had a ferry range of 4,630 miles as against 3,935 for G.D.–Grumman, the next competitor, which meant it stood alone in being able to fly a bomb from the U.S. to friendly bases in Japan without refueling; its lift-to-drag ratio, an indication of the wing efficiency that gave it this extreme range, was 20 vs. G.D.–Grumman's score of 16.50. In addition, it was clearly superior at treetop level — of prime importance to the Air Force — and on an 800-mile mission could fly 173 miles at mach 1.2 versus 141 miles for the nearest competitor, G.D.–Grumman. On loiter time, Boeing's Navy version could remain on station for 4.11 hours, the next best, G.D.–Grumman, 3.66 hours. With all this, the teams raised some warning signals about giving Boeing a clear track. The engine-evaluation group reported that G.E.'s MF295, the foundation of Boeing's design, could not meet the TFX timetable, a factor of rising importance since the Tactical Air Command was determined to keep the plane strictly on schedule. Moreover, Boeing's design, while considered the best of all submitted, still fell short of the capability that both the Navy and the Air Force wanted. Nevertheless, on January 19, 1962, the Source

[2] Source Selection Boards are ad hoc service groups convened to recommend a winner from among the contestants for a particular weapon contract. This one was made up of Rear Admiral Frederick L. Ashworth (Navy), Brigadier General Allman T. Culbertson (Systems Command), Major Generals William W. Momyer (Tactical Air Command), T. Alan Bennett (Logistics Command), and the nonvoting chairman, Major General W. Austin Davis (Systems Command).

Selection Board voted unanimously to recommend Boeing as the winner of the TFX contract.

Under normal circumstances this recommendation would have gone up through channels, gathering endorsements as it went, for the military have not only a high regard for the findings of their Source Selection Boards (the members are typically officers of stature) but an ingrained disposition to believe that what comes up from below is incontrovertible. Boeing, in short, would normally have been awarded the TFX contract at this point, and ordered to rectify the design deficiencies before the specification stage.

This, indeed, was the direction in which things seemed to be heading. The Tactical Air Command declared its approval of the Boeing award and TAC, after all, would be the prime user of the aircraft. The Logistics Command also endorsed the Source Selection Board's recommendation of Boeing. "I sat through two Pentagon briefings with a lot of people from the Navy and Air Force, Harold Brown of McNamara's staff, A. F. Under Secretary Joe Charyk, and some others from [Air Secretary] Zuckert's office," said a veteran of the TFX competition. "In neither was there any indication that there'd be a reversal of the board's recommendation. You can't tell what's in people's minds, of course, but I came away from those briefings feeling the contract would go to Boeing."

What was in people's minds, however, was the very thing that was just about to upset Boeing's applecart. In the first place there was that embarrassing business about the MF295 engine. TAC was insisting on holding the TFX to schedule. Boeing would therefore have to switch to Pratt & Whitney's TF-30. But that meant very substantial changes in design. The propulsion people at Wright-Patterson were already beginning to blush at the recollection of how they had ebulliently approved the MF295's eligibility in September, only to turn around in December and decide that it really wouldn't meet the time schedule. And the Pentagon's civilian bosses felt their own faces would be even redder if, in one breath, they declared Boeing's design had won on the basis of what it could do with the MF295, then in the next breath announced the winner would have to go through substantial redesign, and probably degradation of performance, to accommodate a different power plant (the TF-30).

Second, there was that business of commonality so dear to the civilian hearts. Over and over Air Secretary Zuckert had repeated his manifesto: "The name of the game is a single plane for *two* services." Harold Brown, Defense research chief, had carried the same message from McNamara. Brown had forced the Navy and Air Force to compromise their requirements enough so one plane was possible. Boeing's design had very low commonality — the two versions were little over 50 percent similar. Zuckert and Brown suspected that what tended to be two planes at the start would likely become two planes in fact, under the pressure of each service to get its own TFX. These two civilians found they had a powerful fellow skeptic in Lieutenant General Bernard Schriever, chief of the Air Force Systems Command and officer in charge of new program developments. After going over the Source Selection Board's findings with General Davis, Schriever weighed in with a strong recommendation that Boeing not be awarded the contract until it had produced a more complete design and a higher degree of commonality.

And finally there was the Navy's strong suspicion that if Boeing got the award then and there, the Navy might not get all that it wanted in the way of a naval TFX. The Navy had no "family" relationship with Boeing such as it had with Grumman. Therefore, it reasoned that if there was really going to be a bi-service TFX, it might be smart to have everything nailed down and all deficiencies satisfied before awarding the contract, particularly since there seemed to be no prospect of a backup plane.

Thus the stage was already set for a reversal when on January 24 the Air Council, plus the Navy's representative, Vice Admiral Robert Pirie, met to consider the Source Selection Board's vote. Admiral Pirie said he'd go with Boeing if the decision had to be made that minute, but the Navy would prefer to have the substantial design problems hammered out in six to eight weeks of additional competition. Lieutenant General Dean Strother, the acting chairman, broke precedent to go behind the board's recommendation and ask Colonel Charles A. Gayle, officer in charge of the TFX evaluation teams, what *he* thought should be done. Colonel Gayle's opinion tallied with that of his boss, General Schriever, who recommended a runoff between Boeing and General Dynamics–Grumman, on grounds that this might avert the familiar trouble connected with rushing complicated weapons into development before designs had been adequately worked out. The Air Council's decision, arrived at with no loss of composure, was to reject the board's recommendation. Instead it proposed the eight-week extended competition between Boeing and G.D.–Grumman. . . .

Nothing had occurred to lessen the Washington pressures. Secretary McNamara was still hell-bent on proving that a well-designed TFX could save $1 billion over the cost of giving the Air Force and Navy separate fighter planes. The Air Force Tactical Command, which had asked for the plane in the first place, was still complaining that every delay was a delay in strengthening U.S. capability in an area where it was woefully weak. The two services remained united only in the common desire to hamstring a bi-service weapon that promised more bi-service weapons to come. Rumors of political pressure flew as thick and fast as before: Boeing was alleged to be doomed before heavy Texas politicking; General Dynamics–Grumman was reported tottering to defeat as Washington Senators Magnuson and Jackson pulled the strings. But perhaps the greatest pressure was the fact that McNamara's Defense Department had simply junked the time-honored service procedure of awarding a contract to the top scorer in a competition, and then granting time for the winner to correct his deficiencies. Instead the Pentagon had decided to gamble that protracted competition between a pair of finalists would get it exactly what it wanted.

At the start of the second race, the two finalists stacked up about like this: Boeing's design had been adjudged far superior to anybody else's; indeed, the company might already have been declared the winner had it not been led down the garden path by the Air Force and designed its plane around the wrong engine. Boeing would now have to redesign around a completely different power plant, Pratt & Whitney's modification of the TF-30. G.D.–Grumman, on the other hand, had had the good fortune to pick the P. & W. engine from the first, but even so would have to go fast and far to overcome Boeing's long technical lead.

The corporate strategies for winning the contract remained substantially the same. General Dynamics–Grumman's strategy was to come as close as it could to giving Secretary McNamara what he wanted, one plane for the two services. This meant sticking by McNamara's insistence on commonality and resisting Navy and Air Force pressure for two TFX's, separate planes designed solely to satisfy each service's requirements. Boeing continued to gamble that the defense industry's old way, pleasing the services, was still the best way, and that McNamara's dream of a bi-service TFX would ultimately be recognized as unattainable. Boeing would again go all out to satisfy the Air Force's requirements, for it had long been an Air Force-oriented company; at the same time, it would do the best it could to woo the Navy, which was mistrustful of the fact that Boeing had never made a modern Navy fighter. . . .

This time, as on January 19, the bi-service Source Selection Board at Wright-Patterson Air Force Base found in favor of Boeing. This time, moreover, the Air Force's top-level Air Council went along with the board. Boeing's strategy of pleasing the Air Force appeared to have been a resounding success.

Then the Navy opened up. Though it had never wanted a TFX at all, the Navy had decided earlier that — if faced with the inevitable — its best chances for a tailored naval version lay in getting an old-line Navy plane maker into the deal. G.D.'s partner, Grumman, had filled that bill. But now the G.D.–Grumman design had been officially judged inferior to Boeing's, and the Navy faced the bitter prospect of having to accept what it considered a straight Air Force airplane. On top of this seeming denial of the seagoing distinctiveness of naval aviation, something else was sticking in the Navy's craw. For years its custom had been to concentrate on *design* competitions, hammering the design out with a few time-tested contractors like Grumman, or Douglas, then relying on past experience (rather than contemporary analysis) to pilot the new plane through such tricky byways as costs or production plans; the Air Force's method, in-augurated with the Atlas missile in 1956, was to hammer out *everything* — design, costs, planning, etc. — during the competition. Now, the ad-mirals were asking themselves, what was going to happen to the Navy's procurement and development system if the Air Force's newborn Systems Command was allowed to bring off this, the biggest fighter program since World War II? So began a concerted effort, led by Vice Admiral Robert Pirie, Deputy Chief of Naval Operations for Air, and supported by other admirals, to get the Navy a TFX of its own or at the very least a version that would not give precedence to Air Force requirements.

The Navy's initial point of attack was weight: Boeing's design was 7,000 pounds heavier than the specifications called for. "This is ridiculous," said the Navy spokesmen, in voicing their protest to the Defense Department's Office of Research and Engineering. "We wanted a 40,000-pound plane but you talked us into accepting one of 55,000 pounds. Now the thing weighs 62,000 pounds. We just can't handle it on our carriers. The arrest-ing gear won't take it and the catapulting equipment isn't powerful enough to launch that much airplane." Defense's engineers pointed out that the Navy had had no difficulty handling a 70,000-pound carrier-based bomber, the A-5 (nee A3J), but the admirals shrugged this off with the observation that such big planes overcrowded their flight decks. "This was an emotional problem," said Dr. John McLucas, the young Deputy Director of Defense Research and Engineering. If it was, it wasn't *blind* emotion, for the Navy next attempted to confound design plans by redefining the kinds of mis-sions it wanted the TFX to fly. This was like inviting everybody to start all over again, since it was only because Navy and Air Force missions had been painfully reconciled in months of heated discussions during 1961 that the *bi*-service TFX was even put out to contract competition. In conse-quence there was an altering of the design away from Air Force require-ments, away from a bi-service TFX, and toward what the Navy had hankered after all along: a lower-performance, slower airplane of much less weight. Or, as a disgusted NASA designer put it, "a big black Packard."

All this time Secretary McNamara had stayed some distance from the battle. He had watched approvingly while Navy Secretary Fred Korth and Air Force Secretary Eugene Zuckert backed up the Air Council's orders for the twelve-week runoff between Boeing and G.D.–Grumman. Now, how-ever, there was a split between the military and the service secretaries. Both Zuckert and Korth felt the designs of the two contestants were still un-satisfactory, while the Air Council wanted Boeing. McNamara decided that the time for direct intervention had arrived. His faith in a bi-service plane had recently been reinforced by his success in getting the Air Force to buy the Navy's spectacular new fighter, the McDonnell Phantom II, instead of reordering its veteran Republic F-105 — and the initial Air Force growls had turned to murmurs of pleasure once the airmen had begun to fly the Phantoms. If the multiservice idea had worked for the Phantom, a plane already built, it should certainly work for the TFX, which was being specially designed to suit the Navy and Air Force. "But here I realized," he said, recalling the occasion, "that after eight months of work we'd come up to May and the Navy was *still* saying *neither* design met its require- ments. That was a terrible setback. My first reaction was disappointment, and then disbelief, because in mid-1961 we had finally got the services to agree on a set of requirements that were basically similar."

And, being McNamara, he was concerned about something else in the bids — i.e., the estimates of costs. Both Boeing and G.D.–Grumman had submitted "hungry" bids, and Boeing in particular had bid extremely low. These estimates, as McNamara measured them against Defense's own analyses, were full of wishful thinking.

"I asked the Secretaries of the Navy and Air Force to tell the contractors that their cost estimates were completely unreasonable," said McNamara recently. "We weren't going to accept anything like that; they were without foundation. It appeared that they were following a practice that is evident elsewhere in our society of trying to entangle a customer by a low initial bid, keeping the thought in back of the mind that it can be raised later." Why did he attach so much importance to realistic costs? Fundamentally because a significant cost overrun on a $7-billion program like the TFX not only would have to be borne by the taxpayers, but if it amounted to, say, $3 billion, this might raise the total price of the TFX to a level where it would have been wiser to put the $10 billion in a different weapon system, one that had had to be rejected on grounds of cost. "I had learned that final costs on major systems had exceeded the original estimates by between 300 and 1,000 percent. Although changes accounted for some of these overruns, this is the point: if the estimates had been better, we might not have bought those particular systems. I'm not saying we wouldn't spend what it costs to get adequate defense, but we might have bought different things. I know it is difficult to estimate costs, but there's no excuse for errors of this sort — 20 to 30 percent maybe, but not 300 percent."

So the recommendation of the Source Selection Board and of the Air Council for Boeing went flying back with an emphatic disapproval. In- credibly, the race went into a third lap. Instructions were sent out that both Boeing and General Dynamics–Grumman would have to continue the competition in the interests of a better design — and sounder costs.

Needless to say, McNamara's decision was received with mixed feelings by almost everyone concerned. Boeing had gained the support of the in- fluential Air Council, but now the extra time would allow its competition to catch up. G.D.–Grumman, having risked its all on McNamara's commonality, wondered if it shouldn't hedge its bets. The Air Force was furious at this further erosion of the TFX's time lead over Soviet aircraft; the Navy was delighted with the success of its tactics. The third lap thus began in a swirl of emotions, with the contractors sternly adjured to get more commonality in their designs and at the same time to meet the Navy's specifications, weight in particular.

The Defense engineers suggested a number of ways of accomplishing the latter — e.g., thinner-gauge stainless steel, the use of titanium, reducing the amount of fuel or weapons carried, altering the missions — and by the June 1 deadline, the groggy contractors were again ready with a whole new batch of proposals.

Then history repeated itself.

For the third time the Source Selection Board recommended Boeing, for the second time the Air Council followed suit. Again the Navy let loose its broadsides. Boeing was admittedly leading in the competition, wrote the Chief of Naval Operations, Admiral George Anderson, but he saw "no indications" that the Navy's requirements had been met. This was too much for the civilian Secretaries. Their analysis of the two proposals indicated that the Navy's demands had reached a stage where they could be satisfied only at the sacrifice of commonality. Further concessions would undoubtedly result in two TFX's instead of the common aircraft McNamara had set his heart on. McNamara read this as a choice between one plane and several admirals, and decided on the former. Into "early retirement" went Vice Admiral Pirie, Deputy Chief of Naval Operations for Air, and out to new jobs went a number of other Pentagon admirals. Pirie's successor, Rear Admiral William A. Schoech, and the other replacements were soon demonstrating an unsurprising amount of sweet reasonableness.

By this time, however, something akin to desperation had begun to affect all participants. The Kennedy Administration has still to come up with a new weapon system, after all the talk of stirring things up in the Pentagon. Communication between the civilian secretariat and the Source Selection Board at Wright-Patterson had broken down, to say the least, for though each was looking at the same proposals, the Source Selection Board had kept recommending Boeing on one set of standards (operational characteristics), and the civilian Secretaries had kept rejecting Boeing on a different set (costs and commonality). The contractors were in a daze of fatigue and bewilderment; by then even G.D.–Grumman had begun to think of a bi-service TFX as "a philosophical concept" technologically impossible of fulfillment. McNamara considered the companies' new cost estimates to be, if anything, more optimistic than before; in fact, so unrealistic that he had little hope the "brochuremanship" could be worked out of them within the time span of an additional race. Something clearly had to give. In the military view there had been far too much delay already so far as security was concerned; moreover, cold-war situations such as Viet-Nam and, potentially, Cuba cried out for a plane like the TFX. Hardware-hungry Curtis LeMay, Air Force Chief of Staff, told the Secretary: "I for one don't pay much attention to cost estimates in a competition at this time." Admiral Schoech had concurred; so had General Schriever, chief of the Air Force Systems Command, whose doubts about Boeing's costs had carried considerable weight in the Air Council's January recommendation for a runoff. McNamara decided to have one more try and one only. He insisted, however, that this final competition be held under quite a different set of rules.

Heretofore the contractors had been competing blindfolded, not knowing precisely how short of meeting specifications they were. Customarily, such measurements are withheld until after the competition is over, then the losers are told exactly where they fall short and the winner is advised what he still must do to come up to standard. Now, on McNamara's orders, both teams were to be treated as if each had actually won the competition. Air Force Secretary Zuckert and Navy Secretary Korth got off a joint letter for Colonel Charles Gayle, the TFX program officer at Wright-Patterson, telling him to loosen up. "I told Gayle," said Zuckert, recapitulating the instructions, "to give each of the contractors his impressions of the costs they used as against those he had worked up himself — so they're not in the position of competing in the dark. Put everything on the table. He would say on design, for example, we don't think the engine arrangement minimizes the danger of foreign objects, but if you just did thus and so you might solve the problem. We permitted our people this kind of talk in order to have the best plane we could get." In early July the contractors were themselves notified of the new ground rules and told that the previously secret "payoff points" — those given the most important weightings — were structural design, commonality, and reliable costs.

Boeing's reaction to the change of plan was to crowd on even more speed, still confident that the wider the margin of its technical superiority the more certain its ultimate victory. Yet some members of Boeing's top management could not down a sense of foreboding. Many of the disquieting rumors they had heard since the project's beginning had been subsequently borne out by events. G.D.–Grumman's choice of engine, the Pratt & Whitney TF-30, *had* won Pentagon approval over Boeing's choice, the G.E. MF295. The Navy *had* stalled for a better design, providing G.D.–Grumman the time needed to perfect its own. In light of the Pentagon's reversals of the Source Selection Board and Air Council recommendations, it had even begun to look as if there might be substance to the prediction that Boeing's intelligence had picked up from a Texas politician: G.D.–

Grumman would beat Boeing out of the contract, no matter how good a TFX the latter came up with. Now, under the changed rules, G.D.–Grumman was bound to get information about the Boeing design that would help equate the two. Not that there would be an outright leakage to G.D.–Grumman at the Wright-Patterson briefings; nevertheless some hints were bound to come out in the "corridor sessions" (to use the euphemism of a retired admiral) and more would emerge by the very nature of things. "If any design contest is dragged out," explained an official of the Defense Research and Engineering staff, "the designs tend to approximate each other, through the exchange of 'helpful' ideas on what one service or the other finds deficient. There is no way of avoiding a gradual drawing together toward a common design." In fact, at this stage of the game, that would appear to be precisely what the Pentagon wanted. . . .

On September 11, 1962, Boeing and G.D.–Grumman submitted their fourth and last set of technical proposals to the Source Selection Board. On October 15, Admiral Anderson reported the momentous news that the Bureau of Naval Weapons, at long last, had found a design satisfactory to the Navy; indeed, both designs were satisfactory. On November 9, Air Force Secretary Zuckert got a brightly wrapped present for his fifty-first birthday: the military's ultimate report on the competition. Both contractors were now judged capable of designing and producing the TFX, but Boeing was chosen unanimously to do so. The Source Selection Board recommended that company over G.D.–Grumman on the basis of lower quoted costs, greater weapon selectivity and carriage capability, less chance of engine damage from foreign objects, a better deceleration mechanism (thrust reversers), and superiority in all major operating characteristics. The Air Council went on record with the flat statements (1) that the winning proposal (Boeing's) provided a substantial improvement in the capabilities of the Tactical Air Command, and that of the Navy as well, where G.D.–Grumman's would not provide as much, and (2) that there was a manifest and substantial advantage in Boeing's proposal over G.D.–Grumman's in limited war actions from primitive airstrips.

The report further noted that all items, costs in particular, could not be completely corrected to the satisfaction of the military and would have to rest on the contractor's say-so until further refinements were made. Time, the report added nudgingly, was of the essence: even if approval of Boeing were immediately forthcoming, there would be a slippage of roughly six months in the initial operating capability of the first tactical wing. Lined up behind Boeing was undoubtedly the most glittering array of top brass since the Japanese surrender ceremonies aboard the battleship *Missouri:* General LeMay, Chief of Staff of the Air Force; ten assorted generals and admirals of the Air Council; General Walter C. Sweeney of TAC; General Mark E. Bradley of Logistics Command; Lieutenant General Bernard

Schriever of Systems Command; Admiral Anderson, Chief of Naval Operations; Admiral William E. Ellis, Assistant Chief of Naval Operations for Air; Rear Admiral Kleber S. Masterson, Bureau of Weapons; plus the five general and flag officers of the Source Selection Board itself.

Such a show of interservice solidarity was most impressive — especially when viewed through the battle smoke of the preceding fourteen months; the realization that both contractors now had the capability of building the TFX hung like a rainbow in Secretary Zuckert's office. McNamara's hopes for a bi-service weapon finally had substance behind them. But Zuckert had long since learned not to approach the boss with somebody else's un-evaluated conclusions. As he remarked recently, "I had the problem of having this guy downstairs with the bad habit of going back into the basic documents; so after two years and many ulcers I've learned. I can't get him just to accept the fact that four Selection Boards and umpty-ump Air Force generals have said it's O.K. to go with a certain contractor. He'll ask me if I've personally looked into the thing and if I say, 'Yeah, I heard the briefing,' that doesn't fly: I have to support everything I say, whether I disagree with the conclusions or go along with them. McNamara demands a different philosophy and approach to the source-selection problem, a different degree of presumption you favor the experts with." And the more Zuckert poked about behind the report's conclusions, the more he got an uneasy feeling that this final recommendation for Boeing might be the occasion when the civilians would have to reverse all those glittering echelons of gold braid.

The next morning, Saturday, he and Navy Secretary Korth talked it over, and Zuckert put in a couple of hours questioning the TFX program officer. Then Zuckert and Korth went down to see McNamara. Despite the military's unanimous recommendation for Boeing, it was a very close race, the Air Secretary said; in the raw score comparison, Boeing stood at 172.1, G.D.–Grumman at 175.6, only 3.5 points or less than 2 percent apart. Boeing's prime appeal to the services was that it had designed for *maximum* specification (i.e., capability), but the company had been able to achieve this only at the expense of commonality. G.D.–Grumman's lesser appeal for the services stemmed from a design of *minimum* specification, the price it had had to pay for achieving a high degree of commonality. The chances were that Boeing's design would become even less common in the production stage, and Zuckert, recalling Bomarc and Minuteman, was also apprehensive about Boeing's costs: if they were as wrong as they seemed to be at the start, experience had taught they'd be much worse at the finish.

McNamara contented himself with a "that's very interesting," but over that weekend both he and Deputy Defense Secretary Roswell Gilpatric pored over Zuckert's material. McNamara first satisfied himself on the fundamental point that both the Navy and Air Force now considered they had designs which met their requirements, then he turned his attention to a point-by-point comparison of the competing designs. He noted the Air Force had given a significant edge to Boeing on the basis of its greater ferry range, more firepower, and the employment of thrust reversers for increased maneuverability. But he noted that the Navy, though also giving precedence to Boeing in operational features, did so to a much lesser degree. As for G.D.–Grumman, in Navy eyes its slight inferiority in weapon selectivity (the number of attachment points for bombs, missiles, etc.) and in carrying capacity was overcome by its superior supersonic performance. McNamara proceeded to an examination of the other two prime "payoff points," costs and commonality.

He soon concluded that both contractors were still unrealistic on costs, but since there just wasn't time at that stage of the game to insist that they develop more reliable figures, it came down to a matter of choosing the lesser of two unreliabilities. . . .

With that thought in mind, he began to compare the production plans of the two contractors, for he had always held that invalid cost estimates were the result of imprecise production planning. He found that G.D.– Grumman had adopted a conservative approach in that it expected the TFX development program to demand a high level of engineering and test effort. Boeing, on the other hand, was clearly optimistic that few major problems or engineering changes would arise to challenge the validity of its extremely low engineering and cost estimates; it obviously believed that the development of the thrust reversers would give it little trouble, that the variable-sweep wing could be easily applied to the TFX configuration, the use of well over a ton of an exotic metal, titanium, to hold the wing on would cause no important manufacturing difficulties, and there would be only minor problems with its unique design for housing the engines. Maybe, but to McNamara the wish seemed father to the thought; it looked to him as if Boeing had seriously misjudged the difficulties to be expected in this aircraft. Then he turned to the section on commonality and Boeing's stock sank even further. There, flatly stated, was the evaluation group's opinion that Boeing was, "in effect, proposing two different airplanes from the structural point of view." Boeing's total program costs for producing the Navy and Air Force versions of a common TFX showed that it expec- ted a saving of only $397 million in comparison with its cost of developing the two versions as separate aircraft; G.D.–Grumman reported a saving nearly twice that, $623 million.

Bright and early the following Tuesday, November 13, McNamara, Gil- patric, Zuckert, and Air Force Under Secretary Joseph Charyk met for breakfast in Zuckert's dining room, Tuesday being the Air Force's regular day for such gatherings, and over the orange juice and scrambled eggs set themselves to weighing the relative merits of both proposals. McNamara opened with the observation that since both the Boeing and G.D.–Grumman aircraft could perform the missions required by either the Navy or the Air Force and there was no overriding margin in favor of one design as opposed to the other, the choice of contractor could be made on other grounds than design. Gilpatric thought the commonality comparison was critical: on final evaluation G.D.–Grumman had many fewer parts in its design than Boeing. The General Dynamics total stood at 14,423, and the Fourth Evaluation Report had found that 83.8 percent of these were identical in both versions. Boeing, on the other hand, had 18,653 parts, only 60.4 percent of which were identical; so it was going to build the aircraft about halfway to completion, then "hog out" (machine away) enough of the remaining elements to suit its Navy version. Gilpatric had never heard of this being done before, he said, and neither had the tooling experts he'd talked to; he was afraid a mere 60 percent commonality would prevent Boeing from making good on the crucial $1-billion saving.

Zuckert agreed. He'd spotted the fact that Boeing intended to have two static test programs for its two versions and to him this meant the likelihood the Pentagon would eventually be confronted with two separate aircraft. Moreover, he was disturbed over the optimism of Boeing's costs; this was not a proved plane; nobody would really *know* what he was in for until it had been flown. Yet if Boeing got into difficulties and missed its estimates by 50 percent, that was a couple of billion dollars! As the talk moved on, it became clear that they were all of one mind: G.D.–Grumman should get the contract on grounds of a higher degree of commonality and the greater likelihood that it would produce the plane on schedule and within the funds earmarked for it.

The next question was, who would prepare a memorandum of record justifying the award? Plainly this would be a ticklish job, for many Air Force noses would be out of joint over the rejection of Boeing, and if Senator Jackson, No. 2 man on the McClellan investigating subcommittee, chose to investigate the award through the committee (as he has), he'd probably get plenty of sub-rosa expertise: Zuckert appropriately enough, volunteered for the job. Then, late that afternoon, McNamara and Gilpatric trotted over to the White House to inform the President that G.D.–Grumman had won the award, and the program would soon be under way. What did Kennedy say? Nothing. Either way, he'd be getting a headache from someone, from the unemployed citizens of Fort Worth or those of Wichita, from Washington Senators Jackson and Magnuson or Texas politicos Governor John Connally, Congressman Jim Wright, and possibly even Vice President Johnson.

The Memorandum for the Record was some eight days in preparation, as Zuckert went behind the Selection Board reports to the basic findings of the evaluation teams. It received McNamara's approval on Wednesday, November 21. Public announcement was scheduled for 11:00 A.M., the twenty-fourth, a Saturday, and the Secretary issued explicit instructions on just how the news was to be broken. The press was to get it first, the politicos next. Moreover, McNamara made a point of telling Navy Secretary Korth, of Fort Worth, that no Texan was to be informed prior to eleven, and that this applied most particularly to the notification of Korth's Navy predecessor, Governor Connally. But the ink was hardly dry on the memorandum of record before at least one politician showed unmistakable signs that he sensed something conclusive in the wind. Congressman Wright armed his Fort Worth office with lists of people to be notified and pecked about nervously like a mother hen all day Thursday and Friday. On Saturday at 10:59 A.M. Major General Hoisington sent the announcement down to the Pentagon's press room and at eleven sharp he and a half-dozen other officers of the Air Force's Legislative Liaison Office started ringing up the politicians. Congressman Wright heard the glad tidings at home with a face full of shaving lather and was soon bubbling over the telephone to G.D.'s Fort Worth Division. There the operator screamed, "Did we get it?" as soon as she heard who was on the line, then cut him off while she herself spread the news. The competition that had cost the military 250,000 man-hours for evaluation, and cost Boeing and G.D.–Grumman some $25 million in the ten months of run-offs, was finally all over but the shouting.[3] . . .

JOSEPH PORTER CLERK, JR.

The Art of the Memorandum

Governments, as Joseph Porter Clerk notes, move on memoranda. His half-humorous description of the art of the memorandum includes serious and important insights into a major arena of bureaucratic maneuvers and arguments. In theory, the memorandum is merely the vehicle for authoritative communication in the nominally hierarchical structure of the foreign policy bureaucracy. In fact, as Clerk shows, memoranda are employed by supporters and opponents of policy change at all levels of the bureaucracy in efforts to stimulate or block change, to gain or be refused permission to act,

[3] By special ruling the two contractors are to be reimbursed for their expenses incurred in the ten-month runoff period.

Reprinted from *The Washington Monthly*, 1, 2 (March 1969), pp. 58–62 with the permission of the author. Joseph Porter Clerk, Jr., is pseudonymous.

to signal or to build support for one's position. As with most maneuvers and arguments, the memo may serve a variety of functions and seek several objectives.

Armies move on their stomachs; governments on their memoranda. Memoranda are the devices by which bureaucrats communicate, make decisions, and record what has happened. You cannot succeed in government without mastering the art. Nor is it easy to come by. After seven years in government, I am just gaining a beginner's command over this indispensable tool of deceptively simple appearance.

When I entered government, I assumed a memorandum was an official document that bureaucrat A wrote to bureaucrat B when A wanted B to do something. This was naive. B's usual response is to do nothing.

This may be because B is too busy writing his own memoranda or, more likely, because B is one of those public servants whose impulses to action are thoroughly controlled by their awareness of the accompanying risks.

In either event, the primary rule of the memorandum is to expect no action from its recipient.

This rule, when first learned, tends to be dispiriting, but its advantages soon become apparent. Other men's inertia can be the secret of your power to act and to influence policy.

Consider a simple example. As a novice you would have written to your superior asking his permission to do such and such. You would have received no answer and therefore not had the authority to do what you had proposed doing. You now know that your memo should say, "Next Tuesday I plan to. . . ." No answer constitutes your authority to act. (The Navy has honored this tactic with the acronym UNODIR — "unless otherwise directed.")

This sort of thing won't work if there is the slightest hint of anything unusual about your proposal. The memorandum must imply, "I'm probably wasting your time to ask you to read what is obviously a matter of course, but I feel I should always lean over backwards to keep you fully informed."

You may, in fact, propose a revolutionary change in policy, but it should always be stated as an interpretation of present policy — an exegesis on scripture in the absence of new revelation.

New ideas are fragile in a bureaucracy. And their chances of survival usually diminish when they are proclaimed as new ideas. Instead, say that you are merely examining the assumptions underlying the status quo. While your reputation for liveliness may suffer, your ideas may succeed.

Occasionally, however, you should advertise the novelty of your proposal. There are some government officials who take great pride in being "open to new approaches." The hazard in dealing with them is that some mean it and some don't. Thus it is crucially important to know your readers. Not only must you know the identity of those few lovers of new ideas for whose benefit you can speak out boldly, but also of that other (not always mutually exclusive) minority, the officials who actually do something when they receive a memorandum.

But you can be assured that most of your readership will be the non-responders. The key fact to realize about them is that everyone who reads your memo and does nothing is to some degree implicated in the action you propose or the policy interpretation you make.

Therefore you want to address the memo to (or at least note "copy to") everyone whose assent you need. Since some of them are likely to be busy and important people who might be able to claim they never read your message in the event its result proves unpopular, you must make sure that they do, in fact, read it.

One device that practically guarantees that B will read it is to add as another addressee someone who is important to B — his superior, perhaps, or the man who controls his budget or his personnel allotment.

Mark the message "Secret" or "Confidential" or "For President's Eyes Only." Security classifications were not devised for their value in catching attention, but that only makes them more useful for the purpose.

Make your message stand out from the others. If blue paper is required for memos, use pink. If most messages are in the form of official cables (as is the case in U.S. embassies overseas), use a commercial cable or write a letter. If messages are in letter form (as is generally true in domestic agencies), send a telegram.

Another way to gain attention is to use concise English. However, there is a risk here: you may be regarded as a dangerous eccentric. It should never be tried by a new man, for he will be looked upon with pity as a novice who simply lacks the appropriate vocabulary.

Sometimes you will want to make sure that a recipient does *not* read your memorandum. He may be one of those unpredictable action-takers mentioned earlier, or he may be a man you know to be totally dedicated to shooting down any idea of yours. Nevertheless, you need to have him implicated in this one. How do you manage it without having him read the memorandum? Make it long and dull. Make the subject sound highly technical. Send a faint carbon or a bad Xerox. See that it is delivered late Friday afternoon. It will join large piles of written material behind the executive's desk, where it will testify to his good intentions until the day of his retirement. Or it will travel thousands of miles in the bottom of his briefcase, waiting for a moment that will never come.

When I was working in the General Counsel's office at AID, I once recommended that we send a complaint against a construction firm to the Department of Justice for suit. The firm had built a road in Southeast

Asia which collapsed. It was important to get the case to the Department of Justice not so much because several million dollars of taxpayers' money was involved, but because once the problem was at Justice we could stop wasting our time answering inquiries from Congress and the General Accounting Office. We could simply reply that Justice was considering suit and that we had been asked not to comment.

My memorandum recommending suit had to do with the kind of decision that the General Counsel would feel he should make himself but would never find time for. To get my memorandum through him I knew that I would have to persuade him at the outset that he would never study the matter. Assembling the relevant (and not so relevant) papers having to do with the case and labeling them exhibit 1, 2, 3, etc., I piled the whole mass in a shopping cart borrowed from the General Services Administration and wheeled it into his office, with my memo on top. I urged a personal study of the problem. I got his initials in three minutes.

Success with the memorandum can depend just as much on your fellow senders as on the recipients. Mustering others to join in sending a memorandum accomplishes two things: it displays wider support for the message and, more important, it diffuses responsibility for it. The desirability of the latter becomes clear when the memorandum outrages a higher official.

Multiple authorship is ordinarily effected by a device known as "clearance." This process consists of obtaining on the yellow copy of the memorandum the signatures or initials of persons other than the nominal sender of the memorandum. The most extraordinary thing about the process is that no one knows exactly what "clearance" means. Some degree of affirmation is presumed to be involved. The vagueness of that affirmation may make it easier to get B to clear a memorandum than to act upon it. He can mean "yes, in principle" without assuming an obligation to do anything. An additional advantage is that you can more easily pressure for a quick initialing, so as not to "hold up the memo."

Of course the reverse may also be a good tactic. Instead of asking such known sympathizers as P and Q to clear the memorandum, put them down as addressees. This places them in the position of being able to initiate a favorable response. This device can even be extended to having someone else send to you the memorandum you would have liked to write (or maybe did in fact write) so that you can respond favorably. This is the only sure-fire method of assuring prompt action by the addressee.

Suppose all this art has been directed at you and there is now a memorandum on your desk from someone else proposing an action or supporting a policy about which you are doubtful but don't wish to commit yourself, even by implication.

Reply that the proposal is so interesting that it deserves to be the subject of a large task force study. This will guarantee a six-month delay at the very least.

WARNER R. SCHILLING

The H-Bomb Decision: How to Decide without Actually Choosing

President Truman's "decisions" in early 1950 regarding the H-bomb program suggest both how "grand strategy" is likely to be the cumulative result of a sequence of individual minimal decisions about relatively narrow problems and how participants in the process exploit occasions for such decisions in an effort to achieve their particular interests and objectives.

The relatively narrow issue of whether to increase efforts aimed at developing a thermonuclear weapon afforded one more occasion for interested members of the national security bureaucracy to address the much broader policy concerns of national strategy, control of atomic energy, and foreign policy objectives in Europe. Their stands on the issue under discussion derived from their stakes on these and other issues. The President's inclination to decide as little as possible afforded ample opportunity for the participants to engage in maneuvers and arguments designed to move actions in the directions they preferred.

Although the H-bomb had received detailed consideration as early as 1942, advocates of a large-scale effort to develop the weapon consistently failed in their efforts to receive a priority equal to or greater than the A-bomb program. The explosion of the first Russian atomic device — an event under the control of none of the United States participants — provided another occasion to seek a policy change.

Proponents of an accelerated H-bomb program were opposed by the Atomic Energy Commission (AEC) and by its General Advisory Committee (GAC) in particular. The advocates maneuvered to keep the issue narrow — whether or not to begin a crash program of development — in an effort to minimize the number of opponents and the arguments which might be employed against them. Those who opposed the crash program maneuvered to redefine the issue and to include participants who might become allies in terms of the redefined issues.

For example, one opponent, the AEC, called for interdepartmental consideration of the proposal at the NSC level. This maneuver involved many

Reprinted from the *Political Science Quarterly*, 76 (March, 1961), pp. 24–46 with permission.

This article is based on part of the research conducted on the H-bomb decision by the present writer in connection with the Civilian-Military Perspectives Project of the Institute of War and Peace Studies, Columbia University. Research and article have both benefited greatly from the guidance and criticism of the Institute's Director, William T. R. Fox. Earlier versions of the article were prepared for discussion at the Arms Control and National Policy Seminar, California Institute of Technology, and the December 1960 meeting of the American Historical Association.

more actors and many more definitions of what was "the" issue. Thus those advocates of international control of atomic energy in the State Department, who through the NSC were now included in the policy decision, might feel that the development of an H-bomb would foreclose any hope of success. Perhaps simply including a diversity of interests and objectives would lead to a stalemate and therefore no change in policy.

The H-bomb opponents also redefined and broadened the issue, not only to involve new actors but also to alter the consequences for each of them. Thus, in an effort to engage the interests of those whose organizational mission required atomic weapons and to keep the military services divided, the trade-off between H-bomb production and A-bomb production was emphasized. The GAC also sought to require an agreement on a single strategic doctrine as a prerequisite for decision.

The maneuvers and arguments of the H-bomb opponents were largely unsuccessful, in part because the motives of the AEC were suspect and in part because of the skill displayed by the advocates' counter-maneuvers and arguments. Thus the Army could not be swayed by Lilienthal's appeal for more conventional weapons, both because it did not trust Lilienthal and because the appeal seemed to be an example of the AEC meddling in the Army's business.

The NSC recommendation submitted to Truman in January 1950 included a series of arguments which represented the "greatest common denominator of agreement" among the supporters of the H-bomb program as well as arguments which neutralized the opponents. The coalition between the State and Defense Departments in support of the H-bomb program in large measure determined the shape of the final recommendation. Significantly, the two departments supported the recommendation for quite different reasons and sought very different objectives.

Finally, it should be noted that for Truman, "the" issue was, in large measure, one of minimizing conflict and of building consensus within his own bureaucracy; he had made *his* decision regarding the H-bomb the previous October.

President Truman made his first H-bomb decision on January 31, 1950. He ordered the Atomic Energy Commission to continue its efforts to determine the technical feasibility of a thermonuclear weapon. The rate and scale of the effort were to be fixed jointly by the AEC and the Department of Defense. He also ordered the Department of State and the Department of Defense to re-examine the nation's strategic objectives and plans, both diplomatic and military, in light of the forthcoming developments to be expected in Soviet nuclear weapons capabilities. Both directives had been recommended to the President in a report submitted the same day by a special committee of the National Security Council, composed of the Secretaries of State and Defense and the Chairman of the Atomic Energy Commission.[1]

[1] See Harry S. Truman, *Memoirs* (1956), II, p. 309.

The report of the special committee and the President's subsequent decision marked the first resolution of a policy discussion that had begun in September, 1949, with the discovery that the Russians had exploded a fission bomb. This discussion had been broadly concerned with the implications of the Soviet explosion for American security and with the question of what actions the United States should undertake as a result of it. The first purpose of this article will be to contrast the content and form of the President's decision with that of the policy discussion that had preceded it. The point of this contrast will be to illustrate the "minimal" character of the decision made on January 31st. Of all the courses of action considered and debated during the preceding five months, that chosen by the President represented one which seemed to close off the least number of future alternatives, one that left the most issues still undecided. The second and third purposes of this article will be to advance an explanation for the minimal character of the decision and to indicate some of the policy consequences that followed from its having been made in this manner.

THE POLICY BACKGROUND

The explosion by the Russians of a fission bomb on August 26, 1949, was an event which took American policy-makers by surprise and one for which they had prepared neither specific plans nor a general strategy. The Joint Chiefs of Staff, taking what many believed to be a pessimistic view, had not expected the Soviet Union to detonate a fission weapon until 1952. Although steps had been taken prior to August, 1949, to provide for the detection of such an explosion, nowhere in the government had any formal attention been given to the question of what actions might be appropriately taken once the evidence of an explosion had been detected. The absence of forward planning can be attributed in part to the absence of any formal deadlines or pressures compelling planning groups in State, Defense, or the Commission to undertake it. It can also be attributed to the absence of any generally agreed-on body of strategic thought regarding the foreign policy implications of nuclear weapons which could have served as a point of departure and frame of reference for more specific plans.

Since the end of the Civil War, the continental security of the United States had been doubly insured. First, by virtue of its superior military potential which completely overshadowed that of the other Great Powers, the United States had no need to fear any nation. The weapons of World Wars I and II and the distribution of the people, skills, and resources necessary to make and use these weapons were such that no single foreign nation could conceivably mobilize enough military power from inside its own frontiers to assault successfully the American continent. Secondly, by virtue of the balance of power abroad, the United States could afford to leave its potential largely unmobilized. The interests and arms of the other

Great Powers were so committed one against the other that none was free to direct its strength against the United States. In time of peace these powers did not dare turn their backs on more immediate enemies, and in time of war their hands were full fighting them. The American continent was subject to only one serious military threat: the possibility that through conquest and alliance the people, skills, and resources of the Old World might be gathered together into one hostile combination. Only in this event could the United States be confronted with a military potential roughly equivalent to its own. The result, if not in all instances the intent, of American intervention in World Wars I and II had been to remove this contingency from the realm of reality.

Following World War II two revolutionary changes occurred in this security position. The first was the inability of the European Powers to re-establish a balance of power on the European continent. The nations of Western Europe were in no position to prevent the Russians from achieving at their ease what had just been so painfully wrested from the hands of the Germans: an empire from the Urals to the Atlantic embracing all the peoples, skills, and resources of the Old World. The United States moved resolutely to meet this situation, both through policies designed to substitute American power for European (the Truman Doctrine, the North Atlantic Treaty) and through policies designed to restore to the Western Europeans themselves the capacity to balance the Russians (the Marshall Plan, the Mutual Defense Assistance Program).

These policies, which constituted the main burden of American security policy between 1945 and 1949, were addressed to a real and immediate problem. They were, however, essentially pre-nuclear in their rationale. The advent of nuclear weapons had not influenced the American determination to restore the European balance of power. It was, in fact, an objective which the United States would have had an even greater incentive to undertake if the fission bomb had not been developed. Nor were nuclear weapons believed to have qualitatively altered the military problem of achieving that objective. The American monopoly of the atomic bomb was seen as greatly facilitating the task of defeating the Red Army (and hence in deterring an attack by it), but in the judgment of at least two of the three services it would still be necessary to maintain sufficient ground strength on the continent to permit the mounting of the large-scale land offensive which they believed would be required in order to terminate the war.[2]

---

[2] For the rationale of the American interest in restoring the European balance of power, see Walter Millis and E. S. Duffield (eds.), *The Forrestal Diaries* (1951), pp. 341, 349–351. For military doctrine regarding a war in Europe, see e.g. General Omar Bradley, "This Way Lies Peace," *Saturday Evening Post* (October 15, 1949); and Walter Millis, Harvey C. Mansfield, and Harold Stein, *Arms and the State* (1958), pp. 237–245, 247–249.

In the summer of 1949 the second revolutionary change in the American security position, that occasioned by the advent of Soviet nuclear weapons-systems, had yet to occur. This was a development destined to change completely the strategic significance of the traditional components of American security. The new weapons were so cheap and so destructive, relative to the old, that the Soviet Union would have the ability to mobilize from inside its own frontiers enough military power to accomplish what had heretofore been beyond the means of any single foreign nation: the capacity to strike a mortal blow at the American continent. The consequences were twofold: the industrial superiority that had guaranteed victory in two World Wars was no longer the equivalent of overwhelming military potential, and the United States could no longer afford to leave its potential largely unmobilized during time of peace. Unlike the case of the Kaiser's or Hitler's Germany, the conquest of the people, skills, and resources of the Old World would not be a necessary first step in a Soviet attack on the United States. As a result, the United States would no longer be able to count on the unfolding of such conquest (1) to provide time for Americans to alert themselves to danger and to arm to meet it, and (2) to provide allies to preoccupy the enemy until they were ready. In fact, the import of the second revolution was to diminish that of the first. The more developed Russian transcontinental nuclear striking power, the less important would be the addition of Western Europe's people, skills, and resources for a Soviet attack on the United States and, perforce, the less significant the distribution of power on that continent for the security of the United States.

The implications of the advent of nuclear weapons for American security were stark. American policy between 1945 and 1949 had by no means been blind to these possibilities, and two major policies had been formulated to meet them. The first was the proposal made for international control of atomic energy, which by the fall of 1947 appeared to have little prospect of being accepted by the Soviet Union. The second was the development of a military doctrine to cope with the contingency of two-way nuclear war. The character of this doctrine can be seen in the report released in January, 1948, by the President's Air Policy Commission. Bluntly entitled *Survival in the Air Age*, the Finletter Report called for a "new strategy" to provide victory in an atomic war if it came and, hopefully, by confronting the enemy with the "prospect of a counterattack of the utmost violence," to persuade him not to attack in the first place.

According to the Report, this strategy would require an Air Force capable of smashing the Russian cities and factories. The prospect of such a "devastating price" would make the Soviets hesitate to attack. The Air Force would also need the capability of launching a counteroffensive against the Russian air forces "at the earliest possible moment" in order "to silence the attack on the United States mainland and give us the time again to build up our industrial machine and our manpower to go on to win the war." The Soviet objective, on the other hand, would be to smash American industrial power "at the outset" and to destroy the American air defense and counterattack forces. Basically, however, what was outlined in the Finletter Report was not so much a "new strategy" as the problems and choices over which the discussion of strategy was to ponder for years thereafter. The Report took no note of the possible conflicts between a strategy designed to deter atomic attack and a strategy designed to win an atomic war. Neither did the Report confront the question of why, if the United States could achieve a counteroffensive blow of the magnitude described against Russian cities and delivery forces, the Russians could not do the same or better with their attacking blow, and, in this event, against what and with what would the United States launch its counterattack? [3]

These, then, were the three major postwar security policies that the United States had evolved by the eve of the Russian explosion: the effort to restore the European balance of power; the effort to secure international control of nuclear weapons; and the effort to evolve a force for two-way atomic war and a strategy to guide it. The three objectives were by no means carefully interrelated. Just as the strategy to restore the European balance of power made no provision for the time when American security would cease to turn on the stability of that balance, so the strategic doctrine outlined in the Finletter Report, while correctly anticipating that the future pivot would be the stability of the Soviet-American balance of terror, made no provision for the possibility that the United States would continue to have a political and military stake in the independence of Western Europe. As for the proposal for international control, this, if accepted, would require a substantial revision of the forces required to implement both of the other objectives. It should also be noted that each of these three policies had the potential of pointing the American response to the Russian explosion in a different direction. With the passing of the American monopoly on the atomic bomb, the defense of Western Europe might now require a larger commitment of ground forces than had heretofore been necessary. The need to prepare for two-way atomic war, on the other hand, would seem to call for the allocation of additional resources to the weapons for air attack and defense and an expansion in the size of the nuclear stockpile. Finally, the development by the Russians of their own nuclear weapons could be seen as the proper occasion to reopen and redouble the effort to secure their control by an international agency.

[3] See *Survival in the Air Age: A Report by the President's Air Policy Commission* (1948), pp. 6, 10, 12, 14, 20, 23–25.

It was against this background of policy that discussion began in September, 1949, on the question of what should be done now that the Soviet Union had exploded an A-bomb. The major participants in this discussion came from five government institutions: the Departments of State and Defense; the Atomic Energy Commission (including a number of scientists employed in full or in part by the Commission or its subcontractors); the Office of the President; and the Joint Committee on Atomic Energy of Congress. By far the bulk of the policy discussion among these participants took place informally, and the degree and effect of the initiative exercised through these informal contacts fully support the insight of the observer who commented that the Federal Government is the last stronghold of private enterprise in the United States. Although a number of the participants had begun by December, 1949, to leak some of the subject matter of the discussion to the press, the policy discussion was for the most part closed to the general public.

The formal development of the policy discussion was tied to the bureaucratic history of a particular issue, that of whether to undertake an intensive effort to make a thermonuclear weapon. This matter was placed on the agenda of the Atomic Energy Commission on October 5th for reference to the Commission's main scientific advisory body, the General Advisory Committee. Both the report of the GAC, submitted on October 30th, and that submitted by the five Commissioners to the President on November 9th made it clear that the issue was hardly one that could be decided without reference to political and military as well as technical considerations. For this reason, and because he was well aware of the differences that were developing both between and within the major governmental bodies involved in the issue, the President referred the issue on November 10th to the previously noted special committee of the National Security Council. Under the auspices of this committee a working group was set up, composed of representatives from each of the three Executive agencies concerned: State, Defense, and the AEC. In addition to the work done jointly by this group, each agency also conducted a variety of independent studies into aspects of the problem, and the ultimate products of this activity were the recommendations submitted by the special committee to the President on January 31, 1950. It should be noted that throughout this period the Joint Committee on Atomic Energy was active in exploring the issue and voicing its views, through letters and personal visits by the Chairman to the President.

It will be the purpose of the following section to present a summary description of the issues and alternatives that were developed during the course of these proceedings. Although there will be occasional references to individual or institutional views, the purpose of the section is not to describe in any detail the positions held by particular individuals or government bodies with regard to the issues and alternatives discussed. The views of most of the individuals concerned were quite complex, and individual views within the same government bodies were by no means uniform. Many individuals and agencies took similar policy positions but for quite different reasons, and the views of some individuals and agencies changed over the time period involved. The summary is meant to delineate not individual or institutional positions but rather the range and content of the major policy proposals and considerations that were produced as a result of these five months of debate and deliberation.[4]

ISSUES AND ALTERNATIVES

The discovery that the Soviet Union had exploded an A-bomb several years before it had been expected to do so suggested to many that one response should be to step up the pace of America's own nuclear weapons program. Since plans had just been completed to provide for a major expansion in the facilities for producing fissionable material and to undertake the development of fission weapons of much larger power and varied size than those heretofore fabricated, the focus of attention turned to the prospects for making a fusion weapon. The possibility of such a weapon had first received detailed study in 1942, and it had been a continuing concern of the atomic energy program ever since. It had proved, however, a recalcitrant technical problem and, both during the war and after, work on it had been given a much lower priority than work on the development and improvement of fission weapons.

The idea, in the fall of 1949, that a greater effort to make a fusion weapon was now in order received some stimulus from what were believed at the time to be some promising new technical approaches to the problem, but the major motive for reconsidering the state of the program was provided by the Russian explosion. Those who advocated a greater effort were moved by two considerations. One was the idea that if the United States could develop a bomb with thousands of times the energy release of the Hiroshima bomb, it would be able to maintain its qualitative

[4] The information in the preceding paragraphs and the sections that follow can largely be found in two published sources: Truman, *Memoirs,* Vol. II, chap. 20; and United States Atomic Energy Commission, *In the Matter of J. Robert Oppenheimer: Transcript of Hearing before Personnel Security Board* (1954). The article also draws upon extended personal interviews during 1956–1958 with sixty-six of the participants in the events discussed. Given the character of interview data and the particular focus of this article, it is the present writer's conclusion that the best way to meet scholarly obligations to both readers and participants is by omitting citation for the points that follow. The same considerations are responsible for the fact that these pages omit reference to individuals except where stylistically infeasible. Detailed description and citation will, of course, be later available with the publication of the whole study of the H-bomb decision.

lead over the Soviet program and thereby minimize the political and military disadvantages of the loss of its fission monopoly. Even more compelling, in the minds of most advocates, was the possibility that if the United States did not move more energetically to explore this possibility, the Soviet Union might be the first to achieve such a capability.

This reasoning seemed so persuasive to its advocates that many did not bother to think through in much detail, especially in September and October, exactly what advantages the United States could get from such a weapon that it could not secure through its superior stockpile of fission bombs or, for that matter, just what it was that the Russians might do if they secured an H-bomb first. It seemed sufficient and obvious that in the first instance American interests would be advanced, and that in the second they could only be hurt. Nor were the advocates of a greater effort very definite during September and October with regard to the rate and scale of the effort they had in mind. The analogy of the effort made during the war to develop the A-bomb came naturally to mind, and it was in these terms that the proposal was formally placed on the agenda of the Commission.

The issue of the rate and scale of the program could not be left in such ambiguous terms. The particular thermonuclear design which most of the participants had in mind, the so-called "Super," required as one of its major components a large amount of tritium. The most feasible method of making tritium was to bombard lithium with neutrons, and neutrons which were used to make tritium would not be available to make plutonium. Accordingly, the manufacture of tritium for the Super would mean foregoing the manufacture of fission bombs. Moreover, the scientific talent of the nation, as well as its supply of neutrons, was limited. Scientists put to work on the Super would be scientists not available to work on the new fission weapons. A more intensive effort to make an H-bomb would, in short, involve costs to the nation's A-bomb program.

The discussion that developed among the participants about the costs that an expanded H-bomb program would entail for the A-bomb program proved to be one of monumental confusion and misunderstanding. The least of the difficulties was that no one knew just how much tritium the Super would require. The major difficulty was that (a) the participants were reasoning from diverse premises about the kind of effort to be made and about the value of the weapons involved and (b) the divergent character of these premises were by no means always made clear in the arguments that were then joined.

Thus, the development of any consensus with regard to the plutonium costs involved was handicapped by the fact that some participants were thinking in terms of making only enough tritium in the Hanford reactors to support a test program, others contemplated a larger diversion of those piles in order to have a stockpile of tritium immediately on hand with which to fabricate a number of usable weapons in case the Super proved feasible, and still others were thinking in terms of building a number of new reactors for the production of the tritium stockpile, and it was not always clear whether they expected those reactors to be in operation before or after a demonstration of feasibility. The discussion of the talent costs was similarly complex. Some scientists did not see how additional talent could be put to work profitably on the problem even if it was made available. In their view the Los Alamos Laboratory was already doing about all that could be done. Others were convinced that the problem had been starved for talent all along. The development of a consensus on this point was further complicated by the fact that some thought the additional talent could be secured by bringing in scientists not then working on fission weapons, and others believed that if more people were put to work on the Super they would have to come mainly from those already engaged in fission work.

Difficult as it was for the participants to reach any common conception of what kind of expanded H-bomb program they were talking about and what kind of cost it would bring to the A-bomb program, this was only half the problem in reaching a conclusion about the rate and scale of the effort to be made. A judgment about the desirability of foregoing any given number of plutonium bombs or incurring the delay or loss of any given number of improvements in the development of fission weapons would depend on the application of some criteria for comparing the relative military utility of A-bombs and H-bombs. One of the major reservations expressed by the scientists on the GAC about the idea of embarking on a large-scale H-bomb program was the result of the application of such criteria. They were by no means confident that the Super could be delivered by air, and they thought there would be few targets for which a bomb of such large yield would be suited. They concluded that the military purposes of the United States would be much better served by the A-bombs and A-bomb developments which would otherwise have to be foregone or postponed.

Illustrative of how different participants were talking about different things is the fact that the GAC judgment cannot be directly compared to that of the Joint Chiefs of Staff. At the time of the GAC report, the Chiefs were on record before the Joint Committee as desiring an accelerated effort to develop the Super, but they had not been specific about the rate and scale of the effort they had in mind and, hence, the A-costs they were willing to incur. When the Commissioners submitted their report, guidance on this point had yet to be produced by the military, and this was one of the questions to which they urged the President to secure an answer before making his decision.

The issue of the rate and scale of the effort to be made on the H-bomb thus turned, in part, on the issue of the relative military utility of H- and A-bombs. The discussion of this issue was conditioned, in turn, by the issue of what strategic doctrine should guide American military policy. It was here, at the level of general strategy, that some of the most significant differences existed among the participants. The three issues were so inter-related, however, that the participants were not always able to distinguish against what (and even for what) they were arguing.

The GAC report is a case in point. Many of its members were by no means persuaded that the doctrine of strategic bombing was a desirable military policy. Their views were not far removed from those of the Admiral (who was also a member of the Military Liaison Committee to the AEC) who had argued before the House Armed Services Committee in October, 1949, that strategic bombing was militarily unsound, morally wrong, and not suited for achieving the kind of political conditions the United States would want to obtain at the conclusion of a war. The GAC's recommendation against the development of the H-bomb was grounded, in part, on the belief that its only utility would be for the bombing of large cities and the objection to a military doctrine which would lead to the mass slaughter of Russian men, women, and children. The point was blurred, however, by their failure to carry through and make clear that they had equivalently strong objections to the use for this purpose of the products of the expanded fission program which they did support.

Another issue of doctrine interjected into the debate related to the condi-tions under which the United States would use nuclear weapons. It was argued by some that a decision with regard to the H-bomb program could not be rationally made until it was first decided for what purpose the United States was accumulating nuclear weapons: for the purpose of de-terrence and retaliation only, or with the intent of so incorporating them into military plans and structure that the United States would initiate their use regardless of whether they had been employed by the enemy. The point to the argument was the idea that if weapons were being accumulated for the first purpose only, given the great value which the Russians attached to their industrial plant, a limited number of fission bombs would be sufficient to serve it.

The preference for a strategy based on last-resort use and for a clear-cut rejection of the principle of first use was strong among those who had major reservations about the desirability of strategic bombing and those who doubted the capacity of the American public to conduct itself ratio-nally in a world in which conflict with the Soviet Union would continue to be deep and basic but in which a resort to violence would become increas-ingly suicidal. Among the participants in the Department of Defense, however, these arguments received a different reception. There was no great interest in adopting a strategy which seemed to bind the United

States to fight only on terms of the enemy's choosing, and there was determined opposition to the idea that the need for an H-bomb program turned on the making of such a choice. It was the judgment of these and other participants that for an effective performance of the task of deterrence as well as that of fighting a victorious war the armed services would need the most powerful weapons they could secure.

The idea that an over-all review of national policy and a decision with regard to these strategic issues should precede the further development of the H-bomb was energetically pressed at the NSC level by the Chairman of the AEC, David Lilienthal. One reason why he did so relates to still another issue: that of the relative utility of conventional as compared to nuclear weapons. During the NSC discussions, Lilienthal was shocked to learn just how dependent the military were on nuclear weapons, and he became convinced that what the United States needed far more than the H-bomb was a large-scale increase in conventional armaments. This conclusion was influenced in part by the prevailing military judgment that nuclear weapons alone could not win World War III, but it also reflected Lilienthal's own conviction that the foreign policy purposes of the nation would be better served by a military posture that was not so dependent on the use of large bombs against urban targets.

It was Lilienthal's contention that the decision on the Super should be delayed until an effort had first been made to review the nation's strategic doctrine and to consider the desirability of reducing the nation's dependence on large-yield nuclear weapons by increasing the size of its conventional forces. He believed that if the decision to press for the Super was made first it would prejudice the chances for a later review of that choice and greatly lessen the opportunity to secure conventional rearmament. There would be little prospect of persuading Congress and the public to support an expensive conventional rearmament program, he argued, once the Super program was announced, for most would conclude from the announcement that the security of the United States was in good shape and that the answer to the Russian A-bomb had been found.

One other major issue was raised in connection with the H-bomb debate and that was the question of its relationship to the effort to secure international control of atomic energy. The feeling was strong among many, especially the GAC and members of the Commission, that with the development of the Russian A-bomb the world had reached a crossroads in history. From this point it stood fair to continue into the mounting tensions of a nuclear arms race and perhaps, in time, into the horrors of nuclear war. The most appropriate thing to do at this time, so it seemed, was not to rush to try to make even bigger bombs but rather to make a last determined effort to reverse the direction that international politics had been taking since 1945. To those who thought in these terms the urgency of those who advocated a more intensive H-bomb program seemed both intemperate and short-sighted. To those who thought negotiation with the Russians fruitless, the insistence on delay seemed quixotic and dangerous.

The specific ideas advanced by the GAC and some of the Commissioners as to what might be done to reopen the international control negotiations or to otherwise try to move the world away from a nuclear arms race were, however, most indefinite and not very clearly stated. Some suggested that the United States increase the scale of its research on the H-bomb but not go all-out on the H-program without first reopening the international control negotiations with the Russians. Others recommended not pushing ahead at all on the H-bomb until it and the control of nuclear weapons in general had been first discussed with the Russians. (The minority annex of the GAC report suggested, in this connection, that the two Powers might agree not to make the H-bomb. Since its successful development was believed to require a test, violation of the agreement could be easily detected.) The most extreme position was that taken by the majority of the GAC, which recommended that the United States unilaterally announce that it was not going to make the weapon.

This last recommendation illustrates the interconnection among all the issues involved in the discussion. The judgment of those who made it was that the United States would not be losing much: a weapon that looked as if it would be very hard to make; one which would cost more in A-bombs than its military utility was worth; and one which if used would be employed in a manner highly repugnant to the values for which American culture was supposed to stand. It was believed that the Russians would not try very hard to make it themselves, given the cost of the weapon, the uncertainty that it could even be made, and the American example. Renunciation, so it was thought, was an opportunity for America to gain considerable moral prestige at very little cost and to make some contribution to the possible limitation of warfare in the future.

THE DECISION EXAMINED AND EXPLAINED

It is appropriate at this point to recall the content of the President's decision on January 31st: that an effort be made to determine the technical feasibility of a thermonuclear weapon; that the rate and scale of the effort be fixed jointly by the AEC and the Department of Defense; and that the State and Defense Departments undertake concurrently to review the nation's foreign and military policies in light of the prospective nuclear capabilities of the Soviet Union.

This decision stands in some contrast to the issues and alternatives just described. Had the President decided the issue of the rate and scale of the H-bomb program? Had he decided that the military utility of the Super would be worth the A-costs involved? Had he made a decision about the military and political desirability of strategic bombing? Had he decided whether military doctrine with regard to nuclear weapons was to be governed by the principle of first use or that of last resort? Had he decided that the nation needed bigger nuclear weapons more than it needed large-scale conventional rearmament? Had he decided not to renew negotiations with the Soviet Union on the subject of international control?

The President had decided none of these things. This is not, of course, to say that he had decided nothing at all. He had quite definitely decided that the United States would not unilaterally renounce the effort to make an H-bomb. Although a literal reading of his directive with regard to the determination of feasibility would indicate that he had ordered the AEC and Defense only to continue what they had already been doing, there was certainly an implication that they should approach the task with a greater sense of urgency than had heretofore been the case. The directive also made it evident that the President had not endorsed an intensive H-bomb program. The directive said nothing about production facilities for the Super; nor did it even specify that the determination of feasibility was to include a test program.

The President had also decided to order the re-examination of the nation's strategic plans that so many had urged. He further decided not to wait until the completion of that review before making his H-bomb choice. He had similarly decided against two other alternatives which involved a delay in his making that choice: the alternative of first exploring the possibility of international control, and the alternative of first endeavoring to secure a large increase in conventional arms.

The President did make choices, but a comparison of the choices that he made with those that he did not make reveals clearly the minimal character of his decision. It bears all the aspects of a conscious search for that course of action which would close off the least number of future alternatives, one which would avoid the most choice. Thus the President had affirmed his interest in exploring the feasibility of an H-bomb, but he had said nothing about testing a device if one were fabricated, nothing about producing a weapon if the device were ever tested, nothing about how many weapons would be produced if any were made, nothing about whether such weapons would ever be used if produced, and nothing about the purposes for which such weapons would be employed if ever used.

An explanation for the minimal character of this decision is to be found partly in the views and power of those who shaped the recommendations of the special committee of the NSC, partly in the character of the American governmental process, and partly in the perspectives with which the participants approached the problem of choice. With regard to the first factor, the decisive influence on the outcome of the H-bomb discussion proved to be that of the State Department. It was the Secretary of State who spoke with authority, so far as the President was concerned, with regard to the various foreign policy hopes and fears that had conditioned the views of many of the other participants. It was also the Secretary of State who held the balance of persuasion, so far as the President was concerned, on those issues on which the representatives of the Department of Defense and the Atomic Energy Commission were divided.

The State Department was responsible for rejecting the various alternatives which involved some approach to the Russians with regard to international control before undertaking to accelerate the American H-bomb program. It was, in the opinion of Secretary of State Dean Acheson and those who assisted him on the NSC committee, simply not a time period in which the Russians were interested in serious negotiations. All that could be expected from approaching them would be stalling tactics which might embarrass or perhaps even completely inhibit the American program while leaving the Russians free to push ahead on their own.

The State Department sided with the Secretary of Defense, Louis Johnson, in stressing the importance of not delaying in the effort to discover whether the Super could be made, although the reasoning in the two Departments was somewhat different. A number of planning groups within the Department of Defense had given careful study to the military utility of the Super, and the suggestions that it was in all probability not worth making struck them all as unsound, to say the least. (One member of the GAC was later to observe that the GAC report had the unprecedented effect of unifying the services.) If the judgments of some of the scientists were grounded on a concern for what the world would look like after an H-bomb war, and those of the military on a concern for what it would be like to have to fight an enemy who had a monopoly on such a powerful weapon, those of the State Department representatives reflected a concern for the diplomatic opportunities the Russians would gain from such a monopoly for political blackmail around the Soviet periphery. Most of Acheson's advisers took this possibility very seriously, as did the Secretary himself.

The State Department's strong interest in avoiding the possible consequences of the Russians getting the H-bomb first also led Acheson to side with Defense with regard to the alternatives of reviewing the nation's strategic plans and of securing an increase in conventional weapons before making a choice about the H-bomb program. Acheson was quite willing to undertake such a review concurrently (as was Defense), and, as the Department's work on this review in the spring of 1950 was to show, he was prepared to push hard for an increase in conventional weapons. But he wanted no delay on the H-bomb research.

Lilienthal's arguments for the priority of a conventional weapons program might plausibly have been expected to win him some allies in the

Pentagon, especially in the Army. They did not, largely because they were suspect. The fact that they associated Lilienthal with many of the GAC views led most of the military representatives to discount his argument as a device to delay the H-bomb for what were, really, other reasons. There was, moreover, a history of AEC-Defense disputes over the rôle of the AEC in determination of military requirements that made the defense representatives especially unresponsive to what was considered AEC meddling. President Truman, who had the greatest stake in not dissipating the persuasive lever that the Russian A-bomb gave him if he was later to press for a large-scale rearmament program, was not in the habit of examining the decision immediately before him for its implications for his future choices, and he, too, proved unresponsive to the argument.[5]

The character of the President's decision owes much to the coincidence of State and Defense views. It must also be attributed, however, to one of the major necessities of the American political process: the need to avert conflict by avoiding choice. The distribution of power and responsibility among government elites is normally so dispersed that a rather widespread agreement among them is necessary if any given policy is to be adopted and later implemented. Among the quasi-sovereign bodies that make up the Executive the opportunities to compel this agreement are limited. Agreement must be given, and it will not long be given for nothing. This condition of mutual dependence, the need, as it were, to "build a consensus" that includes one's enemies as well as one's friends, produces a strain toward agreement in the political process that is as fully characteristic of that process as the conflicts in which the participants are continually engaged.

There are many occasions when the necessary amount of cooperation can be achieved only by the device of avoiding disagreement, that is, by postponing the consideration of issues over which long and determined conflicts are certain to be waged. The H-bomb decision is a case in point. The issues which the President did *not* decide were all matters which, if he had endeavored to resolve them, would have pushed one group or another of his subordinates into passionate opposition. The President's position in the political process, however unique, is one which finds him, too, dependent upon the cooperation of others for the success of his policies, and Truman, in this instance, saw no reason to go out of his way to stir up a momentous struggle within his administration. Although he carefully read all the documents involved, from the GAC report through the NSC studies, Truman's own position on the H-bomb issue was the same in January as it had been in October when he first heard of it. If the bomb could be made, he did not see how the nation could afford to

[5] For Truman's decision-making style in this respect, see Richard E. Neustadt, *Presidential Power* (1960), pp. 172–173.

let the Russians get it first, and he was therefore prepared to back whatever program made sense to the Departments concerned.[6]

If the President had no interest in maximizing conflict, neither had the members of the special committee. Acheson was quite aware of the gulf between Lilienthal's views and those of Johnson. Indeed, he was obliged to meet each separately, since Lilienthal's and Johnson's personal relationship had deteriorated to the point where they could not profitably meet together. He was therefore consciously searching for the common ground between them. The military representatives on the NSC working group, for their part, proved not only willing but eager to follow the lead of the State Department and back a recommendation that called for only a determination of the feasibility of the Super. The responsible officials in the Department of Defense had never been among those demanding an H-bomb program on the scale of the Manhattan District. They were determined primarily in their opposition to the views and recommendations that had been advanced by the GAC and some of the Commissioners.

The final factor conditioning the character of the decision was the nature of the perspectives with which the participants approached the problem of choice. The influence of Truman's "one decision at a time" approach has already been noted. The perspective that the military members of the NSC working group brought to the decision was: "what needs to be decided *now*?" What needed to be decided now, in their view, was whether the government would make an urgent effort to determine the feasibility of the weapon. This would settle the immediate problem of defeating those who argued for delaying the program, for one reason or another, and those who argued that the weapon was of insufficient value to justify diverting any more neutrons and talent to pursue it. What need at this point, they reasoned, to stir up discussion regarding the production or use of the weapon. By avoiding these issues, Defense would avoid certain conflict with the AEC and possible conflict with State. Avoiding these issues would also permit the Department to present a unified front to its enemies. The Army and Navy were as persuaded as the Air Force that the nation had to have this weapon, if it was to be had, and that it should be secured before the Russians got it. But there was real potential for disagreement among the services once the issues of production and use became operational. If very large amounts of tritium were to be manufactured, the plutonium foregone might well cut into that which the Army and Navy hoped would soon be available for their use, and at this point the doctrinal

---

[6] The analysis in these two paragraphs owes much to the stimulation of Gabriel Almond, *The American People and Foreign Policy* (1950), pp. 143–145; Neustadt, *Presidential Power*, esp. chap. 3; Roger Hilsman, "The Foreign-Policy Consensus: An Interim Report," *Conflict Resolution* (December 1959); and Samuel P. Huntington, "Strategic Planning and the Political Process," *Foreign Affairs* (January 1960).

issues that divided the services with regard to the relative importance of strategic bombing as compared to other approaches to victory would be certain to arise.

The perspective with which the State Department representatives approached the decision was one that worked, in this instance, to the same end as that of the military but was significantly different in its rationale. Instead of asking "what has to be decided *now*," they asked: "what is the *least* possible that can be decided." The purpose was not so much to avoid conflict as it was to keep as many alternatives open for the future as possible, in order to be in a position to take maximum advantage of new information or changed conditions. It was with this perspective in mind that State drafted the recommendations that the special NSC committee later submitted to the President.

Of the three agencies, the perspective of the Commission representatives came closest to that of "what is the *most* that has to be decided." In fact, both State and Defense representatives had the feeling that the Commission was deliberately holding up the H-bomb program as a means of trying to force them to confront some of the major choices involved. The end result of the tactics of State and Defense, however, was to leave Lilienthal with very little to argue against or to argue for. Rate and scale? No one was urging an all-out program that would entail extremely large fission costs. Military utility? All that was being advocated was an effort to determine whether and at what expense the Super could be made; what better way to treat the question of its military value. Issues of strategic doctrine? State and Defense were to start immediately to review them, and an H-program so modest as not even to specify the conducting of a test could hardly be said to prejudice the results of such a review in advance. International control and the need for conventional weapons? Both of these matters would be given intensive study by the State-Defense review. Lilienthal could not shake the feeling that even in its minimal form the decision would prejudice the opportunity to depart from a big bomb strategy and he so argued to the end, but he had by now the feeling that there was no one at the NSC level with whom to argue.

CONSEQUENCES OF THE DECISION

One consequence of the minimal character of the President's decision was that all the issues on which he had avoided making any choice came back at him again. Thus, by the winter of 1951–1952 the disputes and dissatisfaction regarding the rate and scale of the program had reached such proportions that Air Force officials were considering setting up a weapons laboratory of their own. Similarly, in 1950 new investigations indicated that the tritium required for the Super would be much greater than that estimated at the time of the President's decision. This information, together with the concern that the Korean War might soon develop into all-out war with Russia, served in December, 1950, to reopen the discussion of the military utility of H- as compared to A-bombs and the desirability of incurring significant costs to the fission program in the effort to make it.

The State-Defense review, which became NSC-68, addressed itself boldly to the need to increase America's conventional weapon strength, but it did not really come to grips with the issues of nuclear strategy that had been raised during the H-bomb debate. Thus in December, 1951, when a group of scientists were active in urging the development and production of a large number of A-bombs for tactical use in the ground defense of Western Europe, the rationale for the proposal was in part the search for a strategy that would serve American security without requiring the bombing of cities. Their hope was that if the Red Army could be defeated through the battlefield use of A-bombs, the Strategic Air Command would be relieved of the burden of deterring a Soviet ground attack and free to exercise an option as to whether it struck the Soviet cities and initiated, thereby, an exchange that would bring bombs down on European and American cities as well. The issue of strategic bombing remains partly unsettled even today, as does the issue of last-resort use versus the principle of first use, although the terms are now "city-busting" versus "counterforce" and "second-strike" versus "first-strike" strategies. Similarly, the issue of conventional weapons versus nuclear weapons constituted a major source of debate during the whole of the Eisenhower administration.

The H-bomb decision is hardly the only occasion on which the policy process has produced a minimal decision. The continuous winnowing and worrying of the same old issues is an inevitable consequence of a political process that depends on the voluntary cooperation of independent and competing elites for the formulation and conduct of policy. Major policy changes can, for the most part, be effected only through slow and incremental change. However, as the same issues come around for the second, third, and nth time, they do so in a context slightly altered by the previous minimal choices to which they have been subjected.

The unilateral renunciation idea, for example, could hardly be advanced, after the President's decision, in the same form that the GAC had recommended it in October, 1949. It had to reappear in the form advanced by some other scientists in February, 1950: that the United States pledge itself not to be the first to initiate the use of H-bombs. Similarly, when the international control issue reappeared in November, 1952, with the proposal that the United States not set off its hydrogen device until it had first tried to negotiate an agreement with Russia not to test H-bombs, the conditions of the problem were not quite those that had prevailed when the same proposal was made in the minority annex of the GAC report. In place of an agreement on a device which no one even knew how to make, agreement would now have to be made with regard to a device which one side knew how to make and the other, presumably, did not.

The question might well be asked if there is not a possibility that through a sequence of minor "tactical" or minimal decisions the Government might some day find itself occupying a new "strategic" position without ever having made the major choice to get there. The answer, in a word, is yes, and again the H-bomb decision provides an illustration. On February 24, 1950, scarcely three weeks after the President's decision, the Joint Chiefs of Staff submitted a memorandum to the President requesting "an all-out development of hydrogen bombs and means for their production and delivery." The Chiefs, Johnson reported, wanted to undertake quantity production of the H-bomb as soon as possible.

Once again, Truman summoned the special committee of the NSC, with Sumner Pike now serving in place of Lilienthal, who had submitted his resignation in November, 1949, but had stayed on to see the H-bomb decision through. On March 1st, this committee recommended that, without prejudice to the State-Defense review which was still under way, the research program should proceed to a test stage as soon as possible and that preparation be made for the quantity production of the H-bomb without waiting for the results of the test. The President so ordered on March 10th, and construction began shortly thereafter on the Savannah River reactors.

So far as those who in the fall of 1949 had advocated an intensive H-bomb effort were concerned, the program instituted in the spring of 1950 represented all that they had ever had in mind. The AEC and the Department of Defense had no basic policy disagreements in the design of this program. Although initially skeptical of the military need for an all-out H-bomb program, Pike believed that if a determined effort was going to be made to make an H-bomb a parallel production program should accompany it. Having alerted the Russians to the fact that the United States was urgently trying to make the bomb, it was to be expected that the Russians would move fast themselves and the United States had therefore better do the same.

So far as the Department of Defense was concerned, the memorandum of February 24th was designed to "button down" the decision of January 31st. What had to be decided *now* was the issue of production. Defense had no more interest than Pike in ending up in 1951 or 1952 with a handful of successful test devices and no plant with which to make the weapon. Neither did it want weapons without carriers, although in this respect the February memorandum was somewhat redundant since the January decision had also authorized the Air Force to undertake a carrier program.

Unlike the Department of State, Defense had no interest in keeping the issues of production and use open. The orderly development of military plans and programs required a clear and early decision, not the flexibility and freedom sought by State. The February memorandum was, then, an invitation to State and the AEC to dispute now, if they wished, the decision to produce the H-bomb in quantity and to develop a capability to use it.

For the reasons noted, there was no dispute from the AEC. What of the Department of State and the idea that the decision to determine feasibility left open the decisions to test, to produce, and to use? There was no dispute from the Department of State either, despite the fact that the State-Defense review of strategic plans was not completed. Some of the State Department representatives have advanced the argument that a decision to produce the means for production was not yet a decision to produce the weapon, but this is to stretch words further than reality. A more accurate reading of the reasoning in the State Department would be that, whilst their responsibilities did not dispose them to push for quantity production, they saw no good reason for opposing it. In retrospect, it would seem that Lilienthal's sense of what was afoot on the 31st of January was not mistaken. The minimal decision permitted the Department of Defense to achieve its objectives in two bites and to take its possible opponents one at a time, and while the January decision might not have prejudiced the chances for an unfettered look at the H-bomb program, the March decision certainly did.

One cannot draw a straight line from January-March, 1950 to the present. The decisions here discussed are but two of the points from which one would have to plot the course of American policy from then to now. Whether the subsequent choices with regard to nuclear weapons policy were of the same order as those just described is, so far as the present writer is concerned, an unknown matter. Given, however, the propensity of the political process for minimal decisions, it would be plausible to expect that they were.

The H-bomb decision is essentially a tragic story. The GAC was "right" in sensing that the development of the H-bomb would drive twentieth-century man deeper into the box that he has been building for himself with his military technology, doctrine, foreign policy, and cultural ethos. The GAC was also "right" in asserting that it was a time to stop, look, and think. But the GAC was not alone in seeing the dimensions of the box. It was every bit as apparent to most of the advocates of the Super program. The trouble was that no one had any good ideas of how to get out of the box. Nor are they apparent today.

Basically, the H-bomb decision is a story of international rather than domestic politics. It affords a classic example of the traditional security dilemma. Both the Soviet Union and the United States would no doubt have preferred a world in which neither had the H-bomb. Each, however, wished to avoid a world in which the other had the H-bomb and it did not. Both rushed to make it, and they ended in a worse position than that in which they had begun.

VINCENT DAVIS

The Development of a Capability to Deliver
Nuclear Weapons by Carrier-Based Aircraft

The Navy's post-World War II efforts to develop a capability to deliver nuclear weapons with carrier-based aircraft suggests that crucially important national security decisions sometimes are made without the involvement of senior officials and without serious attention to the international environment which they will affect. The impetus for this particular innovation is to be found in the power of the Navy's organizational routine and the relative parochialism of some of its officers. The officers' success in securing approval for a program to establish the Navy's role in strategic nuclear bombing was due primarily to the organizational environment and astute bureaucratic maneuvering by some of the participants.

The two officers primarily responsible for the proposal for a nuclear bombing capability were aviators, and both had careers which included training in nuclear physics and duty with the wartime Manhattan (atomic bomb) Project. Desiring to give the Navy the capacity to deliver atomic weapons was, for these men, a natural outgrowth of their experiences, and they thought in terms of improving already existing Navy routines and enhancing the position of aviators within the Navy. Their proposal was, in one sense, innovation by inadvertence.

Their project's success required overcoming two sets of obstacles — one within the Navy and the other from the President and Congress. Resistance within the Navy was subdued in large measure because senior Navy officers believed that their service's very existence was threatened by the growing dominance of the Air Force and that the naval aviators represented the best available counter. The potential threat posed by the Soviet Union apparently played little role in their calculations.

Recognizing the need for ultimate approval from the President and the Congress, the project's supporters engaged in a series of bureaucratic maneuvers designed to present these actors with a virtual *fait accompli*. Navy Secretary Forrestal averted Presidential attention from the still-

Abridged by the editors. Reprinted from Vincent Davis, *The Politics of Innovation: Patterns in Navy Cases,* Monograph No. 3, Monograph Series in World Affairs. Denver: The University of Denver, 1967, by permission of the author.

organizing program (and thereby a low-cost negative decision) by deciding that the necessary aircraft modifications did not require White House
approval.

Efforts were made to present the issue to the President and the Congress
not as one of *creating* the necessary capability but rather of merely *improving* an *already existing* capability. Vice Admiral Sherman maneuvered
to make resources available to the project in order to construct a primitive
capability from items then in the inventory. Men, money, and equipment
were marshaled to demonstrate that the Navy already could deliver nuclear
weapons. The Atomic Energy Commission was persuaded to assign a
nuclear weapon to the service and thus to increase the credibility of the
Navy's capability. The outcome was a set of circumstances which had the
appearance to the President and Congress of the relatively marginal decision of continuing and expanding existing missions.

A set of interrelated ideas became widely popular in Congress and in
many other powerful places in the American government and among the
American people at large in the final months of 1945 after the end of
World War II.[1] The first of these ideas was that the American monopoly
on nuclear weapons could and should be used to pose a threat of devasta-
tion against any adversary, with the Soviet Union rapidly becoming the
potential adversary uppermost in most people's minds. Second, it was
believed that this threat would be so effective that it would deter virtually
all kinds of military threats that would concern the United States, although
most people at that time suffered from an extension of the Pearl Harbor
syndrome leading to the conclusion that the next war involving the United
States — if such a war could not be deterred — would begin with an adversary initiating a massive surprise air attack directly against most major
industrial and population centers within the United States. Third, it was
therefore believed that the capability to deliver nuclear weapons was virtually the only military capability that the United States needed. Fourth, it
was believed that the U.S. Air Force was the ideal — indeed, many believed that it was the only — American military service that could and
should possess this capability. Fifth, it was believed that nuclear weapons
had rendered all surface military forces — i.e., armies and navies —
intolerably vulnerable to attack and therefore obsolete.

A number of Navy men consequently foresaw rather quickly that the
Navy would need to accomplish two goals very soon if the Navy were
going to succeed in remaining in existence. First, it would have to be
demonstrated that ships were not excessively vulnerable to atomic attack,

[1] Most of the information presented in this case study is drawn from the author's
book: Vincent Davis, *Postwar Defense Policy and the U.S. Navy, 1943–1946* (1966),
pp. 240–259 *et passim*. For further details and documentation on this case, see the
book.

contrary to a rapidly growing belief in many important political quarters. Second, it would have to be demonstrated that Navy carrier aircraft could be at least as useful and valuable as Air Force bombers for the delivery of nuclear weapons. Secretary of the Navy James Forrestal understood these problems very well — to be sure, he understood them before many naval officers came to these conclusions — and he took a number of steps including the establishment of the Office of Special Weapons (Op-06, as it was called according to the number-coded system for designating the agencies within the overall Office of the Chief of Naval Operations). Forrestal gave to Op-06 broad responsibility for developing not only naval applications of atomic energy but also missiles and other foreseen new technologies.

Op-06 played a prominent role in the "Bikini tests" in the summer of 1946. The Navy men hoped that these tests would achieve the first of their two urgent goals: a demonstration that ships were not excessively or peculiarly vulnerable to atomic attack. Though the tests were in many respects inconclusive, public and political pressure against the Navy eased after the tests (in large part for other reasons) to the extent that the Navy men felt that their service at least was going to be allowed to remain in existence for awhile longer. This seemed to afford time — a breathing space — in which to pursue the second urgent goal: a demonstration that the Navy had the capability to deliver as well as to endure an atomic attack.

By the spring of 1947, however, the Navy had appeared to win most of its points in the longstanding struggle with the Air Force in the so-called "unification of the armed forces" dispute. Most senior naval officers were exhausted from this struggle, and wanted to avoid anything that might further antagonize the Air Force, in order to turn their full attention to a number of urgent but neglected problems within the Navy. Under the category of Navy actions that would surely antagonize the Air Force was any further effort at that moment to develop a Navy capability for delivering nuclear weapons. Accordingly, there was little sympathy in high Navy circles in the spring of 1947 for pushing ahead with such efforts, although such efforts had thus far made very little progress. On the other hand, and at somewhat lower rank levels within the Navy, there were a number of younger officers who did not share the sanguine mood of inter-service disengagement and a narrow focus on internal problems that appeared to characterize the more senior officers. The younger men were more than ever convinced that the Navy's very existence remained at stake, and that the development of a nuclear delivery capability was probably the only thing that could save it. Navy appropriations were going ever downward and the Bureau of the Budget had denied the Navy its request to initiate the so-called "supercarrier" building program in fiscal year 1948. At the same time, the trend of authorizations and appropriations for the Air

Force seemed to foreshadow a long-range commitment by the Congress and the President to make it the dominant service that it wanted to be.[2]

This inter-service acrimony between the Navy and the Air Force (it did not begin in the post-World War II period — on the contrary, it had been a steady fact of life within the American armed forces from the moment that Billy Mitchell returned from World War I in 1919) and the persistent feeling in the Navy for the first few post-World War II years that the Air Force was threatening the Navy's continued existence, served as a backdrop for the efforts of two younger officers between 1945 and 1949 to persuade the Navy to go all-out to develop a nuclear delivery capability with carrier aircraft. These two were Commander Frederick L. "Dick" Ashworth and Commander John T. "Chick" Hayward, and the details of their story will be briefly chronicled later, but first it is necessary to suggest why the term "backdrop" has been cautiously and advisedly used here.

A stronger term than "backdrop" would be "cause," and some might think it accurate enough to suggest that the Navy's fear for its organizational life within the midst of the broader and longstanding Navy–Air Force acrimony did in fact cause Ashworth and Hayward to press their proposal after World War II regarding a carrier nuclear delivery capability. The chronological sequence of events and other relevant details, however, do not precisely support a simple causal connection. Ashworth initiated his efforts in the early fall of 1945 as a direct continuation of his key role in the Manhattan District Project — he was one of the very few naval officers working for the Project — in which he had been significantly responsible for adapting and fitting the first atomic bombs to the large B-29 bombers of the Air Force. But, precisely because he had worked for the Project during most of the war, Ashworth was effectively isolated from most of the swirling storms of controversy between the Navy and the Air Force. Unlike many naval officers of his generation, his earlier career recorded no significant involvement in the overall "unification of the armed forces" conflict within which all Navy–Air Force disputes took place. He therefore undertook his efforts in late 1945 largely innocent of the nature and dimensions of the inter-service quarrel, beginning his work with the straightforward reasoning that the first atomic bombs were fitted to Air Force rather than to Navy planes for largely coincidential rather than inherent circumstances. Given the manner in which atomic bombs could increase the offensive punch of an aircraft, Ashworth merely concluded that they now ought to be adapted and fitted to Navy planes as well as to Air Force bombers. Hayward, who initiated his efforts in the spring of 1947 and to some degree independent of Ashworth's earlier efforts although

---

[2] For further details on the high point of the Navy–Air Force dispute after World War II, see the excellent case study by Paul Y. Hammond, "Super Carriers and B-36 Bombers: Appropriations, Strategy, and Politics," in Harold Stein (ed.), *American Civil-Military Decisions* (1963).

proceeding from them, appeared to be primarily motivated by essentially the same kind of reasoning.

More will be said later about the motivations of Ashworth and Hayward, but at this point the arguments above still leave dangling the important question: What was the relationship between the external environment — that is, the Navy–Air Force conflict and the developing preferences for a national military strategy then emerging among most key government policymakers — and the actions of Ashworth and Hayward? The answer seems to be that this backdrop, while it did not *cause* Ashworth and Hayward to proceed as they did in the first place, served to create a climate of thinking in the Navy that made the Navy generally more receptive to proposals for innovation than might otherwise have been the case. In other words, the need to ensure the Navy's survival encouraged many Navy people to look with favor on new ideas that might be of help in this cause. Looked at in a broader frame of reference and at a higher level of generalization . . . it may be suggested that any circumstances prompting the Congress to legislate a build-up in the strength of any part of the armed forces — and such circumstances have generally occurred when there was a growing national perception of some other nation as an increasingly threatening adversary — have tended to encourage a heightened degree of receptivity within the Navy to proposals for innovation in weapons systems. But, returning to the case in hand, the conviction persists in this author's mind that the innovation advocates themselves — Ashworth and Hayward — would doubtless have done precisely as they did even if no Air Force had existed and the Navy was therefore the only service that could have entertained the possibility of using nuclear weapons. For Ashworth and Hayward the original and overriding stimulus was the thought that atomic bombs would give the Navy an enhanced capability for carrying out missions that the fast carrier task forces had extensively conducted during the war. In short, these two officers were mainly concerned to give the Navy an improved ability to carry out old missions that they thought had been well established for the Navy by the war, although Hayward was later one of the large number of naval officers swept into the swirling vortex of the Navy–Air Force dispute and he accordingly was not averse to using aspects of this dispute to help him sell his proposed innovation within the Navy.

The capability to deliver a nuclear weapon from carrier-based aircraft depended on a suitable combination of three basic components: a ship, a plane, and a bomb. As for the ship that would be required, the Navy Department had already initiated planning for the envisaged new "supercarriers" before World War II was over — a new class of aircraft carriers that could accommodate a range of new and much heavier carrier airplanes that the Navy also had in mind. But in the fall of 1945 when Commander Ashworth began his efforts to persuade and help the Navy to acquire this capability, the supercarriers were still little more than a gleam in the eye, the nature of atomic bombs then in existence also seemed to be a fixed factor for the short-range future, and Ashworth was not sure what kind of airplanes might be available and adaptable. The first step he took, therefore, was a visit to the Navy's Bureau of Aeronautics in Washington to learn about existing or soon-to-be-available new carrier aircraft that could be adapted to carry and deliver an existing nuclear weapon.

Commander Ashworth possessed virtually unique technical qualifications in the Navy for the kind of role he was about to play. Because he had achieved a brilliant academic record as a midshipman at Annapolis with special distinction in physics, he was given opportunities in his duty assignments in the 1930's that allowed him to maintain his contact with developments in the sciences — particularly physics. Therefore, when the Manhattan District Project was created at the outset of the war as a War Department activity assigned to the Army's Corps of Engineers but actually designed to draw on the capable people in all of the armed forces, Ashworth was one of the very few naval officers who were qualified. He and Navy Captain W. S. "Deke" Parsons were thus the only two regular naval officers who were assigned to the Manhattan District for most of the war and who had important major responsibilities at Los Alamos.[3] The first crude atomic bombs had to be armed by hand immediately before release from the bombing aircraft over the target, and the man who did this job was called the "weaponeer." Parsons was the weaponeer for the first atomic bomb dropped on Hiroshima, and Ashworth performed the same role a few days later for the second atomic bomb dropped on Nagasaki. As soon as the war ended and he was released from his duties with the Manhattan District, Ashworth was assigned along with Parsons to the Navy's new Office of Special Weapons (Op-06). He immediately became the Officer in Charge of Naval Vessel Tests for the Bikini test series in 1946, as part of his responsibilities in Op-06 and, when the Atomic Energy Commission was created in 1947, Ashworth became the first Executive Secretary of the AEC's crucially important Military Liaison Committee. In short, he was a young officer as of the end of World War II who had already enjoyed a brilliant early career not only because of his competence in nuclear physics but also as a naval aviator, and he seemed destined for a further career of continuing distinction. That promise was fulfilled; at the time of this writing he is Vice Admiral Ashworth serving in one of the Navy's choice sea duty billets as Commander of the U.S. Sixth Fleet in the Mediterranean. But, as young Commander Ashworth in October of 1945, he had been back in Washington only a few weeks fol-

---

[3] Parsons was promoted to rear admiral just after the war ended and was named as the first Director of Op-06, the Office of Special Weapons. He died of cancer at a relatively young age several years later, one of the most respected and well-liked among the Navy's younger flag officers.

lowing release from his duties with the Manhattan District and was just getting into his new duties with Op-06 at a time when the whole future of the development of atomic energy and weapons was uncertain, pending Congressional and Presidential decisions.

When Ashworth went to the Bureau of Aeronautics in October of 1945 to inquire what kind of existing or soon-to-be-available airplanes the Navy possessed that might be suitable for a special configuration for delivering existing atomic bombs, he learned that in mid-1945 BuAer had asked the North American Aviation Company to initiate the development of a heavy new attack bomber for use aboard carriers; it was called the AJ. He met and talked with Captain Joseph N. Murphy (later, Rear Admiral Murphy, in charge of the Navy's Aviation Test and Development Center at Johnstown, Pennsylvania). Murphy was BuAer's expert on planes of this type, and Ashworth recruited Murphy to his little personal project. In specific, he persuaded Murphy to accompany him on a visit to the North American Aviation Company's main plant then located in Los Angeles. The trip took place in early 1946, and by that time the AJ was already in the mock-up stage. Ashworth's hope was that the AJ could be sufficiently redesigned so that its bomb compartment could carry the Mark 4 "Fat Man" atomic bomb — the same primitive nuclear weapon that had been used on Nagasaki. Working only from his memory of the exact size and shape of the bomb (secrecy was still so tight at that time that Ashworth was unable to obtain the blueprints and other detailed figures on the bomb although he himself had been a key figure in developing it and then dropping it on Nagasaki), he and Murphy were quickly convinced that the AJ could be redesigned around this requirement. With Murphy's support he sent a letter through channels intended for Secretary Forrestal's signature, asking President Truman to authorize the Navy to proceed on this. But several key officers in the channel of communications, including BuAer's Vice Admiral Arthur Radford (later a full Admiral and Chairman of the Joint Chiefs of Staff in the Eisenhower Administration), had a number of reservations about the Navy's possible acquisition of a nuclear delivery capability and they stalled the Ashworth letter on its way to Forrestal. When it finally did reach the Secretary, Forrestal decided that he possessed the authority to approve the required modifications in the design of the AJ without the President's concurrence — at that stage leaving open the question whether the President would ever actually approve assigning atomic bombs to the Navy. Armed with this Secretarial endorsement, Ashworth then succeeded in getting clearance for North American to obtain the exact specifications of the Mark 4 bomb, and in June of 1946 the Navy let a contract to North American to put the AJ into limited production redesigned as Ashworth wanted it.

The AEC shortly after it was created in early 1947 went to work to design and build improved atomic bombs (i.e., smaller in size but with more powerful warheads). The original Hiroshima "Little Boy" bomb yielded only 14 kilotons. The Nagasaki "Fat Man" bomb around which the new AJ aircraft had been redesigned was somewhat more efficient, yielding 20 kilotons, but it weighed 10,000 pounds (most Navy carrier airplanes did not themselves weigh that much at that time) and was a huge 60 inches in diameter. New weapons on the drawing boards would yield in the 100-plus kiloton range and would be as small as 22 inches in diameter. Such devices would be far more suitable for carrier aircraft, but they were still a substantial way from being in the operational hardware stage in early 1947.

By early 1947, however, Commander Ashworth was quickly becoming heavily involved in his new duties with the Atomic Energy Commission and was therefore unable to give much more time to his personal project to help persuade the Navy to develop a nuclear delivery capability. It was at this point that Commander John T. Hayward decided to pick up the crusade and to make it his personal mission, apparently without any collusion or specific arrangement with Ashworth although he and Ashworth were old friends with remarkably similar career patterns. Hayward, the product of a not exactly affluent family in the New York City area, had once been a bat-boy for the New York Yankees baseball team in an effort to help finance his high school education. But it was not until many years later, after he had graduated with honors from Annapolis and had largely completed his doctoral studies in nuclear physics that he was finally awarded his high school diploma on an ex post facto basis. In his early Navy career and during the first part of World War II he acquired a reputation as one of the Navy's most skilled (and most decorated) aviators. He was assigned to the Manhattan District Project late in the war, and, although his role was not as significant as Ashworth's, he nevertheless assumed important responsibilities for the Manhattan District. Early in 1947 he was named to the key new position of Plans and Operations Director of the Armed Forces Special Weapons Project (AFSWP), an agency within the new AEC. Thus, he and Ashworth were both in crucial AEC jobs in 1947, although Hayward apparently found more spare time to devote to the task of helping the Navy to develop a nuclear delivery capability than Ashworth could manage in the 1947–1948 period. Thus, Hayward's early career in the Navy as of the end of World War II, like Ashworth's, was quite distinguished and seemed to portend a further career of growing distinction. As in Ashworth's case, that promise was fulfilled. By 1960 Hayward had already served as the first three-star admiral in the new position of Deputy Chief of Naval Operations for Research and Development (DCNO for R&D), with Ashworth as one of his immediate assistants, and in 1961 he was widely publicized as a leading candidate for the Navy's number one job for a uniformed officer, Chief of Naval Operations. At the time of this writing he is Vice Admiral Hayward in the coveted position of President of the Naval War College.

When Hayward picked up the ball from Ashworth in early 1947, his first action was to go see Vice Admiral Forrest Sherman, then the Deputy Chief of Naval Operations for Plans and later the Chief of Naval Operations. Sherman enjoyed a reputation in the Navy as one of the most able aviation admirals, one of the most astute thinkers, one of the most sophisticated practitioners of bureaucratic politics, and one of the few senior naval officers generally receptive and responsive to new and innovative proposals. Hayward requested that Sherman go to Congress specifically to ask for an endorsement of the Navy's plans for the AJ aircraft and more generally for approval of the Navy's overall plan for developing a nuclear delivery capability. Sherman told Hayward that this would be politically unrealistic, in view of the growing Congressional faith in the Air Force's guarantee of its exclusive talents in the strategic bombing field. This, of course, had been a primary claim in the Air Force as far back as Billy Mitchell, but it was never a claim that the Navy aviators had accepted. Although the naval aviators had not been given much opportunity to develop their capabilities in the 1920's and 1930's when the Navy was dominated by the "battleship admirals," they nevertheless had achieved a few things. For one example, the B-17 "Flying Fortress" used so widely as an Air Force bomber during World War II had originally been designed by and for the Navy but was then turned over to the Air Force when it proved unsuitable for naval uses. The naval aviators also recalled that, although Air Force aviators got the assignment, the first strategic bombing attack on Japan during the war was the famous "Doolittle Raid" launched from a Navy carrier. For these and other reasons the Navy fliers felt that many kinds of strategic bombing missions were just as much within the Navy's field of established competence as within the preserve of the Air Force.

Sherman and Hayward both shared these convictions that were characteristic of naval aviators, but Sherman gave Hayward a little lesson about how to do business with Congress. In response to Hayward's request that Sherman get from Congress a general endorsement of Navy plans within the area of nuclear weapons delivery systems, Sherman told him that Congress might conceivably buy the Navy idea but only after the Navy had first demonstrated on its own initiative a clearcut capability — although perhaps quite crude at the outset — for long-range strategic bombing with airplanes that could carry then-existing atomic bombs. It was a rich-get-richer-and-poor-get-poorer theory of Congressional largesse, but it was probably not inaccurate in this case. Sherman therefore concluded that the Navy would have to use ships and planes already on hand to devise some sort of system, no matter how primitive originally, for delivering atomic bombs already in existence, before it would be realistic to ask the Congress to approve Navy plans for better ships and planes especially designed for this purpose.

Hayward accepted Sherman's advice, and immediately made a request of him: assign to Hayward several of the Navy's huge P2V antisubmarine patrol bombers, which were used on land fields, and Hayward would figure out some way to fly them on and off of aircraft carriers already in existence. Sherman managed to work out a way to grant this request, and in addition, gave Hayward permission to round up a team of top Navy men to join the project.

The P2V's were about as much intended and designed for carrier use as were the DC-6 commercial airliners then in use, but they were nevertheless the smallest planes possessed by the Navy at that time with bomb bays large enough to hold the huge World War II atomic bombs that were still the only nuclear weapons in the nation's inventory. Hayward calculated that a P2V could take off and land on the deck of a *Midway*-class carrier (the largest carriers that the Navy then owned) with a few inches of clearance between the starboard wingtip and the superstructure "island" at the right side of the deck *if* extremely careful flying could be achieved and *if* there were no untoward circumstances. Even so, the plans would have to be greatly modified, and this was the next step in Hayward's project. Each of the twelve planes assigned to him was stripped of all expendable equipment to bring it down to a minimum weight, and tailhooks were installed for carrier landings. The bomb bays were modified to match the configuration of the "Little Boy" Hiroshima bombs. The flight decks of the three *Midway* carriers were considerably strengthened to support the vast weight of these planes and their bombs. Throughout all of this work Hayward also had to start training special assembly teams, because 48 hours were required to put together a "Little Boy" — and this had to be done immediately before installing the weapon in the aircraft just before sending it on its mission.

By early 1948 Hayward and his group were ready to start actual flight tests and on April 27, with himself at the controls, one of the 60,000-pound P2V's took off from the 986-foot flight deck of the U.S.S. *Coral Sea* (one of the three *Midway*-class carriers). Landing and takeoff techniques were modified and practiced again and again during the rest of that year but, by December, Hayward had proved his concepts sufficiently that the Navy Department allowed him to commission his development group under the nonedescript name Composite Squadron (VC-5). He was the first commanding officer and, appropriately, Ashworth was his executive officer. In January of 1949 a part of VC-5 was split off and formed into a second squadron, VC-6, with Ashworth as the commanding officer. Admiral Sherman meanwhile succeeded in getting the Atomic Energy Commission to reserve one or two "Little Boy" bombs (some people have said that the national inventory of atomic bombs at that time came to a total of three) for issue to one or both of these Navy squadrons in the event of a national emergency. By the end of 1948 it was therefore possible to say that the Navy had achieved its capability — no matter for the time being how crude — to deliver an atomic bomb with planes from a regular operational carrier squadron. There were, it is true, a number of important episodes during the following year. For example, in September of 1949 just before the "supercarriers vs. B-36 bombers" and the "revolt of the admirals" controversy reached its peak in the ever intensifying conflict between the Navy and the Air Force, Hayward and his project team undertook an incredible publicity stunt designed to prove to Congress and other important doubters that the Navy had in fact achieved its capability. The episode featured a day on the *Midway* demonstrating the Navy's P2V capabilities for a select audience of highly prominent guests. The guests included Secretary of Defense Louis Johnson, Secretary of the Air Force Stuart Symington, Secretary of the Army Gordon Gray, Secretary of the Navy Francis Matthews, and Chairman of the Joint Chiefs of Staff Omar Bradley. At the end of the improbable day Hayward flew these guests back to Washington from the carrier, which was located about a hundred miles off the Atlantic coast, in one of the P2V's, with Secretary Johnson sitting in the co-pilot's seat so that he could get a close-up view of the takeoff from the carrier. He also would have had a close-up view of the crash if the takeoff had been unsuccessful and, given the record of crashes as Hayward and his group had tried to perfect the techniques for using the huge lumbering planes on the carriers, a perfect flight was by no means assured. The chances in favor of wiping out virtually the entire high command of the U.S. military establishment in one quick moment did not appear altogether offset by the chances of making a favorable impression on this group of Navy-critical VIP's, but a flair for the dramatic gamble was a part of the Hayward style. . . .

Several things are worth noting in this case. First, Ashworth and Hayward were relatively young officers at a middle-rank level in the Navy, senior enough to have acquired a Navy-wide perspective and concern but not senior enough to have acquired the kind of cautious restraint often accompanying positions at the very top in the uniformed Navy, where perspectives and concerns cutting across the entire Washington bureaucracy may make a man more sensitive to problems than to opportunities. This attitude of cautious restraint characterized Vice Admiral Arthur Radford and a number of senior officers who emerged as a kind of high-level horizontal alliance opposing the efforts of the low-level horizontal alliance composed of Ashworth, Hayward, Murphy and their associates. Radford and his associates had grown skeptical about the so-called "flush-deck supercarrier" that was a part of the vision entertained by the younger group, and Radford and the older group were also not sure that the Navy ought to press ahead with the effort to get into the atomic bombing business at a time when the Navy already had its hands full in persistent old conflicts with the Air Force.

Ashworth, Hayward, their friend Captain Murphy and others who sided with their efforts possessed technical expertise relevant to their innovative proposal that was not generally shared by their fellow officers, and they had been fortunate in receiving duty assignments that gave them some extra leverage and additional expertise relevant to their purposes. Ashworth's and Hayward's assignments in connection with the new Atomic Energy Commission were particularly useful in keeping them abreast of developments in the overall national atomic energy policy area. Their reputations as distinguished naval aviators were also an asset in the particular cause that they were promoting. Although at the outset they did not consciously join forces to promote their shared cause — on the contrary, they at first worked independently each on his own initiative — their work converged to the extent that they and such supporters as Captain Murphy constituted a tacit horizontal political alliance at the middle-ranks level.

This middle-ranks alliance formed around Ashworth and Hayward was not making notable progress, however, until it acquired a strong vertical dimension in the form of crucial high-level support from Admiral Sherman and, behind Sherman, the tacit but strong support of Forrestal. As early as September of 1945 Forrestal and other key Navy spokesmen had testified in public before a Congressional committee that the Navy planned to develop a capability to deliver nuclear weapons with carrier-launched aircraft.[4] It seemed little more than political rhetoric at the time, to counter Air Force claims of an exclusive mission in the field of atomic bombing, but it did coincide with Forrestal's strong determination to build the postwar Navy around carrier aviation, and everyone in the Navy knew that Forrestal was moving in this direction. It was therefore unnecessary for Forrestal to come out openly on the side of the Ashworth-Hayward alliance, because they were in effect moving to implement something that he had much earlier declared to be a Navy goal. Sherman was therefore the key man, facilitating what amounted to an end run by Ashworth and Hayward around Radford's blocking position. Radford, as the Chief of BuAer, would have been the logical man to assist the Ashworth-Hayward alliance, but, because he was playing the game in the other direction, they needed Sherman to run their interference for them and to obtain for them the men and planes necessary to move ahead with their project.

[4] See Davis, *op. cit.*, pp. 194–195 *et passim*.

It is also worth noting that the Ashworth-Hayward alliance did not attempt to justify their cause in terms of any new grand strategy. There was no great strategic vision, no talk of a revolution in naval warfare, no talk of a revolution in warfare in general. As far as Ashworth and Hayward and Sherman and Forrestal and most other naval aviators were concerned (Forrestal too had been a Navy flier, in World War I), the revolution in naval warfare had already taken place in World War II, had been successfully won, and they were merely taking the next logical steps The revolution in naval warfare, as the aviators saw it, was the departure during World War II from the old conviction that had dominated the Navy for decades before the war, i.e., the conviction that navies existed primarily to fight other navies, to the new view that ships at sea were merely launching platforms for projecting military force against an adversary wherever the adversary might be located on land or on sea within the range of carrier aircraft.

The Ashworth-Hayward alliance did not engage in the kind of sophisticated analyses that characterized the late 1950's and 1960's when new weapons systems were under consideration. Those later analyses sought to predict what new weapons systems might do to international politics, power balances, and possible counterweapons produced by adversaries. Rather, these key members of the alliance justified their cause primarily in terms of simply a better way to perform a Navy mission that they had argued for throughout a period well before World War II and which they felt had been clearly established within and for the Navy during the war itself. In this sense the Ashworth-Hayward alliance was primarily an action in response to factors internal to the Navy; stated more specifically, it was part of the consolidation of the naval aviators' triumph as they assumed dominance of the postwar Navy in place of the battleship admirals who had dominated it for almost half a century before the war. It was in this light that it was possible to suggest a few pages earlier in this monograph that the naval aviators would doubtless have sought a capability to deliver nuclear weapons even if the Air Force and the Navy conflict with the Air Force had not existed. But those factors did have a bearing on the success or failure of the Ashworth-Hayward alliance even if they were not a part of what stimulated them to undertake their project.

The Navy conflict with the Air Force, as suggested earlier, helped the Ashworth-Hayward alliance in the sense that many naval officers who under other circumstances might not have favored innovative proposals were willing to tolerate these new ideas if they would help the Navy to survive in the face of the Air Force challenge. Moreover, the fact that the Air Force had attempted to embody the new consensus national strategy emphasizing nuclear bombing had assisted the Ashworth-Hayward team not only in making the Air Force threat seem more dangerous to their fellow naval officers but also in providing a potentially favorable climate in the Congress and in the White House if these advocates could demonstrate that naval carrier planes were at least as useful as Air Force bombers in nuclear strike missions.

There was little or no specific regard to any particular adversary in the thinking and arguments of the Ashworth-Hayward team within the Navy. Naval officers, primarily due to prodding from Secretary Forrestal, gradually came to view the Soviet Union as the primary new international menace during the period beginning in early 1945 (actually, late 1944) and carrying into 1947 when Hayward began his efforts in behalf of a Navy nuclear delivery capability. But neither Hayward nor other naval officers argued for this capability primarily or even secondarily in terms of a response to the Soviet danger. Looking back from the perspectives of the 1960's, it seems curious that this argument was not strongly used by the Ashworth-Hayward team. The Soviet Union possessed a negligible navy in the immediate post-World War II period and was not greatly dependent on maritime commerce. Therefore, if the U.S. Navy was going to play a major role in American responses to the Soviet threat, that role in the late 1940's would necessarily have had to be constructed around a capability to penetrate the Soviet land mass with long-range strikes using carrier aircraft. Forrestal understood this as early as late 1944, but substantial numbers of naval officers did not really begin to understand it until several years later.[5] Members of the Ashworth-Hayward alliance accordingly based their arguments for a nuclear delivery capability mainly on the simple and broadly general proposition, derived from the far-ranging and diverse uses of carrier aircraft in World War II, that anything which improved the long-range striking power of the fleet was vitally necessary for the Navy and would be of potentially great use against almost any adversary.

In summary, only in the sense of the general proposition noted above did the Ashworth-Hayward alliance pay any explicit attention to international factors in analyzing and arguing the case for a Navy nuclear delivery capability. Their thinking and their efforts were primarily an outgrowth of the Navy's experiences in World War II, not an explicit and carefully formulated response to new threats foreseen in the postwar world. The bitter conflict between the Navy and the Air Force was neither the stimulus for nor a major initial part of the arguments for the Ashworth-Hayward proposal, but the conflict related to the eventual success of the Ashworth-Hayward proposal within the Navy in that it encouraged naval officers to be receptive to new ideas — especially a new idea that seemed in keeping with the major emphasis in defense policymaking in the Congress and in

[5] *Ibid.*, pp. 100–118, 219–225 *et passim.*

the White House. In all of these ways it seems fair to conclude that the Ashworth-Hayward proposal was far more a response to considerations internal to the Navy and internal to the national policymaking environment in Washington than a response to explicitly recognized and analyzed factors in the international political environment.

MORTON H. HALPERIN

The Gaither Committee and the Policy Process

The Gaither Committee serves as an illustration of a Presidential commission that backfired. Ostensibly, Eisenhower's objective in appointing the Gaither Committee was to obtain a fresh and unbiased report on continental defense. However, the formation of the Gaither Committee was, at least in part, a maneuver by the Eisenhower Administration to substitute the symbolic action of study by outside experts for the fiscal action it felt it could not afford. The Gaither Committee, from Eisenhower's perspective, got completely out of control. Because the Committee members were independent of the bureaucracy, they felt relatively free both to broaden the scope of their mandate and to pursue their investigation to a final conclusion no matter how disruptive of the status quo. The President's subordinates within the bureaucracy who had lost in previous policy disputes found a new conduit for the renewed expression of their views and positions. Eisenhower thus was confronted with expensive, controversial recommendations he did not want from the prestigious and potentially influential committee he had created.

The members of the Gaither Committee were so convinced of the importance of their recommendations that they themselves embarked on a series of bureaucratic maneuvers designed to enhance the prospects for implementation of their report. Some of their activities suggest their awareness of the fact that commissions composed of outsiders are themselves virtually impotent to change policies and actions. However, their over-all analysis and strategy imply a certain naiveté regarding the operations of the national security bureaucracy. Their report was the product of outsiders who had given minimal attention to the "bureaucratics" of the problem.

The Committee appears to have decided that the changes sought re-

Reprinted by permission from *World Politics*, 13, 3 (April, 1961), pp. 360–384. Copyright © 1961 by Princeton University Press.

quired any one or some combination of three components: (a) support from the President's subordinates in the national security bureaucracy, (b) public awareness of the dangers, and (c) Presidential commitment on behalf of their recommendations. The structure of their report virtually doomed their first objective to failure. Unlike most National Security Council papers, which represented carefully negotiated agreements among the bureaucratic participants, the Gaither Committee's recommendations were unconstrained by past bureaucratic understandings and took no account of the diverse needs of the actors. As a result, every important participant found something in the report which was objectionable and the Committee's recommendations stirred no support within the national security bureaucracy.

The Committee members concentrated their efforts on winning Presidential support, perhaps under the common — but mistaken — assumption that this was a necessary and sufficient condition for changing policy and behavior. But the Committee apparently understood Eisenhower's view of his problems and goals no better than it did the interests and objectives of the bureaucratic participants below the President: its recommendations explicitly called for sharply accelerated defense spending at a time when Eisenhower was seeking to constrain expenditures.

The Committee members next engaged in a series of maneuvers to get a version of their report made public. This may have reflected their acceptance, at face value, of Eisenhower's assertion that the public would not accept the burden of increased spending, or possibly the Committee intended to change the domestic political consequences for the President, thereby making it more expensive for him if he failed to act. In any event, the domestic political interests of the President and his advisers, particularly in view of the upcoming Congressional election, led to strong and largely successful efforts to suppress official publication.

The history of the Gaither Committee and its report offers instructive lessons in bureaucratic maneuvers designed to change national security policy and to influence outcomes: a group of outsiders were free to discover inadequacies in the defense posture but, largely because they were outsiders, were unable to exert influence on the foreign policy bureaucracy.

Despite the extensive government apparatus for policy-making on problems of national security, the American President in the postwar period has, from time to time, appointed groups of private citizens to investigate particular problems and report to the National Security Council.[1] Some of these groups have performed their task without the public's ever becoming aware of their existence; others have in one way or another come to public

[1] The first such Presidential Commission was appointed by President Truman in January 1948 to make a general survey of foreign intelligence activities (see U.S. Senate, Subcommittee on National Policy Machinery, Committee on Government Operations, *Organizational History of the National Security Council*, 86th Cong., 2d sess., 1960, p. 10).

attention. Among the latter are those which have become known under the names of their chairmen: Finletter, Gray, Paley, Sarnoff, Gaither, Draper, Boechenstein, and Killian. President Truman made use of such groups, and the variety of tasks for which they were appointed grew steadily during the Eisenhower Administration.[2]

Some analysts have seen in this development an indication that the government is exploiting all possible sources of policy recommendations, and have praised the use of such private groups.[3] Others have argued that their use reflects the bankruptcy of the NSC procedure.[4] There is agreement that the committees have often made imaginative and valuable recommendations, but the degree to which such advice can and should be fitted into the Executive decision-making process has been the subject of some dispute.

Perhaps the most publicized and controversial of such groups was the Gaither Committee, which, in 1957, presented a report on the nation's defense requirements. The Report remains a classified document, but the effects of the Committee and its work continue to be mentioned in the nation's press. The Gaither Report was probably the most general study of the nation's defense effort to be undertaken by an *ad hoc* civilian group. Much of its contents and the events surrounding its drafting and presentation have become public, shedding a good deal of light on the national security decision-making process.

In this article I will attempt to trace and analyze the series of events connected with the Gaither Report. While explicating an important political incident, I will use the Gaither episode to generate hypotheses about the use of civilian study groups, about the Executive decision-making process, and about the role of information in the public debate about national security policy.

I. Drafting the Report

In the spring of 1957 the Federal Civilian Defense Administration (FCDA) submitted a report to President Eisenhower recommending that the government spend 40 billion dollars over a period of several years to erect shelters which would provide protection against the blast-effect of nuclear weap-

---

[2] See the following articles by former NSC staff members reprinted in U.S. Senate, Subcommittee on National Policy Machinery, Committee on Government Operations, *Organizing for National Security, Selected Materials*, 86th Cong., 2d sess., (cited hereinafter as *Selected Materials*): Sidney W. Souers, "Policy Formation for National Security," p. 32; Robert Cutler, "The Development of the National Security Council," p. 58 and Gordon Gray, "Role of the National Security Council in the Formation of National Policy," p. 65.

[3] See the articles by Bowie, Cutler, and Gray in *ibid*.

[4] See the articles by Kissinger, Nitze, and Jackson in *ibid*.

ons.[5] The FCDA proposal was discussed by the National Security Council, and the President ordered a study to be made by an *ad hoc* committee of private citizens. The sense of the NSC meeting had been that before the Administration considered spending a sum equal to its annual military expenditure, it should investigate other possible uses of the 40 billion dollars. It was argued that if the government were prepared to increase spending for defense, it should explore the advantages of increasing its active defense effort.

The Eisenhower Administration had come to rely on the use of private consultants and this was the type of situation in which an *ad hoc* group was likely to be most helpful. An alternative would have been to set up a committee of the interested Executive agencies, but such a group would either have been unable to agree or would have drafted a "compromise" split of the proposed 40 billion-dollar expenditure. A committee of private citizens might be expected to take an unbiased look at the situation. The FCDA proposal was too serious to be rejected out of hand and it was too expensive to be adopted. Formation of an expert committee was an effective way of handling the proposal.

Reflecting the NSC discussions, the directive asked the committee to evaluate the shelter-building proposal as part of a study of American active and passive defense capability. It anticipated that the committee would find it necessary to explore other aspects of national security as they impinged on the nation's defense effort. The committee was titled the Security Resources Panel of the Science Advisory Committee to the FCDA, but in fact it was directly subordinate to the NSC and its members were considered NSC consultants.

The President, acting with the advice of his Special Assistant for National Security Affairs, Robert Cutler, called in H. Rowan Gaither, Jr., a West Coast lawyer and chairman of the boards of the Ford Foundation and The RAND Corporation, and asked him to head the Committee. Robert C. Sprague, an industrialist and an expert on continental defense, was asked to serve as co-director of the study. Together they recruited an eleven-man panel which included experts on various aspects of military policy.[6] In addition to Gaither and Sprague, it included William C. Foster, a former Deputy Secretary of Defense and an expert on defense organization; James A. Perkins and William Webster, who had studied civil defense extensively; and, as staff director, Jerome Wiesner, an expert on weapons systems evaluation who is now President Kennedy's science adviser. Sup-

---

[5] *New York Times,* December 21, 1957, p. 8:4; Chalmers M. Roberts' article in the *Washington Post and Times Herald,* December 20, 1957, reprinted in the *Congressional Quarterly Weekly Report,* XV (December 27, 1957), 1328–1330, and in the *Congressional Record,* 85th Cong., 2d sess., 1958, p. 858 (Roberts citations hereinafter refer to the *Congressional Quarterly Weekly Report*).

[6] The membership of the Gaither Committee and its advisory panel was released by the White House and printed in the *Congressional Record, loc. cit.*

plying additional technical competence for the panel were Robert C. Prim and Hector R. Skifter, and rounding out the group were Robert Calkins, John J. Corson, and James Baxter, who provided some of the expertise of the social scientist, particularly in economics and history.

The panel met briefly in the spring of 1957 and set in motion a series of technical studies by the large scientific staff which it had brought together.[7] Much of this work was completed over the summer, and the Committee members arrived in Washington in the fall to devote full time to a study of defense policy. At this point the Committee appointed as special advisors Colonel George A. Lincoln of West Point and Paul H. Nitze, a former head of the State Department Policy Planning Staff and now Assistant Secretary of Defense (International Security Affairs).[8]

No public announcement had been made of the existence of the Committee as it set to work in the old State-War-Navy Building on the study which was, in a few months, to come to public attention as the Gaither Report.[9] The first decision taken by the group was to broaden the scope of its inquiry to cover the whole range of defense problems facing the country.[10] This is a phenomenon which seems to typify such *ad hoc* studies. In the absence of agreed American policy on most aspects of national security, it is difficult for any group to evaluate a proposal in any one area without considering other problems. In this case the panel had been asked in effect how the United States could best spend an additional sum for continental defense. But clearly defense is only one part of the deterrence strategy and hinges on how well other parts function. It might very well be true that the greatest payoff for continental defense would come, for example, from investing in ballistic missiles. In the absence of any priority plans for spending additional sums for various systems, the Committee was forced to study the whole problem. In addition, the members were so prominent and had such definite opinions on the problems of American military policy that it was natural for them to decide to use the rare opportunity of drafting a paper for the NSC to present their views on a wide range of topics.

Just as the Committee was beginning its study, Gaither was taken ill and was hospitalized for several weeks.[11] Direction of the study fell to

---

[7] A part of this staff was supplied by the Institute for Defense Analyses (IDA). See *IDA Annual Report II*, March 18, 1958, pp. 6–7.

[8] Also serving as advisors to the panel were Albert C. Hill, General James McCormack, and Edward P. Oliver of The RAND Corporation.

[9] The only leak regarding the Gaither study had come in August when Stewart Alsop reported that the President had asked Gaither to study the possibility of employing new technological means of defense against atomic attack. He noted that the Committee was attracting "top level" talents, but he warned that "it remains to be seen whether anything solid comes of Gaither's assignment, in the present national mood of complacency" (*New York Herald Tribune*, August 26, 1957, p. 12).

[10] Interview with Gaither, *New York Times*, December 25, 1957, p. 24.

[11] *Ibid.*, p. 24.

Sprague and Foster, who became co-directors.[12] Each member of the Committee took responsibility for a particular section of the Report, but they all met frequently as a group to discuss each other's work. The Committee drew on the technical studies which had been prepared for it and had clearance to reports of the Defense Department and other agencies concerned with national security.[13] It also held frequent sessions with high military officials, including the Joint Chiefs of Staff. In addition, it consulted with a number of private experts on national security policy and with quasi-public experts, including members of The RAND Corporation.

An advisory panel for the Gaither Committee, appointed by the President, met periodically with the Committee members to fill in gaps in their expertise. Among the panel's eleven members were retired military officers; Frank Stanton, the president of CBS; two prominent Republican financiers, Robert Lovett and John J. McCloy, now head of the United States Disarmament Agency; and I. I. Rabi and Ernest O. Lawrence, two of the nation's top scientists.[14]

As the Committee members sifted through this mass of material, it became clear to them that the top echelons of the government did not fully appreciate the extent of the Soviet threat as it was described by the Pentagon and the CIA.[15] With a real sense of urgency, the Committee set to work to draft a summary report based on the individual studies prepared on various aspects of military policy. Just as the Report was being completed, the nation was shaken out of its complacency by the Soviet Union's announcement on October 4, 1957, that it had launched Sputnik. This event gave the Committee greater hope that the Administration would accept its recommendations.[16] A week later the Report was finished and presented to the President for discussion at an NSC meeting.[17]

II. Presenting the Report

On November 7, 1957, the President presided over one of the largest NSC meetings in history. Over forty people gathered in the White House for the presentation and discussion of the Gaither Report. In addition to

[12] *Ibid.*, December 21, 1957, p. 8.

[13] Press release by Presidential Press Secretary James Hagerty, *ibid.,* December 22, 1957, p. 4.

[14] The other members of the advisory panel were Admiral Robert C. Carney, General James H. Doolittle, James B. Fisk, General John E. Hull, Mervin J. Kelly, and James R. Killian.

[15] Testimony of Dr. James R. Perkins in U.S. Senate, Subcommittee on National Policy Machinery, Committee on Government Operations, *Hearings,* 86th Cong., 2d sess., 1960, Pt. II p. 293 (cited hereinafter as *Jackson Hearings*).

[16] Roberts, *loc. cit.*, p. 1328.

[17] Perkins testimony, *Jackson Hearings*, Pt. II, p. 294.

the dozen top officials who regularly attended, the civilian secretaries of the services and the Joint Chiefs of Staff joined members of the Committee and its advisory panel and other top government officials. Almost everyone present had read the Report in the three weeks between its completion and the meeting, and chief interest was focused on what the reaction of the President would be.

The briefing on the contents of the Gaither Report was opened by Sprague, and in turn Wiesner, Foster, Corson, and Webster came up to the podium to discuss different sections of the Report. Graphs and charts were used extensively to illustrate the points that it made.

The Report presented to the NSC was in many ways not a typical NSC document. Unlike most NSC papers, the Gaither Report did not result from a compromise of the views of a number of departments and agencies. It did not represent an amalgam of considerations, including those of domestic finance. Furthermore, it was not bound by previous government policy decisions and specifically was not within the framework of budgetary limitations laid down by the President. The Report was thus able to call for measures which the Committee thought to be necessary and to present them in a dramatic fashion to the President and his top advisers. It deviated from government policy in a number of ways, but most fundamentally in the estimation of the danger facing the country and the amount of money which the United States should spend for defense.[18]

The Report began with an analysis of Soviet and American capabilities. It compared the economic situation in the two countries, pointing out that the Soviets devoted 25 per cent of their GNP to defense, while the United States invested only 10 per cent. This meant that both countries were spending the same absolute amount and suggested that, given the faster Soviet growth rate, Russia would soon be devoting much larger sums to defense.[19] Tables were presented comparing Soviet and American industrial capability and military forces, and projecting relative strength into the future on the basis of present growth rates.[20] The Report contrasted

---

[18] The text of the Gaither Report has not been made public. This account relies entirely on published sources. It draws heavily on Roberts' article (see n. 5 above), about which Senator Clark declared on the Senate floor: "The importance of the article arises from the fact that it is well known by many Members of this body, including myself, that this newspaper account accurately and clearly states the major findings and conclusions of the Gaither Report" (*Congressional Record, loc. cit.* p. 859). The information in the Roberts article has been supplemented and checked with news and news analysis articles in the *New York Times* and *Herald Tribune*, as well as columns by Arthur Krock, James Reston, Drew Pearson, and Stewart Alsop, and various magazine articles. In addition, speeches by members of the Committee and its Advisory Panel after the Gaither Report was presented, and their testimony at the Jackson Hearings, provided confirmation of the major points made in the Report.

[19] Cf. testimony by Robert Sprague, *Jackson Hearings*, Pt. I, p. 50.

[20] Roberts, *loc. cit.*, p. 1329.

America's armed forces of two and one-half million men equipped and trained only for general nuclear war with the larger Russian army supplied with weapons for both nuclear and conventional warfare.

After drawing this rather grim picture of comparative capabilities, the briefing moved on to an analysis of the situation and a series of policy proposals. The major danger facing the country, according to the Committee, was the vulnerability of the American strategic force.[21] The briefing dwelt at length on the problems of maintaining an effective second-strike force. It was pointed out that what must deter the Russians was not the force which the United States had, but the force which was capable of surviving an all-out Russian attack. The vulnerability of SAC was stressed. The planes of America's strategic force were exposed and concentrated in a way that made it extremely unlikely that they could survive a nuclear attack. The Committee warned that by the early 1960's, when Russia had an operational ICBM, she would be capable of destroying the American retaliatory force.[22]

The Gaither Report argued that the United States must give overriding priority to the development of an invulnerable second-strike force. It urged that for the short run everything possible be done to enable SAC to survive an attack.[23] It also called for an acceleration of the IRBM program.[24] For the longer run the Report urged that the missile production program be greatly accelerated. It warned that there was little value in acquiring missiles which were difficult to fire and which were exposed to enemy bombing. It urged therefore that American missiles be hardened and dispersed.

The Report laid the greatest stress on this point, reflecting the feeling of the Committee members that top Administration officials did not have a complete understanding of the problem of effectively deterring a Russian strategic strike.[25] The Report stressed the need to look at the problem in terms of the vulnerability of the force rather than its initial destructive capacity.[26] This was the problem which most bothered the Committee and

[21] The Committee's proposals on strategic vulnerability were heavily influenced by a classified RAND report prepared under the direction of Albert Wohlstetter. For a discussion of the RAND report, see Joseph Kraft, RAND: Arsenal for Ideas," *Harper's*, CCXXI (July 1960), 71–73.

[22] Alsop, *New York Herald Tribune*, November 25, 1957, p. 18, and *idem*, November 23, 1957, p. 1; Claude Witze, "Classified Report Says Soviets Can Neutralize SAC by 1960," *Aviation Week*, LXVII (December 2, 1957), 28.

[23] Such a program would presumably include dispersal of SAC, some planes in the air, and a ready alert for the rest of the command.

[24] Drew Pearson, "Gaither Report Release Sought," *Washington Post and Times Herald*, December 18, 1957.

[25] Cf. the testimony by Sprague, Baxter, and Perkins in *Jackson Hearings, passim*.

[26] For an unclassified but well-informed discussion of the problem of maintaining a stable strategic balance, see Albert Wohlstetter, "The Delicate Balance of Terror," *Foreign Affairs*, XXXVII (January 1959), 211–234.

gave its members the feeling that the government was dangerously under-estimating the gravity of the Russian threat.

The Committee Report reflected the feeling that the vulnerability of the American strategic striking force was *the* great danger facing the country, but it also indicated that this was not the only military danger. The Report advised that, once the United States had recovered its full retaliatory capacity, the military develop a capacity to fight limited wars.[27] The establishment of a nuclear balance would mean that local aggression would be the likely form of warfare. The Committee found that the American military force was unprepared to engage in limited wars. The Report suggested that the Middle East and Asia were the most likely areas in which local wars might erupt and it discussed the importance and the problems of keeping a war limited.[28] The second recommendation of the Committee was therefore that the United States train and equip its forces for conventional local warfare.

The Gaither Committee had considered the FCDA proposal to spend 40 billion dollars for blast shelters, and while conceding that such shelters would save some lives in the event of war, it assigned a very low priority to such construction. In making policy proposals to the NSC, the Committee ranked its suggestions, giving top priority to the need to revitalize the strategic force and improve America's limited-war capability. In the civil defense field, the Report gave first priority only to a comparatively modest proposal to spend several hundred million dollars in the following few years for research on various aspects of shelter construction and other non-military defense measures.[29] The Committee assigned secondary priority to a proposal to spend approximately 22 billion dollars for the construction of radiation (rather than blast) shelters. It was anticipated that any construction program would follow the research phase.

Foster briefed the NSC gathering on the defence reorganization proposals contained in the Gaither Report. He urged that the military command structure be organized to place primary reliance on joint and specified commands. The Report urged that a joint limited-war command be established. It suggested that most planning and research be carried on directly under the Joint Chiefs of Staff. Orders, it was argued, should go from the Secretary of Defense through the Joint Chiefs to the commands, and the services should concentrate on logistics and training operations.

---

[27] "Leak — and a Flood," *Newsweek*, December 30, 1957, p. 14; *New York Times*, November 23, 1957, p. 8; *New York Herald Tribune*, November 23, 1957, p. 1.

[28] Krock, *New York Times*, December 22, 1957.

[29] The Committee's analysis of the civil defense problem reflected the influence of Herman Kahn of the RAND Corporation. The alternative civil defense proposals sketched here are elaborated in *Report on a Study of Non-Military Defense*, RAND, R-322-RC, July 1, 1958.

The Report also urged that the layers of Pentagon committees be eliminated and the Secretary of Defense be given his own military staff.[30]

Although it was only forty pages long,[31] the Gaither Report also touched briefly on other subjects. It urged the government to increase spending for basic scientific research and stressed the importance to military policy of other areas of foreign policy. It also discussed the potential immediate impact on the American economy of the proposed increase in defense spending. The Report did not provide an exact estimate of the cost of all of its recommendations, but it indicated the need for rapid increases in the military budget to about 48 billion dollars per year in the 1960's.[32]

The entire NSC paid close attention during the presentation of the Report. The President had a copy of the written text balanced on his knee and alternated between following along in the Report and watching the speaker.[33] When the briefing was concluded, a general discussion followed. The President thanked the group and indicated that he was impressed with the arguments contained in the Report and wanted to implement them. However, he expressed a nagging fear that the American people would not be willing to pay the bill.[34] For reasons which I shall explore in the next section, none of the department heads present was willing to give support to the proposals as a whole. In fact, Secretary of State John Foster Dulles spoke out strongly in opposition to the Report's recommendations. Support came from some members of the Committee's advisory panel. John J. McCloy and Robert A. Lovett, both prominent members of the American financial community as well as former Defense Department officials and active Republicans, argued that the American economy could afford to pay for the vitally needed measures outlined in the Report. They predicted that the people as a whole and the business community in particular would support the President if he urged increased spending for defense.[35]

The session broke up without any sense of the meeting having been arrived at. According to standard NSC procedure, the Report was formally sent to the departments concerned for their information and comments. In general, with reports of this nature nothing further happens. The reports are either used or rejected at the departmental level and the consultants

[30] That the Gaither Report included proposals on defense reorganization was indicated by Defense Secretary McElroy (*New York Times*, January 22, 1958, p. 15). The proposals were spelled out by Foster in a speech before the Student Conference on United States Affairs (SCUSA), IX, printed in *Proceedings of the Conference*, West Point, N.Y., 1957, p. 9.

[31] Cutler testimony in *Jackson Hearings*, Pt. IV, p. 594.

[32] *New York Times*, December 21, 1957, p. 8.

[33] Charles J. V. Murphy, "The White House since Sputnik," *Fortune*, LVII (January 1958), p. 230.

[34] Roberts, *loc. cit.*, p. 1328; *Newsweek*, December 30, 1957, p. 14.

[35] Roberts, *loc. cit.*, p. 1328.

return to their civilian jobs. However, in the case of the Gaither Report, there were significant further developments which throw considerable light on the policy process. Some of the Committee members made a determined effort to have their proposals implemented and at the same time they joined with others in seeking to have the Gaither Report made public.[36]

III. The Effect of the Report

Even in the early stages of their work on the Gaither Report, the members of the Committee were aware of the great discrepancy between the danger which was being described to them by the CIA and the military, and the sense of complacency at the top levels of the government. At least some of the Committee members became convinced that they had an obligation to make a strenuous effort to obtain the implementation of their proposals. Even as they worked on the Report, they were concerned with how best to proceed to secure its adoption by the Administration. In discussions with top civilian and military leaders, the Committee sought support for the types of recommendations it was considering. In the office of the President it attempted to make clear the nature of the problem facing the country.[37]

In seeking to influence national security policy-making at the Executive level, the Committee was dealing with a complex and bewildering decision-making process. It was clear, however, that in seeking to influence policy in a number of agencies, the most direct route was through the President. Some days before the NSC presentation, several of the most prominent members of the Committee and its advisory panel, including Gaither (who had just rejoined the group), Sprague, and Foster, met with President Eisenhower to discuss the content of the Report.[38] Again, at the NSC meeting the Committee members had several hours in which to present him with their views.

The difference in tone of two speeches delivered by the President suggests that these briefings had at least a momentary impact on his thinking. On the evening of the NSC meeting of November 7, he gave the first of two scheduled addresses on the state of the nation's security.[39] The tone of this speech was one of reassurance. President Eisenhower stressed the present military strength of the United States:

> It is my conviction [he declared], supported by trusted scientific and

---

[36] Some of the Committee members, including Gaither, returned to their civilian jobs and took no part in the campaign discussed below.

[37] Sprague testimony, *Jackson Hearings*, Pt. I, pp. 49–51.

[38] Murphy, "White House since Sputnik," p. 230; Cutler testimony, *Jackson Hearings*, Pt. IV, p. 594.

[39] Reprinted in *New York Times*, November 8, 1957, p. 10.

military advisers, that . . . as of today the over-all military strength of
the free world is distinctly greater than that of the Communist countries.

• • •

It misses the whole point to say that we must now increase our expenditures on all kinds of military hardware and defense. . . .[40]

The President recognized the need "to feel a sense of urgency," but he
was determined that the United States not "try to ride off in all directions
at once." The speech stressed the need to support a sound economy and
to keep down the level of defense expenditure.

A week later in Oklahoma City the President delivered the second part
of his talk, entitled "Future Security." [41] While this speech did not directly
contradict the first, its tone was completely different. He discussed again
the problems of balancing expenditures and receipts and keeping the
budget low, but this time he asserted: ". . . now, by whatever amount
savings fail to equal the additional costs of security, our total expenditures
will go up. Our people will rightly demand it. They will not sacrifice security
to worship a balanced budget." [42] The President recalled one of his statements of the previous week, but made a significant addition: "I assure you,
as I did last week, that for the conditions existing today they [U.S. military
forces] are both efficient and adequate. But if they are to remain so for
the future, their design and power must keep pace with the increasing
capabilities that science gives both to the aggressor and the defender." [43]

In spelling out the strategic requirements for the future, the President
showed most clearly the effect which the Gaither Report was having, at
least momentarily, on his thinking. He seemed to be recognizing that the
country *did* have to ride off in many directions at once. The first requirement was, he declared, to maintain a nuclear retaliatory force such that an
attack by the Soviets "would result, regardless of damage to us, in their
own national destruction." In addition, forces were needed to deal with
any form of local aggression, and home defense had to be improved.
And, the President continued, more money must be spent on SAC dispersal
and an acceleration of the missile program. "The answer," President
Eisenhower asserted, "does not lie in any misguided attempt to eliminate
conventional forces and rely solely upon retaliation. Such a course would
be completely self-defeating." [44]

The members of the Gaither Committee quickly realized that the in-
corporation of some of their ideas into a Presidential speech did not mean

[40] *Ibid.*
[41] Reprinted in *ibid.*, November 14, 1957, **p. 14.**
[42] *Ibid.*
[43] *Ibid.*
[44] *Ibid.*

that their proposals were about to be adopted by the Administration. The President might forward the Report to his writers with the suggestion that they use some of its ideas, but he was not likely to impose policy decisions on the operating agencies. Under the staff system used by President Eisenhower, policy proposals had to come up through the regular channels before he would act upon them. The Gaither Report had not sufficiently impressed or convinced the President for him to seize the initiative. He was not only reluctant to upset routine staff procedures but also not eager to embark on the large-scale spending programs urged in the Report. The President was anxious to maintain his image as a man of peace and had no wish to approve a major expansion in the American military forces. He sought from his advisers assurance that the problems were being met rather than programs for new action.

After the failure of the initial attempt to alter Aministration policy, the Gaither Committee, led by Foster, considered and to some extent implemented three courses of action. These were: further attempts to reach the President directly, efforts to enlist the support of operating agencies, and measures to arouse the American public and elite groups to the dangers facing the country. The operating agencies were perhaps the most likely allies of the Gaither Committee, and the failure to gain the support of a single department suggests the built-in forces for stability in the process.

The Gaither Report had recommended across-the-board increases in spending. While assigning some priorities, it had not made any really hard choices among weapons systems. Here was seemingly a document which might have been acceptable to everyone. Why then was no support forthcoming?

The Gaither Committee had taken seriously the question which, in effect, had been put to it: how the government should spend vastly increased sums of money. It was clear, however, to the operating agencies who were at the time wrestling with limitations imposed by the Budget Bureau that the "pie" was, in fact, not going to get bigger. The military services, the AEC, and the FCDA could only look upon the Report as a proposal to redivide the pie.[45] As such, they were naturally highly suspicious of its recommendations. The civil defense proposals caused the most difficulty. The FCDA was unwilling to accept a report which rejected its major proposal for blast shelters and which accepted implicitly the notion that civil defense spending should be weighed against possible military uses of the same funds. The military services were unwilling to support a plan which recommended a further splitting of the military-spending pie by including

---

[45] In considering the reaction of Executive agencies, it should be kept in mind that the Administration placed very tight restrictions on access to the Report. For example, NATO Supreme Commander General Lauris Norstad did not see it (*New York Herald Tribune,* January 8, 1958, p. 2).

civil defense spending. The Report had given secondary priority to a 20 billion-dollar spending program within the next few years. The military could not have been expected to advocate such spending when their assumption was that it would come out of their funds.

In terms of individual proposals, the Committee members found some support within the services.[46] The Army, for example, was eager to endorse the proposals for a limited-war force. However, the individual recommendations were not new and only provided some additional leverage for the service viewpoints.[47] In addition, the services were reluctant to endorse a paper which suggested that they had been derelict in their duty of keeping the country militarily strong. Although the Army would continue to argue for larger limited-war forces, it would never be ready to agree that it was not in a position to win a limited war. Similarly the Air Force was not willing to concede that its forces were as vulnerable as suggested by the Gaither Report. The military services could not admit the extensive deficiencies outlined by the Report. The formal comment of the Joint Chiefs was reportedly that the study did not contain any new proposals, but was "largely a summation and endorsement of steps under way or under consideration." [48]

The military services were also reluctant to commit themselves to what was in effect a new, more "rational" method of splitting up the defense pie. Under the "political" method the services could pretty well predict what their per cent of the defense budget would be. There was no way to tell just what budget-making by outside experts would look like. There is a general distrust among operating officials of this type of advice. In discussing the weakness of private expert committees, Nitze explicated one of the problems facing the Gaither group: "The most serious of these disadvantages is the possibility that the committee may be too far removed from executive branch responsibility to be fully effective. Those members

---

[46] The recommendations of the Gaither Committee were broken down into groups. The agencies concerned prepared papers on these proposals and they were discussed at a series of NSC meetings. See Cutler testimony, *Jackson Hearings*, Pt. IV, p. 594.

[47] Cf. General Maxwell Taylor, *The Uncertain Trumpet* (1959). Taylor, in discussing policy papers drafted for the NSC while he was Army Chief of Staff, makes it clear that most of the strategic concepts and recommendations of the Gaither Report were discussed frequently by the Joint Chiefs and the NSC before and after the Gaither Report was presented, although he does not mention the Report itself.

[48] *New York Times*, December 21, 1957, p. 8. This phenomenon clearly needs greater study. The strait jacket which has confined the military chiefs, preventing them from admitting extensive weakness even while pressing for more funds, has surely been an important restraint on the flow of information to the White House and to Congress. A comparison of the statements to Congress made by Army Chiefs of Staff on, for example, the adequacy of our capability for limited war and the statements they make after retiring indicates vividly the reality of this phenomenon. (I am indebted to Paul Hammond and Louis Kushnick for bringing this point to my attention.)

of the executive branch who are actually responsible for carrying out policy
. . . feel, perhaps rightly, that such groups are out of touch with the real
problems with which the officials, in the end, must always deal. In any
case, it is obvious that the committee, once its report has been presented,
is in a poor position to help fight its recommendation through the decision
stage. *Both of these difficulties characterized the reception of the Gaither
Report* two years ago. . . ." [49]

This fear of civilian expertise and the inability of the Gaither group to
put any influence back of its recommendations combined with the motives
discussed above to explain the failure of administrative agencies to support
the Gaither proposals. There were, however, two men in the government
who might have been expected to take the over-all view necessary to
endorse the recommendations of the Report. For vastly different reasons,
however, neither the Secretary of State nor the Secretary of Defense was
prepared to do so. Defense Secretary Neil McElroy viewed his job as that of
an administrator. He refused to be drawn into strategic discussions or
debates about the level of defense spending. He felt that he had been
appointed because of his ability to run an organization efficiently and
refused to deal with subjects about which he had no expertise.

Secretary of State John Foster Dulles was in no sense reluctant to discuss military matters. He had in fact become closely associated with the
policy of massive retaliation which the Report indirectly, but clearly,
challenged. Dulles was not prepared to endorse a program which called
for large-scale spending and which committed the United States to local
defense in the peripheral areas. In addition he felt that a shelter program
would frighten America's allies. He feared that the Gaither proposals
would use funds that otherwise could be used to increase foreign aid.[50]
Dulles' influence with the President on foreign affairs suggests that his
opposition must have been a major stumbling block in the efforts to
convince the President to implement the Gaither proposals. Both the
Treasury and the Budget Bureau were of course opposed to the Gaither
recommendations because of the large-scale increase in spending proposed. With the Secretaries of State and Treasury and the Director of the
Budget opposed to them and the Secretary of Defense refusing to express
an opinion, the Gaither group members had to try either to influence the
President directly [51] or to arouse American public opinion.

Following the presentation of their Report, the members of the Gaither

---

[49] Paul H. Nitze, "Organization for National Policy Planning in the United States,"
Selected Materials, p. 168 (italics added).

[50] Cf. Dulles' testimony before the Senate Foreign Relations Committee, *New
York Times*, January 10, 1958, p. 1.

[51] For an excellent discussion of the kinds of problems that President Eisenhower
would have faced in seeking to impose the recommendations of the Gaither Report
on the operating agencies, see Richard Neustadt, *Presidential Power* (1960).

Committee discussed possible courses of action among themselves and with experts on American foreign policy and defense. Following these weeks of informal discussions, a dinner meeting was held in Foster's Washington home in mid-December. Joining Foster were Frank Stanton and Paul Nitze, who had worked on the Gaither Report, and others, including Laurance Rockefeller and Elmo Roper.[52] Vice-President Richard Nixon attended on his own initiative but, according to one report, with the approval of the President.[53] Part of the evening was taken up with a further briefing of the Vice-President. In addition, Foster made two proposals to the group. He suggested that it aim at publication of a "sanitized" version of the Gaither Report.[54] He also urged the formation of a committee which would seek to convince the American people of the need for greater sacrifices in light of the grave Soviet threat. Foster argued that the release of the Report was essential to mobilize public opinion to support new programs. At the same time that it was trying to arouse public opinion, Foster suggested that his proposed committee continue the fight within the Executive for the implementation of the Gaither proposals.

In the discussion that followed, a general feeling was expressed of the need to do whatever was possible to alert the Administration and the people. Although Foster's proposal to set up a committee was received with much sympathy, the consensus was that the crucial problem lay with the President. If President Eisenhower could be convinced of the need to take bold action, he would have no difficulty arousing the American people. On the other hand, without the leadership of the President, it was felt that no group, whatever its composition, could reach the public.[55] Other members of the Gaither Committee shared this viewpoint. In testifying before the Jackson Committee, Sprague expressed his own opinion and in effect summed up the feeling of the meeting at Foster's home. In answer to a question as to what could be done to arouse the public,

[52] *New York Times, December* 11, 1957, p. 8; *New York Herald Tribune,* December 11, 1957, p. 1.

[53] *New York Times,* December 12, 1957, p. 11.

[54] *Ibid.,* December 13, 1957, p. 26.

[55] This feeling that the President constituted the key to the problem was reflected in a report by Samuel Lubell on a field trip made soon after Sputnik II. Lubell reported that "one thing I found especially striking was how closely the public's reactions corresponded to the explanatory 'line' which was coming from the White House. Relatively few persons repeated the criticisms which were being printed in newspaper editorials or were being made by members of Congress or by scientists. In talking about Sputnik, most people tended to paraphrase what Eisenhower himself had said. . . . The public generally tended to follow the President's lead. In no community did I find any tendency on the part of the public to look for leadership to anyone else — to their newspapers or radio commentators, to Congressmen or to men of science. Nor, with some exceptions, could people be said to be in advance of the President, or to be demanding more action than he was." (Samuel Lubell, "Sputnik and American Public Opinion," *Columbia University Forum,* I (Winter 1957, p. 18.)

Sprague replied: "Senator, a citizen like myself, *or a group of citizens*, can do very little about this. I think there is one man in the United States that [*sic*] can do this effectively, and that is the President. I do not think there is anybody else." [56] Sprague's testimony reflected the bewilderment of the Foster group as to the position of the President. The Gaither Committee members were not sure whether the problem was to convince the President that their analysis was correct, or to get him to act on the basis of the information which he now had. As Sprague explained it: "I believe . . . that the danger is more serious than the President has expressed himself to the American public. I do not know whether he feels this or whether he does not. But I do not believe that the concern that I personally feel has as yet been expressed by the President to the American public. This is a complicated matter." [57]

The gathering at Foster's home broke up without a firm decision on whether or not to form a committee, but with a commitment on the part of those present to work for release of the Gaither Report to the public.[58] The efforts of members of the Gaither Committee [59] to have their Report released coincided with the demand of other groups.

IV. The Public Debate

The Gaither Committee had drafted its Report for the President without Congress' or the public's being aware of its existence. When the Report was presented to the NSC on November 7, 1957, the *New York Times* simply stated that an extraordinary meeting of the Council had been held and that members of the President's Science Advisory Committee were in attendance.[60] On November 9 the *New York Times* indicated that a special committee headed by Rowan Gaither had presented a report.[61] The contents of the Report leaked out slowly to the press. On November 23, 1957, the *Herald Tribune* published a fairly complete account of the contents of the Gaither study [62] and on December 20 the *Washington Post and Times Herald* ran a story by Chalmers Roberts which

---

[56] *Jackson Hearings*, Pt. 1, p. 55 (italics added).

[57] *Ibid.*

[58] Ultimately no committee was set up reflecting the view expressed by Sprague. A leak to the press about the gathering and its purpose made further action by the group more complicated and, in addition, embarrassed the Vice-President.

[59] Not all of the Gaither Committee joined in this effort. Gaither, for example, told a news conference that "a report like this to the Security Council and to the President is never made public. If all or part of it is made public, it would be an exception, and the first time such a thing was ever done." (*New York Herald Tribune*, December 25, 1957, p. 3).

[60] *New York Times*, November 8, 1957, p. 10.

[61] *Ibid.*, November 9, 1957, p. 11.

[62] *New York Herald Tribune*, November 23, 1957, p. 1:8.

contained the most accurate report of the study's contents that had appeared to date.[63] As the nature of the Report and its sober conclusions came to the attention of the public,[64] a number of groups called for release of the official text. Thus, when the group meeting in Foster's home decided to press for publication of the Report, they were echoing the demand of others.

The group's desire to have the Report released coincided with a similar request from Congressional Democrats and some Republican Senators, including Styles Bridges.[65] The debate over making the Report public attracted wide interest in the press and among the attentive elites. As Senator Clark made clear on the Senate floor, those demanding release of the Report were not concerned with learning its contents. Anyone with this goal had only to turn to one of several newspaper and magazine accounts. To make this task easier, Clark inserted in the *Congressional Record* the Roberts article, and assured the readers of the *Daily Record* that it was accurate.[66]

Congressional Democrats, particularly those Senators who had been advocating higher defense spending, viewed the Report as a vindication of their views. The declaration by a group of distinguished citizens, including a number of prominent Republicans, that the Eisenhower Administration had failed to act in the face of a grave danger to the survival of the country was excellent political ammunition. The Democrats had been trying to paint a picture of an inactive President failing to respond to the challenges of the time. Since it would be difficult to publish the Report without creating the impression that its findings were valid, release of the Report by the Administration itself could not fail to bolster this image, with important political advantages for the Democratic Party in the next Congressional election. Apart from the partisan political advantage which they saw in publication of the Report, the Senate Democrats were concerned about the state of the nation's defenses. The Preparedness Subcommittee was conducting extensive hearings and an official request for the Report came from Senator Lyndon Johnson, the majority leader and chairman of the Subcommittee. The Johnson Subcommittee was briefed on the substance of the Report [67] but nevertheless pressed for its publication, apparently feeling that it would aid its case regarding the need for the nation to make greater sacrifices.

The Senate debate over release of the Gaither Report followed the

[63] See n. 5 above.

[64] The leaks apparently came from both within the Administration and from members of the Gaither Committee.

[65] *New York Herald Tribune*, December 13, 1957, p. 1; *Washington Post and Times Herald*, December 21, 1957, p. 1.

[66] *Congressional Record, loc. cit.*, p. 858.

[67] *New York Times*, December 23, 1957, p. 6.

presentation to Congress of the President's budget message. The proposed spending for national defense had greatly disappointed those who held the views outlined in the Report. In his State of the Union Address on January 9 the President had declared that the United States must act "wisely and promptly" to maintain the capacity to deter attack or defend itself, and he had added: "My profoundest conviction is that the American people will say, as one man: No matter what the exertions or sacrifices, we shall maintain that necessary strength." [68] But while the budget message had called for some increase in spending, it was not enough in the opinion of those demanding release of the Gaither Report. The budget called for modest acceleration of the missile and SAC dispersal programs but, while recognizing the need for conventional forces and civilian defense, it called for a curtailment of these programs to save part of the amount needed for the expanded activities. It specifically ruled out a substantial increase in the defense budget. [69]

Once again there was a sharp contrast between what was included in the President's speech and the actual policy position of the Administration. Any possibility that the President would have overruled his subordinates on this issue was eliminated by Eisenhower's stroke. He was not working during most of the period between presentation of the Gaither Report and the submitting of his budget to Congress.

Senators and Representatives urging release of the Report felt it would strengthen their hand in trying to convince the Congress to increase defense expenditures substantially and to generate pressures on the Administration to spend the money which was appropriated. As Senator Clark declared on the Senate floor: "That [Gaither] report should have caused this Administration to have a far greater sense of urgency than it presently gives any indication of having." [70] He urged a reading of the Roberts article in order to "have an understanding of the very critical situation which confronts our country, and which I must say in all good conscience the President's budget does so little to remedy." [71]

Echoing this Congressional demand for release of the Report were newspapers and magazines which argued that the public was entitled to read this study by a group of distinguished citizens. [72] It was pointed out that various distortions had appeared in print, including one that suggested

---

[68] Paul Zinner (ed.), *Documents on American Foreign Relations, 1958* (1959), p. 2.

[69] Portions of the budget message relating to national security are printed in *ibid.,* pp. 15–23.

[70] *Congressional Record, loc. cit.,* p. 860.

[71] *Ibid.*

[72] See, for example, the editorials in the *New York Times,* December 13, 1957, p. 26; *New York Herald Tribune,* December 23, 1957, p. 16; and *Washington Post and Times Herald,* December 30, 1957, p. 14.

that the Committee had advocated preventive war.[73] Only the full publication of the Report would stop the rumors and give the people an opportunity to evaluate this Report which, it was stressed, had been written by an extremely able group of private citizens. Members of the Gaither Committee pressed for publication of the "sanitized" version of the Report which Foster had offered to prepare. Publication would indicate that the Administration took the Report seriously and was prepared to implement it. It also would would be an effective first step in what they hoped would be a Presidential campaign to arouse the American people to meet the crisis facing the nation. Those within Adminstration who favored more spending for defense were pressing for release of the Report for the same reasons and leaked its contents. Private citizens concerned about the nation's defense effort were also seeking publication of the Report.

Despite these intense efforts, the President refused to yield. The official Administration position was set forth in a letter to Senator Johnson: ". . . From time to time the President invites groups of specially qualified citizens to advise him on complex problems. These groups give this advice after intensive study, with the understanding that their advice will be kept confidential. Only by preserving the confidential nature of such advice is it possible to assemble such groups or for the President to avail himself of such advice."[74] To publish this Report, the letter concluded, would violate the privacy of this relation and also the standing rule that NSC documents are not made public.[75]

Earlier, at a press conference, the President had made it clear that he considered the Report confidential and had no intention of making it

---

[73] In his column in the *New York Times* on December 20, 1957, p. 26, Arthur Krock inferred from what he knew about the Gaither Report that it recommended a "first strike" strategy and speculated that this was why the Report was being kept secret. Two days later he was able to write that "it is authoratatively stated that this point was not included in the report" (*ibid.*, sec. 4, p. 3:2).

The Communists sought to exploit this and other distortions of the Gaither Report. On December 26, Moscow and Peking broadcasts monitored in London charged that the "authors of the report are proponents of a limited war which would be fought with all types of modern nuclear weapons" (*New York Times*, December 27, 1957, p. 4). Then Soviet Premier Bulganin in a note to President Eisenhower on March 7, 1958, wrote that "the American press had been discussing for the past few weeks the idea of 'preventive war' against the USSR which, according to such well-known American commentators as Hanson Baldwin, Arthur Krock, and Drew Pearson, was advanced in a secret report to the National Council of Security [*sic*] by the so-called Gaither Committee" (*ibid.*, March 8, 1958, p. 2).

[74] *Ibid.*, January 23, 1958, p. 10.

[75] This was not an unimportant consideration. It undoubtedly heavily influenced the President's Special Assistant for National Security Affairs, Robert Cutler, who argued against the release of the Report. Cf. Robert Cutler, "Organization at the Policy Level," *General Electric Defense Quarterly*, II (January-March 1959), pp. 12–13. For a general discussion of this problem, see Francis E. Rourke, "Administrative Secrecy: A Congressional Dilemma," *American Political Science Review*, LIV (September 1960), pp. 691–693.

public.[76] A Presidential press release noted simply that "the report is, of course, a highly classified document." [77] James Reston, analyzing the Eisenhower Administration's refusal to publish the study, termed the Report an indictment of Eisenhower's policy and noted that publication would have weakened the President as well as the Republican Party.[78] The desire to withhold political ammunition from the Democrats undoubtedly played a part in the decision not to release the Report, as did the need to maintain the tradition of privacy for such reports. Probably more important, however, was the President's oft-repeated fear that the American people, if panicked, would ride off in all directions and demand spending which would be unwise and would damage the economy.[79] Thus, after Sputnik the President moved to calm the nation and ultimately rejected the fundamental assumption of the Gaither Report that the country was in grave danger. To take the unusual course of releasing the Report would imply that it presented an accurate picture and would increase pressures, which the Administration was fighting, to step up defense spending substantially.

The Eisenhower Administration continually denied that the Gaither Report showed the United States to be weak at the time the document was being written. It asserted that the government was already dealing with the problems outlined in the Report and that adequate measures were being taken on the basis of this and other reports to assure the nation's survival.[80]

Although they failed to have their Report released, many of the Gaither Committee members spoke out in an effort to alert the nation to the imminent dangers. Foster, in particular, appeared before numerous groups to argue the need for greater sacrifices. Sprague told the Jackson Committee that he had spoken to thirty or forty groups since serving on the Gaither panel, but, he continued, "I do not think this is very effective. I have done all that I can." [81] After a while the Committee members gave up the effort to arouse the public, with the realization that they could not compete against the President's words of reassurance.

V. CONCLUSION

The dispute about releasing the Gaither Report was a short episode in the continuing political debate over American defense strategy and the level of military spending necessary to implement the foreign and military

[76] *New York Times*, January 16, 1958, p. 14.
[77] *Ibid.*, December 22, 1957, p. 4.
[78] *Ibid.*, January 22, 1958, p. 10.
[79] *Ibid.*, December 22, 1957.
[80] *Ibid.*, December 29, 1957, p. 1.
[81] *Jackson Hearings*, Pt. 1, p. 56.

policies of the United States. While the Report did not substantially alter the course of the struggle, it helped to bring some of the issues and pressures more sharply into focus. The fight over the release of the Report reflected almost exactly the larger dispute over defense spending. The American political process may be viewed as a struggle between clusters cutting across governmental structure, political parties, and interest groups and forming and reforming around various causes or specific proposals.[82] The defense debate which followed the launching of the Russian earth satellites brought into action two groups. One, which included the President, members of his Cabinet, some Congressional leaders, and members of the attentive elite, reacted to Sputnik with programs for modest increases in national security spending but continued to assert that no large increase in spending or re-evaluation of strategy or governmental structure was needed. The other group, which included members of the Gaither Committee, Congressional Democrats and some Republicans, directors of mass media, and national security experts, saw in the Sputniks an affirmation of its belief that the United States was faced with a grave threat to its survival and an opportunity to have its views prevail. Its members urged substantial increases in government spending and an awakening to the serious military, economic, and political challenge facing the United States and its allies. The Gaither Committee included a number of men who even before Sputnik had been arguing for substantial increases in defense spending. The other members of the Committee were won over to this view by the intellectual climate of the Committee as well as their review of the military situation. The Gaither Report provided a guide for the "pro-spending cluster," [83] presenting a rationale for its position and a blueprint for the expenditure of the additional sums which were to be made available. It hoped that the Administration could be pressed to accept the Report drawn up by a committee of the NSC as a guide for a substantially increased military effort.[84]

[82] For a similar model spelled out, see Roger Hilsman, "The Foreign Policy Consensus: An Interim Research Report," *Journal of Conflict Resolution*, III (December 1959), pp. 361–382. I am indebted to H. Bradford Westerfield for the model used here.

[83] The term "pro-spending cluster" is not meant to imply that its members favored spending for its own sake. While some people supporting the Gaither proposals were willing to back any plan for larger government spending, others (notably Sprague) were reluctant to endorse any spending programs; most of this cluster supported the Gaither proposals without being influenced by the spending implications.

[84] NSC 68 provides some interesting parallels to the Gaither Report and suggests the role it might have played if Sputnik had led to an Administration decision to increase the defense budget substantially. NSC 68 was drafted by a joint State Department–Defense Department committee, but it was, like the Gaither Report, prepared without considering domestic economic or political factors and without regard to the budget level set by the President. It included a complete review of the

The Gaither Report was valuable to the pro-spending cluster in a number of ways. Within the Administration it provided an excuse for a further review of the American defense position, and brought before the President and his top advisers in a dramatic fashion the arguments for spending substantially larger sums of money. It contributed to an awareness, on the part of the President and his top advisers, of the vulnerability problem and of the crucial importance of the dispersal of SAC and the development of mobile, hardened missile systems. The Report was instrumental in convincing the Air Force of the need to develop invulnerable second-strike forces. In the longer run it was probably partly responsible for the acceptance by both the Eisenhower Administration and the Air Force of programs for SAC dispersal and missile hardening. It also undoubtedly contributed to the growing acceptance by the Administration of the need to have forces for limited war (although it did not alter the failure to implement this decision in the military budget). It contributed to the pressure which raised military spending slightly.

By leaking the Report, those in the Administration arguing for higher spending aided those with similar views in the legislature and the attentive public. For these groups the Report provided substantiation from a source with access to all government intelligence of the arguments frequently offered by critics outside the government.[85] The Report made it clear that Executive optimism was based not on additional information but on a different reading of the facts available to the public. The data and reasoning of the Gaither Report could be used to bolster the case for increased spending, the need to overcome the missile gap and to develop a limited-war force. In addition, the struggle over publishing the Report was dramatic and helped to publicize the somewhat technical arguments over military strategy and the demands for greater expenditure on defense. Their service on the Gaither Committee substantially increased the prestige and influence of its members. Some continued in advisory capacities in the Eisenhower Administration, and all are looked to as experts on national security problems.

---

national security situation and called for a large increase in defense spending — providing a blueprint for the use of the funds. The Report was presented to the NSC just prior to the outbreak of the Korean War. It was initialed by President Truman just after the war started and served as the government's rationale for the expanded defense effort. It enabled the Administration to assert that spending was being guided by a long-range plan drafted prior to the war. See Paul Hammond, "NSC 68: Prologue to Rearmament," in Warner R. Schilling, Paul Y. Hammond, and Glenn H. Snyder, *Strategy, Politics, and Defense Budgets* (1962).

[85] For example, in the Rockefeller Brothers study on defense problems, whose recommendations closely parallel those of the Gaither Report; see Rockefeller Brothers Fund, *International Security: The Military Aspect* (1958), reprinted in *Prospect for America: The Rockefeller Panel Reports* (1961), pp. 93–155.

The Report had a significant influence on the analysis of strategic problems by national security experts. The recent emphasis in the military policy literature on the problems of vulnerability and second-strike forces stems partly from the impact of the Gaither Report and the members of the Committee and its advisory panel.

While the Gaither Report served temporarily as a rallying point for those favoring increased spending, the anti-spending cluster was quick to recognize the danger which the Report posed. The President, battling the pressures for greater military expenditures, refused to make the Report public and stressed that it was just one of a number of reports made to him. Senate Republicans opposed to large spending urged that the Report be kept secret, noting with alarm the influence it had already had in increasing the pressures on the Administration. Had the Report been made public, it would have represented a significant victory for the pro-spending cluster and would have probably indicated that the group was gaining the upper hand in the Administration.

The complexities of military planning and strategy are such that public debate (and even the Congressional appropriations process) plays a limited role in making critical decisions. The failure of Congress to have the Gaither Report published indicated the ability of the Executive to limit Congress' role by cutting off vital information. Insofar as Congressional and public debate play a role in the process of national strategy, the Gaither incident was of some value. The public debate had an important educational function in bringing to the attention of the Administration an analysis of the situation different from that provided by operating agencies. By calling attention to problems of vulnerability and limited war, the Gaither Report increased public understanding of these crucial questions.

In part, Congressional activity on defense matters can be viewed as a massive lobbying effort to influence the political decision-making process of the Executive branch.[86] The analysis of the Gaither Committee added to the ability of Congress to influence the process and to press for increased and more rational spending. If the public dispute over the Gaither Report contributed to the political climate which has influenced President Kennedy, it may well have made a vital contribution to the nation's security.

Although when the contents of their reports are leaked or released, the work of civilian *ad hoc* NSC committees is of value to Congressmen and private citizens, such groups are primarily instruments of the President and need to be evaluated in terms of their possible contribution to the Executive decision-making process. Within the Executive the Gaither Report provided a fresh look at the nation's defense posture. It served

[86] Cf. Samuel P. Huntington, "Strategic Planning and the Political Process," *Foreign Affairs*, XXXVII (January 1960), 285–299.

as an effective communication procedure to bring before the attention of the President and his principal advisers concerns which were being felt at the middle and upper levels of the operating agencies but which had not filtered through to the White House.

The Committee Report provided clear, well-reasoned statements of the problems of vulnerability and limited war, of the role of dispersal and hardening, and of the problems and opportunities of civil defense. It undoubtedly made a major contribution to the understanding of these problems by top officials. The panel was able to point out serious deficiencies where it found them because it was not responsible for past policy action, and the President could receive such advice because he anticipated being able to keep it private. The Committee also advanced a number of new policy proposals, particularly in the field of defense reorganization, which were not likely to come from the armed services themselves.[87]

Having made its proposals, the Gaither Committee found that it lacked the power base to fight for their implementation. But clearly the value and activity of such a group are not measurable in terms of its political influence on the decision process. The Committee furnished the President with a program, which, while perhaps not very precise or well thought-out in detail, could have served as a guide for action. The Committee thus fulfilled its primary purpose of providing an additional source of information for the President, unencumbered by future and past policy responsibility. The operating agencies can only view such committees as threats to their prerogative. But to a strong, vigorous President they could prove to be a powerful tool for overcoming bureaucratic and political opposition to the implementation of new, vitally needed programs.

BRUCE L. R. SMITH

Strategic Expertise and National Security Policy: A Case Study

The report of a Rand study group on strategic air bases offers a useful contrast to the experiences of the Gaither Committee. Although the Rand Corporation stands in a somewhat different relationship to the Air Force

---

[87] Some of its proposals were adopted in the 1958 reorganization of the Defense Department.

Abridged by the editors from *Public Policy*, 13 (1964), pp. 69–108, with the permission of the author and publisher.

than does an ad hoc Presidential commission to the incumbent administration, the similarities outweigh the differences. Both the Gaither Committee and the Rand study group were composed of "outsiders." Both expanded their relatively narrow mandates to consider the broadest questions of strategy and national security policy. Both reached conclusions which convinced them of the need to have their findings accepted and their recommendations implemented, and both worked to get the government to change its policies. Yet, the Gaither Committee essentially failed, and the Rand group substantially succeeded.

The Rand team, headed by Albert Wohlstetter, showed awareness of the bureaucratic realities of changing policies and behavior and carefully planned their strategy to accommodate those realities. They recognized that, as an outside group, it was not sufficient for them to present their findings and to assume that somehow these automatically would be implemented. Rather, it was deemed necessary to spend a great deal of time in selling their report to their client. The Rand group did enjoy one advantage compared to the Gaither Committee: its client, the Air Force, was the operating agency which would be responsible for any implementation which did occur. They also knew that it was not enough to persuade the top echelons of their findings and recommendations. If behavior were to change, officers up and down the hierarchy had to be persuaded that it was in their interest to implement the recommendations.

The Rand group demonstrated great sensitivity to the Air Force's organizational objectives and bureaucratic needs. Their findings could and, to some extent, did excite SAC's concern for its organizational autonomy, force admissions of error from the Air Force, undermine morale, and require substantial changes in standard operating procedures. To counter these problems, Wohlstetter worked to present the report in as non-threatening a manner as possible. Thus, he cultivated informal contacts within the Air Force to establish his credibility and trustworthiness and to win allies. He started his persuasion campaign with SAC, since it was potentially the most threatened organization within the Air Force. He was careful to restrict circulation of the "preliminary" report to the Air Force in order to give the service an opportunity to respond without pressure from its bureaucratic opponents, and he changed the tense of verbs in the "final" report to signal that it had done so. When bureaucratic opposition did develop, Rand's position as an outsider was *exploited*, and the formal chain of command was short-circuited. Even then, Wohlstetter remained within the Air Force rather than briefing the Secretary of Defense. Rand's role was publicly minimized, and the Air Force received most of the credit.

One of the most striking phenomena in postwar defense organization in the United States is the growth of the non-profit research or advisory corporation. The "non-profits" form a significant portion of the small but influential community of scientific strategists, made up to a considerable degree of civilian researchers and advisers, that has come to play a role in defense policy formation scarcely imaginable as recently as several decades ago.[1] Struck by the phenomenon, one foreign observer reportedly remarked that "representatives of certain U.S. research organizations stalk the Pentagon like the Jesuits in the chancelleries of 18th century Europe." Each of the three military services has at least one of the novel advisory corporations performing policy and operations research or systems analysis for it on a contractual basis. . . .

What are the implications of this development for the process of national security policy formation in the United States? Is the non-profit corporation an answer to the ills of bureaucracy? A form of government organization particularly well-adapted to an era of science and technology? Or a threat to the established executive agencies and to orderliness and accountability in the conduct of public policy? . . .

The objective of this study is to contribute to a broad understanding of the scientific adviser's role in national policy formation through a careful look at the operations of one of the chief advisory corporations working in the defense area: The RAND Corporation. I will approach the task by undertaking a case study of the origins, execution, and eventual communication to Air Force policy-makers of one of the most significant studies ever done at RAND: the Strategic Bases Study (Rand Report 266).[2] An incidental advantage of selecting the basing study (R-266) for analysis is the fact that most of the relevant materials are now free from security restrictions and can be discussed in the open literature. More important, the study offers an excellent illustration of what a useful RAND systems analysis is and how it can influence public policy. Tracing the study's evolution also throws important light on the nature of RAND and how it has operated. . . .

ORIGINS AND EARLY HISTORY OF THE STRATEGIC BASES STUDY

The origins of R-266 go back to May 1951, when the Air Force addressed a request to RAND for a study of the selection of overseas air bases.[3] Military construction authorized by Congress for the fiscal

[1] For a general description of the Community of "scientific strategists," see Bernard Brodie, "The Scientific Strategists," in U.S. Senate, Committee on Government Operations, Subcommittee on National Security Staffing and Operations, *Administration of National Security: Selected Papers*, 87th Cong., 2d sess., pp. 190–201; Joseph Kraft, "The War Thinkers," *Esquire* (September 1962), pp. 102–104; and Kathleen Archibald, "Social Science Approaches to Peace: Problems and Issues," *Social Problems*, No. 11 (Summer 1963).

[2] A. J. Wohlstetter, F. S. Hoffman, R. J. Lutz, and H. S. Rowen, *Selection and Use of Strategic Air Bases*, RAND R-266, April 1, 1954, declassified 1962.

[3] The request came from Col. L. C. Coddington, Deputy to General Maddux, Assistant for Air Bases. The original request for the study included a tentative formulation of the problem and posed a number of questions for analysis in a short supporting staff paper.

year 1952 included some 3½ billion dollars for air base construction, almost half of which was for overseas base construction, and the prospect was that a much larger volume of new construction would be planned in the next several years. It appeared to the Air Force officer responsible for the request that RAND might make a useful contribution by studying the most effective ways for acquiring, constructing, and using air base facilities in foreign countries. The criterion then in use for guiding decision on basing questions was a very crude one, having to do principally with minimum cost for given facilities. There was no concern shown to total systems costs which, as it turned out, were markedly different under alternative basing policies. The request was referred to Charles J. Hitch, head of RAND's Economics Division.

In keeping with the general RAND practice, Hitch sought to interest some of his staff in researching the area rather than attempting to thrust the project on anyone. The interest or lack of interest shown in a proposed study by the research staff would be an important factor in determining whether or not RAND would accept the Air Force's request. One of the men approached by Hitch was Albert Wohlstetter, a consultant of diverse background and interests newly added to the RAND Economics Division. Wohlstetter was not very interested in working on the project. "It did not look to me at the time," Wohlstetter recalls, "like a very interesting or challenging study . . . dull, full of nuts-and-bolts, the kind of thing one normally associates with logistics." [4] For a time, it appeared that the request for the base study would be one of those Air Force requests that RAND turned down. However, before giving a definite "no," Wohlstetter asked for a week or two to think about the matter. The week's reflection brought Wohlstetter to the conclusion that some potentially major problems might be raised by such a study. He opted to work on the study, and RAND informed the Air Force that it was willing to undertake the project.

Throughout the spring and summer of 1951, Wohlstetter was the only one formally working on the project. At this stage, Wohlstetter spent most of his time trying to formulate what exactly was the problem. He asked questions of himself and others constantly, and spent long hours familiarizing himself with Air Force procedures and current basing policies. He became convinced that the real task lay in discovering what were the right questions to ask instead of accepting the client's tentative formulation of

[4] All direct quotations used in this study that are not otherwise documented are based on personal interviews. My special thanks are due to Albert Wohlstetter, formerly of The RAND Corporation and currently Ford Research Professor at University of California, for giving generously of his time and cooperating fully in this case study's preparation. I also benefited greatly from interviews with Henry S. Rowen, Fred S. Hoffman, Robert Belzer, Frederick Sallaghar, L. J. Henderson, Jr., of The RAND Corporation.

the problem and providing answers to ready-made questions. Conversations with Henry S. Rowen, a RAND economist with engineering training, were particularly helpful at this stage. Rowen was then engaged in several RAND projects related to Wohlstetter's field of interest, which made him a particularly valuable collaborator in the research. Later another economist, Fred S. Hoffman, and an aeronautical engineer, Robert J. Lutz, joined Wohlstetter and Rowen. . . .

A Draft of the Study Appears: The Hard Job of Filling in the Gaps and Checking the Analysis

By the late fall of 1951, Wohlstetter's thinking had crystalized to a point where he felt able to put some ideas down on paper. With Rowen, he drafted a "D" — or internal working paper — for internal RAND consumption which was completed on December 29, 1951 — D-1114, "Economic and Strategic Considerations in Air Base Location: a Preliminary Review." This paper, though a document of some 100 pages in length and containing 40 pages of graphs and tables, represented only a sketchy summary of some useful approaches to the basing problem. But it did lay down in preliminary form what were to become the central concerns of R-266. Among the most important of these was the question of the vulnerability of aircraft on the ground to surprise atomic attack. It occurred to Wohlstetter that the past thinking on strategic bombing and basing posture had not given adequate attention to a question that could become of vital importance in the future: what would happen if the enemy struck first, hitting U.S. bombers on the ground before they reached enemy air space? The full importance of this question was only vaguely seen at this point, but certain uncomfortable conclusions emerged even from the preliminary analysis. It was found, for example, that Air Force regulations on base installation called for the concentration of facilities to minimize the costs of utilities, pipelines, roads, and normal peacetime operational costs. Wohlstetter and Rowen discovered that such a system was highly vulnerable to enemy nuclear attack and suggested tentatively that a policy of dispersing facilities on bases would be preferable.

D-1114 contained many gaps and was inconclusive at points, but it had at least raised some significant questions and suggested new approaches to the problem of basing policy. For a variety of reasons, the study encountered considerable opposition and skepticism within RAND. Earlier RAND strategic bombing studies had dealt with such questions as: what is the best way to penetrate enemy fighter defenses? How high should bomber aircraft fly? What kind of aircraft, turboprop or turbojet, should be used? The question of where the strategic strike force should be based was not considered a very important issue. The offensive capability the Soviet

Union had at the time was considered likely to be used only against cities, not bases, and this could be taken care of by appropriate air defense measures. It was assumed that we could base U.S. aircraft at a variety of points within range of enemy targets at minimum risk. Because of this assumption many RAND people did not consider D-1114 to be dealing with a very significant or vital problem. Some at RAND even believed the project was a waste of time and money, and should be discontinued. On the other hand, a few RAND staff members were impressed by D-1114, and thought the matter important enough to be briefed at the Pentagon without delay.

At this juncture, RAND's permissive and decentralized management policies played an important role in preventing either a premature cut-off of the project or a hasty effort to bring the findings to the Air Force without adequate verification. The decision was made at the divisional level by Economics chief Hitch that the study raised enough interesting possibilities to warrant further investigation. Top RAND management served a useful function in not intervening and forcing a decision on the research staff at this early point. The decision of when to bring the results of the research to the attention of the Air Force was left to Wohlstetter himself for the time being. Wohlstetter opposed any effort to communicate the findings of D-1114 to the Air Force at this point, on the grounds that further work was needed before any firm policy recommendations could be drawn from the research.

For the next several months, Wohlstetter and his small team (by now Rowen and Lutz were working more or less full-time on the study) spent long hours rechecking the assumptions of D-1114; calculating the effectiveness and costs of alternative basing postures under a variety of different conditions; injecting new variables into the analysis and estimating their effect on the data; and determining which base systems would be most affected by errors in assessments of uncertainties (e.g., if enemy capabilities were greater than anticipated by a factor of 10, or if mechanical failures were to cause a much higher rate of aborts than expected). The RAND team throughout was concerned only with *gross differences* in system cost and system performance, i.e., differences that would still be important despite large elements of uncertainty in the analysis.

By the end of the spring of 1952, Wohlstetter and Rowen had completed a draft of the study. The 400-plus pages of the draft, and the numerous supporting papers used in its preparation, attest to the extensive detailed and empirical work required to carry out a complex study. This time the results of the work appeared to be conclusive and to contain far-reaching policy implications. The analysis pointed toward the shattering conclusion that in the last half of the 1950s the Strategic Air Command, the world's most powerful striking force, faced the danger of obliteration from enemy surprise attack under the then-programmed strategic basing system.

Meanwhile, concern had gradually begun to grow in the Air Force over the implications of the Soviet A-bomb for the security of U.S. forces and problems such as Air Defense were receiving increased attention. A group around Secretary of the Air Force Thomas Finletter was particularly active in calling attention to the potential dangers of the Soviet Union's acquisition of a nuclear capability and in urging that the United States begin planning for the time when the Soviet Union would have developed a substantial force of long-range bombers. In late 1951 Secretary Finletter wrote to Air Force Chief of Staff Hoyt S. Vandenberg suggesting that the Air Force undertake a major study of the vulnerability of SAC bases to enemy nuclear attack. In May 1952, a request came to RAND from General Craigie (which carried the imprimatur of the Air Force Chief of Staff) for RAND to study the problem of SAC base vulnerability. Like the original request for a study of basing policies, the Air Force request only vaguely groped to define the issues. But as in the basing study case the request showed the responsible government official's genuine concern and sense for what is important which often generates significant problems for detailed study. A special RAND study team on vulnerability was thereupon formed under the direction of mathematician Igor Ansoff. Although this team's work was eclipsed by the base study and no final report was ever published or issued to the Air Force, some of its work provided useful data for integration into the final version of the basing study. One of the researchers active in the other project also proved useful in the process of communicating the base study's findings to the Air Force.

It is also important to point out here the occurrence of a natural disaster in the fall of 1952 that indirectly had a bearing on the basing study's fate.[5] As often only disaster can, the event aroused high-level concern and dramatized the importance of a problem that was hitherto only dimly recognized. The event in question was a tornado that ripped through a major U.S. military airbase, completely destroying 12 B-36 heavy bombers. Since the bombers were thought to be secure, the disaster added to the worry over aircraft vulnerability already present in some Air Force circles and helped fashion a frame of mind receptive to the basing study's suggestions.

The last phase of work on the study marked the beginnings of the stage of communicating the research results to the client (and also the beginning of the sizable feedback of questions for further study). In talking to large numbers of Air Force officers during the middle and late months of 1952,

---

[5] The historical records at headquarters SAC report that the disaster occurred at Carswell Air Force Base on September 1, 1952. Personal correspondence, R. L. Belzer, The RAND Corporation.

Wohlstetter and his associates began injecting the ideas of the study into the Air Force hierarchy and through personal contact forming allies who were later to prove important in getting the results of the study incorporated into Air Force policy. . . .

The research strategy involved an exhaustive examination of four alternative basing systems in terms of their costs and their effectiveness in destroying enemy targets: (1) as a point of departure, the then-programmed system of bombers based in time of war on advanced overseas operating bases; (2) bombers based on intermediate overseas operating bases in wartime; (3) United States-based bombers operating inter-continentally with the aid of air-refueling; and (4) United States-based bombers operating intercontinentally with the help of ground-refueling at overseas staging areas. The examination of each of these four alternative systems was carried out by taking certain principal factors which are important determinants of system cost and effectiveness and applying them to each system. These principal factors were the distances the bombers must fly from base to targets, to favorable entry points into enemy defenses, to the source of base supply, and to the points from which the enemy could attack these bases. The analysis was concerned with the joint effects of these respective factors on the costs of extending bomber radius; on how the enemy might deploy his defenses, and the number of our bombers lost to these defenses; on logistics costs; and on base vulnerability and our probable loss of bombers on the ground. The analytical treatment of the four critical base location distances presented intricate problems and required skillful handling. On its face the problem appeared to involve contradictory elements. Considerations of logistics costs and ease of penetrating enemy defenses argue for locating bases close to the Soviet Union. Nearness to the source of supply and reduced vulnerability to enemy attack, on the other hand, argue for locating bases in or near the United States and away from the Soviet Union.

The results of the study showed that the preferred system was alternative (4): United States operating bases for the strike force with the assistance of overseas refueling bases.

The then-programmed system of advanced overseas operating bases proved to be decidedly inferior to the U.S.-operated system with overseas bases used only for staging and refueling purposes.[6] R-266 demonstrated that this system would be extremely vulnerable to enemy attack in 1956 (even under very conservative estimates of Soviet forces). It would, in

---

[6] The then-programmed system envisaged the bulk of the U.S. strategic force being located in 30 bases on the continental United States in peacetime and then, upon the outbreak of war or a sharpening of international tension which presaged war, being moved overseas, to operate from a base system consisting of about 70 bases. Fighter defense and anti-aircraft battalions would be provided but there was relatively little emphasis given to the passive defense of this system.

consequence, have the least destruction potential of enemy targets of any of the systems. Most of the projected overseas bases would be easily within the range of Soviet bombers. Moreover, warning time of an enemy attack would not be sufficient to permit evacuation of our aircraft in time to escape destruction. Furthermore, even under favorable assumptions about the size of enemy stockpiles of atomic weapons and the yield of the weapons and the state of U.S. base-defense capabilities, it was found that, by a first strike, the enemy could destroy almost our entire combat force while it was still on the ground. And the attack would make it unlikely that the small surviving part of our force could respond effectively and penetrate enemy defenses in a retaliatory strike. The cornerstone of U.S. policy at the time — deterrence of aggression through the nuclear striking power of the Strategic Air Command and destruction of enemy industrial targets if deterrence failed — was thus seen to be jeopardized by the projected basing system. Indeed, the whole concept of deterrence as it was then conceived seemed in need of revision. "Deterrence" was thought of largely as deterring a massive assault on Europe. R-266 showed that a vital part of any viable deterrence policy had to be deterrence of an attack on the deterrent forces themselves through the provision of a second-strike strategic capability. Thus the basing study contributed to important changes in U.S. strategic thought and doctrine.

The second alternative of intercontinental operation with the aid of air-refueling (which had some strong advocates in the Air Force) was shown to buy lower base vulnerability at so high a cost that total striking power would be drastically reduced. Air-refueling, the study demonstrated, was much more expensive than conventional ground refueling for any one of a number of different possible air campaigns. Here one sees what is meant by *gross differences* in systems cost and performance that was referred to above as one of the study's operational principles. The differences in cost between the air- and ground-refueling systems were not of a marginal nature — they were of the order of magnitude of 10–15 billion dollars over the life of the system.

The third alternative of intermediate overseas operating bases proved to be the worst of all the systems in that it combined some of the major disadvantages of the advanced overseas operating system and the air-refueling system. It would be almost as vulnerable as the former because even intermediate distance operating bases would be within range of enemy attack and not within the warning network that permitted evacuation of our aircraft in time to escape destruction. And, like the air-refueling system, it would be costly to operate because supplies and personnel would have to be moved overseas and expensive facilities at the bases constructed to accommodate the maintenance, bomb-loading and manifold other functions of an operating base.

The system relying on overseas bases for staging and refueling purposes was shown to be the "best" system on the grounds, first, that it was relatively invulnerable to enemy attack either before or after the strike against the enemy. U.S. bombers would only be on the ground a very short time for refueling either before and/or after striking their targets, making it very difficult for the enemy to destroy them on the ground. Routes could also be varied so that the enemy would never be sure which base the U.S. bomber force would use. Moreover, the base would not need the large-scale construction of expensive and vulnerable facilities that would be necessary in an operating base. Modest expenditures on underground storage for fuel would radically reduce vulnerability to almost any atomic attack within the enemy's capabilities at that time. This conclusion was not sensitive to unfavorable resolution of some of the uncertainties of the analysis. The results would hold true even if, for example, the estimates of the number of A-bombs in the enemy's stockpile were underestimated by a factor of 10 or if the bombs were of a larger yield than anticipated. Further, the overall costs of the system were lower than the other three systems, thus freeing additional resources for the performance of the mission. Considered in all its complex aspects, the overseas staging base system appeared to be markedly superior to the other three systems.

COMMUNICATING THE RESEARCH RESULTS TO THE FOCAL POINTS OF DECISION

In policy-oriented research the communication of results is almost as important a task as the research — and sometimes hardly less difficult and demanding. Paradoxically, the client agency may be strongly motivated not to use the research that it has sponsored. As a recent study comments:

> Offhand, it might be expected that the client, by virtue of his role, would function wholly to foster utilization. Having commissioned a research project, he, among all the parties concerned, would be the most highly motivated to use its results. Where utilization does not occur, therefore, one would be tempted to look elsewhere for an explanation. However, an examination of the record suggests, perhaps surprisingly, that the client is very often directly responsible for the nonutilization of the results of research which he sponsors.[7]

At the outset it is important to recall that decision-making in the defense establishment (as elsewhere in the government) is a *process*. Phrases like the "decision-making process" and the "process of policy formation" are not mere incantation: they refer to the continuous flow of decisions, large

---

[7] Charles Y. Glock, "Applied Social Research: Some Conditions Affecting Its Utilization," *Case Studies in Bringing Behavioral Science into Use* (Studies in the Utilization of Behavioral Science, Vol. I [Institute for Communications Research, Stanford University, 1961]), p. 7.

and small, that make up the seamless web of policy formation and administrative action in our federal government. The dynamic flux of the process makes the job of the adviser particularly difficult. It means that there is no orderly procedure whereby the adviser can state his views or explain his research and then retire from the scene confident that his advice will receive systematic consideration. Decisions once made can become unmade a week later. *Continuity* is thus an essential attribute of effective communication of policy-oriented research.

A corollary of this is that the advice cannot simply be given to the top levels if favorable decision and effective implementation of the advice is desired. Take the case of a high-level decision-maker accepting the recommendation of an advisory group and making a "policy" decision designed to implement the advice. Unless the subordinates carry out the decision effectively, the whole intent of the policy decision can be defeated.[8] Comprehension of the basis for the decision reached at the higher level can be a vital factor in winning the consent and enthusiasm of those who must execute the decision and, in doing so, make a myriad of other decisions which can determine the success or failure of the original decision. It follows therefore that it is often desirable to communicate the research or advice to the working levels of an organization as well as to the higher policy levels.

In the case of R-266, the task of communicating the findings of the analysis to the Air Force lasted from about the fall of 1952 through most of 1953. By the end of 1952, the study had begun to assume final form. For some months, Wohlstetter and his colleagues had been in close contact with Air Force officers, checking out the assumptions of the study and beginning to circulate its potentially revolutionary conclusions. In January of 1953, the research had progressed to the point where Wohlstetter now felt confident that RAND should present the findings formally to the Air Force. Hitch at the division head level agreed, and so did top RAND management. Pressure also began building up within the Air Force from sympathetic officers for an early release of the findings. The question then became one largely of tactics.

A first concern felt by RAND management was the need for some special device or tactic to dramatize the study's importance so as to maximize its impact on Air Force policy. Accordingly, it was decided that the results of the study, by now nearly completed, would be disseminated to

---

[8] Good discussions of this theme include: Henry Wriston, "The Secretary and the Management of the Department," and Don K. Price, "The Secretary and Our Unwritten Constitution," in Don K. Price (ed.), *The Secretary of State* (American Assembly, 1961), pp. 76–112, 166–190; Seymour Martin Lipset, *Agrarian Socialism: A Cooperative Commonwealth Federation in Saskatchewan* (1959); Peter M. Blau, *Bureaucracy in Modern Society* (1956), pp. 85–101; and Paul Appleby, *Policy and Administration* (1949).

the client in preliminary form. This staff report (R-244-S) amounted to a condensed version which summarized the essential findings and policy recommendations of the larger study, and would be distributed solely to the Air Force.

With the publication and distribution of 75 copies of R-244-S through-out the Air Force on March 1, 1953, the dissemination of the basing research findings entered into its most intensive phase. This phase lasted until approximately November of the same year.

Wohlstetter had made several trips to Washington in January and February 1953 in preparation for the report's release, but after the March 1 date of publication he was almost constantly in Washington. A large portion of that time was consumed in briefings. The briefing can often be a very effective technique of communication because it permits interaction between the researcher and the decision-maker, and the researcher can answer objections to the study that the decision-maker might raise. In the present case, the importance of the subject meant an extraordinarily large number of briefings, and its startling conclusion foretold a vigorous interchange of views.

In fact, Wohlstetter gave 92 briefings (most of them during the period from March to the end of October). Some idea of the considerable interaction between briefer and audience is suggested by the fact that 16 charts were used for the main briefing, whereas it was found necessary to prepare 70 charts for use during the question period. The question period also typically lasted longer than the main briefing.

The initial briefing began with the Strategic Air Command (SAC), the functional command most directly affected by the study's recommendations. The immediate response was enthusiastic. The briefing (and report) came as a "shocker" and aroused great interest within SAC. Increased support was added to the initial group of sympathetic officers who shared Wohlstetter's conclusion that the vulnerability of SAC under the programmed base system was a serious threat to the nation's security. Surprisingly, very little opposition to the study was encountered at this point on the basis of its being done by civilians without "military experience." Next Wohlstetter and his team went to the Pentagon to brief a group of about 40 senior colonels representing various directorates of the Air Staff. The reception was generally favorable. It was determined that a "saturation" campaign of briefings should be undertaken throughout various commands and major components of the main Air Force directorates with a view to testing the research findings and generating the momentum to bring them eventually to the Air Force Council.[9] The

9 The Air Force Council was attached in the Air Force hierarchy to the Vice Chief of Staff's office; it acted as a staff arm and decision-making aid to the Vice Chief of Staff. The Chief of Staff had the final authority to act or not to act on Air Force Council advice. Typically, however, a recommendation by the Air Force

saturation campaign of briefings continued through the end of May. Then in early June a significant briefing was arranged with officers of general rank. This was the highest ranking group that Wohlstetter had briefed thus far, and it was at this briefing that an important decision was taken. The generals decided to create a special Ad Hoc Committee of the Air Staff to check out the component parts of the study in terms of their accuracy, reasonableness of assumptions, and feasibility of implementation.[10] The general intention was that the Ad Hoc Committee would examine the study in depth, and prepare a report for submission to the Air Force Council. If the Ad Hoc Committee submitted a favorable report, the prospects looked bright for favorable decision and action on the study's recommendations.

A number of factors, however, cautioned against any easy optimism. As happens frequently with review committees, the Ad Hoc Committee decided to operate on the basis of parceling out specific areas of interest to particular committee members. This meant that something of a system of "concurrent majorities" would obtain, with the Wohlstetter team having to persuade each Committee member (and the Directorate or functional command he represented) to endorse the study. It was important to persuade each Committee member (and each Directorate) because separate "concurrences" were to be solicited from each Directorate to form a major part of the Ad Hoc Committee's Report. In effect, each member to some extent could exercise a check or veto on the Committee's recommendations.

Meanwhile, the momentum that had developed toward a rapid decision on the study's recommendations at this point had begun to slow down. Jurisdictional questions arose, for example, which presented new obstacles to early decision on the study. SAC, as a specified command, was responsible to the Joint Chiefs of Staff (JCS) for policy guidance. But at the same time it was still tied closely to the Air Force and had certain ill-defined responsibilities to the Air Staff. This divided responsibility between JCS and the Air Staff raised difficult questions as to the exact nature of SAC's relationship to the Air Staff. Elements within SAC began to fear that the study could be used as an opening wedge for the Air Staff to interfere with internal SAC operations and responsibilities.

Council met with the Chief of Staff's approval, and where possible the Chief of Staff encouraged consideration of important issues by the Council. It might be noted, parenthetically, that it was at this briefing of senior colonels where Wohlstetter encountered his only serious objection to civilians proferring advice to military professionals. But several officers with extensive combat experience successfully rebutted their colleagues' objections to civilian assistance of this kind.

[10] The Ad Hoc Committee was also to absorb another Air Staff Ad Hoc Committee which had been organized separately in March 1953 to analyze the vulnerability question.

Elsewhere pockets of resistance developed as it was realized that acting on the study would involve drastic changes in programmed activity.[11] The inertia of established programs proved difficult to overcome even in the face of strong evidence arguing for innovation. A point of concern also was the prospect that substantial changes might be interpreted by rivals as an admission of error on a vast scale. The RAND team as well encountered opposition from a number of Air Force officers who genuinely feared that the drastic revision in policy suggested by the study could undermine the confidence and morale of their units. Conceivably the Air Force could also be embarrassed before Congress and might even become involved in a Congressional investigation. Thus even some Air Force officers who agreed with the RAND study's recommendations felt it desirable to straighten out the error as unobtrusively as possible at some future date. In this general atmosphere, critics saw the special Ad Hoc Committee as a convenient vehicle for delaying action. Studying the study, it should be noted, often affords the decision-maker a minimum risk course of action: he can thereby avoid or postpone action that might create enemies and at the same time appear to be doing something to satisfy critics. Hence those who, for one reason or another, did not favor adopting the study's recommendations now largely adopted the tactic of delay and attrition and opposition to any immediate action or decision on the study's main recommendations.

The delaying tactics had a notable success in July and August of 1953. Wohlstetter had the feeling that his "wheels were spinning" during this period. "It looked as though we would convince everybody intellectually," he recalls, "but that nothing would get done." Some of the sense of urgency had departed, and the RAND team found that something of a reverse "bandwagon effect" was beginning to take effect. A number of original Air Force supporters reversed themselves and either lined up with the opposition or adopted a noncommittal position.

---

[11] This is consistent with the March-Simon contention that organizational innovation will occur more easily if the proposed changes are of a gradual incremental nature — "when the carrot is just a *little* way ahead of the donkey — when aspirations exceed achievement by a small amount." If the proposed innovation is too drastic a departure from current doctrine or procedure, frustration results and "neurotic reactions interfere with effective innovation." James G. March and Herbert A. Simon, *Organizations* (1958), p. 184. To allay doubts, the Wohlstetter team on occasion sought to underplay the novelty of their recommendations. The subject of organizational change and innovation has recently attracted increasing scholarly interest. It is widely recognized that organizations, and especially large organizations, have great difficulty in effecting change in their policies and procedures. For a good theoretical discussion of organizational innovation, see March and Simon, *Organizations*, chap. 5. For an application of the March-Simon conceptual schema to strategic program innovation in defense agencies, see Samuel P. Huntington, *The Common Defense* (1961), chap. 5. A comprehensive general treatment of innovation is Everett M. Rogers, *Diffusion of Innovations* (1962).

In the face of these setbacks, the RAND team and the Air Force group favoring the study intensified their efforts to communicate the research results. A planning exercise was even carried through which tested the recommended system's capacity to handle a complex strike. Despite redoubled efforts, the fortunes of the study continued in doubt. By the end of the summer, Wohlstetter was convinced that some drastic step was necessary to assure that the study reached the Air Force Council for consideration. Consequently, he proposed to RAND Vice-President Henderson that a special visit be made to General Thomas S. White, acting Chief of Staff of the Air Force,[12] to focus high-level attention on the study and to guard against a permanent tie-up in delays and jockeying at lower levels. Henderson agreed, and an interview was arranged between General White and a delegation from RAND consisting of Wohlstetter plus the top echelon of RAND management (President Collbohm, Vice-President Henderson, and Vice-President J. R. Goldstein). This interview proved to be an important turning point.

The RAND team was now assured of consideration of the study by the Air Force Council; and in any event they could now count on an appeal to the highest decision-making level in the Air Force. From this point on, the prospects for favorable decision brightened and the opponents of the study were placed on the defensive. Ironically, Wohlstetter and his colleagues also received a fortuitous assist from an unexpected quarter: Premier Malenkov's announcement that the Soviet Union had detonated a hydrogen bomb.[13] Though intelligence estimates at this time were uncertain, there was little disposition in the Air Force after the Malenkov announcement to doubt that the Soviet Union had a substantial nuclear capability. Wohlstetter and his colleagues capitalized on this announcement in the late summer briefings to dramatize the dangers of an enemy first strike against vulnerable overseas staging bases.

Several aspects of the interview with General White deserve additional comment. First, White was influenced in his decision to place consideration of R-244-S on the Air Force Council Agenda in part by the pressure of the budgetary cycle. For the advisory group interested in timing the release of reports and briefing campaigns to maximize their impact on policy, this is an important factor. Though the decision-making process is diffuse and tends to be geared to crises which are by their nature unpredictable, there is always the assurance that the pressure of budget preparation will pose important policy choices and in general serve as a stimulus to decision.

[12] General Hoyt S. Vandenberg, Chief of Staff, was ill with cancer.
[13] The Malenkov announcement more than offset the negative effect of former President Truman's famous comment after he had left the White House that he doubted whether the Russians really had the A-bomb.

Second, the fact that it was even possible to approach General White, when seemingly blocked or delayed at lower echelons, deserves notice. RAND's existence *outside* the Air Force hierarchy, and its reputation for independence and objectivity, is seen as playing an important role. It is doubtful whether an Air Force officer, an "in-house" advisory group made up of Air Force career personnel, or even a civilian advisory group attached to a unit within the normal chain of command, would have the same opportunity or incentive to by-pass immediate superiors and press for the adoption of controversial ideas at higher levels. The data here thus support the tentative hypothesis of Merton and others that the utilization of expert advice in the behavioral sciences will be positively influenced by location of the adviser outside the organization for whose procedures or policies he is suggesting innovation.[14]

In this connection it should also be stressed that location of the research or advisory unit outside the organizational framework of the decision-making agency allows greater scope for truly original and creative ideas to emerge in policy-oriented research. Within an agency responsible for policy-making and operations, there are strong and understandable pressures to ensure agency-wide policy coordination and orientation of the work effort toward clearly-defined and shared objectives. It is difficult for anything but "symbolic" research, i.e., research that is innocuous, does not reflect unfavorably on agency policies or procedures, and raises no disruptive problems to be conducted in such an organizational setting. Thus it would appear both on grounds of accessibility to the various points of decision scattered throughout the client organization and on grounds of effective use of scarce creative research talent that a strong case can be made for contracting many policy research and advisory functions to an outside organization. . . .

Last, it should be noted that there was no "end run" of the sponsor in this case. Clearly, problems of a fundamentally different and more complex nature would have been presented had RAND sought to by-pass the Air Force in the present case and bring the study results directly to the Secretary of Defense's attention. A striking feature of this incident, indeed, is the fact that strategic decisions of enormous importance were made solely by a military service. Now that more and more the OSD [Office of the Secretary of Defense] level is assuming primary responsibility for strategic policy it is doubtful that such decisions could be made without involving OSD agencies and personnel. . . .

[14] Robert K. Merton, "The Role of Applied Social Science in the Formation of Policy," *Philosophy of Science,* XVI (July 1949), 168; Ronald Lippit, "Two Case Studies in the Utilization of Behavioral Research," *Case Studies in Bringing Behavioral Science into Use* (Studies in the Utilization of Behavioral Science, Vol. I [Institute for Communications Research, Stanford University, 1961]), pp. 34 ff.

THE IMPACT: R-266 REFLECTED IN AIR FORCE
POLICY CHANGES

Distinguishing between the stage of communicating the research results and the stage of their actual reflection in Air Force policy is somewhat arbitrary. One could say that in a sense the study began to have an "impact" even before the RAND team distributed copies of the special staff report R-244-S and initiated the program of formal briefings. Numerous informal contacts existed between the RAND team and various parts of the Air Force, and the thinking of many Air Force officers had already been affected by contact with the ideas contained in the study. While the mental set of the policy-maker doubtless may have important implications for policy, it does not follow that a "policy" change will necessarily result from a change in attitude or outlook.

The fact that a policy change follows in a temporal sequence the submission of advice does not, of course, necessarily imply a causal relationship between the two. It is also evident that influential advice often may come from different sources. Witness, for example, the decision to accelerate plans for the development of the ICBM as a military weapon. A RAND scientist, Bruno Augenstein, and scientists of the Von Neumann Committee independently arrived at the conclusion that smaller weight warheads could make such a weapon system feasible. In such a case, it clearly becomes difficult to assign weights to the relative impact of the different advisers.

Added to these general considerations is the fact that the effective advisory group usually goes to great pains to conceal its impact on policy. It is not a sensible tactic to claim credit for particular decisions, since this will likely irritate, annoy, and even frighten those who must assume final responsibility for decisions. On the contrary, one of the most important tasks of the advisers is to elicit the decision-maker's involvement in the study's fate. Clearly, this can be accomplished more readily in most circumstances by making the decision-maker feel the ideas are really reflections of his own thinking than by making him appear obtuse and intransigent. In the present case, the final publication of R-266 was held up to 1 April, 1954, in part to permit the Air Force to implement some of the suggested changes on its own prior to the report's formal release. An opportunity was thus afforded for the decision-makers to have already initiated policy changes at the time R-266 was being circulated generally within the defense establishment. The final wording of the report also reflects this concern with the sensitivities of the decision-makers. Phrases like "the *formerly*-programmed" and "the *then*-programmed system" were used to refer to the base system originally planned for the 1956–1961 period, and care was taken to note the efforts made by the Air Force to revise the original plans.

Nonetheless, despite these difficulties which must accompany any effort to identify the policy impact of a research product or item of advice, the evidence in the present case clearly indicates that the RAND base study was the catalyst to major Air Force policy changes.

A chain of personal interaction establishes beyond doubt that the ideas developed in the base study were brought to the attention of Air Force decision-makers. Furthermore, an unmistakable causal relationship seems to exist in this case between the advice and the policy changes. The evidence suggests that the distinction between a first strike and a second strike capability — perhaps *the* central contribution of R-266 — originated with the Wohlstetter team. The concept was essentially a novel one. No other study or other group had so clearly recognized its importance and spelled out its implications for U.S. policy. Several previous studies had dealt generally with the problem of vulnerability, but none had drawn explicit attention to the need for developing a deterrent force capable of surviving an initial enemy atomic assault and still inflicting unacceptable damage on the enemy. Nor had the operating procedures and strategic doctrines of the defense agencies reflected a clear appreciation prior to the base study of the need to achieve a secure deterrent capability. . . .

It remains to complete the story of the basing study's impact on Air Force policy. In September 1953 an important breakthrough occurred when the Air Staff Ad Hoc Committee reached agreement and endorsed the study's broad policy suggestions. Its report concurred with the RAND findings that the programmed base system would be extremely vulnerable in the 1956–1961 period, and found the RAND-proposed overseas re-fueling base concept generally the most feasible approach to maintaining a high strike capability with reduced vulnerability. Of particular importance in the Ad Hoc Committee's report was the estimate in the Installations Section of the report that the overseas refueling base system would save at least $1,000,000,000 over the programmed system in construction costs alone. This augured well for the disposition of the RAND study. For it held up the prospect to the top Air Force decision-makers of achieving a more secure capability *and actually saving money in the process.*

In October, the issues went to the Air Force Council as General White had promised. There the Ad Hoc Committee appointed to evaluate the RAND study presented its report, after which Wohlstetter briefed the Council for an hour and a half.

The Air Force Council continued its deliberations for some three weeks. Quite properly, only Air Force officers participated in these final deliberations of exactly how the RAND research would be translated into Air Force policy. In late October 1953, the Council reached a decision on the following essential points: (1) That the vulnerability of air base facilities be recognized in all Air Staff planning and action; (2) That a hardening program be initiated on critical facilities in overseas bases; (3) That new overseas bases be constructed to the specifications of ground-refueling functions; (4) That exceptions to these instructions will require special justification; and (5) That vulnerable stocks of material on overseas bases be reduced. Shortly thereafter, in early November, the Air Force Chief of Staff ratified the Council action.

Changes were quick to follow. Air Force's plans no longer called for the deployment of the bulk of the strike force in overseas bases at the outbreak of hostilities. Instead, Operation Full-House, a new system employing the RAND proposed overseas staging base concept, was adopted. The construction program on overseas bases was modified significantly; some critical facilities were dispersed and hardened. Runways at some new bases were made narrower so as to reduce construction costs and make possible the addition of more bases to the system (in keeping with the RAND suggestion that a larger number of cheaper bases would complicate the enemy's problem in launching a surprise attack). Measures designed to safeguard key personnel at overseas bases were put into effect. And plans for an expensive major depot in Alaska, on which it would be possible to do long-term maintenance of SAC bombers, were cancelled.

In all, the base study had made several dozen specific suggestions. Some of these were adopted in toto by the Air Force, some were partially adopted, and some were never adopted. In addition, the Air Force initiated certain changes on its own that did not relate to any specific RAND suggestion, but that indirectly grew out of the Air Force's consideration of the problem raised by the basing study. The changes affected many parts of the Air Force hierarchy, including the functional command level and the Air Staff units responsible for war plans, logistics, installations, personnel and even the Directorate for Medical Requirements. The changes also were distributed over a time span: some went into effect almost immediately, while others were adopted only at various later points. Follow-up research to the basing study by Wohlstetter and Hoffman led to further specific changes in Air Force policies and procedure. The "fail-safe" procedure now employed by SAC, whereby SAC bombers are sent winging toward enemy targets on receipt of even ambiguous warning only to return automatically to their bases unless given an explicit Presidential order to proceed to target, was recommended in the next major study. The concept of the airborne alert and increased readiness of SAC forces also originated from the later RAND research. RAND suggestions on the importance of warning of enemy nuclear and thermonuclear attack, too, contributed to important changes in Air Force policies. Later RAND studies also pointed out certain problems of command and control under wartime conditions and the need for hardening ICBM sites which influenced Air Force policies.

In the end, the Air Force does not come out badly as a user of advice in the present case. It was neither uncritically receptive nor hostile to the suggestions. Though made uncomfortable by the findings of the RAND study, the Air Force recognized the need for innovation. And it acted with discretion and reasonable expedition in taking the steps necessary to guard against the dangers brought to light in the study even though this involved substantial changes in its plans and operating procedures. The delay and opposition that developed was hardly surprising in view of the magnitude of some of the proposed changes. . . .

PATRICK J. McGARVEY

DIA: Intelligence to Please

The senior players in the national security bureaucracy are dependent upon their subordinates for the information and analysis upon which their decisions are based. However, the bureaucratic organizations which supply the information and analysis frequently have interests and objectives which diverge from the needs of their superiors and which influence the form and content of the data they communicate. The impact of organizational interests and objectives on the responsiveness of subordinates to their superiors is illustrated by the operations and practices of the Defense Intelligence Agency (DIA) in the Pentagon.

The intelligence reports of the individual military services tend to supply information and analysis which support and justify their respective positions on the issue under consideration. DIA was established in large measure to counter this tendency and to minimize the influence of the services' organizational interests on military intelligence. As Patrick McGarvey demonstrates, the efforts have been substantially unsuccessful, and the output from DIA is more inclined to serve the interests of the military services than the needs of good decisionmaking by their civilian superiors. The Secretary of Defense remains dependent upon DIA for intelligence, while the incentives for those who serve in DIA remain those of advancing their careers by supporting the positions and advancing the objectives of their military superiors.

At the least, recognizing that the information supplied is unreliable, the Secretary may rely on alternative sources (where available) or proceed on the basis of deficient data. At the worst, the Secretary will fail to recognize

Reprinted with permission from *The Washington Monthly* (July, 1970). Copyright 1970 by The Washington Monthly Company.

the particular distortions in the intelligence reports he receives. To this extent, he will make decisions based on information designed less to reflect reality than to enhance careers and protect organizations.

Among a multitude of examples of the Pentagon's proclivity for laboring mountainously and bringing forth mice, an instructive one is the Defense Intelligence Agency. DIA is responsible for providing the Secretary of Defense, and ultimately the President, with up-to-date facts about military matters of all kinds and with dispassionate assessments of what those facts portend. Presumably, it is because statesmen possess this crucial secret information that they can resolve so much more wisely than an uninformed man in the street such issues as, say, whether or not to send American soldiers into Cambodia. However, the assiduous cultivation by the diplomatic and military establishment of the presumption that it is on the basis of "having all the facts" that a President acts, does not mean that it has much basis in reality. Leaving aside the fascinating question of the extent to which any secret intelligence, as compared with political calculation or predilection or dogma, influences decisions, the secret intelligence dispensed by DIA is all too often of a quality that makes it more of a hindrance than a help to rational decision-making.

Two kinds of defects are pervasive in DIA — an outfit commonly referred to in the intelligence community as "the taxi squad" or "the country club" or "the old people's home." One, probably the less injurious of the two because it is so common a Washington phenomenon that most officials are bound to suspect it and try to compensate for it, is the tendency of any operating agency's evaluation arm to justify the agency's operations. Thus, DIA's reports — which to some extent are necessarily guesses — about, for example, the amount of damage bombing the Ho Chi Minh trail inflicts and how much that damage limits Hanoi's capability to fight, are almost certain to be the highest possible guesses, not so much through slovenliness or mendacity as in accordance with natural bureaucratic law. Or, to cite another example, in determining whether or not the F-105 that the Chinese shot down in May, 1966, had really strayed into Chinese air space as the Chinese claimed, there were two basic sources of data: radar plots and the accounts of the pilots of the other planes in the mission. The radar plots, which had an impressive record of previous accuracy and no personal ax to grind, showed that the flight had flown well into Chinese territory. The returned pilots, who if they were human had some inclination to exonerate themselves, said the flight had done no such thing. DIA resolved this conflict in accordance with the natural law: it took the word of the pilots.

This kind of self-justification, which is by no means an exclusively military vice, may be absurd; but a good deal of the time its sheer blatancy insures that it won't be taken very seriously. Much harder to detect and guard against are the workings of DIA's policy of compromise and of blandness, of pleasing everybody and therefore of informing or edifying nobody. For example, during the early days of the bombing of North Vietnam, the Army, which was pushing for a big buildup of ground forces, wanted to show that North Vietnamese forces were pouring into the South at unprecedented rates. However, the Air Force's interest was to show that very few northern troops were getting through its barrage. In theory DIA was set up to choose among such conflicting claims; in practice it generally refuses to admit that a conflict exists and comes up with something like "Enemy infiltration continued at a rate higher than last month. However, the cumulative effect of U.S. bombing has seriously degraded his ability to mount a large-scale offensive" — never mind whether mounting a large-scale offensive was what the enemy had in mind. It is hard to imagine how such an evaluation could help produce a reasoned bombing policy or, indeed, anything but an intellectual miasma.

Perhaps one reason DIA is so proficient at compromise is that it is a product of compromise itself. It was formed in October, 1961, by former Secretary of Defense McNamara in the hope that he would receive intelligence appraisals without service bias and to eliminate some of the duplication of intelligence activities in the Department of Defense (DOD). Pitched battles took place as the agency was formed. The Army was totally against it. It fought every suggestion, preferring to hang onto the responsibility of producing its own intelligence. The Navy, too, was against the formation of DIA but fought less vehemently. The Air Force seized the ball and ran with it. As a result most of the top management jobs at the beginning went to blue suiters. This brawling forced a crucial compromise between McNamara and the service intelligence staffs. To quiet the opposition McNamara finally allowed the DIA to be placed under the supervision of the Joint Chiefs of Staff. In short, it was agreed that DIA would serve the civilians through the military rather than report to the Secretary through a (civilian) Assistant Secretary of Defense for Intelligence.

By charter, then, the DIA serves two masters — the JCS and the Secretary of Defense. What this entails with respect to the JCS is providing intelligence background and assessments for just about every decision paper that is put out by the chiefs, briefing the JCS daily on overnight developments and keeping them abreast whenever necessary of longer-range developments worldwide, and working closely with every component of the Joint Staff, the working arm of the JCS. If, for example, the J-5 Plans Staff is drafting a contingency planning paper on Africa, DIA must provide as much detail as is necessary, which could include data on coast and landing beaches, urban maps that show key installations, political, sociological, and economic studies of the countries involved, and, of course, in-depth assessments of the country's military capabilities. In other areas, such as science and technology, DIA must keep the JCS informed on such technical breakthroughs as are achieved by any and all potential enemies around the world. The discovery of a new radar site in the Soviet Union, for example, can generate more paper in the Pentagon than the rational mind can comprehend. If the J-3 Operations Staff wants to plan a bombing campaign, the DIA must come up with suitable lists of targets, pinpointing them on maps and assessing the likely effect the destruction of the targets would have on the target country — a service that reached new heights of absurdity, which will be touched on later, during the bombing of North Vietnam.

The responsibilities the DIA has to the Secretary of Defense are not so easy to define because they depend on the Secretary's attitude. McNamara was a demanding taskmaster. To date, Melvin Laird has chosen not to be one. Several functions, however, persist under Laird. Public affairs people in the Secretary's office relay a lot of foul balls DIA's way. A hot flyer will come winging down with a photocopy of a press article stating, for example, that the Soviets are flying MIGs over Egypt. DIA will be asked to provide, by noon, "a complete assessment of the details. How do they stack up with classified holdings? How did they get this information (as if DIA knew)? Give me a classified reply and an unclassified reply." At one time the Secretary's staff demanded and got detailed information on all matters that had intelligence relevance. This, of course, put DIA squarely in the middle of controversies between the Secretary's staff and the JCS. For example, it had to provide the JCS with enemy infiltration data that would support a request for more troops for Vietnam, and, on the other hand, it had to provide the Secretary's staff with an assessment of Vietnamese troop strength, U.S. "body count" claims, and the results of the bombing of North Vietnam, all of which would be used as ammunition to shoot down the requests.

Indeed, figures are used to support any imaginable position, and often they are the same figures. I was treated to a fine example of number shuffling several months ago. A knowledgeable source in DIA informed me that the personnel office was concerned about the attrition rate among the agency's college trainees and had called a conference of young men who had gone through the year-long training program to find out what was on their minds. At this session the personnel staffers disclosed that better than 60 per cent of college trainees in the past two years had quit. A confidential survey among those remaining indicated that 55 per cent were actively seeking employment elsewhere. When I published an article containing these figures, DIA quickly denied it. It stated that the figure was approximately 27 per cent, normal attrition rate in government and industry. Further digging revealed that in the "refining" of the original 60 per cent figure DIA had:

1. diluted the issue by "broadening the data base" to take into account all hirings and resignations during the period, including clerks, messengers, and secretaries;

2. included in the total only those who quit within 12 months of completion of training; resignations after 12 months were deemed immaterial to the question at hand;

3. omitted from its new figures men who had resigned to return to school for graduate work;

4. dropped from the total all men who had been drafted and failed to return to DIA after discharge;

5. included in its new figures only those men who had resigned while in grades GS-7 and GS-9; higher grade resignations were not included.

Another function DIA performs for the Secretary of Defense is to prepare detailed fact sheets for his trips and interviews. DIA also keeps him informed daily of worldwide developments and provides him with estimates of likely future developments. Most important to the Secretary, DIA is expected to serve as arbiter among the services' divergent points of view on intelligence matters. It has presumably been given the clout to do this since its director wears three stars and thus outranks the two-star chiefs of the service intelligence branches.

Indeed, DIA's performance with respect to Vietnam should have proved the futility of a joint service approach to intelligence, and in fact Secretaries McNamara and Clifford finally stopped paying any attention to DIA and went to the CIA for answers. From 1964–65, when U.S. involvement in Vietnam began to be considerable, until late 1966 or early 1967, the generals in Saigon worked to build up U.S. troop strength. Therefore, they wanted every bit of evidence brought to the fore that could show that infiltration was increasing. DIA obliged and also emphasized in all reports the enemy's capability to recruit forces from the South Vietnamese population. In 1967 a second period began. The high priests of Saigon decided that we were "winning." Then the paramount interest became to show the enemy's reduced capability to recruit and a slowdown in infiltration due to our bombing. The tune and emphasis of reports from the field changed radically, and so did those put out by DIA.

It should not be concluded that anyone suppressed evidence. No one did. The military in Saigon sent all the facts back to Washington eventually. During the buildup period, infiltration data and recruitment data came in via General Westmoreland's daily cablegram. Data from field contact with enemy units came amid the more mundane cables or by courier up to five weeks later. Cables from Westmoreland, of course, were given higher priority in Washington. When we started "winning," detailed reports high-lighting "body counts" and statistics on how many villages were pacified were cabled with Westmoreland's signature; recruitment studies were pouched or cabled with the reports on the fluctuating price of rice. It was all a matter of emphasis.

During all this time DIA was thoroughly enmeshed in the numbers game. It paid little or no attention to what Hanoi was saying on the radio, dis-counting it as propaganda. It made little effort to perceive the enemy's view of the war. It made little effort to reason out what the enemy's strategy was, why he believed he was winning, what he was saying publicly about how he was going to fight the war, or how the bombing was affecting his morale. It was too busy keeping up with the flow of numbers from Saigon.

As the air campaign crept northward, the Operations people on the Joint Staff wanted bigger and better targets. They didn't ask the intelligence people what was worth hitting or what a rational plan of attack might be. On the contrary, they demanded targets that a certain weapons system could attack. They had a TV-guided missile, and they wanted to use it. "Pick out a building for us to hit," they'd say. DIA could have told the JCS this was the wrong approach, but it played the game. It sent photo-interpreters scurrying to their scanners to find, say, a two- or three-story building in an area open to U.S. raids. If they saw no signs of military activity around the building they would dub it a "possible military storage area," a description that gave J-3 the right to go hunting.

The Operations staff's biggest hangup was over the prohibition on bombing the port of Haiphong. It refused to accept the judgment of the CIA that bombing the port wouldn't stop the flow of goods into North Vietnam. It refused to believe that the North Vietnamese man-packed arms across the Chinese border and imported little by sea. DIA, bowing to J-3's insistence, came up with a list of several hundred small, insignificant targets in and near Haiphong, listing them as crucial and suggesting that the cumulative effect of hitting all 200 or more barge and ferry landings, rail spurs, bridges, and road intersections would be the same as flattening Haiphong — again a triumph for the art of compromise and no doubt small comfort to the pilots shot down in that heavily defended area.

Well before the Tet Offensive of January, 1968, when the enemy buildup at the Khe Sanh first became obvious, two DIA analysts who had been studying enemy tactics and strategy for four years sat down and wrote a paper that concluded that the enemy was planning a feint at Khe Sanh. They based this judgment on their interpretation of General Giap's fighting methods over the past two years. They outlined a likely enemy course of action designed to draw American forces to the Khe Sanh area so that the populous coastal plains would be left thinly defended and concluded that perhaps it would be unwise to react to the Khe Sanh buildup. They presented the findings of their paper at a briefing, much to the amusement of all present. They suggested that the paper be cabled to Saigon as a DIA assessment of the situation and that the JCS be given the benefit of their thoughts. This, too, caused merriment among the assembled. "How could you possibly know more than General Westmoreland?" they were asked. Their boss, an Army Colonel, finally got angry at their persistence and taped the paper to the wall beside his desk, claiming that the analysts had just stuck their professional reputations on the line, and adding he hoped they were wrong. The paper hung there until late in March, 1968, after the Tet Offensive, which occurred largely on the coastal plain, and after the enemy ended the siege of Khe Sanh without ever assaulting it. Then it was taken down quietly. The Colonel never mentioned the subject again. The JCS was never given a copy, and it was never cabled to Saigon.

The pressures on DIA to conform to the views of the military are hard to resist. Take a mechanism known as the National Intelligence Estimate (NIE), which is supposed to represent the best judgment of the intelligence community on a particular issue and is used by the President and his Cabinet in formulating policy. Everyone in the intelligence business has a chance to assert his point of view in these estimates, and it is here that DIA's role is crucial. DIA is well aware that many service judgments are biased and don't reflect reality. Its obligation, in those cases, is to assume its responsibility as arbiter among the services and establish a Defense position on the issue, and it works hard at doing just that. But strong pressures usually come in through the back door.

For one thing, there is something called the "Eyes Only" cable that is sent "back channel" and is severely restricted in dissemination. Usually no more than five people see it. I have seen "Eyes Only" cables come in from the U.S. Commanders in Honolulu and Saigon to the Director of DIA requesting that he give more than a passing consideration to the command viewpoint about this or that. The language is always moving. Such a cable is likely to start off complimenting the recipient for the fine job he is doing and then work in high-sounding phrases which evoke motherhood, apple pie, the American flag, and, of course, the uniform. It then implies that the sender would like to see a particular judgment or set of figures changed to conform to the command view. It rarely offers any evidence to support this request. It is sure to close with a veiled threat that the recipient's career is in jeopardy if he doesn't play the game and "get on the team." Many estimates have been changed or reworded because of an "Eyes Only" cable from a field commander. In one instance the Air Force Chief of Intelligence called my boss at DIA about a nearly completed estimate on U.S. bombing in Laos. He told him that he was sending a team down to change the wording of the estimate and that my boss had better remember what color his uniform was. Of course it was the same as the General's blue. The team arrived, and, over the protests of the DIA analyst, a compromise was reached.

The classic example of command influence on intelligence matters occurred just after the Tet Offensive in January, 1968. In the early weeks of February the JCS insisted that the offensive was total military defeat for the enemy — General Westmoreland told them so in his daily cables. DIA didn't agree with this interpretation, but it watered down every paper it wrote on this subject so that its position was impossible to determine. Then General Wheeler went to Saigon and came back with Westmoreland's request for 206,000 troops to "clean up" the "defeated" enemy. Suddenly it was legitimate to say that the Tet Offensive had really "set us back." Everybody on the service staffs, with DIA leading the pack, started writing gloomy estimates with unaccustomed forthrightness and clarity.

Everyone connected with the DIA is partially at fault for the agency's shortcomings. This includes the military who run it, the civilians who staff it, the Secretary of Defense, the JCS, and the individual service staffs. As far as the military men who manage the agency are concerned, their guilt or incompetence results simply from the fact that they are uniformed men with a parent service. Imagine, if you will, what the prospect of a tour with DIA looks like to a military officer. He knows or soon learns that he will be thrust into a position in which, on occasion, his professional judgment will vary markedly from that of his parent service. He will be expected to defend a position that could enrage his Chief of Staff — but officers who do so more than once get known fast and are accorded an appropriate "reward" at a later date in terms of promotion and assignment. Consider also that a tour at DIA — normally two to three years — is very short when compared to a 20- to 30-year military career. And so most officers assigned to DIA go through a predictable pattern. They come on board as "hard-chargers," ready to set the world on fire. They stick to their principles through one or two scrapes. Then they become a little more circumspect, letting individual issues slide by and rationalizing that it wasn't a crunch question anyway. Finally, they resign themselves to "sweating out" their tours and playing every situation by ear. They avoid committing themselves or making decisions. They refuse to tackle the agency's long-term organizational ills, because doing so would make too many waves.

The shortness of the tours of duty of the military managers of the agency (about nine-tenths of management jobs are filled by military officers) causes some long-term problems. These officers are interested largely in getting good performance out of staff while they are there, not in building up long-run staff or agency capabilities. They want to impress the General, let him know that he's running a "cracker-jack" outfit. The

General, of course, is largely occupied with current problems, so his subordinates gear up to service his needs. This has resulted over the years in the reduction of DIA's long-term research capability to near zero. More than 95 per cent of the effort expended in DIA on Vietnam, for example, is on current problems. Long-term study groups have been disbanded and the staff reassigned to the current problem area. Basic intelligence for detailed studies is simply not getting done or is whipped out with a week-end's furious overtime. The managers who choose to cut the long-term staff don't worry about the ultimate effect because by the time it becomes evident they'll be off on other assignments.

Another problem is the "can do" attitude that prevails among the officer corps. It is unthinkable for an officer to tell his superior that he cannot complete a task. It is a form of heresy. Officers accept a requirement for four or six extra hours' work a day when they know their staff already puts in 12- or 14-hour days. Rarely, if ever, does anyone say no, or point out that certain jobs take time. "Yes, Sir, can do!", is all that is heard. The result is an attitude among DIA staff members that is captured in their motto, "If you want it real bad, you're gonna get it real bad."

There is the age-old military problem of "time in grade" — the tradition that confers genius-like powers on the man who's been around the longest. The impact that this practice has on the efficient functioning of DIA can be illustrated by the fact that I had nine bosses within two years and that each of the first eight was unseated because someone with more time in grade came along. The game of musical chairs goes on constantly. One Army Colonel had been the Commander of the Special Forces in South Vietnam before he was assigned to DIA. He came into the Vietnam division and was contributing tremendously until another Colonel with more time in grade came along. So they transferred the Special Forces Colonel to the Soviet division and assigned the new Colonel to the Vietnam division. The new Colonel was a graduate of the Army's Foreign Area Specialist Training program in Czech affairs.

Then there is the civilian staff. It is second rate, particularly at the middle and upper levels. The military who run the place have made it that way. They have consistently shown over the years that there's no room in DIA for truly capable civilians. They have discouraged original thought, drained the civilian staff of initiative, and inculcated them with the "don't make waves" approach to everything. Very few civilians hold down management slots in DIA, but that doesn't mean they are without influence. Throughout the agency there are civilian deputies at most levels of command. They form an infrastructure that wields a great deal of influence in the day-to-day operation of the organization. The problem is that the ones who have survived that long in the bureaucracy are thoroughly bureaucratized. They are the ones who advise a brash Lieutenant Colonel to "soften his judgment," "temper his language," and "play the game." Their strength, in many cases, comes from their detailed familiarity with the inner workings of the complicated JCS paper mill. They know when to delay a paper, when to react quickly to one, how to kill one, how to insure that it gets through, and, most importantly, how and where to find out exactly what the General wants the paper to say. They then set out to insure that the General's wishes are translated verbatim into the final product, even if those wishes conflict with the evidence on hand or the views of knowledgeable analysts.

Finally, there are half-breed civilians at DIA — retired military officers. These men are generally capable in their areas of job experience, but two factors virtually negate their experience and job skill. The first, and most important, is the fact that they are retired and looking for an easy deal. Their fighting days are over, and they want to take it easy. They never make waves. They simply do what is asked of them. The other factor is simply that they are heavily biased in favor of the military, and they color all of their judgments with this bias. Their attitudes and actions also have a definite influence on the civilians in the agency. For one thing they are hired at the middle grades and clog up the promotion cycle for the younger men. They also have an "in" with the military managers and can frequently be seen on the fairways and greens of the Army-Navy Country Club. Somehow they are always the ones to get the trips abroad.

As far as I can see, the only way to extricate DIA from this morass is to take it altogether out of military hands. There should be an Assistant Secretary of Defense for Intelligence, a civilian. The line of command within the agency should be staffed by civilians — though not those now present, who are too far down the bureaucratic path for salvation. In the think-tanks around the country, in the universities, and in other areas of government, there is a pool of very capable men who could enable DIA to meet its enormous responsibilities. With civilians in the management positions, the chances that service bias would overwhelm, distort, or avoid intelligence judgments would be considerably less. Military men can play an important role in DIA, but not in the management of the agency. In substantive areas dealing with foreign military capabilities, the expertise of U.S. infantrymen or armor specialists, for example, can be put to good use.

Any prediction for the future of DIA has to be grim. One recent glimmer of hope (now fading) came when Secretary Laird directed his assistant for administration, Robert L. Froehlke, to take a hard look at Defense intelligence activities. However, it seems that Froehlke has fallen prey to the military briefings that he was given at DIA. He has set up an office to "coordinate" all DOD intelligence activities — and if there is one thing the DOD can do without, it is another office to coordinate things. DIA probably will grow larger, less productive, and more expensive as time goes on, coordination to the contrary notwithstanding. It will probably continue to drop the ball in emergencies like the Tet Offensive. DIA will doubtless continue to supply the nation's decisionmakers with evaluations that do them little good and potentially much harm. One can only hope that the decisionmakers pay little attention to what DIA tells them.

MORRIS J. BLACHMAN

The Stupidity of Intelligence

The following description of the sources of distortion in the Air Force's reports on the results of bombing targets in North Vietnam is suggestive of the manner in which organizational and personal interests come to dominate less partisan objectives.

The Air Force believes its organizational "essence" to be the capability to deliver bombs on target and to engage other aircraft in combat. In the Vietnam War, opportunities were restricted primarily to the first mission. Therefore its organizational success became operationally defined in terms of apparent progress of the Air Force's bombing campaigns in Indochina. With competition from the Army and Navy, its future prospects, as well as its claims to resources, roles and missions, and organizational autonomy after the war depended upon making a good impression with the civilian decisionmakers during the conflict. Accordingly, when conflicting information on bomb damage emerged, there were strong organizational incentives to rely on the source which reported the most damage — the pilots' estimates — rather than the source presumed to be more accurate — photo reconnaissance. The personal interests of career officers became coincident with the organizational well-being of the service. If the Air Force did not look good in Vietnam, their careers would be stunted by their service's stagnation afterward. Even if some officers did not accept that reasoning, their careers were in the hands of superiors who did. When an order came down to investigate opportunities to expand bombing operations, an officer concerned about his future career would oblige with a long list of new targets.

Thus the organizational interests of the Air Force and the personal interests of career officers tended to generate intelligence reports which exaggerated the effects of the bombing. Then the "success" achieved on

Reprinted from Charles Peters, editor, *Inside the System*: *A Washington Monthly Reader* (New York: Praeger, 1970) with permission.

paper through such reports was cited to press for an expansion of the Air Force mission. The senior players who depended on this information for their decisions regarding war strategy may have unwittingly based their choices on interpretations of reality disguised as factual reports.

When all the intelligence information from Vietnam was fed into a computer, the machine calculated that the United States had destroyed all of Vietnam and had won the war two years earlier. The story is apocryphal, but it might well have happened. Certainly the computer could have reached that conclusion on the basis of the claims made by the military about the effects of its bombing of North Vietnam.

As an Air Force officer attached to Tactical Reconnaissance in Vietnam, I saw at first hand the way the military, and especially the Air Force, gathered and reported the results of its bombing of the North. Those reports greatly exaggerated the effects of the bombing, misleading the American public and, to the extent that they took the reports at face value, misleading both military and civilian policymakers. No one, except the North Vietnamese themselves, knows just how much the Air Force's claims differed from reality. Based on what I saw in my little corner of the air war, the actual destruction was often less than half what the Air Force claimed. (Whether the bombing, or indeed the war itself, was justified on military or moral grounds is a question that lies beyond the scope of this article.)

Yet there was no conscious conspiracy to inflate the numbers of trucks and bridges that supposedly had been destroyed by American bombs. No one, at least no one around me, was systematically lying about the bombing. The Air Force had, in its photo intelligence techniques, remarkably accurate methods of measuring bomb destruction. Those techniques were put to full use in Vietnam, and yet the information they revealed was consistently played down in favor of the far less accurate pilots' reports, resulting in a grossly false picture of the military effects of the bombing. The explanation of this paradox lies, I believe, in the organization of the military and of military intelligence.

This was the system as I saw it. Strikes were ordered against targets in the North selected by us in Tactical Reconnaissance, within the limits set in Washington. As soon as they returned, the pilots reported at their debriefing the effects of the bombs they dropped. Very soon after that — sometimes within an hour or two, sometimes the next day — reconnaissance aircraft flew over the sites and photographed them. Those pictures were developed and analyzed by the photo interpreters. Thus two reports of what happened were available — those of the pilots themselves and the evidence of the photo intelligence.

Usually the general was briefed the next day about the results of the mission. In some cases only the pilots' reports were available. But even when photo intelligence was available, most of the attention was fixed on the pilots' reports. This occurred during most of the briefings I knew about, even though the pilots consistently claimed far greater destruction than the more accurate photo-intelligence reports reflected.

Why was there such a discrepancy? Much of it was inevitable. The pilots were flying at 600 miles an hour and trying to destroy their targets, while dodging ground fire and SAM missiles and sometimes MIG aircraft. Their job was to drop their bombs and try to get back alive. They hardly had time for a critical look at what their bombs had done, and they would be less than human if they understated the accomplishments of missions in which they had risked their lives and on which their future careers depended.

Duplication was another frequent source of error. Four aircraft, for example, would strike a column of trucks moving along a road in the North. At the debriefing, the first pilot might report that he destroyed three trucks and damaged two more. The second pilot might report four trucks destroyed and three damaged, the third pilot four and four, and the fourth pilot five and four. How many trucks were destroyed and damaged? Simple arithmetic provides a total of 16 destroyed and 13 damaged. That's what the general would be told at the briefing. But experience showed that — whenever the pilots' reports could be checked by photo intelligence — the total usually fell far short of the pilots' reports, because two or more pilots would list the same trucks. Most of the time there was no way to determine the extent of such duplication.

Imagine four pilots sent to "interdict" a rail line.[1] The first pilot drops his bomb; he and his fellow airmen see the bombs explode on the tracks and they see what appear to be several "secondary" explosions (things which blow up after being hit by a bomb, such as ammunition, oil drums, or vehicles). Back at the debriefing, the pilots all report that the tracks were destroyed, interdicting the line, and that there were several secondary explosions. Later, when the aerial photos are available, the interpreters see a different picture. Nothing in or around the tracks has been destroyed. The secondary explosions turned out to be large piles of loose dirt blown into the air by the bombs and scattered along the tracks, making the line look as if it had been destroyed. In reality, the railroad can be put back into operation with a few shovels.

For the American public, these distortions create two distinct problems. On the one hand, press briefings about the bombing were invariably

---

[1] Details of specific incidents have been changed to avoid violating security regulations.

condensations of the pilots' reports and were rarely corrected by photo intelligence. Sometimes the results of photo intelligence were not made available to the public. When they were, the newspapers usually concentrated on today's bombing results rather than the correction of yesterday's errors. So the public simply did not have access to accurate information about the bombing.

On the other hand, the public often received strangely contradictory stories. One day a target would be reported destroyed and a day or two later we were bombing it again. A typical example was a three-span bridge we bombed three times in six days. The first time we reportedly destroyed two spans, the second time all three spans, and on the third strike two more spans.

I often wondered if anyone would comment on such an astonishing accomplishment as destroying seven spans of a three-span bridge. But no one said a word, much less questioned our claim, and the bridge remained 233 per cent destroyed. That was the case with many other demonstrably unbelievable claims the Air Force was making for the bombing. Everyone in the system who had access to photo intelligence — from our commanding general down to the enlisted men, and from the general up the chain of command to the Pentagon — repeatedly saw evidence that our bombing reports were at worst false and at best exaggerated. Although a few of us tried to challenge the system, there was no impact on the Air Force's claims. Therefore, those claims, and not what we privately knew to be the truth, became the public record of the bombing of North Vietnam.

There are two major reasons why the system operated as it did: first, intense competition among the services; and second, the system of rewards and punishments inherent in the promotion pattern.

The Air Force exists only to fight in the air or to bomb. The Air Force had to have the bombing of the North — it was the only real Air Force show in the Vietnam war. The career men around me felt keenly that their service was at a disadvantage in the war's inter-service rivalries. The war in the South was an Army and Marine Corps show, with the Air Force supplying important, but little publicized, air support. The Navy had horned in on the air war, and, even if the bombing were to stop, the sailors could always go back to their ships. But for the Air Force, it was bomb — or do nothing. Without the bombing, the Air Force could hope for little publicity and glory — which would mean smaller appropriations and perhaps less attention to Air Force desires. To criticize the bombing claims meant, therefore, to hurt your own organization and to benefit its rivals. Stopping the bombing could be seen as a failure for the Air Force.

Rivalry among these authoritarian systems put great pressure on those within them. On the higher levels, there was frequent sniping between the Air Force and the Navy, with each accusing the other of incompetence in the air war. Another example of this was the military intelligence unit whose commanding officer ordered his men not to exchange information with a nearby unit belonging to another service. Often, also, the Air Force withheld its bombing reports from the Navy.

The promotion system created exceptional pressures for conformity on career officers. Promotion depended heavily on the evaluation report of one's commanding officer; one unfavorable mention in the report could postpone promotion for many years and, perhaps, permanently blight a career. For a colonel a black mark might mean losing his only chance to become a general. So it would have taken a certain amount of courage for the colonel to tell the general that the air strike the general had ordered — and for whose success the colonel felt he would be held responsible — was a failure. (One Air Force general who criticized the bombing was reportedly removed from command and booted upstairs.)

The career officers seemed to fear the role of the messenger who brings bad news. This, of course, is nothing new. At least since Cleopatra, messengers have been punished for bringing news that upset the commanders' preconceptions. Such fears in the Air Force may have been unfounded, or at least exaggerated, but they were real in their consequences. Some organizations compensate for the bad messenger by offering incentives for useful criticism. But I doubt if any Air Force officer thought he would score brownie points by devising an intelligence system that would have reported less destruction from the bombing of the North.

This type of system can lead to distortions at all levels. For example, at some point along the chain of command the decision is made to increase the number of targets. By the time the order gets to the working level — that is, to the men who will actually scan the films of the North for possible targets — it has changed from a stated desire to know about more potential targets to a hard-nosed command to nominate "75 targets" within a couple of days. Once when this happened, one of the men told an officer that they had been unable to find anything of military significance, that they only saw a few villages. The officer retorted: "I think you'd better scan the film again for those suspected 'possible military storage areas.' " Although the order was not explicit, the implication was clear: use a euphemism but produce the target. The airmen felt the pressure very strongly. I remember one of them saying that he just didn't know what to do. If he didn't do what the officer wanted, the officer might give him a bad efficiency report and his career would at best be set back and at worst ruined.

When I was in Vietnam, I wondered at times what the policymakers in Washington believed about our bombings of the North. The Pentagon had access to both the inflated pilots' reports and the much more modest claims of photo intelligence. What did the top military leaders believe, and what kind of evaluation of bombings did they pass on to the civilian leadership? Did the civilian leaders take the Air Force claims at face value, or did they apply some private discount, either because they knew the fallibility of pilot reports or because they had an innate skepticism of any institution's self-evaluation? Were they just allowing the public to be gulled about the effectiveness of the bombing — or were they letting themselves be gulled as well?

The answers to these questions remain shrouded. Recently I had occasion to read through some 475 public statements on the bombing by Lyndon Johnson, Dean Rusk, and Robert McNamara, all made while they were in office. Although these public statements of the leaders of the Johnson Administration, under which the bombing began and ended, do not reveal their private thoughts, they do give us some insight into the level of information the Executive was willing to share with the public. The first impression I got was of the constantly shifting reasons given for the bombing. I counted 30 separate, though often overlapping and even contradictory, justifications for the bombing of the North. They varied from specific military reasons such as to "inhibit, to reduce, to deflect the movement southward of men and material" (McNamara, 1965); to highly generalized ones like "we are bombing North Vietnam because it is violating two solemn international agreements" (Johnson, 1967); to a justification which claims that if we were to stop the bombing "what incentive . . . would [North Vietnam] ever have for making peace?" (Rusk, 1968). What did it mean to talk about the bombing having met all its objectives, as Secretary Rusk did on separate occasions, particularly when he admitted in a hearing before the Senate Foreign Relations Committee in March, 1968, that infiltration had risen from an average of 1,500 per month in 1965 to 5,500–6,000 in 1967? Did Rusk really believe the kinds of publicity that appeared in the newspapers on the success of the air war? He certainly defended the ability of the air war over North Vietnam to accomplish its mission.

By contrast, McNamara showed himself to be skeptical about the bombing in his last year in office. Testifying before Congress in August, 1967, McNamara said that "despite very, very large increases in air strikes, the amount of traffic over the roads had increased, and, as a matter of fact, the whole road network has increased." And then he went on to pull the rug out from under the whole military concept of the bombing of the North: "There are many who believe, and there is much evidence to support the conclusion, that the flow of men and material into the South is not determined by the air campaign in the North . . . in other words, the bottleneck is not on the lines of communication in North Vietnam but is on the lines of communication in South Vietnam."

But at the same hearing, McNamara was repeating some rather unlikely claims. In response to a Senator's question about how many trucks the

North Vietnamese had in operation, McNamara said that there were between 10,000 and 12,000 and that "we have reportedly destroyed 4,100 and reportedly damaged 4,000." Based on my experience, it is impossible to believe that the bombing destroyed anywhere near that number of trucks. The Senators quite naturally wanted to know why North Vietnam had, in McNamara's words, more trucks today than when we started the bombing. McNamara had to say the trucks were imported. This led to additional Congressional pressure for bombing the ports and changing the political character of the war — a consequence of the original false claims.

In this case, the wrong policy decision (the bombing of the ports) was not made. But such wrong decisions are continuing hazards as long as the Pentagon's civilian leadership, the Congress, and the public rely on the military's self-serving intelligence system.

MORTON H. HALPERIN AND TANG TSOU

United States Policy Toward the Offshore Islands

The United States has gone to the brink of war more than once to defend territory which is only remotely related to its national security interests. The formulation of United States policy with regard to the islands of Quemoy and Matsu illustrates both that the sources of particular national security policies and defense commitments are often only distantly related to their public justifications and that the reasons offered by the President's subordinates for a particular course of action may be only tenuously connected to what they believe.

In an important sense, the United States virtually drifted into its commitment to defend the Offshore Islands. Halperin and Tsou highlight the importance of domestic political considerations for an understanding of United States policy. The Truman administration reversed its hands-off policy toward Taiwan in order to secure bipartisan support for the Korean War. The Eisenhower administration strengthened its commitments to the Offshore Islands in part to appear to be consistent with its avowed policy of "liberation." These administrations' need to serve diverse objectives and to communicate with multiple audiences resulted in ambiguous signals, confusion, and important constraints on United States policy toward the Chinese Nationalists.

The manner in which United States policy evolved shows quite well the role and significance of *arguments* within the bureaucracy. When the President's advisers recommend a particular course of action, they are obliged

Reprinted from *Public Policy*, 15 (1966), pp. 119–138 with permission.

to offer a rationale, or arguments, in support of their advocacy. Halperin and Tsou catalogue four of the most common arguments invoked in making foreign policy. The arguments offered do not necessarily reflect what their advocates really believe; rather, they may set forth merely what certain advocates think will persuade the President to do what those advocates want. Since they are not necessarily a reflection of beliefs, arguments serve to build a consensus among those in bureaucracy who prefer the same outcome, but each for his own reasons. Each participant need only subscribe to the common arguments, not to his colleagues' motives.

Recipients of such arguments, if reasonably sophisticated, understand that the rationales are less a perception of reality than a statement of policy advocacy and that in such exchanges arguments serve as a kind of code for communicating policy positions and intensity of commitment. However, even for the most sophisticated, sufficient repetition results in an aura of reality, and the participants come to believe their own arguments and those of previous administrations. Thus, by the late 1950's, Eisenhower could contemplate using nuclear weapons to defend the Offshore Islands, and in 1962 Kennedy felt constrained to respond to threats to Quemoy and Matsu in the same manner as his predecessors.

Few of the foreign policies of the United States in the postwar period have been as controversial or as difficult to explain as the American actions in defense of the Offshore Islands of Quemoy and Matsu. At least once in the 1950's the United States went to the brink of war to defend these small islands off the coast of China and was prepared, according to the later account of President Eisenhower, to use nuclear weapons. Throughout this period, and particularly during the 1958 crisis, the United States acted in the face of widespread domestic and foreign discontent and almost no support from outside the government.

Not only is the continued American commitment to the Offshore Islands difficult to explain, but so also are the arguments with which various administrations have sought, both publicly and privately, to justify their decisions. As discussed below, one of the justifications used rests on predictions of dire consequences. The most extreme instance of predicting "dire consequences" can be found in a planning document drafted, according to President Eisenhower, by himself and his Secretary of State, John Foster Dulles, on September 4, 1958, during one of the Offshore Island crises. That memorandum describes the results of the possible fall of the Offshore Islands as follows:

> The consequences in the Far East would be even more far-reaching and catastrophic than those which followed when the United States allowed [*sic*] the Chinese mainland to be taken over by the Chinese Communists, aided and abetted by the Soviet Union.[1]

[1] Dwight D. Eisenhower, *Waging Peace* (1965), p. 692.

An effort is made here to explain American policy toward the Offshore Islands, first in historical terms and then in relation to the constraints of decision-making in a bureaucracy. We consider the process by which the United States became increasingly committed to the defense of Taiwan and slightly later to the defense of the Offshore Islands without ever being in a position to force the Nationalists off the Islands. We also discuss the stratagems used by those who sought to tie the United States to a defense of Quemoy and Matsu.

THE EVOLUTION OF U.S. POLICY

Prior to the outbreak of the Korean War, the United States had announced that it would not interfere in a Chinese Communist attempt to seize Taiwan. No mention was made of the Offshore Islands, but obviously if no American force was to be used to defend Taiwan, the United States would a fortiori not act to hold the Offshore Islands.

On June 27, 1950, following the outbreak of the Korean War, President Truman issued an order to the Seventh Fleet to begin to patrol the Taiwan Straits to prevent Communist attacks upon Taiwan or attacks from Taiwan against the Mainland. The American statement did not make any mention of the Nationalist-held Offshore Islands, and it is not clear whether in the hectic period at the opening of the war officials gave much attention to these Islands.[2]

In the operations of the Seventh Fleet in the Taiwan Straits, and in the statements of American officials on the scene, it generally appeared that the Offshore Islands were in fact excluded from the U.S. defense perimeter.[3] Moreover, U.S. ships did not try to prevent operations from the Islands directed at the Mainland. Truman was not prepared to defend the Offshore Islands. Nevertheless, having moved to defend Taiwan in order to get bipartisan support for the Korean War, he was unwilling to provoke a partisan row by trying to force a withdrawal from the Offshore Islands. The ambiguity which was to characterize the American commitment to the defense of the Offshore Islands was evident even at this time. Since Truman's statement had not specifically excluded the Offshore Islands from the U.S. defense perimeter, the Chinese Communists could not be sure whether or not the Islands would be defended by the United States.

In February of 1951 under the terms of a bilateral Mutual Defense Assistance Agreement, the United States undertook to provide military assistance to Taiwan with the understanding that the Nationalist govern-

[2] Text in *American Foreign Policy, 1950–1955* (1957), p. 2468. For a discussion of the American decision and the Chinese Communist reaction to it, see Tang Tsou, *America's Failure in China*, 1941–1950 (1963), pp. 558–564.

[3] *New York Times*, November 12, 1950, p. 14.

ment would "use the material to maintain its internal security or its legitimate self-defense." [4] No mention was made of the Offshore Islands in the agreement. Following the signing of the agreement, the United States began to train and give equipment to the troops on Taiwan but with the understanding that they would not be sent to the Offshore Islands.[5] Thus the ambiguity continued.

There is no record of any high-level consideration by the American government of the Offshore Islands question until March of 1952 when John Foster Dulles, then a Special Assistant to the Secretary of State and soon to become Foreign Policy Adviser to Presidential candidate Dwight D. Eisenhower, in a discussion with a group of State Department officials proposed that the Nationalists be authorized to increase their strength on the Offshore Islands.[6] Perhaps triggered by Dulles' remarks, the State Department undertook a study of American policy toward Taiwan including the Offshore Islands. A draft of the study was completed and sent for comment to the American Embassy in Taipei in January of 1953 just before the new Administration took office. In reaction to the study (which has not been made public), the United States Ambassador to the Republic of China, Karl Lott Rankin, proposed that the responsibilities of the U.S. Military Assistance Group (MAAG) on Taiwan be extended to include training and equipment for the 75,000 Chinese Nationalists troops on Quemoy, Matsu, and the Tachen Islands.[7]

Soon after taking office President Eisenhower informed Congress that the Seventh Fleet would no longer be used to prevent the Chinese Nationalists from carrying out operations from Taiwan against the Mainland. He did not refer to the Offshore Islands, however.[8] Rankin made it clear to Chiang Kai-shek that this public statement constituted no change in American policy; the United States would still expect to be consulted before any decision was made by the Chinese Nationalists to attack the Mainland.[9]

While the Offshore Islands were not mentioned in the "unleashing" statement, the action by the United States implied that Quemoy, Matsu, and the Tachens were still put in a different category. The 1950 inhibition on Chinese Nationalist actions against the Mainland applied only to Taiwan and the Pescadores, and the formal release of the Nationalists related as well only to these islands. The United States in early 1953 was

[4] Text in *American Foreign Policy, 1950–1955*, pp. 2470–2471.
[5] Karl Lott Rankin, *China Assignment* (1964), p. 152; *New York Times*, December 7, 1952, p. 72.
[6] Stewart Alsop, "The Story Behind Quemoy: How We Drifted Close to War," *Saturday Evening Post* (December 13, 1958), pp. 85–86.
[7] Rankin, *China Assignment*, p. 152.
[8] Text in *American Foreign Policy, 1950–1955*, p. 2467.
[9] Rankin, *China Assignment*, pp. 154–155.

acting as if the Chinese Nationalist troops on the Offshore Islands were irregular forces whose actions were not subject to the same restrictions as the troops on Taiwan. But this distinction was very soon to erode.

By mid-1953 the American Joint Chiefs of Staff had come to the conclusion that because of the Communist buildup opposite the Offshore Islands the Nationalists would have to improve their defenses if they desired to hold the Offshore Islands. Chiang had been informally advised that the Joint Chiefs of Staff no longer had any objection to the rotating to the Islands of some of the regular American-equipped units from Taiwan. Despite these hints the Chinese Nationalists had taken no action before July when Ambassador Rankin, back from a trip to the United States, met with Chiang to discuss the Joint Chiefs' position and a U.S. MAAG report which proposed a buildup on the Tachens. Rankin urged Chiang to strengthen his forces on the Tachens as well as the other Offshore Islands. Rankin warned the Chinese Nationalist leader that under existing conditions the United States would not intervene quickly in the event of an attack. For precisely this reason he urged the Chinese Nationalists to build up their own forces. In agreeing to the increase in forces on the Offshore Islands, Chiang made three counter-requests to the United States. He asked that renewed consideration be given to a formal integration of the Offshore Islands into the Taiwan defense system and that the U.S. assume direct responsibility to come to their aid. While this move was being considered, he suggested an immediate public statement by the President indicating an interest in the Offshore Islands. Finally, he asked for some military craft for use in the Offshore Islands area.[10]

Rankin told Chiang that it might be some time before his requests could be acted upon. Nevertheless the United States had given advice to Chiang as to how to defend the Islands and had made a specific proposal for an increase in military forces, particularly on the Tachens, which was accepted by the Nationalists. The distinction between Taiwan and the Offshore Islands was eroding.

Soon after the Korean War was terminated by the Armistice Agreement of July 27, 1954, and a Mutual Defense Treaty was initialed by Dulles and Syngman Rhee, Chiang, in an interview, called for the conclusion of a mutual defense pact between the United States and Taiwan. The Nationalists would also have liked to see the conclusion of a Pacific pact similar to the North Atlantic pact.[11] In December of that year, the Nationalist government proposed a security treaty with the United States.[12]

[10] *Ibid.*, pp. 167–169.
[11] *New York Herald Tribune*, August 12, 1953.
[12] Statement by Secretary of State before the Senate Committee on Foreign Relations, February 7, 1955. Text in *American Foreign Policy, 1950–1955*, p. 953.

During 1954 the efforts of the American government to organize a Southeast Asia Treaty Organization led the Chinese Nationalists to press harder for a bilateral Sino-American defense treaty. As Dulles explained to the Senate Committee holding hearings on the treaty, it was difficult to reject the Nationalist request.

> Under these circumstances [of seeking other security pacts] China began to take on significance. It was suggested that the reason for this omission was that the United States desired to keep open the possibility of trading Taiwan (Formosa) and the Pescadores to Communist China as part of a general settlement in the area.
>
> Such ignoble suggestions were damaging to the morale and prestige of the Republic of China and they reflected on the integrity and honor of the United States itself.
>
> The appearance of discrimination against the Republic of China could not be continued without prejudice to moral and political standards that we need to maintain.[13]

At the same time that its desire to establish a ring of military alliances around China led it to accept the Nationalist proposal for a Sino-American treaty, the Administration's policy of "liberation" also precluded any notion of demanding a Chinese Nationalist withdrawal from the Offshore Islands as one of the conditions for American willingness to conclude a treaty. The Administration, already embarrassed by its failure to implement the policy of rolling back the Iron and Bamboo Curtains, was in no position to urge Chiang Kai-shek to withdraw from the Offshore Islands, which both symbolized his determination to return to the Mainland and served as the area from which most of his harassing of the Mainland was carried out.

Thus a major opportunity was lost to force a Chinese Nationalist retreat from the Offshore Islands. Not only did the U.S. not press for a withdrawal, but the Administration suggested a willingness to defend the Offshore Islands. The treaty committed the United States to defend only Taiwan and the Pescadores, but it noted that the provisions of the treaty would "be applicable to such other territories as may be determined by mutual agreement." [14]

Three months before the signing of the treaty, the Chinese Communists launched an artillery bombardment of Quemoy which was preceded by a large-scale propaganda campaign for the liberation of Taiwan. In early November, they shifted their military operations to the Tachens and Ichiangshan Island off the coast of Chekiang and used air and naval forces as well as their artillery. On January 18, 1955, the Communists

---

[13] *Ibid.*
[14] Mutual Defense Treaty between the United States and the Republic of China, December 2, 1954, Article XI. Text in *American Foreign Policy, 1950–1955,* pp. 945–947.

launched an amphibious attack on Ichiangshan and secured the island for two hours of intensive firing. The Communist control of the sea and air around the Tachens made it impossible for the Nationalists to get supplies to the other Offshore Islands, which were also vulnerable to sea attack.[15]

Confronted with this threat before the ink was dry on the Mutual Defense Treaty, the Eisenhower Administration apparently felt that it had no choice but to participate in the defense of at least some of the Offshore Islands. The President, therefore, on January 24, 1955, dispatched a message to Congress which led five days later to Congressional approval of the Formosa Resolution. The Resolution authorized the President

> to employ the Armed Forces of the United States as he deems necessary for the specific purpose of securing and protecting Formosa and the Pescadores against armed attack, this authority to include the securing and protection of such related positions and territories of that area now in friendly hands and the taking of such other measures as he judges to be required or appropriate in assuring the defense of Formosa and the Pescadores.[16]

A few days after the passage of this authorization the United States announced that it was, under the terms of the Resolution, assisting the Chinese Nationalists in the evacuation of the Tachen Islands which had come under heavy fire.

In urging this evacuation, the United States made a secret commitment to the Nationalists to defend Quemoy and Matsu.[17] Eisenhower quoted Dulles as saying at the meeting at which the decision was taken to submit the Formosa Resolution to the Congress:

> I believe we must modify our policy: we should assist in the evacuation of the Tachens, but as we do so we should declare that we will assist in holding Quemoy and possibly the Matsus. . . .[18]

The statement issued by the American government at the time of the evacuation of the Tachens maintained that:

> The U.S. Government has further advised the Chinese Government that with the object of securing and protecting Formosa, in consonance with the congressional resolution approved January 29, 1955, the U.S.

---

[15] After the Ichiangshan campaign, no Nationalist warship reached the Tachen Islands until February 7, when a combined American-Nationalist fleet arrived at the Islands to evacuate the Nationalist forces.

[16] Congressional Authorization for the President to Employ the Armed Forces of the United States to Protect Formosa, the Pescadores and Related Positions and Territories of that Area, House Joint Resolution 159, Public Law 4, 84th Cong., 1st sess. January 29, 1955. Text in *American Foreign Policy, 1950–1955*, pp. 2486–2487.

[17] The evidence for this is overwhelming if circumstantial.

[18] Dwight D. Eisenhower, *Mandate for Change* (1963), p. 467.

Government will extend assistance to the Republic of China in defending such related positions and territories now in its hands as the United States deems to be essential to the defense of Formosa and the Pescadores.[19]

Moreover, Rankin implies by his description of the event that a promise was made. He writes: "The Chinese had hoped for the formal inclusion of Kinmen [Quemoy] and Matsu in this [U.S.] defense area, but they had to accept second best in the shape of informal assurances as to firm intentions." [20] A U.S. commitment to Quemoy and Matsu was further implied on February 22, 1955, when the United States informed the Taiwan government that it would not defend Nanchi Island, which is south of the Tachens but north of Matsu. The Chinese promptly evacuated Nanchi, apparently feeling that at least by implication the United States had committed itself to the defense of the remaining island chains of Quemoy and Matsu.[21] Publicly Secretary Dulles continued to emphasize that the American commitment was to defend only those positions necessary for the defense of Taiwan and the Pescadores.

Thus in a successful effort to get the Chinese Nationalists to evacuate the most exposed of the Offshore Islands, the Tachens, the United States at least in the eyes of the Chinese Nationalists committed itself to the defense of Quemoy and Matsu, and the Formosa Resolution authorized the President to defend those positions should he consider it necessary.

With the crisis passed and the treaty ratified, the United States made what was apparently its only effort in the postwar period to secure Chinese Nationalist evacuation of the Offshore Islands. Assistant Secretary of State Walter Robertson and Chairman of the Joint Chiefs of Staff Admiral Arthur W. Radford were sent to Taipei in April, 1955, to ask the Chinese Nationalists to consider evacuation of Quemoy and Matsu.[22] Radford and Robertson were the two firmest friends of the Chinese Nationalists in the American government. This suggests either that Chiang's best friends were sent to bring the news that he would have to evacuate the Islands or that they were sent to make a passing gesture in order to satisfy critics within the American government who thought that the United States should at least try to get the Nationalists off the Islands. The absence of any signs of bitter debate at the time of the Radford-

[19] "United States Assistance to the Republic of China in the Evacuation of the Tachen Islands," statement by the Department of State, January 5, 1955. Text in *American Foreign Policy, 1950–1955*, pp. 2490–2491.

[20] Rankin, *China Assignment*, p. 221.

[21] *Ibid.*, p. 223.

[22] Eisenhower in his memoirs asserts that Robertson and Radford sought only to persuade Chiang to reduce the size of his garrison and not to evacuate the Islands (*Mandate for Change*, pp. 481, 661–662). Kennedy, both before and after his election, implied that the purpose of the Radford-Robertson trip was to argue for evacuation [*Washington Post*, October 14, 1960; *New York Times*, June 28, 1962).

Robertson visit to Taiwan suggests that if they did propose evacuation of the Islands, they did so in very mild terms. Perhaps they indicated that if the Chinese Nationalists decided they had to stay on the Islands, the United States would understand.

There the matter rested until mid-1958, except that the Nationalists substantially built up their forces on the Offshore Islands with the aid of U.S. military advisers stationed on Quemoy and Matsu. In August and September, 1959, heavy Communist artillery fire against Quemoy brought the United States, according to President Eisenhower, to the brink of nuclear war. Eisenhower reports in his memoirs that he was determined to defend Quemoy and that he had reached the decision to use nuclear weapons if Quemoy were attacked.[23] There were several reasons why the Administration decided not to issue a public statement unequivocally committing itself to defend Quemoy. It was believed that such a statement would stimulate more intensive attacks by critics of American policy. Moreover, the Administration feared that the Chinese Nationalists might use such commitment to draw the United States into a large war. Finally, the Administration was unwilling to defend some of the smaller islands in the Quemoy chain but did not want to invite attack on them by drawing a clear U.S. defense perimeter.[24] By military actions and by their public statements, however, the Secretary of State and the President sought to convince the Chinese Communists that an attack on Quemoy was likely to bring in the United States. The most publicized of these was the Dulles statement issued after his Newport meeting with Eisenhower. Dulles speaking for the President declared that "the securing and protecting of Quemoy and Matsu have increasingly become related to the defense of Taiwan." [25]

The internal memorandum quoted at the outset of this paper stated that the loss of Quemoy would lead ultimately to the collapse of the entire American position in the Far East. If these were the expected results, it is no wonder that the Administration felt that the extensive Congressional and public opposition should carry little weight.

With the ending of the crisis, the Administration apparently made no move to secure evacuation of the Islands, although Dulles, on a visit to Taiwan, did succeed in getting the Chinese Nationalists to agree to rely primarily on peaceful means to liberate the Mainland and persuaded them to cut back slightly the forces on Quemoy.[26]

[23] Eisenhower, *Waging Peace*, pp. 294–295.
[24] *Ibid.*
[25] As quoted in *ibid.*, p. 299.
[26] "United States–Chinese Nationalist Consultations under Article IV of the Mutual Defense Treaty: Joint Communique Issued at Taipei at the Conclusion of Meetings Between the President of the Republic of China and the Secretary of State, October 23, 1958." Text in *American Foreign Policy: Current Documents, 1958* (Department of State Publication 7322 [1962]), pp. 1184–1185.

There was no further public debate or, apparently, private discussion within the Administration of the Offshore Islands until the issue arose during the 1960 Presidential election. At that time in the heat of a TV debate with his Republican opponent Richard Nixon, John F. Kennedy suggested the desirability of trying to persuade the Chinese Nationalists to withdraw from the Offshore Islands. Although in later debates he drew closer to the Eisenhower position, there is no doubt that Kennedy came into office determined to try to find a way out of the Offshore Islands situation.

For a time, numerous press reports predicted that the Kennedy Administration would soon unveil a new China policy. But in fact no changes of policy toward the Offshore Islands were made. When a new crisis in the Taiwan Straits arose in June, 1962, Kennedy was forced by circumstances to state that his position would be the same as that of Eisenhower in 1958. He declared that whatever his own views, the United States would not request the Nationalists to withdraw from the islands under the threat of a gun.[27]

There the matter stands. President Johnson, confronted with a threat in Vietnam which he associates with the expansionist desires of the Communist Chinese, is unlikely to make any move to try to force the Nationalists off the Offshore Islands.

THE RATIONALE

Thus far we have attempted to present historical explanations of why the United States has not tried to force the Nationalists off the Offshore Islands in peacetime and why it twice was prepared to resort to military action to defend the Islands. These explanations can be summarized as follows.

When the Truman Administration first made the decision to defend Taiwan in 1950, it did so to secure bipartisan support for its Korean policy. It was unwilling to jeopardize that support by provoking a fight with the Nationalists over the evacuation of the Offshore Islands. In 1954, when the United States made a treaty commitment to defend Taiwan, the Eisenhower Administration policy of "liberation" made it impossible to surrender additional territory to Communist control or to give up territory which would be useful in attacking the Mainland. In 1958 the view of the Administration as to the disastrous consequences of the fall of Taiwan, together with Dulles' commitment to not retreating under military pressure, made consideration of a withdrawal impossible. Finally, in 1962, before the new Administration could work out a revised China policy, Kennedy was forced to commit himself to the defense of the Islands in the face of renewed military threat.

[27]News conference of June 27, 1962, as reported in the *New York Times*, June 28, 1962.

While historical explanation on the surface accounts for the continuing American commitment to the defense of small islands less than 5 miles from the coast of China, we believe that American behavior can best be understood in light of the fact that the decisions were made by a large bureaucracy. In the remainder of the paper we attempt to say why those within the bureaucracy who opposed withdrawal prevailed. Their arguments, embodying stratagems which had much to do with their success, can be outlined in capsule form: (1) Dire consequences can be predicted. (2) We must not yield to pressure. (3) Now is not the time. (4) The costs are clear but gains uncertain. (5) How would we do it? (6) No one directly responsible is for this.

The Prediction of Dire Consequences. Often during the postwar period the United States has committed itself to the defense of territories whose intrinsic importance to the United States is small. The Offshore Islands represent an extreme case of this type of commitment. Some of the Islands were uninhabited, others had very small populations. If there was to be a justification for the United States defending the Offshore Islands, it had to be found in the consequences of their fall to Communist control. There were many officials who did believe that these consequences made the Islands worth defending.

The particular reasons which led individuals and bureaucratic agencies to support a defense of the Offshore Islands were complex and varied. Those officials who were sympathetic toward the Chinese Nationalist regime believed that the Islands should be held simply because the American pressure to force a withdrawal might provoke a crisis between the two governments which would lead to the collapse of the Chiang Kai-shek government.

Others feared a withdrawal from the Islands would pave the way for a two-China policy. Once off these Islands, the Chinese Nationalists would be 90 miles from Communist guns and would no longer have possession of any territory which was indisputably Chinese. The Chinese Nationalists have been determined to hold the Islands precisely because they see them as a protection against a two-China policy.

Neither the possibility of instability on Taiwan nor the need for a bulwark against a two-China policy are sufficiently serious consequences on which to argue for the use of American military forces, however. Such arguments would not appeal to the President or the public. Thus other warnings had to be advanced. Many officials have discovered that any prediction of the consequences to be expected from a proposed course of action which is not expressed in absolute terms is taken as indication that one does not oppose the policy. Rankin, for example, reports that his assertion that the loss of the Offshore Islands by the Chinese Nationalists would be "very serious but not necessarily disastrous" was taken as meaning that he had withdrawn his very strong opposition to American efforts to force a Nationalist withdrawal from the Islands.[28]

With intelligence estimates taken as policy proposals and with real motivations complex, diverse, and not necessarily persuasive, American officials supporting a defense of the Offshore Islands felt it necessary to resort to the strategy of predicting dire consequences. Thus the President was told by his advisers in 1958 that the American position in Japan, Korea, Taiwan, the Philippines, Thailand, and Vietnam would be seriously jeopardized and the currently neutralist nations, such as Indonesia, Malaya, Cambodia, Laos, and Burma would come under Communist control.[29]

These predictions of dire consequences appear to have served two purposes in the eyes of those making them. First, they convey unmistakably the implicit policy recommendation. If the memorandum drafted for the President and the Secretary of State had said that the danger of subversion in Taiwan would increase if Quemoy had fallen, that steps would have to be taken to assure the continuation of the American presence in the Philippines and elsewhere, and finally that the drift of some Southeast Asian countries toward accommodation with China might be accelerated, the estimate would have appeared more accurate and probably more in line with the actual estimates of the officials. However, their policy proposal would not have been as clear. The President would not have known if these officials were leaving the decision up to him or were implying that the U.S. should not defend the Islands. Predictions of dire consequences served the purpose of implying policy recommendations in what appears to be an accepted bureaucratic shorthand.

Moreover, predicting dire consequences has the advantage of hedging against the actual consequence of an American withdrawal from the Offshore Islands. If the Islands fell with consequences almost as dire as predicted, the officials could have pointed to their warning. On the other hand if the consequences were less severe, the bureaucracy could have taken credit for shoring up American positions after the President had decided not to go to war in defense of what the bureaucracy asserted to be a vital interest. Or perhaps no one would remember the predictions.

The value which officials saw in predicting dire consequences, and their apparent confidence that these predictions would not simply be ridiculed, led those in favor of defending the Islands to agree that they should make such predictions. But ritualistic language comes to be believed by those writing and reading the policy proposals. Thus seven years after the event,

[28] Rankin, *China Assignment*, p. 225. The Ambassador feared that making the absolute prediction would lead to an abandonment of Taiwan once the U.S. decided not to defend the Offshore Islands.
[29] Eisenhower, *Waging Peace*, p. 692.

Eisenhower apparently still claims to feel that it is true that the loss of the Offshore Islands would have had consequences greater than those which followed the fall of China.

The tendency to believe what one reads in formal papers is reinforced by the problem of drafting public speeches explaining American policy. Both in 1954 and in 1958 there were some people who opposed an American defense of the Offshore Islands. In explaining its position, the Administration tended to rely on predictions of dire consequences for reasons analogous to those which led government personnel to such predictions in internal memoranda. That is to say, any public evaluation of the consequences of the fall of the Islands which discussed costs and gains and trade-offs in some detail would appear to undercut the argument that the use of American military policy was necessary and would have suggested that the United States was about to change its position. Thus public exhortation as well as bureaucratic communication requires the prediction of dire consequences which come to be believed and, in turn, influence the actual policy calculations of officials.

We Must Not Yield to Pressure. A second device for coordinating policy views in a bureaucracy with diverse motivations is to seize on an absolute principle of behavior. This is a particularly useful device if some of those involved in the process, particularly high policymakers, actually believe in the principle.

Secretary of State Dean Rusk appears to follow John Foster Dulles in genuinely holding to the principle that it is dangerous and immoral to yield to pressure and permit force to be used to effect political change. For such men, the lesson of Munich is that yielding to military pressure only whets the appetite of an aggressor who then will press for greater conquests. Thus Rusk continues to believe as Dulles did that the United States must if necessary use force to prevent the successful application of force, particularly by Communist China or the Soviet Union. It has, therefore, been possible for the bureaucracy to appeal to the principle that the U.S. cannot yield to pressure when the Offshore Islands have come under the threat of military attack from Communist China.

The principle of not yielding to pressure has been violated by the United States on a number of occasions, even in the Taiwan Straits where the Tachens were evacuated in 1954 under pressure. Nevertheless, the belief in the absolute principle of not yielding to pressure has made the appeal to this principle a useful strategy for those in favor of defending the Offshore Islands.

Now Is Not the Time. Another way to manipulate a policy proposal is to applaud the contrary position but to assert that now is not the time to implement it. Thus those opposed to an American effort to force the Chinese Nationalists off the Offshore Islands could seemingly accept the ultimate value of such a withdrawal while suggesting that it would have to be done at some other time.

Arguing that "now is not the time" has the effect of forcing the advocate of the policy to declare that this is the optimum time rather than talking about the merits of the action. The argument can be used both during crises and in calmer periods. When used at both times, as it has been in relation to evacuation of the Offshore Islands, it is the equivalent of saying there is never an appropriate time.

Apparently during both the 1954 and 1958 crises, as well as at the time of the fear of a Chinese Communist attack in 1962, those who opposed a withdrawal from the Offshore Islands argued that clearly now was not the time to carry out such a policy. This is close to saying that the U.S. cannot retreat under fire but has the added element of saying that the costs of withdrawal will be greater now than they will be at another time.

During a calm period, it is possible to argue that one should not stir up trouble in the area when the other side is leaving well enough alone. If the Chinese Communists are apparently not planning to attack the Offshore Islands, why should the United States stir up trouble by seeking to force a Chinese Nationalist withdrawal? Thus, like the man who will always repair his roof tomorrow, the United States has apparently always come to the conclusion (with the possible exception of the Radford-Robertson visit in 1955) that now is not the time for pressing for an evacuation. The advocates of evacuation have never been able to make the case that any given occasion offered the optimum moment to pursue the policy.

The first two bureaucratic stratagems discussed thus far are applicable only in periods of crisis, while the third is applicable both to crisis and non-crisis periods. We turn now to additional stratagems used to block American pressure for a withdrawal from the Offshore Islands in non-crisis periods.

The Costs Are Clear but the Gains Uncertain. In a crisis period, a major cost of continuing to defend the Offshore Islands is the danger of a nuclear war with China; hence, those desiring to defend the Islands had to predict less obvious but more dire consequences of backing down. At the same time, they were able to assert that standing firm is the way to forestall nuclear war. In quiet periods, those advocating that the United States seek to force the Chinese Nationalists to withdraw from the Offshore Islands confront a situation in which the immediate costs of withdrawal could be clear-cut while any gains are uncertain.

In a situation in which the costs are clear and the gains uncertain, the opponents of the policy will dwell on costs. In the case of withdrawal from the Offshore Islands, they are able to indicate that such a move might provoke a rift with the Chinese Nationalists. They can point out that the President, the Secretary of State, and other high officials will need to spend considerable time on the problem; first evaluating the alternatives and then implementing a policy of forced withdrawal. Opponents of withdrawal discuss the severe morale problems on Taiwan and increased threat of collapse of the regime which would follow a forced withdrawal. Moreover, they point out the United States would have to act to assure its other allies that this move did not presage the withdrawal of the United States from other exposed positions.

The strategy which those advocating a withdrawal would like to adopt would be to point to the extremely favorable consequences which would inevitably result from forcing a withdrawal. But these are difficult to specify. One can argue that withdrawal would make a crisis in the Taiwan Straits less likely. To this argument the answer is that there is no sign of such a crisis developing and the act of attempting a withdrawal might provoke a Chinese Communist attack. Another possible argument is that a withdrawal would make it possible for other governments to associate themselves with the defense of Taiwan. This in itself is not a major gain for the United States, and moreover it is difficult to say which countries would do so and what "associating themselves with the defense of Taiwan" would mean.

There *is* one major consequence which forcing the Chinese Nationalists off the Offshore Islands might have. However, many people in the bureaucracy do not believe that this consequence is a desirable one. A Chinese Nationalist withdrawal from the Offshore Islands would pave the way for the adoption of a two-China policy by the United States. It would be possible for the United States to assert that she recognized the Chinese Nationalist government as the government on Taiwan and recognized the authorities in Peking as the government on the Mainland. It is likely that a number of other states would be prepared to adopt a similar policy. The UN might even be persuaded to find a way to have both Taiwan and China as legal members of the organization even though under present circumstances neither Chinese government would accept such arrangements and actually sit in UN chambers.

The gains reaped from such a policy could be extremely great. And it is likely that only when the President makes it clear that he attaches a very high priority to a two-China policy that the arguments for forcing the Nationalists off the Offshore Islands will carry significant weight.

In the absence of a clear sign from the President that he supports a two-China policy, it is difficult for officials within the bureaucracy to rest a proposal on the assertion that it is good because it will make possible a two-China policy. The obvious answer of the opponents of the policy is therefore that they will consider pressing for a withdrawal from the Offshore Islands only when the American government formally decides that it is in favor of a two-China policy. In the absence of this, the argument that the costs of the proposed action are clear and the gains uncertain will carry more weight than the argument that while the costs are clear, the gains may be great.

How Do We Do It? Another strategy which has been used by those opposing an evacuation of the Offshore Islands is to argue that the United States does not have the power to force a withdrawal. Officials can point out that Robertson and Radford were unsuccessful in 1955. How, they ask, do we do it? They can point out that the Islands are the sovereign territory of the government of the Republic of China and that the United States has neither the right nor the power to decide that an evacuation is necessary.

The answer of those advocating a withdrawal rests on the notion that Taiwan depends on the American security guarantee for its very survival. In such a situation, it is argued, the United States can force a withdrawal if it is prepared to go to the brink of a break. However, the success of such a policy depends on the President and the Secretary of State standing firm in the face of substantial Chinese Nationalist resistance to proposals to withdraw from the Offshore Islands. Thus those in the bureaucracy advocating withdrawal must concede that it is desirable only if the President and the Secretary of State feel very strongly about the issue and are prepared to devote substantial amounts of their own time and energy to the successful implementation of the policy. Given the absence of evidence that the President and the Secretary of State are prepared to devote substantial amounts of their own personal resources, there is no answer to the question: how do we do it?

No One Directly Responsible Is for This. In weighing arguments advanced for or against a policy within a bureaucracy, officials tend to give greater credence to the views of those who would be responsible for implementing a given policy or who would have to deal with the consequences of failure to act. When the proposal to evacuate the Offshore Islands has been made within the government, it has been possible for opponents to argue that no one directly responsible is for this. The Joint Chiefs, for example, are responsible for defending the Islands when they come under attack. Those who conduct American political relations with the Chinese Nationalists have a responsibility for the consequences which would flow from an American decision to withdraw from the Offshore Islands.

It appears to be the case that nobody with responsibility of this sort has pressed for an evacuation of the Offshore Islands. Under the Eisenhower Administration, the Far East Bureau of the State Department had a strongly pro-Chinese Nationalist view and presented the case against withdrawal. The military appear to have counted on the right to use nuclear weapons if necessary to defend Quemoy and in this sense saw the Islands as defensible. Under Kennedy and Johnson, the Far East Bureau has been preoccupied with the Indochinese peninsula and is probably not eager to accept the additional responsibilities which would come from an attempt to secure an evacuation of the Offshore Islands.

Those who advocate the policy of forcing a withdrawal have apparently been in policy-advising roles of various kinds, and hence their views have carried less weight. Moreover, no part of the bureaucracy has seen itself gaining so much from an evacuation that it is prepared to press continually for the implementation of such a policy.

Those who advocate the policy of forcing a withdrawal have apparently tain the status quo in American policy. They constitute a sobering example in the realm of foreign policy of the general proposition that to make a bureaucracy change its position is much more difficult than allowing it to continue a given policy: the bureaucracy prefers the known dangers of an existing course to the uncertain costs and gains of change. If the bureaucracy is unlikely to initiate the proposal to force an evacuation of the Offshore Islands, American policy will move in this direction only if a President or a Secretary of State sees a potentially significant gain from seeking a withdrawal. It has been suggested that only a firm commitment to a two-China policy would lead top officials to envision substantial benefits following from evacuation of the Offshore Islands. Thus any future withdrawal of the American commitment to defend Quemoy and Matsu is likely to stem from and therefore imply a fundamental alteration of American policy toward the acceptance of the existence in the world community of two Chinas.

Part Four

Actions

HERBERT YORK

The Elusive Nuclear Airplane

Any analysis of the making of foreign policy must recognize that the process does not culminate with the announcement of decisions. The story of the program to construct a nuclear-powered aircraft (ANP) illustrates that decisions, including those of Presidents, rarely settle anything permanently and frequently only serve to stimulate increased resistance and new maneuvers and arguments.

The ANP program survived, and for a time even flourished, despite several sharp reductions in its funding and at least one outright cancellation on the authority of the President. Presidential decisions did not result in compliant behavior by subordinates, and the President was, to a substantial degree, unable to control a program over which he had formal authority.

The ANP proponents were able to limit the impact of Presidential decisions by the maneuver of introducing new participants into the game and thereby increasing the domestic political costs to him of denying them their requests. These maneuvers took two related forms. First, prestigious advisory committees and panels were organized to recommend proceeding with the ANP. The President could oppose the nuclear-powered aircraft program only at the cost of appearing to reject the public advice of presumably apolitical experts abetted by congenial intelligence reports and press stories. Second, Congress, and particularly the Joint Committee on Atomic Energy, became actively involved on the side of the ANP supporters. The President requires Congressional support for a wide range of his activities and, as a result, can offend the members' preferences (even regarding decisions in which they have no formal role) only at great peril to his other goals and objectives. Congressional influence over Presidential actions extends far beyond the list enumerated in the Constitution. Moreover, politically powerful contractors exerted influence both on the Congress and directly on the President.

There is no evidence that Presidential subordinates who were ANP supporters ever overtly disobeyed an explicit Presidential directive. What the example of the nuclear-powered airplane illustrates is that noncompliance need not take the form of disobedience. The ANP proponents were able to achieve their objectives by creating pressures on the President to reverse himself and to allow them to continue with their programs. The results, however, were similar: Presidential decisions did not produce implementing behavior among those obligated to discharge a President's orders.

Reprinted from Herbert York's *Race to Oblivion* (New York: Simon and Schuster, Inc. 1970). Copyright © 1970 by Herbert York. Reprinted by permission of the author and Simon and Schuster.

The story of the nuclear airplane is entirely different from the story of the B-70, and a review of that ill-starred program can reveal a great deal about some of the basic forces that drive the arms race. The idea of the nuclear airplane dates back to the waning days of World War II and involves a wedding of two of the technologies which burst forth on the world in the early forties: jet propulsion and nuclear power.

An ordinary jet engine, such as those which propel the large commercial transport aircraft of today, is, in principle, a fairly simple and straightforward device. Air is taken in through a scoop at the front end, compressed by a fan and then mixed with fuel. This mixture then burns and heats itself and in so doing greatly increases its pressure. It then pushes its way toward the rear end of the jet, turning a turbine in the process and finally being exhausted at high speed through a nozzle, giving the aircraft a push in the opposite direction. The turbine extracts some of the energy from the heated air and uses it to drive the compressor fan. The power plant for a nuclear aircraft is, in principle, very similar. Instead of heating the air by mixing kerosene or gasoline with it and then burning the mixture, the air is heated by the energy produced in a nuclear reactor. There are two basic schemes for accomplishing this. In one scheme the air passes directly through the reactor itself and is heated on direct contact with fuel elements consisting of uranium metal which has been clad or "canned" in some suitable material. In the other, heat is removed from the reactor by some intermediate fluid (such as liquid sodium) and taken to another heat transfer unit (crudely similar to an ordinary automobile radiator), where it is transferred from the intermediate fluid to the air, and then the intermediate fluid (the radiator water in an auto) goes back to the reactor for more heat. The first of these schemes is called the direct cycle, and the second is called the indirect cycle.

Work on the nuclear airplane began at an annual rate of $1.3 million in fiscal 1946 and grew steadily to $8.3 million in fiscal 1951. At first only Air Force funds were involved, but by 1949 the AEC had a major piece of the action, which it kept through the end of the program in 1961. The Navy was also involved, but only to a much smaller degree. From the beginning the program had an unusually stormy career. In addition to being beleaguered by extremely difficult technical problems, it was surrounded by political controversy and buffeted by various political power struggles. The program budget oscillated; decisions for early flight of one kind or another were made and quickly rescinded; the AEC concerned itself with what was the Defense Department's business and vice versa; the JCAE, the Joint Committee on Atomic Energy, repeatedly tried to usurp the prerogatives of the executive branch; and through it all the Air Staff and certain major contractors tried to exploit every little bit of confusion and animosity that arose.

Research on the project was begun by the Fairchild Engine and Aircraft Company in 1946 under the rubric of NEPA (Nuclear Energy for the Propulsion of Aircraft). In the next two years, a series of committees urged the project on with glowing testimonials to its importance and optimistic predictions about its possibilities. The Research and Development Board of the Defense Department recommended that it proceed on a priority basis under the supervision of the board and the AEC. The Congressional Aviation Policy Board reported to Congress that NEPA deserved "the highest priority in atomic-energy research and development." An M. I. T. report commissioned by the AEC contended that the nuclear aircraft was feasible and could probably be achieved within fifteen years. (All the early laboratory work and virtually all the theoretical studies were focused on the direct-cycle approach. This was more straightforward and seemed then to offer the surest means for flight in the foreseeable future. Research work on the indirect cycle was not undertaken until 1954.)

Such optimism was not borne out by the initial findings of the researchers. A number of very difficult problems very soon became evident. It turned out that there were then no materials available which would (1) stand up to the high intensity nuclear radiation which necessarily existed throughout the interior of the reactor, (2) resist corrosion by the very hot air which passed through the reactor at great speed, and (3) be guaranteed not to leak any of the highly radioactive fission products into the exhaust airstream.

It also soon became painfully clear that there was a very difficult shielding problem. As with other high-power nuclear reactors, it was necessary to surround this one with a heavy shield in order to protect the pilots, and any instruments or other cargo which the airplane might be carrying, from the intense radiation always generated by these devices. The shielding problem is especially difficult in this case because the shield must be light enough to be flown and because it must be pierced in such a way as to allow large masses of air to pass through it at high speed without creating too large a radiation leak.

A third, very basic set of problems was related to potential operating hazards such as would obviously be associated with a crash landing of such an airplane or even with lesser accidents. While most of the intellectual effort devoted to solving these problems was of the usual serious and straightforward kind, occasionally some bizarre proposals arose. One which was discussed quite seriously was that older men (i.e., men beyond the usual age for begetting children) should be used as pilots so that genetic damage from radiation would be held at a minimum and because older people are generally more resistant to radiation than younger ones.

However, these problems did not daunt those who wanted to have a nuclear plane in flight as soon as possible. At the end of 1950 the Defense

Department recommended that the project aim to put a subsonic aircraft in the air in 1956 or 1957. The project passed from feasibility studies into the development phase. The General Electric Company was commissioned to develop a propulsion plant (using the direct cycle), and General Dynamics was contracted to conduct the "flying testbed" program with the aim of achieving a first flight by 1957. The Joint Committee on Atomic Energy, which eventually held more than thirty-six hearings on the subject, soon became the most vigorous and vocal supporter of the early-flight scheme. It insisted that the Air Force support the program on a massive scale, sufficient to ensure success, or abandon it entirely.

The political pressure to put a plane in flight as soon as possible eventually proved fatal to the program. The part of the program which was supposed to develop reactor materials had by no means reached the point where it could be certain of coming up with something suitable. By demanding that a flight reactor be designed immediately regardless of whether anyone knew how to do so, the politicians and bureaucrats severely inhibited real progress in this vital area. As I will argue, politicians should in general take a strong role in weighing the over-all value of technological programs. But in this particular case, politicians insisted on meddling deeply in the strictly technical elements of the program, and the practically inevitable result was a serious retardation.

In July of 1952 the AEC and the Defense Department announced plans for a flight test of a nuclear-propulsion system between 1956 and 1958 which would use a modified conventional airplane as a "testbed." By then it was widely apparent that no one knew how to build a nuclear engine that could propel an aircraft on its own, but rather than go back to the drawing board the directors bullheadedly insisted on flying something anyway, even if the new device was little more than a passenger in a conventionally powered aircraft.

After Eisenhower's inauguration, all major development programs were reevaluated, including what was by then known as ANP (Aircraft Nuclear Propulsion), and for a while it looked as if good sense might prevail. In March, 1953, an ad hoc committee of the Air Force Scientific Advisory Board recommended cutting the program back fifty percent, on the ground that production activities were premature in the light of the slow rate of progress in research. The following month the National Security Council urged that the program be canceled entirely. Secretary of Defense Charles Wilson issued orders to that effect, calling the nuclear airplane a "shitepike." The "flying testbed" program was terminated, along with most of the work on the direct-cycle propulsion system, and the program was reoriented toward basic research.

Yet only seven months later the ANP enthusiasts were back in action. The Air Force repeatedly told the AEC that it was once again interested in the ANP and asked it to expedite the experimental work. In April,

1954, the director of the ANP project, Air Force General Donald Keirn, claimed that the nuclear-propelled aircraft could be put in flight in half the time originally foreseen, if it were given high priority. The JCAE immediately called for a "crash effort" on the program. At the same time the Pratt and Whitney Corporation was commissioned to begin research on an indirect-cycle propulsion system.

In early 1955, the AEC reported that progress on the direct-cycle system had surpassed expectations and authorized additional funds for it. The Defense Department and the AEC agreed to accelerate the program, with the objective of testing a prototype propulsion plant about 1959. The Air Force insisted that this was a realistic goal. Competition for airframe studies was opened, and General Electric and Pratt and Whitney were directed to proceed with their work on the propulsion systems.

The Joint Committee continued to receive optimistic predictions from the Air Force. In June, 1956, General Curtis LeMay, then commander of SAC, testified that an early flight by a nuclear aircraft was both necessary and possible. The following month, General Keirn told the committee that a ground test of a propulsion system would be possible in 1959, with a flight the following year.

But a review of the technical progress in the program and subsequent budget cuts by the Defense Department led to postponing the flight target date by eighteen months. In December an experimental reactor operated a turbojet in a laboratory for several hours, but not at a temperature suitable for flight propulsion. The accelerated flight program was again canceled, and the research efforts were cut back.

After reviewing the matter, the Air Force Scientific Advisory Board recommended again that less emphasis be put on designing the plane until a suitable reactor had been developed, but the Joint Committee continued to urge the earliest possible flight. Deputy Defense Secretary Donald Quarles agreed with the Air Force Advisory Board that no date should be set for flight until the reactor had been developed. This was an eminently sensible conclusion in my view, but it was not to the liking of the Joint Committee, which continued in letters and testimony to insist to the Defense Department on the importance of immediate flight. In May, 1957, another advisory board, chaired by Air Force General William Canterbury, recommended that a low-level nuclear plane be developed. The reason for specifying a low-level plane was simple: no one knew how to design a reactor suitable for any other kind of flight. Anxious to hold back the budget as much as possible, some Administration officials fought the project, but the Joint Committee, backed up by still another advisory-committee report and a letter from Air Force Secretary James H. Douglas, fought for it. In July, Secretary Quarles relented and approved a program aiming at a test flight in the mid-sixties.

As usual during such periods of political buffeting, little technical progress was made. The date for the test flight was again put off, and complaints were heard that Pratt and Whitney could not carry on adequate research on the indirect cycle effectively without more funds.

At this point the first Sputnik went into orbit, and the Sputnik psychology affected the ANP program just as it did all other high-technology projects. Representative Melvin Price, Chairman of the Research and Development Subcommittee of the JCAE, wrote President Eisenhower that an early flight program was desirable both for military reasons and as a psychological victory to counteract the effects of Sputnik. The AEC recommended that early flight of a nuclear plane be pursued as a means of increasing American scientific prestige in the post-Sputnik era. The Air Force and several Defense Department officials threw their support to the direct-cycle propulsion system in hopes that flight could be achieved as soon as possible, this time suggesting the early sixties as a flight goal.

Eisenhower requested his science adviser, James Killian, to investigate the recommendations, and Killian appointed Robert Bacher to chair a study committee on the matter. The Bacher Committee reiterated the earlier recommendation against accelerating an early flight program and urged that the ANP effort concentrate on developing a suitable reactor. The President expressed agreement with this view. But General Keirn, the Joint Committee, and Congressional ANP proponents attacked the Bacher report and continued to press their case.

When I became Director of Defense Research and Engineering in 1958, by the terms of the position, the ANP program would have come under my jurisdiction; but because of the long, difficult, contentious history of the program, Deputy Secretary Quarles chose to continue himself in direct charge while I was beginning to take up my other responsibilities.

As a result of lack of progress and negative reports on the project, Quarles backed away from his July, 1957 position approving a test flight in the mid-sixties. He continued to maintain this new position despite strong pressures from the Air Force, the AEC, and the Joint Committee, and in the face of very strong lobbying on the part of the larger contractors. A few months later, Quarles died suddenly, and I assumed responsibility for overseeing the program. (The claim was made shortly after Quarles's death that at a meeting in the afternoon before he died he had had a change of mind and had told someone that he wanted to go ahead with a flight vehicle. Unfortunately, Quarles made no written record of this. I was at the meeting; I recall he was beginning to yield to the enormous pressures being applied in favor of early flight, but I do not believe he had quite yet finally decided what to do.)

After carefully reviewing the program with Arthur T. Biehl and others on my staff, I determined that the program objectives for the immediate future should be to (a) continue the development of only such reactors and power plants as would be suitable for militarily useful nuclear flight; (b) increase the effort on the indirect-cycle program so as to determine its potentialities at an earlier date than previously contemplated; and (c) defer initiation of a specific flight program until one of the advanced power plants was established as feasible and potentially useful, and until a flight program could be instituted without seriously interfering with the development of militarily useful power plants.

This decision was very poorly received by those who wanted to "go full steam ahead, damn the technical minutiae," and in the following general questioning by committee members I was very closely cross-examined about my views. The hearings were especially remarkable in that the heads of the contractor programs, D. Shoults of the General Electric Corporation, B. A. Schmickrath of the Pratt and Whitney Corporation, and Andrew Kalitinsky of the Convair Corporation, were also brought in to testify. Shoults and Schmickrath presented prepared statements to the committee, and all three responded to the general questioning of the committee members. To put it simply, Mr. Shoults was there specifically for the purpose of rebutting some of the government witnesses and to testify in behalf of expanding a program which he managed and for which his corporation was receiving approximately $100 million per year.

A more intensive, continuing review of the program in the course of next year revealed that during all this political maneuvering, while there had been substantial progress in the rate of spending money, there had been precious little progress toward solving the basic problems which had been recognized by 1948, well over a decade earlier. After all that time and effort, there were still no materials available with which a useful propulsion reactor unit could be built, the problem of crew and cargo shielding had still not been satisfactorily solved, and potential hazards to the public associated with potential accidents of various kinds were still as bad as ever. The kind of airplane that could perhaps be built and the kinds of uses to which the airplane could conceivably be put appeared to be of no value at all. It was claimed that if we would only build such an airplane and get on with the flight program, somehow in due course these problems would be solved. However, since over ten years of intense laboratory work by some pretty good people had failed to make any real progress at all on these problems, we saw no reason to believe that exposing the reactor prototype then under construction to still more hostile environments (vibrations, etc.) would be useful in solving them.

Therefore, just as the Eisenhower administration was coming to a close, we (my staff and I) determined to terminate further work on the direct cycle and to continue only fairly fundamental work on the indirect cycle at Pratt and Whitney at a level of approximately $25 million per year. I reported all of this to Secretary Gates, but, since it was so late, he suggested that I talk it over with the incoming secretariat. I then discussed the whole matter with Roswell Gilpatric, the Deputy Secretary of Defense designate, and also with Jerome Wiesner, who was about to become President Kennedy's Special Assistant for Science and Technology. If there was any difference between Wiesner's views and mine, he felt more negatively about the program, and, as a result, ANP was canceled in the first months of the Kennedy administration. More precisely, it was not totally canceled: research in the indirect cycle at Pratt and Whitney, essentially along the lines of my earlier recommendation to Secretary Gates, was in fact continued, but under a different rubric.

All during the last two years of the life of this program, the public was bombarded by scare stories and by self-serving intelligence revelations about how the Soviets were just on the verge of accomplishing an ANP of their own and about how dreadful it would be for us if we didn't have one, too. Representative Melvin Price, Chairman of the JCAE subcommittee holding the hearings, commented on "the shattering impact of Russia's Sputniks last fall" and said:

> it became evident that we could ill afford another humiliating psychological defeat in the eyes of the world. Our views were reinforced by our talks with Russian scientists in Moscow last fall, who confirmed that the Soviets were, indeed, pursuing a vigorous development program for a nuclear-powered aircraft.

Later, in the letter to President Eisenhower, Congressman Price wrote: ". . . recent events including the launching of an earth satellite by the Soviet Union have lent urgency to the long-standing need for the United States to develop a flying capability in the field of nuclear-propelled aircraft."

Senator Richard B. Russell of Georgia said in a television statement:

> The report that the Russians have test-flown an atomic-powered aircraft is an ominous new threat to world peace, and yet another blow to the prestige and security of our nation and the free world. It follows in tragic sequence the Russian success of last fall in launching the first earth satellite. If the report is true, it means that we are today faced with a new weapon of terrifying consequences. A plane powered by nuclear energy could have practically unlimited range and load capacity and therefore would be a weapon of incalculable danger to us.

General Keirn (who headed the ANP office) said in a speech, "This emphasis [in the last year] on technical progress has resulted in many suggested proposals to accelerate the ANP program in an effort to beat the Russians to first nuclear flight." In another speech General Keirn said:

> I'm sure each of you is aware of and appreciates the seriousness of any potential threat to our seacoast military installations and industrial

and population centers posed by a large enemy submarine fleet. Imagine in addition to this a fleet of "enemy" high-speed aircraft continuously patrolling the air space just outside our early-warning net capable of air-launching a devastating missile attack followed by high-speed penetration or attack against our hardened installations.

A letter from an employee of one of the contractors was published by the Joint Committee in the record of the hearing; it said:

I believe that an overwhelming majority of American citizens would prefer to be absolutely sure that the amount of national defense available is adequate for security rather than risk even a momentary period of potential collapse in retaliatory deterrent. The nuclear aircraft program can help prevent this potential collapse.

The December 1, 1958, issue of *Aviation Week* carried a signed editorial which said:

On page 28 of this issue we are publishing the first account of Soviet nuclear powered bomber prototype along with engineering sketches in as much detail as available data permits. Appearance of this nuclear powered military prototype comes as a sickening shock to the many dedicated U.S. Air Force and Naval aviation officers, Atomic Energy Commission technicians, and industry engineers who have been working doggedly on our own nuclear aircraft propulsion program despite financial starvations, scientific scoffing, and top level indifference; for once again the Soviets have beaten us needlessly to a significant technical punch.

The story on page 28, datelined Washington and entitled "Soviets Flight Testing Nuclear Bomber," stated flatly:

A nuclear powered bomber is being flight tested in the Soviet Union. Completed about six months ago, this aircraft has been observed both in flight and on the ground by a wide variety of foreign observers from communist and non-communist countries.

There followed all kinds of purported details and even some sketches in which large red stars showed plainly in the side view and the top view of the aircraft. The story ended:

As long as a year ago there were brief but specific mentions in the Soviet technical press of successful ground testing of atomic aircraft power plants. Recent speculative stories in the Soviet popular press suggest conditioning the Russian people to an announcement of a spectacular achievement by an atomic-powered airplane in the near future, probably a non-stop non-fueled flight around the world.

This steady flow of phony "intelligence" came from the missile press, from Congressional sources, from industrial sources, and from the lower levels of the Air Force. General Keirn himself did not specifically claim that he had solid evidence of a Russian program. Rather, in response to a question from Senator Anderson in the hearings referred to earlier, he said only, "I have an intuitive feeling myself that they [the Russians] are quite well along the road." He was then asked (and this was 1959) whether he felt there was any possibility of a Russian nuclear-propelled airplane within two years, and he replied, "I think there is a possibility of it."

President Eisenhower, who, of course, had all intelligence information available to him, as well as the best possible interpretations of that information, said on December 10, 1958, "There is absolutely no intelligence to back up a report that Russia is flight-testing an atomic-powered plane." Today it is quite obvious that no such nuclear aircraft ever existed in the Soviet Union and that stories to that effect were simply one more very clear and very obvious loose attempt to generate what may be called self-serving intelligence, something which can be found again and again in other debates over weapons systems. At the time, the true nature of this "intelligence" was not at all obvious, even to fairly well-informed people, and those of us who had all the facts in the matter and who knew there was no real basis for any of these claims were hamstrung in any attempts we made to deal with them by the secrecy which always surrounds real intelligence information. I do not mean by any of the foregoing that intelligence-type information was deliberately or maliciously falsified. Indeed, if that had been the case, the Administration's problem in dealing with the matter would have had a simple solution: expose the falsifiers. Rather, what happened was that isolated facts and rumors were assembled, and then analyzed and interpreted by zealous amateurs until the result was almost pure wishful thinking and self-delusion. And since the recipients of these phony intelligence analyses were very frequently as eager and as predisposed to believe them as were their purveyors, it was extremely difficult to deal effectively with them.

The story of the ANP, it seems to me, provides a classic illustration of some of the forces that drive the arms race onward. It involves partisan politics: Congress was controlled by the Democrats, the White House by the Republicans. It provides a classic example of the exploitation of the fears and anxieties of the public through the use of imaginary "intelligence." It shows how sincere people who badly want to be misled can easily mislead themselves: the so-called intelligence that was used as one of the arguments in support of a crash program by our side was based in part on technical articles which really did appear in the Soviet press about possible uses of atomic energy, including application of nuclear propulsion to aircraft. These articles were strictly theoretical, but it was quite easy for persons who wanted to believe that the Russians were ahead, to believe it with passion. The ANP story shows how an industrial organization, in this case General Electric, does not merely do what the government asks it to do, but rather works very hard through all possible channels to make sure that the government asks it to do what it wants to do in the first place. It shows how military advocates of programs, especially programs involving more than one agency, attempt to take advantage of all the internal rivalries and tensions which exist in order to find a successful path for the accomplishment of what they — very sincerely, to be sure — believe to be essential, and which they therefore believe justifies the use of any tactics to ensure that administrators will not be able "to put the budget ahead of survival."

BLUE RIBBON DEFENSE PANEL

Report to the President and the Secretary of Defense
on the Department of Defense

Students of the foreign policy process frequently stop their analysis with the conclusion of the decision games, assuming that implementation will be routinely and faithfully forthcoming. More than one participant in the policy process, sharing this mistaken assumption, has struggled to secure decisions supporting his position but has left action games to subordinates. *As a result, he has lost.* As these excerpts from the Report of the Blue Ribbon Defense Panel (Fitzhugh Report) on proposals to reorganize the Pentagon demonstrate, laws of Congress and decisions of Presidents do not ensure that appropriate actions will result.

The National Security Act of 1947 as well as all of the subsequent amendments to that Act have sought to increase civilian control and direction of policies and actions threatening or using physical violence. Today, the Secretary of Defense is encumbered by no legal constraint from making each and every decision in the Pentagon. Yet, as the Fitzhugh Report notes, the fundamental deficiencies which existed in 1947 remain today. The ineffectiveness of the legislation and regulations stands as testimony to the importance of action games in securing favorable outcomes.

The various decisions relating to the organization and administration of the Defense Department have had so little impact in large measure because the uniformed services have managed to ignore, circumvent, or contravene

Excerpted by the editors from Blue Ribbon Defense Panel, *Report to the President and the Secretary of Defense on the Department of Defense,* July 1, 1970, pp. 21–53, 126–128.

their intent in implementation. Despite efforts at increased civilian control, the Secretary of Defense still has no staff with responsibility for military operations, the Joint Staff exceeds the statutory limit on its size by a factor of five, and the Office of the Secretary is responsible for less than one-fifth of the Pentagon's public affairs budget.

Efforts to minimize the effects of service parochialism have been equally futile. The Joint Chiefs of Staff continue to operate as a committee of representatives from each of the separate services, with each Chief dependent upon his service staff for advice and information. The creation of the Defense Intelligence Agency (DIA) to consolidate the intelligence activities of the three services has resulted in increased growth of the individual service intelligence operations. Most dramatically, efforts to remove the services from combat operations have been virtually a total failure, with the operation of the unified and specified commands serving primarily to obscure their continuing participation.

As the report notes, the results have been compliance in form, not substance. As long as senior players continue to devote primary attention to decision games at the expense of action games, and remain highly dependent upon their subordinates for implementation, such outcomes will likely continue.

GENERAL

In approaching its task, the Panel became increasingly aware that no single organization or set of procedures would be adequate for the Department of Defense for all times. The organization and procedures of the Department must be sufficiently flexible to respond to a changing environment and evolving objectives.

Certain principles which guide organizational and procedural objectives do remain constant. First among such principles is the requirement for effective civilian control of the Defense establishment. Under the Constitution, civilian control is exercised through the combined efforts of both the Executive and Legislative Branches. Its effectiveness, however, depends in large measure on the capability of the Secretary of Defense to ensure consistency of Department operations with policy, to surface the viable alternatives on major issues, and to maintain a high degree of visibility to himself, the President and the Congress of the functioning of the national Defense establishment.

Effective control of the military establishment by the Secretary is required not just for the purpose of ensuring the supremacy of civil authority. While the President and the Secretary of Defense must have the benefit of professional military advice based on careers of military training and experience, unified control is essential to provide the Nation with maximum security at minimum costs, and to ensure that military strategy, force structure and operations are consistent with national policy.

Despite the broad authority vested in the Secretary of Defense by the National Security Act of 1947, as amended, experience demonstrates that in practice, the tools available to the Secretary to exercise effective control of the Department are seriously deficient.

The evolution of defense organization since 1947 has not substantially reduced the inherent difficulties arising from the fact that the division of roles and missions among the Military Departments is still based fundamentally on distinctions between land, sea and air forces which have become increasingly less relevant. This results in continued adversary relations between the Military Services, which, although usually confined to the internal paper wars that constitute the Department's decision-making process, severely inhibit the achievement of economy and effectiveness required for adequate defense within available resources. The continuing interservice competition seriously degrades the decision-making process through obfuscation of issues and alternatives, and leads to attempts to circumvent decisions, repeated efforts to reopen issues that have already been decided, and slow, unenthusiastic implementation of policies to which a Service objects.

The results of such "parochialism" are, for example, reflected in: the development of the AX aircraft by the Air Force and the Cheyenne aircraft by the Army for the close air support role; the lack of enthusiasm for airlift expenditures by the Air Force and the Fast Deployment Logistics program by the Navy, both intended to support the Army; the organization of the operational command structure to provide a balance among the Services for senior officer billets; and the continued failure to resolve the issue of the best balance between land and carrier-based tactical air.

It should be noted that inter-Service rivalry fades rapidly in proximity to a zone of combat operations. In Vietnam, despite the encumbrance of a confused, distorted and divided command structure, imposed through a series of Service compromises, the military operates harmoniously as unified armed forces of the United States, due in large degree to the splendid leadership of the senior commanders in the field.

During this study, the Panel was exposed to a broad spectrum of experience-based opinion that deficiencies within the Department of Defense could not be remedied without either integrating or drastically restructuring the Military Services. Significantly, this opinion was not confined to civilians. It is based in no small part on the recognition that the changes made in defense organization since 1947, whether by reorganization plan or by statutory amendment, were all designed primarily to remedy the same or related problems to those which most plague the Department of Defense today. Unquestionably, the phrases in the reports of the Hoover Commission's Task Force on National Security Organization, the Eberstadt Task Force, the Rockefeller Committee of 1953, the President's message to the Congress in 1958, and many other studies made externally and internally to the Department have the familiar ring of applicability to contemporary conditions. . . .

CONTROL AND MANAGEMENT BY THE SECRETARY OF DEFENSE

The National Security Act bestows a broad expanse of authority on the Secretary of Defense to enable him effectively to direct and administer the Department of Defense. There is no serious legal impediment to prevent a Secretary of Defense from making any and every decision within the Department, subject only to Presidential and Congressional policies. Practical, rather than legal, limitations make such an approach impossible. Even the doubling of his time and attention through the person of his alter-ego, the Deputy Secretary, does not significantly increase the decision-making time of the Secretary. A highly centralized decision-making process oriented to a single decision point, whether the decision point consists of one or two men, is inherently inadequate to manage the spectrum of activities required of the Department of Defense.

Indeed, attempts to overcentralize decision-making at the top seriously impair a Secretary's capability to exercise effective control. Under such circumstances, far too many decisions go unmade, critical issues are not addressed, problems are deferred, and the principle of personal accountability is lost in the diffused maze of "staff coordination." . . .

Conceptually, the National Security Act, as amended through 1958, organizationally divides the Department of Defense, below the level of the Office of the Secretary of Defense, between support activities and military operations. The Military Departments were given the responsibility for support matters, and military operations were centered in the Unified and Specified Command structure.

This separation, prescribed by the Congress, has much to commend it. In addition to providing a logical division of the total military power, it permits a Secretary of Defense to fashion his management decision points so as to concentrate on the interfaces between the "suppliers" and the "users" of resources, thereby enhancing his control capability.

The utility of this conceptual division has been impaired in practice. President Eisenhower's message transmitting the 1958 Reorganization Act to Congress said: "Clearly, Secretaries of Military Departments and Chiefs of individual Services should not direct unified operations and therefore should be removed from the command channel." Accordingly, the 1958 Reorganization Act separated the Chiefs of Staff as such from operations, and put the Unified and Specified Commands directly under the command of the President and the Secretary of Defense. However, the Secretary of Defense then delegated to the Joint Chiefs of Staff the responsibility to act as military staff in the chain of operational command to the Unified and Specified Commands. This reinvolved the Chiefs of the Services in combatant operations matters in their capacity as Joint Chiefs. . . .

ORGANIZATION OF THE OFFICE OF THE SECRETARY OF DEFENSE

The Office of the Secretary of Defense (OSD) has more than doubled from approximately 1700 to 3500 personnel since 1956. This growth appears to reflect an attempt at highly-centralized management, undertaken in frequently futile attempts (1) to overcome difficulties arising from Service rivalries; and (2) to manage, in lieu of minimizing, the uncertainties inherent in planning, programming, and budgeting, particularly as related to advanced weapons systems. . . .

The expansion of OSD into many functionally fragmented compartments and their increasing involvement in detailed executory-type activities has resulted in the establishment of a profusion of management information systems and reporting requirements. The excessive detail and duplication of reporting requirements have generated such a sheer mass of informational detail that relevant and important facts are often obscured. Efforts at reports control and limitation have proved largely futile and have added to the already significant load and costs of paper work.

While the process of OSD expansion was occurring, subordinate elements of the Department gradually adjusted. In fact, the diffusion of responsibility and accountability, the freedom to "pass the buck" to the top on hard decisions, and the opportunity to use the extensive coordination process to advance parochial objectives are circumstances to which many in the Department have adapted comfortably. Understandably, this usually resulted in substantial increases in the workload of staffs at subordinate levels to provide information required by and to counter the arguments made by the expanded OSD staff. On the other hand, despite recent improvements made in the Military Departments in such techniques as systems analysis, there is little to indicate that the Department could accomplish its mission if there were a reversion to the level and type of decentralization of authority which existed earlier. . . .

For all its size, the OSD has no staff element with significant purview of the area of military operations, despite the fact that the Secretary of Defense, since the 1958 amendments to the National Security Act, is the crucial link in the chain of command between the Commander-in-Chief and the Unified Commanders.

If the Secretary of Defense is to discharge effectively his responsibilities as a key element of the National Command Authority — and the alternative of removing him from the chain of command would, in practice, reduce "civilian control" to a fiction — it is clear that he must have an adequate staff for the purpose.

The present arrangement for providing staff support to the Secretary of Defense for military operations is awkward and unresponsive; it provides a forum for interservice conflicts to be injected into the decision-making process for military operations; and it inhibits the flow of information to and from the combatant commands and the President and Secretary of Defense, often even in crisis situations.

While the Secretary of Defense is constituted by the National Security Act as the link in the chain of command of combatant forces between the President and the Unified and Specified Commanders, the only military staffs presently available for operations staff work are in the Joint Staff — reporting to the Joint Chiefs of Staff — and in the Military Departments. This anomalous situation has been dealt with by the delegation of responsibility to the Joint Chiefs of Staff by the Secretary of Defense to act as his staff for military operations. To perform this responsibility, the Organization of the Joint Chiefs of Staff was enlarged. In addition, each member of the Joint Chiefs of Staff has retained on his military staff within his individual Service a staff element assigned to military operations which is larger than the authorized size of the entire Joint Staff. These are the staff officers who support their Chief of Service in his role as a member of the Joint Chiefs of Staff. There is abundant evidence that it is in these individual Service staff elements, as much or more than in the Joint Staff, that issues dealing with military operations and the recommendations of Unified Commanders to the Secretary are screened, analyzed and shaped.

The National Military Command Center (NMCC) is a facility essential to the functioning of the National Command Authority and is manned by elements of the Organization of the Joint Chiefs of Staff; the NMCC, however, is responsive to the Joint Chiefs of Staff, not to the Secretary of Defense and the President.

This lack within OSD of expertise in military operations critically impairs the civilian control of the military establishment. Virtually all of the combat forces of the United States are assigned to the operational control of the Unified and Specified Commands. There is a statutory prohibition against the transfer of forces in or out of one of the Unified or Specified Commands without the specific approval of the Secretary. It is the Secretary of Defense who, subject to the authority of the Commander-in-Chief, provides the direction and control of the Unified Commanders.

The National Security Act, as amended, clearly contemplated a direct relationship between the Secretary and the Unified and Specified Commanders. It is the Operational Commander of the Unified Command who is in the best position — staffed by officers from all services — to provide military recommendations, alternative courses of action and assessments of short-term military capabilities to the National Command Authority. A staff, preferably military, is necessary in the chain of command between the Secretary and the Unified Commanders; it is imperative that such a staff be responsive to the Secretary of Defense, rather than to the Joint Chiefs of Staff, and through the Joint Chiefs of Staff to the Military Services.

The absence of a staff element for military operations directly responsive to the Secretary of Defense constitutes a deficiency which can be tolerated only at high risk. . . .

Some of the Department's "credibility gap" with the Congress and the public must be attributed to the fragmented, and often confused, functional assignments of responsibilities within the Department for legislative and public affairs.

At present, there are public affairs and legislative liaison offices within the Office of the Secretary of Defense, each of the Military Departments and some of the Defense Agencies, with no effective mechanism for coordination among them. A great many of the matters with which these offices deal affect and are affected by activities of other organizational elements of the Department. Only the public affairs and legislative liaison activities in the Office of the Secretary of Defense have general cognizance of all activities. Representations by other such offices have the potential to be based on partial or incomplete information.

At the present time, the activities of the Assistant Secretary of Defense (Public Affairs) account for less than one-fifth of the public affairs expenditures of the Department. The lack of coordination of all public affairs activities of the Department causes confusion among the public and in the Congress, and at the same time, inhibits the most effective use of available resources.

The Office of the Assistant to the Secretary of Defense (Legislative Affairs) is less than one-half the size of the smallest legislative liaison office of a military Department, and only about one-fourth of the size of the largest. The necessary flow of information attending the budgetary process would be facilitated by direct contacts between the appropriations committees of Congress and the Comptroller of the appropriate department or agency. The use of legislative liaison services in these budgetary matters, where the Departmental sources of data are few and identified, has greater potential for obstruction than assistance. . . .

ORGANIZATION OF THE JOINT CHIEFS OF STAFF
AND THE JOINT STAFF

The Joint Chiefs of Staff

With the exceptions of the relatively minor changes in the authority of the Chairman, the reorganization of the Joint Staff in 1958, and the increases in the limitation on the size of the Joint Staff from 100 to 210 officers in 1949, and from 210 to 400 officers in 1958, there have been no significant changes in the Organization of the Joint Chiefs of Staff and the Joint Staff since 1949.

The Joint Chiefs of Staff are still composed of the Chairman, appointed by the President, with the advice and consent of the Senate, from the officers of the regular components of the Armed Forces; the Chief of Staff of the Army; the Chief of Naval Operations; the Chief of Staff of the Air Force; and as a practical matter, the Commandant of the Marine Corps, unless the Secretary of Defense determines that a particular matter under consideration by the Joint Chiefs of Staff does not concern the Marine Corps.

Both the organizational characteristics and the performance capability of the Joint Chiefs of Staff have been sources of concern almost since the inception of the organization.

From an organizational standpoint, concern has been created by the reliance on a "committee" for the performance of the important functions assigned to the Joint Chiefs of Staff. Despite the theories which would depict the Joint Chiefs of Staff as a "corporate" body, the near unanimity of the Joint Chiefs of Staff's formal decisions in recent years, and the statutory instruction to the Chairman to report disagreement of the Chiefs to the Secretary of Defense, the Joint Chiefs of Staff must be characterized as a committee.

The "committee" character of the Joint Chiefs of Staff is accentuated by the dual roles of the members, other than the Chairman of the Joint Chiefs of Staff. Each of the Chiefs must bear the load of responsibility for supervision of his own Military Service and for his duties as a member of the Joint Chiefs of Staff.

The excessive workload occasioned thereby was recognized by the report of the Rockefeller Committee in 1953. In the 1958 amendments to the National Security Act, the Chiefs of Staff of the Army and Air Force, the Chief of Naval Operations, and the Commandant of the Marine Corps were authorized to delegate broad responsibilities for supervision of their Services to their Vice Chiefs of Staff. Despite this delegation, the workload of the Joint Chiefs of Staff is still very heavy, and is compounded by the many matters of detail referred to them.

Also, in the 1958 amendments, the Chiefs' authority to "command and supervise" their Services was reduced to the authority "to supervise," and the operational command of combatant forces of all Services was vested in Unified and Specified Commands, responsible directly to the Secretary of Defense and the President. By virtue of the provisions of Department of Defense Directive 5100.1, issued on 31 December 1958, however, the Joint Chiefs of Staff were assigned the duty to serve as advisers and as military staff in the chain of operational command running from the Secretary to the Commanders of the Unified and Specified Commands.

From a practical viewpoint, the roles of the members of the Joint Chiefs of Staff, other than the Chairman, are probably more nearly triple in character than dual. The three roles are: (1) the Chief's supervision of his Military Service; (2) participation in the advisory and planning functions assigned by statute to the Joint Chiefs of Staff; and (3) participation, by delegation, as a member of the Secretary's staff for matters of operational command.

Many consider the dual or triple roles of the Joint Chiefs of Staff to be a fatal deficiency to the effectiveness of the Joint Chiefs. No matter how hard the Chiefs strive to "rise above the particular views of their respective Services" and not to "be restricted by Service positions or instructions," [1] it is very difficult for them to free themselves from their understandable Service loyalties.

The difficulties of the Joint Chiefs of Staff structure are compounded by other factors: (1) the Joint Staff consists of officers assigned from each Service, and they look to their Service for promotions; and (2) the procedures by which major issues addressed by the Joint Chiefs of Staff, require that the issues first be coordinated by the Joint Staff with each of the Military Services.

President Eisenhower referred to these difficulties in his message to the Congress on the Defense Reorganization Act of 1958. The President stated: "These laborious processes exist because each military department feels obliged to judge independently each work product of the Joint Staff. Had I allowed my interservice and interallied staff to be similarly organized in the theaters I commanded during World War II, the delays and resulting indecisiveness would have been unacceptable to my superiors."

The increase in frequency of unanimity in the recommendations and advice of the Joint Chiefs of Staff is by no means conclusive proof of subjugation of particular Service views. Such frequency of unanimity can just as cogently support a conclusion that the basis of such recommendations and advice is mutual accommodation of all Service views, known in some forums as "log rolling," and a submergence and avoidance of significant issues or facets of issues on which accommodations of conflicting Service views are not possible. . . .

Despite the many changes, the members of the Joint Chiefs of Staff have retained their involvement, in one or the other of their roles, in operational command matters. Prior to 1953, the Joint Chiefs of Staff designated one of their members as their executive agent to exercise operational command in a specified geographical area. From 1953 to 1958, the Secretary of Defense designated a Military Department as executive agent for a particular unified command and the Service Chief acted for the Secretary of his Military Department, so that for any particular unified command, the

[1] Report of the Rockefeller Committee, 1953.

chain of operational command ran from the President to the Secretary of Defense to the Secretary of the designated Military department to the Service Chief to the unified command. The 1958 change was intended to shorten and clarify the chain of operational command, by making the channel run from the President to the Secretary of Defense directly to the unified command. Because of the delegation from the Secretary of Defense to the Joint Chiefs of Staff to act as military staff in the chain of command to the unified commands, this change proved to be largely one of form, rather than substance, for it merely "changed the hat" the Chief of Service wears during his involvement in military operational matters.

The numerous functions now assigned to members of the Joint Chiefs of Staff impose an excessive workload and a difficult mix of functions and loyalties. Some of these functions must consequently suffer, and the evidence indicates both the strain on individuals who have served in such capacity and a less than desirable level of performance of the numerous functions assigned. This result has occurred despite the outstanding individual ability and dedication of those who have served on the Joint Chiefs of Staff and despite the attempts to shift a portion of the load from the Chiefs of Service to their Vice Chiefs. The difficulty is caused by the system, not the people.

The excessive workload of the Joint Chiefs of Staff has also resulted in a perceptible shift of responsibilities for the performance as staff of the Secretary of Defense in operational control of combatant forces from the Joint Chiefs of Staff to the Chairman of the Joint Chiefs, acting individually and "keeping the members of the Joint Chiefs of Staff informed." This trend, while usually increasing efficiency, imposes a severe workload on the Chairman, and does not appear entirely consistent with either the statutory prohibition against the Chairman exercising command functions or the repeated rejection by the Congress of the Single Chief of Staff concept.

Of the varied functions assigned to the Joint Chiefs of Staff, those involving operational command are least compatible with the organizational character of the Joint Chiefs of Staff. A committee is inhibited in its performance of any function by its very nature, but it is most deficient as a decision-mechanism in matters which are time-critical, such as operational control of combatant forces.

The recommendation of the Rockefeller Committee to eliminate the Joint Chiefs of Staff from duties involving operational command of combatant forces is as well taken today as in 1953, if not more so, but this time the change should be made in such a clear and unequivocal way that it cannot be circumvented. . . .

The Joint Staff

The Joint Staff is placed by statute under the Joint Chiefs of Staff and is limited in size, currently to 400 officers.

These statutory limitations have proved to be of no practical consequence, deterring neither the growth past the magic number of 400 officers serving on the central military staff, nor the creation of additional military staff. With the apparent, but statutorily silent, acquiescence of all concerned, including the Congress, the limitations of the statute have been circumvented by the creation of an entity called the "Organization of the Joint Chiefs of Staff."

The title, "the Organization of the Joint Chiefs of Staff" was used to include the Joint Chiefs of Staff, the Joint Staff and various committees formed by the Joint Chiefs of Staff prior to 1953. These "committees" were, for the most part, disestablished effective June 7, 1958, in response to President Eisenhower's message to the Congress on defense reorganization transmitted on April 3, 1958. Four committees not so disestablished were redesignated in name from "Committee" to "Council" or "Group" for compliance in form, if not in substance.

Despite the "elimination" of the committees included in the Organization of the Joint Chiefs of Staff, the number of personnel serving as staff and staff support for the Joint Chiefs of Staff increased from approximately 486 in 1958 to 2,145 in 1969, of which some 900 are military officers. The size of this organization is projected to diminish to some 1,996 in 1970. The "staff" character and its interrelationship to the officially designated Joint Staff is in no way disguised nor camouflaged, and nothing surreptitious can or should be implied from its constitution. The official Joint Staff, maintained with the 400 officer-size limitation, is organized under five directorates and one office of Special Assistant as follows: J-1 (Personnel), J-3 (Operations), J-4 (Logistics), J-5 (Plans and Policy), J-6 (Communications-Electronics), and the Special Assistant for Counterinsurgency and Special Activities. In the overall Organization of the Joint Chiefs of Staff, but outside the officially designated Joint Staff, are a large number of staff elements, variously entitled Directorates, Agencies, Special Assistants, etc., all of whom report either through the J-3 (Operations), the J-5 (Plans and Policy), or directly to the Director of the Joint Staff, the same as do elements of the official Joint Staff.

Less obvious "extensions" and "additions" to the Joint Staff also exist. For instance, the Defense Atomic Support Agency (DASA) performs the staff function for maintaining inventory control of nuclear weapons, and in fact, an element of the DASA staff is located contiguous to the National Military Command Center, operated by the Organization of the Joint Chiefs of Staff. Also, the some 400 or more personnel, a number of whom are military officers, working in the National Military Command System Support Center, are assigned to the Defense Communications Agency.

Size alone, nor even a substantial and continuing growth of staff, does not provide evidence of a deficiency in organizational composition or performance. Nevertheless, such artificial structuring of organization, in an effort to circumvent arbitrary limitations, however benign because of the passage of time, can hardly fail to perform less adequately than an organization functionally structured for efficiency of performance. . . .

Defense Intelligence Agency

The Defense Intelligence Agency (DIA) was established in 1961 in an effort to create a mechanism to solve the problems presented by the disparate intelligence estimates being produced, and the duplicative efforts being engaged in by the Military Department.

DIA is assigned the responsibility for:

1. The organization, direction, management, and control of all Defense intelligence resources assigned to or included within the DIA.

2. Review and coordination of those intelligence functions retained by or assigned to the Military Departments.

3. Supervision of the execution of all approved plans, programs, policies, and procedures for intelligence functions not assigned to DIA.

4 Obtaining the maximum economy and efficiency in the allocation and management of Defense intelligence resources.

5. Responding directly to priority requests levied upon the DIA by the United States Intelligence Board (USIB).

6. Satisfying the intelligence requirements of the major components of the Department.

Its charter reveals that DIA was originally intended to (1) provide for the assembly, integration, and validation of all Defense intelligence requirements, the policies and procedures for collection, and the assignment of relative priorities to the requirements, and (2) develop and produce all the Department's intelligence estimates and information and contribution to the National Estimates for the USIB. It was intended that the Military Departments would retain the resources to collect and process intelligence information, under the supervision of DIA.

Concurrent with the establishment of DIA, the Directorate of Intelligence (J-2) of the Joint Staff was disestablished, and its functions assigned to the Director of DIA. The established reporting line for DIA was and is through the Joint Chiefs of Staff to the Secretary of Defense.

The principal problems of the Defense Intelligence Agency can be summarized as too many jobs and too many masters.

Two areas of conflict are apparent. In addition to his administrative responsibilities as the Director of a Defense Agency, the Director of DIA must provide the staff assistance on intelligence matters to the Secretary of Defense and must also provide staff assistance on intelligence matters to the Joint Chiefs of Staff. On many intelligence issues, particularly procedural issues with jurisdictional implications, the positions of the Secretary of Defense and the Joint Chiefs of Staff can be and often are diverse. As staff officer and adviser to both, the Director of DIA finds himself in an impossible position. The result can be delays in staff work that, in turn, result in unresolved issues of significant moment.

The second area of conflict is between DIA and the Military Services. DIA is charged with responsibilities to supervise the collection and processing of intelligence by the Military Services, specifically by prescribing procedures, allocating requirements, and reviewing the total intelligence programs of the Services. Yet the Director of DIA reports directly to the Joint Chiefs of Staff, comprised in four-fifths majority by the Senior Officers of the four Military Services for whose intelligence programs the Director of DIA is charged with the responsibility to provide coordinated supervision. In addition, the Services determine which officers of what qualification are assigned to DIA, and the services also retain the power of promotion and future assignment over those so assigned. In consequence, the "supervision" by DIA of intelligence collection and processing by the Services, and DIA's fiscal control is largely impotent and its visibility of the Service intelligence programs obscured.

While the DIA was established primarily to consolidate the intelligence activities at the Washington level, each Military Department currently has a larger intelligence staff than it had before the creation of DIA. Each departmental staff is still engaged in activities clearly assigned to DIA. The Military Departments justify these activities on the basis that DIA does not have the capability to provide the intelligence they need. It is paradoxical that DIA cannot develop a capability to perform its assigned functions while the Military Departments, which provide a large proportion of DIA personnel, maintain the required capability to produce intelligence estimates — or more properly, threat assessments — which are crucial to decisions on weapon systems research and development. DIA is charged with the responsibility, but has never been organized to discharge it. The Military Departments produce such estimates and the Air Force, at least, intends to enlarge its capability.

Each Military Department has a large organization devoted primarily to Mapping, Charting, and Geodesy (MC&G) activities: The Army Topographic Command of the Corps of Engineers; The Naval Oceanographic Office under the Oceanographer of the Navy; and The Aeronautical Chart and Information Center reporting to the Chief of Staff of the Air Force.

DIA attempts to coordinate these activities to eliminate duplication and set priorities for production. However, DIA coordinates through the intelligence elements of the Departmental staffs and only the Air Force MC&G agency is within the staff purview of its intelligence staff. The Army and Navy MC&G elements are in agencies which are not a part of the intelligence community.

While MC&G activities make use of intelligence information, they are not intelligence activities. Savings can be accomplished in personnel and equipment by consolidating the three Service MC&G agencies in a single agency reporting to the Secretary of Defense.

ORGANIZATION OF THE COMBATANT COMMANDS

The Combatant Forces of the United States and their direct support are assigned to eight Unified and Specified Commands: Alaskan Command, Atlantic Command, Continental Air Defense Command, European Command, Pacific Command, Southern Command, Strategic Air Command, and Strike Command.

This Unified and Specified Command structure has evolved during the period since World War II. As now designated and assigned the Alaskan Command is the oldest of the existing Unified Commands, dating from January 1, 1947, and Southern Command the newest (June 1963). . . .

The existing structure consists of functional and area commands, and a mixture of both.[2] Command is distributed among the Military Departments as follows: Army — European Command (EUCOM), Southern Command (SOUTHCOM), and Strike Command (STRICOM); Navy — Pacific Command (PACOM), and Atlantic Command (LANTCOM); and Air Force — Strategic Air Command (SAC), Continental Air Defense Command (CONAD), and Alaskan Command (ALCOM). Interestingly, very few Navy forces are assigned to Unified Commands in which the Unified Commander is not a Naval Officer, except for the 6th Fleet assigned to EUCOM. Equally significant, all of the Army Forces in PACOM, which are commanded by a Naval Officer, fall under sub-unified commands commanded by other than Naval officers and the overwhelming proportion of Army forces in PACOM fall under sub-unified commands which are commanded by Army officers. . . .

Serious questions persist about the suitability of the Unified Command structure for the conduct of war, either general or localized, for the conduct of peacetime activities, or for the handling of recurring crises. An examination of the primary missions of the present commands and some of the specific problems indicates that the present structure is not effective, and probably would have to be radically changed to support a major war effort.

CONAD is charged with responsibility for the defense of the North American Continent. Although CONAD prepares plans for such defense, strategic offensive forces operate in the same geographic area under SAC.

---

[2] Continental Air Command and Strategic Air Command are functional; Southern Air Command, area; Alaskan Command, Atlantic Command, Pacific Command, European Command, and Strike Command, mixed.

The Commander-in-Chief, CONAD also serves as Commander of the North American Air Defense Command, which is a joint United States–Canadian Command.

SAC, the only Specified Command, is charged with the primary responsibility for the strategic offensive mission. However, since the deployment of Polaris submarines, a strategic offensive mission has been assigned to the Atlantic, European, and Pacific Commands. The Joint Chiefs of Staff have established a joint planning group to effect better coordination in target planning and assignment. The Commander-in-Chief, SAC also serves as Director of this joint planning activity.

Each of the other six Unified Commands has a mission oriented to a designated geographic area, and each Unified Commander is charged with preparing contingency plans for his area. The Unified Commander, however, is not given adequate guidance as to what forces will be available to him over and above those assigned. As a result, the plans of two or more Unified Commands for contingencies which can materialize simultaneously, may well be based on the assumption that each will employ the same forces. The Joint Chiefs of Staff review the contingency plans of the Unified Commands, but do not effectively resolve the basic problems of conflict in force requirements.

An example of the confusion that can be created in the present Command structure occurred in the Arab-Israeli War of 1967, when the U.S. Military was directed to evacuate U.S. Nationals. The crisis was in the area of responsibility of STRICOM; however, a decision was made to perform the evacuation with airlift assets assigned to EUCOM. In anticipation of commanding the evacuation, STRICOM sent a command aircraft with a command and control element aboard to Europe. Because of indecisions as to whether STRICOM should command the evacuation, the aircraft was first stopped at the Azores, then was allowed to proceed to Greece, at which point it was decided that EUCOM should command. The STRICOM command aircraft was assigned to EUCOM, and EUCOM was directed to execute the STRICOM evacuation plans.

The Alaskan Command is assigned a geographic area of responsibility, but the principal mission of the Commander-in-Chief, ALCOM is not as a Unified Commander, but rather as a subordinate commander under NORAD in the defense of the North American Continent.

The Atlantic Command has no Army or significant Air Force forces assigned (one small Air Force unit, designated Iceland Defense Force) and tends to be oriented towards a general war maritime role as distinguished from a perhaps more probable contingency involving land operations in its geographic area of responsibility. The Commander-in-Chief, LANTCOM (CINCLANT) is also the Supreme Allied Commander, Atlantic, under NATO, and is responsible for operations in support of EUCOM on a unilateral U.S. basis, if required. CINCLANT also has a strategic offensive mission resulting from the assignment of Fleet Ballistic Missile submarines to his Command.

EUCOM and PACOM are primarily oriented to contingencies in their respective geographic areas, although each has Fleet Ballistic Missile submarines and a resulting strategic retaliatory role. The Commander-in-Chief, EUCOM, is also Supreme Allied Commander, Europe, under NATO, and is responsible for planning for the defense of Europe with U.S. forces integrated with other NATO forces or for unilateral U.S. operations, as required. CINCPAC is engaged heavily in military assistance and advisory activities.

SOUTHCOM is primarily responsible for the defense of the Panama Canal, military assistance activities in Latin America, and planning for contingency operations which might be required in Latin America.

STRICOM was established to provide a capability for the rapid deployment of combat forces to overseas areas as required. In addition, STRICOM is assigned responsibility for the Middle East/Southern Asia and Africa South of the Sahara.

Within the major Unified Commands, there are sometimes created "Sub-Unified Commands." A number of such "Sub-Unified Commands" now exist, such as the Military Assistance Command, Vietnam (MACV), the Military Assistance Command, Thailand (MACTHAI), and the U.S. Forces (Korea) Command, all of which fall under the Commander-in-Chief, Pacific (CINCPAC), the major Unified Command.

The responsibilities for forces assigned to the Unified and Specified Commands are divided between the Commanders and the Military Departments. The Commanders exercise "full operational command" which includes the responsibility to specify the composition of subordinate forces, assign tasks to these forces, designate objectives and exercise full authoritative direction necessary for accomplishment of their assigned missions. The Military Departments provide the operational forces to the Unified and Specified Commands and have the responsibility to select, train, equip, supply, administer (e.g., handle assignments, rotation and promotions), and discipline such forces.

Each Unified Commander has a joint staff, comprised of officers from all Military Services which have forces assigned to the Command. The staff of the Unified Commander is the only element within the command over which the Unified Commander has total command authority — including disciplinary authority and administrative and logistics responsibility. The Unified Commander has no direct responsibility for such functions as supplying, administering, and disciplining the combatant and direct support forces assigned to his command, but only exercises "operational command," or as it is more descriptively used, "operational control" over these forces. The Unified Commander reports through the

Joint Chiefs of Staff to the Secretary of Defense, and receives his directions through the same channel.

For each Military Service which has forces assigned to the Unified Command, there is a component command, to which the forces provided by a Military Department to the Unified Command are actually assigned. The Unified Commander exercises "operational command" through the component commander. On matters other than "operational command," such as supply, equipping, maintenance, administration, and discipline, the component commander receives supervisory direction from and reports to the Military Department to which he and his assigned forces belong. With respect to the latter functions, the component commander's chain of authority runs up to the Chief of his Service and to the Secretary of his Military Department and does not run through the Unified Commander.

This deficiency was pointed out clearly by President Eisenhower in his message to the Congress on the Defense Reorganization Act of 1958. He stated: "Because I have often seen the evils of diluted command, I emphasize that each Unified Commander must have unquestioned authority over all units of his command. . . . Today a unified command is made up of component commands from each military department, each under a commander of that department. The commander's authority over these component commands is short of the full command required for maximum efficiency."

What President Eisenhower referred to as "Diluted Command" was at that time defined officially as "Operational Control." In response to President Eisenhower's message, the Defense Reorganization Act of 1958 vested in the Unified Commander "full operational command," clearly indicating a Congressional intent to overcome the deficiencies of authority for the Unified Commander cited by President Eisenhower. In *Unified Action Armed Forces* (JCS Pub. 2) which sets forth principles, doctrines, and functions governing the activities and performance of forces assigned to Unified Commands, the JCS now define "Operational Command" as being synonymous with "Operational Control."

Despite the establishment of the unified command concept in the Defense Reorganization Act of 1958, as requested by President Eisenhower, the relationship and relative authority between the Unified Commander and the component commander, and between the component commander and his Military Department, remain substantially unchanged.

The net result is an organizational structure in which "unification" of either command or of the forces is more cosmetic than substantive. The resultant organizational structure is also layered with large headquarters and headquarters' staffs.

In the case of a Sub-Unified Command, such as MACV, the "operational command" runs from CINCPAC directly to MACV, not through CINCPAC's component commanders (U.S. Army Forces, Pacific

(USARPAC), U.S. Air Forces, Pacific (PACAF) and the Pacific Fleet (PACFLT)), as it does to most other forces in the Pacific. The "supervisory" direction for such matters as supply, maintenance, administration, and discipline, however, passes down a line from the Military Departments to the appropriate major component command (USARPAC, PACAF or PACFLT) and to the corresponding component command of the Sub-Unified Command (e.g., U.S. Army, Vietnam; Navy Forces, Vietnam; or the 7th U.S. Air Force).

One of the most significant factors relating to the internal organization of the Unified Command is the fact that only at the single-Service component command level of either the major or Sub-Unified Command is the total command authority which can be vested in a military commander brought together by merging the "supervision" originating in the Military Department and the "operational command" flowing from the Secretary of Defense through the Joint Chiefs of Staff and the Unified Command.

It is of more than passing interest to note that General Creighton Abrams, and before him General William Westmoreland, as the Sub-Unified Commander in Vietnam (COMUSMACV) chose to be his own Army component commander. . . .

The organizational structure of the major Unified Commands contributes significantly to deficiences in two procedural areas.

The channel for submission of requirements which can lead to material developments (variously called Operations Capability Objectives by the Army, General Operational Requirements by the Navy, and Required Operational Capabilities by the Air Force), to the extent they originate at all with operating commands, bypasses the Unified Commander and the "Operational Command" chain. To the extent there is one, the requirements flow is from the major component commander to the Military Service. As a consequence, the senior elements of the "operational command" chain — now the Secretary of Defense, the Joint Chiefs of Staff and the Unified Commander — who have the total mission awareness, have no opportunity for review and coordination of the requirements submissions, until after the requirements submissions have been processed and validated by the Military Services, if at all.

Secondly, there is no effective means for the Unified Commanders to participate in the programming and budgeting process. Presumably, the Unified Commander would be the most knowledgeable source of advice on the force structures, strengths, and equipments necessary to perform the mission assigned to his command for execution. The component commanders participate to an extent in some review processes of the Service budget submissions prepared by the Military Departments. Also, the Joint Chiefs of Staff solicit the views of the Unified Commanders on their requirements prior to the beginning of the Joint Chiefs' annual planning process which culminates in the Joint Strategic Objectives Plan. Neither of these processes, however, provides the senior joint commanders of combatant forces — the Unified Commanders — with any effective mechanism for influencing the programming and budgeting process, nor for materially affecting the planning process except in the area of contingency plans.

The existing command structure provides little flexibility and a considerable potential for confusion in crisis situations. For example, misunderstandings concerning forces to be used and to whom they are assigned; command relationships which are ambiguous, and which require extensive coordination between parallel commanders; confusion over the lines dividing areas of responsibility and jurisdictions; and the increased potential for mishaps created by the assignment of one command to execute the plans prepared by another. The inevitable delays occasioned by the layering of commands literally invite National Command Authorities to bypass some elements of the command chain.

The present combatant command structure does not facilitate the solution of many serious problems which materially affect the security of the nation: there is inadequate coordination between the strategic defensive and strategic offensive forces which must operate in the same physical space; the strategic offensive mission is split between four commands, SAC, EUCOM, LANTCOM and PACOM; the six area commands do not individually have a proper purview to permit realistic contingency planning.

The present structure of eight Unified and Specified Commands and a large number of subordinate Unified Commands has proved cumbersome, imposes too broad a span of control for a single decision point in time of peace, is excessively layered, unwieldy and unworkable in crises, and too fragmented to provide the best potential for coordinated response to a general war situation. Without exception, every crisis within the last decade that has involved the movement of forces has required both an ad hoc organizational rearrangement and ad hoc planning.[3] . . .

THE JOINT CHIEFS OF STAFF DECISION-MAKING PROCESS

The decision-making process of the Joint Chiefs of Staff (JCS) is highly formalized. It is a system based not only on coordination with, but also on concurrence by, the Military Services. The Flimsy-Buff-Green System (so called because the first draft was originally on onion skin, the second on buff-colored paper and the third on green paper) is a negotiation mechanism designed to exploit every opportunity for compromise and resolution of disagreement.

A JCS action may be initiated by the Secretary of Defense, the Deputy

[3] Vietnam, Cuba Missile Crisis (1962), Panama Riots (1964), Tonkin Gulf Crisis (1964), Congo Rescue Mission (1964), Dominican Republic Crisis (1965), Arab-Israeli War (1967).

Secretary of Defense, an Assistant Secretary of Defense, a Unified or Specified Command, a Military Service, the Chairman of the Joint Chiefs of Staff, or the Director of the Joint Staff.

A normal JCS action — not involving a study — takes about three weeks to process.

An action officer from the Joint Staff is appointed for each action. His immediate task, after receipt of a directive, is the preparation of a Flimsy, the purpose of which is to develop an approach to the problem and to resolve as many divergencies of view as possible before the formal phases of the process are entered. The action officer may either write the Flimsy and send it to the other Joint Staff and Military Service action officers for comment, or he may call a meeting of such action officers to discuss the problem before writing the Flimsy himself, or may request submission from the other action officers.

Once prepared, the Flimsy must be sent to the other action officers, after which a period of 24 hours must be permitted to elapse before the scheduling of a meeting of the action officers. After all differences are resolved among the action officers, the paper becomes Buff.

The Buff must first be coordinated with the Joint Staff Agencies, and changes by these Agencies are published as an appendix to the Buff report. The Buff is then forwarded to the Military Services where it receives wide circulation and the attention of more senior officers, the "planners." The Joint Staff action officer is responsible for the Buff's coordination and if there are no dissents by the Military Service "planners," the paper moves to the next phase and turns Green. However, if any Service dissents (a dissenting Service comment is called a "Purple"), the dissent must be circulated to all the Military Services, and unless all concur and the differences are resolved, a "planners' meeting" must be scheduled. The "planners' meeting" is at the senior Colonel level and is chaired by the Joint Staff "planner," usually a Brigadier General. The Joint Staff action officer having the initial responsibility may attend this meeting, but may not participate unless specifically requested by the Chairman. If differences can be resolved at this level, the paper is rewritten and the Buff turns Green. Where differences cannot be resolved, the dissenting Military Services prepare formal statements of nonconcurrence which are attached to the paper. The Joint Staff action officer who originated the report must then prepare an originator's consideration of the nonconcurrence(s) which is also attached, and the resultant package becomes a formal, numbered JCS green paper.

At this point, the Chairman of the Joint Chiefs of Staff, or the Director of the Joint Staff, may request a briefing, and when changes are suggested by either, they too are appended to the Green. The Green then goes to the Operations Deputies (which consist of the Director of the Joint Staff, the Deputy Chief of Staff for Military Operations of the Army, the Deputy Chief of Staff for Plans and Operations of the Air Force, and the Deputy Chief of Naval Operations (Plans and Policies) of the Navy). If, when the Operations Deputies consider the paper, they can resolve the disagreement, they approve it and remove it from the Joint Chiefs of Staff agenda; and such agreement constitutes approval by the Joint Chiefs of' Staff, unless the Operations Deputies consider the subject of the paper to be one of major importance, in which case they may send it to the Joint Chiefs of Staff. If agreement is not reached, the subject goes to the Joint Chiefs of Staff. The Joint Chiefs of Staff themselves may approve a report as written, approve modifications, return a report for rewrite by the Joint Staff and Military Service Staff planners, or disagree and forward it to the Secretary of Defense. In the latter case, the Chairman of the Joint Chiefs of Staff customarily prepares a covering memorandum explaining the nature of the disagreement and, perhaps, his own view.

Several procedures are authorized to expedite the process in certain cases.

Under the standard procedure described above, the Buff phase may be omitted and the Flimsy processed directly to a Green if (1) there are no substantive issues in the report, and (2) the report is urgently required.

Memorandum of Policy 97 (PM 97) permits actions taken on JCS matters by the Joint Staff to become decisions and to be implemented, provided that (1) actions are unanimously concurred in by the Services and the Directors of the pertinent Joint Staff Divisions, and (2) during the five days following submission of the report to the Joint Chiefs of Staff, no member of the Joint Chiefs nor the Director of the Joint Staff requests consideration of the matter by the Chiefs. If all involved agree, the report is not scheduled for an agenda, but is instead turned Green, with the cover carrying a date on which the report will automatically become a decision. If, prior to this date, a request for consideration should be made, the report will be put on an agenda.

On a matter of urgency which is not sufficiently substantive to warrant consideration of the Joint Chiefs of Staff, a phone vote may be employed. At the time of the vote on the Buff, the Services may indicate their willingness to use a phone vote instead of a formal meeting, and if there are no nonconcurrences during the phone vote, the report becomes a decision.

Memorandum of Policy 133 (PM 133) authorizes the Chairman of the Joint Chiefs of Staff to take actions for the Joint Chiefs of Staff and to inform them on (1) matters involving operations of the forces where a decision is urgent and time does not permit formal consultation with the Chiefs; (2) matters on which Joint Chiefs of Staff policy, plans, procedures, or guidance has been previously established; (3) matters on which the "corporate" views of the Joint Chiefs of Staff on a similar problem are known to the Chairman of the Joint Chiefs of Staff; and (4) matters not important enough for Joint Chiefs of Staff consultation. PM 133 also authorizes the Directors of Divisions of the Joint Staff to issue instructions in the name of the Joint Chiefs of Staff which are in accord with Joint Chiefs of Staff approved plans, policies, and procedures.

While a majority of the decisions made by the Joint Chiefs of Staff employs one of the alternate decision methods, contentious issues follow the Flimsy-Buff-Green route. The use of the PM 133 alternative reached a peak in 1966, and has since steadily declined in both absolute number of issues and as a percentage of total issues.

The Flimsy-Buff-Green procedure is ponderous and slow, but its most serious deficiency is the incentive created for unanimity, compromise and mutual accommodation of the views of the Military Services. So strong are the pressures for unanimity that in 1969, the Joint Chiefs of Staff were unanimous on all but eight-tenths of one percent of the issues considered, and in 1966, 1967 and 1968, the Joint Chiefs of Staff split on only two-tenths of one percent of the issues considered.

The process militates against the likelihood of the Joint Chiefs of Staff clearly facing-up to difficult and potentially divisive issues. The repetitious, committee-type negotiations tend to reduce issues to a level of compromise which will either avoid the potential conflicts or substitute a solution that can be accepted on a quid-pro-quo basis.

Lost in the process is the advantage of a joint staff, which, ideally, should be able to provide a more national viewpoint than staffs which are Service-oriented. This is because the procedure injects the joint participant into the process as little more than a coordinator of the views of the several Services.

Part Five

Interaction among Nations

RICHARD E. NEUSTADT

White House and Whitehall

Although the formal political system and the informal rules of the game result in concrete variations from country to country, the analytical description of the bureaucratic process remains applicable. While real-world British Prime Ministers may strive to behave more like the stereotypical American President who *decides*, real-world Presidents are obliged to behave very much like the stereotypical PM who presides over collegial decisionmaking by a Cabinet of equals. Although the particular arguments and maneuvers vary among political systems, both Prime Ministers and Presidents must negotiate with and maneuver around those who can block or delay their objectives, whether they be located in the British Cabinet or in the American executive branch and U.S. Congress.

However, any analysis of interaction among nations, which depends upon a knowledge of the bureaucratic process, must be careful to distinguish form from function. The formulation and execution of foreign policy in Britain is, as it is in the United States, a process of bureaucratic politics. However, the framework outlined in the Introduction to this book cannot be transferred mechanically from the American context to the British. The players and organizations who are the participants in the British bureaucratic process do not have the same official titles, nor do they occupy the same formal roles, as their American counterparts. Although their maneuvers and arguments are similarly constrained by rules of the game, these rules have several distinctive British characteristics.

To locate the British equivalent of the politically appointed "inners-and-outers" in the United States, one must look to the senior career civil servants, particularly the Permanent Secretaries of the Cabinet and Treasury. As Neustadt's description makes clear, they behave very much like the American political appointees who are the junior and senior players in the American foreign policy bureaucracy. To assume that they resemble career civil servants in the United States would result in serious errors of interpretation and prediction.

The rules of their game also are somewhat different. Once consulted, these senior civil servants acquiesce in the decision, whether or not they agree. Unlike their American counterparts, they do not attempt end-runs around their ministers to the back-benches of Parliament (no doubt in large part because Parliament is not receptive to such maneuvers). Ministers reciprocate by remaining aloof from the civil servants' pursuit of their personal interests and objectives: ministers do not interfere in the civil service's policies of recruitment and promotion.

These differences among bureaucratic systems mean that efforts by one

Reprinted from *Public Interest*, No. 2 (1966), pp. 50–69. Copyright 1965 by National Affairs, Inc., with the permission of the author and publishers.

nation to influence the behavior of another must begin with a keen appreciation of the fact that the other nation's actions also result from bureaucratic compromises. But beyond that generalization, the policymaker must
also bear in mind the *distinctive* structure and process of bureaucratic
politics in each nation that he hopes to influence.

Cabinet government, so-called, as practiced currently in the United Kingdom, differs in innumerable ways — some obvious, some subtle — from
"presidential government" in the United States. To ask what one can learn
about our own system by viewing theirs may seem far-fetched, considering
those differences. But actually the question is a good one. For comparison
should help us to discriminate between shadow and substance in both
regimes. A look down Whitehall's corridors of power might suggest a lot
of things worth noticing in Washington.

For a President-watcher, who tries to understand the inner workings of
our bureaucratic system by climbing inside now and then, and learning on
the job, it is no easy matter to attempt a comparison with the internal life
of Whitehall. How is one to get a comparable look? Those who govern
Britain mostly keep their secrets to themselves. They rarely have incentive
to do otherwise, which is among the differences between us. Least of all are
they inclined to satisfy the curiosities of academics. Even we colonials, persistent though we are and mattering as little as we do, find ourselves all too
frequently treated like Englishmen and kept at bay by those three magic
words: "Official Secrets Act." Why not? Nothing in the British Constitution
says that anyone outside of Whitehall needs an inside view. Quite the
reverse. If academics know, then journalists might learn, and even the
back-benchers might find out. God forbid!

In Britain governing is *meant* to be a mystery. And so it is. Only in the
memoirs of participants does one get glimpses, now and then, of operational reality. And even the most "indiscreet" of recent memoirs veil the
essence of the modern system: the relations between ministers and civil
servants in the making of a government decision.

For four years I have made a hobby of attempting to poke holes in
Whitehall's defenses, and to take a closer look than either interviews or
books afford. Partly this has been a "busman's holiday": having roamed
one set of corridors, I find the temptation irresistible to look around
another. Partly, though, I have been tempted by the thought that a comparison of set likenesses and differences would add a new dimension to
President-watching.

To test that proposition, let me raise two simple points of difference
between their system and ours.

First, we have counterparts for their top civil servants — but not in our
own civil service.

Second, we have counterparts for their cabinet ministers — but not exclusively, or even mainly, in our cabinet.

If I state these two correctly, and I think I do, it follows that in our conventional comparisons we all too often have been victims of semantics. Accordingly, in our proposals for reform-by-analogy we all too often have confused function with form. I find no functions in the British system for which ours lacks at least nascent counterparts. But it is rare when institutions with the same names in both systems do the same work for precisely the same purpose. Thus, the most important things that I bring back from my excursioning in Whitehall are a question and caution. The question: what is our functional equivalent? The caution: never base analysis on nomenclature. These seem to be embarrassingly obvious. But it is astonishing how frequently they are ignored.

I

"Why are your officials so passionate?", I once was asked in England by a bright, young Treasury official just back from Washington. I inquired with whom he had been working there. His answer: "Your chaps at the Budget Bureau."

To an American, those "chaps" appear to be among the most *dis*-passionate of Washingtonians. Indeed, the Budget staff traditionally prides itself on being cool, collected, and above the struggle, distant from emotions churning in the breasts of importunate agency officials. Yet to my English friend, "They took themselves so seriously . . . seemed to be crusaders for the policy positions they thought made sense . . . seemed to feel that it was up to them to save the day. . . ." If this is how the Budget Bureau struck him, imagine how he would have felt about some circles in our Air Force, or the European Bureau of the State Department, or the Office of Economic Opportunity, or the Forest Service for that matter, or the Bureau of Reclamation, or the National Institutes of Health!

His inquiry suggests two further queries. First, out of what frame of reference was he asking? And second, is it sensible of him (and most of us) to talk of our own budgeteers as though they were his counterparts? These questions are pertinent because I think we are very far from candid with ourselves about the way we get *his* work done in *our* system.

This young man was a Principal-with-prospects at the Treasury. By definition, then, he was a man of the Administrative class, the elite corps of the British civil service. More important, he was also an apprentice member of the favored few, the elite-of-the-elite, who climb the ladder *in* the Treasury. With skill and luck and approbation from his seniors he might someday rise to be a Mandarin. And meanwhile he would probably serve soon as personal assistant to a Cabinet minister. In short, he had the frame of reference which befits a man whose career ladder rises up the central pillar of the whole Whitehall establishment toward the heights where dwell the seniors of all seniors, moulders of ministers, heads of the civil service, knights in office, lords thereafter: the Permanent Secretaries of the Cabinet and the Treasury.

English civil servants of this sort, together with their foreign office counterparts, make up the inner core of "officials," civilian career men, whose senior members govern the United Kingdom in collaboration with their ministerial superiors, the front-bench politicians, leaders of the parliamentary party which commands a House majority for the time being. Theirs is an intimate collaboration, grounded in the interests and traditions of both sides. Indeed it binds them into a Society for Mutual Benefit: what they succeed in sharing with each other they need share with almost no one else, and governing in England is a virtual duopoly.

This is the product of a tacit treaty, an implicit bargain, expressed in self-restraints which are observed on either side. The senior civil servants neither stall nor buck decisions of the Government, once these have been taken in due form. "Due Form" means consultation with these senior civil servants, among other things; but having been consulted, these officials act without public complaint or private evasion, even though they may have fought what they are doing up to the last moment of decision. They also try to assure comparable discipline in lower official ranks, and to squeeze out the juniors who do not take kindly to it.

The senior politicians, for their part — with rare and transient exceptions — return this loyalty in full measure. The politicians rarely meddle with official recruitment or promotion: by and large, officialdom administers itself. The politicians preserve the anonymity of civil servants both in Parliament and in the press. Officials never testify on anything except "accounts" (an audit of expenditures), and nobody reveals their roles in shaping public policy. Ministers take all kudos for themselves — likewise the heat. They also take upon themselves protection for the status of officialdom in the society: honors fall like gentle rain at stated intervals. They even let career civil servants run their private offices, and treat their personal assistants of the moment (detailed from civil-service ranks) as confidentially as our department heads treat trusted aides imported from outside. More important, the politicians *lean* on their officials. They *expect* to be advised. Most important, they very often follow the advice that they receive.

This is an advantageous bargain for both sides. It relieves the politicians of a difficult and chancy search for "loyal" advisers and administrators. These are in place, ready to hand. And it relieves civil servants of concern for their security in terms both of profession and of person. No wonder our career men appear "passionate" to one of theirs; theirs have nothing at stake except policy!

So a Treasury-type has everything to gain by a dispassionate stance, and nothing to lose except arguments. To be sure, since he feels himself with reason to be one of an elite, ranking intellectually and morally with the best in Britain, this is no trifling loss. If parliamentary parties were less disciplined than they now are, or if he had back-benchers who identified with him, he could afford to carry arguments outside official channels, as his predecessors sometimes did a century ago — and as *military* officers still do, on occasion. But party discipline calls forth its counterpart in his own ranks. And party politicians on back-benches have no natural affinities with civil servants — quite the contrary. The civil servant really has no recourse but to lose his arguments with grace and wait in patience for another day, another set of ministers. After all, he stays, they go. And while he stays, he shares the fascinating game of power, stretching his own mind and talents in the service of a reasonably grateful country.

The Treasury-type is a disciplined man; but a man fulfilled, not frustrated. His discipline is the price he pays for power. Not every temperament can take it; if he rises in the Treasury, he probably can. But there is more to this than a cold compromise for power's sake. Those who rise and find fulfillment in their work do so in part because they are deliberately exposed at mid-career to the constraints, the miseries, the hazards which afflict the human beings who wield power on the political side. They know the lot of ministers from observation at first hand. Exposure makes for empathy and for perspective. It also makes for comfort with the civil servant's lot. Whitehall's elites gain all three while relatively young. It leaves them a bit weary with the weight of human folly, but it rids them of self-righteousness, the bane of *our* career men — particularly endemic, of course, among budgeteers.

A Treasury-type gains this exposure through that interesting device, the tour of duty in a minister's private office as his personal "dogsbody." The private secretary, so called, serves his master-of-the-moment as a confidential aide, minding his business, doing his chores, sharing his woes, offering a crying towel, bracing him for bad days in the House, briefing him for bad days in the office. Etcetera. Remarkably, by our standards, the civil service has preempted such assignments for its own. (Do not confuse a minister's private secretary with mere *parliamentary* private secretaries who are drawn from the back-benches of the House.) Still more remarkably, the politicians feel themselves well served and rarely dream of looking elsewhere for the service. I know an instance where a minister confided in his private secretary a secret he told no one else save the Prime Minister, not even his Permanent Secretary, the career head-of-department, "lest it embarrass him to know." The Permanent Secretary was the private secretary's boss; yet the secret was kept as a matter of course. This, I am assured, is not untypical: "ministerial secrets" are all in the day's work for dogsbodies.

Accordingly, the one-time private secretary who has risen in due course to be permanent secretary of a department knows far more of what it feels like to perform as a politician than his opposite number, the department's minister, can ever hope to fathom in reverse. A William Armstrong, for example, now joint-head of Treasury, whose opposite number is the Chancellor of the Exchequer, spent years as private secretary to a previous Chancellor who was among the ablest men in the cabinets of his time. Draw the contrast with our own career civil servants.

Our budgeteers imagine that they are the nearest thing to Treasury civil servants. For this, no one can blame them. Much of our literature suggests that if they are not quite the same as yet, a little gimmickery could make them so. Many American political scientists have bemused themselves for years with plans to borrow nomenclature and procedures from the British side, on the unstated premise that function follows form. But it does not.

Functionally, our counterparts for British Treasury-types are *non*-career men holding jobs infused with presidential interest or concern. They are "in-and-outers" from the law firms, banking, business, academia, foundations, or occasionally journalism, or the entourages of successful Governors and Senators — along with up-and-outers (sometimes up-and-downers) who relinquish, or at least risk, civil servant status in the process. Here is the elite-of-the-elite, the upper-crust of our "Administrative class." These are the men who serve alongside our equivalents for ministers, and who share in governing. One finds them in the White House and in the *appointive* jobs across the street at the Executive Office Building. One finds them also on the seventh floor of State, and on the third and fourth floors of the Pentagon; these places among others.

Let me take some names at random to suggest the types. First, the prototype of all: Averill Harriman. Second, a handful of the currently employed: David Bell, William Bundy, Wilbur Cohen, Harry McPherson, Paul Nitze. Third, a few recent "outers" almost certain to be back, somehow, sometime: McGeorge Bundy, Kermit Gordon, Theodore Sorensen. Fourth, a long-time "outer" who is never back but always in: Clark Clifford. Three of these men got their start as government career men, two as academics, two in banking, two in law, and one on Capitol Hill. The numbers are but accidents of random choice; the spread is meaningful.

The jobs done by such men as these have no precise equivalents in England; our machinery is too different. For example, McGeorge Bundy as the President's Assistant for National Security Affairs was something more than Principal Private Secretary to the Prime Minister (reserved for rising Treasury-types), a dogsbody-writ-large, and also something different from the Secretary of the Cabinet (top of the tree for them), a post "tradition" turns into an almost Constitutional position, certainly what we would call an "institutional" one. Yet the men in those positions see a

Bundy as their sort of public servant. They are higher on the ladder than my young friend with the question; they do not take budgeteers to be their counterparts; they know a Senior Civil Servant when they see one.

Every detail of our practice is un-English, but the general outline fits. One of our men appears on television; another testifies against a bill; a third and fourth engage in semi-public argument; a fifth man feeds a press campaign to change the President's mind; a sixth disputes a cabinet member's views in open meeting; a seventh overturns an inter-agency agreement. So it goes, to the perpetual surprise (and sometimes envy?) of the disciplined duopolists in Britain. Yet by *our* lights, according to *our* standards, under our conditions, such activities may be as "disciplined" as theirs, and as responsive to political leadership. The ablest of our in-and-outers frequently display equivalent restraint and equal comprehension in the face of the dilemmas which confront our presidential counterparts of their Cabinet politicians.

The elite of our officialdom is not careerist men in the British sense (although, of course, our in-and-outers have careers); why should it be? Neither is it the President with his department heads. They, too, are in-and-outers. We forget that the duopoly which governs Britain is composed of *two* career systems, official and political. Most ministers who will take office through the next decade are on the scene and well identified in Westminster. The permanent secretaries who will serve with them are on the Whitehall ladders now; a mere outsider can spot some of them. Contrast our situation — even the directorships of old-line bureaus remain problematical. Who is to succeed J. Edgar Hoover?

We have only two sets of true career men in our system. One consists of Senators and Congressmen in relatively safe seats, waiting their turn for chairmanships. The other consists of military officers and civil employees who are essentially technicians manning every sort of specialty (including "management") in the Executive establishment. Between these two we leave a lot of room for in-and-outers. We are fortunate to do so. Nothing else could serve as well to keep the two apart. And *their* duopoly would be productive, not of governance, but of its feudal substitute, piecemeal administration. We can only hope to govern in our system by, and through, the Presidency. In-and-outers are a saving grace for Presidents.

II

Since 1959, English commentators frequently have wondered to each other if their government was being "presidentialized." In part, this stemmed from electoral considerations following the "personality contest" between Harold Macmillan and Hugh Gaitskell in that year's general election. In part, too, it stemmed from the impression left by Macmillan's active premiership —

reinforced this past year by the sight of still another activist in office, Harold Wilson.

Despite their differences of style, personality, and party, both Macmillan and Wilson patently conceived the Cabinet Room in Downing Street to be the PM's office, not a mere board-room. Both evidently acted on the premise that the PM's personal judgment ought, if possible, to be decisive. Both reached out for the power of personal decision on the issues of the day. Macmillan did so through offstage maneuver, while avowing his fidelity to cabinet consensus. With perhaps a bit more candor, Wilson does the same. Hence discussion about trends toward "presidential" government.

Yet between these two Prime Ministers there was another for a year, Sir Alec Douglas-Home. And by no stretch of the imagination could his conduct in office have been characterized as presidential. On the contrary, by all accounts he was a classic "chairman of the board," who resolutely pushed impending issues *out* of Number 10, for initiative elsewhere, by others. He managed, it is said, to get a lot of gardening done while he resided there. I once asked a close observer what became of the initiatives, the steering, the maneuvering, which Home refused to take upon himself. He replied:

> When ministers discovered that he really wouldn't do it, they began to huddle with each other, little groups of major figures. You would get from them enough agreement or accommodation to produce the main lines of a government position, something they could try to steer through Cabinet. Or if you didn't get it, there was nothing to be done. That's how it began to work, outside of Number 10, around it.

That is how it would be working now had there been but a slight shift in the popular vote of 1964.

The British system, then, has *not* been presidentialized, or not at least in operational terms. For, as we learned with Eisenhower, the initiatives a President must take to form "the main lines of a government position" cannot survive outside the White House precincts. Toss them out and either they bounce back or they wither away. A President may delegate to White House aides ("ok, S.A."), or to a Foster Dulles, but only as he demonstrates consistently, day-in-and-out, that they command his ear and hold his confidence. Let him take to his bed behind an oxygen tent and they can only go through motions. Eisenhower's White House was a far cry from 10 Downing Street in the regime of Douglas-Home. That remains the distance Britain's system has to travel toward a presidential status for prime ministers.

But even though the system did not make an activist of Douglas-Home, his predecessor and successor obviously relished the part. The system may not have required them to play it, but they did so, and the system bore the weight of their activity. In externals, Number 10 looks no more like the

White House under Wilson than it did a year ago. But, in essence, Wilson comes as close to being "President" as the conventions of *his* system allow. He evidently knows it and likes it. So, I take it, did Macmillan.

How close can such men come? How nearly can they assert "presidential" leadership inside a cabinet system? Without endeavoring to answer in the abstract, let me record some impressions of concrete performances.

First, consider Britain's bid for Common Market membership four years ago, which presaged an enormous (if abortive) shift in public policy, to say nothing of Tory Party policy. By all accounts, this "turn to Europe" was Macmillan's own. The timing and the impetus were his, and I am told that his intention was to go whole hog, both economically and politically. As such, this was among the great strategic choices in the peacetime politics of Britain. But it never was a "Government decision." For those, by British definition, come in Cabinet. Macmillan never put the issue there in candid terms. Instead he tried to sneak past opposition there — and on back-benches and in constituencies — by disguising his strategic choice as a commercial deal. The Cabinet dealt with issues of negotiation, *en principe* and later in detail, for making Britain part of Europe's economic union without giving up its Commonwealth connections (or farm subsidies). One minister explained to me:

> Timing is everything. First we have to get into the Common Market as a matter of business, good for our economy. Then we can begin to look at the political side. . . . Appetites grow with eating. We couldn't hold the Cabinet, much less our back-benchers, if we put this forward now in broader terms. . . .

Accordingly, the move toward Europe had to be played out in its ostensible terms, as a detailed negotiation of a commercial character. This took two years; and while the tactic served its purpose within Tory ranks, these were the years when France escaped from the Algerian war. By the time negotiations neared their end, Charles de Gaulle was riding high at home. Macmillan tiptoed past his own internal obstacle, but took so long about it that his path was blocked by an external one, the veto of de Gaulle.

Second, take the Nassau Pact of 1962, which calmed the Skybolt crisis between Washington and London even as it gave de Gaulle excuses for that veto. Macmillan was his own negotiator at the Nassau Conference. He decided on the spot to drop his claim for Skybolt missiles and to press the substitution of Polaris weaponry. He wrung what seemed to him an advantageous compromise along those lines from President Kennedy. Then and only then did he "submit" its terms to the full Cabinet for decision (by return cable), noting the concurrence of three potent ministers who had accompanied him: the Foreign, Commonwealth, and Defence Secretaries.

With the President waiting, the Cabinet "decided" (unenthusiastically, by all accounts) to bless this *fait accompli*. What else was there to do? The answer, nothing — and no doubt Macmillan knew it.

Third, consider how the present Labour Government reversed its pre-election stand on Nassau's terms. Within six weeks of taking office, Wilson and his colleagues became champions of the Polaris program they had scorned in opposition. Their back-benchers wheeled around behind them almost to a man. It is no secret that the Prime Minister was the source of this reversal, also its tactician. So far as I can find, it was his own choice, his initiative, his management, from first to last. He got it done in quick-time, yet he did it by maneuvering on tiptoe like Macmillan in the case of the Common Market (with just a touch of the shot-gun, like Macmillan in the Nassau case). When Wilson let Polaris reach the Cabinet for "decision," leading ministers, both "right" and "left," already were committed individually. By that time also, Wilson had pre-tested back-bench sentiment; he had "prematurely" voiced to an acquiescent House what would become the rationale for Cabinet action: keeping on with weapons whose production had already passed a "point of no return."

Superficially, such instances as these seem strikingly unpresidential. In our accustomed vision, Presidents do not tiptoe around their Cabinets, they instruct, inform or ignore them. They do not engineer *faits accomplis* to force decisions from them, for the Cabinet does not make decisions; Presidents decide. A Kennedy after Birmingham, a Johnson after Selma, deciding on their civil rights bills, or a Johnson after Pleiku, ordering the bombers north, or Johnson last December, taking off our pressure for the multilateral force, or Kennedy confronting Moscow over Cuba with advisers all around him but decisions in his hands — what contrasts these suggest with the maneuvers of a Wilson or Macmillan!

The contrasts are but heightened by a glance at their work-forces: Presidents with twenty-odd high-powered personal assistants, and a thousand civil servants in their Executive Office — Prime Ministers with but four such assistants in their Private Office (three of them on detail from departments) and a handful more in Cabinet Office, which by definition is not "theirs" alone. Differences of work-place heighten the effect still more: 10 Downing Street is literally a house, comparing rather poorly with the White House before T.R.'s time. The modern White House is a palace, as Denis Brogan keeps reminding us, a physically cramped version of the Hofburg, or the Tuileries.

Yet beneath these contrasts, despite them, belying them, Americans are bound to glimpse a long-familiar pattern in the conduct of an activist Prime Minister. It is the pattern of a President maneuvering around or through the power-men in his Administration *and* in Congress. Once this is seen, all contrasts become superficial. Underneath our images of Presidents-inboots, astride decisions, are the half-observed realities of Presidents-in-sneakers, stirrups in hand, trying to induce particular department heads, or Congressmen or Senators, to climb aboard.

Anyone who has an independent power-base is likelier than not to get "ministerial" treatment from a President. Even his own appointees are to be wooed, not spurred, in the degree that they have their own attributes of power: expertise, or prestige, or a statute under foot. As Theodore Sorensen reported while he still was at the White House:

> In choosing between conflicting advice, the President is also choosing between conflicting advisers. . . . He will be slow to overrule a cabinet officer whose pride or prestige has been committed, not only to save the officer's personal prestige but to maintain his utility. . . . Whenever any President overrules any Secretary he runs the risk of that Secretary grumbling, privately if not publicly, to the Congress, or to the press (or to his diary), or dragging his feet on implementation, or, at the very worst, resigning with a blast at the President.

But it is men of Congress more than departmental men who regularly get from Pennsylvania Avenue the treatment given Cabinet ministers from Downing Street. Power in the Senate is particularly courted. A Lyndon Johnson (when he served there), or a Vandenberg in Truman's time, or nowadays an Anderson, a Russell, even a Mansfield — to say nothing of a Dirksen — are accorded many of the same attentions which a Wilson has to offer a George Brown.

The conventions of "bipartisanship" in foreign relations, established under Truman and sustained by Eisenhower, have been extended under Kennedy and Johnson to broad sectors of the home front, civil rights especially. These never were so much a matter of engaging oppositionists in White House undertakings as of linking to the White House men from either party who had influence to spare. Mutuality of deference between Presidents and leaders of congressional opinion, rather than between the formal party leaderships, always has been the essence of "bipartisanship" in practice. And men who really lead opinion on the Hill gain privileged access to executive decisions as their customary share of "mutual deference." "Congress" may not participate in such decisions, but these men often do: witness Dirksen in the framing of our recent Civil Rights Acts, or a spectrum of Senators from Russell to Mansfield in the framing of particular approaches on Viet Nam. Eleven years ago, Eisenhower seems to have kept our armed forces out of Indo-China when a projected intervention at the time of Dien Bien Phu won no support from Senate influentials. Johnson now maneuvers to maintain support from "right" to "left" within their ranks.

If one seeks our counterparts for Wilson or Macmillan as Cabinet tacticians, one need look no further than Kennedy or Johnson maneuvering among the influentials both downtown *and* on the Hill (and in state capitals, or among steel companies and trade unions, for that matter). Macmillan's caution on the Common Market will suggest the torturous, slow course of JFK toward fundamental changes in our fiscal policy, which brought him to the point of trying for a tax cut only by the end of his third year. Macmillan's *fait accompli* on Polaris brings to mind the Southeast Asia Resolution Johnson got from Congress after there had been some shooting in the Tonkin Gulf — and all its predecessors back to 1955, when Eisenhower pioneered this technique for extracting a "blank check." Wilson's quiet, quick arrangement for the Labour Party to adopt Polaris has a lot in common with the Johnson coup a year ago on Federal aid to education, where a shift in rationale took all sorts of opponents off the hook.

British government may not be presidential, but our government is more prime-ministerial than we are inclined to think. Unhappily for clarity of thought, we too have something called a Cabinet. But that pallid institution is in no sense the equivalent of theirs. Our equivalent is rather an informal, shifting aggregation of key individuals — the influentials at both ends of Pennsylvania Avenue. Some of them may sit in what we call the Cabinet as department heads; others sit in back rows there, as senior White House aides; still others have no place there. Collectively these men share no responsibility nor any meeting ground. Individually, however, each is linked to all the others through the person of the President (supported by his telephone). And all to some degree are serviced — also monitored — by one group or another on the White House staff. The former "Bundy Office," or the "Sorensen Shop" which one might best describe now as the Moyers "sphere of influence," together with the staff of legislative liaisoners captained until lately by Lawrence O'Brien — these groups, although not tightly interlocked, provide a common reference-point for influentials everywhere: "This is the White House calling. . . ." While we lack an institutionalized Cabinet along British lines, we are evolving an equivalent of Cabinet Office. The O'Brien operation was its newest element, with no precursors worthy of the name in any regime earlier than Eisenhower's. Whether it survives, and how and why, without O'Brien become questions of the day for Presidency-watchers.

The functional equivalence between a British Cabinet and our set of influentials — whether Secretaries, Senators, White House staffers, Congressmen, or others — is rendered plain by noting that, for most intents and purposes, their Cabinet members do the work of our congressional committees, our floor leaderships, and our front-offices downtown, all combined. The combination makes for superficial smoothness; Whitehall seems a quiet place. But once again, appearances deceive. Beneath the surface, this combine called "Cabinet" wrestles with divergencies of interest, of perspective, of procedure, of personality, much like those we are used to witnessing above ground in the dealings of our separated institutions. Not only is the hidden struggle reminiscent of our open one, but also the results are often similar: "bold, new ventures" actually undertaken are often few and far between. Whitehall dispenses with the grunts and groans of a Washington, but both can labor mightily to bring forth mice.

It is unfashionable just now to speak of "stalemate" or of "deadlock" in our government, although these terms were all the rage two years ago and will be so again, no doubt, whenever Johnson's coat-tails shrink. But British government is no less prone to deadlock than our own. Indeed I am inclined to think their tendencies in that direction more pronounced than ours. A keen observer of their system, veteran of some seven years at Cabinet meetings, put it to me in these terms:

> The obverse of our show of monolithic unity behind a Government position, when we have one, is slowness, ponderousness, deviousness, in approaching a position, getting it taken, getting a "sense of the meeting." Nothing in our system is harder to do, especially if press leaks are at risk. You Americans don't seem to understand that. . . ."

In the Common Market case, to cite but one example, the three months from October to December, 1962 were taken up at Brussels, where negotiations centered, by a virtual filibuster from the British delegation. This drove some of the Europeans wild and had them muttering about "perfidious Albion." But London's delegates were not engaged in tactical maneuvering at Brussels. All they were doing there was to buy time for tactical maneuvering back home, around the cabinet table. The three months were required to induce two senior ministers to swallow agricultural concessions every student of the subject knew their government would have to make. But Britain could not move until those influential "Members of the Government" had choked them down. The time-lag seemed enormous from the vantage point of Brussels. Significantly, it seemed short indeed to Londoners. By Whitehall standards this was rapid motion.

One of the checks-and-balances in Britain's system lies between the PM and his colleagues as a group. This is the check that operated here. A sensible Prime Minister is scrupulous about the forms of collective action: overreaching risks rejection; a show of arbitrariness risks collegial reaction; if they should band together his associates could pull him down. Accordingly, the man who lives at Number 10 does well to avoid policy departures like the plague, unless, until, and if, he sees a reasonable prospect for obtaining that "sense of the meeting." He is not without resources to induce the prospect, and he is at liberty to ride events which suit his causes. But these things take time — and timing. A power-wise Prime Minister adjusts his pace accordingly. So Macmillan did in 1962.

Ministerial prerogatives are not the only source of stalemate or slow motion in this system. If members of a Cabinet were not also heads of great departments, then the leader of their party in the Commons and the country might be less inclined to honor their pretensions in the Government. A second, reinforcing check-and-balance of the system lies between him and the senior civil servants. To quote again, from the same source:

> The PM has it easier with ministers than with the civil servants. The ranks of civil servants do not work for *him*. They have to be brought along. They are loyal to a "Government Decision" but that takes the form of action in Cabinet, where the great machines are represented by their ministers.

The civil servants can be his allies, of course, if their perceptions of the public interest square with his; then all he needs to do is to bring ministers along. Something of this sort seems to have been a factor in the Labour Government's acceptance of Polaris: Foreign Office and Defence officials urged their masters on; Treasury officials remained neutral. The PM who first manages to tie the civil servants tighter to his office than to their own ministries will presidentialize the British system beyond anything our system knows. But that day is not yet. It may never come.

So a British Premier facing Cabinet is in somewhat the position of our President confronting the Executive Departments and Congress combined. Our man, compared to theirs, is freer to take initiatives and to announce them in *advance* of acquiescence from all sides. With us, indeed, initiatives in public are a step toward obtaining acquiescence, or at least toward wearing down the opposition. It is different in Downing Street. With us, also, the diplomatic and defense spheres yield our man authority for binding judgments on behalf of the whole government. Although he rarely gets unquestioning obedience and often pays a price, his personal choices are authoritative, for he himself is heir to royal prerogatives. In Britain these adhere to Cabinet members as a group, not to the Prime Minister alone. True, he can take over diplomacy, as Neville Chamberlain did so disastrously, and others since, or he can even run a war like Winston Churchill. But Chamberlain had to change Foreign Secretaries in the process, and Churchill took precautions, making himself Minister of Defense.

Still, despite all differences, a President, like a Prime Minister, lives daily under the constraint that he must bring along *his* "colleagues" and get action from *their* liege-men at both ends of the Avenue. A sensible Prime Minister is always counting noses in Cabinet. A sensible President is always checking off his list of "influentials." The PM is not yet a President. The President, however, is a sort of super-Prime Minister. This is what comes of comparative inquiry.

III

For over half a century, a great number of studious Americans have sought to fasten on our system, frankly imitating Britain, both a senior civil service drawn from career ranks and a Cabinet drawn from Congress. Meanwhile, without paying much attention to such formulations, our governmental practice has been building *ad hoc* counterparts. I have given two examples and could offer many more, but I hope these suffice to make the point.

The in-and-outers on whom we depend to do at presidential level what the Treasury-types of Whitehall do at Cabinet level deserve much more notice than they have so far received. They are a political phenomenon to study. They also are a political resource to nurture. Their care-and-feeding should concern our schools of public service not less but rather more than that of civil servants who remain in career ranks. (At least this is a proposition we shall test at Harvard with the new resources we are to obtain in memory of that notable recruiter, John F. Kennedy.)

As for our Cabinet-substitute, the shifting set of influentials, few things are more interesting in our system than the still inconclusive signs that we *may* now be on the verge of a new institutional breakthrough, a pragmatic innovation in our Constitution which might match those of the Roosevelt-Truman years. For White House staffing in the years of Kennedy and Johnson, combined with Johnson's tendency to use some senior Senators as though they were Executive advisers — these together, if sustained, could lay the basis for new patterns of relationship we someday would discover had become an institution. It is, of course, too soon to tell. Truman, in his early years, also leaned a lot on certain Senators. Eisenhower's staffing innovations mostly were a flash-in-the-pan. Influentials on the Hill are not yet tied into the presidential circle with anything like the firmness or the mutual satisfaction (relatively speaking) of the ties which bind their counterparts downtown. Perhaps they never will be. But if they ever are to be, the Johnson years appear a likely time.

These among others are the thoughts a look at Whitehall can suggest to a watcher of Washington — provided one is careful to distinguish form from function.

HENRY BRANDON

Skybolt

Analysts of international relations who conceive of nation-states as unitary purposive actors either would be at a loss to explain the near crisis in Anglo-American relations occasioned by the cancellation of the Skybolt air-to-ground missile or would attribute it to some vague notions of a breakdown in communications between the two countries. As we have seen, however, the "United States" did not support and then cancel Skybolt; nor did the "United Kingdom" want and need the missile. Rather, a variety of participants within each country's national security bureaucracy saw different faces of the issue and assumed positions in support of or opposition to Skybolt for a broad range of reasons. Research into bureaucratic decisionmaking makes the analyst aware of the importance of disaggregating the nation-states into separate actors and organizations and directs his attention to the interaction among these participants, both within each nation and between them. Viewed in this manner, the potential crisis which accompanied the Skybolt cancellation is somewhat less mysterious.

Definitions of what the Skybolt issue represented varied, depending upon the participant; each actor had a different problem and pursued varying objectives. The Conservative government in Britain, which wanted to maintain an independent nuclear deterrent in part for domestic political reasons, saw Skybolt as a relatively inexpensive way to do so. The Royal Air Force, like the U.S. Air Force, saw Skybolt as extending the lease on life of the manned bomber. The Royal Navy perceived in Skybolt a device to avoid diverting its precious budget resources to expensive, unwanted Polaris submarines. For some in the State Department, Skybolt was an obstacle to European integration that would include Britain. The U.S. President and Secretary of Defense saw Skybolt as an expensive inefficient weapon system which, if permitted to proceed, not only would waste money but would vitiate their campaign to exert strong control over military procurement. Thus, part of the problem was, in a sense, a failure of communication: all of the participants looked at Skybolt but saw different problems and opportunities. To the extent that each did not understand the others' needs, efforts to communicate clearly and avoid tensions were likely to fail.

Most approaches to international relations assume that the primary focus of attention of foreign policy bureaucracies is the foreign governments with which they have to deal. But the operation of bureaucratic politics suggests that the predominant source of problems and threats for each of the participants is *intra*-national. The incumbent Conservatives were especially concerned about the electoral consequences of a Skybolt cancellation,

Reprinted from the *London Sunday Times*, December 8, 1963 with permission of the author.

while Kennedy and McNamara were worried about Air Force obstruction and Congressional opposition. The internal focus had two consequences which promoted the potential for crisis. First, since none of the participants saw Skybolt primarily as a problem in international relations, they devoted relatively little time to that aspect. Second, even such efforts as were made to minimize the international complications were encumbered by the fact that neither side could risk being candid with the other, let alone correct misread signals, lest its domestic adversaries listen and react.

Little did President Eisenhower suspect how premonitory was his gesture when he presented Harold Macmillan with a table model of a Polaris submarine at Camp David in 1960. It was at that meeting that the United States promised to supply Britain with the ill-fated Skybolt missile, a promise which less than two years later led to the most perilous crisis between these two Allies since the Suez affair.

How two such men as President Kennedy and the Prime Minister, who kept their special telephone line between London and Washington fairly "hot," could so miscalculate each other's reactions — especially with Sir David Ormsby Gore, close friend of Mr. Kennedy, as British Ambassador in Washington — how, in fact, two Allies in constant touch at so many levels, civilian and military, could fall out so badly and misjudge each other's aims and psychology so glaringly is still a mystery.

It perturbed and puzzled President Kennedy so much that he asked Professor Richard E. Neustadt, of Columbia University, to conduct an inquest to try to determine what went wrong. I have not seen Professor Neustadt's study, which is secret. But after weeks of extensive research in Whitehall and in Washington I have tried myself to piece together the story of this failure in transatlantic communications. It is an intriguing story, full of forebodings and uncertainties, of high political stakes dependent on technological progress, of a chain of errors of judgment carefully kept from the public gaze, and, finally, at Nassau, one of the great confrontations in the history of Anglo-American relations.

The opening setting to the drama was as it should be: serene and informal in the best tradition of Anglo-American cooperation and friendship. The proceedings in the rustic and unpretentious atmosphere of Camp David in March, 1960, were amiable and predictable. All the ingredients for the crucial Skybolt Agreement had been prepared well in advance.

The request for Skybolt came shortly after the British Government had decided to jettison the Blue Streak missile. Its selection was based on the desire to prolong the life of the V-bombers, badge of Britain's independent deterrent, whose effective life span was likely to expire in another five to seven years. It was, therefore, not difficult for the Royal Air Force, which can always count on encouragement from the United States Air Force for anything that will also be to its own advantage, to persuade the British Government that what was needed was Skybolt — a new venture to which Thomas Gates, then Secretary of Defense, under heavy pressure from the Strategic Air Force, had given the go-ahead only one month earlier.

This two-stage ballistic missile system, which was to have the advantage of being launched from under the wing of a bomber some 1,000 miles from the target, was originally devised to offset the growing enthusiasm within the Pentagon for another new missile system — the United States Navy's Polaris. Skybolt, as Thomas Gates remembers, was at first nothing but a paragraph and a concept derived from the Polaris and originally called the "Polaris of the sky." Although Britain's decision in favor of Skybolt had already been settled by the Cabinet in London, the U.S. Navy, which hated to be outdone by the Air Force, made a last-minute effort (alas, an unsuccessful one) on behalf of Polaris among the British contingent at Camp David, through President Eisenhower's own naval aide.

If Britain at that time had opted for Polaris, at least one principal involved in these negotiations told me, it could have had it on terms similar to those for Skybolt, especially since at that time the United States was already furnishing Britain with information about nuclear-powered submarines. Skybolt, for anyone taking the long view, was a faulty gamble.

Mr. Harold Watkinson, then Britain's Defence Minister, at the time advised Mr. Macmillan that if the U.S. offered Polaris, it would be tied to NATO; that only Skybolt would keep Britain's deterrent independent; that Polaris had the disadvantage of being useful only in nuclear war, whereas the aeroplane also had its uses in "brushfire" wars.

The first formal agreement between the United States and Britain was embodied in a memorandum stating that the United States was prepared to sell Skybolt missiles, minus warheads, to the United Kingdom in 1965 or later. The offer was specifically designed to help extend the effective life of the V-bomber force and was necessarily to be dependent on the successful and timely completion of the program. The only hint that some sort of bargain had been struck in the privacy of that luxury log-cabin at Camp David was muffled with the gentlemanly delicacy one would expect from Eisenhower and Macmillan. It was Britain's commitment to put a naval base in Scotland at the disposal of the United States for its nuclear-powered Polaris submarines.

It was never referred to by such a vulgar name as "bargain," and each item was negotiated without specific reference to the other. But it is clear from later evidence (however much confusion and soul-searching the question of this link between the two caused the Kennedy administration) that each side considered the other's commitment morally binding.

In fact it was the United States which first reminded the British Government of this commitment when Mr. Dillon, then Under-Secretary in the State Department, complained to the British Ambassador, Sir Harold Caccia, about the delay in London caused by various political problems arising out of some fear that Polaris submarines might be a rather dangerous beast to harbor in a British port. Despite massive protest, however, the British Government was not to be deterred from going ahead with the agreement; difficulties were overcome, and on Holy Loch was conferred what seemed to many in Britain — and particularly in Scotland — a dubious distinction: the first Polaris base in European waters.

The Skybolt Agreement between the United States and Britain was an extraordinarily advantageous "deal" from the Prime Minister's point of view. The research and development of Skybolt remained exclusively an American technical and financial responsibility, at no cost whatever to the British Government. Britain was committed to pay only for whatever number of operational Skybolt missiles it decided in the end to acquire, and for the minor costs of their adaptation to the V-bomber.

There was much skepticism about Skybolt from the very beginning. The most influential doubters on the American side were Thomas Gates, as Secretary of Defense, and his deputy, James Douglas. But both approved of Skybolt although the Fletcher Committee, a review board inside the Pentagon, had recommended against it because at the time there was still great doubt as to what other missile systems would become available — only the Atlas missile was then operational.

On the British side Sir Solly Zuckerman, the scientific adviser to the Prime Minister, was also a doubter from the start, and his role and advice in the Skybolt affair are therefore puzzling, especially since he is anything but a true believer in the independent deterrent. Either he could not assert his point of view against the Royal Air Force position, or he was overruled on political grounds. At any rate it would seem that as Skybolt was building up into a political issue, expert advice carried less and less weight.

Under the Camp David compact the United States allowed several RAF experts to sit in on various briefings dealing with Skybolt's progress, and some were directly stationed at Wright Field and the works of the Douglas Aircraft, the contractors for Skybolt. There was no mystery about how Skybolt progressed; it was merely that different people offered different estimates according to their point of view. The Douglas people and the U.S. Air Force, not surprisingly, were persistently optimistic. Thomas Gates, on the other hand, became increasingly pessimistic and at times impatient, and he occasionally warned his opposite number in London, Mr. Harold Watkinson, not to exclude failure.

In many ways it was the most complex ballistic missile system the U.S.

had yet undertaken — more so than Minuteman or Polaris. The missile had to be launched over an altitude range of several thousand feet, to be able at high speed to resist shock, vibration, and noise from a hostile environment, and to be integrated in a unique way with the mother ship which, with its computer system, contains about 130,000 parts.

In June, 1960, Mr. Gates and Mr. Watkinson drew up a supplementary Memorandum of Understanding in which the U.S. agreed to make any reasonable effort to ensure the successful and timely completion of Skybolt development, and in September, 1960, a detailed termination clause was inserted in another unpublished technical agreement providing that either party might terminate its interest in the project at any time but neither would do so without prior consultation with the other. It reflected just a little more American doubt and uneasiness about the Skybolt agreement with Britain.

Later that year, at a lunch in Washington, Mr. Gates asked Sir Solly Zuckerman to warn Mr. Watkinson that nobody would gain much from making a political issue out of Skybolt, for it was impossible to know what would happen to it, especially since in the eyes of American scientists its prospects were deteriorating and Polaris was fast becoming the Pentagon's *Wunderkind*. Sir Solly accordingly counseled London to play it in low key.

Shortly afterwards, in December, 1960, Mr. Gates visited London. Mr. Watkinson gave him the full flavor of British reaction to possible abandonment of Skybolt. He minced no words in explaining the missile's importance to Britain, and added a judicious reminder of the connection between Skybolt and Holy Loch. At the same time he also acknowledged that the British Government had always understood Skybolt to be a development project subject to uncertainties.

Mr. Gates did not abandon Skybolt, but in sharply reducing funds for it in Eisenhower's final Budget he slowed down the development program. President Kennedy meanwhile, resting in Palm Beach after his victory over Richard Nixon, was beginning to acquaint himself with the problems he would have to face in drawing up his own first Budget.

In a dispatch to the *Sunday Times* from Washington on November 27, 1960, I wrote that in a confidential report prepared by a committee of experts at the request of Mr. Kennedy serious doubts were expressed about continuing the development of Skybolt. However, Mr. McNamara, the new Secretary of Defense, did not follow the recommendation of this report (in which the chapter on defense had been written by Paul Nitze, who became his Assistant Secretary for International Affairs). He was worried by the "missile gap" between the Soviet Union and the United States which Mr. Kennedy had repeatedly played up during the election campaign, and wanted to take out an insurance, so to say, in case it turned out to be serious. He therefore decided to restore the funds which Gates had withdrawn and actually increased them somewhat. Whitehall took a deep breath and relaxed again.

Through various technicians and particularly one RAF group captain at the Pentagon, whose sole task it was to follow the tantalizing progress of Skybolt, the British Government was as well informed as the U.S. Government. There were always the opposition background noises in the Pentagon, weighing Skybolt against other competing weapons systems, but there was also the U.S. Air Force which said, in effect: Don't worry. We will in the end force the necessary appropriations as long as you, the British Government, also keep the pressure on Washington. And London rated the power of Strategic Air Command in the Pentagon power structure as very high.

Nobody in London, at least in 1961, realized that McNamara, once an industrial manager himself, could not be intimidated by what President Eisenhower in his farewell address called the "military-industrial complex." He gave Skybolt time: he himself needed time to decide which fights with the Services and Congress he would take on. Having introduced the so-called "cost-efficiency" system to establish criteria on weapons to keep and those to cut out, he had some hard fights ahead of him.

In the autumn of 1961 several such people as Dr. Harold Brown, Director of Defense Research and Engineering, Professor Jerome Wiesner, the President's Scientific Adviser, and David Bell, Budget Director, tried to persuade McNamara to abandon Skybolt. Warnings were telegraphed to London and messages indicating British concern were quickly sent to Washington.

The American critics of Skybolt repeated that what mattered from the U.S. point of view was reliability. In the American armory Skybolt's task was limited to neutralizing the enemies' defenses or, as the experts call it, "defense suppression"; while for the U.K. it was purely a weapon for attack, and whenever the British political argument cropped up about the need to maintain an independent deterrent, Washington suggested earnestly and with raised eyebrows that defense was a serious business — not merely symbolic.

But instead of canceling the whole program, Mr. McNamara that winter made a "pact" with Eugene Zuckert, Secretary for Air, to the effect that total Skybolt development costs must stay below a 500-million dollar ceiling in 1962. Thus Skybolt was given another reprieve.

By January, 1962, reports reached the British Embassy in Washington that Skybolt's unpopularity at the Pentagon was rising. That same month, over what was assumed would be a quiet lunch at the White House for Julian Amery, Britain's Minister of Aviation, sparks began to fly when President Kennedy casually wondered out loud whether Skybolt would ever work, and he added cautiously, "One should not bank on it too much." Amery almost fell off his chair, as the President put it later, and red in the face as he easily gets, insisted that it *must* be made to work: "It's the basis of our nuclear defence," he said, "it's part of an understanding. It could have far-reaching effects on Anglo-American relations!" The President, surprised at this outburst, then reassured his guest that every effort was being made to make Skybolt work, that more money than ever before was being spent on it and that his layman's doubts did not mean that he would not give the project every support.

That spring of 1962, however, it became clear that the monthly rate of expenditure was being exceeded and that the development time-lag was widening. By the summer the Minuteman missile was only six months away from leaving the production line, and Polaris was exceeding expectations. Moreover, not only had the missile gap blissfully vanished, according to all intelligence estimates, but the Russians were also behaving as if they had acquired a second strike capability.

When Mr. Thorneycroft, the new Minister of Defence, came to Washington in September Mr. McNamara told him that Skybolt in terms of "cost-effectiveness" was becoming an increasingly poor investment. But in those days London was still innocently unaware of the full meaning of this new-fangled term that the Pentagon "whiz-kids" had introduced as their chief criterion for assessing the value of every weapon.

Mr. McNamara at this stage did not risk telling Mr. Thorneycroft that he was seriously considering the cancellation of Skybolt, because he feared that through him the U.S. Air Force would hear of it, and would then mobilize Congressional opinion for a bitter, last-ditch public battle. But when at some point he asked Mr. Thorneycroft how many Skybolt missiles Britain was planning to buy, he left him, at least superficially, reassured.

Early in October, however, serious warnings reached London across the technical network that Skybolt might have its throat cut in the new Budget. Still most people in London thought that with Strategic Air Command fully behind Skybolt, in addition to the heavy American commitment to Britain, the opposition would once again be overcome. How often in the past, after all, had it happened in Pentagon history that weapons for which a funeral had already been arranged were in the end given a new lease on life?

In mid-October the decisive days for Skybolt began, delayed only by the Cuban crisis, which suddenly swept it out of everybody's mind. But not for long. Mr. Thorneycroft at that point smelled a rat, and when Mr. John Rubel, Deputy Director of Defense Research and Engineering, visited London he invited him to his house on November 3. He asked Rubel whether it was true that Skybolt was about to be canceled; at that moment Rubel, quite truthfully, had no certain knowledge and said so. The following day, just as McNamara was preparing to lower the Budget guillotine on Skybolt, he got a cable from Thorneycroft congratulating him on what the

Minister of Defence had erroneously interpreted as the start of its production phase. It was probably meant less as an expression of joy than as an attempt to smoke out Mr. McNamara's intentions. Thus in spite of the various channels of information there was a hide-and-seek quality about Skybolt communications between London and Washington. Where was the customary candor? Was it frustrated by the complicated maneuvers of the impending American Budget cut?

On November 7, three days after receiving Thorneycroft's cable of congratulations, McNamara reported to the President, with Secretary of State Dean Rusk present. He told them that he was very seriously considering the cancellation of Skybolt. He suggested, in view of the serious impact this would have on the British Government, that he first discuss the matter with the Ambassador, Sir David Ormsby Gore, and then with Mr. Thorneycroft. Mr. Rusk raised no objection and counseled that something should be done to help the British without upsetting other European Allies. But nobody seriously delved into the political aspects of this decision. The President seemed to have forgotten Julian Amery's shocked reaction and Dean Rusk was content to leave negotiations about something as technical as a weapons system to his Pentagon colleague, Mr. McNamara.

No one at this stage felt that this would develop into a real political crisis; no one made any attempt to place himself in British shoes to discover how and where they would pinch. The subject, in fact, was dropped relatively soon, and most of the meeting was occupied with another crisis — the Chinese invasion of India.

Mr. McNamara, in volunteering to negotiate the Skybolt case, struck out into a new field. It is not easy successfully to mix politics and cost-efficiency, and to Mr. McNamara and almost everybody else on the American side Skybolt was a technical rather than a political problem at this stage. His outstanding quality is managerial, and people often refer to his brain as a computer. But few know that he has another very important side to him, and that is a deeply-felt universal humaneness; underlying both is courage. These three qualities have enabled him to establish tight control of the Pentagon, the world's most unwieldy ministry, and also to grasp the stakes involved in modern warfare. But the authority he now had — to call in first Sir David Ormsby Gore to put the British Government on notice as to what was in the offing — was unusual, because it by-passed the State Department.

When on November 8, Sir David called on Mr. McNamara, it was the beginning of the final dénouement.

The Defense Secretary went at length into the entire history of the Skybolt missile: how its costs had "sky-rocketed," how the schedule had fallen behind, that he was now seriously reconsidering the worth of the weapon, and that he had asked the Joint Chiefs of Staff for a recommendation on whether to continue with Skybolt. He mentioned possible alternatives open to the British Government should Skybolt be canceled, but he said that the final decision about the fate of the weapon was still three to four weeks off.

The Ambassador saw the writing on the wall: "Dropping Skybolt," he said, "would be political dynamite in London." He also stated that it was his impression that none of the alternatives mentioned would be acceptable.

Before leaving he suggested that Mr. McNamara send a memorandum directly to Mr. Thorneycroft, but Mr. McNamara said he would telephone him instead the following day to make sure that he knew the contents of the Ambassador's cable. Thus the U.S. Government began tiptoeing toward that part of the agreement stipulating that "either party might terminate its interest in the project at any time but neither would do so without prior consultation with the other."

Perhaps if at this point the President had called the Prime Minister personally on the transatlantic telephone he might have realized sooner that he had a major crisis on his hands. Perhaps the traumatic experience of the Cuban crisis had dulled his usually very sensitive political antennae; perhaps it was the belief that so long as an alternative were found — and that, he assumed, should not be too difficult — a crisis could be avoided. At any rate, Skybolt still had a low rating as crises go in Washington.

Mr. McNamara telephoned Mr. Thorneycroft in London twenty-four hours after he had seen Sir David Ormsby Gore, and repeated more or less what he had already told the Ambassador, taking care to point out that in the event of cancellation — the final decision had not yet been reached — there would be several alternatives open to the United Kingdom. Mr. Thorneycroft was appreciative of the advance notice and said that he for his part would immediately arrange for his Department to consider how the V-bomber force might be operated without Skybolt. He did imply, however, that among the alternatives the British Government would like to discuss was the Polaris missile, if the loss of Skybolt made the V-bomber force obsolete.

About a week later Sir David Ormsby Gore saw the President and reminded him that cancellation of Skybolt could stir up a real crisis in Anglo-American relations. But the gravity of his warnings still did not seem to have quite sunk in; possibly only a direct confrontation between McNamara and Thorneycroft could have accomplished it. It did not sink in perhaps because Washington thought this was London's crisis and London felt exactly the opposite: the U.S. was canceling Skybolt, and it was therefore up to the U.S. to make amends, to live up to a commitment.

For the U.S., however, the commitment had a clear limitation: the technical success of Skybolt. Thus Mr. McNamara, while conceding that Britain had a problem and that the U.S. must do its best to help, was nevertheless also convinced that it was up to Britain to determine just what should be done about it. Mr. McNamara, who was quite prepared, for example, to give Polaris to Britain so long as this force was assigned to NATO, did not for some time fully realize what an "independent" deterrent meant to the British Government.

The State Department never really got into the act. The two points Mr. Dean Rusk emphasized were that Anglo-American relations must remain unharmed and that any new agreement must not upset the rest of the NATO alliance. This was in contrast to some in the State Department who agitated that this was the time to force Britain into a multilateral nuclear arrangement. The President himself had not by then had time to study the matter thoroughly, but he promised the Ambassador that he would take all the Skybolt papers with him to Hyannis Port for the Thanksgiving weekend (November 22–25).

Budget discussions meanwhile twice delayed Mr. McNamara's trip to London, and much valuable time was lost. The only point on which there was complete agreement between London and Washington was the importance of avoiding leaks about cancellation, to prevent the affair from mushrooming prematurely into an international crisis, and all queries were fended off with the excuse that the entire defense Budget was under review.

A test of Skybolt had been scheduled for November 27, and there was some fear that a failure might bring the issue into the open. The test was a complete failure, but somehow escaped the attention of the Press. But it made it all the more important in the eyes of officials to keep the matter under wraps. To make doubly certain of this, Mr. McNamara decided on November 29 to pay another installment of 20 million dollars to Douglas Aircraft.

As events went their course throughout November the U.S. feeling was that it had given the British Government enough of the facts for the latter to come up with an alternative to Skybolt; London on the other hand was still hoping to pressure the U.S. into continuing with it. And so both sides waited, allowing the crisis to feed on itself.

The U.S. Joint Chiefs of Staff meanwhile had recommended the continuation of Skybolt, but Mr. McNamara, on the advice of his civilian experts, overruled them. In London many people still believed that the "military-industrial" complex might yet force McNamara's hand. Both SAC and the Douglas Aircraft people reinforced this conviction, no doubt hoping that if only Britain held out it would bolster their own positions.

This and the belief that Britain could lose little by waiting — any new deal was likely to be less advantageous than the Skybolt arrangement, whose development cost the British nothing — must account for Whitehall's continued passive attitude. There was also the reluctance of the Services: the

RAF did not want to lose Skybolt, and the Navy did not want Polaris because it was bound to cut its own budget to shreds. A similar situation in
Washington would have created a flurry of contingency planning, whereas
in London this art was virtually still unknown.

On December 4 I reported in the *Sunday Times*: "There is a growing
doubt in the Pentagon whether to proceed with the development of Skybolt.
. . . No decision has yet been taken here, but those who have for some time
been skeptical about Skybolt are now in the ascendancy. . . ." Among the
reasons for junking it, I gave: failure of the tests, costs pushing above the
established ceiling, and the desire of some "who see in the failure of Skybolt's development a logical way to ease Britain out as a Power with an
'independent' nuclear deterrent."

As the first rumblings about Skybolt's uncertain future were hitting the
front pages of Britain's newspapers Mr. Dean Acheson weighed in with a
speech critical of England, delivered at the Military Academy at West
Point. "Great Britain has lost an empire and has not yet found a role . . ."
were the words that struck lightning on the other side of the Atlantic. In
political London many thought the speech was officially inspired and might
even have had some sinister connection with the tottering Skybolt. I am
confident it had not. Mr. Macmillan nevertheless felt compelled through
the device of a letter to the Institute of Directors to give a stinging rebuke.
Plainly the atmosphere between London and Washington had become
electric.

On the eve of Mr. McNamara's arrival in London on December 10 the
atmosphere was highly charged. The British Press, as America's United
Press agency put it, "bristled with claims that the abandonment of Skybolt
could finish Britain as an independent nuclear power." The *Washington
Post* said that news dispatches based on "leaks" from official British sources
hinted at an "agonizing reappraisal in London and suggests that abandonment of the Skybolt could lead to the voiding of the agreement to give the
United States bomber and nuclear submarine bases in Britain." It also took
the editorial line that "unless our Government is welshing on some undis-
closed but firm commitment, the British reaction to possible cancellation of
the Skybolt project is extraordinary to say the least."

Mr. McNamara did not improve the situation with a statement that was
distributed on his arrival in London recalling that "all five flight tests of
Skybolt attempted thus far have failed." As the *Times* concluded: ". . . he
sounded the death knell of the Skybolt missile." What embarrassed the
British Government about his statement was that it ruined "the virginity of
the lady" in public, for at this stage the Prime Minister, particularly, was
still hoping to get another reprieve for Skybolt. There was obviously a
shortage of cool heads. Mr. Macmillan for various other reasons was none
too firmly in the saddle. Skybolt was rapidly becoming a domestic political
crisis first and Anglo-American crisis second.

When Mr. McNamara and Mr. Thorneycroft faced each other across a long table the atmosphere was one of polite reserve. Mr. McNamara presented his case in a cool, fluent matter-of-fact tone based on a "talking paper," a copy of which he had handed to the British Minister of Defence before the meeting began.

His argument was that budgetary and above all technical problems had most decisively influenced his decision to cancel Skybolt. There was a list of the technical shortcomings, the time slippage, the mounting costs. Skybolt, in short, was an unsound use of American resources. Was Thorneycroft faced with a *fait accompli*? In effect he was, but Mr. McNamara declared his immediate readiness to discuss how best to solve the resulting British problem.

The ball was now in Mr. Thorneycroft's court. He began quietly and earnestly. He did not want to argue the technical and financial aspects, he said: he was certain he could find technical experts who could argue either side with conviction. "What I would *like* to discuss," he declared, "are the political implications of your decision — they are of the gravest character."

As he developed his theme Mr. Thorneycroft worked himself gradually into a crescendo of emotion. "Skybolt," he stressed, "is the principal example of Anglo-American complementarity." He warned that, whatever the technical reasons given, those who had been saying for some time "you can't rely on the United States" would throw this into the face of those who had always stood up for close Anglo-American relations.

Mr. Thoneycroft was gradually building to the attack. He claimed that a recent speech by Mr. McNamara at Ann Arbor, rightly or otherwise, had created the impression that he, too, was against the British independent deterrent; that that at least was the impression left with many people in England. He loaded this political thrust with the reminder that Skybolt was closely tied to Britain's acceptance of basing Polaris missile submarines at Holy Loch, a risk both political and military because it made her an enemy target.

Finally he demanded from Mr. McNamara an answer to the question: did the United States want to deprive Britain of its independent deterrent role, and, if such were not the case, was the U.S. willing to do everything possible to assist Britain in maintaining an independent role, and to say so publicly?

This was one of the bluntest talks ever given by a British Minister to his American opposite number. It was a brilliant forensic display, the Americans felt, but it was not the reply Mr. McNamara had expected or hoped for. He had come to this meeting to find a technical alternative to help the British out of a dilemma. Was the United States being asked to change a technical decision for political reasons? Did Britain think that by throwing the fate of Anglo-American relations on to the scales it could move mountains — even salvage Skybolt?

To bring the conversation back on his track, Mr. McNamara asked whether he could assume that Britain would want to proceed with Skybolt on her own, in which case he would be ready to turn over £150 million-worth of research and development free of charge to Britain, adding perhaps another £30 million in cash. But gradually it emerged that Mr. Thorneycroft did not think any of the alternatives offered by Mr. Mc-Namara was viable. Suddenly he raised Polaris, which Mr. McNamara had not mentioned.

Mr. McNamara pointed out some of the legal and financial problems, and the repercussions it might have in Europe if the United States gave Britain such an advanced missile system, but he added that he was willing to give Britain all the necessary facts to study the matter; he did not seem opposed to the idea but remained non-committal.

What was important to Mr. Thorneycroft, however, was whether Britain could use British Polaris submarines independently if they became part of a multilateral force. He did not get an answer — obviously Mr. McNamara's instructions and authority did not stretch that far — and the meeting broke up without conclusions. But Sir Solly Zuckerman, accompanying John Rubel in a car to the airport, discussed a one-page paper on Polaris. It was obvious that the British needed more facts and information about Polaris, and these were immediately promised.

Was Polaris Britain's chosen alternative? The Americans doubted it. The costs, they thought, would be too high: it involved constructing expensive submarines and buying the A-3 Polaris missile from the U.S. — alone about twice as expensive as Skybolt would have been.

In Paris, meanwhile, the Defense and Foreign Ministers were gathering for a NATO Council meeting. Both McNamara and Thorneycroft went there direct from London. Thorneycroft, who was known to be "messmerised" by some of the views of the French Minister of Defense on the possibility of some sort of European nuclear deterrent, saw M. Messmer on the eve of Mr. Macmillan's arrival at what was expected to be just a routine meeting. Mr. Macmillan was to see General de Gaulle at Rambouillet, and there were further meetings between McNamara and Thorneycroft and between Dean Rusk and (as he then was) Lord Home.

But it was quite clear that little could be done now about Skybolt — the showdown would come when Kennedy and Macmillan met, as they were soon to do, at Nassau.

On Saturday night, three days before the Nassau meeting, over an intimate dinner at the American Embassy with only a few top American officials present, Walt W. Rostow, the highly articulate chief of the State Department's Planning Staff, made an impassioned plea that this was the historic moment to close Britain's door to an independent deterrent, leaving only one choice: multilateralism. While some disagreed with the idea, there were a good many nods around the table. It was Mr. Rostow's staff which, with one or two experts from the Pentagon, had developed the idea for a sea-borne multilateral Polaris fleet.

The Prime Minister's meeting that day with de Gaulle went badly. General de Gaulle clung to his view that Britain did not "belong" in Common Market Europe, that her whole outlook was still ambivalent. Mr. Macmillan nevertheless stayed for the second day, for he was anxious for General de Gaulle to understand that his one aim at Nassau was to preserve the independent deterrent.

He went into some detail in explaining the Skybolt dispute and he reassured the General that if necessary he would buy American weapons to save Britain's independent nuclear capacity. He did not touch on the problem of a European nuclear deterrent, at which he had faintly hinted during his last meeting with the General in May. He then indicated that if Britain became a member of the Common Market, after the economic questions were settled, certain political and military consequences would, of course, flow from this new constellation.

In Washington, meanwhile, the Kennedy team that weekend was busy preparing its position paper for Nassau. On Sunday afternoon Mr. McGeorge Bundy, the Special Assistant for Security Affairs and one of the President's most trusted aides, was asked on *Meet the Press,* a television show, whether Britain would have to get out of the "nuclear business."

He fended his questioner off by stressing on the one hand the need to decide "what is the best way of organizing a missile force for NATO as a whole," and on the other how the Americans and British conduct their affairs with each other "so that we do not entangle our relations with the great countries of the Continent." With consummate skill he refused to show the American hand before the Nassau meeting, but essentially he set the two issues that needed reconciliation.

The following evening, before his departure for Nassau, President Kennedy gave a television interview. Asked about Skybolt, he pointed out that it was just another case where the U.S. would have borne all the costs while Britain would have paid only for the purchase of a hundred missiles.

December 18 was a clear and pleasantly warm day. It was Nassau at its best. Even the arrival of a horde of VIP's and an even bigger horde of reporters did not really disturb the serenity of the island. Still, it did not placate the mood in which the British delegation had landed, a mood of nagging exasperation and bitter indignation.

The Prime Minister's precarious political position at home, the complete uncertainty about how the conference would end and the statements of the President and McGeorge Bundy on television — ill-timed in the eyes of the British delegation — all added to resentment and suspicion of American intentions such as I have never experienced in all the Anglo-American conferences I have covered over the past twenty years.

There had been no advance exchange of position papers; the British

Ambassador in fact left Washington on President Kennedy's plane unaware that the British Government had decided at the last minute to opt for the Polaris missile. The time he spent with the President was therefore wasted in developing a new American offer to continue the development of Skybolt as a joint Anglo-American enterprise, with each country bearing equal share of the future costs. This offer, mentioned in the final communiqué, was turned down "because of the doubts that had been expressed about the prospects of success of this weapons system and because of uncertainty regarding date of completion and final cost of the program."

President Kennedy, Mr. McNamara and Mr. Bundy had all spoken the death warrant for Skybolt, and it was useless for the Prime Minister to cling to it. The only real alternative left in his mind therefore was Polaris.

Originally the President and the Prime Minister had planned to discuss the great world issues at Nassau, but these had now been overshadowed by Skybolt or, more precisely, by the question whether Britain would be able to claim that she had an independent deterrent. That, in a nutshell, was the basis of the dramatic fight, and it was one of Mr. Macmillan's finest hours — a true political tight-rope trick. But then, this kind of drama, by the time the communiqué is written, is usually willingly forgotten. . . .

As the conference opened Mr. Macmillan began like a Marcus Antonius — though with muffled pathos — giving the funeral oration. Even some of Antony's lines (*I come to bury Skybolt, not to praise it . . .*) would have fitted, though this particular point came later. Mr. Macmillan can be a master of the dramatic crescendo. He opened with some of his nostalgic memories of better days in Anglo-American relations, of the greater days in Britain's position as a world Power (his memory, after all, went back much further than anyone else's in the room).

There were the proud days when it was chiefly due to British scientists that the Bomb was developed, when later their work was shifted from beleaguered Britain to the United States and, he mused, in the light of all this the two countries in a sense owned an equal share in this equity. He moved on through the history of Anglo-U.S. nuclear relations to Camp David and its agreement "based on a broad, honorable understanding" and involving the stationing of Polaris submarines in Scotland.

It was his impression at Rambouillet that General de Gaulle would not be upset by a switch from the lame horse Skybolt to Polaris. Nor did he feel that there was any contradiction between the concept of independence and interdependence, for after all under NATO national forces are placed under an international command but can, in certain circumstances, be used for national purposes. As to Polaris being a different system, to him the only difference was that one was fired from the air, the other from the sea.

And Allied reaction? Did this matter more to the United States than Britain? He had reached what was to him the central issue: his concern that Anglo-American relations would be severely hurt if the U.S. came under suspicion in England of wanting to deprive Britain of her nuclear capacity.

The President still tried to fight off the political argument. The decision to cancel Skybolt was basically a technical one: why therefore should it have such dire political repercussions, especially since the U.S. was offering Britain several quite favorable alternatives? The two were now approaching the heart of the argument: the future of the independent deterrent, which Mr. Macmillan insisted could not be blurred.

With something of a Churchillian palette he painted the future of Anglo-American relations in gloomy colors. Britain, he said, certainly would not welsh on any of the past agreements with the U.S. The Polaris depot could remain at Holy Loch, the advanced radar station would be allowed to operate from Fylingdales, the bomber bases would remain at the disposal of the U.S. but — having said all this — he felt obliged to add that the United Kingdom had run and was still running risks by harboring these bases.

Would the President really want Britain to take these risks yet exercise none of the powers? If this seemed to be so, it would inevitably shatter U.S.-U.K. relations, and public opinion, fickle as it is, could get out of control.

The President was visibly impressed, but he had some cogent arguments on his side. The British Government, it should be remembered, had been on notice for at least nine months, beginning with the exchange with Julian Amery, that Skybolt was a very uncertain gamble. It was not his fault that British public opinion was unprepared for this situation. Moreover, weren't the three alternative offers generous enough to convince the British public that the United States was genuinely anxious to help? Britain could still proceed with Skybolt. . . .

But with his shrewd political instincts Kennedy soon realized that there was only one alternative left to Macmillan: to find an acceptable compromise — or return home in a huff. Nor was he unaware that a break with Britain would be unpopular at home. The *Washington Post* on the eve of the Nassau Conference, scolded his Administration for seeing Skybolt solely as a weapons problem and attacked the State Department for failing to "perceive signs of decay with its closest ally." This was the kind of criticism that could snowball.

After the first day most members of the British delegation could discern a silver lining, but Mr. Thorneycroft remained a pessimist. He thought the strings tied to the Polaris offer would be too much. Certainly one American proposal, the idea of postponing a decision and of setting up a study group until the Common Market negotiations were completed, was unacceptable.

The following day it had become clear that what mattered to Kennedy most was Anglo-American relations. He was now ready to switch to Polaris; on what conditions remained to be thrashed out.

I have ample reason to think that neither Mr. Kennedy nor Mr. Mc-Namara nor Mr. Rusk, who kept in touch with Nassau from Washington and added a useful third dimension to the discussions from a distance, meant to use the Skybolt affair to deprive Britain of its independent deterrent. In their minds it really had been purely a technical decision until now, when the political problem had come home to them with a vengeance.

So, gradually, the President steered his delegation towards a compromise formula which would not contradict his own policy on multilateralism and the prevention of the spreading of nuclear weapons, yet would also make it possible for Macmillan to claim that he had saved Britain's independent deterrent. Thus Kennedy paved the way for a graceful transition in British history.

He was also concerned about French reaction, though the prevailing view was that the Polaris agreement would not decisively influence Common Market negotiations. It did, in the end, serve de Gaulle as an excuse to keep Britain out — ironically, not because Macmillan succeeded in preserving his independence, but because in the General's view he had lost it. When Kennedy proposed to extend the Polaris offer to France, it was finally rejected, a decision which in retrospect will probably prove to have been a major mistake.

Whether the United States in quiet backstage negotiations could have been persuaded to give Britain Polaris under the conditions agreed to at Nassau is difficult to determine. It might not have been possible to forge this compromise except in the heat of a great crisis and at the summit. Whatever one may think about the reality of the independent deterrent, the Nassau agreement was a *tour de force* for the Prime Minister, but Macmillan was too badly wounded politically to have a success like Nassau judged fairly.

On Friday evening the President, unusually tired, reached Palm Beach for what he hoped would be an undisturbed weekend. Early on Saturday morning the Pentagon announced out of the blue a successful flight test of Skybolt. It was like the final twitching of the tail of a dead lizard.

RICHARD E. NEUSTADT

Memorandum on the British Labour Party and the MLF

If the bureaucratic perspective yields additional insights to analysts of foreign policy and international politics, it follows that foreign policy advice which is based on this approach should be far richer than planning based on the assumption that other governments behave as unitary purposive actors. In 1964, President Johnson sent Richard Neustadt to Britain to assess British sentiments regarding the pending proposal for the Multilateral Force (MLF). When he returned, Neustadt prepared for the President a memorandum assessing the consequences of an electoral victory by Harold Wilson and the Labour Party and recommending courses of action designed to avert another Skybolt-like crisis. Neustadt's analysis and recommendations are a model of policy advice which takes bureaucratic politics into account.

Neustadt's description of the probable Labour government resembles a full-scale bureaucratic analysis including an inventory of the major actors on the British side and the stakes and interests of each. He draws attention to the unique features of the British governmental system which would have an impact on Wilson's treatment of MLF and gives special consideration to the new government's domestic and Parliamentary political problems. And he describes *their* view of *our* system, players, positions, and stakes.

On the basis of this analysis, Neustadt offers suggestions of possible courses of action available to the American government. They all depend on the central assumption that the United States would be more likely to achieve its objectives if it appreciated Wilson's view of his problems and needs and took actions which met his expectations, improved his bargaining position relative to the other participants in the British bureaucracy, and anticipated his domestic political problems. The essence of Neustadt's advice is based on his dictum regarding Presidential power and applies that view to international relations: persuading those whom you want to act that their own interests require that they do so.

Everyone I saw in London during June brought up "MLF," usually with curses. I looked sympathetic and listened hard, trying to judge whether we might have another "Skybolt" brewing if Labour comes in: another situation where the differences of interest are compounded by each side's misreading of the pressures and procedures on the other side. I think we might. I also think we have a good chance to avoid it. On both scores, here is why.

Reprinted with the permission of the author.

What follows has been drawn from conversations with *politicians* (mainly Wilson, Gordon Walker, Healy, Brown, Mulley, Jenkins — and Heath), with *officials* (mainly Hardman, Cary, Palliser, Armstrong, Bligh), and with *spectators* (mainly Gwynn-Jones, Buchan, Beedham, Duchene). Before I left I swapped appraisals at our Embassy with Bruce, Irving and Newman. They will speak for themselves but I think we agree.

I. Assessment

Regarding Labour's look at *us* if they win in October and we in November, I think it safe to say that *as of now* both the prospective ministers and the civilian top officials in MOD, FO, and Number 10, see three things pretty much alike:

1. President Johnson *personally* wants negotiations wrapped up, with the British in if possible, before the CDU right-wing steps up its sneers at Erhardt (and Erler too) in the German campaign period.
2. Otherwise the President confronts a *concrete* "German problem," a pressing question for which he lacks answers: "If not MLF, what?"
3. Judged on his form as a Senate Leader, our President — newly and well elected — can be expected to press hard for what he feels he needs, and to reward a helping hand but not forget a hindrance.

When Wilson raised the subject at our first talk in mid-June, I told him that I understood the President himself did seek to see the MLF brought to fruition, for good reason from his point of view considering where he took up the issue, and that after the two elections Wilson, if in office, might want to ponder Johnson's Senate record. "Oh," said Wilson, "a deal."

But while these things are seen, it does *not* follow that a Labour Government will promptly seek a "deal." No member of the front-bench is impressed with MLF in its own terms; none really buys our line on Europe or on Germany; the best of them still pursue McNamara's line of some two years ago; the others flounder. Also, most of them worry about Eastern European reaction. Moreover — more important — all the internal forces in their system press the other way, to put off the issue, or better still (were Johnson willing) to evade it altogether. As viewed in June the pressures for delay *after* a Labour victory include the following:

1. Transition Bureaucratics. Wilson's first cabinet will be nothing to brag about in terms either of intellect or of experience. He is aware of this and means to take all key decisions into his own hands. He wants not merely to make ultimate decisions but to pass issues through his own mind early, sitting at the center of a brains-trust, with himself as first brains-truster on the model, he says, of JFK.

This suggests that much of his attention at the start will be devoted to machinery-building and administrative management (it fascinates him) and to getting hold of issues in economic management which may present themselves the moment he takes office. Besides, he has to oversee the drafting of the Queen's Speech (however banal) and the scheduling of work for Parliament (however routine) as it sits after election, unable to rise until the Christmas recess.

Also, more importantly, he has to keep one step ahead of all his colleagues in the precedent-making first encounters and arrangements which set tone and style for their relationships. "I shall be chairman of the Board, not President," he says, "but Managing Director too, and very active at it."

All these concerns are bound to turn his mind from MLF. Wilson will take office quite unready to decide his course on *that*.

Moreover, at the start of Wilson's Government, the issues posed by MLF will be as unripe for decision as he is unready. His new Ministers, fresh from campaigning as an opposition, will confront a deeply divided officialdom which has been marking time in an unprecedented fashion through a long "American" campaign, and is unsettled further by the prospect of a Cabinet less experienced than any known since 1923.

When officials get their hands on the new Ministers, Foreign Office briefs presumably will urge affirmative response to us (assuming we stand firm) and then hard bargaining with us about terms and conditions (and the name) of the new mixed-manned force. Assuming Gordon Walker is the Foreign Secretary (he almost certainly will be), I expect he will submit with little struggle and become the advocate of his official "line," since he seems quite incapable of taking a coherent line himself and has no source of strength, politically, beyond what he can draw from his machine. On the other hand, Defence Ministry briefs presumably will urge resistance to expenditures on seaborne forces and will propose alternatives along the lines worked out for Thorneycroft last month. The Navy still wants Indian Ocean carriers above all else, is reconciled I gather to Polaris submarines, but fears the bite of MLF ships on its manpower *and* money as much as it once feared those submarines. The Air Force and the Ministry of Aviation (and the industry) are fighting to secure a lasting mission (and orders) for manned aircraft. TSR-2 [Aircraft] is to them what the B-70 and Skybolt were to the USAF. Top Defence civilians, borrowing "Hitchcraft" from us, find MLF of no account on military grounds and see no budgetary compensation in it, quite the contrary.

Assuming Denis Healy is Defence Secretary (he seems confident he will be), his own interest in a mission East of Suez (and in sales of British aircraft), his mistrust of continentals, his disdain for MLF, comport well with the bulk of these official views. Despite some surface differences on such things as Polaris subs, the likelihood is that this minister and his machine will find their outlooks basically comparable. They probably will come into agreement rather readily for reasons more substantial than in Gordon Walker's case — which gives Healy an advantage over Walker, an advantage enhanced by intellect and drive.

The prospect then is for perpetuation in the new regime of present differences between FO and MOD on MLF *per se*. The issue will be Wilson's to resolve. Neither minister could resist him; neither has an independent power base politically.

But this is not an issue to be met in isolation. Budgeting and politics alike require that it be decided in the context of Polaris subs, TSR-2's, carriers, Aden, arms control, East-West "detente," and Anglo-American relations. This is not the context for snap judgment. Nor is it the context for a judgment based on Healy *versus* Walker. Wilson being Wilson (as above), he'll almost surely want to reach beneath his Ministers to their machines and form his own views before they have frozen theirs. For this he will need time.

Gordon Walker gave me the opinion that a Labour Government could easily be ready to confer with the Americans by late November. Maybe so, in FO terms. But I asked Cary (now at Navy) when official briefs on East-of-Suez plans could be expected to get serious ministerial attention. His reply: about six weeks after election (early December). I asked Wilson when he thought that Ministers and their machines would be fully engaged with one another and with him. His reply: Christmas recess (late December-January). And I asked Healy when he thought they'd have decided, as a Government, what they might do for us and wanted from us. His reply: late January. Considering how long it took the Tory Government — some four months, I surmise — to bargain out internally their current "supplementary" MLF proposals, Wilson is an optimist (and Gordon Walker silly).

2. Parliamentary Politics. As Wilson now is going, back-bench opposition from his own side to a Labour Government (no other kind of opposition threatens British Cabinets) can arise only on the left. The right will not be troublesome for a long time to come. Its leaders, to a man, will be in office.

A Labour victory should leave the left unorganized and leaderless (Wilson *was* its leader) with its prospective size unknown either to its own hard-core or to the party leadership — underlying attitudes of many freshman MP's will be hard to gauge.

The problem posed for Wilson by this latent opposition is a matter to be estimated *after* the election. Everything depends upon the size and composition of his overall majority. At present, the left-wing in its most general sense numbers about one-third of Labour MP's, with a hard-core of 15–20 who are often very close indeed to the Communist line. Were Labour to win but a bare majority in Commons, that hard-core could become a pressing problem. Were Labour to sweep in (which nobody expects), the general leftish group might rise to half the party membership (with hosts of screwballs riding on the tide), also a pressing problem. If Labour wins a middle-sized majority, comfortable and not too big (70 is the the front-bench ideal), left-wing opposition can become a problem only as the Government decides to make it so by forcing issues which give hard-core leftists wide appeal outside their own ranks.

But MLF may well be such an issue. Krushchev and Zorin are making it so. It is indeed the best such issue, in left terms, now visible on the horizon — far better than Polaris subs which have a solid jingoist appeal, especially now that CND [Committee on Nuclear Disarmament] is dead. "MLF" means literally nothing to the general public now and little more than that to most back-benchers, but it might be made to mean "pro-German, anti-Russian," when the time comes, with "American arm-twisting" as an added feature. Hence, the potential wide appeal which won't be lost on leftists.

Whatever the dimensions of his victory, Wilson will need time to assess it, to count noses in the House, to decide which sort of problem he confronts and how he wants to meet it. MLF is inextricably involved in these decisions. The circumstances may suggest an early challenge to the left for disciplinary purposes, in which case MLF becomes an interesting possibility, one among others. Or the circumstances may suggest leaving the opposition latent and unorganized as long as possible, in which case MLF becomes a sheer embarrassment. In neither case will Wilson want to rush his calculations.

His need for caution can only be enhanced by the status of that other opposition, the official Opposition, the late Government, which will confront him with a front-bench better informed at the outset than his own. Home, Heath, Thorneycroft could not unseat him, but they certainly could embarrass him if he puts a foot wrong.

3. Pre-election Postures. As of now neither Party seeks to make the MLF a campaign issue. The Tory Cabinet can't afford public commitment now, over Thorneycroft's dissent and Mountbatten's scorn. So long as the Government does not officially endorse it, the opposition has no reason to oppose it. And the voters remain free to ignore it, as they do, which suits the front-bench on both sides since both want their hands free after election.

But Wilson, Healy, Gordon Walker, Brown (among others) all have taken personal positions ranging from extremely skeptical to very negative. These, although unnoticed by the *general* public, are on record with assorted special publics: the press corps, back-benchers, continental Socialists, and in Wilson's case, Krushchev. (In the Kremlin he apparently defended us against the charge that MLF was meant to arm the Germans, but he didn't defend MLF as such). Wilson talks of arms control and detente. He and Healy — and especially Gordon Walker — talk of Atlantic consultation on strategy and policy "up to the final decision on the trigger, which is yours and must remain so." All three talk of "getting back to McNamara's doctrine at Ann Arbor, which made sense." And all this talk, however imprecise, revolves around a *substitute* for MLF: they may be fuzzy on exactly what they do want but they don't want that — and everyone who cares to listen knows.

This raises the problem of eating words after election — and the season for *campaign* words hasn't yet begun.

Moreover, in a related sphere, other words which made more public impact may cause quite a lot of pain as the campaign proceeds: words about Polaris subs and the "independent deterrent." With one exception, every Labour MP I encountered (about 20) expressed worry over Tory charges two months hence that "they want to hand our deterrent to Goldwater," a nice point since if he is nominated his defeat will not have happened by the time of their election. Wilson was the exception: he professed himself unworried: "I'll reply that the Tories have so little judgment as to count Johnson out, and Johnson won't like that." (How this helps *Wilson* is unclear to me). I asked Heath how he saw the issue. He grinned: "They got themselves into it, didn't they?"

As things stand even now, I sense little disposition among Labour frontbenchers to scrap Polaris if they do come in, though they'd be glad to scrap Macmillan's escape clause as a sop to "Ann Arbor" — and their left — since it is meaningless in substance and they don't need it politically. Indeed, I get the clear impression that the main reason they still toy with canceling Polaris is that they think *we* want to end their national deterrent and would pay a price for that — in short, a bargaining point with us. This contrasts oddly with our State Department view that MLF is a "way out" for them, a way to rid themselves of a political embarrassment. But CND *is* dead, and Tories shortly may be breathing down their necks — and Thorneycroft is trying (via contracts) to give them the easier out of crying "*fait accompli*" after election.

In the whole sphere of nuclear deterrence and allied relations there may be lots of words to eat by next October. The conjunction of our two campaigns helps not at all. Such eating calls for sugar-coating first. And that takes time (and sugar, some of it ours).

4. Dreams of Glory (Retrospective). Labour has been out for twelve years. Few of its prospective Cabinet ministers have ever been "in." Their vision of the place and power in the world which they hope to assume as HM Government has rather more to do with 1951 than 1964, judging by the overtones when they discuss their prospects. Many of the educative shocks which Tories and officials have encountered in the interim do not seem to have registered in full on these outsiders. Roy Jenkins estimates that it will take a year at least for his front-benchers, once in office, to get up to date about the "multi-racial Commonwealth," for instance, let alone "Europe." Regarding the Commonwealth, Atlee's old concepts persist, and Wilson says, "We must make a new try in terms of economics, not politics." Regarding Europe there is real ambivalence. Wilson and Healy evidently share the deep distrust of Frogs and Wogs (to say nothing of Huns) which was characteristic of Atlee, Bevin, even Gaitskell — and remains in character for lots of Labour voters. On the other hand, temptations toward a continental policy, free from Americans, are never wholly lacking and might grow apace if only there were socialist regimes to join. Healy can't play Thorneycroft and knows it, but I gather that he does think now and then of what it would be like (at least for bargaining with us) if there were Social Democrats in power on the Continent.

And Wilson evidently has his own dreams of a role as honest broker in East-West relations (shades of 1945). Currently he is "the man who knows Krushchev."

Power breeds realism, no doubt. But there *is* a gestation period. Meanwhile, Her Majesty's new ministers are bound to be a rather proud and touchy lot, mindful of prerogatives and eager to believe that they have other options than a deal with us.

To summarize the foregoing four points: there will be no internal pressures on a Labour Government after election to spur it toward an early deal with us. Quite the contrary. The *only* spur we can expect is their perception of our need and fixed intention to proceed with *or* without them.

Accordingly, the first thing they will test is our intention, in the context of events after our own election. Although they know *now* that the President wants MLF, they'll seek to satisfy themselves that he still wants it. Maybe events in Southeast Asia, say, or in East-West relations, will have altered his priorities. Or maybe he's been firm only because of a "one-sided presentation" from the "cabal" (British for Rostow, Owen, Schaetzel, Bowie, whose positions are identified and classified in London). Maybe he would shift ground in the winter if he heard "the other side" presented properly by Labour (a Healy speculation).

If and as their testing shows us still determined, then and only then will they turn their minds in full seriousness to the key questions: What is the least they have to do for Johnson? and What is the most they might get in return?

Subsumed under the first of these two questions are at least three issues on which nobody in Labour *now* appears to have a firm grip or a clear understanding: Would we really go ahead without them, even if Rome held out too? Would we really assent to a voting formula which risks *their* veto over *our* abandonment of our veto? Does it take a German-sized financial contribution to obtain full voting status, and, if so, what else but money might be made to count? After election, when they try to gauge our "quid," these issues will come up for clarification.

Regarding the second question, the "quo" in any bargain, shadow-ministers *now* voice assorted notions, none of them precise, none "jelled." Few of these are firmly held, some are scarcely serious, but all together do suggest the range within which they'll begin to think after election. These notions include the following (items are *not* mutually exclusive):

1. A new disarmament approach to the Soviets *before* decision on an allied mixed-manned force.

2. New inter-allied consultative mechanisms (*and symbols*) as substitute (or supplement) for any mixed-manned force.

3. A mixed-manned force of aircraft, Pershings, ground forces, what-have-you, with few if any surface ships to start (variations on the present government's proposal).

4. With any mixed-manned force, assurance of some form of U.S. veto into perpetuity (or of British veto over our withdrawal from our veto).

5. American orders for British aircraft, or some variant which serves the same purposes (unless these have been served by item three above).

6. American support for and assistance to new forms of British presence East of Suez — carriers, etcetera — including diplomatic support with Nasser for an unimpeded, unexploited, phase-out from the Aden base.

Beyond these notions one goes around the world, touching speculatively on South East Asia (including Indonesia), British Guiana, Cuba, and the like, as places where the U.S. might be threatened or the U.K. rewarded in the course of bargaining over MLF. The talk grows less substantial as one goes.

But in the talk there is a hint: if we harm them, they are not without resources to retaliate in kind. Whether *we* think they actually can afford to hurt us matters less than whether *they* think they can. As of now they do.

David Bruce predicts that Wilson almost surely will try out on Johnson item two above (consultative machinery), perhaps combined with item one (disarmament talks) as a substitute for MLF. Only when Johnson said "no" *except* in the context of action on MLF would Wilson come to grips with other items on this list and seriously contemplate a deal. Bruce thus suggests that a two-stage negotiation is in prospect, with Wilson being turned down at the first stage. Such an outcome adds materially to the risks of Skybolt-type misunderstandings. We should improve upon this prospect if we can.

II. RECOMMENDATIONS

Wilson told me that after the two elections he expects to bring a team to Washington, introducing the regimes to one another in the context of exploratory talks across-the-board, "as Macmillan did with Eisenhower in 1957." Regarding Britain and the MLF, we should begin to plan *now* for the timing and the content of those talks. I suggest the following:

1. Pre-election Restraint. We've got one message across: Johnson wants MLF, and if they seek fruitful Anglo-American relations (as they must), they'll have to reckon with that fact. Enough argued for the time being. Americans should now confine themselves to listening. Let *Englishmen* like Harlech, Gwynn-Jones, and other close observers needle Wilson and the rest on how to do their reckoning. *We* should not be caught with needles in our hands. Especially not members of the "cabal." At the same time, we should — of course — keep contact. We need to know as best we can what reckoning they do, or leave undone, and why, before election.

2. Post-election Gestures. If Wilson is elected in October, Johnson (still running) can't do much more than send formal congratulations. But immediately after *our* election, the President — assuming he remains of the same mind on MLF — might well send Wilson a warm, personal communication, inviting him to come and bring his team for talks in every sphere, "as soon as you are ready," perhaps suggesting the last week in January "after Inaugural" as a good time, and saying with respect to the defense sphere that Johnson is determined to get action on the MLF, if possible in company with Wilson: no pressure, no gun-to-the-head on timing, but explicit determination.

This letter should be hand-carried, preferably by Mac Bundy (cover story: "arrangements for a meeting," with a one-day trip to Bonn regarding further meetings, if need be). Wilson and his colleagues regard Bundy as close to the President, completely reliable, and not a "cabal" member. A cabinet officer would be too prominent, a "cabal" member fatal. Bundy is our best bet. He could effectively enlarge upon the message that he carried in at least the following respects:

   a. Our interest in their cancellation of Polaris sub. If we *haven't* any interest and it's *not* a bargaining point with us, the sooner they know that the better.

   b. Our view on trading off the MLF for something from the Russians which would interest the Germans. If we think there is no prospect of a useful exploration until after we have got MLF launched, the sooner they know that the better. And the sooner they know what we think the Russian "quo" might have to be, the likelier they are to see our point on timing.

   c. Our view on consummating MLF without them if need be, however much we'd rather have them in. If we really mean to go ahead, should they find, after reasonable thought and talk, that they can't join, the sooner the better again.

A Bundy trip conceivably could save us the whole first stage of Bruce's predicted two-stage negotiation.

3. Planning for a Deal. We have four months before we can make post-election contracts. This is ample time to clarify our own minds on the range of responses we could make to Wilson's probable requests. When we see how *his* reckoning progresses, we can adjust our planned responses, provided we have planned them in advance. We might start by identifying every element of bureaucratic, political and personal pressure *against* MLF, which Wilson once in office may encounter, and then see what we could devise to temper each such element, as follows:

a. The British Navy East of Suez: Do we want a Western presence of substantial capability in the Indian Ocean area? Are we prepared to see it wear a British label, thus perpetuating a non-European mission for Great Britain? If so, here is a promising route to a new joint venture linking our interests for years ahead in a relationship which can't be criticized on grounds that it discriminates against the rest of Europe. British resources alone, even in the most ambitious naval plans, evidently won't produce a force which could do more than enter friendly harbors, on request, for police actions. But British naval hearts, I think, would quicken to the notion of a layer mission under British management with joint support. Healy's interests would, I think, become engaged. And even if we did no more than befriend a restricted British presence, our support, if tangible, might ease the pain of MLF in British naval circles. Either way, what support could we offer?

b. The British Aircraft Industry: RAF is eager for TSR-2 as a matter of manned-bombership. The Ministries of Defence and Aviation accept the idea of its multilateralization to produce more orders, thereby cutting unit costs and adding work for British manufacturers. This expensive, problematical new weapon (still under development) locks up a lot of defense funds which otherwise might cover MLF and carriers too. But TSR-2 also is the only thing in sight to sustain Britain's aviation industry. This is the crux of the matter. RAF aside, the interests of those Ministries (and of Wilson's projected Ministry of Technology) run with new orders — and employment — for that industry. Either in the context of a mixed-manned force or separately, new orders for *some* aircraft (whether TSR-2 or not) would compensate these interests for support of MLF. This is virtually sure to be an item in their bargaining. Granting our own industry's concerns, what might we do for theirs?

c. The American Veto: Labour front-benchers say they'd never take a control formula for MLF which hints at an American withdrawal (their eyes are on back-benchers, and on anti-Germans, and on Moscow). But Germans — and Europeans — want to point toward the day when a United Europe could "buy us out." Their need to do so must be balanced against Labour's need to say "not without British consent." My *guess* is that a form of words which subjects changes in control, a dropping of *our* veto, to consent by every member (thus to HMG's consent) will do the trick especially if Wilson could go home and claim a victory while Erhardt could express himself still satisfied. Have we the words to produce this result?

d. Consultative Mechanisms: A Labour Government will need some symbols both for public satisfaction for Gordon Walker's *amour propre* (to say nothing of Wilson's). But it presumably could also use some substance, and the closer symbols can relate to substance the better. Symbolically, if there are British colonels now at Omaha, could we have them ostentatiously replaced by generals? If the Berlin task force is a useful mechanism, could we ostentatiously enlarge its mandate? If the Board of Governors of MLF is to preside over a nuclear force, could we formally put it into the business of discussing allied strategy, or arms control, or both? Other comparable questions will suggest themselves. Substantively, I would hope there is some real work to be done behind facades like these. And perhaps we could go beyond these to some further ventures of decided usefulness to Britain in real terms even if not symbolically. I think particularly of a joint review from ministry to ministry concerning our projected force levels, roles, missions around the world, with Bonn's Defense Ministry brought in for a tripartite look at Europe. Conceivably this might become an annual exercise geared to our respective "budget seasons." Whether publicized or not it would have undoubted meaning, substantively, for the British (there's more in it for them than for us). Is this something else Wilson might gain from talks with us?

e. East-West Relations: Wilson will need protection from the charge that by support for MLF he enters a pro-German, anti-Soviet, anti-detente, capitalist plot. He will also need to be convinced in his own mind that he is doing no such things, and that the Russians know it. How do we *convince* him, once we have informed him (if we do) that consummation of the MLF must precede any thought of explorations looking toward a trade-off with the Soviets? I think of several things which might well help. He'll want to tell the President about Krushchev; the President could listen with attentive interest. He'll want to hear the President discourse upon the cause of reduced tension, East and West, with as much seriousness as the late President displayed to him in April 1963. This should be no problem. As a Kremlinologist he'll want to hear strong reasons why that cause can be *advanced* by action on the MLF. He'll want to hear them because if he makes a deal with us, he'll need to use them. And he'll want the MLF he joins to wear a different look — perhaps be called a different name — than it has worn since Moscow started to attack it. This as a matter of conviction *and* protection. These things do not exhaust the list. What else? Or what instead?

f. Atmospherics: Wilson's first contact with Anglo-American relations came in the Second World War, when he was a young civil servant. His last official contact came in Atlee's government. As Prime Minister I would expect him to arrive in Washington with recollections of the Anglo-American relationship and hopes for his own personal relationship which are quite different from perceptions of reality held by many American officials. Numbers of things can be done on the cheap to avoid shocking his sensibilities. For one, the President might ask his advice on a short list of replacements for David Bruce. For another, Averell Harriman might figure prominently among his hosts. If these don't serve, there are sure to be others. They are worth thought and attention.

These suggestions all rest on one underlying premise — that it will be worth our while to ease the path for Wilson, pay him a good price, leave him no possible excuse we can foresee for failing to proceed toward MLF in company with us and with the Germans. That assumption is subject to challenge, I know. I make it because I surmise that if we get over this hurdle in good style, the stage will be well set not only for effective Anglo-American relations but for increasingly productive Anglo-German ones. And I can think of nothing likelier to speed a Labour Government's approach toward the European *and* Atlantic attitudes *we* favor, than productive, firm relations with both Washington and Bonn. There is, besides, an opposite side to the coin. And I don't like the look of *that*.

Suggestions for Further Reading

MEMOIRS

Presidents

Eisenhower, Dwight D. *Mandate for Change, 1953–1956*. Garden City: Doubleday and Co., 1963.

Eisenhower, Dwight D. *Waging Peace, 1956–1961*. Garden City: Doubleday and Co., 1965.

Johnson, Lyndon Baines. *The Vantage Point: Perspectives of the Presidency, 1963–69*. New York: Holt, Rinehart and Winston, 1971.

Truman, Harry S. *Memoirs: Year of Decisions*. Garden City: Doubleday and Co., 1955.

Truman, Harry S. *Years of Trial and Hope*. Garden City: Doubleday and Co., 1956.

Presidential Advisers

Cutler, Robert. *No Time for Rest*. Boston: Little, Brown and Co., 1965.

Hughes, Emmet John. *The Ordeal of Power: A Political Memoir of the Eisenhower Years*. New York: Atheneum, 1963.

Larson, Arthur. *Eisenhower: The President Nobody Knew*. New York: Popular Library, 1968.

Reedy, George E. *The Twilight of the Presidency*. Cleveland: World Publishing Co., 1970.

Schlesinger, Arthur M., Jr. *A Thousand Days*. Boston: Houghton Mifflin Company, 1965.

Sorensen, Theodore C. *Kennedy*. New York: Harper and Row, 1965.

Departments and Agencies

Acheson, Dean. *Present at the Creation: My Years in the State Department*. New York: W. W. Norton and Co., 1969.

Frankel, Charles. *High on Foggy Bottom: An Outsider's Inside View of the Government*. New York: Harper and Row, 1968.

Hilsman, Roger. *To Move a Nation: The Politics of Foreign Policy in the Administration of John F. Kennedy*. Garden City: Doubleday and Co., 1967.

Kennan, George F. *Memoirs, 1925–1950*. Boston: Little, Brown and Co., 1967.

Lilienthal, David E. *The Journals of David E. Lilienthal,* Vol. II. New York: Harper and Row, 1964.

Lilienthal, David E. *The Atomic Energy Years, 1945–1950*. New York: Harper and Row, 1964.

Millis, Walter (ed.). *The Forrestal Diaries*. New York: Viking Press, 1951.

York, Herbert. *Race to Oblivion: A Participant's View of the Arms Race*. New York: Simon and Schuster, 1970.

Ambassadors

Attwood, William. *The Reds and the Blacks*. New York: Harper and Row, 1967.

Cleveland, Harlan. *NATO: The Transatlantic Bargain*. New York: Harper and Row, 1970.

Galbraith, John Kenneth. *Ambassador's Journal*. Boston: Houghton Mifflin Company, 1969.

Martin, John Bartlow. *Overtaken by Events: The Dominican Crisis from the Fall of Trujillo to the Civil War*. Garden City: Doubleday and Co., 1966.

Murphy, Robert. *Diplomat among Warriors*. Garden City: Doubleday and Co., 1964.

Rankin, Karl Lott. *China Assignment*. Seattle: University of Washington Press, 1964.

Smith, Earl E. T. *The Fourth Floor: An Account of the Castro Communist Revolution*. New York: Random House, 1962.

Military Officers

Clark, Mark W. *From the Danube to the Yalu*. New York: Harper and Bros., 1954.

Ridgway, Matthew B. *Soldier (Memoirs)*. New York: Harper and Bros., 1956.

Taylor, Maxwell D. *The Uncertain Trumpet*. New York: Harper and Bros., 1959.

ANALYTICAL STUDIES

Cornford, F. M. *Microcosmographia Academia: Being a Guide for the Young Academic Politician, Second Edition*. London: Bowes and Bowes, 1922.

de Rivera, Joseph. *The Psychological Dimension of Foreign Policy*. Columbus: Charles E. Merrill Pub. Co., 1968.

Downs, Anthony. *Inside Bureaucracy*. Boston: Little, Brown and Co., 1967.

Lindblom, Charles. *The Intelligence of Democracy*. New York: Free Press, 1965.

March, James G. and Simon, Herbert A. *Organizations*. New York: John Wiley and Sons, 1958.

Neustadt, Richard E. *Presidential Power: The Politics of Leadership.* New York: Wiley Science Editions, Inc., 1962.

Sapin, Burton M. *The Making of United States Foreign Policy.* New York: Frederick A. Praeger, 1966.

Tullock, Gordon. *The Politics of Bureaucracy.* Washington, D.C.: Public Affairs Press, 1965.

Waltz, Kenneth N. *Foreign Policy and Democratic Politics: The American and British Experience.* Boston: Little, Brown and Co., 1967.

Wilensky, Harold L. *Organizational Intelligence.* New York: Basic Books, 1967.

CASE STUDIES

Abel, Elie. *The Missile Crisis.* Philadelphia: J. B. Lippincott, 1966.

Allison, Graham T. *Essence of Decision: Explaining the Cuban Missile Crisis.* Boston: Little, Brown and Co., 1971.

Armacost, Michael H. *The Politics of Weapons Innovation: The Thor-Jupiter Controversy.* New York: Columbia University Press, 1969.

Art, Robert J. *The TFX Decision: McNamara and the Military.* Boston: Little, Brown and Co., 1968.

Cohen, Bernard C. *The Political Process and Foreign Policy: The Making of the Japanese Peace Settlement.* Princeton: Princeton University Press, 1957.

Dunn, Frederick S. *Peace-Making and the Settlement with Japan.* Princeton: Princeton University Press, 1963.

Edgerton, Russell. *Sub-Cabinet Politics and Policy Commitment: The Birth of the Development Loan Fund.* Indianapolis: Bobbs-Merrill Co., 1970.

Hammond, Paul Y. "NSC-68. Prologue to Rearmament." In Schilling, Warner, Paul Hammond, and Glenn Snyder, *Strategy, Politics, and Defense Budgets.* New York: Columbia University Press, 1962.

Johnson, Haynes, et al. *Bay of Pigs.* New York: Dell Publishing Co., 1964.

Jones, Joseph M. *The Fifteen Weeks: Feb. 21–June 5, 1947.* New York: Viking Press, 1955.

Lambright, W. Henry. *Shooting Down the Nuclear Plane.* Indianapolis: Bobbs-Merrill Co., 1967.

Neustadt, Richard E. *Alliance Politics.* New York: Columbia University Press, 1970.

Paige, Glenn D. *The Korean Decision: June 24–30, 1950.* New York: Free Press, 1968.

Robinson, James A. *The Monroney Resolution: Congressional Initiative in Foreign Policy Making.* New York: Henry Holt and Co., 1959.

Schilling, Warner R. "The Politics of National Defense: Fiscal 1950." In Schilling, Warner, Paul Hammond, and Glenn Snyder, *Strategy, Politics, and Defense Budgets.* New York: Columbia University Press, 1962.

Snyder, Glenn H. "The 'New Look' of 1953." In Schilling, Warner, Paul Hammond, and Glenn Snyder, *Strategy, Politics, and Defense Budgets.* New York: Columbia University Press, 1962.

Stein, Harold (ed.). *American Civil-Military Decisions*. University, Ala.: University of Alabama Press, 1963.
Wicker, Tom. *JFK and LBJ*. Baltimore: Penguin Books, 1968.

INSTITUTIONAL STUDIES

Beichman, Arnold. *The "Other" State Department*. New York: Basic Books, 1967.
Caraley, Demetrios. *The Politics of Military Unification*. New York: Columbia University Press, 1966.
Clark, Keith C. and Legere, Laurence J. (eds.). *The President and the Management of National Security*. New York: Frederick A. Praeger, 1969.
Cohen, Bernard C. *The Press and Foreign Policy*. Princeton: Princeton University Press, 1963.
Enthoven, Alain C. and Smith, K. Wayne. *How Much Is Enough? Shaping the Defense Program*. New York: Harper and Row, 1971.
Harr, John Ensor. *The Professional Diplomat*. Princeton: Princeton University Press, 1969.
Huntington, Samuel P. *The Common Defense*. New York: Columbia University Press, 1961.
Krock, Arthur. *Memoirs: Sixty Years on the Firing Line*. New York: Funk and Wagnalls, 1968.
Smith, Bruce L. R. *The Rand Corporation*. Cambridge, Mass: Harvard University Press, 1966.